Progress in IS

Progress in IS encompasses the various areas of Information Systems in theory and practice, presenting cutting-edge advances in the field. It is aimed especially at researchers, doctoral students, and advanced practitioners. The series features both research monographs, edited volumes, and conference proceedings that make substantial contributions to our state of knowledge and handbooks and other edited volumes, in which a team of experts is organized by one or more leading authorities to write individual chapters on various aspects of the topic. Individual volumes in this series are supported by a minimum of two external reviews.

Jorge Marx Gómez • Anael Elikana Sam •
Devotha Godfrey Nyambo
Editors

Smart and Secure Embedded and Mobile Systems

Selected Papers from the First International Conference on Embedded and Mobile Systems (ICTA-EMOS), 24-25th November 2022, Arusha, Tanzania

Springer

Editors
Jorge Marx Gómez
University of Oldenburg
Oldenburg, Germany

Anael Elikana Sam
The Nelson Mandela African Institution
of Science and Technology
Arusha, Tanzania

Devotha Godfrey Nyambo
The Nelson Mandela African Institution
of Science and Technology
Arusha, Tanzania

ISSN 2196-8705 ISSN 2196-8713 (electronic)
Progress in IS
ISBN 978-3-031-56605-9 ISBN 978-3-031-56603-5 (eBook)
https://doi.org/10.1007/978-3-031-56603-5

This Springer imprint is published by the registered company Springer Nature Switzerland AG
The registered company address is: Gewerbestrasse 11, 6330 Cham, Switzerland

Acknowledgement

The Organizing Committee of the 1st International Conference on Technological Advancement in Embedded and Mobile Systems (1st ICTA-EMoS) 2022 thanks all the implementing partners of the dSkills@EA Project for support and collaboration to host the conference.

EAC
JUMUIYA YA AFRIKA MASHARIKI

INTER-UNIVERSITY COUNCIL FOR EAST AFRICA
IUCEA
QUALITY EDUCATION FOR DEVELOPMENT

german
cooperation
DEUTSCHE ZUSAMMENARBEIT

DAAD
Deutscher Akademischer Austauschdienst
German Academic Exchange Service

giz
Deutsche Gesellschaft
für Internationale
Zusammenarbeit (GIZ) GmbH

Contents

A Machine Learning Internet of Agro Things (IoAT)—Adaptive Smart Cloud Farming System for Small-Scale Farmers in Tanzania

Alcardo Alex Barakabitze and James Robert

1 Introduction

Crop cultivation is the main agricultural activity of Tanzanian small-scale farmers (SSFs), which consist on average of more than five household members with a mean land holding capacity of around 1.2 hectares. An average small family farm in Tanzania generates a gross income of about USD 5032/year [1]. On-farm activities contribute 56% of this income while the growing and selling of crops contribute to 47%. Although on-farm income is still the most important source of livelihood, poverty remains high and 39% of the smallholders in Tanzania live below the national poverty line. Despite ongoing agricultural growth in the country, there are poor farm management techniques that do not proactively solve current agricultural problems, for example by forecasting risks such as those affecting crop performance due to mismanagement of resources. Environmental factors such as soil fertility, moisture, and weather conditions adversely affect crop production and need urgent attention whenever detected [2]. Unfortunately, farmers who attempt to improve the condition use local techniques to identify and forecast pests and disease outbreaks and perform irrigation schedules that depend on abstract weather and soil conditions information [3].

Sensor technology using the Internet of Things (IoTs) in agriculture offers good support and allows farmers to simply map their areas. Researchers in the agriculture field use the latest technology, such as multispectral cameras, satellite photography, remote sensing, and drones, with the help of the IoTs and cloud computing, to

A. A. Barakabitze (✉)
AI4D Research GROUP, Department of Informatics and Information Technology, Sokoine University of Agriculture, Morogoro, Tanzania
e-mail: alcardo.alex@sua.ac.tz

J. Robert
Department of Research and Innovation, Neggrow Company Ltd, Morogoro, Tanzania

J. Marx Gómez et al. (eds.), *Smart and Secure Embedded and Mobile Systems*,
Progress in IS, https://doi.org/10.1007/978-3-031-56603-5_1

rely heavily on sensor technologies for monitoring and manage on-farm and crop performance. The introduction of sensor technologies that improve crop and soil quality, food safety, sustainability, and profitability has resulted in an increase in the production level of agriculture [4]. Farmers may be relieved from the duties of owning servers by implementing IoT networks across Tanzania that are utilized by remote servers or cloud computing technologies [4]. Open-source Long Term Evolution (LTE) modem that utilizes the technology to send the data from a distant location and solar-powered allows us to send text and multimedia data in Tanzania. Therefore, this chapter proposes a Machine Learning (ML) IoT-based smart farming system with cloud computing for farmers in Tanzania by implementing remote sensors like soil moisture sensors, imaging sensors, and weather sensors. Cloud computing will be used to store and interpret data that is received from individual sensors and use the ML algorithm to forecast crop performance, predict pests and disease outbreaks, detect crop stress, and recommend irrigation schedules for farmers. The expected impacts and outcomes of this innovation include (a) increased crop productivity and (b) training and imparting modern farming techniques to smallholder farming groups (e.g., women farming groups) in Tanzania.

1.1 Research Challenges and Motivation

Smallholder farmers employ about 70% of the world's population and produce 70% of the world's food. Tanzania's agriculture sector accounts for 26.7% of GDP and employs more than 80% of the population, with women accounting for 60% of the farm workforce. Most small and medium-sized farmers in Tanzania, on the other hand, cannot afford to embrace such advanced equipment for sustainable agriculture, which goes against the UN Sustainable Development Goals (SDG) tenet of "leaving no one behind." Although the use of digital technologies can help address some of the issues, success in this area has been limited and has not been scaled up sufficiently [1]. The agriculture sector in Tanzania is confronted with the following issues [5]: pests and diseases which are the critical burning issues for SSFs in Tanzania. Small and marginal farmers own less than two hectares, resulting in insufficient farm revenue and poverty. Soil degradation and water stress are the outcome of unsustainable farming methods. Lack of data at the farm, farmer, and sector levels, resulting in greater service costs; Food waste is increasing due to a lack of food processing, logistics, and warehousing infrastructure near farm gates. Financial and digital inclusion challenges; Gaps in market linkages, difficulties in price discovery for farmers, and market price volatility; due to financial constraints and farm mechanization which is inadequate [5–7]. This chapter addresses these gaps by implementing a ML-IoT-based management system for increasing agricultural productivity. The developed AI/ML-IoT-based solution will be able to monitor and manage in real-time crop performance and provide decision support tools for Small-scale farmers (SSFs) in Tanzania.

1.2 Research Objectives and Contributions

The main objective of this chapter is to develop a ML-based adaptive smart farming management system with an open IoT solution over cloud computing to increase agricultural productivity of SSFs in Tanzania. The main contributions of this chapter are twofold:

- We propose and develop an efficient ML-driven IoT-based cloud computing farm management and monitoring system to monitor in real-time crop performance and provide decision support tools for SSFs.
- We provide the implementation of the proposed using real-time devices that send and receive data for the farmers' recommendations.
- We develop measures and recommendations that that will support decision-making in terms of policy and intervention strategies in the context of spreading crop diseases among plants in the farms belonging to these regions.

2 Related Work

Rapid developments in the IoT, cloud computing, robotics, and AI are accelerating the transition to smart farming and the promotion of big data and precision agriculture to improve agri-food sustainability [2]. Previous works investigated the application of ML and IoT technologies for improving agriculture [2, 8]. Aworka et al [8] propose three prediction models: crop random forest, crop gradient boosting machine, and crop support vector machine where data on crop productivity, the use of pesticides, and the climate are combined to create a decision-making system based on cutting-edge machine learning algorithms. Authors suggested a decision system that can forecast crop yields at the country level in 14 East African countries despite the limited availability of agricultural data in Africa. Ayaz et al [2] provide the potential of IoT and wireless sensors in agriculture, as well as issues that are anticipated when integrating this technology with conventional farming methods. The authors present state-of-the-art IoT-based architectures and platforms used in agriculture. However, the authors do not provide any implementations and prototypes of IoT/ML for agriculture. Lufyagila et al [9] propose the IoT technology for low-resource smallholder farmers to monitor environmental conditions in chicken houses. Compared to the conventional approach, the system saves time (84%) and labor costs (66.7%) since the farmer can remotely monitor and regulate the conditions with security and dependability. Additionally, the chapter suggests an algorithm for the system's online and offline functionality (i.e., synchronizing with the cloud server when Internet access is available). However, these works are limited in the implementation aspects of integrating ML and the IoT devices in monitoring and managing crops performance. There is also no real-time implementation in these works stated above, making serious concerns for their adoption by smallholder farmers in Tanzania. There has been a limited study in the area of providing a real-time implementation and a prototype of AI/ML-IoT-based solution to monitor and manage crop performance and provide decision support tools for Small-scale farmers (SSFs) in Tanzania.

3 Research Methodology

3.1 Study Area

This study was carried out in Morogoro at SUA farming sites. The study area was selected based on climate-related conditions and easy monitoring of study implementation. We utilized a group of weather, soil, and environmental sensor nodes positioned at different locations in the farms/plots to communicate with the gateway over local telecommunication systems to measure the growth and performance of root activity of crops in the farms.

3.2 A Proposed Architecture for ML-Driven Agriculture IoT-Based Farming Monitoring and Management System in Tanzania

The proposed IoT-based ML farming management system using cloud computing, virtualization, and big data analytics employs weather, soil, and environment sensors to monitor crops growth and predict diseases and pests, detect crop stress, and predict yield based on the following components: the gateway, cloud infrastructure, pests and disease prediction, crop stress prediction, and smartphone application.

3.2.1 A Network Gateway

A network gateway acts as an interface between the field sensors (soil moisture sensors, weather stations, humidity sensors, and crop health sensors) and the central server or cloud-based platform, allowing data to be transmitted, processed, and acted upon. It enables the collection, transmission, and analysis of data related to agricultural activities in order to optimize crop production and facilitate efficient farm management. Advanced algorithms and ML techniques can be applied to derive meaningful insights from the collected data. This analysis can help identify patterns, predict crop growth, detect diseases, and optimize resource usage. Based on the analyzed data, the gateway system can generate alerts, notifications, and recommendations for farmers and agronomists. For example, it can send alerts about soil moisture levels dropping below a certain threshold, indicating a need for irrigation. These alerts can be delivered through mobile apps, SMS, or email (Fig. 1).

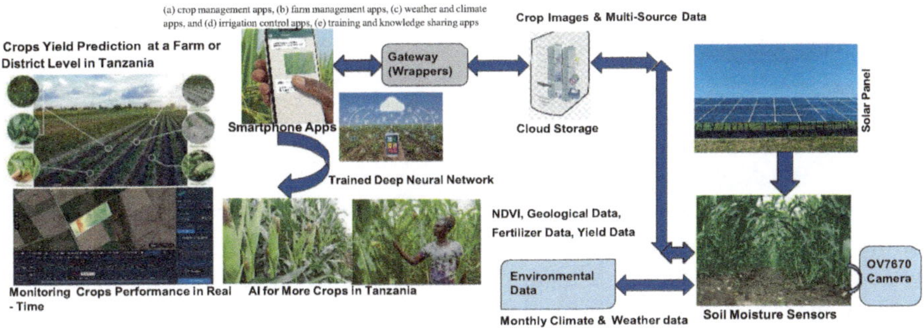

Fig. 1 The ML-driven IoAT-based farming monitoring and management architecture in Tanzania

3.2.2 Environmental Data

The environmental data from different IoT devices (sensors) is collected and filtered using the gateway. We employ an OpenIoT Extended Global Sensors Network (X-GSN) component to perform data ingestion and to facilitate the deployment and programming of sensor networks [10]. We also use wrappers to encapsulate the data received from the data source into the standard X-GSN data model. Note that the wrapper is an interface that allows the gateway to pull/push data from/to the underlying IoT device (sensor). We deploy gateways at various sites or locations in farms/plots consisting of sensors.

3.3 ML-Driven IoAT Prototype Implementation in Real-Time

3.3.1 Cloud Storage Infrastructure

We use ThingSpeak (https://thingspeak.com/) to store and manage the data that are generated by sensors. ThingSpeak allows you to aggregate, visualize, and analyze live data streams in the cloud [11]. ThingSpeak provides instant visualizations of data posted by IoT sensors. To handle a large volume of data streams from different IoT devices both (virtual and physical) implements publish/subscribe queues and stores the sensor data in the resource description framework (RDF) format. Different metadata, functional data for small-scale farmers' accounts, and ontology are stored in the cloud infrastructure. The ontology refers to farmers' plots descriptions, types of crops cultivated (e.g., maize and tomato), and different treatments (e.g., plots/farm irrigated or not irrigated) applied to the plots. Using these ontologies, farmers can perform basic operations (reading, updating, deleting) data from IoT devices (sensor) using a Smartphone Application interface. Then, interactive data analytics and interpretation will be delivered to farmers' smartphones after specifying specific information such as crop species selected, amount of crops soil moisture contents in the farm, types of predicted disease/pests, health and unhealthy crops, and roots activity of crops.

3.3.2 OV7670 Camera

It is used to capture the leaf images throughout the growth period of crops in the farms. We define four collection windows (1-h window, 1-day window, 1-week window, 1-month window, 2-month window) of leaf images based on the root activity measured using the soil moisture sensors. Each of these windows holds data points collected from leaf images which are then used as inputs for developed (a) pests and disease predictions ML algorithm, and (b) crop yield prediction algorithms. For predicting the health of the crop, a camera is also interfaced with the solar panel module. Then, we employ an open-source software namely, OpenIoT (http://www.openiot.eu/) which is deployed in a JBOSS application container. We use it to provide real-time scalable analytics on the sensor data generated from captured crops. The sensor data to be analyzed is delivered to the cloud infrastructure using a local gateway. Weather station: it collects information such as rainfall, humidity, wind speed and direction, and temperature. Soil moisture and temperature sensor: the paper uses the DHT11 Sensor type to measure soil temperature, conductivity, and estimates the amount of water in the soil/farm where crops are cultivated. We use both stationary sensors and portable soil moisture probes in the implementations. We place 40 soil-moisture sensors at multiple locations at depths (e.g., 15 cm–1.5 m) below the soil surface in the farms. The deployed sensors will help us to know the water extraction of crops' roots from the soil throughout the cultivation season.

3.3.3 A/ML-Driven Crop and Farm Monitoring Using IoT

Real-time monitoring of farm operations is performed using the processed data. Farmers can access this information through intuitive dashboards or mobile applications as indicated in Fig. 2. They can monitor various aspects/parameters such as soil moisture, temperature, humidity, light intensity, weather conditions, water levels in reservoirs or tanks, energy consumption, and equipment status. AI algorithms can leverage historical and real-time data to provide predictive analytics. Multiple factors such as weather forecasts, soil conditions, and past trends can be used by the AI/ML algorithms to forecast crop growth, disease outbreaks, or irrigation needs. This allows farmers to plan and make informed decisions in advance. IoT devices and sensors can be integrated with automated control systems to enable remote monitoring and control of farm operations.

AI-driven crop and farm monitoring using IoT technologies offer immense benefits to farmers, including improved resource management, early detection of issues, optimized operations, and enhanced productivity. By leveraging real-time

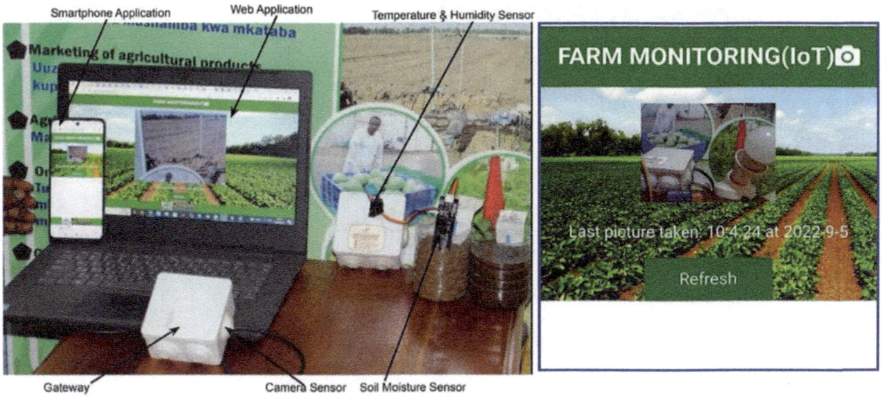

(a) Configuration of various IoT devices. smartphone apps and web application

(b) Crops and farming monitoring and management

Fig. 2 The prototype implementation of the ML-driven agriculture-IoT-based farming monitoring and management system

data and intelligent algorithms, farmers can make data-driven decisions to maximize yields, minimize risks, and promote sustainable agricultural practices.

3.3.4 Smartphone Application for Crops and Farm Monitoring

This App is developed using Android Studio, Keras, and PyTorch, open-source libraries to provide various options for farmers to select the crop, monitor the status of crops growth. The App also predicts crop pests and diseases in maize or sorghum fields using the pests and diseases prediction algorithm/component. The prediction results and the performance analysis of crops will be shared with farmers, growers, commercial organizations, and researchers through the Smartphone App (see Fig. 1). This allows them to visualize and make recommendations for supporting smart farming techniques in the country leading to improved agriculture productivity. The data used for pests and diseases are collected by the sensors. In addition, the web application creates different views for the data from the sensor readings and provides opportunities for interacting with devices like water pump and valve on the cloud (Fig. 1).

4 Initial Implementation Results, Outputs, and Discussion

Our initial implementation results include the prototyping and helping smallholder farmers to see different farm attributes like temperature, humidity, and soil moisture which are directly seen or observed through a farmer's smartphone using a mobile App. We have also been able to progam the hardware by imbedding and linking them

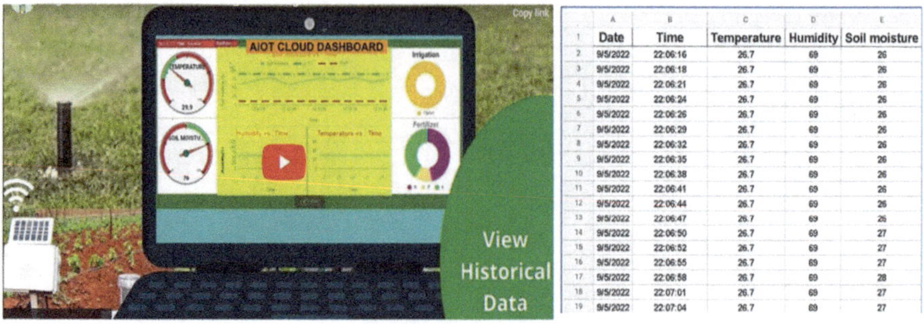

	A	B	C	D	E
1	Date	Time	Temperature	Humidity	Soil moisture
2	9/5/2022	22:06:16	26.7	69	26
3	9/5/2022	22:06:18	26.7	69	26
4	9/5/2022	22:06:21	26.7	69	26
5	9/5/2022	22:06:24	26.7	69	26
6	9/5/2022	22:06:26	26.7	69	26
7	9/5/2022	22:06:29	26.7	69	26
8	9/5/2022	22:06:32	26.7	69	26
9	9/5/2022	22:06:35	26.7	69	26
10	9/5/2022	22:06:38	26.7	69	26
11	9/5/2022	22:06:41	26.7	69	26
12	9/5/2022	22:06:44	26.7	69	26
13	9/5/2022	22:06:47	26.7	69	26
14	9/5/2022	22:06:50	26.7	69	27
15	9/5/2022	22:06:52	26.7	69	27
16	9/5/2022	22:06:55	26.7	69	27
17	9/5/2022	22:06:58	26.7	69	28
18	9/5/2022	22:07:01	26.7	69	27
19	9/5/2022	22:07:04	26.7	69	27

Fig. 3 Soil, temperature, and humidity data collected from IoT Sensors in Real-time to the Cloud

with web applications. The developed prototype has been tested at SUA farming sites available at the Sokoine University of Agriculture, Edward Moringe Campus in Morogoro. Figure 3 indicates the data that is collected in real time by sensors after every 1 min and sent to the cloud storage. The data is collected after a time threshold of 1 min, which is a threshold that we set for IoT sensors to upload the data to the cloud storage. The IoT data pushed to the cloud storage can be also available to a smartphone for a farmer to visualize and take the necessary actions of performing irrigation/fertilizing applications in the farm, see Fig. 3. As indicated in Fig. 3, the soil moisture is 27 and 28 while the humidity and temperature values are 29, 29, and 26.7 at 22:06:55 and 22:06:58, respectively. It is worth mentioning that, the implemented systems provide a starting point toward the adoption of ML-driven IoT technologies in Tanzania. The SSFs can apply the proposed solution in their farming activities individually or in groups because the sensors used are of low cost.

4.1 Real-Time IoAT Dashboard for Data Visualization

Figure 3 also shows an IoAT dashboard on the left-hand side that connects various types of sensors in the farm to provide real-time data and measure environmental parameters such as temperature, humidity, soil moisture, light intensity, and air quality. These sensors can be integrated into the IoT dashboard to provide real-time data. This allows farmers to quickly analyze the data and make informed decisions. The dashboard sets customizable alerts and notifications based on specific thresholds or conditions. For example, if the temperature exceeds a certain limit or the soil moisture drops below a certain level, the system can send alerts to the farmers via email, SMS, or push notifications.

4.2 *Recommendations for Policy and Intervention Strategies for AI/ML and IoT in Agriculture*

- The Government should establish a regulatory framework that addresses the ethical, legal, and social implications of AI/ML and IoT in agriculture. This framework should encompass data privacy, security, transparency, accountability, and fairness to protect the rights and interests of all stakeholders.
- The Government should develop standards and protocols that facilitate interoperability among different AI/ML and IoT systems used in agriculture. This will ensure seamless integration, data sharing, and compatibility between various technologies, enabling effective decision-making.
- The Government should implement robust data governance practices to manage the vast amounts of data generated by AI/ML and IoT systems in agriculture. Define data ownership, access rights, data quality standards, and data sharing policies to enable secure and responsible data utilization.
- The Government should invest in training programs and initiatives to enhance the digital literacy and technical skills of farmers, agricultural workers, and policymakers. This will empower them to understand, adopt, and effectively utilize AI/ML and IoT technologies in agriculture.
- The Government should encourage the establishment of testbeds and pilot projects to assess the feasibility, scalability, and impact of AI/ML and IoT interventions in agriculture. These initiatives provide valuable insights and data for evidence-based decision-making.
- The Government should foster collaboration between researchers, industry experts, and policymakers through workshops, conferences, and knowledge-sharing platforms. Encourage the exchange of ideas, experiences, and lessons learned to promote collective learning and better decision-making.

Decision makers can make well-informed choices regarding policy and intervention strategies for AI/ML and IoT in agriculture, leading to sustainable and beneficial outcomes for the agricultural sector.

5 Conclusion

This chapter proposes and develops an efficient IoT-based cloud computing farm management and monitoring system using ML to monitor real-time crop performance and provide decision support tools for SSFs. We provide the implementation of the proposed using real-time devices that send and receive data for the farmer's recommendations. We develop measures and recommendations that that will support decision-making in terms of policy and intervention strategies in the context of spreading crop diseases among plants in the farms belonging to these regions.

Acknowledgments This research has received funding from the International Development Research Centre (IDRC) through the African Technology Policy Studies Network (ATPS) and partners (iCIPE and KUMASI HIVE) and co-funded by the SUA Research and Innovation Funds from the Government of Tanzania.

References

1. WFP: World Food Programme United Republic of Tanzania: Current Issues and What the World Food Programme is Doing. (2021). Preprint at https://www.wfp.org/countries/tanzania
2. Ayaz, M., Ammad-Uddin, M., Sharif, Z., Mansour, A., & Aggoune, E. M. (2019). Internet-of-things (iot)-based smart agriculture: Toward making the fields talk. IEEE. *Access, 7*, 129551–129583.
3. Gupta, A., Gupta, H. P., Kumari, P., Mishra, R., Saraswat, S., & Dutta, T. (2018). A real-time precision agriculture monitoring system using mobile sink in wsns. *IEEE International Conference on Advanced Networks and Telecommunications Systems (ANTS), 7*, 1–5.
4. Ram, S. K., Sahoo, S. R., Das, B. B., Mahapatra, K. K., & Mohanty, S. P. (2021). Eternal- thing: A secure aging-aware solar-energy harvester thing for sustainable iot. *IEEE Transactions on Sustainable Computing (TSUSC), 6*(2), 1–22.
5. Barakabitze, A., Kitindi, E., Sanga, C., Shabani, A., Philipo, J., & Kibirige, G. (2015). New technologies for disseminating and communicating agriculture knowledge and information: Challenges for agricultural research institutes in Tanzania. *Electronic Journal of Information Systems in Developing Countries, 70*, 1–22.
6. Sanka, M. B., & Nkilijiwa, A. L. (2021). Access to agricultural credit for smallholder farmers in Shinyanga region–Tanzania. *East African Journal of Social and Applied Sciences, 3*, 181–191.
7. Simbakalia, J. L. (2012). The role of financial sector in agriculture development and industrialization. *Economic and Social Research Foundation, 3*, 3–6.
8. Rubby Aworkaa, L., Saadio, C. W., & Hamilton, Y. (2022). Agricultural decision system based on advanced machine learning models for yield prediction: Case of east african countries. *Smart Agricultural Technology, 2*, 1–9.
9. Lufyagila, B., Machuve, D., & Clemen, T. (2022). Iot-powered system for environmental conditions monitoring in poultry house: A case of Tanzania. *African Journal of Science, Technology Innovation and Development, 14*(4), 1020–1031.
10. Codeluppi, G., Cilfone, A., Davoli, L., & Ferrari, G. (2020). Ai at the edge: A smart gateway for greenhouse air temperature forecasting. In Proceedings of the 2020 IEEE International Workshop on Metrology for Agriculture and Forestry (MetroAgriFor) 14, 348–353.
11. Varshney, L. R., & Richardson, D. (2017). Intelligent infrastructure for smart agriculture: An integrated food, energy and water system, pp. 1–8. https://arxiv.org/abs/1705.01993abs/1705.01993

Barriers to Using Open Data in the Innovation Process

Ifeoluwapo Fashoro, Antonieta Alcorta de Bronstein, and Jantje Halberstadt

1 Introduction

The data revolution spurred by the proliferation of new technologies such as urban sensors, social media, mobile phones, and the Internet has made it easier and cheaper for organizations to access, store, and analyze large volumes of data. Public and private sector organizations have recognized the importance of data for competitive advantage, economic growth, sustainable development, and good governance, which has led to an increase in data availability and advanced data analytics through Information Communication Technologies (ICT) [1]. The phenomenon of open data has grown parallel to this growth in data availability.

Open data involves the release of previously private data from the public sector and private organizations for public use [2, 3]. Data release is an essential driver for a sustainable economy, innovation, and creativity bridge in developing a new ecosystem with Industry 4.0 and smart cities [4]. Both public and private sectors have been increasingly adopting measures to make data open, which is evidenced by the increasing number of open data online portals currently available. Provided by government authorities and private organizations, these portals provide access to numerous datasets for public use. According to the Open Data Maturity Report, all 27 European Union countries have a national open data portal [5], the United Nations' (UN) e-government report states that 153 countries have open government portals [6], while the Open Knowledge Foundation offers a list of 597 private and public data portals [7].

I. Fashoro (✉)
Nelson Mandela University, Gqeberha, South Africa
e-mail: ife.fashoro@mandela.ac.za

A. A. de Bronstein · J. Halberstadt
University of Vechta, Vechta, Germany
e-mail: antonieta.alcorta-de-bronstein@uni-vechta.de; Jantje.Halberstadt@uni-vechta.de

J. Marx Gómez et al. (eds.), *Smart and Secure Embedded and Mobile Systems*,
Progress in IS, https://doi.org/10.1007/978-3-031-56603-5_2

Although governments have been the biggest drivers of open data in terms of providing data, setting up policies, and regulating the use of open data, private institutions and citizen groups have also invested in open data projects, collecting and releasing data for reuse. For example, Sensor.Community is a citizen platform that provides data on air quality collected by individual citizens [8]. Such platforms empower citizens to collectively provide solutions to problems that affect them as a community.

The use of open data has many advantages. Some of the cited benefits for governments include enhanced transparency, accountability, citizen participation, and opportunities to commercialize developed products and services which lead to economic benefits, employment opportunities, improved quality of life for citizens, and better decision-making that positively impacts real-life issues [2, 9, 10]. According to the United Nations, open data provided by the government stimulates people-centric innovation, eliminates redundancies and red tape, and hastens the provision of publicly requested information, while allowing academics, businesses, and citizens the chance to offer insights into complex policy issues [6]. As early as 2013, McKinsey predicted the economic value of open data to be as high as $3 trillion, with stated benefits for consumers and businesses [3].

Whether in the private or public sector domain, the most articulated benefit of open data is innovation. There is a basic assumption that releasing data publicly is beneficial and leads to innovation [2, 11]. The innovation process itself is complex comprised of different stages. Each of these stages has its unique characteristics and actors who are involved. This process also comes with its own set of barriers. However, little is known about how open data and innovation barriers influence each stage of the innovation process. In addressing the issue of barriers to open data, Ruijer and Meijer [12] point out that previous studies have not considered the timing of these barriers, indicating that each one affects the innovation process at different stages (timing). The timing of each barrier, therefore, needs to be considered and understood. This paper will consequently explore how the open data and innovation barriers influence the different stages of the innovation process.

We propose a conceptual framework that maps out the open data and innovation barriers related to the different stages of the innovation process. The proposed framework intends to lay a foundation to better understand how using open data in the innovation process might be impeded. The conceptual analysis method proposed by Jabareen [13] was used to design this framework. The paper is structured as follows: the following section presents the conceptual analysis method as the research method for this paper. This is followed by a literature review relating to open data and the innovation process which are findings from the conceptual analysis. A review of relevant theories is presented as part of the conceptual analysis process. The conceptual framework is then presented, and the final section of this paper concludes by reflecting on key points and recommendations for further development. The primary contributions of this paper are (1) a synthesis of open data and innovation barriers from existing literature and (2) the conceptual framework.

2 Conceptual Analysis Process and Literature Review

A conceptual framework is described by Jabareen [13] as a network of interlinked concepts that together provide a thorough understanding of a phenomenon while not seeking to predict an outcome or explain hard facts about a phenomenon. Instead, it provides an "interpretive approach to a social reality" [13]. The conceptual analysis method of building a conceptual framework is an iterative process consisting of eight phases: mapping the selected data sources, extensive reading and categorizing of the selected data, identifying and naming concepts, deconstructing and categorizing the concepts, integrating concepts, synthesis, re-synthesis, and making it all make sense, validating and rethinking the conceptual framework.

The first four phases incorporate the mapping and categorization of the concepts. This was done through a critical literature review. The selected databases for the literature search were Google Scholar, Web of Science, Elsevier, and ScienceDirect. The search terms used were "Open Data Barriers," "Open Data for Innovation," "Open Data for Innovation Process," and "Innovation Barrier." The selection criteria included papers published between 2018 and 2022. The initial papers selected were from conference proceedings and journal articles. The initial search was augmented with articles identified from the reference list of relevant articles. This led to the inclusion of articles outside the initial publication year criteria. The search resulted in 2653 papers which were evaluated for relevance using the titles. A further analysis was done based on the abstract of these papers, 1973 papers were excluded because their focus was on open innovation theory or data-driven innovation rather than open data for innovation. Duplicate studies (42) published in different conferences or journals were also excluded. Content analysis of the remaining papers led to a further exclusion of papers that did not meet the inclusion criteria. At the end of the analysis process, 20 papers were deemed relevant as they focused on open data and innovation barriers. These phases enabled the identification and categorization of the initial concepts which are presented in the literature review. The next two phases involved the integration and synthesis of the concepts into a framework which is presented in the conceptual framework section below where related concepts are grouped and relationships between identified concepts are established. This paper will focus on the first six phases of the process, while the last two phases will be covered in a different stage of the research study.

3 Open Data and Innovation

Innovation is key to solving complex problems, including society's greatest challenges, and therefore enhancing sustainable development as a result. Innovation is defined as "the implementation of a new or significantly improved product (good or service), or process, a new marketing method, or a new organizational method in business practices, workplace organization or external relations" [14].

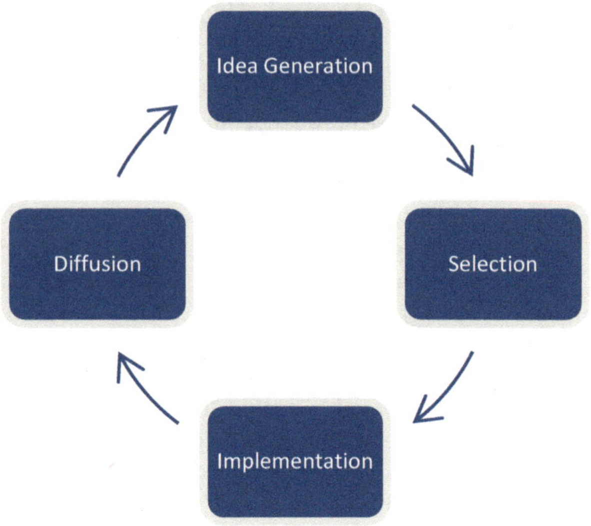

Fig. 1 The innovation process based on Sørensen & Torfing [15]

This paper adopts the innovation process as stipulated by Sørensen & Torfing [15], the stages of which are identified as: idea generation, selection, implementation, and diffusion [15]. Each of these stages has its unique characteristics and therefore unique challenges. For example, idea generation involves nurturing, presenting, and developing the initial designs or prototypes of potential new solutions for an identified problem. Idea selection involves decisions about viable ideas. Idea implementation involves actions to develop initial designs into fully functional services, practices, and programs, while managing changes introduced by innovations in individual behavior and organizational structures. Idea diffusion additionally involves the propagation of innovation within an organization or externally to other organizations. This process of innovation shown in Fig. 1 is described as complex, non-linear, and iterative. Each of these stages has its specific characteristics and complexities and is therefore impacted by different barriers.

Open data is seen as an essential raw material and basis for product and service innovations that have the potential to solve complex problems, create new companies, and provide employment opportunities [2]. The innovation process in this study refers to the process of using open data to create a product or service. In the case of open data, idea generation would involve the process of ideating solutions to a real-life problem identified in a community using open datasets available to the public. This is mostly done through hackathons and citizen challenges. Here, the selection process involves determining the most viable solution to the problem based on the results emerging from these hackathons and challenges. The selected solution would then be implemented in the community and diffused to citizens by raising their awareness of it [12].

4 Open Data and Innovation Barriers Influencing the Innovation Process

While the promise of open data is optimistic, there are barriers to its use that might hinder the innovation process. Furthermore, there are barriers arising not only from open data but also from the complex nature of the innovation process. We therefore combine two bodies of literature: studies on open data barriers, and on innovation barriers [11, 16–20]. In our literature review, we found barriers to open data and to innovation which we further synthesized here. The synthesis identified 78 barriers which we grouped into six categories: collaboration, cultural, economic, legal, organizational/administrative, and technical.

As mentioned above, several innovation studies have found that barriers affect the innovation process in different stages [19, 21]. Ruijer and Meijer [12] refer to this as the timing of the barriers. Based on this, this study adopted the innovation process as a basis for analyzing the barriers listed in Table 1.

5 Conceptual Framework on Open Data and Innovation Barriers Affecting the Innovation Process

The framework presented in this section links the categorized barriers from Table 1 to each stage of the innovation process. The barriers reflected in Fig. 2 are the main barriers after a process of further synthesizing the original 78 barriers from the literature. Some barriers affect the entire innovation process, such as administering the process and slow bureaucracy in organizations. Figure 2 shows the open data and innovation barriers relating to each stage of the innovation process. The framework has been color coded according to the categories of barriers previously mentioned, with pink, green, blue, yellow, purple, and orange representing cultural, collaboration, economic, legal, organizational/administrative, and technical barriers, respectively. The barriers specific to innovation are indicated with the ♦ symbol.

Barriers relating to culture are identified in literature typically in the idea generation stage. The culture of the organization can hamper or stimulate innovation. According to Rakšnys et al. [22], organizational culture should be favorable to innovation and learning and be one of the first steps for effective innovation processes. Aspects of organizational culture identified in literature are risk-averse culture, top-down managerial thinking, lack of learning culture, closed government culture, and slow bureaucracy [11, 16, 18, 19]. In relation to collaboration barriers, inadequate communication, lack of agreement on common goals, a lack of accountability between collaborators and community engagement for building capacities, and finding agile solutions are essential to the idea generation stage. Economic barriers in this stage include those related to funding the innovation process, fees related to paying for data, perceived economic risks, and a lack of incentives for data users. Legal barriers involve issues around government regulation, policies, and licenses

Table 1 Open data and innovation barriers (Authors' construct)

Category	Code	Barrier	Author
Collaboration	B1	Ensuring sustainable change through "ecosystems" of key actors	[18]
	B2	Lack of shared understanding between collaborators or network members ♦	[19]
	B3	No agreement on common goals, common decisions, common vision, and mission ♦	[19]
	B4	Inadequate communication and knowledge sharing between public organizations ♦	[19]
	B5	A lack of effective network governance ♦	[19]
	B6	Inappropriate accountability between public sector organizations ♦	[19]
	B7	Inadequate involvement of citizens or NGOs ♦	[19]
	B8	Public doubt and opposition towards an innovation ♦	[19]
	B9	Inadequate or failed contractors ♦	[19]
	B10	A lack of trust ♦	[17, 19]
	B11	Engaging with the wider community in a two-way conversation to build capacities and find agile solutions	[18]
Cultural	B12	Risk-averse culture	[11, 19]
	B13	Top-down managerial thinking	[19]
	B14	Slow bureaucracy	[19]
	B15	Lack of organizational learning culture	[19]
	B16	Closed government culture	[16, 18]
Economic	B17	Fees and funding	[11, 17, 18, 20]
	B18	Existing charging models	[11, 16]
	B19	Uncertain economic impact	[16]
	B20	Lack of incentives for the users ♦	[11, 18, 19]
	B21	Excessive perceived economic risks	[11, 20]
	B22	Unexpected, escalated costs	[11]
	B23	Direct innovation costs are too high ♦	[20]
	B24	Having to pay a fee for the data (users)	[11]
Legal	B25	Litigation and liability	[11, 17]
	B26	Privacy legislation and violation	[11, 16–18]
	B27	Prior written permission required to gain access to and reproduce data	[11]
	B28	Need to meet government regulations	[20]
	B29	No license for using data	[11]
	B30	Lack of procedures and standards on how to deal with open data	[18]

(continued)

Table 1 (continued)

Category	Code	Barrier	Author
	B31	Limitation on reuse arising from copyrights and changes for commercial use	[11, 18]
	B32	Copyrights may result in lack of clarity over who owns data	[18]
	B33	Complexities of the various national legal frameworks for copyright and related rights	[18]
Organizational/ Administrative	B34	Lack of standardization of open data policy	[16]
	B35	Security	[16–18]
	B36	Lack of leadership ♦	[19]
	B37	Lack of business case	[11]
	B38	No process for dealing with user input	[11]
	B39	Ambitious or unclear goals ♦	[19]
	B40	Resistance or lack of support from specific actors	[18, 19]
	B41	Lack of available resources in terms of money, time, and IT infrastructure	[17, 19, 20]
	B42	Losing enthusiasm ♦	[19]
	B43	Inappropriate organizational structure and culture	[19]
	B44	Lack of skills, knowledge, and expertise ♦	[19]
	B45	Balancing autonomy and control	[17, 18]
	B46	Registration is required before being able to download the data	[11]
	B47	No time to delve into the details or no time at all	[11]
	B48	No time to make use of the open data	[11]
	B49	Administering the innovation process ♦	[19]
	B50	Uncertain demand for innovative goods/services ♦	[20]
Technical	B51	Debatable/limited quality of user input	[11]
	B52	Quality of data	[11, 16, 18]
	B53	Lack of data	[18]
	B54	Information overload	[16]
	B55	Limited user-friendliness of portals	[16]
	B56	Digital divide	[16]
	B57	Network overload	[16]
	B58	Absence of standards	[11, 17]
	B59	No central portal or architecture	[11]
	B60	Complexity of an innovation ♦	[19]
	B61	Incompatibility of innovation ♦	[19]
	B62	Lack of meta data standards	[11]
	B63	Obsolete and non-valid data	[11]
	B64	Lack of information on markets ♦	[20]

(continued)

Table 1 (continued)

Category	Code	Barrier	Author
	B65	Lack of information on technology ♦	[20]
	B66	Un-harmonized datasets, formats, and standards	[11, 18]
	B67	Poor data management practices	[18]
	B68	No tooling support or help desk	[11]
	B69	Data formats and datasets are too complex	[11]
	B70	No access to the original data (only processed data)	[11]
	B71	Making public only non-value-adding data	[11]
	B72	Contradicting outcomes based on the use of the same data	[11]
	B73	Lack of the necessary capability and knowledge to use the information	[11]
	B74	Similar data stored in different systems yields different results	[11]
	B75	Difficulty in searching and browsing due to no index or other means to ensure easy search for finding the right data	[11, 18]
	B76	Apps hide the complexity, but also potential other uses of open data	[11]
	B77	Inadequate information technology infrastructure	[18]
	B78	No standard software for processing open data	[11]

♦ Innovation Specific Barriers

relating to using data, as well as the risk of litigation in the case of its violation. Cinar et al. [19] highlight risk aversion and lack of funding as barriers in this stage. Some of the organizational/administrative barriers in this stage have been previously discussed in relation to the other categories of barriers, and include a lack of business case, lack of skills, knowledge, and expertise, and ambitious and unclear goals which introduce uncertainty and delay the innovation process [23]. Technical barriers in this stage include the digital divide and lack of information on markets for innovation.

Economic barriers in the selection stage include existing payment models, uncertain economic impact of an innovation, and having to pay a fee for an innovation. These barriers impact the decision to continue with the development of an idea. Issues around licensing and permission to use open data impact the selection stage as users become hesitant to commit to developing innovations using these data. Organizational/administrative barriers in this stage are similar to those discussed in the idea generation stage. Technical barriers in this stage are related to publicized data, its availability, quality, format, and complexity.

The implementation stage has the most barriers, with collaboration barriers being the most prominent. Collaboration barriers include inadequate communication, lack of agreement on common goals, and a lack of accountability between collaborators. Economic barriers include funding for the innovation, and lack of incentives and

Fig. 2 Open data and innovation barriers in the different innovation process stages (Authors' construct)

fees related to data use. Legal barriers are similar to previous stages and revolve around regulations, licenses, copyrights, and standards for using open data. Users encounter barriers related to time involved in searching for and exploring data. The need to register on open data portals is also considered a barrier to users. Other organizational/administrative barriers are linked to a lack of resources, skills, and technology infrastructure. Technical barriers are the most common in the implementation stage. These include inadequate skills and capability to use and understand the data, inadequate technology infrastructure, including standardized software and barriers concerning the data such as incomplete data, poor quality, lack of metadata, obsolete or invalid data, and contradicting outcomes when the same dataset is used. Poor data management practices also hinder innovation in the implementation stage.

Collaboration barriers in the diffusion phase include a need to ensure sustainable change through ecosystems of key actors, inadequate support from citizens, a lack of trust, and opposition to an innovation. Economic barriers make users hesitant to use an innovation, and include fees, funding, and incentive issues. Legal barriers arise from issues regarding the use and reuse of data and innovations developed from this data. The main organizational/administrative barriers involve the provision of feedback to data publishers, users providing products and services from this data, as well as a loss of enthusiasm for the innovation. Feedback has been identified as an essential part of the open data process [2, 11]. In the diffusion stage, technical barriers include the complexity and incompatibility of an innovation, and the lack of end-user support.

Slow bureaucracy and administering the innovation process are described as crucial barriers evident in all stages of the innovation process [19]. Slow bureaucracy can lead to delays in the innovation process especially relating to decision-making at each stage of the process [17]. The different activities executed at each stage of the innovation process involve varied actors and resources and require administration which can become complex and give rise to barriers if not handled efficiently.

6 Conclusion

The use of open data for innovation has been lauded by numerous authors. It enables people-centric solutions to society's problems, enabling the development of products and services in both public and private organizations. Innovation is not a simple process, and the nature of open data adds a level of complexity to it. Barriers to innovation and open data have been presented separately in other studies. This paper explores the barriers that affect the use of open data in each stage of the innovation process by analyzing in conjunction both types of barriers (innovation and open data). The barriers are synthesized into collaboration, cultural, economic, legal, organizational/administrative, and technical categories.

As the results of the study are based on a literature review, the proposed framework so far must be seen as a collection of barriers that appear in the different steps of the complex innovation process. The analysis does not yet include information on the importance of the respective barriers, e.g., the strength and directions of influences on open data-based innovation processes. It needs meta-analyses and additional empirical work to derive insights on possible issues and how they may be related. We also call for more work on combining open data as a promising source for innovation and this specific innovation process with its challenges. The framework can be used as a basis. It shows the variety of barriers that can appear and provides arguments for diving deeper into the topic of analyzing related problem fields. Based on that solutions can be generated for overcoming these barriers and thereby improve the number and quality of open data-driven innovation. The work is, therefore, relevant for both researchers and practitioners, e.g., for open data producers, users, and especially those using open data for innovation. Even though the work focuses on barriers, by shedding light on the advantages of using open data for innovation and pointing at deriving solutions for overcoming the barriers we want to motivate both research and practice to follow up and use data available, share experiences, and conduct empirical studies delivering additional insights.

Acknowledgment This work is based on the research supported by the TWAS-DFG Cooperation Visits Programme for scientists from Sub-Saharan Africa.

References

1. Temiz, S. (2018). Open data and innovation adoption: Lessons from Sweden.
2. Mergel, I., Kleibrink, A., & Sörvik, J. (2018). Open data outcomes: U.S. cities between product and process innovation. *Government Information Quarterly, 35*(4), 622–632. https://doi.org/10.1016/j.giq.2018.09.004
3. Manyika, J., Chui, M., Groves, P., Farrell, D., van Kuiken, S., & Doshi, E. A. (2013). The McKinsey Global Institute. [Online]. www.mckinsey.com/mgi
4. Nikiforova, A. (2021). Smarter open government data for society 5.0: Are your open data smart enough? *Sensors, 21*(15), 5204. https://doi.org/10.3390/s21155204
5. van Hesteren, D., & van Knippenberg, L. (2021). Open data maturity report.
6. United Nations. (2020). E-government survey 2020 digital government in the decade of action for sustainable development with addendum on COVID-19 response.
7. Open Knowledge Foundation. (2022). DataPortals.org. Retrieved August 24, 2022, from https://dataportals.org/
8. Sensor Community. (2022). Sensor community. Retrieved August 29, 2022, from https://sensor.community/en/
9. Kitsios, F., Kamariotou, M., & Grigoroudis, E. (2021). Digital entrepreneurship services evolution: Analysis of quadruple and quintuple helix innovation models for open data ecosystems. *Sustainability (Switzerland), 13*(21), 12183. https://doi.org/10.3390/su132112183
10. Khurshid, M. M., Zakaria, N. H., Rashid, A., Kazmi, R., Shafique, M. N., & Nazir Ahmad, M. (2019). Analyzing diffusion patterns of big open data as policy innovation in public sector. *Computers and Electrical Engineering, 78*, 148–161. https://doi.org/10.1016/j.compeleceng.2019.07.010

11. Janssen, M., Charalabidis, Y., & Zuiderwijk, A. (2012). Benefits, adoption barriers and myths of open data and open government. *Information Systems Management, 29*(4), 258–268. https://doi.org/10.1080/10580530.2012.716740
12. Ruijer, E., & Meijer, A. (2020). Open government data as an innovation process: Lessons from a living lab experiment. *Public Performance and Management Review, 43*(3), 613–635. https://doi.org/10.1080/15309576.2019.1568884
13. Jabareen, Y. (2009). Building a conceptual framework: Philosophy, definitions, and procedure.
14. OECD. (2005). Oslo manual guidelines for collecting and interpreting innovation data.
15. Sørensen, E., & Torfing, J. (2011). Enhancing collaborative innovation in the public sector. *Administration and Society, 43*(8), 842–868. https://doi.org/10.1177/0095399711418768
16. Huijboom, N., & van den Broek, T. (2011). Open data: An international comparison of strategies. *European Journal of ePractice, 12*(1), 4–16.
17. Barry, E., & Bannister, F. (2014). Barriers to open data release: A view from the top. *Information Polity, 19*(1–2), 129–152. https://doi.org/10.3233/IP-140327
18. Ubaldi, B. (2013). Open government data: Towards empirical analysis of open government data initiatives. https://doi.org/10.1787/5k46bj4f03s7-en.
19. Cinar, E., Trott, P., & Simms, C. (2019). A systematic review of barriers to public sector innovation process. *Public Management Review, 21*(2), 264–290. https://doi.org/10.1080/14719037.2018.1473477
20. D'Este, P., Iammarino, S., Savona, M., & von Tunzelmann, N. (2012). What hampers innovation? Revealed barriers versus deterring barriers. *Research Policy, 41*(2), 482–488. https://doi.org/10.1016/j.respol.2011.09.008
21. Meijer, A. (2015). E-governance innovation: Barriers and strategies. *Government Information Quarterly, 32*(2), 198–206. https://doi.org/10.1016/j.giq.2015.01.001
22. Rakšnys, A. V., Valickas, A., & Vanagas, R. (2020). Challenges of creation and implementation of collaborative innovations in public sector organisations. *Public Policy Adm, 19*(1), 9–21. https://doi.org/10.5755/j01.ppaa.19.1.25989
23. Stockstrom, C., & Herstatt, C. (2008). Planning and uncertainty in new product development. *R&D Management, 38*(5), 480–490.

The IoT Based Newborn Room Temperature Control System with Fire Detector (A Case of Mount Meru Hospital)

Juma O. Salim, Ramadhani Sinde, and Shubi Kaijage

1 Introduction

A Newborn Room Temperature Control System is an electronic system that automatically monitors and controls the surrounding temperature of the room. The design intends to stabilize the newborn temperature and prevent hypothermia. Hypothermia is one of the problems facing infants worldwide [1]. As this problem threatens infants, premature and low birth weight (LBW) are the most affected groups [2]. The average temperature of the babies has been recommended to be maintained at 36.5 and 37.5 °C. Below this range, the baby is said to have hypothermia; however, the effect can be classified as mild hypothermia for body temperatures ranging from 36 and 36.4 °C, the temperature ranges from 32 and 35.9 °C falls in moderate hypothermia, and severe hypothermia at a temperature below 32 °C [3]. Thus, hypothermia reduces the body's core temperature, which may occur immediately after birth.

Maintaining a neutral temperature environment is one of the most complex physiological hurdles facing newborns. Care is critical in lowering morbidity and mortality in newborns. Once after birth, hypothermia in newborns occurs by heat exchange from the skin to the environment due to conduction, convection, evaporation, and radiation [4]. Although the hypothermia problem is considered worldwide, low-income countries such as the East African region are among the most affected [5].

According to infant health professionals, all babies should be resuscitated and stabilized in delivery rooms equipped with radiant warmers following birth [4, 5].

J. O. Salim (✉) · R. Sinde · S. Kaijage
School of Computational and Communication Sciences and Engineering, Nelson Mandela African Institution of Science and Technology, Arusha, Tanzania
e-mail: salimj@nm-aist.ac.tz

J. Marx Gómez et al. (eds.), *Smart and Secure Embedded and Mobile Systems*, Progress in IS, https://doi.org/10.1007/978-3-031-56603-5_3

Like other nations in the East African Community (EAC), Tanzania continues to struggle with the effects of infant mortality brought on by various factors, including infection and other causes. At the same time, hypothermia accounts for 19% of newborn deaths [2]. Despite progress, there are still issues with infant room temperature control systems worldwide, such as poor communication between nurses and technicians, a lack of a failsafe system, and high costs. In a case study at Mount Meru Hospital, this project aims to improve the methods undertaken to fight the hypothermia problem. The hospital uses an overhead heater to warm the room. Still, the system lacks control facilities, communication with nurses and technicians, and an alerting unit. Therefore, according to the operator setting, the project aims to regulate the room temperature and humidity by automatically turning the ON/OFF heater when necessary. To do this, the system should be very accurate, as the temperature exceeding the maximum rating (37.5 °C) will result in hyperthermia [6]. The system comprises backup heaters that will turn ON automatically whenever the fault occurs and a fire detection capability that will alert the users (people in a room) about the fire early. It communicates between the system in the controlled room and the nurse's room through wireless communication and sends a short message (SMS) to technicians whenever a fault is detected. Thus, according to the test results, shown on page 8, the system is performing as aspected and hence, can highly reduce the heater fault and prevent infants' hypothermia.

2 Related Works

Thermal reduction in newborns is a complicated natural phenomenon that impacts their development. Using technology breakthroughs, diverse equipment has been designed to prevent and treat neonatal thermal impairment in various infant diseases. The panda warmer is one of the more modern technologies in use today. This infant warming device regulates the temperature of the nearby surrounding to keep them warm [7]. A similar design was implemented by Unicef [8] called the newborn mobile resuscitation table. The system consists of a radiant warmer, overhead light, X-ray slot accessories, and other features to help infants transition from birth to adulthood. These technologies offer thermal support for newborns in the birth room and critically unwell infants who require constant nursing care [8]. Although high-tech equipment such as these are available, they are only designed to be used by one child at a time. Furthermore, these machines are not cost-effective for using healthy term newborns in situations where more than one child must be placed in the same room simultaneously.

Another form of room temperature regulation is free-standing heaters. This type of heater has oil-filled fins that allow heat to travel freely throughout the device, resulting in highly uniform heat distribution across the room [9]. These designs include Manchester-based VonHaus Oil Filled Radiator, Donyer Power Convector Radiator, Dimplex Cadiz, and others [9]. These systems include thermal cut-off and safety switches to facilitate overheat protection for peace of mind [10].

However, the units have no wireless communication between the system and nurses or technicians.

Electrical radiators mounted on the wall are also employed. The designs of such heaters are thin, powerful, and cost-effective, with a maximum output of 2KW and WIFI enabled [10]. However, the system can be intermittently unavailable due to the bandwidth issue. In addition, the WIFI network reliability is not suitable due to weak signal experienced by obstacles resulting in loss of connectivity. Also, these systems are designed to have overheat protection for user safety, but they don't have fire detection capabilities.

Sharmin [11] presented a cutting-edge method and implementation for room temperature management and automatic switching speed electric heater. These circuits rely heavily on temperature and humidity sensors, providing them with the most functionality [11]. However, this system lacks communication, making it impossible for users to access malfunctioning information. Yusarelan [12] created a similar technique to control room temperature. In this work, the system automatically controls the speed of a fan according to changes in the surrounding temperature and can be controlled remotely through a web browser and Apps [12]. However, the system may introduce some running costs due to internet service and can be unreachable when there is no network.

Another system has been created to manage an electric fan and a heater. A PIC microcontroller with an LM35 controlled the room temperature [13]. Another project uses Arduino Uno and LM35 temperature sensors to control the room temperature using the PWM technique [14]. The limitation of these systems is that they seem capable of measuring only the room temperature, not the humidity of the surroundings, and no fire detection.

The author [15] employed the Node MCU ESP8266 WiFi module and the DHT11 temperature and humidity sensor. The project reads environmental parameters and sends data to the cloud. The technology can broadcast the current environmental conditions, and any abnormalities can be updated in the cloud. These systems' limitations are running costs due to internet service, which can be unreached when there is a network breakdown.

The suggested low-power batteries LoRa-based system with a mobile App is used to monitor the temperature and humidity of the surrounding air, spot fires, and regulate how appliances turn on and off [16]. However, the system can drop down due to low battery capacity. A similar approach was created, which made communication between the LoRa Client and LoRa Server using LoRa Dragino 915 MHz module [6].

3 Methodology

This part explains the methodologies and techniques used to accomplish this study. It describes the study area, system requirements, and system development.

3.1 Case Study

The room temperature control system is one of the crucial parts of the maternity sector and the newborn resuscitation room. It helps to keep the room in a convenient condition that maintains the body temperature of pregnant mothers and their children. However, some of the warming equipment in our hospitals lack these control mechanisms and information systems, leading to the unavailability of warming services and low quality of the working environments. This study focused on innovating the current warming system by developing and implementing an IoT-based automatic room temperature control system to ensure a stable warm environment and an excellent information-sharing approach.

The study was conducted in Arusha, Tanzania, at Mount Meru Regional Referral Hospital in conjunction with the biomedical engineering department and maternity ward. Currently, the hospital uses an overhead heater for resuscitation purposes. However, it has been known that there is some problem with the warming system that occurs from time to time due to heater faults. This heater fault causes some trouble for healthcare workers. Observations show that this repeated heater fault results from the heaters having no control mechanism, leading to overwork of the heater. Figure 1 shows the overhead heater used to warm the room for newborns.

Fig. 1 Manual overhead heater that is used to warm the room for newborns

Table 1 Newborn Room Temperature Control System Specifications

	Item	Description
1	Area of the room	$\approx 20m^2$
2	No. of heaters in a room	Two heaters
3	The power rating of each heater	2KW
4	Operating temperature of the room	25–28 °C
5	Normal humidity	30–50%
6	Type of babies nursed in the room	Term babies from normal and cesarean delivered
7	Time takes for the baby to stay in the room	Time is taken for a mother to get her body clean or take medical care after delivery

3.2 *System Requirements*

The room temperature control system has various parameters such as room size, number of heaters, and wattage of each heater. Table 1 shows the essential requirement used in designing the system.

3.3 *System Development*

The system comprises an atmega328 microcontroller, which processes the information it receives from sensors. The temperature and humidity sensor DHT22 measures the surrounding temperature and humidity, while the MQ2 flame sensor detects any fire indication, such as smoke. The system uses a GSM module to establish communication between the system and technicians, specifically when a heater fault arises. The fault detection was made possible with the help of the ACS712 current sensor. Relays as an actuator with ULN2001 relay driver deployed to switch the heaters ON/OFF when necessary. To facilitate the communication between the main control unit and the remote one, the LoRa module has been used. Therefore, the two units wirelessly communicate. Hence, the nurses can see the room condition through a remote unit installed in the nurse room with the help of a system display. If the doctor/nurse needs to set the system operating condition, they will use the keypad attached to the system's central control unit.

4 Results and Discussions

4.1 Proposed System Block Diagram

Figure 2 depicts how different hardware parts used in this system were integrated. The system has two units, the central control unit on the left side, which communicates wirelessly with the remote unit shown on the right side. The main control unit consists of a sensor that takes room information and sends it to CU, which does the needful after processing. The microcontroller instructs the switching unit employed here to turn the ON/OFF the heater. The GSM and LoRA modules provide system communication, while the keypad helps the user set the operating condition of the system.

4.2 Flow Operations of the Developed System

The designed system's flowchart diagram is shown in Fig. 3.

This flow diagram is an algorithm representing the information process for both system activities.

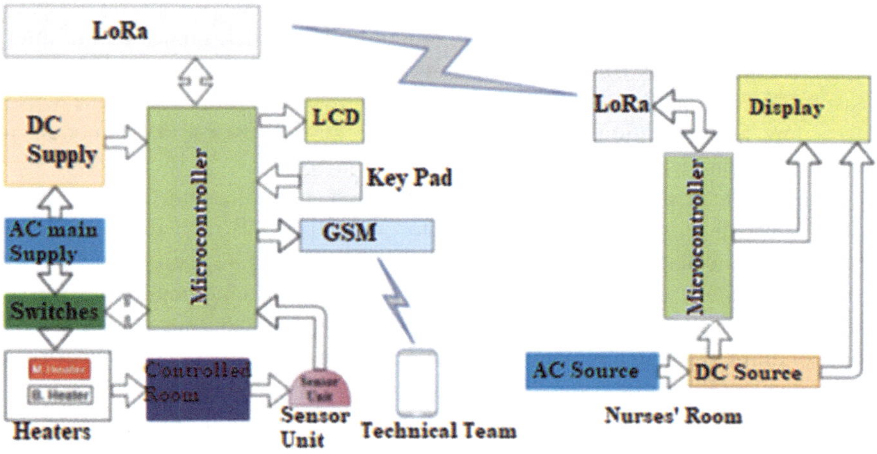

Fig. 2 System block diagram

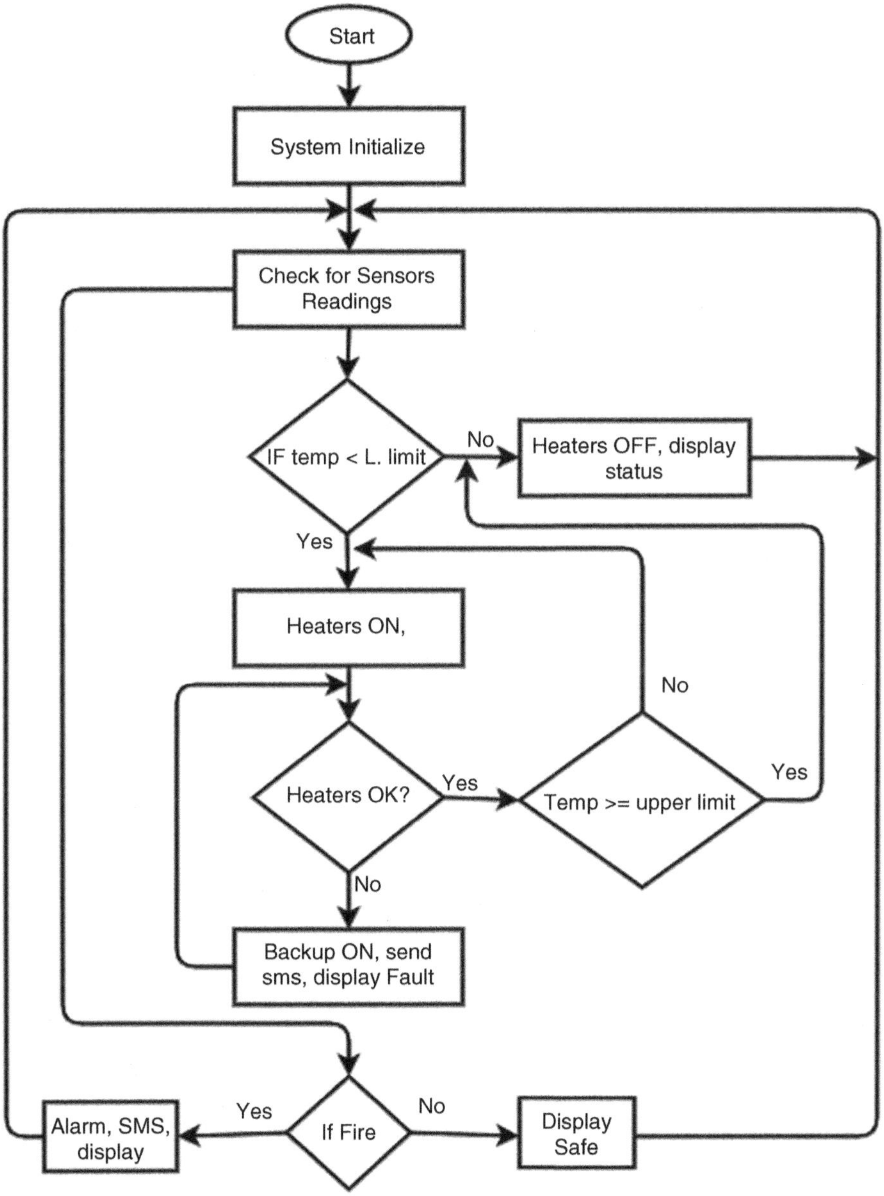

Fig. 3 Flowchart of the developed system

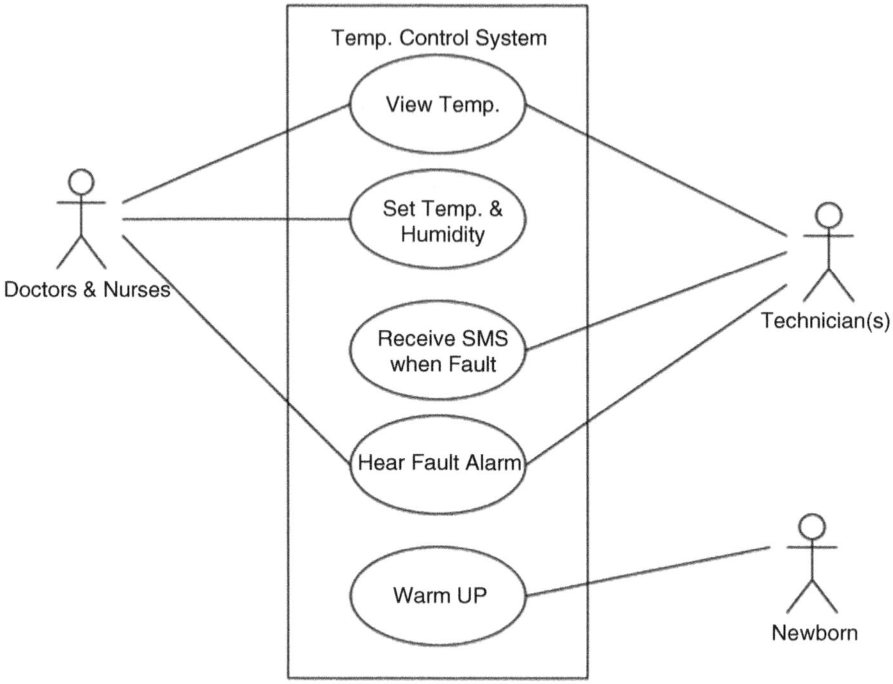

Fig. 4 System use case diagram

4.3 System Use Case Diagram

The designed system comprises many users, such as doctors/nurses, technicians, and newborns. The system use case in Fig. 4 describes how each user can act to/from the system.

4.4 Temperature and Humidity Measurement Test Results

This test was based on measuring the temperature and humidity of the controlled surrounding using the DHT22 temperature and humidity sensor. Different operating temperature ranges were set in a system, and the system was commanded to operate. The results showed that the system passed to measure the proposed operating temperature and humidity accordingly. Figure 5 shows the temperature and humidity in the central control and remote unit displays.

4.5 Communication Unit Test Results

The system comprises the main control unit and a remote unit designed to communicate wirelessly using LoRa technology. This test was to observe if the communication between these two units was adequately established. Every 2 to 5 seconds, the remote unit receives updates from the main control unit. The result showed that the units are communicating correctly, as shown in Fig. 5. In this case, the same information that was designed to share is the very one that was precisely articulated. On the other hand, the system also proved that whenever there is a fault, the GSM network effectively sends an SMS to technicians requesting a repair, as indicated in Fig. 6.

Fig. 5 Load test results system display

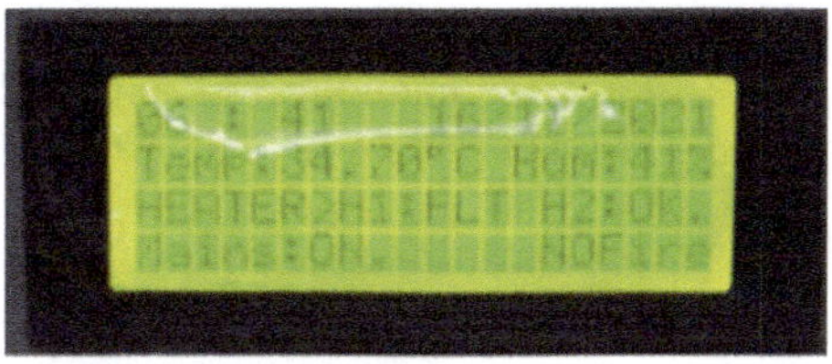

a. Main control unit

b. Remote control unit

Fig. 6 Communication testing results

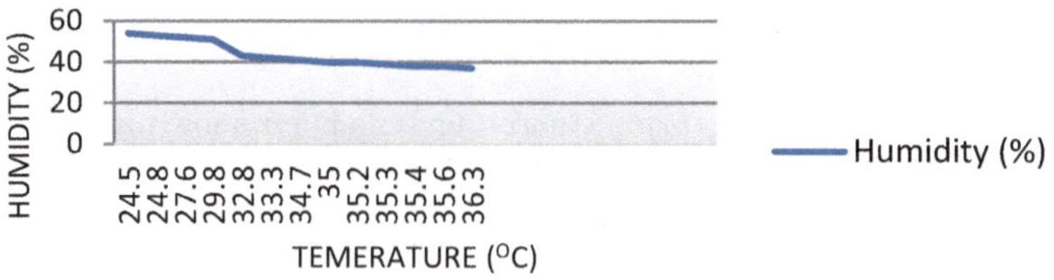

Fig. 7 Room temperature and humidity test results

4.6 Discussion

According to test results, the system conceded to keep the room temperature and humidity within an acceptable range. For example, at room temperatures of 24.5 °C and 36.4 °C, the humidity was 54% and 38%, respectively. The fields seemed to change at other values, as indicated in Fig. 7, which shows the temperature and humidity are moving opposite.

Sharmin [11] categorized the room humidity as 0—to—30% as dry, 31 to 79% as moderate, and 80 to 100% as wet temperature. As the temperature increases, the humidity decreases and vice vassal. According to the organization [16], the optimal thermal condition for a term baby is 25 °C. A room temperature higher than 25 °C is better for maintaining the core temperature of the babies, but this might be uncomfortable for the adults and healthcare workers within the room [17]. Although a room temperature higher than 25 °C is better for the newborn, it should not be too high as it can cause a new baby's hyperthermia [16]. Therefore, for this criterion, the system proved that it passes to maintain the room humidity at a moderate level which is more convenient and safer for human health. On the other hand, the system passed to alert the surrounding whenever there is a fire indication. In addition to that, the communication between the system, nurses, and the technician was well established, see Figs. 5 and 6.

5 Conclusion and Recommendations

5.1 Conclusion

Thermal management for infants is crucial during the first time of delivery since its reduction leads to affecting their health and growth. This study contributes to 'infants' room temperature and humidity control to reduce hypothermia in neonates. The control is achieved by automating the heaters so that they are switched ON/OFF only at specified conditions. That is, when the temperature falls to 25 °C and when it raised above 28 °C respectively while still maintaining humidity at a preferred value. By doing so, the system reduces the working time of the heater and thus avoids frequent heater faults. Due to different tests, the developed system proved that it could minimize the problems and issues facing the existing systems. As the method comprises a communication facility, it provides an instant call for repair to technicians when a fault occurs, and can reduce the problem that faced the nurses from the current system. The system can be installed in any room, and its capacity is four heaters, each having a maximum power rating of 2000 W.

Furthermore, as fire disaster is still a challenge in society, the system is comprised of early fire detection and warning mechanism which can recognize the presence of fire and alerts the surrounding peoples at an early stage to avoid unnecessary injuries and improves life assurance. The system is user-friendly and contains no complications. The following issues were addressed in this effort in response to the limitations of the existing systems:

- The designed system can rapidly identify a malfunction and turn ON the backup heater to keep the infant safe.
- It keeps the temperature and humidity within specified conditions set by the user.
- It turns off the heater when the maximum set temperature is reached to prevent infants with hyperthermia as well as skin effect (burn).
- It can call for repair to technicians once the failure occurs.
- It provides instant awareness to nurses through the remote unit utilizing wireless communication.
- It reduces the fault rates and hence increased reliability.

5.2 Recommendations

The utilization of the created system will successfully enhance the warming system's current approach. The following are the suggestions for managing neonatal room temperature:

- To use this automated system as it is highly reliable and can control humidity and temperature in a space.
- In case of management wants to change the heater types, the system will be able to handle any kind with a power rating within 2KW. For those exceeding 2KW, the technical team should consider changing only the relays or may use a solenoid corresponding to that heater's current rating.
- The scope of this work didn't provide a mobile app for the developed system, so it is recommended that someone can further extend the system by creating a mobile app.

References

1. Yip, W. Y., et al. (2017). *A quality improvement project to reduce hypothermia in preterm infants on admission to the neonatal intensive care unit., 29*(7), 922–928.
2. Winkler, L. A., et al. (2020). *A multi-year analysis of kangaroo mother care outcomes in low birth weight babies at a Nyakahanga Hospital in rural Tanzania., 20*(1), 498–508.
3. Organization, W.H. Thermal control of the newborn: A practical guide. 1993. *World health organization.*
4. Lin, D., Y. Guo, and Q.J.Z.y.L.q.x.z.z.C.J.o.M.I. Zhu, Research and Application of Quality Inspection Information System in Medical Device Manufacturers. 2021. 45(1): p. 17–21.
5. Jia, Y. S., et al. (2013). Effect of delivery room temperature on the admission temperature of premature infants: A randomized controlled trial. *Journal of Perinatology, 33*(4), 264–267.
6. Organization, W.H. (1997). *Thermal protection of the newborn: A practical guide.* World Health Organization.
7. Solutions, H. PANDA WARMER. 2021.; Available from: http://healthsolutions.com.ph/shop/panda-warmer/.
8. Unicef. Resuscitation & Anaesthesiology Equipment 2018; Available from: https://supply.unicef.org/s0002035.html.
9. HeatingForce. 7 Best Free Standing Electric Radiators (Reviews) in 2021. 2020 1 July, 2020; Available from: https://heatingforce.co.uk/blog/free-standing-electric-radiators/.
10. highreview. THE 17 BEST ELECTRIC RADIATORS AND CENTRAL HEATING OPTIONS FOR 2021. 2020 15 July; Available from: https://highreviews.co.uk/best-electric-radiators/.
11. Sharmin, F., et al. (2019). Humidity based automated room temperature controller using IoT. In *In 2019 third international conference on I-SMAC (IoT in social, Mobile, analytics and cloud)* (p. I-SMAC). IEEE.
12. Yusarelan, M., et al. (2020). IoT based temperature control for smart mosque. In *IOP conference series: Materials science and engineering*. IOP Publishing.
13. Zungeru, A. M., et al. (2018). *Design and simulation of an automatic room heater control system., 4*(6), e00655.
14. Junizan, N. A., et al. (2019). *Design and implementation of automatic room temperature controlled fan using Arduino uno and LM35 heat sensor., 1*(2), 8–14.
15. Razali, M. A. A., et al. (2020). A ThingSpeak IoT on real time room condition monitoring system. In *In 2020 IEEE international conference on automatic control and intelligent systems (I2CACIS)*. IEEE.
16. Ahsan, M., et al. (2021). *Smart Monitoring and Controlling of Appliances Using LoRa Based IoT System., 5*(1), 17.
17. Dubos, C., et al. (2020). *The newborn infant's thermal environment in the delivery room when skin-to-skin care has to be interrupted.*, 1–7.

A Web-Based Human Resource Management System with Machine Learning Techniques

A Case Study of the Inter-University Council for East Africa (IUCEA)

Gideon Muleme, Shubi Kaijage, and Ben Ruhinda

1 Introduction

Human Resources Management (HRM) is a key factor in ensuring that a company achieves its strategic objectives through maximization of employee performance. It involves tactical approaches to managing employees in an organization or business entity effectively and efficiently so that they can gain a competitive edge over its competitors [1]. Furthermore, employees' experience can be enhanced while also bolstering organizational operations with effective HRM policies in place.

HRM is the centre of any business as without it, firms wouldn't be able to effectively attract and retain talent, grow and improve, or maintain an acceptable workplace environment [2]. Manual HR operations and procedures result in wastage of time spent in carrying out monotonous and less productive repetitive tasks, increased risk of data inaccuracies, and growing cases of non-compliance.

Due to the growing use of technology in company operations across the globe, Human Resources (HR) activities are becoming more automated and many enterprises have opted to integrate as well as streamline their HR operations via various digital platforms [3]. This has improved the efficiency of HR departments by releasing its personnel from time-consuming manual tasks and letting them to focus on more sophisticated responsibilities such as strategy formulation and decision making [4].

G. Muleme (✉) · S. Kaijage
School of Computational and Communication Science and Engineering (CoCSE), Nelson Mandela African Institution of Science and Technology (NM-AIST), Arusha, Tanzania
e-mail: mulemeg@nm-aist.ac.tz; shubi.kaijage@nm-aist.ac.tz

B. Ruhinda
Department of Information, Communication and Technology (ICT), The Inter-University Council for East Africa (IUCEA), Kampala, Uganda
e-mail: bruhinda@iucea.org

J. Marx Gómez et al. (eds.), *Smart and Secure Embedded and Mobile Systems*,
Progress in IS, https://doi.org/10.1007/978-3-031-56603-5_4

Application of machine learning in some of the HR processes such as recruitment, employee attrition detection, talent management doesn't only minimize time wastage and human errors through elimination of loads of paperwork but also increases internal productivity and operating effectiveness as a result of a more efficient HR experience for both the institution and employees.

2 Literature Review

There are a number of existing works in relation to a web-based human resource management system with machine learning techniques and a few of them are described below.

Shukur et al. [5] developed an efficient paperless-based human resource management system for a university that streamlines organizational procedures, eliminates challenges of a paper-based system, saves time and cost as well as improves the quality of services. The system was developed using the Laravel framework and is made up of 14 modules that provide services grouped in four categories i.e., applicant services e.g., online recruitment, staff services e.g., registration, annual premium, leave management, payroll management, institution and presidency services e.g., post and statistics, university services e.g., post and statistics.

The creation of a centralized human resource information system was advocated by Jeffrey F. Papa [6]. The Human Resource Information System, the Fingerprint Attendance System, and the Payroll Alert System were among the three (3) key application software or modules. In the HR office, the Human Resource Information System is utilized to process employee records. Employees' time-in and time-out for attendance are recorded using the Fingerprint Attendance System. The Payroll Alert System is used to remind accounting personnel to generate payroll on time.

Jawad [7] proposed a human resource management system that comprises of a Graphical User Interface (GUI) and a database with its main functionality as management of employee data such as registration, salary and promotions. The system was tested in a typical working environment and exhibited a high level of performance as well as efficiency in regards to data storage and control.

Faliagka & Ramantas [8] described a machine learning approach for assessing job candidates in online recruitment platforms. The system extracts a set of unbiased criteria from the candidates' LinkedIn profiles and uses linguistics analysis to infer personality traits from their blog posts. Furthermore, the system was deployed in a real-world recruitment scenario and performed more consistently in comparison with the human recruiters.

Mgbeafulike & Nnaemeka [9] proposed an e-HRM, biometric authentication and verification system. This software allows the administrator to make changes to employees, add new ones, transfer, promote, and fire them. Each employee in the database is given a biometric identity number. To authenticate identification, authentication systems collect information about unique human attributes and compare it to previously submitted data. Most significantly, the employer can assign tasks to employees and track their progress in order to maintain track of their performance. The system was limited in terms of functionality, and it lacked automated notifications like emails for onboarding new employees, leave approval, and so on.

Jagan Mohan Reddy et al. [10] presents a machine learning model that predicts job applicants that are likely to join a company once the entire recruitment process is complete. The model utilizes several qualitative as well as quantitative attributes such as work experience, age, current salary, gender for prediction and ensures time and cost savings by not selecting candidates that are likely not join the firm even if they are successful in the job application.

Based on the related work, most of the existing HR management systems don't incorporate machine learning in their operations. A number of machine learning applications to HR management exist but majority of them operate as stand-alone modules and are not integrated in the centralized HR management systems. Furthermore, most of the models employed in these systems are not applicable in the African context.

3 System Design

The system was designed on the basis of the conceptual framework in the Fig. 1 where requirements from stakeholders guided the development of the system.

The system consists of six modules as detailed in the block diagram in Fig. 2.

4 System Development

The case study of the research was the IUCEA in Kampala, Uganda. The system comprises of a web application with six core HRM modules and machine learning models for the recruitment module as detailed below.

4.1 Web Application

This system component incorporates six core HRM modules i.e., employment management, recruitment, employment onboarding and administration, payroll management and reporting along with a centralized dashboard. The User Interface (UI) of the web application was developed using Hyper Text Mark Language (HTML) and was styled using Cascading Style Sheets (CSS) as well as Bootstrap. The backend logic of the web application was developed using the open-source PHP-based CodeIgniter framework and JavaScript. The XAMPP server was

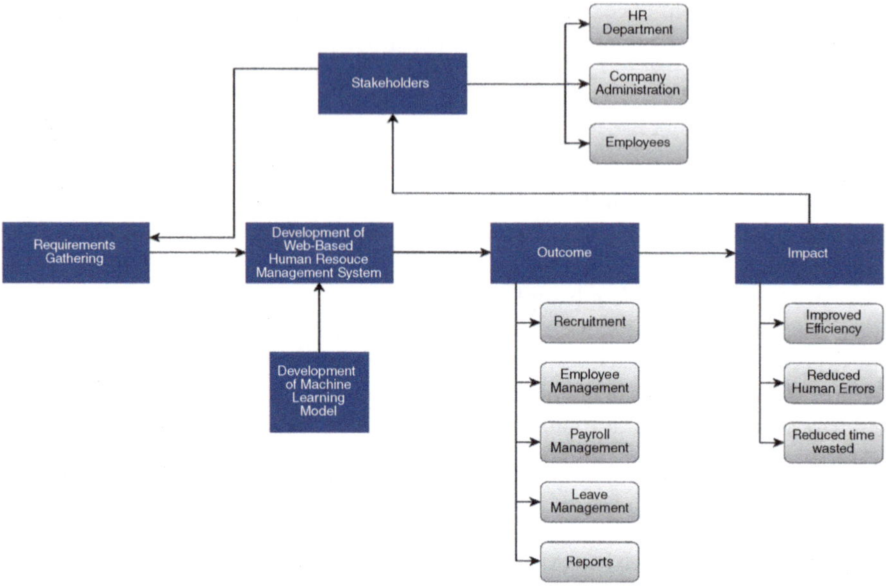

Fig. 1 Conceptual framework illustrating the relationships between different system variables

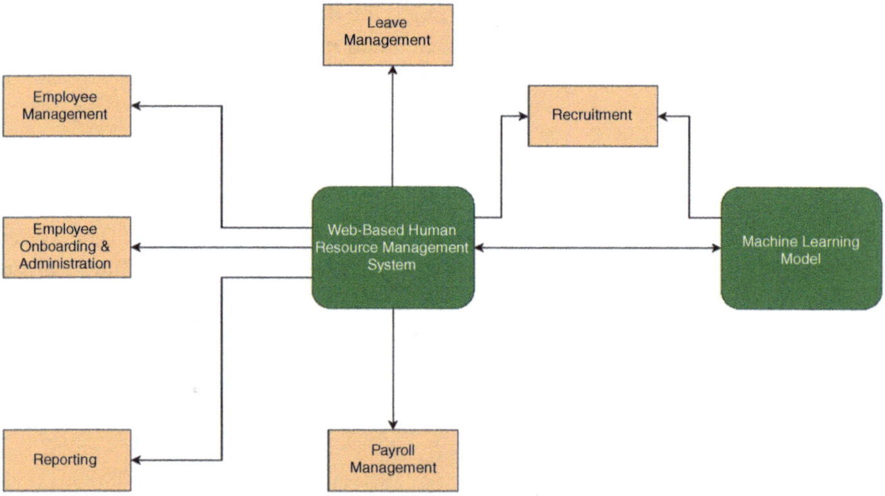

Fig. 2 Block diagram illustrating the system modules

employed as the web server while the MySQL database was utilized for data storage and retrieval.

4.1.1 Employee Management

The module provides employees access to personal information, work and income history, and leave requests. It keeps all of the employees' data linked to the main record, which simplifies tracking and reporting.

4.1.2 Recruitment

The recruitment module facilitates submission of online job applications. Furthermore, it utilizes the developed machine learning models to automatically sort the submitted job applications based on pre-defined job requirements. The recruitment prediction system as illustrated in Fig. 3 takes input in form of a CSV file and outputs a CSV file with the predicted labels.

4.1.3 Employment Onboarding and Administration

This module enables HR to onboard employees as well as send them various essential company communication through automated email updates so as to keep them in sync with the daily operations of the organization.

4.1.4 Payroll Management

The payroll management module provides accurate financial records of employees with details of their salaries, incentives, benefits, bonuses, deductions, and net pay.

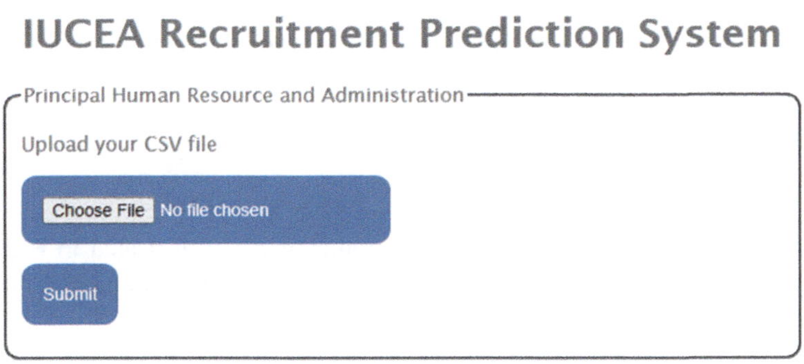

Fig. 3 Recruitment prediction UI

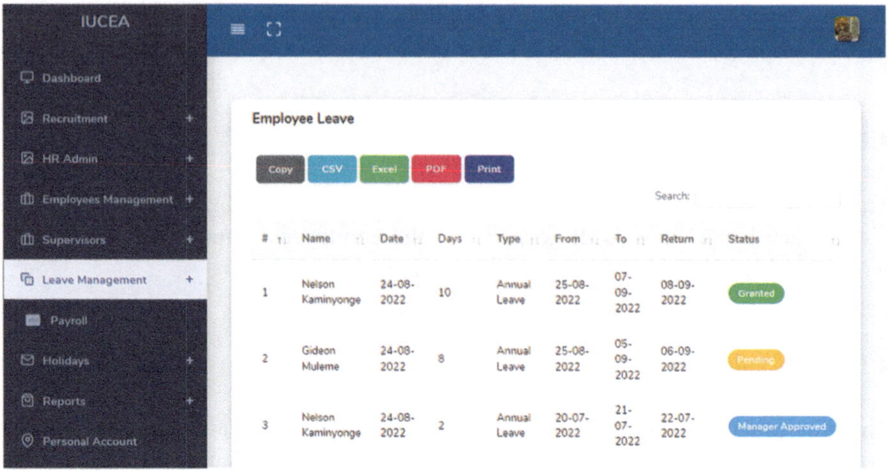

Fig. 4 Leave management module UI

It also streamlines company financial workflows and simplifies payroll processes for the employer.

4.1.5 Leave Management

This module aids in management of leave days for both the HR department and the employees as depicted in Fig. 4. It allows employees to request leave and supervisors as well as managers to approve requests made by employees. In addition, it provides notifications in regards to the response towards each employee leave request.

4.1.6 Reporting

This module enables the HR personnel to generate customized reports about the existing data from the other modules in three different formats i.e., pdf, csv and excel. It also allows printing of the generated reports directly.

4.1.7 Dashboard

This provides data summarizations and visualizations as illustrated in Fig. 5 that provide quick insights into vast amounts of HR data thereby aiding HR managers and admins in making well-informed decisions.

Fig. 5 Web application dashboard

4.2 *Machine Learning*

This system component involved data acquisition, synthetic data generation, data labelling, data preprocessing, modelling and evaluation.

4.2.1 Data Acquisition

An existing dataset was acquired from the IUCEA HR department. It was based on applications from three job positions i.e., executive secretary, principal human resources and administration and principal internal auditor. The data was inspected and it consisted of 18 features (columns) and 98 observations (rows). The features that were not relevant to the developing the machine learning models were dropped. 12 features were dropped and only 6 features were retained. The data obtained from the HR department was insufficient for machine learning and therefore there was need to generate synthetic data that mimics the original dataset that would be used for training of the machine learning models.

4.2.2 Synthetic Data Generation

The preprocessed data from the HR department was divided into 3 datasets based on the job position being applied for i.e., executive secretary, principal human resources and administration and principal internal auditor. Respective synthetic datasets with 11,200 observations were generated using the DataSynthesizer module. The details of the datasets are summarized in Table 1.

Table 1 Dataset description

S/N	Feature	No of Observations
1	Highest level of education	11,200
2	Job position	11,200
3	Professional course	11,200
4	Field of qualification	11,200
5	Years of experience	11,200
6	Previous job position	11,200
7	Label	11,200

4.2.3 Data Labelling

The generated synthetic data was labelled based on the different IUCEA predefined job requirements and with the help of expertise insights from the Human Resources Personnel. This involved assigning each job application a rating of 0 for those that don't qualify for the job and 1 for those that qualified for the job.

4.2.4 Data Preprocessing

Each dataset was inspected and was found to consist of 7 features (columns) and 11,200 observations (rows). The features were Highest Level of Education, Job Position being Applied for, Professional Course, Field of Qualification, Years of Experience, Previous Job Position and Label. The data was checked for missing data and there were missing values for the Professional course feature for all the three datasets i.e., 3832 for the principal internal auditor dataset, 582 for the principal human resources and administration dataset and 7339 for the executive secretary dataset. The missing values were replaced with 0 s. Other features/columns were found to have no missing values in all the three datasets.

4.2.5 Exploratory Data Analysis

More insight about each dataset was obtained through visualization using seaborn and matplotlib libraries. Focus was placed on individual feature distributions as well as correlation of exploratory features and target feature.

4.2.6 Modelling

Data Reduction

Job Position being Applied for, Previous Job Position and Label features were dropped for the principal human resources and administration and principal internal auditor datasets while Job Position being Applied for, Professional Course, Field of

Qualification, and Label features were dropped for the executive secretary dataset. The dropped features were found not to be relevant for training of the respective models. This is because they were not defined in the required job requirements for the respective job positions and therefore would not influence the model outcome to a larger extent.

Feature Engineering/Data Transformation

Categorical features i.e., Highest Level of Education, Professional Course, Field of Qualification, Previous Job Position were encoded using the pandas get dummies function. Categorical encoding converted the categorical features to numeric values that the models can work with.

Model Training

Highest Level of Education, Professional Course, Field of Qualification, Years of Experience were selected as the exploratory features and Label as the target feature for the principal human resources and administration and principal internal auditor model. Highest Level of Education, Years of Experience and Previous Job Position were selected as the exploratory features and Label as the target feature for the executive secretary model. The three datasets were split into train and test datasets in a ratio of 0.7 to 0.3 respectively. Three classification algorithms i.e., Random Forests, Support Vector Machine (SVM) and Logistic Regression algorithms were employed in the training of the models.

4.2.7 Evaluation

The performance of each algorithm was evaluated based on accuracy, log loss and confusion matrix metrics for each trained model when tested on unseen test data as illustrated in Tables 2, 3 and 4;

Table 2 Performance evaluation of the algorithms for the principal internal auditor job position

Metrics	Logistic Regression	Random Forests	SVM
Accuracy	94.81	98.43	98.58
Log loss	1.79	0.54	0.49
Confusion matrix	[[6030 315][15 0]]	[[6014 69][31 246]]	[[6045 90][0 225]]

Table 3 Performance evaluation of the algorithms for the executive secretary job position

Metrics	Logistic Regression	Random Forests	SVM
Accuracy	99.70	99.98	99.70
Log loss	0.10	0.01	0.10
Confusion matrix	[[6132 1][18 209]]	[[6150 1][0 209]]	[[6132 1][18 209]]

Table 4 Performance evaluation of the algorithms for the principal human resource and administration job position

Metrics	Logistic Regression	Random Forests	SVM
Accuracy	92.01	98.74	98.74
Log loss	2.76	0.43	0.43
Confusion matrix	[[5852 508][0 0]]	[[5846 74][6 434]]	[[5846 74][6 434]]

5 Conclusion

HRM is a very critical component of any company handling various important aspects such as recruitment, professional growth of employees, creation of a suitable work environment. In this paper we have described a web-based human resource management system with machine learning techniques. The system streamlines HR processes of recruitment, employee onboarding and administration, employee management, payroll management, leave management and reporting. This will in turn reduce time wasted in doing monotonous manual tasks as well minimize human errors thus enhancing the overall efficiency of the HR department. Additionally, utilization of machine learning in the recruitment process will assist in the timely and fair sieving of qualified candidates from a pool of job applications.

References

1. Zeebaree, S. R. M., Shukur, H. M., & Hussan, B. K. (2019). Human resource management systems for enterprise organizations: A review. *Periodicals of Engineering and Natural Sciences, 7*(2). https://doi.org/10.21533/pen.v7i2.428
2. What Is HRIS? System, Model, and Application | Spiceworks," Spiceworks, [Online]. Available: https://www.spiceworks.com/hr/performance-management/articles/what-is-hris/. [Accessed 22 March 2022].
3. S. Kim, Y. Wang, and C. Boon, "Sixty years of research on technology and human resource management: Looking back and looking forward," Hum Resour Manage, vol. 60, no. 1, 2021, doi: https://doi.org/10.1002/hrm.22049.
4. T. V. Bondarouk and H. Ruël, "Human resource management via the web: Opportunities and threats," in Webist 2007 - 3rd international conference on web information systems and technologies, proceedings, 2007, vol. SEBEG, no. EL/-. doi: https://doi.org/10.5220/0001290301790187.
5. Shukur, H. M., Zeebaree, S. R. M., Zebari, R. R., Hussan, B. K., Jader, O. H., & Haji, L. M. (2021). Design and implementation of electronic Enterprise University human resource management system. *Journal of Physics: Conference Series, 1804, no. 1*. https://doi.org/10.1088/1742-6596/1804/1/012058

6. J. F. Papa, "Development of a Centralized Human Resource Information System of Cavite State University," Asia Pacific Journal of Multidisciplinary Research, vol. 4, no. 3, 2016.
7. W. K. Jawad, "Design and Implementation of E-Human Resource Management," International Journal of Scientific Research and Engineering Development, vol. 7, 2020.
8. E. Faliagka and K. Ramantas, "Application of machine learning algorithms to an online recruitment system," 2012.
9. Ike, M., & Frances, N. (2020). Design and implementation of a biometric authentication for a web based human resource system. *COOU Journal of Physical Sciences, 3*(1), 7.
10. D. Jagan Mohan Reddy, S. Regella, and S. R. Seelam, "Recruitment prediction using machine learning," 2020. doi: 10.1109/ICCCS49678.2020.9276955.

A Digital Twin Approach and Challenges for Real-Time Automated Surface-Drip Irrigation Monitoring: A Case of Arusha Tanzania

Joseph Wangere, Ramadhani Sinde, Mussa Ally, and Omary Mbwambo

1 Introduction

Agriculture is pivotal as a backbone of food security. It dominates socio-economic activities in third-world countries among continents such as Africa, that face income disparities emanating from overpopulation and climate change [1]. An upward trajectory in global population in recent years has worsened the situation of food insecurity. An increase in hunger prevalence was reported in 2019 by 60 million more people compared to 2014 [2]. Changes in climate due to factors such as global warming have resulted in a shift toward rainfall inconsistencies. Studies reveal that drought will be more hazardous in the coming days [3]. Therefore, there is a need for climate-smart agricultural methods to ensure continuous yield despite harsh climate [4]. Irrigation is among the potential methods for combatting water scarcity. Irrigation entails artificial application of water to plants using a network of pipes, valves, pumps, and any other relevant technology. Manual irrigation systems are less efficient due to high water consumption per square meter compared to their automatic counterparts [5].

There has been ongoing research in recent years regarding automation of irrigation processes. Application of Internet of Things (IoT) has become a hot topic in this subject globally. IoT describes a blend of sensing devices, connectivity media, data storage, and visualization platforms [6].

In this epoch of the fourth industrial revolution (4IR), wireless sensor networks have gained global popularity from the development of infinitesimal, low-cost sen-

J. Wangere (✉) · R. Sinde · M. Ally
Nelson Mandela African Institution of Science and Technology, Arusha, Tanzania
e-mail: wangerej@nm-aist.ac.tz; ramadhani.sinde@nm-aist.ac.tz; mussa.ally@nm-aist.ac.tz

O. Mbwambo
World Vegetable Center, Arusha, Tanzania
e-mail: omary.mbwambo@worldveg.org

J. Marx Gómez et al. (eds.), *Smart and Secure Embedded and Mobile Systems*, Progress in IS, https://doi.org/10.1007/978-3-031-56603-5_5

sors that can detect, and transmit desired parameter data while occupying minimum space on circuit boards, with low power requirements due to their sleep-mode capabilities. Furthermore, advanced algorithms have been proven for minimizing the energy consumption of these wireless sensor networks while enhancing their lifetime with minimal interruptions [7].

There are different irrigation methods depending on factors such as the size of land, type of crop, availability of resources, and the type of soil. Surface irrigation, drip irrigation, and sprinkler irrigation represent the common methods. Drip is the most preferred following its water-saving capabilities and efficiency as it involves the application of water directly at the crop root zone [8].

Farmers in low-income countries in Africa such as Tanzania rely on manual irrigation systems to supplement the inadequacies in sporadic rainfall patterns. In isolated cases, pressurized systems are applied, where water is pumped from reservoirs using diesel or electric pumps and channeled to irrigation zones. Each irrigation zone is controlled by gate valves that are manually operated.

These manual operations are tedious and inefficient. A lot of time is spent moving across the farm locating valves in order to switch them on or off. Additionally, there lacks a formal method of aggregating data regarding amount of water utilized in irrigation as well as an accurate way of meeting crop water demands. Lack of data-driven methodologies results in erroneous irrigation, causing over- or under-irrigation. Over-irrigation potentially damages crops, while at the same time, water which is a valuable natural resource is wasted. Figure 1 represents different irrigation zones around Arusha, most of which are manual based.

2 Related Works

Humanity is dependent on nutrients to thrive and lead healthy lives. Nutrients are obtained from food substances. Both human beings and animals rely on plant foods to obtain these necessary nutrients directly or indirectly, hence the need to uphold farming, while conserving natural resources such as water.

Irrigation can be classified as an efficient attempt to conserve water resources [10]. There are different factors that determine plant water requirements and irrigation methods to use. Such include plant type, soil properties, depth of water table, plant growth stage, climatic conditions, availability of funds, skilled labor, and the availability of water [11–13].

Irrigation automation systems have been suggested by different researchers. Key technologies for irrigation automation revolve around the use of the Internet of Things, Wireless Sensor Networks, Artificial Intelligence, and Embedded Systems.

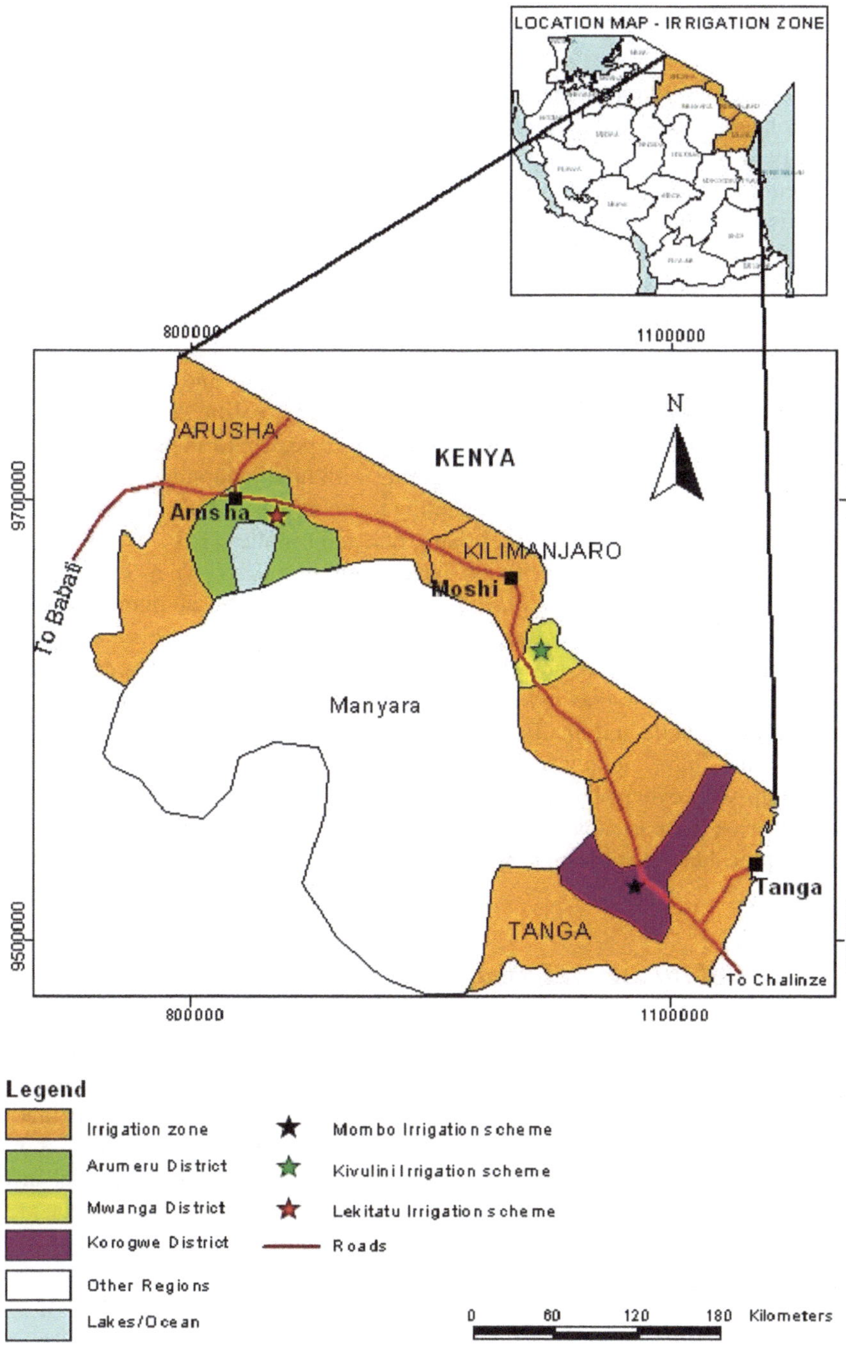

Fig. 1 Irrigation zones around Arusha [9]

2.1 Digital Twins

The concept of digital twins is an upcoming trend from the fourth industrial revolution and is expected to dominate the projected fifth industrial revolution (5IR). Digital twin is a virtual model of a complex physical phenomenon, which depicts that phenomenon's interaction and communication with its environment. Through digital twins, human beings can interact with physical or industrial environments virtually as though they were interacting with them physically. Data is generated that can give valuable insight regarding the physical phenomena under observation, and can be fed back into the system as feedback in a loop to generate predictions that can facilitate autonomy [14]. Industry 4.0 was characterized by industrial process improvement using automation, cyber-physical systems, and interconnectivity-enabling technologies such as Internet of Things and Artificial intelligence. The fifth industrial revolution on the other hand is expected to capitalize on human expert creativity and how they will collaborate with intelligent machines to enhance efficiency. Digital twin is among the enabling technologies of Industry 5.0, including other key technologies such as blockchain, 6G, and robotics [15].

Different types of Digital Twins have been proposed. They can either be imaginary, monitoring Digital Twin, predictive, prescriptive, autonomous, or recollection [16]. Scientific literature is already pointing to the use of digital twin frameworks in smart farms, however, missing out on the crucial component of data transmission using low-power wireless communication technologies from the farm to a coordinator node and finally to the cloud [17].

Researchers have already found useful applications of digital twin technologies to come up with cyber-physical systems that simulate the actual behavior of real-time scenarios such as canals, thus providing insights regarding flooding as well as hydrographical characteristics [18].

2.2 State of the Art in Irrigation Automation

Conventional irrigation methods have received criticism over concerns of inefficiency in terms of time and water wastage. Following recent rapid technological evolution, many researchers are formulating mechanisms for automating irrigation. Automatic drip irrigation has exhibited potential for minimizing water consumption in irrigated fields by up to 15%. Soil moisture sensors have been crucial in the process of automating irrigation, by measuring the real-time water content in the soil and relaying the data to a central controller that initiates the process of applying water [19].

Different research works and proof of concept systems have been developed to automate irrigation for different crops. To achieve optimum results, a variety of technologies have been proposed. These range from Wireless Sensor Networks (WSNs), Internet of Things (IoT), Unmanned Aerial Vehicles (UAV), Artificial

Table 1 Comparison of wireless communication technologies used for smart irrigation

Reference	Technology	Strengths	Limitations
[21]	Sigfox	Small packet size (12 bytes),	Limited number of messages for uplink and downlink
[22]	Narrowband IoT	Deep coverage, minimal energy consumption, less complex, supports numerous connections	Interference with LTE, restricted coverage in rural regions, high latency hence unsuitable for real-time applications
[23]	LoRA, LoRaWAN	Long distance transmission	Poor response if gateway is indoor while end-node is outdoors
[24]	ZigBee	Offers security through data encryption, mesh capabilities, energy efficiency using TDMA and CSMA, support for multiple nodes per network	Short outdoor range compared to LoRa, low transmission rate
[25]	Wi-Fi	Bandwidth is high, high transmission rate, non-line-of-sight transmission requirements, longer transmission distance compared to ZigBee	Energy consumption is high due to the increased transmission rate

Intelligence (AI) as well as cloud computing [20]. Emerging low-power wireless communication technologies for WSNs range from ZigBee, Long-Range wide area networks (LoRa WAN), Narrow-band IoT (NB-IoT), Sigfox, Bluetooth Low Energy (BLE) as well as radio frequency (RF) communication as presented in Table 1.

An agricultural smart system for irrigation using the drip method was proposed in a different study. The primary operation involved detecting moisture content in the soil and activating water supply to the soil as per the requirements. The technology used included an ATmega328 microcontroller, GSM module, humidity sensors as well as soil-moisture sensor. However, in this work, remote data processing component was missing as it was a purely SMS-based system. There was no provision for accessing real-time or historical moisture-related data [26].

In a study to review how varied technologies of smart irrigation are applied in different research areas such as precision irrigation control models, it was discovered that farmers perceive these technologies as utilities for improving irrigation efficiency. The most desirable features for farmers range from automated notifications, control using hand-held devices, integrating irrigation systems with weather forecasting and alerts as well as the use of soil moisture sensors and model tools for gathering crop water requirements [27].

Meshed wireless sensor networks using radio frequency modules such as nRF24L01 have been suggested for collecting soil moisture data and actuating pumps. However, these radio modules have a higher power consumption compared to other wireless technologies such as ZigBee due to lack of support for sleep mode, making them unsuitable for mesh wireless sensor networks [28].

There are proposals as to what parameters are important to monitor in order to automate irrigation systems. They include soil data, forecasting, plant data, water as well as weather. Soil moisture still holds a high number of publications globally, being the most monitored parameter [29]. A framework has been proposed for utilizing digital twins in managing pressurized irrigation systems, to enhance water efficiency through limiting overflow and monitoring water delivery to farmers [30]. However, critical details regarding low-power wireless communication technologies for providing near real-time data have not been addressed.

2.2.1 Observation

This review investigated the latest trends in irrigation automation from published research work. So far, from the work reviewed, researchers do not seem to acknowledge the capabilities of digital twin technology in combining all the sophisticated smart systems to create virtual experiences that can allow for remote monitoring as well as autonomous operation of irrigation systems. There is little to no exploitation of this new technology in harnessing its capabilities for automating and monitoring irrigation [31], which forms the basis of this study.

3 Materials and Methods

3.1 Materials

This section is an outline of the hardware selected for the development of the proposed system. Table 2 represents the different hardware components and their respective model numbers where applicable.

3.1.1 Software

An open-source approach is proposed for development of the digital twin in this study. Raspberry pi operating system is selected for the coordinator node. Node-red is proposed for visual presentation of flows for the users on a dashboard. Circuit design tools for hardware development include fritzing for first-level prototypes and KiCad for advanced schematic layout and printed circuit board production. XCTU software is recommended for configuring the XBee modules in API mode, which supports mesh networks as opposed to AP mode which is not scalable as it is suitable for peer-to-peer communication between two nodes only.

Table 2 Hardware selection

Component	Model
Soil moisture sensor	ICStation
Soil temperature sensor	DS18B20
Ambient temperature humidity sensor	AM2303
Rainfall sensor	Cytron
UV sensor	GY-ML8511
Ball valve	½" DN15 Brass Motorized Ball Valve
Water pump	Seaflo 750GPH
Mini-solar panels	Generic 6 watts
Rechargeable battery	Li-ion
Water flow sensor	YFS-201
ZigBee radio modules	XBee S2C Pro
Raspberry pi	4 model B
Sensor node MCU	STM32F103C8T6
LCD display	2004 Liquid Crystal Display
I2C display adapter	PCF8574

3.2 System Development Methodology

An agile approach has been selected for the development of the proposed system. The extreme programming method of agile is proposed due to its focus on high-quality software as well as flexibility in adapting to changing requirements, giving room for collaboration with intended customers throughout the iterations [32]. Agile is growing as a preferential project management standard in the technology ecosystem. This can be attributed to reduced development cycle times, early release of a usable product and low risk [33].

4 Results and Discussion

4.1 Results

4.1.1 Proposed Design

This study proposes the design of a digital twin, based on a wireless sensor network using XBee modules for field sensor nodes. These leverage the high computing power of an STM32F103C8T6 module running on an ARM Cortex-M3 processor to collect soil and weather data, and further relay this to a Raspberry Pi 4 minicomputer running ARM Cortex-A72 for processing. Node-red software platform is proposed for creating visual flows that a user can interact with via a graphical user interface locally or remotely. This virtual experience allows users to bypass automatic pump

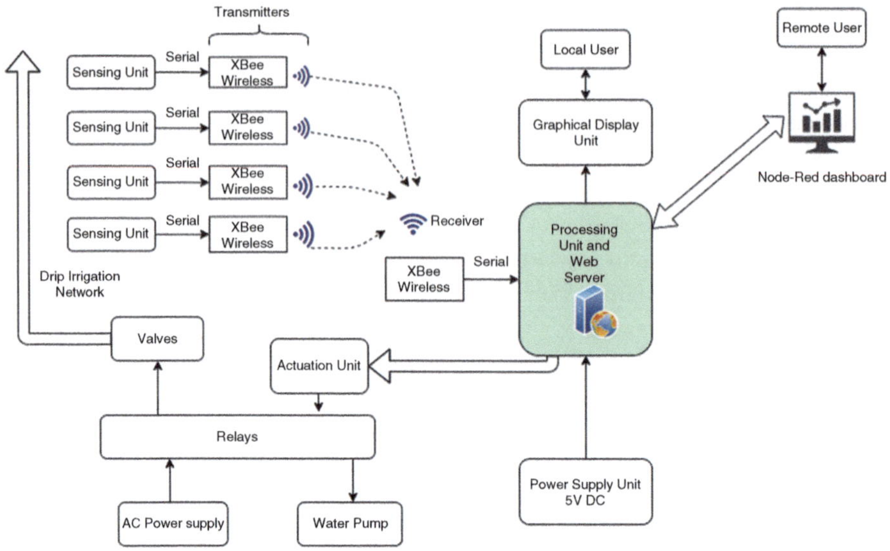

Fig. 2 Conceptual design

and valve operations and control them remotely on a case-by-case basis, factoring in parameters like crop growth stage and availability of rainfall. The overall system design is described in the subsequent sections. Figure 2 represents the overall conceptual design of the proposed digital twin.

4.1.2 Sensor Node System Design

An ARM Cortex-M3 STM32F103C8T6 befits the wireless sensor nodes owing to its availability, low cost, fast processing speed, and sufficient number of GPIO pins. The sensor node circuit simulation results are presented in Fig. 3.

Solar is proposed for charging the node's battery power supply since they will be deployed in the field hence power considerations have to be optimized. An I2C display adapter is proposed to minimize the number of connection pins required for the system. An XBee radio module is connected to the microcontroller unit using one of the three UART serial interfaces it has. A DS18B20 soil temperature sensor is used for monitoring soil temperature to approximate evaporation of moisture from the soil. A non-corrosive soil-moisture probe is used for monitoring soil moisture values. The wireless Sensor Node prototype is illustrated in Fig. 4.

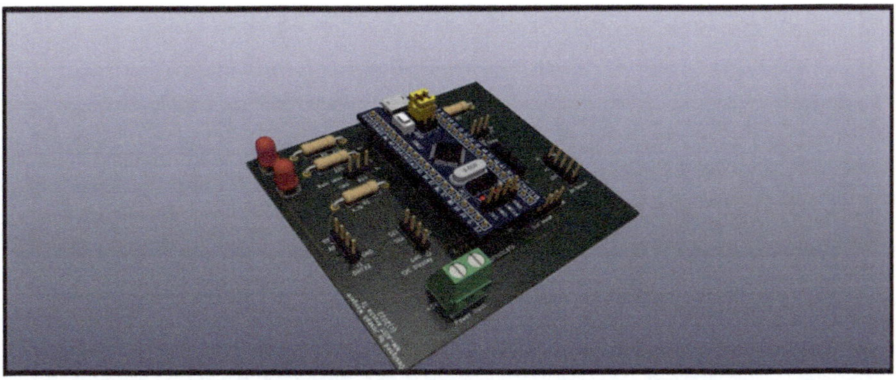

Fig. 3 Sensor node circuit simulation

Fig. 4 Wireless sensor node prototype

4.1.3 Coordinator Node System Design

The proposed coordinator node consists of a raspberry pi 4 model B interfaced with an XBee module configured as a coordinator for receiving data from the wireless sensor nodes. Additionally, the coordinator node regulates the automatic opening and closing of water pump and valves, while at the same time monitoring the flow rate through each connected valve to account for water consumption in each irrigation zone. The coordinator node provides the digital interface to mirror the states and behavior of the water pump and gate valves that allow water flow to each irrigation zone. For water to flow to a specific zone, the water pump state has to be on and the gate valve for the particular zone has to be on as well.

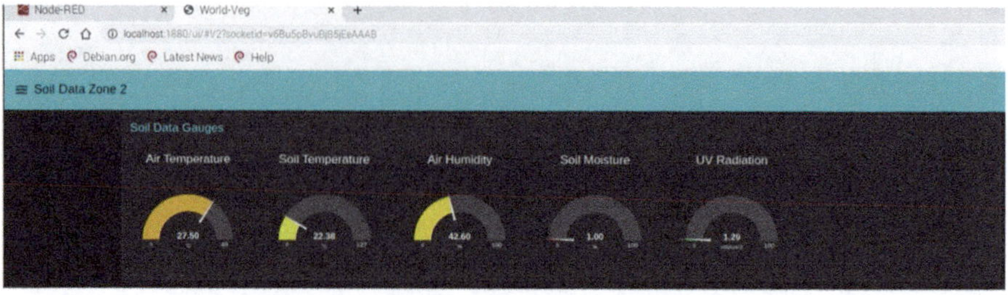

Fig. 5 Dry soil data visualization dashboard

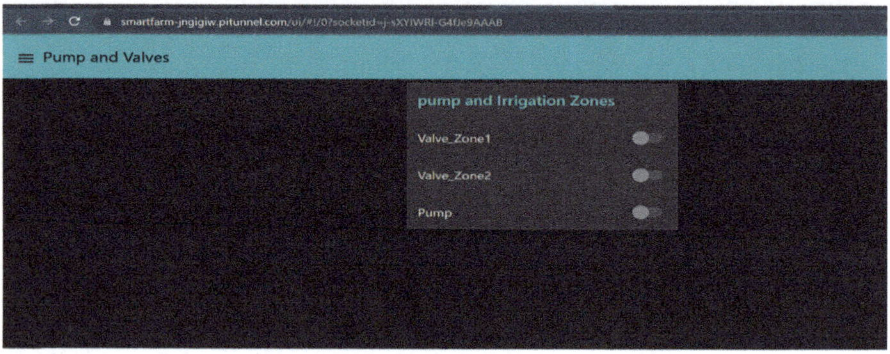

Fig. 6 Pump and valve remote-control interface

4.2 System Development

The soil data for the monitored parameters can be accessed wirelessly through a web browser, as represented in Fig. 5 where the Raspberry pi acts as a server. Optionally, the pump and valves can be controlled remotely from the web interface via Node-red, hosted remotely using pitunnel remote ssh platform.

To override automatic control of pumps and valves, a control panel can be accessed remotely via a web browser. A user can then turn on or off specific irrigation sections by triggering the opening of valves via relays connected to the raspberry pi pins. The web monitoring platform has two interfaces, one for control of pump and valves as presented in Fig. 6, while the other is for visualization of sensor data.

4.3 Discussion

This study demonstrates the capabilities of digital twin technology that can be incorporated into the automated monitoring of irrigation systems. Sensor node design was proposed, integrated with ZigBee wireless sensor network for sensor data transmission. Solar power was emphasized with an inclination towards renewable energy, for the devices deployed in the field.

An interactive user interface based on Node-red, that can be accessed remotely for monitoring and control of irrigation equipment was developed.

4.3.1 Challenges

This study unearths several challenges that could potentially be exploited to make digital twins more robust. Firstly, integrating Internet of Things devices poses another debate regarding updating firmware remotely. For the microcontrollers selected for implementation, there has to be a wireless connectivity media that can provide for seamless rollout of updated firmware remotely. Additionally, remote updates must be scheduled within durations in which the farm equipment are inactive, with the possibility of quick roll-back to an earlier stable version in case of bugs in a new release.

Safety is also a critical aspect of digital twins, given irrigation deals with high-voltage pumps. It is important to ensure that remote control mechanisms do not potentially result in hazards, for instance, in the case of users accidentally turning on pump control buttons on the graphical user interfaces.

5 Conclusion and Future Works

In this paper, the concept of digital twin and how it is applicable in control and automation of irrigation was highlighted. Different wireless communication technologies were compared in relation to irrigation monitoring. The challenges that could be explored to build more powerful irrigation digital twins have been outlined and can be a starting point for further studies. A prototype for an affordable digital twin for irrigation monitoring was presented.

In the future, this work will be advanced by testing out the developed digital twin in a real farm set-up with different irrigation zones. The model can further be improved by introducing a feedback loop into the system to provide data that can be used for machine learning and prediction. Further, water leakage detection mechanisms can be added to ensure loss of water is kept at a minimum. Firmware over the air updates (OTA) can be enabled as a feature to minimize the need for visiting the farm physically to update firmware on the microcontrollers.

As a recommendation, more virtual reality features can be incorporated in the system to enhance the digital twin and provide users with a virtual experience that is similar to the actual farm environment. This can be done by adding GIS mapping component as well as utilizing live camera feeds for on-farm imagery from unmanned aerial vehicles as well as satellite imagery.

Acknowledgments This work is financed by the CENIT@EA Project (Center of Excellence for ICT in East Africa), funded by the German Federal Ministry for Economic Cooperation and Development (BMZ), and implemented by the Deutsche Gesellschaft für Internationale Zusammenarbeit (GIZ) and the German Academic Exchange Service (DAAD).

References

1. Pawlak, K., & Kołodziejczak, M. (2020). The role of agriculture in ensuring food security in developing countries: Considerations in the context of the problem of sustainable food production. *Sustainability, 12*(13), 5488. https://doi.org/10.3390/su12135488
2. F. A. O. (2021). *World Food and Agriculture - Statistical yearbook 2021*. Food & Agriculture Org.
3. Wu, G., Chen, J., Kim, J.-S., Gu, L., Lee, J.-H., & Zhang, L. (2022). Impacts of climate change on global meteorological multi-year droughts using the last millennium simulation as a baseline. *Journal of Hydrology (Amst), 610*, 127937. https://doi.org/10.1016/j.jhydrol.2022.127937
4. Dorward, A., & Giller, K. E. (2022). Change in the climate and other factors affecting agriculture, food or poverty: An opportunity, a threat or both? A personal perspective. *Global Food Security, 33*, 100623. https://doi.org/10.1016/J.GFS.2022.100623
5. Ançay, A., Michel, V., & Baroffio, C. A. (2017). Comparison of manual and automatic irrigation systems in strawberries. *Acta Horticulturae, 1156*, 263–268. https://doi.org/10.17660/ActaHortic.2017.1156.40
6. Abbassi, Y., & Benlahmer, H. (2021). The internet of things at the service of tomorrow's agriculture. *Procedia Computer Science, 191*, 475–480. https://doi.org/10.1016/j.procs.2021.07.060
7. Sinde, R., Begum, F., Njau, K., & Kaijage, S. (2020). Refining network lifetime of wireless sensor network using energy-efficient clustering and DRL-based sleep scheduling. *Sensors, 20*(5), 1540. https://doi.org/10.3390/s20051540
8. Rai, R. K., Singh, V. P., & Upadhyay, A. (2017). Irrigation methods. *Planning and Evaluation of Irrigation Projects*, 353–363. https://doi.org/10.1016/B978-0-12-811748-4.00010-8
9. Mkojera, E. (2009). Economic analysis of farmers-managed irrigation schemes in Tanzania: A case of Mombo, Kivulini and Lekitatu irrigation schemes.
10. Casadei, S., Peppoloni, F., Ventura, F., Teodorescu, R., Dunea, D., & Petrescu, N. (2021). Application of smart irrigation systems for water conservation in Italian farms. *Environmental Science and Pollution Research, 28*(21), 26488–26499. https://doi.org/10.1007/s11356-021-12524-6
11. Walker, W. R. (1989). *Guidelines for designing and evaluating surface irrigation systems*. Food and Agriculture Organization of the United Nations.
12. Ali, M. H. (2010). *Fundamentals of irrigation and on-farm water management: Volume 1*. Springer New York. https://doi.org/10.1007/978-1-4419-6335-2
13. Southorn, N. (1997). *Farm irrigation: Planning & management*. Inkata Press.
14. Stavropoulos, P., & Mourtzis, D. (2022). Digital twins in industry 4.0. In *Design and operation of production networks for mass personalization in the era of cloud technology* (pp. 277–316). Elsevier. [Online]. https://linkinghub.elsevier.com/retrieve/pii/B9780128236574000105
15. Maddikunta, P. K. R., et al. (2022). Industry 5.0: A survey on enabling technologies and potential applications. *Journal of Industrial Information Integration, 26*, 100257. https://doi.org/10.1016/j.jii.2021.100257
16. Verdouw, C., Tekinerdogan, B., Beulens, A., & Wolfert, S. (2021). Digital twins in smart farming. *Agricultural Systems, 189*, 103046. https://doi.org/10.1016/J.AGSY.2020.103046
17. Alves, R. G. et al. (2019, October). A digital twin for smart farming. In *2019 IEEE Global Humanitarian Technology Conference (GHTC)*, pp. 1–4. https://doi.org/10.1109/GHTC46095.2019.9033075.

18. Ranjbar, R., Duviella, E., Etienne, L., & Maestre, J.-M. (2020). Framework for a digital twin of the Canal of Calais. *Procedia Computer Science, 178*, 27–37. https://doi.org/10.1016/j.procs.2020.11.004
19. Panigrahi, P., Raychaudhuri, S., Thakur, A. K., Nayak, A. K., Sahu, P., & Ambast, S. K. (2019). Automatic drip irrigation scheduling effects on yield and water productivity of banana. *Scientia Horticulturae, 257*, 108677. https://doi.org/10.1016/j.scienta.2019.108677
20. Abdollahi, A., Rejeb, K., Rejeb, A., Mostafa, M. M., & Zailani, S. (2021). Wireless sensor networks in agriculture: Insights from bibliometric Analysis. *Sustainability, 13*(21), 12011. https://doi.org/10.3390/su132112011
21. Klaina, H., et al. (2022). Analysis of low power wide area network wireless technologies in smart agriculture for large-scale farm monitoring and tractor communications. *Measurement, 187*, 110231. https://doi.org/10.1016/j.measurement.2021.110231
22. Rastogi, E., Saxena, N., Roy, A., & Shin, D. R. (2020). Narrowband internet of things: A comprehensive study. *Computer Networks, 173*, 107209. https://doi.org/10.1016/J.COMNET.2020.107209
23. Saban, M., Aghzout, O., Medus, L. D., & Rosado, A. (2021). Experimental Analysis of IoT networks based on LoRa/LoRaWAN under indoor and outdoor environments: Performance and limitations. *IFAC-PapersOnLine, 54*(4), 159–164. https://doi.org/10.1016/J.IFACOL.2021.10.027
24. Baronti, P., Pillai, P., Chook, V. W. C., Chessa, S., Gotta, A., & Hu, Y. F. (2007). Wireless sensor networks: A survey on the state of the art and the 802.15.4 and ZigBee standards. *Computer Communications, 30*(7), 1655–1695. https://doi.org/10.1016/j.comcom.2006.12.020
25. Li, L., Xiaoguang, H., Ke, C., & Ketai, H. (2011). The applications of WiFi-based wireless sensor network in internet of things and smart grid. In *2011 6th IEEE Conference on Industrial Electronics and Applications (ICIEA)*, pp. 789–793. https://doi.org/10.1109/ICIEA.2011.5975693.
26. Vimal, S. P., Sathish Kumar, N., Kasiselvanathan, M., & Gurumoorthy, K. B. (2021). Smart irrigation system in agriculture. *Journal of Physics Conference Series, 1917*(1), 012028. https://doi.org/10.1088/1742-6596/1917/1/012028
27. Masseroni, D., Arbat, G., & de Lima, I. P. (2020). Editorial—Managing and planning water resources for irrigation: Smart-irrigation systems for providing sustainable agriculture and maintaining ecosystem services. *Water (Basel), 12*(1), 263. https://doi.org/10.3390/w12010263
28. Tiglao, N. M., Alipio, M., Balanay, J. V., Saldivar, E., & Tiston, J. L. (2020). Agrinex: A low-cost wireless mesh-based smart irrigation system. *Measurement, 161*, 107874. https://doi.org/10.1016/j.measurement.2020.107874
29. García, L., Parra, L., Jimenez, J. M., Lloret, J., & Lorenz, P. (2020). IoT-based smart irrigation systems: An overview on the recent trends on sensors and IoT Systems for Irrigation in precision agriculture. *Sensors, 20*(4), 1042. https://doi.org/10.3390/s20041042
30. Moreira, M., Mourato, S., Rodrigues, C., Silva, S., Guimarães, R., & Chibeles, C. (2021). Building a digital twin for the management of pressurised collective irrigation systems. In *Proceedings of the 1st international conference on water energy food and sustainability (ICoWEFS 2021)* (pp. 785–795). Springer International Publishing. https://doi.org/10.1007/978-3-030-75315-3_83
31. Nasirahmadi, A., & Hensel, O. (2022). Toward the next generation of digitalization in agriculture based on digital twin paradigm. *Sensors, 22*(2), 498. https://doi.org/10.3390/s22020498
32. Douglass, B. (2013). Agile development for Embedded Systems. In *Software Engineering for Embedded Systems* (pp. 731–766). Elsevier. [Online]. https://linkinghub.elsevier.com/retrieve/pii/B9780124159174000219
33. Srinivasan, J., Dobrin, R., & Lundqvist, K. (2009). 'State of the Art' in using agile methods for Embedded Systems development. In *2009 33rd Annual IEEE International Computer Software and Applications Conference*, pp. 522–527. https://doi.org/10.1109/COMPSAC.2009.186.

IoT-Based-System for Telecom Tower Fire Detection and Aviation Obstruction Light Monitoring

Thierry Ndayitezibiganza, Devotha Nyambo, Sinde Ramadhani, and Anael Sam

1 Introduction

The rapid growth of the mobile phone sector and Internet usage in the communication sector are resulting in the construction of millions of telecommunication towers in different parts of the world [1]. Trade and investment liberalization have both contributed to the expansion of Tanzania's telecom industry due to population growth [2]. In the same manner, in Tanzania, the statistics showed that in January 2022 the number of internet users was 15.60 million of the population using telecommunication companies such as Airtel, Halotel, Smile, Tigo, Ttcl, Vodacom, Zantel, and Habari node, and other services like calls and SMS [3] which means that when there is an interruption of any things in those telecommunication services or any issue, it is a big loss even economically depended on what kind happens [4]. Through the use of telecom towers, people can do business over long distances by using the Internet and other services.

Many places where the towers are installed, like parks, villages, and forests, are not easy to reach. Over the years, automated systems as remedial mitigations against challenges have not been effectively deployed [5], other than to ping the Internet and consequent Internet breakdown [6]. Generally, there is a technological system put in place to detect issues regarding fire outbreaks or aviation obstruction light status. Research shows the attendant limitations of manual systems, especially the use of monitoring the tower remotely [7]. These limitations include high time consumption, human errors, cost intensiveness, the difficulty of auto-report generation, and real-time information. The current limitations on the use of manual

T. Ndayitezibiganza (✉) · D. Nyambo · S. Ramadhani · A. Sam
The Nelson Mandela Africa Institution of Science and Technology (NM-AIST), Arusha, Tanzania

School of Computational and Communication Science and Engineering, Arusha, Tanzania
e-mail: ndayitezibiganzat@nm-aist.ac.tz

J. Marx Gómez et al. (eds.), *Smart and Secure Embedded and Mobile Systems*,
Progress in IS, https://doi.org/10.1007/978-3-031-56603-5_6

approaches to tackle the challenges necessitated the use of an IoT-based system. The use of this system in telecom fire prevention and aviation light monitoring provides appreciable features of maximization of time, prevention of fire, overcurrent control, increased security, sending alerts like calls and messages and monitoring the status of the aviation obstruction lights in the tower when there is a problem.

2 Related Works

Telecommunications towers are structures that hold communication equipment used in wireless applications such as mobile telephony, television, radio, and public safety communications networks [8]. Various methods have been used to resolve the same issue, with a focus on fire detection and aviation obstruction light monitoring separately. The following are the most relevant researches in that field.

A study was conducted in Bangladesh by developing remote real-time monitoring and fire detection based on the Internet of Things to maintain safety and prevent fire against electrical short-circuits, which can cause damage to many things [9]. The system was using thingSpeak to record as a means of monitoring. Using the Arduino Uno flame sensor, NodeMcu Esp8266, relay, and buzzer, the system was able to detect fire and shut down the power when there were electrical faults. However, the system was not able to extinguish the fire detected and no notification to the concerns when a fire was detected, except to check on thinkSpeak cloud.

A study was conducted deeply in Tanzania, due to the frequent occurrence of fires in several East African countries, resulting in the loss of property and lives for the purpose of developing an early fire detection system [10]. Flame sensors and wireless sensors were connected to the Internet of Things to monitor the situation with real-time notifications. However, the system was designed for monitoring, as well as delivering notifications to the concerned parties, but it lacked a real-time extinguisher for quick intervention.

Alqourabah et al. [11] implemented a smart fire system using IoT technology with an automatic water sprinkler to protect against fire accidents. Therefore, some sensors were used to detect the cause of the fire. The system was using the IoT platform to make the data exchangeable from that cloud. It is minimizing false alarms and turning on automatically the water sprinkler, which was making this system to be active. However, the system was for monitoring and auto intervention using water but no notification was sent to any concern about the issue.

Another study was conducted in Habari node by focusing on a battery voltage level monitoring system based on embedded systems to monitor the voltage level, the current level of the batteries and fire [12]. Users were able to access the system remotely through the Mobile application with real-time notifications. However, that system was unable to extinguish the fire detected in the telecommunications tower cabinet. Furthermore, an implemented IoT-based Automatic Email and Audio Message Notification System for Electric Light Failure Detection against the Electric Light failures that were common in unknown circumstances inside the holy mosques in Saudi Arabia [13]. The system developed a BMS solution that could be applied for light failure detections under circuit breakers and notifications related to the issue. However, compared to the existing systems of light failure detection, the developed system was simple and non-invasive. Therefore, various work has been done to monitor tower usage using IoT. However, the work done did not consider monitoring the fire, over current control, and aviation obstruction light in the telecommunication tower.

Automatic Damaged Light Fault Detection and Management System was implemented in India because people were complaining about the street lights down when they are passing in the colony (street) [14]. The system was for monitoring and identifying those lights that have been damaged. Therefore, using wireless sensors, the system tracks the lights which are not working remotely without human interaction and sends notifications related to them. However, the system was for monitoring only, when the electrical contactor is down there was no remote access for switching ON.

3 Materials and Methods

3.1 Case Study

The developed system has been carried out at Habari Node Public Limited Company in Arusha, Tanzania, by focusing on the tower which is near Kilimanjaro Airport (see Table 1). Therefore, fire detection, aviation obstruction light status, and other parameters that can intervene in its safety were the main purposes of the developed system. The telecommunication tower was an aid in monitoring and controlling some causes of tower destruction. As a result, having an automatic fire extinguisher to extinguish the fire when there is a fire in the tower with some alerts using GSM to stakeholders of the Tower, firefighters, and the nearest environment using the buzzer to take quick action. Moreover, the system will report to the technician Manager the aviation obstruction light status, especially when it is not.

3.2 System Development Approach

The agile software development methodology (ASDM) was used from the stage of problem identification, solution design, development, and evaluation. The ASDM

Table 1 Habari node tower GPS tower location

GPS location	Coordinates of the tower	
Kilimanjaro Tower	Latitude (LAT)	Longitude (LONG)
	−3.426949	37.074913

was selected to develop the IoT-based fire safety warning system and real-time aviation light monitoring because it can quickly and easily adapt to new changes and has a clearer sense of how a project is running as well as how it is working [15]. It also allows continuous improvement at each stage of the system [15]. However, Extreme Programming (XP) which is the branch of agile was used because it is a branch of the agile system development life cycle [16]. The selected technology is more efficient for small projects compared to the Scrum Method. The scrum method is the most popular, but it is more useful when there is a need of working on large projects and it focuses on teamwork and organizing work [17]. For the developed system, XP was more applicable because it helped in the development of the prototype. It focuses on efficiency, concerns feedback, and the quality of the product. The Extreme Programming methodology was used because it includes the following steps (activities): planning, designing, coding, and testing [18].

3.3 Software Tools Integration

The software tool after data collection for the developed system, EasyEDA (standard) 6.4.31 was used for simulation and design with a microcontroller that connects all sensors and actuators. The Arduino IDE came with all of the required libraries for Microcontroller ESP32-WROOM-32D programming and the cloud platforms (software and APIs) to facilitate data storage, visualization, and remote control with relays automation [19]. Moreover, SQL and PHP are for the server-side and HTML, CSS, and JavaScript are for the front side. The ThingSpeak was used to plot on the web the sensory data with remote visualization of lights, fire, current, and remote control using through relays.

3.4 Hardware Tools Integration

ESP32-WROOM-32D was selected due to that it is a low-cost SoC microcontroller made by the same company that made the ESP8266 SoC [20]. The 32-bit Xtensa LX6 Microprocessor from Tensilica is the replacement for the ESP8266 SoC. It has built-in Wi-Fi and Bluetooth and comes in both single and dual-core versions.

The chemical fire extinguisher when there was a fire detected in the tower to pin 28 and the second was to control the aviation obstruction Light connected to the pin 15. In terms of aviation Light monitoring, LDR Sensor turns OFF and ON the Light during the night or daily to pin 23 and the BH1750 sensor for luminosity monitoring to pins 21 and 22.

The transmitter (Tx) and receiver (Rx) pins of GSM module were connected to pins 19 and 18 of the microcontroller. Therefore, short message notifications and a call were used as alert to concerns with the help of the Bulk SMS and GSM module. The GSM SIM800L was powered by 5 V and other components to 3.3 V from the

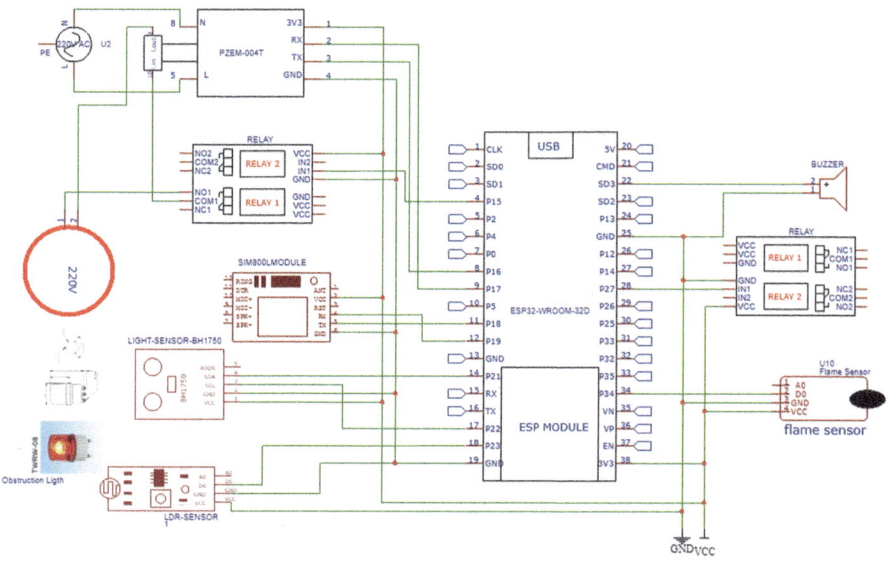

Fig. 1 Circuit diagram of the developed system

ESP32 (see Fig. 1) showing the prototype integration of the microcontroller, all the sensors and actuators.

4 Results and Discussion

4.1 Results

4.1.1 The Functionality of the Developed System

After the system had been switched on, constant iterative runs were performed so that the sensors and other components could begin functioning and begin the process of initializing settings. The Pzem-004t was used in this project to manage the power supply of the tower by turning OFF the contactor if the current was more than 22 A. Therefore, the Flame sensor was for to detect fire at any time happens and activate the fire extinguisher automatically and trig ON the buzzer by giving an alert to the nearest environment. Furthermore, the darkness and luminosity of the Obstruction Light were controlled which means that if the Light-dependent resistor detected the darkness and the BH1750 sensor is measuring the ambient luminosity as less than 2.5 lux. The microcontroller received the data that had been gathered from the sensors, and it proceeded to process and examine the information. Following the completion of the data processing, each output data set was evaluated in light of the predetermined threshold. In this particular instance, technicians and firefighters

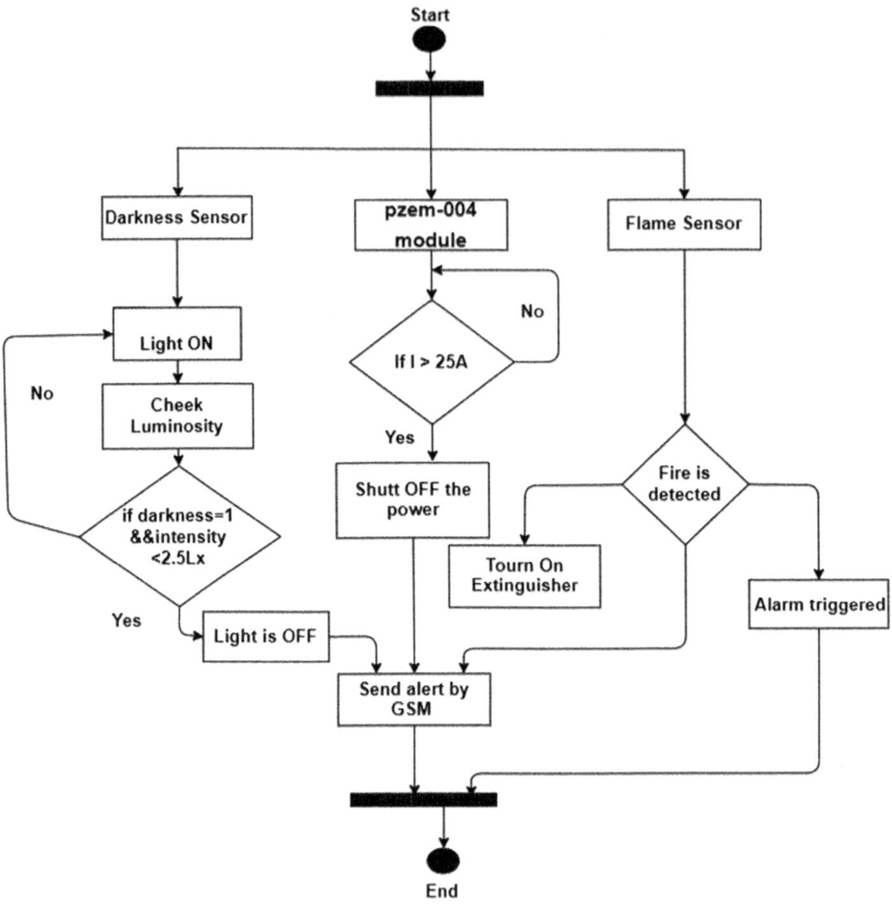

Fig. 2 Flowchart of the developed system

were made aware of the situation through notification (SMS and call), which was sent via Bulk SMS API and GSM SIM800L as a backup (see Fig. 2). In addition to that, the data were analyzed from the developed prototype (see Fig. 3) on an ongoing basis in the cloud storage (Database) that was housed inside of the ThingSpeak platform.

4.1.2 System Validation

Continuously monitored the aviation obstruction light, fire, and power. As the aviation light on the top of the mast, an increase of luminosity during the night symbolized that it was working properly. Therefore, indicates a dangerous condition if it is decreased that the lux during the night, An SMS notification and call were

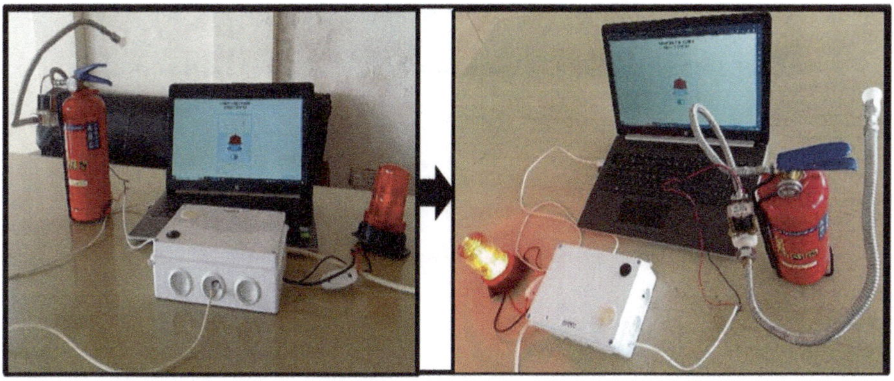

Fig. 3 Developed prototype

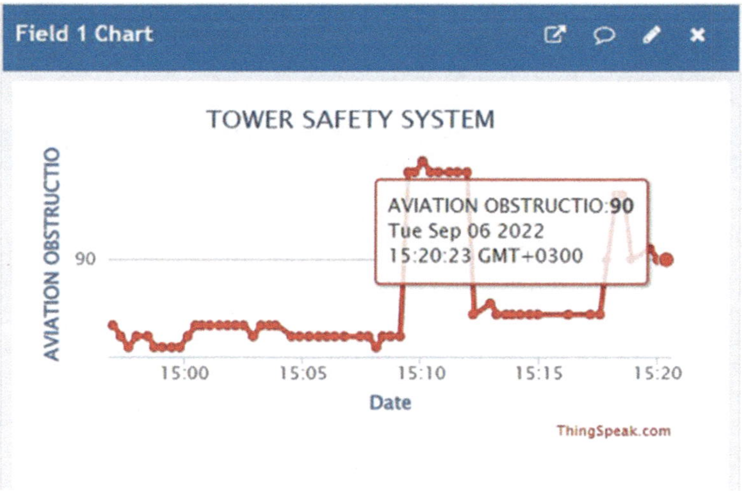

Fig. 4 Visualization of the aviation obstruction from BH1750 sensor

triggered when the fire and the light as there is a dangerous condition in the tower (Fig. 4). Besides, the sensed fire (see Fig. 5), luminosity (see Fig. 4), voltage, and current (see Fig. 6) were updated after every 15 s.

During the testing, the system was sending the notification. Findings from the study of the system were revealed on the dashboard and controlled as a record of the tower condition status, as it was installed in the tower near Kilimanjaro Aeroport (see Table 1). However, this did not indicate any negative effects because there was no serious fire and the aviation obstruction light was working see Fig. 7.

Fig. 5 Visualization of the fire from flame sensor

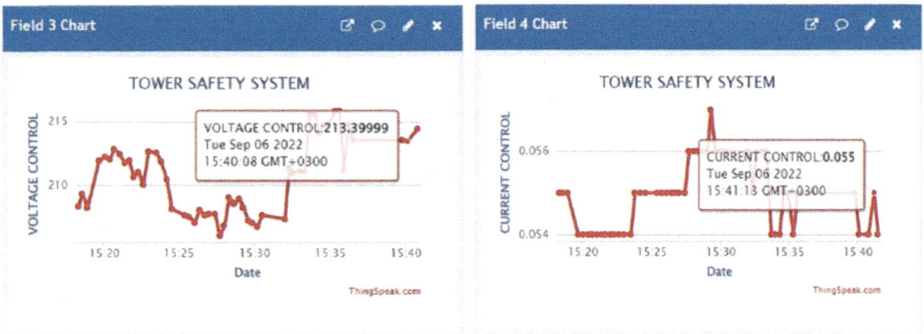

Fig. 6 Visualization of the current and voltage from Pzem-00t

4.2 Discussion

Experiments performed demonstrated the reliability of the status information of all telecommunication towers for safety purposes: the existence of fire, voltage and current regulation, and aviation obstruction light were monitored, and the likelihood of maintenance delays was decreased. Figure 7 depicts the monitoring and access to the aviation obstruction light and fire detection through mobile phones during the test case period. Data analyzed by the sensor were sent in real time to the cloud and an alert was generated in the event of a fire or aircraft light anomaly.

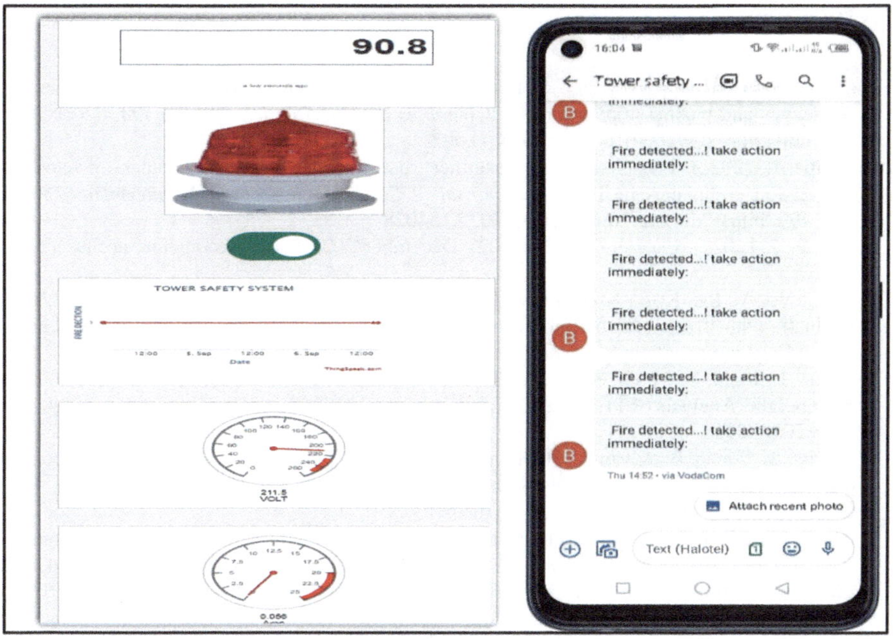

Fig. 7 Visualization of the tower and notifications

5 Conclusion and Future Work

The developed system lays the foundation for IoT-based system for telecom fire detection and aviation obstruction monitoring systems for tower technicians to ensure the suitable safety of the tower. The development of the system consisted of the integration of sensors for remotely monitoring and control through the mobile phone or web based. The system can send notifications (call and SMS) to all technicians of the company via using the GSM module. Remote monitoring using thingspeak platform connected to the cloud through the Internet. The platform allows real-time access and monitoring in all towers. Future researchers can continue by integrating machine learning when the fire is detected so that the fire extinguisher can extinguish focally and protect the tower against lightning.

Acknowledgment I would like to use this opportunity to extend my deepest gratitude to the Center of Excellence in East Africa (CENIT@EA) for their unwavering support of the scholarship fund. Their careful direction, support, and encouragement during the duration of my internship from both the academic supervisor and the industrial host supervisor, along with the facilitation they offered, were all essential to the success of this project.

References

1. Imtiaz, S. Y., Khan, M. A., & Shakir, M. (2015). Telecom sector of Pakistan: Potential, challenges and business opportunities. *Telematics and Informatics, Elsevier Ltd, 32*(2), 254–258. https://doi.org/10.1016/j.tele.2014.09.002
2. Pasape, L. (2022). Key elements of customer trust towards retaining customers of telecommunication companies in Tanzania. *Journal of Service Science and Management, 15*(04), 476–499. https://doi.org/10.4236/jssm.2022.154028
3. Quarter 2. (2022). Quarter 2–2021 / 2022 December 2021 Table of contents, no. December 2021.
4. Adekunle, A., Ibe, K. E., Kpanaki, M. E., Umanah, I. I., Nwafor, C. O., & Essang, N. (2015). Evaluating the effects of radiation from cell towers and high tension power lines on inhabitants of buildings in Ota, Ogun State. *Communications in Applied Sciences, 3*(1), 1–21.
5. Zlatar, T., Lago, E. M. G., Soares, W. D. A., Baptista, J. D. S., & Junior, B. B. (2019). Falls from height: Analysis of 114 cases. *Production, 29*, e20180091. https://doi.org/10.1590/0103-6513.20180091
6. Gerrits, B., Topan, E., & van der Heijden, M. C. (2022). Operational planning in service control towers—Heuristics and case study. *European Journal of Operational Research, 302*(3), 983–998. https://doi.org/10.1016/j.ejor.2022.01.025
7. Alladi, T., Chamola, V., Parizi, R. M., & Choo, K. K. R. (2019). Blockchain Applications for Industry 4.0 and Industrial IoT: A Review. *IEEE Access, 7*. Institute of Electrical and Electronics Engineers Inc., 176935–176951. https://doi.org/10.1109/ACCESS.2019.2956748
8. Faisal, M. M. A., Mortuza, M. G., & Alam, T. (2018). Cell tower radiation and effect on human body: Bangladesh perspective. In *2018 international conference on innovations in science, engineering and technology, ICISET 2018* (pp. 423–426). Institute of Electrical and Electronics Engineers. https://doi.org/10.1109/ICISET.2018.8745560
9. Kibria Badhon, M., Ranjan Barai, A., & Zhora, F. (2019). Remote Real Time Monitoring and Safety System for Earthquake and Fire Detection Based on Internet of Things. In *3rd International Conference on Electrical* (pp. 41–44). Computer and Telecommunication Engineering, ICECTE. https://doi.org/10.1109/ICECTE48615.2019.9303575
10. Hilary, R., Rotich, P., Geofrey, A., & Sam, A. (2020). Early fire detection system in Tanzania markets. *Engineering Proceedings, 2*(1), 50. https://doi.org/10.3390/ecsa-7-08215
11. Alqourabah, H., Muneer, A., & Fati, S. M. (2021). A smart fire detection system using IoT technology with automatic water sprinkler. *International Journal of Electrical and Computer Engineering, 11*(4), 2994–3002. https://doi.org/10.11591/ijece.v11i4.pp2994-3002
12. Uwamahoro, R., Mduma, N., & Machuve, D. (2021). A battery voltage level monitoring system for telecommunication towers. *Engineering, Technology & Applied Science Research, 11*(6), 7875–7880. https://doi.org/10.48084/etasr.4550
13. Misbahuddin, S., Mohsen, M., Abdulqudus, M., Ahmed, A., & Bin Jahlan, A. K. (2020). IoT based automatic email and audio message notification system for electric light failure detection inside Harmain Sharifain of Makkah and Madinah. In *2020 International Conference on Computing and Information Technology* (pp. 225–229). ICCIT. https://doi.org/10.1109/ICCIT-144147971.2020.9213811
14. Nanduri, A. K., Kotamraju, S. K., Sravanthi, G. L., Babu, S. R., & Pavan Kumar, K. V. K. V. L. (2020). IoT based automatic damaged street light fault detection management system. *International Journal of Advanced Computer Science and Applications, 11*(8), 412–416. https://doi.org/10.14569/IJACSA.2020.0110853
15. Mahnic, V. (2019). A capstone course on agile software development using scrum. *IEEE Transactions on Education, 55*(1), 99–106. https://doi.org/10.1109/TE.2011.2142311
16. Rai, A. K., Agarwal, S., & Kumar, A. (2018). A novel approach for agile software development methodology selection using fuzzy inference system. *Proceedings of the International Conference on Smart Systems and Inventive Technology, ICSSIT, 2018*(1), 518–526. https://doi.org/10.1109/ICSSIT.2018.8748767

17. Adi, P. (2015). Scrum method implementation in a software development Project Management. *International Journal of Advanced Computer Science and Applications, 6*(9), 198–204. https://doi.org/10.14569/ijacsa.2015.060927
18. Azdy, R. A., & Rini, A. (2018). Penerapan Extreme Programming dalam Membangun Aplikasi Pengaduan Layanan Pelanggan (PaLaPa) pada Perguruan Tinggi. *Jurnal Teknologi Informasi dan Ilmu Komputer, 5*(2), 197. https://doi.org/10.25126/jtiik.201852658
19. Baig, M. J. A., Iqbal, M. T., Jamil, M., & Khan, J. (2021). Design and implementation of an open-Source IoT and blockchain-based peer-to-peer energy trading platform using ESP32-S2, Node-Red and, MQTT protocol. *Energy Reports, 7*, 5733–5746. https://doi.org/10.1016/j.egyr.2021.08.190
20. Akyildiz, I. F., Kak, A., & Nie, S. (2020). 6G and beyond: The future of wireless communications systems. *IEEE Access, 8*, 133995–134030. https://doi.org/10.1109/ACCESS.2020.3010896

IoT and Health Systems in Developing Countries: A Review

Doudou Dione, Idy Diop, Demba Faye, Ibrahima Gueye, and Sidi Mohamed Farssi

1 Introduction

Health is one of the major concerns for populations in developing countries [1]. Solutions focusing on the use of the Internet of Things are becoming more and more common in the healthcare field for remote patient monitoring [2]. The implementation of a successful architecture can significantly improve business processes. More and more healthcare practices are oriented toward innovative technologies such as the Internet of Things and artificial intelligence. In this context, especially in view of the great upheaval in the healthcare sector, it is imperative that the stakeholders (patients and physicians) join forces to take advantage of the many opportunities offered by these emerging technologies in the healthcare environment. The demand for healthcare in developing countries is growing. This problem is most palpable in the countryside. In Senegal, more than 60% of the population lives in rural areas. Patient follow-up is one of the major problems of hospitals in third-world countries. The capacity of health facilities in these countries is very low compared to the demand for basic care [3]. In the field of health, the Internet of Things is intervening to solve a set of challenges related to hospital management and permanent patient monitoring. More and more applications are being developed ranging from monitoring patients and hospital staff to monitoring the conditions of medicines or even vaccines [4].

The IoT is now used to enable better healthcare management with more autonomy and proactivity on patients' well-being to improve safety and quality of life. This technology can also help with prevention and, above all, reduce costs. However, even if the benefits are numerous, the use of Internet of Things technology

D. Dione (✉) · I. Diop · D. Faye · I. Gueye · S. M. Farssi
Cheikh Anta Diop University, Dakar, Senegal
e-mail: doudou2.dione@ucad.edu.sn

J. Marx Gómez et al. (eds.), *Smart and Secure Embedded and Mobile Systems*,
Progress in IS, https://doi.org/10.1007/978-3-031-56603-5_7

in the health sector has a number of risks and drawbacks. Data confidentiality and integration of data networks between devices and protocols, internet connection, but also the problem of access to electricity in remote areas are all constraints for the development of medical IoT.

In this chapter, we present and discuss the main aspects and challenges related to medical connected objects in developing countries. Our work is structured as follows:

In Sect. 2, we discuss the work that has been done in the field of health, in the second part, the contribution of IoT in healthcare and in the last part, challenges related to the design of an IoT system suitable for developing countries for healthcare are discussed.

2 Related Works

Much work has been done on monitoring the vital signs of patients using connected objects with machine learning or deep learning.

A temperature and relative humidity monitoring system for the maintenance of products in hospitals or pharmaceutical entities is developed by J. Cabra et al. [5]. The system consists of three parts: a WSN, a management component, and the cloud.

These intelligent sensors allow a large area to be mapped in real time. The electrocardiogram (ECG) represents the electrical activity of the heart due to depolarization and repolarization of the atria and ventricles. An ECG provides information about the basic rhythms of the heart muscles and acts as an indicator of various cardiac abnormalities. These abnormalities include arrhythmia, QT prolongation, myocardial ischemia, etc. The use of IoT technology has found application in the early detection of cardiac abnormalities through ECG monitoring [6].

The DNN is proposed in [7] to classify four categories of disease based on real-time ECG images.

S. Raj et al. in [8] have created an IoT-based ECG monitoring prototype. This system provides data to identify heart diseases from ECGs in real time. It is a conceptual device for monitoring a possible arrhythmia. Their prototype allows real-time remote monitoring and automatic recognition of different rhythm classes. Doctors can monitor the ECG in real time through IoT and mobile devices with the complete system. This immediate and efficient information can provide medical staff with the most effective information to facilitate further relevant diagnosis and treatment.

Increasingly, cloud-based data centers are providing e-health services. In low-income countries, there is a large disparity between urban and rural areas in terms of health infrastructure. These cloud-based services can enable people in remote areas to benefit from basic health services [9].

A. Mwangi et al. in [10] proposed a system that provides early warning of asthma attack emergencies. It is an IoT-based system and consists mainly of a keyboard interaction unit. The system emits a sound signal to alert the neighborhood and also sends a text message to the doctor. However, their study does not take into account cases of asthma whose triggering origin may be related to the environment.

An IoT-based e-health model is developed by C. Raj et al. in [11]. This model is intended for telemedicine practice and remote patient monitoring in developing countries, especially in remote areas. In addition to sensors to monitor vital signs, their system includes a real-time camera for telemedicine. An application to send notifications and prescriptions. It also includes a dialogue box.

N. Kamal and P. Ghosa have proposed a system to address the lack of qualified personnel in developing countries, especially the infrastructure problems in rural and remote areas. Their platform provides real-time data in graphical form such as body temperature and rhythm and performs analysis of the parameters. However, it takes into account a few parameters [12].

A. Das et al. [3] present a system that takes into account several physiological parameters. The system is designed via the ThingSpeak IoT platform, and in addition to displaying, processing, and recording the collected data, sends real-time notifications.

Kumar SP. et al. in [13], also use this open-source server which is accessible everywhere. They provide a system that allows real-time monitoring of vital parameters and the position of a patient.

A. D. Acharya and S. N. Patil [14] have developed a telemedicine framework combining several sensors for physiological parameters and a video monitoring system. The main advantage of the system is that it is able to function in case of Internet connection failure. This can perfectly meet the expectations in villages and remote areas.

The authors of [15] developed a system to combat the pandemic situation using Internet of Things (IoT) and Machine Learning (ML). The developed system helps to track the infected persons from the previous data and isolates them from the uninfected person.

3 IoT and Healthcare

3.1 IoT Architecture

The technologies that make up the IoT architecture are: the node layer consisting of the wireless sensor network (WSN), the local management layer of the WSN, and the cloud-based layer to enable remote monitoring [5]. The components involved in an IoT architecture include four main components (Fig. 1).

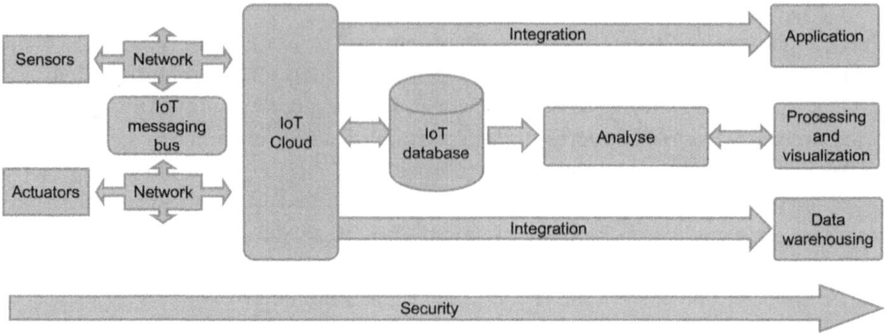

Fig. 1 IoT system architecture

The applications and analysis component are the part that processes and displays the information collected via the IoT. It includes analysis tools, AI, machine learning, and visualization capabilities.

There is the component that ensures that the applications, tools, security, and infrastructure integrate effectively with the existing enterprise-wide ERP and other business systems, also known as the integration part.

We have the security and management component which includes securing the physical components of the system through embedded firmware and security providers.

And finally, the infrastructure component which includes the physical devices (the IoT sensors, which capture information, and the actuators, which control the environment). It also includes the network on which the sensors or actuators reside such as Bluetooth, Wi-Fi, 4G, or 5G.

3.2 Communication Protocols

Communication in IoT networks is defined based on the exchange or sharing of information between users, devices, or even the exchange of information between different IoT layers. Considering the wide applications of IoT devices in different fields, several communication protocols have been used in IoT networks.

WBANs represent one of the main IoT health technologies, where the development of reliable sensors is essential for the proper functioning of a complete system [16]. IEEE 802.15.6 is a reference standard for WBANs and aims to provide low-power, short-range, and highly reliable wireless communication outside and inside the human body.

There are several varieties of protocol but ZigBee, Bluetooth Low Energy (BLE), and Wi-Fi have received the widest adoption. In addition to LR-WPAN technologies and standards, in recent years LP-WAN technologies have been developing rapidly, such as LoRaWAN, Sigfox, NarrowBand-IoT, Thread, Random Phase Multiple Access (RPMA), and Machine Type Communications (LTE-M).

Recently, IEEE 802.11ah, marketed as Wi-Fi HaLow, has emerged as an amendment to the IEEE 802.11-2007 wireless networking standard, particularly suited for better coverage and energy-efficient IoT and M2M applications [17].

3.3 Security

Communication devices handling sensitive data such as connected objects in the field of health require special security. Data confidentiality but also reliability must be emphasized to establish a system of trust.

The major concern in smart health systems is related to data security and privacy issues [18]. Only authorized health personnel should have access to patient data. The implementation of an access control system can solve this problem.

Y. Zhang et al. in [19] introduced a Privacy-Aware S-Health (PASH) access control system. PASH is based on the CP-ABE (Ciphertext-Policy Attribute-Based Encryption) scheme and the attribute values of access policies are hidden in encrypted s-health records (SHRs) and only the attribute names are revealed. The authors added an efficient decryption test that requires a small number of bilinear matches before full decryption to improve efficiency. Theoretical analysis and experimental results indicated that PASH is more secure, efficient, and expressive than existing schemes.

Camara, C. et al. in [20] present a number of security threats against implantable medical devices (IMDs). This is particularly interesting as these threats can generally be projected onto WBAN-like medical devices.

In [21], the authors proposed a secure edge computing solution for IoT applications based on the security gateway deployed at the edge to manage devices, data, IoT clients, and IoT services aimed at providing secure access and visualization services to users.

To address these security and privacy challenges, Guo et al. [22] proposed an improved symmetric homomorphic cryptosystem to monitor delay-sensitive applications. Finally, they experimented with their solution with two attack sets to indicate the improvement of privacy and security. The experimental results demonstrated the effectiveness of the proposed solution compared to existing related approaches.

3.4 IoT in Health Systems

The use of this technology increased sharply with the COVID-19 pandemic in the West to help staff counter the spread of the virus. Several applications have been developed in China and India. Indeed, the pandemic has shown the limits of our hospitals and even of our health system in general. Even if the African continent is little affected by COVID-19 compared to Europe and the United States, rethinking the system is a necessity to face diseases in the future that may appear at any time. This will require a resilient health system.

This chapter focuses on the impact of connected objects in the health sector with the implementation of intelligent systems for treatment and diagnosis to enable doctors to monitor the disease in an individual.

The Internet of Things is accompanied by advanced technologies such as artificial intelligence, cloud computing, and big data for monitoring vital signs.

Smart healthcare allows patients in poorly populated rural areas to access treatment and diagnosis using connected wearable devices. For example, wearable devices collect heart rate and blood glucose as well as oxygen saturation and transfer them to the caregiver via patients' mobile applications [23]. Recent advances in healthcare technology increasingly offer many features and functionalities for medical sensors based on software implementation. The use of software to operate such devices has made it possible to offer more complex functions, as well as features that increase, improve, and revise the usability of the device. This functionality involves remote access and control of the device, cloud-based cross-faces, and remote data collection. Figure 2 shows the general architecture of a healthcare system based on medical connected objects. Inertial sensors, heart rate and blood pressure monitoring sensors, and blood glucose meters provide patients with per-personalized healthcare. These objects can track patient parameters over long periods of time in real time and store the data in the cloud. These devices are used to track patient health parameters in real time and even perform local data analysis in addition to storing historical data in the cloud. Based on these measurements, patients receive personalized suggestions on how to improve their health status, while at the same time potentially life-threatening conditions can be detected in time. This should have a strong impact on people's lives, especially for those who live alone and improve their sense of health security.

These objects provide doctors with important information on the state of health of patients internally or externally. And thanks to the large amount of data collected by these objects, the use of intelligent techniques such as machine learning allows us to know more about the patient's health condition but also about the treatment and its evolution.

Analysis of this data could provide hospitals with new insights into how to improve the overall organization and use of resources. Figure 2 shows an example of a patient monitoring system with an interface that allows data visualization.

The Internet of Things combined with artificial intelligence can be used to improve the overall clinical workflow, from the preventive and diagnostic to the prescriptive and restorative stages of health management:

- Collection of signals of any kind
- Data transmission
- Checking information
- Health data storage and analysis
- Data visualization

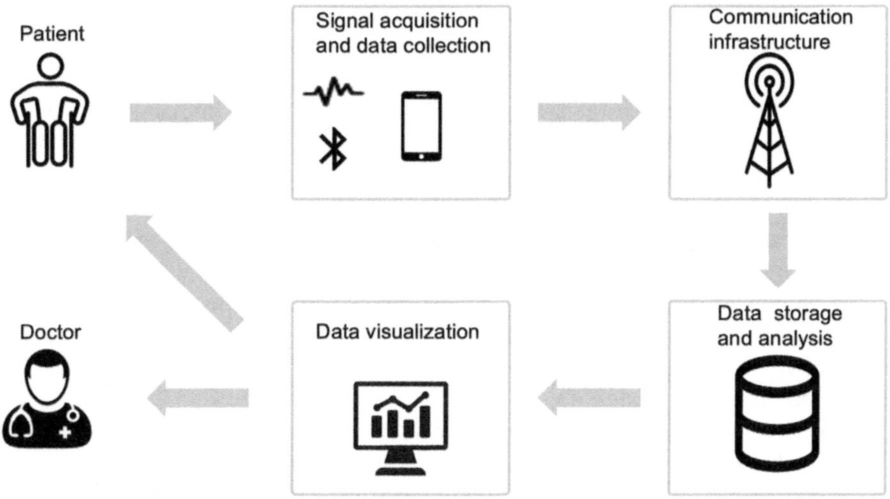

Fig. 2 IoT-based real-time monitoring system

4 The Challenges of IoT in Healthcare

Security and privacy are the main challenges of data in healthcare IoT as described in several works. Collecting and transmitting information exposes these devices to a high-security risk.

Blockchain proposes smart service subscriptions based on contracts to provide a more secure and reliable system for healthcare management. The concept of blockchain can enable the healthcare sector to provide an intelligent system by using their resources more efficiently without worrying about the security of the data collected.

The ability of a system to work with parts of other systems is also a challenge in the IoT ecosystem. Device vendors are not reaching a consensus on common communication protocols and standards.

There is also the challenge of analyzing the massive data from devices deployed in these environments as well as from body sensors on patients.

Once the challenge of data storage and retrieval is solved, there is still a need to perform automatic analysis of patient data and provide meaningful results and recommendations. Data analysis is typically performed using machine learning techniques that take advantage of the vast amount of patient data available to provide more accurate results and even draw conclusions not possible using other, simpler data analysis techniques. In particular, ML can be used to help health professionals diagnose diseases that may be difficult to diagnose. This includes early-stage cancer by analyzing MRI and microscopic images.

With the rapid growth of mobile technology, new healthcare applications are being added every day. Although a large number of mobile applications are available for healthcare applications, the types of diseases for which these applications have been designed are still limited. Therefore, there is a need to include more diseases that have been either neglected or insufficiently addressed in the past. This will add to the diversity of IoT applications in health.

Increasingly, nanosensors are being developed that can be implanted in the body and function as normal sensors by recording all data. These sensors would be able to produce a detailed history of daily activities.

The implementation of an IoT architecture adapted to the health sector, taking into account all the players and realities, will allow for better patient care in developing countries.

Although the security challenges are important, there are specific challenges, particularly in developing countries, which are often linked to the lack of infrastructure accompanying these technologies, such as poor network coverage or even a lack of electricity in some places.

Cloud technology is of great help in the development of IoT. Indeed, the large amount of data generated by the Internet of Things in the field needs to be stored and processed. This data is multiplying because of the interaction that exists today between health structures, insurance companies, and mutual health insurance companies. These clouds have the capacity to process several types of data coming from different places in real time in order to perform appropriate analyses.

The strength of such a system lies in the sensors that continuously collect and interact and transmit information to dedicated clouds. Cross-platforms are created to make it easier for doctors and patients to access information in real time. Insurers can also access certain information via a cloud platform (Fig. 3).

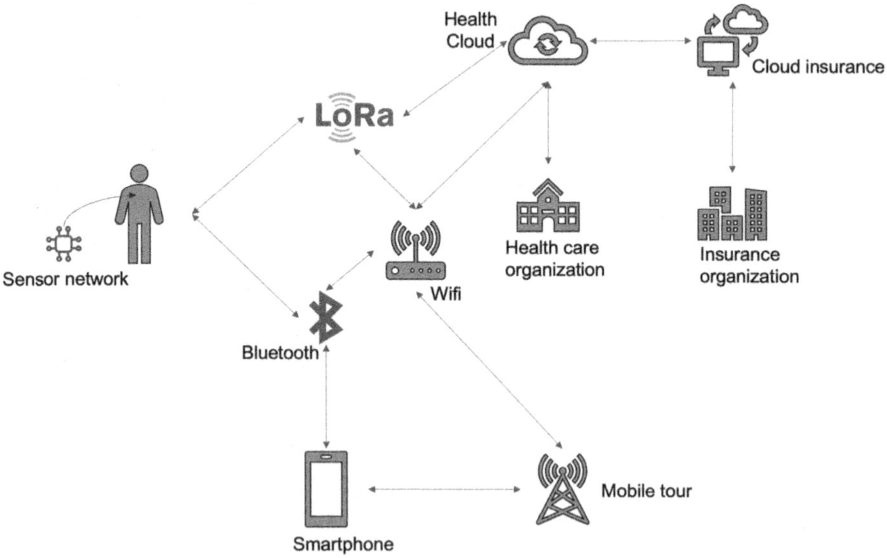

Fig. 3 A multi-functional, cloud-based health system [24]

5 Conclusion

One of the most important applications of the IoT era is in the field of healthcare. Based on IoT, the concept of smart healthcare has greatly revolutionized healthcare practice. This chapter focuses on the study of IoT technology in the health sector and gives an overview of the overall challenges they face. We consider that technologies such as AI, and the Internet of Things with the integration of security techniques such as blockchain can significantly improve healthcare practices in our healthcare facilities and provide a confidential platform for patients. This will be most important for developing countries to alleviate a failing health system, especially in rural areas.

Acknowledgments This work is supported by the African Centre for Technology Studies (ACTS) and the International Development Research Centre (IDRC) / Swedish International Development Cooperation Agency (SIDA).

References

1. Trivedi, S., & Cheeran, A. N. (2017). Android based health parameter monitoring. In *2017 International conference on intelligent computing and control systems (ICICCS)* (pp. 1145–1149). IEEE.
2. Alsalan, P., Tariq, A., & Hussain, A. (2020). IoT based health monitoring system. *Journal of Critical Reviews, 7*(4), 739–743. https://doi.org/10.31838/jcr.07.04.137
3. Malapane, T., Doorsamy, W., & Paul, B. S. (2020). An intelligent IoT-based health monitoring system. In *2020 international conference on intelligent data science technologies and applications (IDSTA)* (pp. 95–100). IEEE. https://doi.org/10.1109/IDSTA50958.2020.9264102
4. Fagroud, F. Z., Toumi, H., Ben Lahmar, E. H., Talhaoui, M. A., Achtaich, K., & Filali, S. E. (2021). Impact of IoT devices in E-Health: A Review on IoT in the context of COVID-19 and its variants. *Procedia Computer Science, 191*, 343–348. https://doi.org/10.1016/j.procs.2021.07.046. Epub 2021 Sep 8. PMID: 34512818; PMCID: PMC8424414.
5. Cabra, J., Castro, D., Colorado, J., Mendez, D., & Trujillo, L. (2017). An IoT Approach for Wireless Sensor Networks Applied to e-Health Environmental Monitoring. In *2017 IEEE international conference on internet of things (iThings) and IEEE green computing and communications (GreenCom) and IEEE cyber, Physical and Social Computing (CPSCom) and IEEE Smart Data (SmartData)* (pp. 578–583). IEEE. https://doi.org/10.1109/iThings-GreenCom-CPSCom-SmartData.2017.91
6. Pradhan, B., Bhattacharyya, S., & Pal, K. (2021). IoT-based applications in healthcare devices. *Journal of Healthcare Engineering, 2021*, 6632599. https://doi.org/10.1155/2021/6632599
7. Yeh, L.-R., Chen, W.-C., Chan, H.-Y., et al. (2021). Integrating ECG monitoring and classification via IoT and deep neural networks. *Biosensors, 11*(6), 188.
8. Raj, S. (2020). An efficient IoT-based platform for remote real-time cardiac activity monitoring. *IEEE Transactions on Consumer Electronics, 66*(2), 106–114. https://doi.org/10.1109/TCE.2020.2981511
9. Joshi, M., & Pant, D. (2016). Role of cloud enabled data center for transforming E-health services in Uttarakhand. In *2016 international conference system modeling & advancement in research trends (SMART)* (pp. 209–212). IEEE. https://doi.org/10.1109/SYSMART.2016.7894521

10. Mwangi, A., Ndashimye, E., Karikumutima, B., & Ray, S. K. (2020). An IoT-alert system for chronic asthma patients. In *2020 11th IEEE annual information technology, electronics and mobile communication conference (IEMCON)* (pp. 0012–0019). IEEE. https://doi.org/10.1109/IEMCON51383.2020.9284816
11. Raj, C., Jain, C., & Arif, W. (2017). HEMAN: Health monitoring and nous: An IoT based e-health care system for remote telemedicine. In *2017 International Conference on Wireless Communications, Signal Processing and Networking (WiSPNET)* (pp. 2115–2119). IEEE. https://doi.org/10.1109/WiSPNET.2017.8300134
12. Kamal, N., & Ghosal, P. (2018). Three tier architecture for IoT driven health monitoring system using raspberry pi. In *2018 IEEE International Symposium on Smart Electronic Systems (iSES) (Formerly iNiS)* (pp. 167–170). IEEE. https://doi.org/10.1109/iSES.2018.00044
13. Kumar, S. P., Samson, V. R. R., Sai, U. B., Rao, P. L. S. D. M., & Eswar, K. K. (2017). Smart health monitoring system of patient through IoT. In *2017 International conference on I-SMAC (IoT in social, mobile, analytics and cloud) (ISMAC)* (pp. 551–556). IEEE.
14. Acharya, A. D., & Patil, S. N. (2020). IoT based health care monitoring kit. In *2020 Fourth international conference on computing methodologies and communication (ICCMC)* (pp. 363–368). IEEE. https://doi.org/10.1109/ICCMC48092.2020.ICCMC-00068
15. Sitharthan, R., & Rajesh, M. (2021). Application of machine learning (ML) and internet of things (IoT) in healthcare to predict and tackle pandemic situation. *Distributed and Parallel Databases, 40*(4), 1–19. https://doi.org/10.1007/s10619-021-07358-7. Epub ahead of print. PMID: 34393377; PMCID: PMC8349240.
16. Wu, T., Wu, F., Redouté, J., & Yuce, M. R. (2017). An autonomous wireless body area network implementation towards IoT connected healthcare applications. *IEEE Access, 5*, 11413–11422. https://doi.org/10.1109/ACCESS.2017.2716344
17. IEEE. (2017). Standard for information technology—Telecommunications and information exchange between systems—Local and metropolitan area networks—Specific requirements—Part 11: Wireless LAN medium access control (MAC) and physical layer (PHY) Specifications amendment 2: Sub 1 GHz license exempt operation; IEEE Std 802.11ah-2016; IEEE: Piscataway, NJ, USA, pp. 1–594.
18. Solanas, A., et al. (2014). Smart health: A context-aware health paradigm within smart cities. *IEEE Communications Magazine, 52*(8), 74–81. https://doi.org/10.1109/MCOM.2014.6871673
19. Zhang, Y., Zheng, D., & Deng, R. H. (2018). Security and privacy in smart health: Efficient policy-hiding attribute-based access control. *IEEE Internet of Things Journal, 5*(3), 2130–2145. https://doi.org/10.1109/JIOT.2018.2825289
20. Camara, C., Peris-Lopez, P., & Tapiador, J. E. (2015). Security and privacy issues in implantable medical devices: A comprehensive survey. *Journal of Biomedical Informatics, 55*, 272–289.
21. Jin, W., Xu, R., You, T., Hong, Y. G., & Kim, D. (2020). Secure edge computing management based on independent microservices providers for gateway-centric IoT networks. *IEEE Access, 8*, 187975–187990. https://doi.org/10.1109/ACCESS.2020.3030297
22. Guo, C., Tian, P., & Choo, K. K. R. (2021). Enabling privacy-assured fog-based data aggregation in E-healthcare systems. *IEEE Transactions on Industrial Informatics, 17*(3), 1948–1957. https://doi.org/10.1109/TII.2020.2995228
23. Tiwari, A., Dhiman, V., Iesa, M. A. M., Alsarhan, H., Mehbodniya, A., & Shabaz, M. (2021). Patient behavioral analysis with smart healthcare and IoT. *Behavioural Neurology, 2021*, 4028761., 9 pages. https://doi.org/10.1155/2021/4028761
24. Kaur, A., & Gupta, A. K. (2019). E-health approaches for developing countries. In *2019 5th international conference on signal processing, Computing and Control (ISPCC)* (pp. 269–274). https://doi.org/10.1109/ISPCC48220.2019.8988421

Evaluating the Impact of Energy Pricing Policies on Household Consumption Behavior in Light of Global Pandemics Using a Theoretical System Dynamics Model

Mohamad Hamed and Jorge Marx Gómez

1 Introduction

COVID-19 was first discovered in Wuhan, China, in December 2019, and on March 11, 2020, the World Health Organization declared it a global pandemic [1]. The pandemic had significant effects on energy demand, with a substantial decrease in services and industry, but an increase in home energy consumption due to global lockdown measures [2]. While global CO_2 emissions dropped by approximately 5.4% from 2019 to 2020, the reduction is deemed insufficient for meaningful climate change mitigation without substantial climate policy actions beyond the pandemic, because short-term emission reductions have no real influence on the store of greenhouse gases in the atmosphere [3]. For example, the 2008–2009 Global Financial Crisis caused a − 1.4% decrease in global CO_2 emissions in 2009, followed by a + 5.1% increase in emissions in 2010, well above the long-term average. Emissions quickly returned to pre-crisis levels [4]. The shift towards renewable energy (RE) sources increased during the pandemic, driven partly by lockdown measures and seasonal effects affecting renewables' availability [1] whereas the most critical factors influencing RE share are wind and solar parks in operation, weather conditions, and total demand [5]. However, disruptions in global supply chains impacted some renewable energy projects [6]. while it is crucial to prioritize commitment to the health sector and emergency assistance during a crisis like the COVID-19 pandemic [3]. Governments around the world have implemented measures to combat the coronavirus, influencing energy markets and prices, and affecting renewable energy production [7], and learned from the COVID-19 crisis about their societies' ability to deal with a global crisis in the healthcare, economic,

M. Hamed (✉) · J. Marx Gómez
Department of VLB, University of Oldenburg, Oldenburg, Germany
e-mail: mohamad.hamed@uni-oldenburg.de; Jorge.Marx.Gomez@uni-oldenburg.de

J. Marx Gómez et al. (eds.), *Smart and Secure Embedded and Mobile Systems*,
Progress in IS, https://doi.org/10.1007/978-3-031-56603-5_8

After the first lockdown measures were implemented in the United States, demand decreased while RE outperformed the contribution of conventional power plants and the EU. The same thing happened in India and China. Lockdown periods have seen new highs in variable renewables contribution as a share of electricity demand in several EU countries, particularly Italy, Spain, and Germany [3]. Despite these efforts, the interaction between energy pricing policies and household consumption patterns remains poorly understood, as pricing policies may have varying effects on energy-consuming behavior [8].

This chapter is introduction research for series that employs a system dynamics methodology to assess the effects of energy pricing policies on household consumption patterns during global crises and pandemics. The objective is to make consumption behavior more flexible and compatible with renewable energy production. The proposed theoretical system dynamic model evaluates the impact of energy pricing policies on household consumption behavior in Germany, focusing on government measures to combat COVID-19. It analyzes householder responses to energy pricing policies, considering the factors influencing consumption during pandemics and crises, while also considering the generation patterns of renewable energy resources, particularly solar and wind energy, which account for the majority of renewable energy output.

The chapter aims to address the following research questions:

What are the key characteristics of energy pricing policies that should be considered to achieve the long-term strategic goals of renewable energy policies?

Which energy pricing policies impact household consumption and lead to changes in consumption behavior under stable and pandemic conditions?

In conclusion, this study seeks to shed light on the complex relationship between energy pricing policies and household consumption patterns during global crises and pandemics, with the ultimate goal of facilitating a more sustainable and renewable energy-oriented consumption behavior.

2 The Peculiarity of the Electricity Market

Balancing electricity production with demand in conventional power plants is an automated process [9]. However, this task is challenging due to the non-storability of electricity, leading to significant impacts on real-time balancing with any fluctuations in demand or supply. Even small changes in electricity generation or demand can result in substantial shifts in electricity prices within just a few hours in competitive power markets [10]. These markets exhibit seasonality, volatility, and mean-reversion, leading to seasonal pricing behavior [8].

In addition to commercial, industrial, and household electricity activities, climatic conditions such as temperature and daylight hours influence electrical energy consumption behavior. Consequently, electricity prices become seasonal and cyclical. During periods of increased demand, electricity generating stations with higher marginal costs (e.g., oil and diesel) are brought into the supply side, leading to higher spot electricity prices [8].

2.1 *Energy Pricing Policies*

Pricing policy generally refers to how a company determines the pricing of its products and services in relation to costs, value, demand, and competition. In contrast, pricing strategy governs how a company uses pricing to achieve its strategic objectives [11]. Many countries around the world have liberalized their electricity markets with the primary goal of enhancing efficiency, competition, and transparency [10].

2.2 *Factors Affecting Electricity Prices*

While some theoretical studies suggest the classification of electricity markets based on demographic and consumption behavioral factors, practical verification of these concepts remains limited [10]. As previously mentioned, electricity, being non-storable, is subject to various influential factors, which can be classified as follows:

- Outer Events: Events such as power plant outages, non-availability or stoppage of supply chains for oil, gas, and coal for thermal power stations, and accidents or failures in electrical transformers and transmission grid reliability can have a significant impact on electricity prices.
- Primary Factors: These factors include fuel prices, the cost of producing electricity per unit, weather conditions, and time indices such as the day of the week, month, and season [12].
- Operational Factors: Factors related to power transmission, congestion, power system operation and condition, electricity production (deficit/surplus), network maintenance, and electricity load also play a crucial role in determining electricity prices [10].
- Strategic Factors: These factors involve power purchase agreements, bilateral contracts, power exchange mechanisms, bidding strategies, and market design [10].
- Historical Factors: Historical price data and demand patterns also contribute to shaping electricity prices [10].

Thus, understanding the complexities of the electricity market and the factors affecting electricity prices is essential for policymakers and participants in the energy market. This knowledge becomes even more critical during global crises and pandemics when electricity consumption patterns and pricing behavior may experience significant changes.

2.3 Types of Pricing Policies

This section highlights various aspects of electricity pricing, including strategies to reduce peak demand, opportunities to lower electricity bills, and changes in consumption patterns through different pricing types [13]. Electricity pricing policies can be classified into the following concepts:

- Flat Tariffs: Under this pricing policy, the electricity price remains fixed and unaffected by any changes in demand or other factors. Regardless of supplier-side fluctuations, consumers are charged a constant tariff. This approach provides consumers with a sense of stability and no financial incentive to alter their electricity consumption habits. It shields customers from unexpected high-value electricity bills [14].
- Block Rate Tariffs: This type of pricing policy categorizes consumption into blocks, with each block having a different price. As consumption increases within larger blocks, prices also rise, while they decrease when consumption falls below certain thresholds [14].
- Seasonal Tariffs: Seasonal pricing involves setting different electricity prices for different seasons to manage varying demand levels. Prices are increased during high-demand seasons like winter and reduced during low-demand seasons like summer [12].
- Time-of-Use (TOU) Tariffs: TOU or TOD (Time-of-Day) rates offer pre-announced prices that vary throughout the day. This pricing type relies on Smart-Meters and sets higher prices during peak hours and lower prices during off-peak hours [13].
- Critical Peak Pricing (CPP): CPP represents a dynamic pricing policy with higher prices during defined peak hours of high demand and normal prices during the rest of the day. The primary goal of this pricing strategy is to encourage peak load reduction and prompt customers to modify their electricity consumption behavior [15].
- Variable Peak Pricing (VPP): Similar to CPP, VPP also features peak prices that change daily. Customers receive advanced communication about peak prices [16].
- Real-Time Pricing (RTP): RTP is an advanced form of dynamic pricing with significant risk to consumers. Prices in this market fluctuate regularly, often changing every few minutes or every hour [17].

So, electricity pricing policies come in various forms, each with its implications for consumer behavior and demand management. By understanding these different pricing strategies, policymakers, and consumers can make informed decisions to optimize their electricity consumption patterns and manage electricity costs efficiently.

3 System Dynamic

System Dynamics (SD) is a simulation method used for describing, building, testing, and studying complex issues and systems, considering processes, information, organizational boundaries, and strategies [18]. The SD model is composed of interconnected stocks and flow variables, where a stock represents an accumulation, integration, or level, using terminology from different fields [19]. SD serves as a systematic methodology to study and define complex practical problems, and it has the potential to significantly contribute to the current understanding and management of general systems [20].

3.1 System Dynamic Methodology

The SD methodology follows the following steps to simulate a system [18]:

- Formalizing the System: This step involves clearly defining and structuring the system under study. It identifies the key components, interactions, and feedback loops within the system, providing a formal representation of its dynamics.
- Modeling the System: Based on the formalized understanding, a mathematical model is constructed to depict the behavior and relationships of the system's elements. This model typically employs differential equations and feedback loops to capture the dynamic nature of the system.
- Experimenting with Policies: Using the constructed model, different policies and scenarios can be tested to observe their impacts on the system's behavior. This experimentation allows for an understanding of how various policies influence the system's outcomes.
- Discussion of Policies: The results of the experiments are analyzed and discussed. This step involves evaluating the effectiveness of different policies and considering their implementation in the system.

By employing the System Dynamics methodology, researchers can gain valuable insights into the behavior of complex systems, such as those related to energy pricing policies and household consumption patterns. The use of SD modeling facilitates the understanding of how pricing policies affect energy consumption, especially during global crises and pandemics. Moreover, it aids in devising effective strategies for the adoption of renewable energy and the promotion of sustainable practices in response to the challenges of today's world.

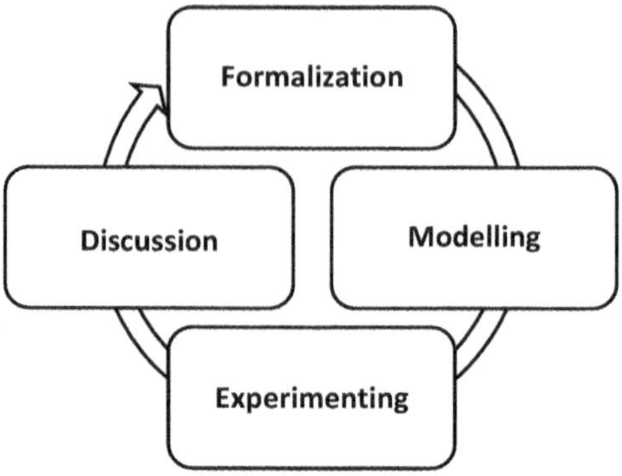

3.2 *Why System Dynamic? A Literature Review*

System Dynamics (SD) has emerged as a powerful tool for simulating and understanding the dynamic relationships within complex energy systems. It can effectively model various components of energy systems, including energy growth, technology adoption, renewable energy limitations, fluctuating prices, environmental concerns, and political factors [20]. SD is particularly well-suited for modeling complex environments with time-dependent variables and multidimensional scales, such as ecosystems and human activities.

Over the last four decades, SD modeling has been widely applied for strategic planning and policy analysis in the energy sector. It has been utilized to analyze the impact of climate change on renewable energy resources, study renewable energy behavior, and allocate resources accordingly [18]. Several studies have employed SD to support decision-making in the field of energy generation:

In the north-western United States, SD was used to support wind energy generation by simulating price patterns for tradable green certificates [21]. Agent-based simulation approaches were suggested for estimating policies for solar energy generation systems in the United States, aiming to create decision-making support tools for distributed photovoltaic (PV) systems and stabilize electricity prices [22]. In Iran, SD modeling was utilized to understand the impact of policy changes on the future development of wind power, emphasizing the importance of supportive policies and industry vision revision [23]. Germany and Spain also adopted SD models to support their transition to green energy. In Germany, a system dynamic model was developed to facilitate the transition until 2025, while in Spain, a model analyzed the dynamic behavior of the photovoltaic sector under various scenarios [20]. Additionally, a theoretical system dynamic model in Iberia was used to investigate the long-term impact of wind power generation on electricity prices in the market [24].

The versatility and ability of SD to capture complex dynamics make it an attractive approach for studying energy systems and devising effective policies to address various challenges, including renewable energy adoption and environmental sustainability. Through SD modeling, researchers and policymakers can gain valuable insights into the interactions between different energy system components and make informed decisions to shape a more sustainable and efficient energy future.

4 Conclusion

This chapter has introduced the application of system dynamics methodology to evaluate the impact of energy pricing policies on household consumption patterns during global crises and pandemics, with the aim of fostering flexibility and compatibility with renewable energy production. System dynamics has proven to be a widely used and valuable tool in the studies reviewed, particularly in analyzing energy policy issues and understanding their long-term effects ranging from 1 month to 100 years. The literature review revealed commonalities among related studies, where dynamic aspects were modeled to optimize power plant planning, production, and utilization in the electricity field. SD's role in supporting decision-making processes in the energy sector was also highlighted in the review. Additionally, it was evident that system dynamics not only allows for studying the causal dynamics within diverse energy systems but also enables specific analyses of energy transitions. The literature emphasized the importance of evaluating energy pricing policies to address concurrent market failures, ensure grid stability, and load distribution during renewable energy production periods.

For the next study, the focus will shift to the practical application of the system dynamics methodology, providing a detailed explanation of building a system dynamic model. By combining theoretical insights with practical implementation, researchers and policymakers can further leverage system dynamics to devise effective strategies for promoting sustainable energy consumption and transitioning to a greener and more resilient energy future.

References

1. Belesova, K., Heymann, D. L., & Haines, A. (2020). Integrating climate action for health into COVID-19 recovery plans. *BMJ, 370*, m3169.
2. Markard, J., & Rosenbloom, D. (2020). A tale of two crises: COVID-19 and climate. *Sustainability Science Practice and Policy, 16*(1), 53–60.
3. OECD. (2020). COVID-19 and the low-carbon transition: Impacts and possible policy responses. 1 OECD 2020 Eval. Initial impact COVID-19 contain. Meas. Econ. Act. httpsreadoecd-Ilibraryorgviewref126126496-Evgsi2gmqjtitleEvaluatingtheinitialimpact ofCOVID-19containmentmeasuresoneconomicactivity.
4. Le Quéré, C., et al. (2020). Temporary reduction in daily global CO2 emissions during the COVID-19 forced confinement. *Nature Climate Change, 10*(7), 647–653.
5. IEA. (2021). COVID-19 impact on electricity, IEA, Paris. [Online]. https://www.iea.org/reports/COVID-19-impact-on-electricity

6. PV, M. (2020). BNEF lowers 2020 global PV outlook due to coronavirus concerns. [Online]. https://pv-magazine-usa.com/2020/03/16/bnef-lowers-2020-global-pv-outlook-due-to-coronavirus-concerns/
7. Volton, E. (2021). COVID-19 impact on electricity. [Online]. https://voltonelektrik.com.tr/blog-detail/COVID_19_impact_on_electricity/
8. Correia-da-Silva, J., Soares, I., & Fernández, R. (2020). Impact of dynamic pricing on investment in renewables. *Energy, 202*, 117695.
9. Basit, A., Hansen, A. D., Altin, M., Sørensen, P., & Gamst, M. (2014). Wind power integration into the automatic generation control of power systems with large-scale wind power. *Journal of Engineering, 2014*(10), 538–545.
10. Girish, G., & Vijayalakshmi, S. (2013). Determinants of electricity price in competitive power market. *International Journal of Business and Management, 8*(21), 70.
11. McWilliams, A., & Siegel, D. S. (2011). Creating and capturing value: Strategic corporate social responsibility, resource-based theory, and sustainable competitive advantage. *Journal of Management, 37*(5), 1480–1495.
12. Keles, D., Hartel, R., Möst, D., & Fichtner, W. (2012). Compressed-air energy storage power plant investments under uncertain electricity prices: An evaluation of compressed-air energy storage plants in liberalized energy markets. *The Journal of Energy Markets, 5*(1), 53.
13. Dutta, G., & Mitra, K. (2017). A literature review on dynamic pricing of electricity. *The Journal of the Operational Research Society, 68*(10), 1131–1145.
14. Shafiee, S., & Topal, E. (2009). When will fossil fuel reserves be diminished? *Energy Policy, 37*(1), 181–189.
15. Herter, K. (2007). Residential implementation of critical-peak pricing of electricity. *Energy Policy, 35*(4), 2121–2130.
16. Suzenski, D. A. (2012). Price response in Connecticut light & power's variable peak pricing option. PhD Duke University.
17. Barbose, G., Goldman, C., & Neenan, B. (2004). *A survey of utility experience with real time pricing*. Lawrence Berkeley National Lab. (LBNL).
18. Hamed, M., Salma, F., Mustafa, O., & Gómez, J. M. (2019). The basic steps of a system dynamics' methodology: Modelling renewable energy decision-making support system. In *Smart Cities/Smart Regions–Technische, wirtschaftliche und gesellschaftliche Innovationen* (pp. 637–650). Springer.
19. Sweeney, L. B., & Sterman, J. D. (2000). Bathtub dynamics: Initial results of a systems thinking inventory. *System Dynamics Review: The Journal of the System Dynamics Society, 16*(4), 249–286.
20. Leopold, A. (2016). Energy related system dynamic models: A literature review. *Central European Journal of Operations Research, 24*(1), 231–261.
21. Lyneis, J. M., & Ford, D. N. (2007). System dynamics applied to project management: A survey, assessment, and directions for future research. *System Dynamics Review: The Journal of the System Dynamics Society, 23*(2–3), 157–189.
22. Zhao, W., Ren, H., & Rotter, V. (2011). A system dynamics model for evaluating the alternative of type in construction and demolition waste recycling center–the case of Chongqing, China. *Resources, Conservation and Recycling, 55*(11), 933–944.
23. Hosseini, S. H., & Shakouri, H. (2016). A study on the future of unconventional oil development under different oil price scenarios: A system dynamics approach. *Energy Policy, 91*, 64–74.
24. Pereira, A. J., & Saraiva, J. T. (2013). A long term generation expansion planning model using system dynamics–case study using data from the Portuguese/Spanish generation system. *Electric Power Systems Research, 97*, 41–50.

Concept Integration of APQC's Process Classification Framework (PCF)® and Enterprise Architecture Frameworks with Signavio

Hans-Jürgen Scheruhn and Pranta Nath

1 Introduction

With the ever-growing world of businesses and information systems, the field of Enterprise Architecture (EA) frameworks and process frameworks are also growing [1–3]. EA serves as a blueprint for an effective IT strategy, guiding the controlled evolution of IT to deliver business value and cost-effectiveness at the same time [4]. While the internal motivation for an organization's strategy to be effectively executed and operations to be optimized forces the organization to adopt an enterprise architecture practice, there are also external pressures such as regulatory frameworks [5].

Considering these increasing needs and complexity of the EA frameworks an integrated enterprise information model based on existing EA frameworks was developed, which is called Enterprise Online Guide (EOG) [6]. Based on 4ITL Information Architecture (IA), EOG was developed to reduce the time and manual effort required to elicit requirements and analyze situations in Enterprise Resource Planning (ERP) projects, in the context of system implementation, maintenance, and further development [6].

Though, the EOG has maintained a vertical relation of process-oriented decomposition similar to APQC's Process Classification Framework® (PCF) [6], there were no clear details about which level of PCF can be compared to which level of EOG. Also, APQC's open standard benchmarking provides process metrics [7] which could have been added to the EOG to give EOG a more holistic view. This

H.-J. Scheruhn
Business Informatics, Media Informatics, Hochschule Harz, Wernigerode, Germany
e-mail: hscheruhn@hs-harz.de

P. Nath (✉)
Technology and Innovation Management, Hochschule Harz, Wernigerode, Germany
e-mail: u36107@hs-harz.de

J. Marx Gómez et al. (eds.), *Smart and Secure Embedded and Mobile Systems*, Progress in IS, https://doi.org/10.1007/978-3-031-56603-5_9

research focuses on the integration of APQC's PCF with EOG and the addition of process metrics to EOG provided by APQC.

In the following, the background section contains information on EA, EA frameworks, EOG, process frameworks, and APQC's PCF. Then, the related works section discusses about the previous studies conducted related to this research. In methodology section, the details about the method followed to conduct this research have been discussed. In the discussion section, the summary and outcome of the research has been discussed. Finally, the limitations and future scope section describes the research gaps and the future possibilities for improvement.

2 Background

In this section, the key concepts used in this research have been described.

2.1 Enterprise Architecture

Enterprise Architecture (EA) can be defined as a set of concepts, methodologies, and models for designing and implementing an organization's organizational structure, business processes, information systems, and infrastructure [8]. Enabling the reduction of wasteful processes through Information Technology (IT) is expected to be EA's greatest value to the firm, according to private sector experience [9].

2.2 Enterprise Architecture Frameworks

On the other hand, an Enterprise Architecture Framework (EAF) offers a systematic design space and a common vocabulary for individuals to collaborate on in order to solve a specific problem [3]. It should not only describe how to design the information system but also a standard of the output of the architecting activity [10, 11]. There are many EA frameworks such as the Zachman Framework for Enterprise Architecture, Department of Defense Architecture Framework (DoDAF), Federal Enterprise Architecture Framework (FEAF), Treasury Enterprise Architecture Framework (TEAF), and The Open Group Architectural Framework (TOGAF) are available today [10, 12, 13].

2.3 *Information Architecture*

Information Architecture (IA) is a focused discipline on the design and building of information systems in support of business strategy in order to facilitate prioritization and decision-making [14]. IA is a component of the EA process that describes the current state, future state, and guidance required to flexibly share and exchange information assets in order to achieve effective enterprise change through a set of requirements, principles, and models [15]. IA provides a holistic overview of a large collection of information based on specific perspectives (also known as views or layers) and levels of abstraction (also known as levels of detail) and integrates all components with each other or in relation to each other [16].

2.4 *Enterprise Online Guide*

Enterprise Online Guide (EOG) is an integrated IA model based on SAP EAF that aids in the organization of variously classified and categorized information of a company and helps to visualize it in a model-based manner in order to obtain a holistic view. This is accomplished through the use of eight company aspects (also known as maps) with four abstraction levels each (also known as zoom factors) [6]. These eight maps are divided into three higher-level maps called, Sustainability Map, Intelligence Map, and Ecosystem Map symbolizing, respectively, the sustainability of the business operations, intelligent human–information system interaction, and networking among the people in the company by means of technology. Also, EOG consists of 32 cells, each of which represents a different fact in a model-based manner depending on the map and zoom factor [17]. Figure 1 shows how the maps and levels are structured in the EOG framework.

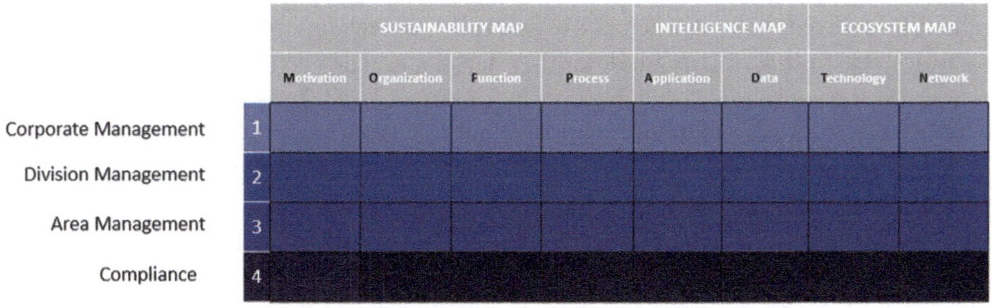

Fig. 1 EOG framework [18]

2.5 *Process Frameworks*

A process framework is a method of categorizing processes [19]. There are several business process frameworks available such as Enhanced Telecommunications Operations Map (eTOM), Information Technology Infrastructure Library (ITIL), Process Classification Framework® (PCF), Supply Chain Operations Reference (SCOR), and Value Reference Model (VRM) [1, 19, 20]. This research was focused on APQC's Process Classification Framework (PCF). APQC's PCF is an open standard developed by the American Productivity and Quality Center (APQC), a nonprofit that promotes benchmarking and best practices worldwide. The PCF is intended to facilitate organizational improvement through process management and benchmarking, regardless of industry, size, or geography. APQC provides not only industry-specific PCFs but also cross-industry versions also [7].

3 Related Works

An enterprise architecture's most essential feature is that it provides a holistic perspective of the organization [8] and is fast becoming acknowledged as the only management and technology discipline capable of producing such designs [21]. On the other hand, ERP systems are software packages that provide cross-organization data integration through business processes consisting of several modules, such as human resources, sales, finance, and production [22].

Thus, ERP case studies are vital as they have a significant impact on knowledge transfer between different entities such as software vendors, lecturers, and users. The case studies, on the other hand, are problematic because they provide little contextual information to the learners aside from the instructions given [23]. Moreover, the diversity of information objects and various a large number of models creates a high degree of complexity in the learning scenario [24]. Also, in an industrial context, companies that use enterprise software, often have to update their software versions as the manufacturers release a newer version of the software and as a result the companies often have to face new project efforts and operational risks that are usually associated with high time and manual effort [6].

To solve these aforementioned issues, an IA called 4 IT Integration Layer Architecture (4ITL) was created [24]. Later, based on 4ITL, a developed version, EOG was created to provide a better learning environment and to analyze ERP systems as automatically as possible while capturing actual processes. EOG was created based on existing EAF and process frameworks which reduced the complexity of learning environment [6].

The EOG distinguishes itself from other architecture concepts by maintaining consistent process orientation across all maps and zoom factors [6]. This research aims to construct a strong and visual relation between a process framework and the EOG to validate the completeness of the EOG.

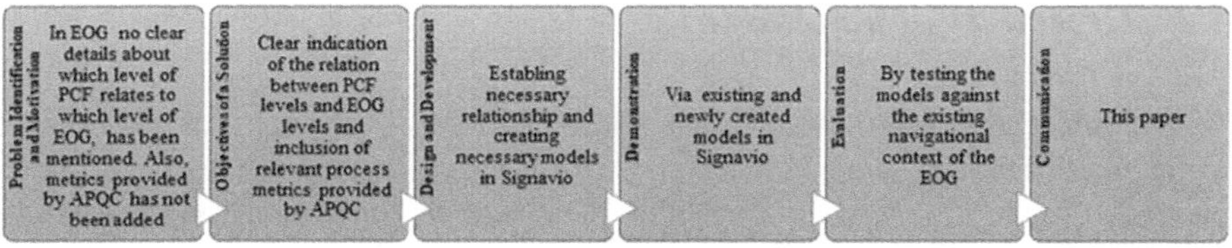

Fig. 2 Design science research process model (own representation)

4 Methodology

This research was done according to the steps mentioned in design science research process model [25]. This section describes all the steps taken to complete this research in detail. Based on other studies [6, 18], an own representation of the design research process model has been shown in Fig. 2.

4.1 Problem Identification and Motivation

The EOG is a combination of redocumentation, process mining, and an IA which was developed to reduce the effort put in by user companies for situation analysis and requirements elicitation in ERP projects [6]. This research paper aims to complement the EOG by indicating the exact similarities with a well-recognized process framework and by adding process metrics.

But, as mentioned, EOG has eight maps and four levels [6]. On the other hand, APQC has five levels across which all process elements are categorized [7]. APQC also has metrics related to these process elements to measure the performance of an organization [7]. The first problem while integrating these two concepts was to determine which level of EOG can be related to which level of APQC. Thus, Research Question 1 (RQ1) was formulated. Is it possible to integrate PCF into specific views and levels of an integrated Enterprise Architecture Framework exemplified by the Enterprise Online Guide (EOG)?

To create the integrated models, a Business Process Management (BPM) tool was needed. For this research, SAP Signavio Process Manager was selected and used. In this cloud-based software, several enterprise architecture modeling languages were available [26]. Among Arcimate 3.0, BPMN 2.0, Event-driven Process Chain (EPC), and several other options available in Signavio, it was necessary to determine which modeling language would serve the purpose of integrating the concepts. Thus, Research Question 2 (RQ2) was formed. How to create the integrated models in Signavio?

4.2 Objectives of a Solution

With the research questions in mind, the objectives of this research paper were to integrate the EOG maps and levels with different levels of APQC and create integrated models in Signavio to establish the validity of the integration. As EOG contains an organization's all the elements and APQC contains all the process elements and process metrics of any type of organization in the world, it was necessary to determine a scope of the research considering the available time and resources. For this research, a typical order-to-cash end-to-end process and corresponding process metrics were considered for a fictitious organization named Global Bike Incorporated (GBI).

At the end of this research, integrated models should be developed and the models should indicate which level of EOG's process and motivation map can be validated by which level of APQC's PCF.

4.3 Design and Development

To integrate the mentioned concepts, first the elements of all the levels of the process map of EOG were analyzed against the five PCF levels. After analyzing the process levels of PCF and EOG, it was found that the PCF level 1 "Category" can be compared with the model "P1 GBI Business Processes" which is in EOG's process map level 1; as for both cases, this level or model represents the highest level of process in the enterprise [7, 27].

Then, PCF level 3 "Process" can be compared with the model "P2 Business Sales Process (SD)" which is in EOG's process map level 2; as for both cases, this level or model represents core elements needed to accomplish a typical order-to-cash end-to-end process [7, 27].

Similarly, PCF level 4 "Activity" can be compared to the model "P3 Sales Process (Process Map)" which is in EOG's process map level 3; as for both cases the level or map represents and identifies the major events that occur during the execution of an end-to-end process [7, 27].

Finally, the PCF level 5 "Task" can be compared to the model "A4 MMBE: SAP S/4Hana Stock Overview" which is in EOG's process map level 4; as in both cases, the level or model represents more fine-grained decomposition than activities [7] or the attribute structure of all associated media or documents which regulates the data input/output process at a physical level of an enterprise [27, 28].

After the existing models had been compared with the PCF's different levels, it was found that no process map level or model of EOG can be compared with PCF level 2—Process Group. For this reason, a new model "P1 Sales and Distribution Process (Process Groups)" was created which can be resembled to PCF level 2. This model groups the similar processes of "P2 Business Sales Process (SD)" and was created using BPMN 2.0 modeling language. This level is established in EOG process map level 1 and has the superiority in terms of hierarchy to "P2 Business Sales Process (SD)" which is in EOG process map level 2.

After, the creation of "P1 Sales and Distribution Process (Process Groups)," it was necessary to indicate which Process Group contains which Processes. For that reason, several other model BPMN models were created in process map level 2 or area management level of EOG's process map.

Now, to find out the relevant metrics for the process elements of the process map of EOG, at first, the processes at level 2 of EOG's process map were listed in an Excel file and then were compared with the process elements of APQC's PCF. The process elements that matched with EOG processes were recorded in the Excel file. Relevant metrics of PCF's process elements were also recorded.

After integrating the individual processes from both PCF and EOG, it was found that not every individual process of a certain level from an organization can be related to a specific level of PCF. As this research was conducted based on an enterprise called Global Bike Incorporated (GBI), an individual process named "Payment Processing" of this certain enterprise, which is in EOG process map level 2, can be compared with an activity of PCF, which lies in PCF level 4. For this case study, it was found that all of the individual level 2 processes of EOG relate to activities from PCF level 4. Thus, the activity metrics developed by APQC's open standard benchmarking were considered as the metrics of the processes of process map level 2 of EOG.

4.4 Demonstration

The research project was demonstrated by BPMN 2.0 and Archimate 3.0 business process modeling languages and by creating several BPMN diagrams, objective diagrams, and technical term models in the SAP Signavio platform.

To demonstrate the relation between the level 2 processes of EOG with the PCF, a technical terms model "O2 Business Vocabulary / Process (APQC)" was created. To establish this technical term model as a level 2 model of organization map in EOG, an additional technical term model "O1 Business Vocabulary / Process (APQC)" was created in level 1 of EOG.

To demonstrate the metrics of the organizational process of GBI derived from APQC's open standard benchmarking, several objective diagrams were created in EOG motivation map level 2. To maintain the hierarchical level, an additional model "M1 Order-to-Cash Process Goals" was created in EOG motivation map level 1 and necessary relationships were established with the objective diagrams in motivation map level 2.

Also, as mentioned in Sect. 4.3, a new BPMN model was created in EOG process map level 1 to establish a relation between PCF level 2 and EOG process map. To demonstrate which process group contains which processes several other BPMN models were created on EOG process map level 2 and hierarchical relationships

Table 1 Comparison between the PCF levels and EOG levels

PCF levels	Relevant EOG levels	Relevant EOG models (Examples)
1 – Category	1	P1 GBI Business Processes
2 – Process Group	1	P1 Sales and Distribution Process (Process Groups)
3 – Process	2	P2 Business Sales Process (SD)
4 – Activity	3	P3 Sales Process (Process Map)
5 – Task	4	A4 MMBE: SAP S/4Hana Stock Overview

were established between the process group model in level 1 and the process models in level 2.

A summary of the relations between the concepts and the list of newly created models in EOG are demonstrated in Tables 1 and 2.

4.5 *Evaluation*

For evaluating this research, three of the four evaluation steps from the proposed framework for evaluating design science research were followed [29]. The evaluation criteria for this research are consistent with the criteria mentioned or used in other research studies [6, 28, 29]. EVAL 1 validates the research need with the help of criterion "Novelty." EVAL 2 justifies the design methodology with the help of criterion "Internal Consistency." Finally, EVAL 3 validates the proof of applicability with the help of criterion "Feasibility." The last step of the evaluation process mentioned in Table 3 was not conducted during this research study. This step is mentioned in detail in Sect. 6.

EVAL 1: Research Need. The validity of the research need can be justified from the Sect. 4.1, where the problem statement, research gap, and design objectives have been described and the previous studies related to that justify the need for this research.

EVAL 2: Logical Reasoning-based Design Methodology. The models created to establish a relation between the PCF levels and EOG process levels are consistent with previous models of EOG. Most of the relations shown between the PCF levels and EOG process levels were done with existing EOG models. Only for process group a new model was created which is also consistent with the EOG models. To maintain the consistency of the navigation several other BPMN models were created to establish a connection between the process group model and consisting processes.

The objective diagrams created during this study are also consistent with the navigation of EOG structure. The metrics introduced as goals in the models are for process level 2. So, the newly created objective diagrams are in motivation map level 2 in EOG and are connected to the corresponding processes. Also, to maintain the hierarchical consistency of the objective diagrams with EOG, an additional model was created in motivation map level 1.

Table 2 List of newly created models in EOG

Position in EOG (in terms of Maps)	Position in EOG (in terms of levels)	Model name
Process	1	P1 Sales and Distribution Process (Process Groups)
Process	2	P2 Accounts Receivable Management Processes
Process	2	P2 Billing Management Processes
Process	2	P2 Inventory Management Processes
Process	2	P2 Master Data Management Processes
Process	2	P2 Sales Management Processes
Process	2	P2 Shipping and Transportation Management Processes
Organization	1	O1 Business Vocabulary / Process (APQC)
Organization	2	O2 Business Vocabulary / Process (APQC)
Motivation	1	M1 Order-to-Cash Process Goals
Motivation	2	M2 Billing Document Processing Goals
Motivation	2	M2 Customer Order Processing Goals
Motivation	2	M2 Inventory Processing Goals
Motivation	2	M2 Invoice Processing Goals
Motivation	2	M2 Quotation Processing Goals

Table 3 Evaluation steps

Evaluation steps (EVAL)	Methodological approach	Evaluation criteria
1	Validation of research need	Novelty
2	Logical reasoning-based design methodology	Internal consistency
3	Feasibility analysis based on demonstration with prototype	Feasibility
4	Surveys and expert interviews (future scope of work)	Impact on artifact environment and user (future scope of work)

The technical term model created is also consistent with the current structure of the EOG and lies in organization map level 2. An additional model was created on level 1 to maintain the consistency of levels.

EVAL 3: Demonstration with Prototype. As mentioned in Sect. 4.5 and demonstrated in Table 1, the recent models were created in SAP Signavio Process Manager using BPMN 2.0 and Archimate 3.0 modeling languages and it successfully establishes connections between APQC's PCF and open standard benchmarking with EOG's levels and maps. Also, with the help of some newly created additional models mentioned in Sect. 4.5 and Table 2, it was also possible to navigate horizontally and vertically between the models in EOG, similarly as the original context of EOG suggests [6].

4.6 Communication

The communication of this research is being done through this paper and previously has been done by presenting the research progress and methods in classes at Hochschule Harz, Germany in front of professors and students.

5 Discussion

The aim of this research was to establish a connection between the APQC's PCF with the EOG so that the development and use of EOG can be more justified as the APQC's PCF is a recognized process framework and is being used around the world by leading industries. Also, APQC's open standard benchmarking provides relevant metrics for the processes which eventually helped to identify relevant metrics for the processes of EOG and particularly in this for the case study of GBI's processes.

Though, in this research, a general connection between the levels of APQC' PCF and EOG's process map levels was made, during the selection of relevant metrics for the processes it was found that for an individual process, the connection between the levels can vary from organization to organization. One of the reasons this happens is because in PCF, lower-level elements are not sub-types of the higher element and instead it is based on the method of functional decomposition. In PCF, until an acceptable level of detail is reached, each higher-level parent function is partitioned into multiple lower-level child functions and relationships between child functions are not taken into account [30]. Another reason is that in PCF all the possible processes available for an industry are listed. But, for a particular case study many processes may not be required, the processes may have different sequences and many processes can have different names than the process names mentioned in PCF [7, 19]. So, for a particular process of a particular organization or enterprise the relative connection between the PCF levels and EOG levels can vary despite a general comparison that has been established in this research.

As mentioned, using SAP Signavio Process Manager the necessary models were created to integrate the mentioned concepts. However, in SAP Signavio Process Manager, it is not possible to establish a hierarchical level directly. If one model is in level 2 of EOG, then the model has to be somehow connected to a model in level 1. For this reason, several additional models were created to maintain the accurate levels of the necessary models. On the other hand, Signavio allows users to integrate APQC PCF directly into the Process Manager with the help of their advanced process modeling tools. This feature is very useful as it allows a user to compare a vast bank of industry standard process models against their own current and future state models [31] and was used during this research to gather ideas about how the process models are designed according to the industry standards provided by APQC.

Overall, this research validates EOG as it can be said that EOG's enterprise architecture framework is supported by a recognized process framework like APQC's PCF because this research has shown, how the PCF levels and EOG levels are related and necessary models were created to establish the relation.

6 Limitations and Future Scope

In the evaluation process of this research, step 4 of the evaluation was not conducted. In future, step 4 of the evaluation can be conducted through surveys and expert interviews in both academic context and industrial contexts. The step 4 of evaluation process will give better insight about the effectiveness of the models and in overall about the EOG.

For this research, the EOG was compared with only one process framework called APQC's PCF. But, in future, the research can focus on other process frameworks such as Supply Chain Operations Reference (SCOR) and Value Reference Model (VRM). Future studies can be focused on integrating these other process frameworks with EOG.

For creating and demonstrating the models, only SAP Signavio Process Manager was used. But, in future other modeling tools can be used and can be compared for the best choice. In this research, because of the limitation of indicating a hierarchy of a model directly, several additional models had to be created. Creating models using other modeling tools may be able to solve this problem.

References

1. Houy, C., Fettke, P., & Loos, P. (2015). Business process frameworks. In J. vom Brocke & M. Rosemann (Eds.), *Handbook on business process management 2: Strategic alignment, governance, people and culture* (pp. 153–175). Springer.
2. Pavlak, A. (2006). Enterprise architecture: Lessons from classical architecture. *Journal of Enterprise Architecture, 2*(2), 20–27.
3. Schekkerman, J. (2004). *How to survive in the jungle of enterprise architecture frameworks: Creating or choosing an enterprise architecture framework*. Trafford Publishing.
4. Hildayanti, S., Putra, R., Suhandi, N., et al. (2018). Enterprise architecture framework selection for higher education using TOPSIS method. *International Journal of Engineering and Technology, 7*, 5327–5330. https://doi.org/10.14419/ijet.v7i4.16140
5. Jonkers, H., Lankhorst, M., ter Doest, H., et al. (2006). Enterprise architecture: Management tool and blueprint for the organisation. *Information Systems Frontiers, 8*, 63–66. https://doi.org/10.1007/s10796-006-7970-2
6. Scheruhn, H.-J., Reiter, C., Biermann, C., & Bayramli, E. (2021). Analyse von ERP-Systemen am Beispiel von SAP. In Brand Lennart; Gräslund K; KD; KH; TK; WH (ed) Proceedings of the SAP Academic Community Conference 2021 DACH. pp. 153–175.
7. APQC. (2019). Process classification framework. Retrieved February 23, 2022, from https://www.apqc.org/resource-library/resource-listing/apqc-process-classification-framework-pcf-cross-industry-excel-7
8. Lankhorst, M. (2005). *Enterprise architecture at work*. Springer-Verlag.
9. Spewak, S. H., & Hill, S. (1992). *Enterprise architecture. Planning*. John Wiley, Sons, inc..
10. Goethals, F. (2005). An overview of enterprise architecture framework deliverables. Available SSRN 870207.
11. The Open Group The TOGAF® Standard. (2022). Version 9.2. Retrieved February 22, 2022, from https://pubs.opengroup.org/architecture/togaf9-doc/arch/
12. Urbaczewski, L., & Mrdalj, S. (2006). A comparison of enterprise architecture frameworks. *Issues in Information Systems, 7*, 18–23.
13. Minoli, D. (2008). *Enterprise architecture a to Z: Frameworks, business process modeling, SOA, and infrastructure technology*. CRC Press.
14. Carter, H. (1999). Information architecture. *Work Study, 48*, 182–185. https://doi.org/10.1108/00438029910286026
15. Enterprise Information Architecture (EIA). (2022). Retrieved February 27, 2022, from https://www.gartner.com/en/information-technology/glossary/enterprise-information-architecture
16. Krcmar, H. (2015). *Information management*. Springer.
17. Scheruhn, H.-J., Weidner, S., & Müller, S. (2021). Case study: Enterprise online guide.
18. Bayramli, E. (2022). *Design eines Konzeptes zur automatisierten Analyse von ERP-Systemen am Bsp. von SAP*. Hochschule Harz.
19. Burlton, R., & Lyke-Ho-Gland, H. (2016). Part three: Frameworks and end-to-end processes. In: BPTrends. Retrieved February 23, 2022, from https://www.bptrends.com/part-three-frameworks-and-end-to-end-processes/

20. Girjatovičs, A., Rizoto-Vidala-Pesoa, L. M., & Kuzņecova, O. (2018). Implementation of SCOR based business process framework for logistics and supply chain in retail company. *Information Technology and Management Science, 21*, 69–74. https://doi.org/10.7250/itms-2018-0011
21. Bernard, S. A. (2012). *An introduction to enterprise architecture*. AuthorHouse.
22. Esteves, J., & Pastor, J. (2001). Enterprise resource planning systems research: An annotated bibliography. *Communication of the AIS, 7*, 1–52. https://doi.org/10.17705/1CAIS.00708
23. Scheruhn, H.-J., Sicorello, S., & Weidner, S. (2012). *Repository-based ERP case studies: A study about chances and benefits of agile case study development*. BIS.
24. Scheruhn, H.-J., Ackermann, D., Braun, R., & Förster, U. (2013). Repository-based implementation of information pyramid: A study based on an ERP case study. In *Proceedings, part III, of the 15th international conference on human-computer interaction. Users and contexts of use - Volume 8006* (pp. 446–455). Springer-Verlag.
25. Peffers, K., Tuunanen, T., Gengler, C., et al. (2006). The design science research process: A model for producing and presenting information systems research. Proc First Int Conf Des Sci Res Inf Syst Technol DESRIST.
26. SAP Signavio Process Manager. (2022). Retrieved February 23, 2022, from https://www.signavio.com/products/process-manager/
27. Scheruhn, H.-J. (2022). Enterprise online guide. Retrieved February 27, 2022, from eog.hs-harz.de
28. Scheruhn, H.-J., Bayramli, E., & Hintsch, J. (2020). An enterprise information model for knowledge transfer with application systems: The current state of Enterprise GPS. In *Proceedings of the 12th international conference on computer supported education* (pp. 278–289). SCITEPRESS - Science and Technology Publications.
29. Sonnenberg, C., & vom Brocke, J. (2012). Evaluations in the science of the artificial—Reconsidering the build-evaluate pattern in design science research (pp. 381–397).
30. Gruchman, G. (2012). Fire and ice. Part 5. BPMN and the forgotten art. In: ARIS BPM blog. Retrieved February 22, 2022, from https://www.ariscommunity.com/users/grzegorzgruchman/2012-03-05-fire-and-ice-part-5-bpmn-and-forgotten-art
31. Signavio. (2022). APQC & Signavio. Retrieved February 28, 2022, from https://www.signavio.com/reference-models/apqc-framework/

A KPI System to Measure Bicycle Attractiveness of a City

Johannes Schering, Jorge Marx Gómez, and Frank Köster

1 Introduction

Quality assessment of traffic infrastructure is important for municipalities. On the one hand, because of environmental problems more action in the direction of sustainable mobility is needed. On the other hand, municipal budgets are limited [1]. That means that efficient measures have to be taken. Although cycling has huge potential to contribute to the solution of these problems, bicycle infrastructure was often neglected in the past: Compared to other countries German municipalities are only middle rated in investments in the bicycle infrastructure [2]. The share of investments in bike infrastructure in relation to other means of transport is very limited [3]. To make the right decisions with a limited budget the city needs to know more about how good or bad a bike path in an overall score is.

If you ask cyclists what bad infrastructure means (and which promotional measures they prefer), you will get a lot of different answers on that. "My bike path on the way to work is too narrow, often I cannot overtake," "I have to stop for 9 out of 10 times at the intersection I have to cross on the inner city main road," "The root damages on this specific road section make the bike trip hardly uncomfortable," etc. A lot of examples can be imagined here. It shows that there is a need for an appropriate performance measurement system that supports the definition of a quality level for specific road sections. Knowledge about specific qualities may help the administration to make the right investment decisions.

J. Schering (✉) · J. Marx Gómez
Department of Business Informatics VLBA, University of Oldenburg, Oldenburg, Germany
e-mail: johannes.schering@uni-oldenburg.de; jorge.marx.gomez@uni-oldenburg.de

F. Köster
German Aerospace Center (DLR), Institute for AI Safety and Security, Braunschweig, Germany
e-mail: frank.koester@dlr.de

J. Marx Gómez et al. (eds.), *Smart and Secure Embedded and Mobile Systems*, Progress in IS, https://doi.org/10.1007/978-3-031-56603-5_10

Several years ago cities and regions started to gather cycling data. A classic example may be the bike counters to measure the amount of bike traffic on a specific road. Many cities provide bicycle apps to get an overview about general bicycle use behavior [4]. In the past few years, many cities have perceived growing numbers of cyclists [5]. Beyond counting and apps, there are quite a lot of cycling data sources that could be potentially used to support the decision-making process. Many Key Performance Indicators (KPIs) could be developed and calculated based on these available data sources. The research question that should be answered in this contribution is which KPIs are relevant to support an efficient planning process. Our goal is to develop a stakeholder-oriented KPI system under consideration of different measurement technologies to enable a continuous assessment of the attractiveness of the bicycle infrastructure. Similar approaches have been developed for the quality assessment of the road infrastructure [6]. Based on the improved knowledge base regarding the attractiveness of cycling road path network cities may be supported on their way to make right decisions in the cycling promotion process.

The paper is structured as follows. We will give a short introduction to cycling data and available data sources that may be applied to the bike infrastructure attractiveness assessment. These data sources have to be categorized according to their related topic and relevance. Some of the identified criteria may be more important than others. As we will see there are already quite a lot of data sources available that may be important in this process. Metrics in the style of KPIs have to be developed and applied for each data set to support the quality assessment. We will make a first attempt to present an integrated and connected KPI system for the bike infrastructure quality assessment. In the final chapter, the discussion and outlook, we will describe the further development steps and discuss about how to evaluate this first approach. More relevant data sources and metrics need to be prioritized in the KPI system development process. Other data sources that were not considered so far may be added.

2 Data Sources

As more and more cities have started the process of gathering bicycle data, we will briefly present our available data sources in this chapter.

2.1 Bike Parking

The availability of cycle racks or other objects that allow to park a bicycle safely may be an aspect that makes cycling attractive in a city. If nowhere is a suitable bike parking facility is available, the cyclist has to care that the (potentially expensive) bike may be stolen when she or he is at work or at shopping. To avoid these kinds of problems attractive and secure bike parking facilities are necessary. The city of

Utrecht in the Netherlands is famous not only for attractive bike paths but also for bike parking. The parking station *Stationsplein* at the central railway station with 12.500 parking spaces on three floors is the biggest bike parking facility in the world [7, 8]. The project that was finalized in 2019 also includes 1.000 public transport bicycles, called OV-bicycle [7]. Citizens can use an app to find available parking spots [8]. The inner city parking stations are equipped with a sensor technology that detects how many people coming in and leaving in a certain amount of time. The attributes include the minimum and maximum number of available (or occupied) bike parking spots. The number of incoming and leaving bicycles (inFlow and outFlow) are also included. As a further development process, we enriched the dataset with the country and city name, the geo-coordinates of the parking facility, and a weather classification as part of the Bicycle Data project [9]. The data may deliver further insights into bicycle use and the demand for bicycle parking.

2.2 *Bike Counting*

To get a first overview about the number of cyclists at (important?) roads or road sections many municipalities have integrated bike counting devices into the asphalt. Induction slopes are very common [10]. As an alternative, rubber tubes are often used for temporary counting campaigns [11]. The newly gathered data can provide an overview to the city administration or decision makers in cycling planning which of the considered locations at intesections or road segments show the highest amount of cyclists. As an example, the city of Oldenburg was running 15 permanent bicycle counting stations in 2021 that are located around the inner city ring road. Figure 1 shows that most people are counted at *Nadorster Straße* which is one of the main roads in the city. *Auguststraße* and *Damm* are at second and third spots. The visualization is related to the measured numbers per day between May 2021 and May 2022. More than 2.000 cyclists were counted per day during that period at the inner city connection of *Nadorster Straße* (only cyclists who are cycling in the city direction were counted). It is obvious that more frequently roads will show higher numbers of bicycle accidents or reportings about infrastructure shortcomings. The number of bicycle traffic amount should be considered in the calculation of related KPIs. Further information about bike counting methods and data analysis results can be found in Schering & Marx Gómez [12].

2.3 *Tracking*

Indeed, the most obvious kind of data collection in the bicycle traffic segment is tracking the trips on a geo-referenced basis. There are many providers of smartphone applications available on the market. Some of these are more concentrating on daily bicycle use, others provide information for the best bike tour at the weekend or

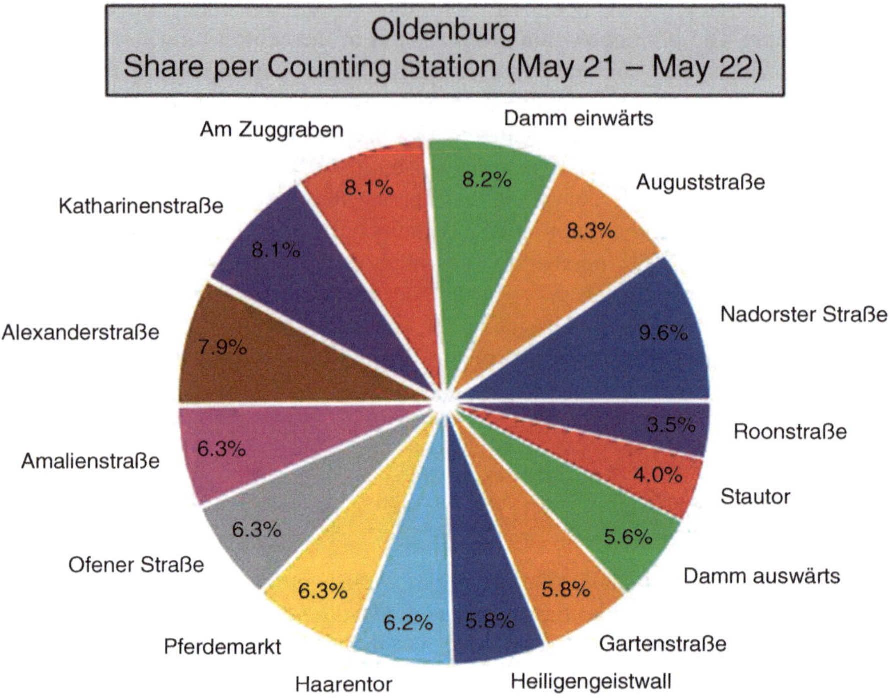

Fig. 1 Share of bicycle traffic amount in Oldenburg at 15 inner city bike counting stations

help you to find points of interest (POI) when you visit a city. The GPS data can be used to learn which roads are frequently used. The data analysis may support the understanding of which road segments cyclists have to stop more often or where the travel speed is reduced because of too much traffic amount or reduced space availability. Bicycle apps are often limited to specific target groups and tend to be more used in leisure time [13]. As an alternative, bike sensor systems are more and more used. Schering et al. [14] give a comprehensive overview about available technologies in this field. The integrated sensors are often very similar compared to smartphone sensors. We have available the data of different smartphone apps [15], ECOSense [16], and Sniffer Bike [15]. In general, if the data measurement frequency is high enough (below one measurement per second) the analysis of brakings or the vibration based on the acceleration sensor is possible. Additional environmental sensors as fine particle concentration in the air, temperature, humidity, or lightning may be integrated into the bike sensor systems. As an example, the Karlsruhe University of Applied Sciences made a study about fine dust pollution and its health influence on babies in bicycle trailers. The sensor measurements revealed that it is healthier for small children to be transported in a car [17].

Another aspect is the bike-sharing system. Many cities have made available a public bike renting system to visitors and citizens as a supplement to public transport services. As an example, the city of Stockholm provides the so-called "Stockholm E-Bikes" service. At this moment it consists of 750 pedelecs which can be parked at 70 stations. The service that only costs around one Euro per day is going to be expanded with e-cargo bikes in the future [18].

2.4 *Bike Infrastructure*

A data collection component with relatively limited availability is bike infrastructure data. That means machine-readable information about the state or the conditions of a bike path. This may include the length of a road, the wideness of a bike path, cleaning intervals, surface types, or road damages. This kind of data is often not available in municipalities. The maximum speed for motorized traffic or the type of alignment of the bike path (if there is one) is often known. Some running research projects as the INFRASense project [19] have started to make prototypical data collections in this field. In addition, many municipalities have used geo-information systems to analyze and visualize bike infrastructure data for many years [20]. These may include bus lines and stops, the incline of a bike path, or the bicycle infrastructure network. More information can be found in Schering et al. [21].

Surface conditions seem to be very relevant to make assessments about the bike path network. What should not be missed here are subjective perceptions of the infrastructure of the cyclists when they cycle in a city. For instance, a cyclist can cross a bike path with many damages (potholes, root damages, etc.) or with seasonal problems (ice and snow in winter periods, leaves and puddles in autumn). To include this kind of user-centered data, it makes sense to take citizen reportings on infrastructure quality into account. At this moment we have available the reportings of the EMSOs portal (EreignisMeldeSystem Osnabrueck). Schering et al. [22] provide an overview about the included information and the potentials of the related data analysis. The data set from 2021 shows that green areas and parking violators are playing a key role in the perceptions.

2.5 *Traffic Safety*

The increasing bicycle use is also reflected by a growing mortality rate of cyclists in Europe [23]. Many cities have formulated the vision zero which means that the number of killed cyclists per year can be reduced to zero. As an example, the city of New York has established a Vision Zero Task force including a Bicycle and Micromobility Working Group to start a dialogue on how to decrease the number of fatalities in the city [24]. A safe infrastructure can motivate more people to use the bike more often instead of the car [25]. Only 7–15% of bike accidents in European countries (e.g. Belgium) are reported to the police [37]. According to Shinar et al. [26], the German police provides a comparable reliable database about different types of bicycle crashes. The datasets provide a first overview about potential problems in the bike infrastructure and include attributes such as accident type, accident severity, and location.

3 KPI System on Bike Infrastructure Quality Assessment

In the next step, all of these bicycle data sources may be divided into different categories. Regarding the data sources that are described above we may differentiate between sources that relate to (1) **Bicycle Use**, (2) **Bicycle Infrastructure**, and (3) **Traffic Safety**. The first category consists of time series data that includes information about cycling behavior. It shows where and how long people are parking their bikes, how long and how fast people are cycling in a city, which are the most frequently used bicycle routes, where they stop or wait at red lights or intersections, etc. As mentioned before, mobile bike sensor systems can be attached with further sensor devices that gather information about the environment as the ECOSense and Sniffer Bike projects did before. The second category consists of all relevant data sets that describe the conditions of the bike path or infrastructure network. These mainly consist of non-time series data and could describe the length, the width, the surface type, or the priority regulation at an intersection. There may be some overlapping with the first category as the sensor systems mentioned above can also provide information about surface conditions (e.g., by acceleration sensors). The third category can consist of every data source that is related to traffic safety. Police statistics about bicycle crashes can provide valuable KPIs. Near accidents deliver further insights into critical spots of the infrastructure (e.g., at intersections) that were not detected as accident hot spots so far. In general, most of the traffic safety-related data sources may include a time stamp.

3.1 DuPont KPI System

The key question of this research is how the described data sources and related metrics can be meaningfully interrelated. In general, in the case of many different criteria stakeholders will have choice problems. The relative importance of the criteria has to be known to solve this problem [27]. It has to be considered that in a closed KPI system may be variables that are interdependent with others. As an example, the cycling speed level may be influenced by the availability and the state of the bike path. The number of accidents on a specific road section may not only depend on the road conditions but also on the number of cyclists—if the route is not attractive for cycling nobody will choose this route and no accident will occur. A low number of accidents does not automatically mean that the road is cycling friendly. If the administration decides to increase the budget for safe bike paths, it can be expected that the satisfaction of the cyclists increases while the number of accidents decreases at the same time. These examples show that there are many interdependencies that have to be taken into account. The KPI system to define the attractiveness of the bike infrastructure should not consist of isolated but of integrated KPIs.

Therefore, there is a need for a causal model to make clear which criteria are influencing each other. This intended model also gives a comprehensive overview about available data sources. At the same time, it can also reveal which data sources are missing and should be gathered in the future to support the further cycling promotion process.

In this context, we suggest a KPI system for the determination of the attractiveness of the cycling network in a city that is inspired by the DuPont System of financial control. This methodological framework has its origin in the financial sector: The return on investment (ROI) calculation which is also known as the DuPont System on financial control is one of the earliest and still one of the most frequently used systems to measure the performance of the financial wealth of enterprises [28, 29]. It provides a comprehensive overview about the business performance of a company in terms of sales and investment. Decision makers in the accounting department get an overview about whether investments are made in the right future segments. At the same time, it may reveal weaknesses in efficiency and performance. Because of the ratio format (e.g., sales/assets), the ROI makes it possible to compare different companies of varying sizes [30]. The investor can determine whether an investment in a company performs better compared to another one of comparable size and structure.

This approach can be easily applied to other fields of interest as the bicycle infrastructure. The related KPIs make it possible to compare different cities of different sizes in different development stages of cycling promotion. It also helps to identify strengths and potential fields of action for further investments in the infrastructure. Figure 2 shows how an interconnected DuPont system-based KPI system for the assessment of bike paths may look like. It includes the sub-topics that were defined above under consideration of the available data sources, the related (potential) KPIs, and its interdependencies.

3.2 Cycling Infrastructure Attractiveness KPIs and its Interrelations

The KPI system for bicycle infrastructure quality shows many related KPIs that are structured according to the classification mentioned above. The metrics in the field **Bicycle Use** show how many people are cycling per day, per month, per year, etc. in total numbers and in average. The example in Fig. 1 reveals how many people use bike per day on specific road sections in Oldenburg. The peak hours may be

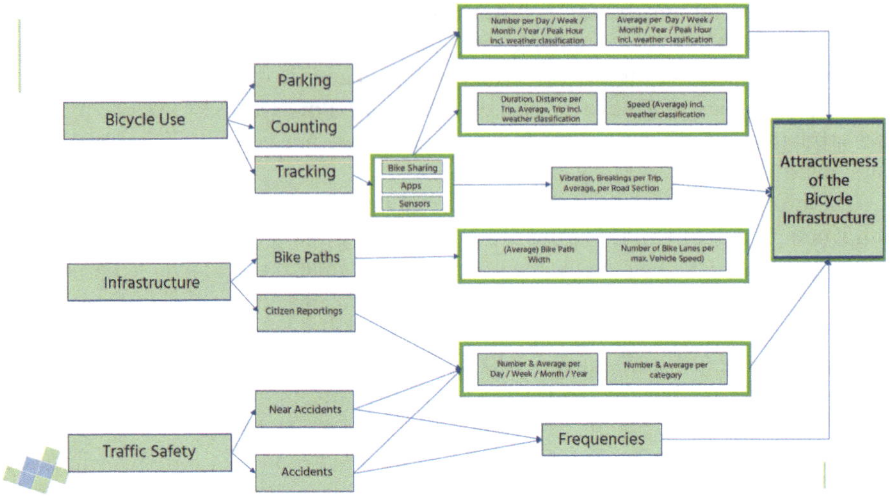

Fig. 2 A prototypical KPI system to assess the attractiveness of the bike infrastructure

observed separately. These can be defined at the time intervals when the majority of bicycle users cycling to work or to school—on working days from 7 to 9 am and 4 to 6 pm. On routes with a tendency to daily life bicycle use as *Nadorster Straße* or *Damm* the highest share of cyclists can be expected. Weather conditions have a strong impact on bicycle use. From many studies, we know that the number of cyclists decreases when it is rainy, windy, or when there are low temperatures outside [31]. Bad weather conditions do not only have an influence on the number but also on the length of the trips. The tracking data of the mobile sensors gives the additional opportunity to look at average distances, durations, and the speed level of the bike trips. As mentioned before, the mobile sensors provide a platform to integrate further sensors. As an example, the acceleration sensor allows to calculate vibrations on a trip. It can be expected that road sections with many bumps can be identified. In addition to the amount of bicycle traffic, the amount of motorized traffic plays also a role to define how attractive a bicycle connection is. If the amount of vehicles is high, the risk of an accident increases. The travel speed will also be reduced, especially in the case of waiting times at red lights.

The metrics in the field **Infrastructure** allow to learn more about the construction criteria of bike paths and lanes. One of the key aspects here is the bike path width. The available space decides when overtaking is possible and is an important determinant about the travel speed. CROW Fietsberaad in the Netherlands has tried to define quality levels for the bike infrastructure based on bike path width in the past [32]. The road lengths can be used to calculate the number of road defects per meter on a specific road. Surface types and conditions should also be part of the KPI system. In general, an asphalt-based surface is more suitable for cycling compared to cubble stone. The distribution of different types will provide further information about cycling attractiveness. Which surface types are more suitable will be discussed with traffic planning experts in the future.

In the case of **Traffic Safety** similar KPIs as in the category Bicycle Use can be imagined. That includes total numbers and averages per day, per month, and per year. It supports the understanding in which city and at which road sections an increased amount of critical situations happen. The results can be used to make specific road sections more safe and convenient. In the case of the accidents different accident types need to be considered. There are turning or crossing accidents—mainly occur at intersections—alone accidents (at railway tracks, slipperiness road), dooring situations, overtaking, etc. [33]. Which of these are more relevant than others is not clarified at this moment. What we know is that turning and crossing is the most common accident type—nearly three out of four cycling accidents in the city of Oldenburg belong to this accident type. The accident severity (not injured, slightly injured, seriously injured, killed) should also be considered in the calculation to identify danger hotspots in the cycling network. In addition to the daily averages, the frequencies could also be calculated. This KPI gives an overview about how many minutes (or hours) it takes until a critical situation happens. In the case of the near accidents this methodology was used to compare traffic safety at several intersections in Antwerp (Belgium) [34] and several Dutch locations [35]. It can be added that critical situations (e.g., evasion movements) on a bike trip can also be detected by smartphone or other mobile sensors [36].

4 Outlook and Conclusion

The presented approach delivers a prototypical implementation of a KPI system to measure the attractiveness of the bicycle infrastructure. The metrics can be applied to the whole city but also to specific road sections or bike paths. In then next step, the approach will be evaluated with traffic planning experts. It has to be discussed which of the identified KPIs are more relevant than others. Maybe some more relevant KPIs that were overlooked are not part of the KPI system so far.

What is only considered at this stage partially in this approach are the interconnections between the three categories that were identified (Bicycle Use, Infrastructure, Traffic Safety). The number of cyclists, the travel speed, and the frequency of bicycle use are not only interconnected with the availability and the quality of the cycling path network but also with the number of (near) accidents. The length and width of a specific road have also to be considered in the analysis process of critical situations. These more detailed interconnections will be specified and discussed with experts in detail and will be considered in the next and more stakeholder-oriented version of the KPI system for the determination of the attractiveness of the bicycle infrastructure.

Acknowledgments This contribution was composed as part of the INFRASense project which is funded by the Bundesministerium für Digitales und Verkehr (BMDV, *German Federal Ministry of Digital and Transport*) as part of the mFUND program (project number 19F2186E) with a funding amount of around 1.2 Mio. Euro. As part of mFUND the BMDV supports research development projects in the field of data based and digital mobility innovations. Part of the project funding is the promotion of networking between the stakeholders in politics, business, administration, and research as well as the publication of open data on the Mobilithek portal.

References

1. Mendgen, A. (2022). Städtetag: Investitionsstau für kommunale Infrastruktur bei 150 Milliarden Euro. Retrieved August 04, 2022, from https://www.rnd.de/politik/staedtetag-150-milliarden-euro-investitionsstau-fuer-kommunale-infrastruktur-4PAGR7FI7VCVPDBN62KMWGUAWY.html
2. Allgemeiner Deutscher Fahrrad-Club ADFC: Interaktive Karte: Wie Europa in die Fahrradinfrastruktur investiert. (2022). Retrieved August 04, 2022, from https://www.adfc.de/artikel/interaktive-karte-wie-europa-in-die-fahrradinfrastruktur-investiert
3. Schmelzer, T. (2022). Mehr Fahrrad wagen! Retrieved August 04, 2022, from https://www.wiwo.de/politik/deutschland/verkehrspolitik-mehr-fahrrad-wagen/19956772.html
4. European Cyclists' Federation: Cycling counting. (2022). Retrieved August 04, 2022, from https://ecf.com/cycling-data/cycling_counting
5. Kraus, S., & Koch, N. (2021). Provisional COVID-19 infrastructure induces large, rapid increases in cycling. *Proceedings of the National Academy of Sciences of the United States of America: PNAS, 118*(15), 1. https://doi.org/10.1073/pnas.2024399118
6. Peter, L., Janko, J., Schick, N., Waßmuth, V., Friedrich, M., & Bawidamann, J. (2021). *Development of an up-to-date, real-time available key performance indicator (KPI) system for the German motorway network. Berichte der Bundesanstalt für Straßenwesen*. Fachverlag NW in der Carl Schünemann Verlag GmbH.
7. City of Utrecht: Bicycle parking Stationsplein. (2022). Retrieved August 18, 2022, from https://www.utrecht.nl/city-of-utrecht/mobility/cycling/bicycle-parking/bicycle-parking-stationsplein/
8. Lücke, B. (2022). Die Zehn-Minuten Stadt. *Radwelt—Das ADFC-Magazin, 1*, 6–10.
9. Bicycle Data. (2022). Retrieved August 04, 2022, from www.bicycle-data.de
10. Rupi, F., Poliziani, C., & Schweizer, J. (2019). Data-driven bicycle network analysis based on traditional counting methods and GPS traces from smartphone. *ISPRS International Journal of Geo-information, 8*(8), 322.
11. Hyde-Wright, A., Graham, B., & Nordback, K. (2014). Counting bicyclists with pneumatic tube counters on shared roadways. *Ite Journal, 84*(2), 32–37.
12. Schering, J., & Marx Gómez, J. (2022). A new research approach to harmonize European bicycle counting data from Germany, Belgium and the UK. In J. Halberstadt (Ed.), *YEEES conference 2021 proceedings*. Springer Nature Switzerland.
13. Garber, M. D., Watkins, K. E., & Kramer, M. R. (2019). Comparing bicyclists who use smartphone apps to record rides with those who do not: implications for representativeness and selection bias. *Journal of Transport and Health, 15*, 100661. https://doi.org/10.1016/j.jth.2019.100661
14. Schering, J., Janßen, C., Kessler, R., Dmitriyev, V., Stüven, J., Marx Gómez, J., van Dijk, E., Brouwer, W., Kamermans, A., Verweij, L., & Janssen, G. (2022). ECOSense and sniffer bike: European bike sensor applications and its potential to support the decision making process in cycling promotion. In J. Marx Gómez & M. R. Lorini (Eds.), *Digital transformation for sustainability. ICT-supported Environmental Socio-economic Development*. Springer Nature Switzerland.

15. Höper, T., Schering, J., & Marx Gómez, J. (2021). Can smartphone generated cycling data contribute to the improvement of the bicycle infrastructure? In *INFORMATIK 2021* (pp. 127–135). Gesellschaft für Informatik. https://doi.org/10.18420/informatik2021-009
16. Schering, J., Janßen, C., Kessler, R., Dmitriyev, V., Marx Gómez, J., Stehno, C., Pelzner, K., Bankowsky, R., & Hentschel, R. (2021). ECOSense and its preliminary findings: Collection and analysis of bicycle sensor data. In A. Kamilaris, V. Wohlgemuth, K. Karatzas, & I. Athanasiadis (Eds.), *EnviroInfo 2020 Environmental informatics—New perspectives in environmental information systems: Transport, sensors, recycling. Adjunct proceedings of the 34th EnviroInfo conference* (pp. 145–153). Shaker Verlag.
17. Sommer, A., & Prinzing, B. (2022). Radfahren mit Baby: Messung der Feinstaubbelastung in Fahrradanhängern. In J. Eckart, C. Hupfer, R. Kriesten, P. Nenninger, & J. Riel (Eds.), *Fahrradlabor Hochschule Karlsruhe* (pp. 39–48).
18. Busch, L. (2022). Leihräder in Stockholm—Mit E-Bikes zur Verkehrswende, Retrieved July 31, 2022, from https://www.tagesschau.de/ausland/europa/e-bikes-stockholm-101.html
19. German Federal Ministry of Digital and Transport. (2022). Entwicklung einer Softwareanwendung zur Qualitätsbestimmung kommunaler Radverkehrsanlagen auf Basis von Crowdsourcing-Daten—INFRASense. Retrieved August 18, 2022, from https://www.bmvi.de/SharedDocs/DE/Artikel/DG/mfund-projekte/infrasense.html
20. Aultman-Hall, L., Hall, F., & Baetz, B. (1997). c. *Transportation Research Record, 1578*, 102–110.
21. Schering, J., Marx Gómez, J., Büsselmann, L., Alfaro, F., & Stüven, J. (2022 September, 26–30). Potentials of bicycle infrastructure data lakes to support cycling quality assessment. Informatik 2022, Betriebliche Umweltinformationssysteme, 52. Jahrestagung der Gesellschaft für Informatik (2022) (in publication process). In D. Demmler, D. Krupka, & H. Federrath (eds.) Informatik 2022, Informatik in den Naturwissenschaften (pp. 783–794). https://nextcloud.gi.de/s/4HZNzZGRxrrxGLs
22. Schering, J., Marx Gómez, J., & Alfaro, F. (2022). Citizen reportings and its application to bike infrastructure quality assessment. In: Proceedings of the 3rd International Conference on Next Generation Computing Applications, NextComp. IEEE Xplore. https://doi.org/10.1109/NextComp55567.2022.9932249. https://ieeexplore.ieee.org/stamp/stamp.jsp?tp=&arnumber=9932249.
23. Walker, L. (2022). Growing popularity of cycling reflected in road fatalities. Retrieved August 18, 2022, from https://www.brusselstimes.com/234202/growing-popularity-of-cycling-reflected-in-road-fatalities
24. New York City. (2022). Vision zero task force. Retrieved August 04, 2022, from https://www1.nyc.gov/content/visionzero/pages/vision-zero-task-force
25. Allgemeiner Deutscher Fahrrad-Club ADFC: Neue Studie: 42% bemängeln Sicherheit für Radfahrende. (2022). Retrieved August 18, 2022, from https://www.adfc.de/presse/pressemitteilungen/pressemitteilung/neue-studie-42-bemaengeln-sicherheit-fuer-radfahrende
26. Shinar, D., Mora, P. V., van Strijp Houtenbos, M., Haworth, N., Schramm, A., et al. (2018). Under-reporting bicycle accidents to police in the COST TU1101 international survey: Cross-country comparisons and associated factors. *Accident Analysis and Prevention, 110*, 177–186.
27. Parida, A., & Chattopadhyay, G. (2007). Development of a multi-criteria hierarchical framework for performance measurement (MPM). *Journal of quality in maintenance engineering, 13*(3), 241–258.
28. Yadav, N., & Sagar, M. (2013). Performance measurement and management frameworks: Research trends of the last two decades. *Business Process Management Journal, 19*(6), 947–971.
29. Stricker, N., Echsler Minguillon, F., & Lanza, G. (2017). Selecting key performance indicators for production with a linear programming approach. *International Journal of Production Research, 55*(19), 5537–5549.
30. Phillips, M. (2022). The DuPont invention that forever changed how things work in the corporate world. Retrieved November 06, 2022, from https://qz.com/569738/the-dupont-invention-that-forever-changed-how-things-work-in-the-corporate-world

31. Wessel, J. (2020). Using weather forecasts to forecast whether bikes are used. *Transportation Research Part A: Policy and Practice, 138*, 537–559. https://doi.org/10.1016/j.tra.2020.06.006
32. Veroude, B., & van Boggelen, O. (2021). *Discussienotitie - Actualisatie aanbevelingen voor de breedte van fietspaden*. CROW Fietsberaad.
33. Gesamtverband der Deutschen Versicherungswirtschaft e.V.: Unfalltypen-Katalog: Leitfaden zur Bestimmung des Unfalltyps. (2016). Unfallforschung der Versicherer, Berlin. https://www.udv.de/resource/blob/80022/89b4d80028aacf8cab649d3a3c6157a0/unfalltypenkatalog-data.pdf
34. Schering, J., Marx Gómez, J., Soetens, S., Verbeek, K., & Singh, A. (2021). How to measure safety risks for cyclists at intersections? In J. Halberstadt, J. Marx Gómez, J. Greyling, T. K. Mufeti, & H. Faasch (Eds.), *Resilience, entrepreneurship and ICT - Latest research from Germany, South Africa, Mozambique and Namibia* (pp. 263–278). Springer Nature Switzerland.
35. Schering, J., & Marx Gómez, J. (2022). BITS: A key performance indicators (KPIs) supported approach to assess traffic safety for cyclists at intersections in The Netherlands. In V. Wohlgemuth, S. Naumann, H.-K. Arndt, G. Behrens, & M. Höb (Eds.), *EnviroInfo 2022, short–/ work in Progress-papers, September 26–28 2022, Hamburg* (pp. 248–257). Köllen Druck+Verlag GmbH.
36. Temmen, M., Eckart, J., Merk, J., Karakaya, A.-S., & Bermbach, D. (2022). Crowdsourcing in der Radverkehrsforschung—Erfahrung aus der wissenschaftlichen Begleitung der SWR-Mitmachaktion #besserRadfahren. *Internationales Verkehrswesen, 74*(1), 66–69.
37. Vandenbulcke, G., Int Panis, L., & Thomas, I. (2017). On the location of reported and unreported cycling accidents: A spatial network analysis for Brussels. Cybergeo: European Journal of Geography [En ligne], Systèmes, Modélisation, Géostatistiques. http://journals.openedition.org/cybergeo/28073. doi: https://doi.org/10.4000/cybergeo.28073

Assessment of ICT Infrastructure in Rural Areas to Support the Use of Websites to Disseminate Crop Production and Management Information: Case of Tanzania

Victor Ngessa, Kisangiri F. Michael, Kelvin Mark Mtei, and Mawazo Mwita Magesa

1 Introduction

Studies show that Internet access is very important in rural areas [1–5]. For example, [2] indicates that mobile phones and the Internet stimulate agricultural development, which, in turn, boosts mobile penetration and Internet usage even further. This means that mobile phones and the Internet play significant roles in agricultural development, as agricultural development also plays an important role in the expansion of mobile phones and Internet usage. Van Hook and Meetwa [6] emphasize that the Internet provides social benefits in rural areas such as communication, information, and education, as well as economic benefits such as time and money savings and new opportunities. It is also urged that Internet access is even more important in rural areas as compared to urban areas, as rural areas lack alternatives such as telephone lines, public transport, newspapers, roads in good condition, and libraries [6]. Inadequate coverage of Internet services in rural areas as compared to urban areas creates what is known as digital divide [7–9], which deprives the rural population of knowledge. Also, people who live in rural areas and use the Internet are less likely to be in multidimensional poverty [5],

V. Ngessa (✉) · K. F. Michael
School of Computational and Communication Science and Engineering, Arusha, Tanzania
e-mail: ngessav@nm-aist.ac.tz; kisangiri.michael@nm-aist.ac.tz

K. M. Mtei
School of Materials, Energy, Water and Environmental Sciences, Nelson Mandela African Institution of Science and Technology, Arusha, Tanzania
e-mail: kelvin.mtei@nm-aist.ac.tz

M. M. Magesa
Department of Informatics and Information Technology, College of Natural and Applied Sciences, Sokoine University of Agriculture, Morogoro, Tanzania
e-mail: magesa@sua.ac.tz

J. Marx Gómez et al. (eds.), *Smart and Secure Embedded and Mobile Systems*,
Progress in IS, https://doi.org/10.1007/978-3-031-56603-5_11

which is defined by [10] as not having enough money, education, or access to basic infrastructure. Ma et al. [3] study suggest more interventions and policy programs to boost the Internet service and telecommunication infrastructure in rural areas as well as facilitate rural users' uptake and use of the Internet as an instrument for attaining valuable goals and performing significant roles, thereby positively affecting the economy and quality of life.

E-Agriculture is an example of Internet use in rural areas where Information and Communication Technology (ICT) and other digital solutions are used in innovative ways to boost the agricultural sector—thereby improving the livelihoods of rural communities, fostering sustainable agriculture, and driving socioeconomic development while also allowing environmental protection [11]. Appropriate infrastructure should be in place for Internet access to be available. Mobile broadband technology is an example of a technology that facilitates the availability of the Internet. The technology allows for a wireless wide area network (WWAN), i.e., Internet access to portable devices by way of radio towers. Internet access is enabled wherever a Global System for Mobile Communications (GSM) or Code-division Multiple Access (CDMA)-based cellular service is available [12].

A person accessing information on a website would need an Internet-enabled device like a mobile phone with 3G or 4G or higher capabilities. In this case, the Internet connection is sent to a user's device by mobile phone towers over a mobile phone network. The Internet-enabled mobile device can then use this connection.

The trend worldwide is toward providing Internet services to underprivileged societies, and in Tanzania, a number of initiatives have been launched to improve Internet access in rural areas. Stakeholders in the agriculture sector have taken this opportunity to develop websites and other ICT applications, like mobile applications, that target the rural population. Ngessa et al.'s [13] study found stakeholders in the agriculture sector develop websites aimed at providing farming skills and knowledge as well as other necessary information to farmers. IMF [14] mentions four pillars that can help guide policies aimed at improving the state of digitalization in sub-Saharan countries, which are infrastructure, policy frameworks, skills, and risk management frameworks to address cyber security risks. This study intends to make an assessment of one of these pillars, infrastructure, available in rural Tanzania to support the use of websites to disseminate crop production and management information to smallholder farmers. Specifically, among others, this study will look at: devices used in rural areas that can access the Internet; Internet access availability; interest in learning agricultural production practices using the Internet; and policies and regulations available in the country to support the use of ICT services by smallholder farmers.

2 Methodology

The study focuses on assessing the ICT infrastructure available in rural areas to support the usage of websites in the provision of crop production and management information to smallholder farmers. Five (5) out of seven (7) of Tanzania's main agro-ecological zones were involved in the study. The five zones (the northern zone, southern-highland zone, central zone, eastern zone, and lake zone) were selected randomly. To be included in the study, the respondent had to be a smallholder, male or female, and own at least one electronic communication device. From this population, a sample of 736 respondents was drawn randomly.

A questionnaire was designed with the help of stakeholders in the agriculture sector (smallholders and agricultural extension officers). The questionnaire had five parts to cover: demographics, electronic communication devices used, skills to use devices, charging of devices, and willingness to use the web to learn crop production and management. Interviews were conducted with selected smallholder farmers to get detailed clarification on some of the questions. Documentary reviews were conducted to learn about the ICT policies and regulations available in Tanzania to support or influence the availability and usability of ICT in agricultural production in rural areas.

3 Findings and Discussion

3.1 Demographics of Respondents

Age of Respondents. As shown in Table 1, of the respondents from this study, 3% were aged below 18 years, 29% were aged 18–30 years, 32% were aged 31–40 years, 22% were aged 41–50 years, 10% were aged 51–60 years, and 5% were aged above 61 years. This study has found the presence of the "next generation" of farmers as more young people (30 years of age and below) who own mobile phones were found to be involved in agriculture.

Gender of Respondents. Of the 736 respondents for the study, 65% were male and 35% were female (Table 2).

Table 1 Age distribution

Age category	Number of respondents	Percentage
Below 18 years	20	3%
18–30 years	211	29%
31–40 years	235	32%
41–50 years	160	22%
51–60 years	76	10%
Above 61 years	34	5%

Table 2 Gender of respondents

Gender	Number of respondents	Percentage
Male	476	65%
Female	260	35%

Table 3 Education level of respondents

Education level	Number of respondents	Percentage
No. of formal education	28	4%
Primary education	364	49%
Secondary education	224	30%
Certificate	52	7%
Diploma	39	5%
Degree	29	4%

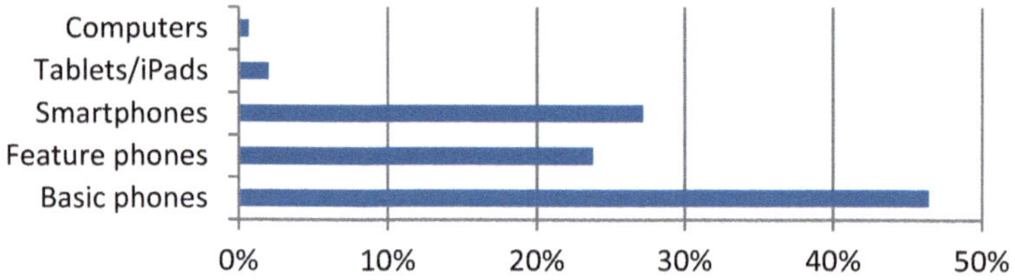

Fig. 1 Electronic communication devices owned by smallholders

Education level of Respondents. The education levels of the respondents were as follows: There were 4% with no formal education, 49% with primary level education, 30% with secondary level education, 7% with certificate level education, 5% with diploma level education, and 4% with degree level education (Table 3).

3.2 *Electronic Communication Devices Owned by Smallholder Farmers*

The findings show that 736 respondents owned a total of 766 electronic communication devices (some of the respondents owned more than one device). Device ownership was found to be: computers (1%), tablets/iPads (2%), smartphones (27%), feature phones (24%), and basic phones (46%); see Fig. 1. A smallholder farmer who own two mobile phones (a smartphone and a basic phone), when asked why he owns two phones, he explained that "*I own two phones and because I have three SIM Cards. I have inserted two SIM Cards in one phone and the other SIM Card in the other phone. I purchased the other phone so that I could use other SIM Cards I was attracted by their packages.*" Researchers found that in the market there exist mobile phones that can accommodate up to three SIM Cards, though most are those that can accommodate two SIM Cards.

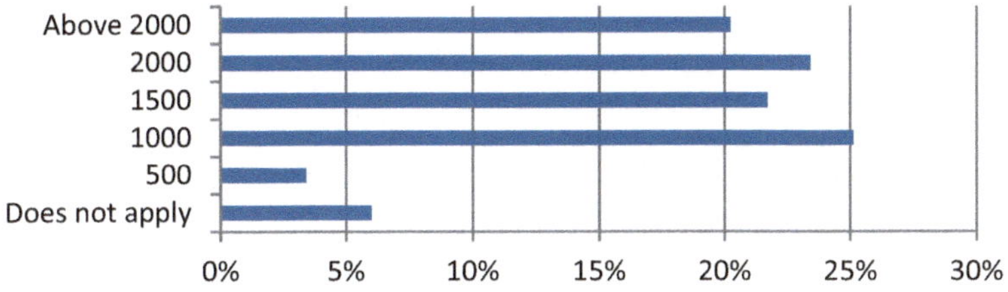

Fig. 2 Internet bundles purchased weekly (in TZS)

The findings of the [15] study, when grouped into two categories—those with Internet capability and those without—agree to a large extent with the findings of this study in terms of the percentage of devices owned by farmers. Mobile phone ownership in [15] was as follows: basic phones 52%, feature phones 13%, smartphones 35%, and iPads 1%.

Our study [15, 16] shows that smallholder farmers own devices that can be used to access the Internet. Internet-enabled devices (computers, tablets/iPads, smartphones, and feature phones) enable users to access websites and other mobile applications. This in turn creates environments for disseminators of agro-information like crop production and management information to reach smallholder farmers via websites or mobile applications.

3.3 *Internet Bundles Purchased Weekly*

The findings indicate the majority of smallholders who own Internet-capable devices purchase Internet bundles weekly (Fig. 2): 20% purchase Internet bundles of more than TZS. 2000/=, 23% purchase Internet bundles of TZS. 2000/=, 22% purchase Internet bundles of TZS. 1500/=, 25% purchase Internet bundles of TZS. 1000/=, 3% purchase Internet bundles of TZS. 500/=, and 6% responded that the question "Does not apply."

The respondent who responded to this question by saying that he uses approximately TZS. 1000/= for Internet bundles weekly explained that: "*I use my phone to make calls, send text messages, and visit social networks. When there is a need, I can use more than TZS. 3000/= per week to buy Internet bundles.*"

Even though it is becoming more affordable in most parts of Africa, according to [17, 18], the cost of Internet access in Africa is still high compared to other places in the world. This hinders mobile phone users from buying airtime and Internet bundles. The study [18] rank Tanzania seventh out of 53 African countries in terms of one gigabyte ($0.71). According to the United Nations, Internet access is considered affordable when the cost of 1 gigabyte is less than 2% of gross monthly income.

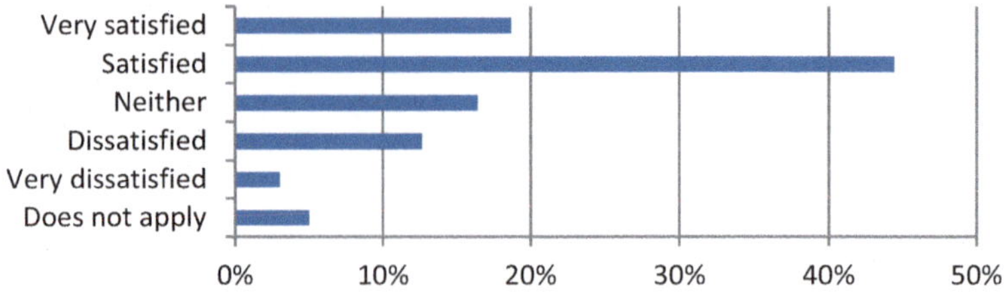

Fig. 3 Internet speed satisfaction level among smallholders

3.4 Internet Speed Satisfaction Level Among Smallholders

Smallholders who own devices that can connect to the Internet were asked about their level of satisfaction with Internet speed. The findings (Fig. 3) show that 19% were "Very satisfied," 44% were "Satisfied," 16% were "Neither," 13% were "Dissatisfied," and 3% were "Very dissatisfied" and 5% responded, "Does not apply."

Researchers used their devices to check for Internet speed by opening websites on their devices and seeing how fast they could open. Smartphones of different specifications and feature phones were used. Also, tools like speedtest.net and speedof.me were used. The speeds of different mobile phone operators (Internet service providers) were compared. Our results concluded that: (1) Internet speed varied from one location to another, with some locations having good Internet speed and others having very poor Internet speed (and this sometimes was the case even within the same village or ward); (2) where we found mobile phone operator A with better Internet speed than mobile phone operator B, it is also where we found the majority of our respondents using SIM Cards for mobile phone operator A; (3) areas close to where there are installations of mobile phone operators' towers have better Internet connectivity; and (4) where there was poor Internet speed, there was poor network coverage in general to the extent that making calls or sometimes sending text messages was a problem.

3.5 Internet Browsing Skills among Smallholders

A total of 736 smallholders responded to the question aimed at learning their Internet browsing skills. A 5-point Likert scale question read, "*I would rate my Internet browsing skills as . . .*" The findings show that 11% have "Very good" skills, 29% have "Good" skills, 18% have "Fair" skills, 11% have "Poor" skills, 22% have "Very poor" skills, and 9% responded to the question as "Does not apply." This question was answered by all respondents who own any kind of electronic communication device, regardless of whether it is Internet-enabled or not. It can be seen that even though some respondents did not have Internet-capable phones like smartphones, they have "Internet skills" because they have owned or used them before. A respondent falling into this category responded that: "*Currently I own a basic phone I purchased for TZS. 30,000/= but before I had a smartphone which I sold to my friend, and I used the smartphone to access Facebook sometimes.*"

The use of digital technologies requires basic literacy and numeracy as well as special technical knowledge and skills [19]. Our study shows a minimal number of respondents (3%) did not have formal education, and therefore a majority of respondents could not have been limited by their level of education to browse the Internet. In Tanzania, prior studies have been conducted to show the use of websites in the provision of agricultural extension services to smallholder farmers, implying that farmers are available who, among others, have skills to use the websites. Sanga et al. [20] are one such study.

3.6 Charging Mobile Phones

Respondents were found to use either solar electricity generated at their homes or electricity supplied by the national electricity company, Tanzania Electric Supply Company (TANESCO) Limited, to charge their mobile phones. On the availability of electricity to charge their devices, 27% said "Excellent," 40% said "Above average," 25% said "Average," 5% said "Below average," and 3% said "Very poor." Charging of the devices was done: "At home" by 55% of respondents, "At neighbor's" place by 35%, "At pay kiosks" by 4%, and "At friends" place by 5%. The frequency of charging devices was as follows: 11% charged their devices "More than once per day," 32% charged "Once per day," 21% charged "Once for every two days," 25% charged "Once per every three days," and 10% charged "Once for every more than three days."

3.7 Smallholders' Willingness to Learn Crop Production Using the Web

Respondents were asked to rate their willingness to learn about crop production using the web. A list of 18 farm activities and other issues related to farming were identified and listed in the questionnaire. The findings in Fig. 4 show that on average, 52% "Strongly agree," 39% "Agree," 3% are "Undecided," 4% "Disagree," and 2% "Strongly disagree" to the willingness to learn about crop production using the web. Researchers conducted a number of interviews with selected respondents to find out why 91% of respondents were willing to use the web to learn about crop production. One of the respondents explained that: "*I am expecting a lot by learning online. There are many things I want to know about what I grow and I think the Internet can give me the information I need.*" Another one said: "*It is important we have*

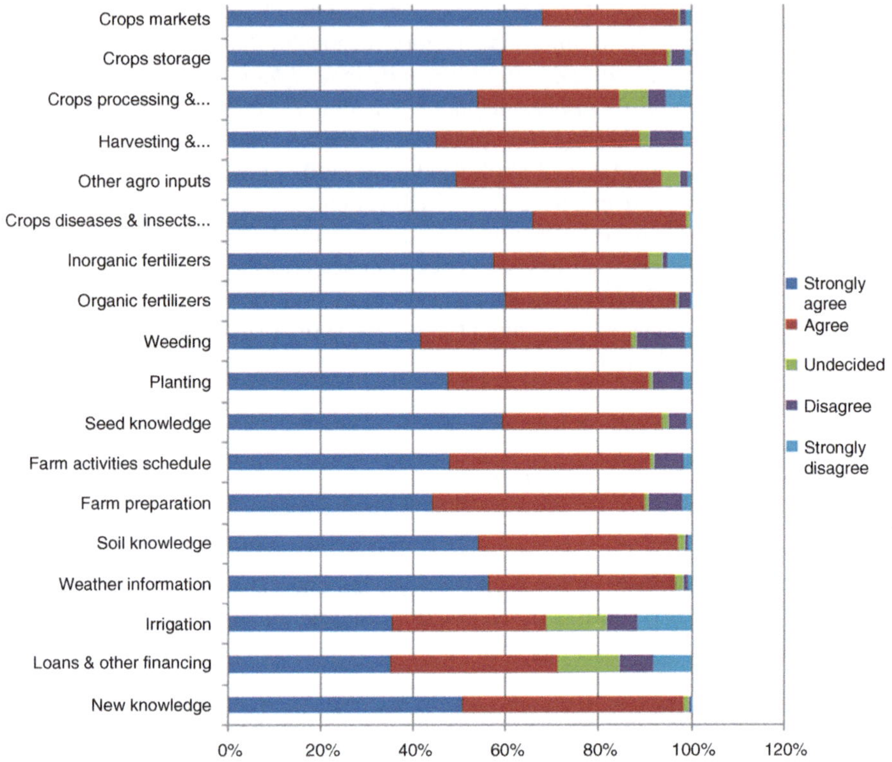

Fig. 4 Crop production information needed by smallholders

many alternatives to getting the right information related to agriculture as this will make us more knowledgeable with what we do in our farms and hence get more produce." Respondents were able to mention a number of current alternatives used to disseminate crop production knowledge and other information to them. One of the respondents in particular explained as follows: "*Currently there are a number of ways we use to learn about how to produce crops and get other information. Among others, we depend on manual documents (like pamphlets and fliers), field farm visits, websites (mostly social networks websites), extension officers, meetings, and radio and TV stations*."

The findings of this study agree with [21, 22] studies that found farmers' information needs ranging from farm preparation to farm management to harvesting and later selling. Rahman, Ara and Khan [21] study also found information needs vary based on the severity of the problems farmers are faced with. In other studies like [23] a high level of interest among farmers in using the Internet (social media) for agricultural extension was found, despite the fact that the majority of them admitted to having never used the technologies before. In the study, farmers indicated time saving, wider coverage, and cost reduction as the major reasons why

Internet-based (social media platforms) were better than non-Internet methods in agricultural extension.

3.8 ICT Policies and Regulations Available in Tanzania

Specific objectives of Tanzania's current 2016 National ICT Policy that align with this study are: improving accessibility and availability of affordable and reliable Internet services to accelerate socioeconomic development; having a reliable, interoperable, and sustainable ICT infrastructure that supports national connectivity; having universal access to ICT products and services to bridge the digital divide; and promoting the effective use of ICT. Some of the ICT regulations found to relate to and support the usage or provision of ICT in rural areas include Consumer Protection Regulations, SIM Card Registration Regulations, and Quality of Service Regulations [24]. Regulations are the rules that users and providers of ICT services must follow. This makes it possible for different players, such as users in the country, to work together in an easy, efficient, and productive way.

A study by [25] notes that for ICT to contribute positively to economic and social development, it is critical that countries adopt policies, legal, market, and social considerations, and other access tools. Access tools are those related to providing adequate access to ICT infrastructure and providing fiscal incentives to encourage wider ownership of electronic devices, among others. However, [26] notes that the policies to promote ICT infrastructure in rural areas are most effective once general knowledge about the benefits of Internet access has already diffused to a more general population. In this way, it is urged that a demand for the Internet will be created by society, which will necessitate building the necessary infrastructure to address the problem. Makoza [27] study recommended African policy makers to integrate monitoring into the ICT policy phases and mechanisms for feedback and learning to address some of the challenges related to their national ICT policies.

4 Conclusion

This study has shown that ICT infrastructure and other supporting environments exist in rural Tanzania that can support the use of websites to disseminate crop production and management information to smallholder farmers. The findings of this study suggest that stakeholders disseminating agricultural information to smallholders in the country can develop websites and other applications like mobile applications for crop production and management. Websites should be mobile friendly, work well on both feature phones and smartphones, cover the whole crop production and management cycle (or the whole activity), be easier to use, and be lighter (looking at education levels, Internet bundles purchased, and Internet skills of smallholder farmers).

References

1. Prieger, J. E. (2013). The broadband digital divide and the economic benefits of mobile broadband for rural areas. *Telecommunications Policy, 37*, 483–502.
2. Evans, O. (2018). Digital agriculture: Mobile phones, internet & agricultural development in Africa. *Actual Problems of Economics, 7–8*(205–206), 76–90.
3. Ma, W., Nie, P., Zhang, P., & Renwick, A. (2020). Impact of internet use on economic Well-being of rural households: Evidence from China. *Review of Development Economics, 24*, 503–523.
4. Magesa, M. M., Michael, K., & Ko, J. (2020). Access and use of agricultural market information by smallholder farmers: Measuring informational capabilities. *The Electronic Journal of Information Systems in Developing Countries, 86*, e12134.
5. Yang, L., Lu, H., Wang, S., & Li, M. (2021). Mobile internet use and multidimensional poverty: Evidence from a household survey in rural China. *Social Indicators Research, 158*, 1065–1086.
6. Van Hoorik, P., & Meetwa, F. (2008). Use of internet in rural areas of Zambia, LinkNet. https://www.semanticscholar.org/paper/Use-of-internet-in-rural-areas-of-Zambia-Hoorik-Mweetwa/ff2f5b59eeed7ad2750e503f19d83071195d9404.
7. Reddick, C. G., Enriquez, R., Harris, R. J., & Sharma, B. (2020). Determinants of broadband access and affordability: An analysis of a community survey on the digital divide. *Cities, 106*, 102904.
8. Vogels, E. A. (2022). Some digital divides persist between rural, urban and Suburban America. Retrieved September 8, 2022, from https://www.pewresearch.org/fact-tank/2021/08/19/some-digital-divides-persist-between-rural-urban-and-suburban-america/
9. Philip, L., Cottrill, C., Farrington, J., Williams, F., & Ashmore, F. (2017). The digital divide: Patterns, policy and scenarios for connecting the 'final few' in rural communities across Great Britain. *Journal of Rural Studies, 54*, 386–398.
10. World Bank Group: Multidimensional Poverty Measure. (2022). Retrieved August 11, 2022, from https://www.worldbank.org/en/topic/poverty/brief/multidimensional-poverty-measure
11. ITU: Connecting humanity: Assessing investment needs of connecting humanity to the internet by 2030. (2020). Retrieved 20, 2022, from https://www.itu.int/dms_pub/itu-d/opb/gen/D-GEN-INVEST.CON-2020-PDF-E.pdf
12. Lenovo: What is Mobile Broadband Technology? (2022). Retrieved October 11, 2022, from https://www.lenovo.com/us/en/faqs/pc-life-faqs/what-is-mobile-broadband
13. Ngessa, V., Michael, K. F., Mtei, K. M., & Magesa, M. M. (2022). Website development: The case of agricultural extension providers in Tanzania. *International Journal of Advances in Scientific Research and Engineering, 08*, 91–102.
14. Simione, F., & Woldemichael, M. T. (2020). Digitalizing sub-Saharan Africa: Hopes and hurdles. Retrieved October 13, 2022, from https://www.imf.org/en/News/Articles/2020/06/15/na061520-digitalizing-sub-saharan-africa-hopes-and-hurdles
15. Krell, N. T., Giroux, S. A., Guido, Z., Hannah, C., Lopus, S. E., Caylor, K. K., & Evans, T. P. (2020). Smallholder Farmers' use of mobile phone services in Central Kenya. *Climate and Development, 13*, 215–227.
16. Quandt, A., Salerno, J. D., Neff, J. C., Baird, T. D., Herrick, J. E., McCabe, J. T., Xu, E., & Hartter, J. (2020). Mobile phone use is associated with higher smallholder agricultural productivity in Tanzania, East Africa. *PLOS ONE, 15*, e0237337.
17. Ehl, D., & Grün, G. (2020). Why mobile internet is so expensive in some African nations: DW: 03.11.2020. Retrieved October 1, 2022, from https://m.dw.com/en/why-mobile-internet-is-so-expensive-in-some-african-nations/a-55483976
18. Kamer, L. (2022). Price for mobile data in African countries 2022. Retrieved October 21, 2022, from https://www.statista.com/statistics/1180939/average-price-for-mobile-data-in-africa/
19. Trendov, N. M., Varas, S., & Zeng, M. (2019). *Digital technologies in agriculture and rural areas, Briefing paper*. FAO.

20. Sanga, C., Mlozi, M., Haug, R., & Tumbo, S. (2016). Mobile learning bridging the gap in agricultural extension service delivery: Experience from Sokoine University of Agriculture, Tanzania. *International journal of Education and Development using Information and Communication Technology, 12*(3), 108–127.
21. Rahman, T., Ara, S., & Khan, N. A. (2020). Agro-information service and information-seeking behavior of small-scale farmers in rural Bangladesh. *Asia-Pacific Journal of Rural Development., 30*, 175–194.
22. Makawia, P. (2018). *Agricultural information needs and their accessibility to sesame producers in Morogoro district, Tanzania. Master dissertation*. Sokoine University of Agriculture.
23. Kimani, A. W. (2019). *Assessment of use of social media among smallholder farmers in Kiambu County, master thesis*. University of Nairobi.
24. TCRA: Kanuni. (2022). Retrieved September 11, 2022, from https://www.tcra.go.tz/documents/regulations
25. Guermazi, B., & Satola, D. (2005). *Creating the 'right' enabling environment for ICT, E-Development: From excitement to effectiveness*. World Bank.
26. Whitacre, B. E. (2010). The diffusion of internet technologies to rural communities: A portrait of broadband supply and demand. *American Behavioral Scientist, 53*, 1283–1303.
27. Makoza, F. (2019). National ICT policy challenges for developing countries: A grounded theory informed literature review. *International Journal of Technology Policy and Law, 3*, 107.

A Loan Application Management System for Efficient Loan Processing: A Case of Muhimbili SACCOS LTD

Luciana Nyaoke Murimi, Marius Siebert, Godwin Salira, Elizabeth Mkoba, and Mussa Ally

1 Introduction

Savings and Credit Co-operative Societies (SACCOS) are member-based cooperative organizations whose primary objective is to encourage saving among their members. SACCOS target members sharing a commonality; this could be living in the same geographical region, working under the same employer, or doing the same type of business. By specifically targeting their members and understanding their businesses, SACCOS have been able to develop products and services well suited for their members. By doing so, SACCOS have gained popularity and are crucial in attaining financial inclusion in Tanzania [1]. The latest comprehensive review of the SACCOS sector was undertaken by Tanzania Co-operative Development Commission (TCDC) in 2021. The TCDC Statistical Bulleting for the quarter ending September 2021 revealed a total number of 3946 SACCOS in the country with an active membership of more than 690,000 [2].

Despite the tremendous achievements by SACCOS in attaining nationwide financial inclusion, SACCOS still face major challenges in their operations such as delayed service delivery and inefficient and ineffective manual business processes. Such business processes include the loan origination process. An ineffective and inefficient loan application process translates into a high loan turnaround time. This means the period from application of a loan by members to disbursal is long. As

L. N. Murimi (✉)
The Nelson Mandela African Institution of Science and Technology, Arusha, Tanzania

German Sparkassenstiftung Eastern Africa, Dar es Salaam, Tanzania

M. Siebert · G. Salira
German Sparkassenstiftung Eastern Africa, Dar es Salaam, Tanzania

E. Mkoba · M. Ally
The Nelson Mandela African Institution of Science and Technology, Arusha, Tanzania

J. Marx Gómez et al. (eds.), *Smart and Secure Embedded and Mobile Systems*,
Progress in IS, https://doi.org/10.1007/978-3-031-56603-5_12

a result, such processes have had an adverse impact on customer satisfaction. In addition to a high loan turnaround time, collection of inaccurate and insufficient member loan application information is another risk introduced by such a process. Basing credit decisions on inaccurate and insufficient loan information results in high levels of non-performing loans and consequently poses a great threat to the sustainability and survival of SACCOS [3].

An empirical study carried out by Marwa [4] on the Tanzanian SACCOS sector revealed that only 14% of the SACCOS were efficient and profitable whereas 49% of the sample SACCOS were not sustainable. Digitalization and automation of SACCOS activities have, therefore, been proposed as one of the ways to achieve sustainability and profitability. Information and Communication Technology (ICT) adoption within the SACCOS sector results in significant cost reduction, increased productivity, and improved customer experience, which translates to increased sustainability and profitability [5]. However, ICT adoption within the SACCOS sector in Tanzania has been slow. The 2018 TCDC Field Data October 2018 report shows that less than 10% of all SACCOS use a fully computerized system while 61% of SACCOS relied on inadequate manual systems at the time of data collection. This is particularly concerning considering the new reporting requirements stipulated in the Microfinance (Savings and Credit Cooperative Societies) Regulations, 2019 [6]. It is therefore crucial that SACCOS embrace digitalization to make their processes much more effective and efficient.

In 2001, Muhimbili SACCOS LTD (MUSACCOS) was established as an employee-based SACCOS with the aim of unifying employees of Muhimbili National Hospital, Muhimbili Orthopedic Institute (MOI), Muhimbili University of Health and Allied Sciences (MUHAS), SISA Health Center, Jakaya Kikwete Cardiac Institute (JKCI), and other health institutions willing to abide by the terms and conditions of MUSACCOS. The primary goal of MUSACCOS was to consolidate economic power through the provision of loans and savings services to its members [7].

As of February 2022, the loan application process, the very first step in the loan origination process was manual and paper-based. MUSACCOS loan origination process begins with the SACCOS member expressing interest in loan at their offices. During this visit, the member brings along their salary slips and SACCOS passbook. The member is then provided with an application form which they fill out with the assistance of a loan officer, providing the required personal and loan information. Upon completion, the loan officer reviews the loan form, salary slip, and passbook before filling in their recommendation on the loan form. The loan officer then generates a template using Excel capturing the employee's check number, name, loan amount, number of loan instalments, total interest, total loan, principal per month, interest per month, and deductions per month. This template is printed out and forwarded to the SACCOS member's respective institution's human resource department. At the respective human resource department, the applicant is verified whether they are a salaried employee of the institution and whether any other deductions are made from their monthly salary. This is key in determining whether the loan repayment will be deducted directly from the salary or by standing order.

Next step, the application is forwarded to the manager who then reviews and comments before forwarding the application to the credit committee which makes the decision on whether to approve; approve at a reduced loan amount or deny the requested loan. If approved by the credit committee the manager signs off the loan application, approves disbursal in the system and the loan is granted to the SACCOS member.

2 Problem

Capturing loan application information on paper increases the probability of human error. Manually filling out loan application forms only to later enter part of the captured data into the SACCOS system not only introduces multiple points where an error can occur but also causes a time delay and consequently increases the loan turnaround time. Physical storage of the loan application forms for later retrieval when needed is not only inefficient but introduces other risks such as misplacement and misfiling of loan application documents, access to the loan application documents by unauthorized persons, potential damage by theft fire or water, and not to mention lack of back up in case these damages do occur.

There is, therefore, a need for a system that achieves a more efficient and effective loan application process. One that lowers the probability of invalid data through data validation during entry. A system that allows for the collection of richer data, such as images and geolocation data. One that allows for storage and easy retrieval of member personal and loan information when needed. A system that reduces loan application costs such as printing of loan application forms, and ensures timely upload of loan information to the Core Banking System in order to realize a lower loan turnaround time and meet member needs as soon as possible.

3 Related Works

Marwa [4] conducted an empirical study to examine the effectiveness and sustainability of SACCOS in Tanzania. The findings of the study indicated that only a meager 14% of SACCOS in Tanzania were profitable, while the majority, about 61%, fell into the low efficiency and low profitability category. Capital constraints, extended loan processing time, manual procedures, inadequate education of members, and insufficient accountability among employers were cited as major setbacks among SACCOS. The focus of this study is therefore to investigate how mobile technologies can address some of these challenges, specifically to enhance the loan application process.

Caruso and O'keefe [8] present the use of an Android-based application by Musoni, Kenya for individual client registration, group registration, and loan application. In a separate case study, Caruso and O'Keefe [9] further give a comparison of the implementation and impact of similar applications at Ujjivan Financial Service, India and Opportunity Bank, Serbia. In all three cases, a significant reduction in loan turn-around time is observed. Increased loan officer productivity and improved customer service experience were among the benefits realized as well. The Android applications developed in these three cases were tailored to fit the specific business requirements and context of the particular microfinance institution.

The use of mobile applications to meet the data collection requirements by different organizations has been explored. Bokonda et al. [10] present an analysis and comparison of four main software solutions used in mobile data collection namely: Pendragon Forms, KoBo Toolbox, Open Data Kit (ODK), and Open Data Kit X (ODK-X). ODK and KoBoToolbox proved suitable in organizations with a relatively ordinary workflow whereas Pendragon Forms and ODK-X were more suitable in organizations with complex workflows. The loan application process within SACCOS involves collection of data (personal and loan information), and such a process would benefit greatly from use of such mobile solutions. Nonetheless, use of such tools in the SACCOS setting remains a challenge. Most of these tools do not accurately fit the business process requirements of SACCOS. Such applications have either provided fewer or more features than required and have therefore not proved to be useful in meeting the SACCOS requirements. The integration of mobile applications used in the loan application process with existing SACCOS systems and Core Banking Systems is also a determining feature when adopting such solutions.

There is, therefore, a need for a custom application built to meet the SACCOS loan application requirements.

4 System Description

In the case of MUSACCOS, a loan application management system was proposed consisting of two modules: a loan officer module and a self-service module. The first module, presented in this chapter, is a tablet-based application for loan officers to file and manage loan applications. Whereas the second module is targeted for the SACCOS members to file their own loan applications from the convenience of their homes.

The context diagram of the loan officer module is shown in Fig. 1.

The manual paper-based loan application process is therefore replaced by the loan application management system whose output can be uploaded to the Core Banking System for subsequent processing of the loan.

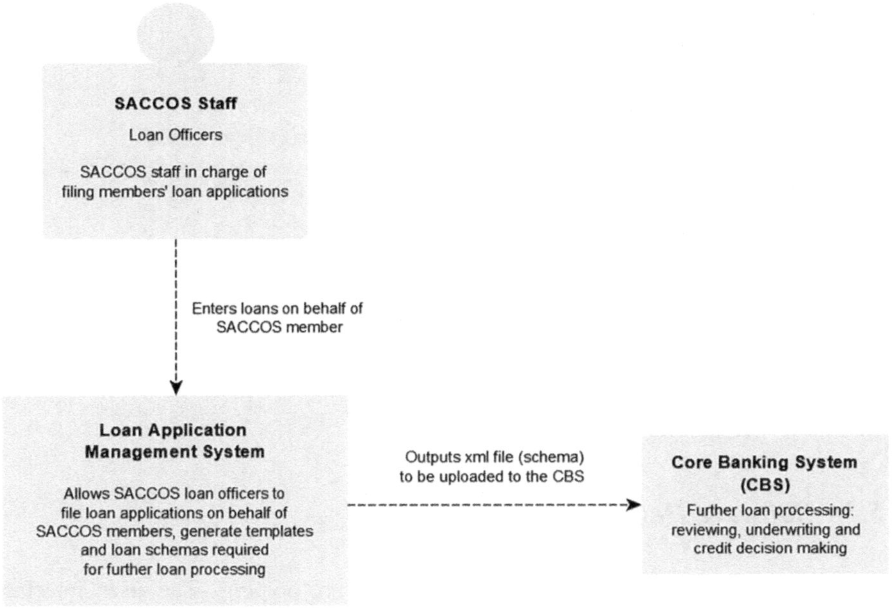

Fig. 1 System context diagram

5 Implementation

This project was carried out in Dar es Salaam region by German Sparkassenstiftung for International Cooperation (DSIK) in partnership with the Savings and Credit Cooperative Union League of Tanzania (SCCULT). MUSACCOS was selected as the participating SACCOS in the project based on its expression of interest and having the resources both technical and human required for the successful implementation of the project.

MUSACCOS staff including the SACCOS manager, IT specialist, and loan officer were interviewed to properly understand the organization, products, and services offered. MUSACCOS business processes specifically the loan application process were studied. From the interview results and after analyzing MUSACCOS lending policy, a comprehensive loan application process was mapped using Bizagi modeler (Fig. 2).

Through follow-up interviews, observations, and document analysis of the lending policy and loan application forms, the system requirements were identified, reviewed, verified, validated, and documented. Following the agile scrum methodology, the requirements were worked on iteratively beginning with the most important functionalities. The functional requirements of the application are shown in Table 1.

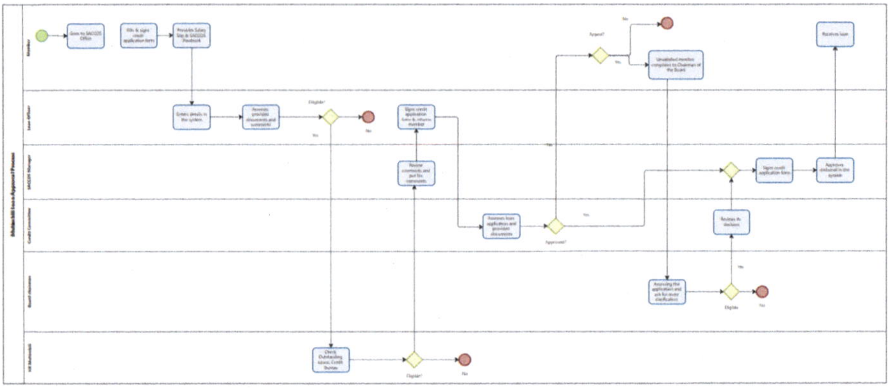

Fig. 2 Loan application process

5.1 *Software Development Tools*

Figma was used in user interface design and prototyping. The user interface was designed to be simple, intuitive, and consistent in order to achieve a good user experience. Flutter Software Development Kit (SDK) was selected for the development of the Android application due to its reduced development time. Firebase was also adopted as the secure backend service (BAAS) so as to further save on development time that would be spent configuring the backend. Both Flutter and Firebase are Google products. Sufficient documentation on the two technologies was therefore available, and their integration was seamless. Being that Firebase uses a NoSQL database; a NoSQL database library had to be also implemented locally to have easier data manipulations. Simple Embedded Application Store Database (SEMBAST) a NoSQL database library was therefore selected for local storage. User management required that the system user has elevated privileges; this could not be achieved using Firebase Client SDK, and therefore this functionality was implemented using Firebase Admin SDK in a trusted environment. An application interface (API) was then implemented for accessing this functionality from the client application. The system architecture overview is shown in Fig. 3.

5.2 *Non-Functional Requirements*

5.2.1 Security

Several measures were put in place to ensure the application's data was safe and secure.

User Authentication. The application user (loan officer) must register before using the application. The email provided during registration is verified, and the

Table 1 Functional requirements

Requirement*:* Registration Actor*:* Loan officer Description: The loan officer should be able to register to use the application. During registration, the loan officer shall provide their personal information, employer information, and login credentials.
Requirement*:* Authentication Actor*:* Loan officer Description: The loan officer should be able to log into the system using their email and password. The application should provide for both online and offline authentication. Through the application, the loan officer should be able to reset their password.
Requirement*:* User management Actor*:* System admin Description: The system admin should be able to view all the registered application users (loan officers). The system admin should be able to enable or disable user (loan officer) accounts.
Requirement*:* Apply for loans Actor*:* Loan officer Description: The application should provide for the application of either: An emergency loan, education loan, or development loan. The application should allow the loan officer to capture the personal information and loan information of the SACCOS member applying for a loan. The application should implement data entry input controls and validate the data during entry. The application should allow the loan officer to capture and attach the applicant's National ID or Passport and Payroll. Through the application, the applicant shall conform to abide by the terms and conditions of the loan. The applicant shall provide their electronic signature as sufficient proof of a legal agreement. The timestamp of signing the agreement shall also be captured. The application should also allow the credit officer to provide their recommendations regarding the loan applied. The credit officer shall be able to provide their electronic signature upon completion of filing an application. Once the loan application is complete and validated, the application shall save the information captured locally. This operation will be logged, and a loan acknowledgment receipt generated upon successful completion of the loan application process.
Requirement*:* Generate templates Actor*:* Loan officer Description: The application shall allow the loan officer to generate the templates required by human resource departments of the institutions under Muhimbili SACCOS for further processing of the loan.
Requirement*:* Upload feedback loan application feedback Actor*:* Loan officer Description: The application shall allow for the capture and entry of loan application feedback from the human resource departments.

(continued)

Table 1 (continued)

Requirement*:* Generate CBS-compatible schema Actor*:* Loan officer Description: The application shall allow the loan officer to generate a schema compatible with KAMA Digital Core Banking System.
Requirement*:* Loan calculator Actor*:* Loan officer Description: The application shall include a loan calculator for accurate calculations of the Equated Monthly Instalments (EMI) as per Muhimbili SACCOS lending policy.
Requirement*:* View and search through loan applications Actor*:* Loan officer Description: The application shall allow the loan officer to retrieve and view the saved loan applications. Using filters such as loan product type, date, and membership number the loan officer should filter through the applications accessing the specific loan applications.
Requirement*:* Upload data to the cloud Actor*:* Loan officer Description: The application shall allow the loan officer to upload the locally stored data to the cloud.
Requirement*:* Localization Actor*:* Loan officer Description: The application shall allow the loan officer to set their language preference as either Kiswahili or English.

user must be approved by the system admin before being able to access and use the application. The system admin oversees user management. They access and view the application users, and approve or disapprove users. By doing so, they control who has access to the application. During login, the user must provide their email and password for authentication before accessing the application.

Encryption of sensitive data. To allow for offline functionality, a copy of login credentials had to be stored locally, and therefore, to ensure security is enforced password hashing was performed before storage.

Firebase was selected as a secure backend service. Firebase encrypts its data both in transit and at rest [11], thus ensuring the application data is not compromised. Firebase also provided an option to enforce rules on who can read and write on the given databases further securing the application data. Furthermore, identifying information such as SACCOS member names were not stored in Firebase (Cloud Firestore) further maintaining confidentiality.

For auditing purposes, the loan officer's identity, membership number, was tied to important operations such as filling loan applications, and generation of schema and templates. This information is timestamped and logged ensuring there is a trail of the loan officers' operations within the application.

Android-scoped storage was enabled to secure the application data. This prevents other applications from accessing and deleting the application data. Also, the

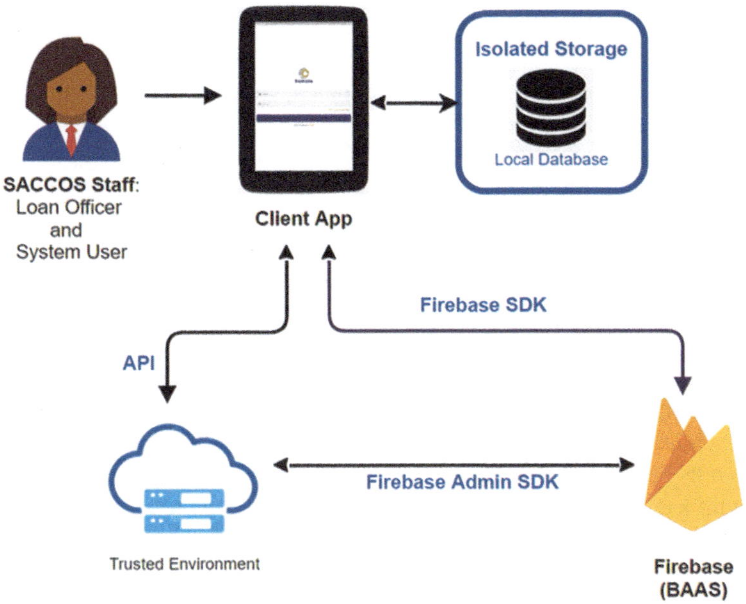

Fig. 3 System architecture overview

directories and files created by the application are only visible when logged into the application, denying access to anyone who is not logged in from accessing application data.

5.2.2 Maintainability

A model-view-view model (MVVM) architecture was implemented in development. This architecture separates the user interface (view) code from the business logic code (view model and model). Through this architecture, a more maintainable and scalable application is achieved.

5.2.3 Availability

Offline and online authentication was implemented. This ensured even in the absence of cellular coverage, the loan officer would still be able to access and use the application. When offline, the data was stored locally within the device, with the option to upload this data to the cloud provided.

5.3 System Outputs

The key outputs of the application were: a loan acknowledgment receipt, respective human resource templates, and a schema.

The loan acknowledgment receipt is a PDF document generated upon successful completion of filling the loan form. This receipt entails the following: applicant's name, membership number, loan summary (loan product requested, loan amount, monthly payments, number of payments, total interest, total payment), and bank account information (name of bank, bank account, account name). The loan officer's name and the electronic signatures of both the loan officer and the applicant are also included in the receipt. This receipt serves as proof of successfully applying for a loan, and a copy is given to the applicant.

The loan officer is also able to generate a PDF template to be forwarded to the respective human resource departments of the applicants. This template entails a list of applicants belonging to the respective institution and their details which include: check number, loan amount, number of loan instalments, total interest, total loan, principle per month, interest per month, and deductions per month.

A schema compatible with KAMA Digital Core Banking System is also generated. This is an XML file with the following attributes: membership number, loan amount, total interest, loan product name, number of instalments, deductions per month, transaction method, name of the bank, bank account, and date. Once generated, the schema can be uploaded to the CBS and the subsequent steps in the loan origination process can then continue.

6 Results and Discussions

The foremost impact of this system is an efficient and effective loan application process. Through data validation during entry, more complete and accurate data is captured. The application provided for capture of richer data. Information such as pictures of relevant documents such as national identity card and payroll that were not previously captured can now be captured. Storage, retrieval, and review of the loan application information has been made more efficient. Using filters such as loan product type, date, membership number, and employment institution, the loan applications are easily filtered and accessed as required. Furthermore, the option to back up this captured data to the cloud is provided. Through the application, the loan officers can now easily generate the required templates and schema and thus enhancing the loan officers' productivity.

However, the loan application forms have not been completely eliminated due to proof of employer information which is mandatory. A reduced form must be printed to be signed by the employer as proof of employment. Nonetheless, the size of the printed document has been significantly reduced saving further on printing costs.

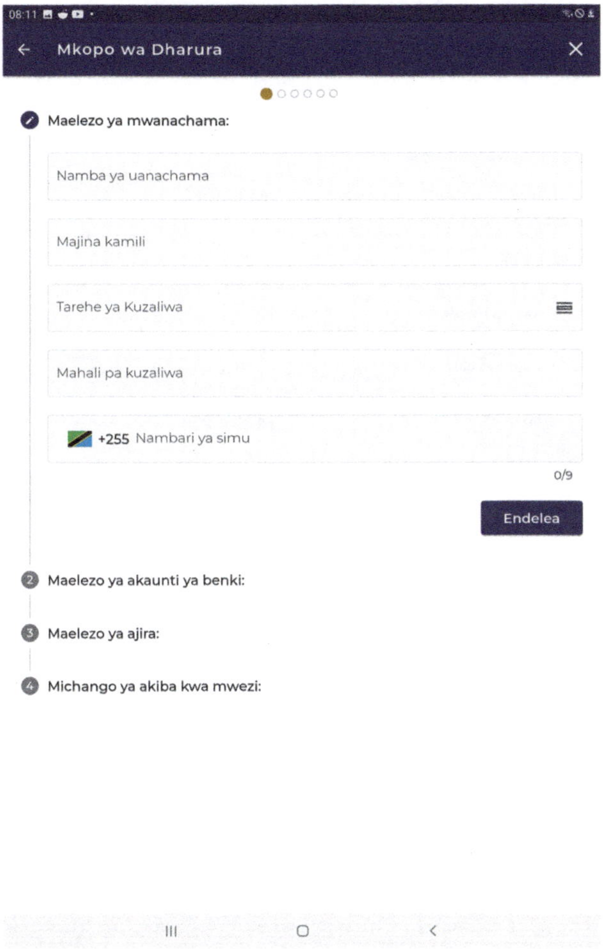

Fig. 4 Loan form screenshot

The application is also available in both English and Kiswahili fitting the Tanzania context. A few screenshots from the application are shown in Figs. 4 and 5.

7 Conclusion

The proposed system aimed to improve the loan application process within SACCOS. The use of the developed tablet-based application as a replacement for the manual paper-based process proved to be beneficial and effective both to

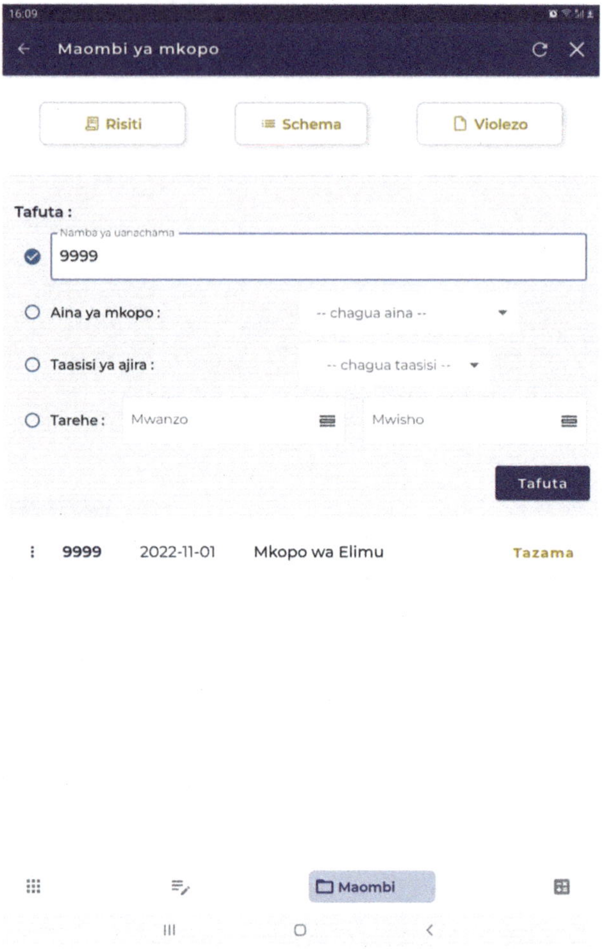

Fig. 5 Screenshot of the loan applications search section

the SACCOS and to its members; improving the loan officer's productivity and customer satisfaction. This project has therefore provided a basic, entry-level solution that can be adopted among employee-based SACCOS to professionalize and make their loan application processes much more efficient.

8 Recommendations and Future Works

After the successful completion of the loan officer module, planning for the next phase of the project, a self-service module, has begun. The self-service module targets the digitally literate SACCOS members, providing them with an option of initiating the loan application process from the convenience of their homes, further improving the customer service experience.

Further work can be done to improve the loan officer module so as to match the complex business processes and products of community-based SACCOS offering products such as agricultural loans. Such SACCOS will benefit greatly from the flexibility in the application process offered by this application. Moreover, the application can be extended to be used by more SACCOS as a shared service.

References

1. Mhlanga, D. (2021). Financial inclusion in emerging economies: The application of machine learning and artificial intelligence in credit risk assessment. *International Journal of Financial Studies, 9*(3), 39. https://doi.org/10.3390/ijfs9030039
2. TCDC. (2021). Statistical bulletin for the quarter ending September, 2021 (July – September 2021). https://www.ushirika.go.tz/index.php/statistics/category/registered-cooperatives
3. Dennis, E., & Mwighusa, N. (2018). Enhancing credit and risk management in saccos and microfinance institutions.
4. Marwa, N. W. (2015). Efficiency and sustainability of Tanzanian saving and credit cooperatives. https://scholar.sun.ac.za
5. Kariuki, L. W. (2019). Effects of adoption of technology on performance of deposit taking Sacco's: A case of K-Unity Sacco
6. BOT. (2019). The microfinance (savings and credit cooperative societies) regulations, 2019. https://www.bot.go.tz/Publications/Acts,%20Regulations,%20Circulars,%20Guidelines/Regulations/en/2020031803513151.pdf
7. Muhimbili SACCOS LTD Board. (2020). Muhimbili SACCOS LTD lending policy.
8. Caruso, C., & O'keefe, G. (2015b). Digital field applications: Musoni case study.
9. Caruso, C., & O'Keefe, G. (2015a). Digital field applications: Case study.
10. Bokonda, P. L., Ouazzani-Touhami, K., & Souissi, N. (2020). A practical analysis of Mobile data collection apps. *International Journal of Interactive Mobile Technologies, 14*(13), 19–35. https://doi.org/10.3991/ijim.v14i13.13483
11. Privacy and Security in Firebase. (2022, March). https://firebase.google.com/support/privacy

Explaining Changes in Short-Term Water Demand Patterns During the COVID-19 Pandemic: An Absorptive Capacity Perspective

Michael Mattern

1 Matching Water Supply and Demand

Humans can get on for weeks or months without food, however, without water, we soon struggle. Water deprivation can be lethal after a couple of days [1]. Furthermore, water is key for the prevention of communicable diseases, for food production, for personal hygiene, for many industrial processes, and—maybe surprisingly—even for keeping the internet up and running [2]. It, therefore, does not come as a surprise that securing its availability is a matter of national security [3–6].

Traditionally, related efforts focus (a) on the supply side and (b) on disastrous yet transitory incidents like terrorist assaults, cyber-attacks, floodings, or earthquakes. However, supply security is not just a matter of protecting the infrastructure but also one of understanding the factors that drive water supply and water demand. Consequentially—and in a world that is affected by environmental uncertainty, more recent government initiatives appreciate the importance of data and information [7].

This chapter sheds some light on how the research community have so far used certain sources of information that became available during the COVID-19 pandemic, to explain changes in the short-term demand for water. We use this specific example to highlight potential absorptive capacity-related issues in light of the growing amount of data produced by embedded and mobile systems. If there is a major gap between available and absorbed information not only in organizations but also in science, measures to reduce that gap could enhance our ability to deal with other external shocks affecting water supply and demand, such as energy price shocks or climate change.

M. Mattern (✉)
Carl von Ossietzky Universität Oldenburg, Oldenburg, Germany
e-mail: michael.mattern@uni-oldenburg.de

J. Marx Gómez et al. (eds.), *Smart and Secure Embedded and Mobile Systems*,
Progress in IS, https://doi.org/10.1007/978-3-031-56603-5_13

1.1 Matching Water Supply and Demand with Water

Water demand is not constant—neither in the long nor in the short run, and a mismatch between supply and demand can have several unfavorable effects:

- Overdimensioned infrastructures are costly [8], thus leading to price increases.
- Reductions in water demand can lead to lower revenues and—depending on the share of fixed costs—to lower contribution margins and higher water prices.
- Unexpected demand peaks may cause higher provisioning costs (because certain resources like energy have to be bought ad hoc and at peak prices) or place additional stress on supply infrastructures thus causing higher wear and tear; in return, both factors can impact prices and supply security.
- As the price elasticity of water demand is low [9], and as scarcity makes water demand even more inelastic [10], mismatches between supply and demand can force people to compromise in terms of quality putting their health at risk [11, 12].
- Using less water than expected can also lead to health-related issues; unused water remaining stagnant in pipes can be a breeding ground for pathogenic germs.

1.2 Information Technology and Absorptive Capacity

To avoid issues like the ones mentioned above, scientists developing predictive and explanatory models for short-term water supply need to recognize, assimilate, and apply valuable yet new information as quickly as possible, that is, have a high absorptive capacity, even more so under uncertainty [13]. As mentioned at the outset, embedded and mobile systems in the guise of—for instance—smart meters or devices tracking human behavior (such as smartphones capturing movement profiles during a pandemic) can provide us with valuable information. However, being able to capture and store information and using it to generate tangible outcomes are two different things.

There is a substantial body of research showing that IT-related capabilities or architectural properties like—for example—the use of business intelligence and analytics have an impact on an organization's absorptive capacity [13–15]. However, the mere presence of valuable information and information processing tools either in the public domain or within an organization does not guarantee its application [16, 17].

1.3 Approach, Method, and Context

Although focusing on "firms" and "commercial ends," Cohen and Levinthal indicated [18] and others later explicitly stated [1] that similar concepts may be applied to individuals, to different types of organizations, or even to nations. Caiazza et al. [3] discussed the absorptive capacity of the economy as a whole in the context of COVID-19, and Farzanegan [2] used healthcare absorptive capacity to explain SARS-CoV-2 mortality, the latter certainly not being a purely "commercial end." Inspired by these publications, we apply the construct (absorptive capacity) to a sub-group of the research community (that is, to researchers that published work dealing with short-term water demand under COVID-19 so far) and then treat the utilization of potentially valuable data sources as an indicator of absorptive capacity.

Ceteris paribus, one can assume (and existing research so far confirms [19]) that governmental measures—so-called non-pharmaceutical interventions (NPIs) like social distancing policies (SDPs) or stay-at-home (SAH) orders—were likely to have an effect on both, the distribution of water demand between the commercial and residential users as well as on weekly or diurnal water demand patterns. Due to the enormous impact of the pandemic, a wide variety of freely accessible data sources related to both NPIs and resulting human behavioral changes soon became publicly available [20–26]. Theoretically, these sources could immediately be used to review, refine, or redesign forecasting models. As we assume that very little was known about the effects NPIs, SDPs, or SAHs might have on—for instance—water demand and water demand patterns before the pandemic, there was very little specific prior knowledge one could build on, thus creating an even bigger challenge in terms of absorptive capacity. We therefore conclude that the utilization of such sources of information can provide an indication of the respective absorptive capacity in research.

2 Factors Driving Water Demand Under COVID-19

In February 2020, the World Health Organization (WHO) declared the COVID-19 outbreak a public health emergency of international concern [27], and governments all over the world responded with a wide variety of measures [28]. As countries were locked down from the beginning of 2020 onward, changes to the short-term residential and commercial demand for water were to be expected—just think of people working from home, of factories being shut down, and of public swimming pools being closed.

2.1 Drivers of Water Demand

Classically, a wide variety of variables and algorithms are used to predict the demand for water. Wybrands [29], for instance, identified 15 different forecasting methods he assigned to seven different forecasting types using 13 types of variables that in return fall into six categories. Many of the forecasting methods (like time series analysis or artificial intelligence) and at least two of these variable categories (socio-demographic data and climatic variables) also play a role in predicting short-term demand [30–32]; and most of the other ones (maybe except "price" under "Economic & Socio-economic Variables")—while unlikely to fluctuate on a short-term basis—may still have modifying effects on short-term demand patterns.

But for obvious reasons, none of the models existing before the beginning of 2020 considered the effect of epidemiological data on governmental NPIs related to a global pandemic, the effect of such governmental NPIs on the behavior of entire populations and the effect of these behavioral changes on the short-term demand for water. And whereas it could be expected that respective work would sooner or later be published, one could only guess which of the newly surfaced data mentioned under "1.3 Approach, Method, and Context" would be utilized for that research.

In the meantime, it has been confirmed that such information can be of value [33]; the question of how many researchers publishing work about short-term water demand have used it so far, however, remained unanswered. In that respect, we consider the publication of data about governmental measures and human behavior during the pandemic a natural experiment. As the respective data were (a) useful [33] and (b) not available before 2020, they represent valuable and new information, and their utilization can provide insights in terms of how quickly such information is absorbed (Table 1).

Table 1 Search strings used, number of results

Source	Search string	Results
Google scholar	https://scholar.google.com/scholar?as_q=water+demand&as_epq=&as_oq=covid+%22cov-2%22+corona+pandemic&as_eq=&as_occt=title&as_ylo=2019&as_sdt=0%2C5&as_vis=1	24
PubMed	"(water[title] AND demand[title]) AND (cov-2[title] OR covid[title] OR corona[title] OR pandemic[title])"	4
Scopus	"(TITLE((water AND demand) AND (cov2 OR covid OR corona OR pandemic)))"	14
Web of science	"TI = ((water AND demand) AND(cov2 OR covid OR corona OR pandemic))"	11

2.2 *Selection and Exclusion Criteria*

To gain some related insights, we performed a brief literature search using the search engines and search strings shown in Table 2 on 2022-08-29.

After removing duplicates and three sources for which the full text was not available plus another four that did not focus on water demand but on water quality, on rainwater harvesting potentials, on a population's willingness to pay for water, and on travel patterns rather than COVID-19, 16 sources of different nature and quality (14 articles, a blog post, and a master thesis) remained. We also excluded the gray literature (the blog post and the master thesis), one more source due to quality issues (research question and conclusions remained unclear), and one because it only collected subjective consumption estimates via questionnaires, thus leading to 12 articles of which one was a literature review. The literature review is not included in Table 2 (because it contained multiple instead of just providing one approach), but we considered its contents in terms of whether any of its sources used the information we specified under "1.3 Approach, Method, and Context."

As shown in Table 2, all remaining sources deal with pandemic-related changes in short-term water consumption but differ in terms of the outcomes they focus on (overall quantity or sectoral/spatial/temporal distribution of demand), and in terms of the independent variables they consider. In summary, the research we reviewed found similar effects of NPIs on short-term water demand:

- The total demand for water remains largely unchanged.
- There are changes in the distribution of that total demand (between residential and non-residential users) and in weekly and diurnal patterns.
- Several other variables (socio-demographic, socio-economic, and socio-technical data) also play a role as mediators or modifiers.

3 Results

While the above findings were to be expected and are well aligned, it comes as a surprise that the sources discussed here as well as those mentioned in the literature review [19] not included in Table 2 make little use of certain data that were freely and publicly available at the time of writing:

1. None of the studies used granular information about governmental responses covering the time from January first, 2020, onward and published by Oxford University [28]. Despite the fact that governmental measures were diverse, multifaceted, and often overlapped [40], many studies treat COVID-related restrictions as binary[1] or categorical/ordinal [42] variables.

[1] This applies to the studies that use date ranges to identify periods with/without restrictions but only rudimentarily differentiate between different levels of restrictions, see Table 2.

Table 2 Short-term water demand under COVID-19: Approaches found in publications

Source	Independent variables	Other factors	Dependent variables	Data collection method
[34]	Date ranges	Commuter balances	Daily demand, weekday, and diurnal patterns	Metering data
[35]	SDPs	Socio-technical data, zones (residential/non-residential)	Daily demand (residential/non-residential)	Metering data
[36]	Date ranges	Socio-economic data	Daily demand, diurnal patterns	Metering data and interviews
[37]	Date ranges		Diurnal patterns	Metering data
[38]	Date ranges	User type (residential, non-residential)	Daily and weekly demand, weekday, and diurnal patterns	Metering data
[33]	Google community mobility reports	Socio-economic data	Daily demand, indoor flow, diurnal patterns	Metering data
[39]	Date ranges	User type (residential, commercial, school)	Monthly demand	Metering data
[40]	Date ranges	User type (residential, commercial, school, ...)	Monthly demand, spatial distribution	Metering data
[41]	Date ranges	Socio-economic data, meteorological data	Daily demand, weekday, and diurnal patterns	Metering data
[8]	Date ranges	Socio-demographic data, fasting (Ramadan)	Weekday and diurnal patterns	Metering data
[42]	SDPs	Building use, occupancy	Monthly water consumption, weekday patterns	Metering data

2. Although behavioral [20, 21] and epidemiological [26] data were available, researchers (except for one study [33]) often speculated about the behavior explaining the observed effects [41].
3. Different methods ranging from mostly descriptive approaches [43] and visual analytics [40] to—for instance—principal component analysis (PCA) [33] and cluster analysis [37] were applied. But in the light of epistemological uncertainty and knowing that multidimensional and non-linear relationships may play a role [33, 44], the rationale behind preferring a certain analytical approach often remains unclear.
4. Although most of the research found seems to have been performed in cooperation with water utilities (suggested by access to metering data), none of it seems to have used an existing analytical environment (such as a data warehouse or a business intelligence solution). Instead, even the most insightful studies had to build their analytical environment from scratch, leading to very heterogeneous, seemingly makeshift, and probably non-reusable architectures consisting of PowerBI, R, and the notorious Microsoft Excel [33].

4 Conclusions

Our quick and—admittedly superficial—search for literature discussing the effect of COVID-19-related measures on short-term water demand indicates that the research community so far has not fully absorbed some new and valuable information published in that context. There are reasons to assume that some of the information we refer to is useful [33], and we did not find any studies claiming the opposite. Hence, we find it a bit surprising that so little of it has been used so far. Furthermore, even though some studies were done in the context of water utilities, it seems as if analytical tools had to be built ad hoc and from scratch on a case-by-case basis. If that observation is correct, one could assume that absorptive capacity when it comes to utilizing new types of information in research related to short-term water demand is not only low but also further hindered due to the lack of pre-existing yet flexible architectures [13] and analytical instruments [33]. We speculate that these findings are not specific to the pandemic but in general to new information generated in the context of regime shifts or black swan events.

Whereas one may argue that the COVID-19 pandemic is a one-off, transient, once-in-a-lifetime event, recent experience suggests that disruptive events (think of climate change or the war in Ukraine) have become the "new normal." Which leads us to the conclusion that we need to think about new ways—maybe also new information architectures—to enable researchers to absorb all the information created by embedded and mobile systems. This need will become even more pressing as the diversity of such data grows rapidly and as higher levels of (so-called "Knightian") ontological or epistemological uncertainty [45, 46] force us to exploit it as quickly as possible.

5 Limitations

From an economic perspective, demand is merely "the quantity of a good or service that economic agents are willing to buy at a given price" [47] and neither a desired quantity nor one limited by resource availability. As with the publications we considered, we assume a practically unlimited supply of water and therefore see water consumption as a proxy for water demand and water demand as a result of conscious or unconscious choices that are—among other things—impacted by the NPIs we discussed.

We have not yet verified the model, we have in mind (NPIs impact behavior impacts demand) but have also not found any related analysis based on the information sources we suggested. And while the data published there may be irrelevant for short-term water demand, one publication [33] seems to point in a different direction; beyond that one source, we also found none that even considered the respective data sources. Nevertheless, due to the superficial nature of our search algorithm which certainly does not constitute a proper and systematic review of the available literature, we may have well overlooked highly relevant pieces of work.

References

1. Popkin, B. M., D'Anci, K. E., & Rosenberg, I. H. (2010). Water, hydration, and health. *Nutrition Reviews, 68*(8), 439–458. https://doi.org/10.1111/j.1753-4887.2010.00304.x
2. Mytton, D. (2021). Data Centre water consumption. *Npj Clean Water, 4*(1), 11. https://doi.org/10.1038/s41545-021-00101-w
3. Janke, R., Tryby, M., & Clark, R. (2014). Protecting water supply critical infrastructure: An overview (pp. 29–85).
4. Was sind Kritische Infrastrukturen? (2022). Retrieved August 18, 2022, from https://www.bsi.bund.de/DE/Themen/KRITIS-und-regulierte-Unternehmen/Kritische-Infrastrukturen/Allgemeine-Infos-zu-KRITIS/allgemeine-infos-zu-kritis_node.html
5. Water Sector Cyber Security Strategy 2017–2021. (2017). Retrieved August 18, 2022, from https://assets.publishing.service.gov.uk/government/uploads/system/uploads/attachment_data/file/602379/water-sector-cyber-security-strategy-170322.pdf
6. Water Infrastructure Resilience. (2020). Retrieved August 18, 2020, from https://www.epa.gov/emergency-response-research/water-infrastructure-resilience
7. Bulk Water Supply Security | Infrastructure Australia. (2022). Retrieved August 28, 2022, from https://www.infrastructureaustralia.gov.au/map/bulk-water-supply-security
8. Rizvi, S., Rustum, R., Deepak, M., Wright, G. B., & S. A. (2021). Identifying and analyzing residential water demand profile; including the impact of COVID-19 and month of Ramadan, for selected developments in Dubai, United Arab Emirates. *Water Science and Technology: Water Supply, 21*(3), 1144–1156. https://doi.org/10.2166/ws.2020.319
9. Bruno, E. M., & Jessoe, K. (2021). Using Price elasticities of water demand to inform policy. *Annual Review of Resource Economics, 13*(1), 427–441. https://doi.org/10.1146/annurev-resource-110220-104549
10. Garrone, P., Grilli, L., & Marzano, R. (2019). Price elasticity of water demand considering scarcity and attitudes. *Utilities Policy, 59*, 100927. https://doi.org/10.1016/j.jup.2019.100927

11. Komarulzaman, A., Ed, J., & Smits, J. (2019). Hidden water affordability problems revealed in developing countries. *Journal of Water Resources Planning and Management, 145*, 05019006. https://doi.org/10.1061/(ASCE)WR.1943-5452.0001051. urn:nbn:nl:ui:22-2066/203841.
12. Li, P., & Wu, J. (2019). Drinking water quality and public health. *Exposure and Health, 11*(2), 73–79. https://doi.org/10.1007/s12403-019-00299-8
13. Mikalef, P., Pateli, A., & van de Wetering, R. (2021). IT architecture flexibility and IT governance decentralisation as drivers of IT-enabled dynamic capabilities and competitive performance: The moderating effect of the external environment. *European Journal of Information Systems, 30*(5), 512–540. https://doi.org/10.1080/0960085X.2020.1808541
14. Mao, H., Liu, S., Zhang, J., Zhang, Y., & Gong, Y. (2021). Information technology competency and organizational agility: Roles of absorptive capacity and information intensity. *Information Technology & People, 34*(1), 421–451. https://doi.org/10.1108/ITP-12-2018-0560
15. Božič, K., & Dimovski, V. (2020). The relationship between business intelligence and analytics use and organizational absorptive capacity: Applying the DeLone & Mclean information systems success model. *Economic and Business Review, 22*, 2. https://doi.org/10.15458/ebr99
16. Todorova, G., & Durisin, B. (2007). Absorptive capacity: Valuing a reconceptualization. *The Academy of Management Review, 32*(3), 774–786.
17. Zahra, S. A., & George, G. (2002). Absorptive capacity: A review, reconceptualization, and extension. *The Academy of Management Review, 27*(2), 185–203. https://doi.org/10.2307/4134351
18. Cohen, W. M., & Levinthal, D. A. (1990). Absorptive capacity: A new perspective on learning and innovation. *Administrative Science Quarterly., 35*(1), 128–152. https://doi.org/10.2307/2393553
19. Cahill, J., Hoolohan, C., Lawson, R., & Browne, A. L. (2022). COVID-19 and water demand: A review of literature and research evidence. *Wiley Interdisciplinary Reviews: Water, 9*(1), e1570. https://doi.org/10.1002/wat2.1570
20. COVID-19 - Mobility Trends Reports. (2022). Retrieved September 15, 2022, from https://covid19.apple.com/mobility
21. COVID-19 Community Mobility Report. (2022). Retrieved September 15, 2022, from https://www.google.com/covid19/mobility
22. TomTom Traffic Index. (2022). Retrieved September 15, 2022, from https://www.tomtom.com/en_gb/traffic-index
23. C3 AI COVID-19 Data Lake. (2021). Retrieved September 15, 2022, from https://c3.ai/products/c3-ai-covid-19-data-lake
24. A Public Data lake for COVID-19 Research and Development. (2022). Retrieved September 15, 2022, from https://aws.amazon.com/de/covid-19-data-lake
25. COVID-19 Government Response Tracker. (2022). Retrieved August 18, 2022, from https://www.bsg.ox.ac.uk/research/research-projects/covid-19-government-response-tracker
26. Ritchie, H., Mathieu, E., Rodés-Guirao, L., Appel, C., Giattino, C., Ortiz-Ospina, E., et al. (2020). Coronavirus pandemic (COVID-19). Retrieved August 18, 2022, from https://ourworldindata.org/coronavirus
27. Organization WH: Timeline: WHO's COVID-19 Response. (2022). Retrieved August 18, 2022, from https://www.who.int/emergencies/diseases/novel-coronavirus-2019/interactive-timeline#!
28. Blavatnik School of Government UoO: COVID-19 Government Response Tracker. (2022). Retrieved August 18, 2022, from https://www.bsg.ox.ac.uk/research/research-projects/covid-19-government-response-tracker
29. Wybrands, M., & Dyck, A. (2021). Long-term water demand forecasting in theory and practice. Die 51 Jahrestagung der Gesellschaft fur Informatikin, INFORMATIK 2021 - 51st Annual Conference of the German Informatics Society, INFORMATIK 2021: Gesellschaft fur Informatik (GI); pp. 207–218.
30. Anele, A. O., Hamam, Y., Abu-Mahfouz, A. M., & Todini, E. (2017). Overview, comparative assessment and recommendations of forecasting models for short-term water demand prediction. *Water, 9*(11), 887.

31. Babel, M. S., & Shinde, V. R. (2011). Identifying prominent explanatory variables for water demand prediction using artificial neural networks: A case study of Bangkok. *Water Resources Management, 25*(6), 1653–1676. https://doi.org/10.1007/s11269-010-9766-x
32. Pacchin, E., Gagliardi, F., Alvisi, S., & Franchini, M. (2019). A comparison of short-term water demand forecasting models. *Water Resources Management, 33*(4), 1481–1497.
33. Fritsche, J. R., Whitby, P., Griffin, E., Norton, J. W. J., Alfahham, N., Kuhns, T., et al. (2022). Changes in water demand resulting from pandemic mitigations in Southeast Michigan. *AWWA Water Science, 4*(3), e1286. https://doi.org/10.1002/aws2.1286
34. Balacco, G., Totaro, V., Iacobellis, V., Manni, A., Spagnoletta, M., & F. PA. (2020). Influence of COVID-19 spread on water drinking demand: The case of Puglia region (Southern Italy). *Sustainability (Switzerland), 12*(15), 5919. https://doi.org/10.3390/SU12155919
35. Bakchan, A., Roy, A., & Faust, K. M. (2022). Impacts of COVID-19 social distancing policies on water demand: A population dynamics perspective. *Journal of Environmental Management, 302*, 113949. https://doi.org/10.1016/j.jenvman.2021.113949
36. Cominato, C., Sborz, J., Kalbusch, A., & Henning, E. (2022). Water demand profile before and during COVID-19 pandemic in a Brazilian social housing complex. *Heliyon, 8*(8), e10307. https://doi.org/10.1016/j.heliyon.2022.e10307
37. Dzimińska, P., Drzewiecki, S., Ruman, M., Kosek, K., Mikołajewski, K., & P. L. (2021). The use of cluster analysis to evaluate the impact of covid-19 pandemic on daily water demand patterns. *Sustainability (Switzerland)., 13*(11), 5772. https://doi.org/10.3390/su13115772
38. Feltman, L. E. (2021). *Effects of COVID-19 lockdown on urban water demand in Cincinnati*. University of Cincinnati.
39. Irwin, N. B., McCoy, S. J., & McDonough, I. K. (2021). Water in the time of corona(virus): The effect of stay-at-home orders on water demand in the desert. *Journal of Environmental Economics and Management, 109*, 102491. https://doi.org/10.1016/j.jeem.2021.102491
40. Kazak, J. K., Szewrański, S., Pilawka, T., Tokarczyk-Dorociak, K., Janiak, K., & Świąder, M. (2021). Changes in water demand patterns in a European city due to restrictions caused by the covid-19 pandemic. *Desalination and Water Treatment, 222*, 1–15. https://doi.org/10.5004/dwt.2021.27242
41. Lüdtke, D. U., Luetkemeier, R., Schneemann, M., & Liehr, S. (2021). Increase in daily household water demand during the first wave of the covid-19 pandemic in Germany. *Water (Switzerland), 13*(3), 260. https://doi.org/10.3390/w13030260
42. Spearing, L. A., Tiedmann, H. R., Sela, L., Nagy, Z., Kaminsky, J. A., Katz, L. E., et al. (2021). Human-Infrastructure Interactions during the COVID-19 Pandemic: Understanding Water and Electricity Demand Profiles at the Building Level. *Acs Es\&T Water, 1*(11), 2327–2338. https://doi.org/10.1021/acsestwater.1c00176. Early Access Date = NOV 2021, EISSN = 2690-0637.
43. Ogunbode TO, & Asifat, J. T. (2021). Comparative assessment of pre-COVID-19 and post-COVID-19 lockdown water demand in selected institutions of learning in a growing Community in Nigeria. *European Journal of Basic Medical Sciences, 11*(1), 38–45.
44. Bich-Ngoc, N., & Teller, J. (2020). Potential effects of the covid-19 pandemic through changes in outbound tourism on water demand: The case of liège (Belgium). *Water (Switzerland), 12*(10), 2820. https://doi.org/10.3390/w12102820
45. Knight, F. H. (1921). *Risk, uncertainty and profit. Hart, Schaffner & Marx prize essays, vol XXXI*. Houghton Mifflin Company.
46. Köhn, J. (2017). *Uncertainty in economics: A new approach*. Springer.
47. Hashimzade, N., Myles, G., & Black, J. (2017). *A dictionary of economics*. Oxford University Press, Incorporated.

Predictors of E-Government Adoption in Developing Countries: A Survey in South Africa

Anass Bayaga

1 Introduction

Several recent studies, both in South Africa and internationally, have focused on the adoption of e-government services, indicating a gradual uptake from various dimensions [1–5]. Research on security risk factors has identified several predictors, including security requirements denoted as SR-SEC [2, 5]. Conversely, it has been recognized that e-government services are affected by security risk predictors, as well as institutional logics, which encompass sociocultural factors [1, 6, 7]. Institutional logic, defined by Thornton and Ocasio [7, p. 804] as "... socially constructed, [and] historical patterns of material practices, assumptions, values, beliefs, and rules by which individuals produce and reproduce their material subsistence, organize time and space, and provide meaning to their social reality," is considered to underpin citizens' and organizational decisions [7–9]. Recent studies suggest the need to consider the effects of institutional logic [9], given that it includes factors such as social and cultural constructs like race, gender, education, income, age, values (privacy beliefs), population density (geo), and employment (empl), among others, as identified in earlier studies. Therefore, institutional logic could be integrated into e-government adoption. This perspective forms the basis of the current study. Previous research has examined the influence of security risk predictors on e-government service adoption. For example, Alharbi, Papadaki, and Dowland [10] discovered that security risk factors affect clients' adoption of online services. Munyoka and Maharaj [6] also recently revealed the bias toward security risk factors in e-government. Others have established a secure payment model using face authentication as a security requirement [11]. Despite these findings, Mawela et al. [2] recently reflected on the implementation of e-government services in South

A. Bayaga (✉)
Nelson Mandela University, Gqeberha, South Africa
e-mail: anass.bayaga@mandela.ac.za

J. Marx Gómez et al. (eds.), *Smart and Secure Embedded and Mobile Systems*, Progress in IS, https://doi.org/10.1007/978-3-031-56603-5_14

Africa and raised concerns about citizens' acceptance of these services, calling for further investigation. What distinguishes the current study from previous research is the need to examine conjoint analysis of both security risk factors and institutional logics simultaneously. Hence, the present study aims to develop hypotheses to guide the discussion and analysis.

2 Research Aims

RA1: To examine the dependency of e-government on predictors such as security risk factors and institutional logic.

RA2: To determine the relevance of security risk factors and institutional logic in predicting e-government services.

3 Literature Review and Hypotheses Development

3.1 Security Risk Predictors and Sociocultural Dimensions

When examining mainstream e-government studies, Heeks and Bailur [12] identified best practices. However, they emphasized the need to acknowledge citizens' sociocultural dimensions as potential influences on e-government service adoption, which are referred to as institutional logics in the seminal work of Thornton and Ocasio [7]. Heeks and Bailur's [12] evaluation is due to the fact that the predictive relevance of institutional logic (or simply social and cultural) constructs, coupled with security risk factors, is not fully comprehended [13]. For example, factors that influence the adoption of e-government services have yet to be fully understood [14], and a critical assessment of potential measurement biases in technology acceptance [15] is also necessary. Specifically, it is yet to be established how certain institutional logics (social and cultural), such as those listed below, primarily predict e-government service adoption [3, 6, 16]:

1. Race.
2. Gender.
3. Education.
4. Income.
5. Age.
6. Population density (geo).
7. Employment (empl).

For instance, it is still necessary to examine how different races moderate the uptake of e-government services while concurrently accounting for security risk factors. Correspondingly, Sarabdeen et al. [13] suggest the importance of examining the relevance of gender. Accordingly, constructs including race and gender, together with security risks, could provide insight into the adoption of e-government services by South African citizens. Other researchers, such as Heeks and Bailur [12], also advocate the need to examine population density (geo) as well as employment (empl) and how such factors moderate e-government service adoption while accounting for security risk factors. For example, Sánchez-Prieto, Hernández-García, García-Peñalvo, Chaparro-Peláez, and Olmos-Migueláñez [17, p. 158] suggest the need to "break the walls and barriers" in terms of population density (location) to facilitate the acceptance of e-government services, particularly among rural communities. Others, such as Sarabdeen et al. [13], suggest that e-government service users' security concerns could be improved based on accessible locations in urban areas and among rural users. Resultantly, there is an indication that, despite the category or forms of e-government services, there is a need to address the risks associated with e-government services in different cultural and social settings [2–4, 6, 16].

It is also not thoroughly examined how education (certificate, diploma) may affect the adoption of e-government services [3, 18, 19]. There is an ongoing debate that citizens with less education do not adopt e-government services, in part, due to e-government security concerns. Additionally, while security risk factors have been considered relevant predictors, it is argued that citizens with different levels of education coupled with high levels of income, as previously identified by Zhao and Zhao [20], may also threaten e-government services adoption. It is assumed that citizens with higher educational levels are more security conscious and are more likely to adopt e-government services than those with lower levels [20]. Based on the reviewed work and various gaps, particularly e-voting, e-tax (e-filing), and e-education, have been identified as conduits to e-government service adoption among South African citizens.

Furthermore, the question remains: will citizens of different income levels experience security risks and control assessments (technologies) in cyberspace differently? Besides income, it could also be argued that citizens of different ages may experience security risks differently when a breach of reliable services in cyberspace occurs [3, 19].

So far, there are several implications of a breach of reliable services in cyberspace [3, 19]. The first is compromising private data, which may occur among different races, genders, education, or income groups, with information being stolen by an attacker or even data being altered, resulting in personal damage. One consequence is that cost recovery expenses may need to be tailored to different races, genders, education, and income groups. A breach in security significantly affects information/data negatively, potentially resulting in financial repercussions for different races, genders, education, and income groups. Such financial repercussions may include the need for new information systems (IS) training and development and acquiring new software or devices for different races, genders, education, and income groups. In some cases, citizens may be involved in a prolonged procedure of restoring lost information and data, resulting in either loss of time or money. Similar to education, population density characterized by rural and urban settings influences e-government differently. The proposed effect regarding population density suggests a lower uptake of e-government services among rural folks than that of urban [3].

Based on the discussion, it could be argued that different races, genders, education, and income groups could influence citizens' needs or perceptions as per population density (rural or urban) regarding adopting e-government services. Adopting e-government services may hinge on the fact that different population density groups are equally concerned with a cost-benefit assessment when deciding whether to disclose confidential information and subsequently adopt e-government services. Thus far, different population density groups may decide against e-government services because the risk level comparable to the benefit is significant in varying population density groups. In addition to population density, researchers are not fully able to comprehend the possible effect of different employment (empl) levels or a combination regarding citizens in South Africa, taking into account security risks. Due in part to e-government initiatives presenting new frontiers of security risks, such challenges concerning different employment (empl) levels are inherently stagnated at all stages, such as government to citizens, government to business, government to government, and government to an employee (G2C, G2B, G2G, and G2E, respectively) of development [13]. For instance, setting up a public web for different employment (empl) levels to download forms and government information in the case of G2C may be sloppy due to inefficiency and poor quality associated with the services [13, 21–23].

Likewise, activities between the local or central government and the commercial business sector (G2B) regarding different employment (empl) levels, as well as employees (G2E), and in some cases, activities within local or central government (G2G) are likely to become stagnant, just as G2C does.

3.2 Institutional Logics and Security Risk Factors

The number of concerns related to predictors of e-governance service adoption over the years has intensified [24–28]. For example, while Nagy et al. [27] were not the first to examine such concerns, this adoption/disruptive literature argues for the need to identify new constructs to examine the effects of innovations on platforms such as e-government services, among others. The assessment of Nagy et al. [27] is significant because Davis and Venkatesh [15, p. 4] had already suggested that identifying such new constructs tends to unpack and thus form the "...critical assessment of [any] potential measurement biases in [any] technology acceptance model." This critical assessment of possible method biases tends to help accurately predict and explain user acceptance of information technologies.

In response, other theories, such as the unified theory of acceptance and use of technology as advocated by Venkatesh, Thong, and Xu [29] have been developed to address potential measurement biases and hence accurate prediction and explanation of constructs. For example, a study among Belgian teenagers (aged 12–18 years) demonstrated numerous cyber-risks affecting users [25]. While not an exhaustive

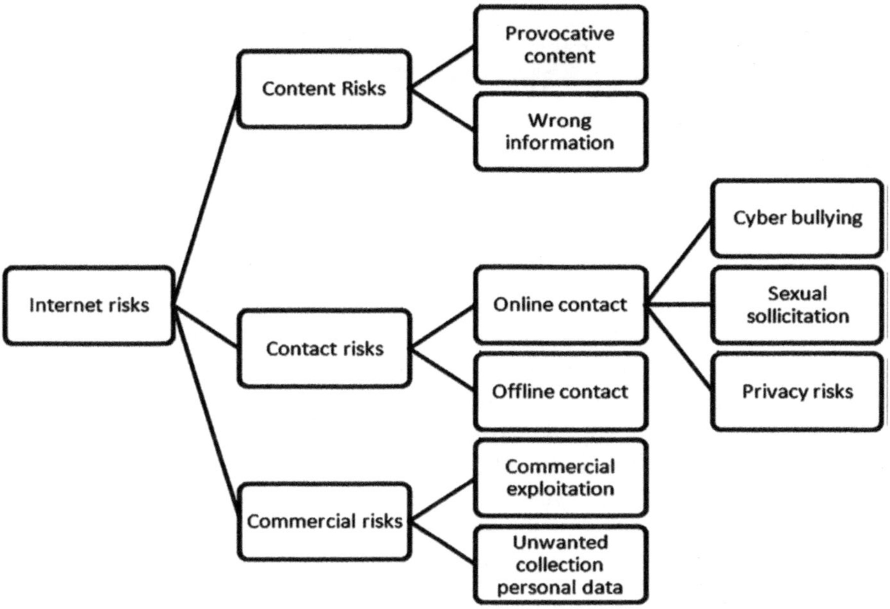

Fig. 1 Flow chart of security risk predictors for clients [28]

list, some cyber-risks include gender, education, income, age, population density (geo), and employment (empl), collectively called institutional logic. Anchored upon the work of De Moor et al. [25], Valcke, De Wever, Van Keer, and Schellens [28] categorized a flowchart of security risk predictors for clients (Fig. 1).

The concerns related to predictors of e-governance service adoption have intensified over the years [24–28]. Nagy et al. [27] were not the first to examine such concerns, but their work argues for the need to identify new constructs to examine the effects of innovations on platforms, such as e-government services. This assessment is significant as Davis and Venkatesh [15, p. 4] had already suggested that identifying new constructs tends to unpack and thus form the critical assessment of potential measurement biases in any technology acceptance model. Such critical assessment of probable method biases helps in accurately predicting and explaining user acceptance of information technologies. Other theories, such as the unified theory of acceptance and use of technology advocated by Venkatesh, Thong, and Xu [29] have been advanced to address potential measurement biases and thus improve the prediction and explanation of constructs.

Several cyber-risks affecting users have been categorized as content risks related to wrong information, contact risks in the form of offline contact and online contact risks, privacy risks, and commercial risks including commercial exploitation and unwanted collection of personal data, as reflected in Fig. 1. However, there are other factors that are not yet known. For instance, the model of Valcke et al. [28] does not explain how those security risk factors influence institutional logic. Young

Fig. 2 Conceptual model: Security risk predictors along with institutional logic in adopting public web

people may visit violent or pornographic internet sites by choice, but they may also be subjected to unpleasant materials and behaviors unwittingly [24, p. 6]. The same may not be accurate for different institutional logics (race, gender, education, income, population density (geo), employment (empl). Therefore, the current study aims to address this unresolved question.

Furthermore, Gámez-Guadix, Borrajo, and Almendros [26] established relationships between different cyber-risks, including adolescent challenges regarding Internet use and their effect on perpetration, exploitation, and unwanted collection of personal data. Different institutional logics may not have the same impact (race, gender, education, income, population density (geo), employment (empl)). Consequently, there is a need to undertake the current study, which is partly a response to ongoing concerns in both developed and developing countries [25, p. 6]. For example, Adeola and Abiodun [25, p. 6] argued that while limited research is conducted in developing nations, far more attempts have been made in developed nations. The current study examines security risk factors and institutional logic model to respond to these gaps, focusing on predictive relevance to e-government service adoption, as depicted in Fig. 2.

3.2.1 Implication and Hypothetical Stance

There are several implications related to the extent to which institutional logics (race, gender, education, income, age, population density (geo), and employment (empl)) tend to moderate the adoption of the public web, such as e-government services amidst security risk factors as reflected in Fig. 2. That is to say, in both practice and theory, the need to adopt e-government services is hampered not only by concerns related to security risks but also by social and cultural dimensions. By implication, not only is adopting e-government associated with data insecurity and costly recovery expenses, but also citizens' social and cultural constructs. In effect, it could be hypothesized that citizens' perceptions of e-government service adoption are dependent not only on security risks but also on social and cultural constructs (race, gender, education, income, age, population density (geo), and employment (empl)).

It may be implied that despite ongoing studies in understanding security risk controls, evidence demonstrates that different citizens in terms of social and cultural settings are persistently concerned about their security and privacy. Given that there is limited citizen-centric research, partly due to a dearth of joint research on the influence of security risk predictors and institutional logic in adopting e-government services, the current research identifies a need to fill the existing gap. Filling the gap is achieved by understanding the adoption and uneasiness of citizens of different cultural backgrounds regarding the security of e-government service adoption. By implication, this study attempts to provide decision makers (theoreticians and practitioners) grounds by extending the work on predicting security and social and cultural settings in adopting e-government services.

Research Hypotheses

Hypothesis H1: Security risks, moderated by age, have an impact on the adoption of public web services, such as e-government services, by citizens.

Hypothesis H2: Security risks, moderated by race, have an impact on the adoption of public web services by citizens.

Hypothesis H3: Security risks, moderated by employment status, have an impact on the adoption of public web services by citizens.

Hypothesis H4: Security risks, moderated by gender, have an impact on the adoption of public web services by citizens.

Hypothesis H5: Security risks, moderated by education, have an impact on the adoption of public web services by citizens.

Hypothesis H6: Security risks, moderated by population density, have an impact on the adoption of public web services by citizens.

Hypothesis H7: Security risks, moderated by income, have an impact on the adoption of public web services by citizens.

These hypotheses aim to examine the impact of security risks moderated by different institutional logics (age, race, employment status, gender, education, population density, and income) on the adoption of public web services, particularly e-government services. These hypotheses seek to address the existing gap in citizen-centric research by exploring the influence of security risk predictors and institutional logic on e-government service adoption.

4 Method

4.1 Outlook, Nature of Constructs in the Instrument (Questionnaire)

The current section explains and examines the general outlook and the constructs employed in gathering data through a questionnaire. Note that the development of the quantitative section was based not only on the hypotheses but also on the reviewed literature. However, a pilot study was conducted to tailor-make and re-assess, thus modifying arguments of previous studies, including the length of the Questionnaire. During the modifications, a wide range of factors was considered. In comparison, some included the Questionnaire, primarily developed in the English language, which used six constructs and 40 indicators, all of which were guided by the hypotheses and literature. Altogether, they were divided into three key sections and finally administered to 420 respondents. In the main, there were different sections. Whereas Section A addressed information related to institutional logic anchored upon previous studies, Section B explored different views on security risk predictors. Section C measured respondents' views on private risk predictors. While the first was the privacy risks process, the second was privacy risks concerns. Additional dimensions explored based on the hypotheses included participants' cultural dimensions (in this case, institutional logic), views related to adopting e-government services, along with information sensitivity. In addressing the outlook and nature of constructs in the instrument (Questionnaire), constructs in Sections B and C comprised a 4-point Likert scale. Predominately the scale assumed 1 = always, 2 = very frequently, 3 = rarely, and 4 = never. However, in section C, privacy risk predators used the following 1, 2, 3, and 4 for very high risk, above-average risk, below-average risk, and very low risk, respectively.

4.2 Specific Outlook of Nature of Constructs in the Questionnaire

Further to the outlook and nature of constructs in the instrument (Questionnaire), a specific outlook related to the nature of constructs in the Questionnaire was also examined. In maximizing the response rate, some participants were recruited using online platforms such as emails. Generally, most scales were adapted from Xu et al. [11] and Dinev and Hart [21]. The reason is that such scales through the seminal work have successfully been used, and credible outcomes and acceptable reliability have been attained. Keenly, they were congruent to the research hypotheses.

4.3 Stages of Analysis

The analysis technique used was partial least squares-structural equation modelling (PLS-SEM) to test the hypotheses, using the SmartPLS 3.2.8 software. PLS-SEM was chosen for several reasons, including its ability to simultaneously reduce residual variances in dependent or latent variables while not just being a regression technique, as suggested by Hair, Ringle, and Sarstedt [30]. Additionally, PLS-SEM provides better latent dependent variables, such as the adoption of e-government services, as suggested by Sánchez-Prietoa et al. [17].

The PLS-SEM process was divided into two main stages: assessing the robustness of the outer (measurement) model and the structural model. To assess the measurement model, a reliability test was used to determine the degree of observable indicators. Item reliability was used to evaluate outer loadings, and variable consistency measured what it does [31]. The outer loadings were iteratively evaluated with a standard value of 0.70 as a guide, and variables with outer loadings below this value were removed, ensuring that the composite reliability (CR) or at least the average variance extracted (AVE) was still above the 0.7 and 0.5 thresholds, respectively.

4.4 Addressing or Controlling Common Method Biases

Despite continuous attempts in the literature to resolve method biases, usually in the form of common method biases, it was still crucial to address one principal concern. As noted by Podsakoff, MacKenzie, and Podsakoff [32], such a concern was the likely sources of method biases and how to control them. The primary reason is anchored upon Podsakoff et al.'s (2003) position that usually, method biases affect the measures used and thus the statistical techniques applied. Consequently, there is a need to consider evaluating the various statistical procedures deemed appropriate for controlling method biases. Noting that method biases lead to sources of measurement errors (whether systematic or random errors), which then threaten the validity of results. To address the aforementioned in terms of techniques for controlling common method biases, while not an exhaustive list/techniques, the current research followed several recommendations from Podsakoff et al. [32]. As described in both general and specific outlooks of the nature of constructs, the first was the need to obtain predictor and criterion measures emanating from different sources (particularly in the demographic cohort for the current study). The reason for the first led to the second, which addresses temporal, psychological, and even methodological separation of measurements. The second simply means the separation of the measurement of the predictor and criterion variables, which included security, privacy risks predictors, as well as institutional logic from their sub-variables. The third step addressed ethics and common method bias to protect interviewees' anonymity and reduce evaluation apprehension. The fourth, that is priming effect, was addressed by counterbalancing question order—thus ordering the questions in a fashion that does not cause ambiguity and thus simultaneously addressing the issue of improving scale item—by defining ambiguous or unfamiliar terms on the first page of the Questionnaire.

5 Data Analysis and Results

This section on data analysis aims to investigate the moderating effects of socio-cultural dimensions, specifically institutional logics, on the relationship between security risks and the adoption of e-government services. Two main goals serve as anchors for predicting the relevance of security risk constructs in this study. Therefore, the question this section aims to answer is: to what degree are security risks affected by institutional logic when citizens adopt e-government services?

To respond to the research question, the moderating effects of age, race, employment, gender, education, population density, and income on the relationship between security risks and e-government service adoption were calculated based on Fig. 2 (conceptual model) and related literature. The security requirements, security risk concerns, and security risks were denoted as SR-EC, SR-AVA, and SR-USE, respectively, as per the literature.

In addition, this section aimed to address the potential moderating effects of institutional logic on the relationship between the exogenous and endogenous variables. The analysis considered the moderating effects of institutional logic on the relationship between security risks and e-government service adoption. The findings from this analysis will help in understanding the significance of institutional logics in shaping citizens' perceptions of security risks and e-government service adoption.

5.1 *The Measurement Model*

Hair et al. [33] recommend estimating the construct's reliability and validity to evaluate the outer (measurement) model. Such estimation was done via the composite reliability (CR) and Cronbach's alpha test. All the CR and Cronbach's alpha values were higher than recommended (0.7). These results confirmed construct reliability, thus indicating that all the constructs were error-free. The AVE and the factor loadings were then used to assess convergent validity. All results show factor loadings greater than the threshold value of 0.7, with AVE values >0.5, thus confirming the convergent validity of all the indicators. HTMT ratio determines discriminant validity, with a ratio below 0.85 [33], thus ascertaining discriminant validity. Consequently, implying constructs were distinct from each other, which generally meant the validity and reliability of the measurement model were considered satisfactory, thus ready for structural modelling.

5.2 *Suitability of the Structural Model*

Once the measurement model's suitability was confirmed, structural modelling was carried out, as recommended by Hair et al. [33]. The authors suggest that several key features are important, including collinearity, coefficient of determination (R-squared), and path coefficients, as well as effect size (f-squared) and predictive relevance (Q-squared). To assess the structural model, all five features are necessary. Collinearity issues were evaluated using VIF measures, with values ranging from 1.022 to 1.111 (all <4), indicating no collinearity issues.

The R-squared value of 0.474 indicated that the model explained 47.4% of the variance in e-government service adoption. Thus, South African citizens' security requirements, concerns, and security risk use related to adopting e-government services contribute to less than 50% (nearly 47.4%) of the variance in adoption. However, Cohen [34] explains that this reflects substantial adoption in a human setting. The bootstrapping procedure of 1000 resamples was also used to test the significance of the path coefficients, as recommended by Hair et al. [33].

Overall, security risk use denoted as (SR-USE) had a beta (β) of 0.629, and SR-SEC with $\beta = 0.140$ ($p < 0.05$, respectively) positively influenced e-government adoption. The f-squared values measured by security requirements and risk use on e-government were 0.679 and 0.034, respectively. Again, Cohen [34] explains that such an f-squared on e-government service adoption is considered substantial. However, the f-squared as measured by security requirements in adopting e-government services is considered moderate, while security risk concerns (SR-AVA) had an insignificant negative effect on adopting e-government services with $\beta = -0.058$, $p > 0.05$.

In assessing the predictive relevance of the model, a construct cross-validated redundancy (Q-squared) value was employed, with a Q-squared of e-government service adoption of 0.327 (<0 as threshold). Therefore, the model can predict the effect of security issues among citizens of South Africa in adopting e-government services.

5.3 Moderation Effects of Institutional Logic

A different approach was considered in moderating institutional logics constructs (age, race, income, education, gender, occupation, and population density) on security risk predictors, as shown in the conceptual model on e-government (Table 1). Starting with age and race, the results of the moderating effects of age and race on the relationships SR-SEC, SR-AVA, and SR-USE to e-government service adoption, respectively, are shown in Table 1. Thus, constructs were of the exogenous variables as they are moderated through age and race on e-government service adoption.

Table 1 shows all the T-values of the moderating variables <1.96 [33], indicating that the effect of all the moderating variables is insignificant. Similarly, the moderating effects of education and population density on the relationships between security requirements denoted as SR-SEC, security risk concerns denoted as SR-AVA, and security risk use denoted as SR-USE to e-government were all insignificant at the 0.05 level Hair et al. [33]. Other evidence is that the moderating effect of income on the paths of security requirements as SR-SEC to e-government, security

Table 1 Moderating effect of age and race

Path	Std Beta	Std error	T-value	P-values	Decision
Age - > e-government	−0.035	0.040	0.885	0.377	Not accepted
Moderating effect1 - > e-government	−0.061	0.063	0.965	0.335	Not accepted
Moderating effect 2 - > e-government	−0.035	0.057	0.616	0.538	Not accepted
Moderating effect 3 - > e-government	−0.050	0.037	1.353	0.176	Not accepted
Moderating effect 4 - > e-government	0.022	0.044	0.484	0.628	Not accepted
Moderating effect 5 - > e-government	0.041	0.058	0.706	0.481	Not accepted
Moderating effect 6 - > e-government	−0.031	0.053	0.576	0.564	Accepted
Race - > e-government	−0.017	0.043	0.408	0.684	Accepted
SR_AVA - > e-government	−0.057	0.042	1.361	0.174	Not accepted
SR_SEC - > e-government	0.106	0.053	1.975	0.049	Not accepted
SR_USE - > e-government	0.632	0.048	13.122	0.000	Not accepted

risk concerns and security risk use denoted as to e-government were generally insignificant ($p > 0.05$). Implying income is not a moderator of the paths of security requirements to e-government.

Conclusively, as moderated by institutional logic, security risks generally do not influence South Africans adopting e-government.

6 Discussion

In line with the two research aims, this section focuses on the moderating effects of institutional logic on security risk factors (exogenous variable) for e-government service adoption (endogenous variable). Based on the conceptual model, the study assessed the moderating effects of age, race, employment, gender, education, population density, and income to address the seven hypotheses. The literature review and conceptual model guided the development of the seven hypotheses, which suggest that security risks moderated by age, race, employment, gender, education, population density, and income are all significant factors that influence e-government service adoption.

6.1 Recap from Literature

The existing literature and theoretical framework suggest a pressing need for further research, both in South Africa and internationally [1, 16]. Despite the importance of institutional logic, there has been a lack of attention paid to security risk predictors that affect citizens' adoption of e-government services. Furthermore, there is limited information on the speed with which South Africans are willing to provide personal data related to any form of electronic (e)-health, education, filing, or banking.

Although South Africans have access to smartphones/computers and Wi-Fi, they are not inclined to install e-government applications for checking the official site applications [16]. Hence, there is minimal South African research on e-government service [16, 35].

It is vital to investigate how South Africans perceive security risks, such as the authorities' use of their data [16, 35]. Additionally, there is a challenge related to security risks via transferred data and mishandling of sensitive data [16]. Other risks include malicious applications, data distribution, mobile SMS vulnerability, hardware, and operating system vulnerability [16]. Without incorporating access and adoption factors influencing technologically under-resourced institutional logic (or simply demographics) into policymaking, there will be no substantial benefits from e-government services [16, 36]. Hence, the current research aims to identify how adoption risks are recognized in South Africa, as little to no evidence exists so far. Moreover, there is a lack of focus on the context and people affected by adopting e-government services in South Africa [36, p. 5].

6.2 Connecting Results As Well as Literature

The discussion revolves around the research objectives and the background information presented so far. An analysis was conducted to determine the moderating effect of institutional logic on exogenous variables (security risk predictors) and endogenous variables (e-government services). The analysis resulted in two research aims: RA1 aimed to examine security risk predictors and institutional logics or sociocultural factors as predictors in terms of adopting e-government services. RA2 aimed to examine security risk predictiveness and sociocultural dimensions in the process of adopting e-government.

RA1 focused on the importance of security risk predictors and sociocultural dimensions (institutional logics) when adopting e-government services. Literature [34] has highlighted the relevance of these factors. The R-squared value of 0.474 indicated that the model explained 47.4% of the variance related to e-government service adoption. Security risk predictors, including security requirements risks concerns and security risks use alone, contributed significantly to citizens' willingness to use e-government. The f-squared values of SR-USE and SR_SEC on e-government were 0.679 and 0.034, respectively. The model was also relevant, with a predictive relevance of security risks and e-government services. This finding contradicts the results of previous studies by Almarashdeh and Alsmadi [1] and Schaupp and Carter [37].

RA2 focused on the moderating effects of institutional logic, including age, race, income, education, gender, occupation, and population density. Unlike previous studies, institutional logic had no relevant predictive power in conjunction with security risk factors. The study revealed that security and privacy risk variables had no direct bearing on institutional logic to adopt e-government services. This finding refutes the predictive relevance of institutional logic suggested by Mbogo

[38]. However, the study suggests that security risk predictors should be carefully addressed to promote e-government services as a major channel for South African citizens to access government services.

6.3 Contribution of Study

The refutation of institutional logic as a moderating effect on e-government adoption is grounded in several explanatory factors concerning cultural traits. Three key explanations have been put forward to support the theoretical refutation. Firstly, the cultural trait of in-group or collectivism suggests that citizens are more concerned with the implications for their group than their individual preferences. This could explain why various logics such as gender, occupation, and population density are not significantly relevant in adopting e-government services [39]. To overcome this challenge, it has been suggested that the South African government should provide more interactive and personalized e-government services to attract citizens to utilize them.

Secondly, Fischer and Derham [39] suggest that in a more collectivistic setting, citizens are not concerned about individual identities such as levels of inclusion in a group, as prescribed by institutional logic (race, age, income, education, gender, occupation, and population density). The reason for this is that individual-group links are stable and non-negotiable. Citizens who adopt e-government services have little choice in whether to stay or leave a group. Therefore, institutional logic has no effect on e-government adoption. Collectivist societies with stable groups have less need for specific identities, as detailed in the discussion on institutional logic.

Thirdly, the cultural trait of high-power distance suggests that less powerful members of such societies adopt e-government services despite the associated consequences. Citizens do not have to identify with specific clusters as suggested by the literature on institutional logic. In conclusion, the theoretical refutation of institutional logic as a moderating effect on e-government adoption is anchored on cultural traits and offers three key explanations to support this perspective [39].

7 Conclusion

The evidence thus far can inspire both theoretical and practical perspectives on e-government adoption. Evidence based on security risk predictors and how they impact the adoption of public sector websites, such as e-government services, tends to depend on security risk factors. Sociocultural dimensions do not influence these factors, also known as institutional logics. Essentially, the South African case highlights the importance of incorporating security and privacy risk factors when adopting e-government services. However, institutional logic and privacy or security risks are independent influencers when it comes to e-government adoption.

7.1 Future Research and Recommendation

A possible direction for future research based on the results is to further explore the concept of different cultural dimensions, in addition to the opportunities for further studies identified in the limitations section. Further analysis could also be conducted beyond the city of Umhlatuze to investigate other factors that were not accounted for in the study but may contribute to the 38.3% unexplained variance in e-government service adoption.

Additionally, other demographics beyond those included in this study could be considered, and other forms of e-government services in South Africa, such as G2B, G2E, and G2G, could also be explored. It may be necessary to examine individual constituents related to e-government services, such as m-Health, m-learning, e-voting, e-tax, and e-banking, as potential areas for future research.

Finally, it may be beneficial to focus on rural populations, as previous studies have largely concentrated on urban settings, and expanding our knowledge of e-government service adoption in rural areas would be valuable.

References

1. Almarashdeh, I., & Alsmadi, M. K. (2017). How to make them use it? Citizens acceptance of M-government. *Applied Computing and Informatics, 13*(2), 194–199.
2. Mawela, T. N., Ochara, M., & Twinomurinzi, H. (2017). E-government implementation: A reflection on south African municipalities. *South African Computer Journal, 29*(1), 147–171.
3. Maharaj, M. S., & Munyoka, W. (2019). Privacy, security, trust, risk and optimism bias in e-government use: The case of two southern African development community countries. *South African Journal of Information Management, 21*(1), 1–9.
4. Ochara, N. M., & Mawela, T. (2015). Enabling social sustainability of e-participation through mobile technology. *Information Technology for Development, 21*(2), 205–228.
5. Pukkasenung, P., & Chokngamwong, R. (2016). Review and comparison of the mobile payment protocol. In J. J. Park et al. (Eds.), *Advances in parallel and distributed computing and ubiquitous services: Lecture notes in electrical engineering* (pp. 11–20). Springer.
6. Munyoka, W., & Maharaj, M. (2017). Understanding eGovernment utilisation within the SADC. In 2017 IST-Africa week conference, IST-Africa.
7. Thornton, P., & Ocasio, W. (1999). Institutional logics and the historical contingency of power in organizations: Executive succession in the higher education publishing industry 1958–1990. *American Journal of Sociology, 105*(2), 801–843.
8. Thornton, P. (2004). *Markets from culture: Institutional logics and organizational decisions in higher education publishing*. Stanford University Press.
9. Thornton, P., & Ocasio, W. (2008). Institutional logics. In R. Greenwood (Ed.), *The SAGE handbook of organizational institutionalism* (pp. 100–129). SAGE.
10. Alharbi, N., Papadaki, M., & Dowland, P. (2014). Security factors influencing end users' adoption of E-government. *Journal of Internet Technology and Secured Transactions (JITST), 3*(4), 320–328.
11. Xu, Z., Zhang, T., Zeng, Y., Wan, J., & Wu, W. (2015). A secure mobile payment framework based on face authentication. In *International multi conference of engineers and computer scientists 2015*. IMECS.

12. Heeks, R., & Bailur, S. (2007). Analyzing e-government research: Perspectives, philosophies, theories, methods, and practice. *Government Information Quarterly, 24*(2), 243–265.
13. Sarabdeen, J., Rodrigues, G., & Balasubramanian, S. (2014). E-government users' privacy and security concerns and availability of laws in Dubai. *International Review of Law. Computers and Technology, 28*(3), 261–276.
14. AlAwadhi, S., & Morris, A. (2009). Factors influencing the adoption of e-government services. *Journal of Software, 4*(6), 584–590.
15. Davis, F. D., & Venkatesh, V. (1996). A critical assessment of potential measurement biases in the technology acceptance model: Three experiments. *International Journal of Human-Computer Studies, 45*(1), 19–45.
16. Nkoyi, A., Tait, M., & Van der Walt, F. (2019). Predicting the attitude towards electronic banking continued usage intentions among rural banking customers in South Africa. *South African Journal of Information Management, 21*(1), 101–112.
17. Sánchez-Prietoa, J. C., Hernández-Garcíab, Á., García-Peñalvoa, F. J., Chaparro-Peláezb, J., & Olmos-Migueláñeza, S. (2019). Break the walls! Second-order barriers and the acceptance of mLearning by first-year pre-service teachers. *Computers in Human Behavior, 95*, 158–167.
18. Kandeh, A. T., Botha, R. A., & Futcher, L. A. (2018). Enforcement of the protection of personal information (POPI) act: Perspective of data management professionals. *South African Journal of Information Management, 20*(1), 917–940.
19. Sutherland, E. (2017). Governance of cybersecurity: The case of South Africa. *The African Journal of Information and Communication (AJIC), 20*, 83–112.
20. Zhao, J. J., & Zhao, S. J. (2010). Opportunities and threats: A security assessment of state e-government websites. *Government Information Quarterly, 27*, 49–56.
21. Dinev, T., & Hart, P. (2006). Extended privacy calculus model for e-commerce transactions. *Information Systems Research, 17*(1), 61–80.
22. Kim, C., Mirusmonov, M., & Lee, I. (2010). An empirical examination of factors influencing the intention to use mobile payment. *Computers in Human Behavior, 26*(1), 310–322.
23. Wu, K. W., Huan, S. Y., Yen, D. C., & Popova, I. (2012). The effect of the online privacy policy on consumer privacy concerns and trust. *Computers in Human Behavior, 28*, 889–897.
24. Opesade Adeola, O., Adetona, A., & O. (2021). An assessment of internet use and cyber-risk prevalence among students in selected Nigerian secondary schools. *Journal of Cybersecurity Education, Research and Practice, 2*(3), 1–14.
25. De Moor, S., Dock, M., Gallez, S., Lenaerts S., Scholler C., & Vleugels, C. (2008). Teens and ICT: Risks and opportunities. Retrieved July 06, 2010, from http://www.belspo.be/belspo/fedra/TA/synTA08_nl.pdf
26. Gámez-Guadix, M., Borrajo, E., & Almendros, C. (2016). Risky online behaviors among adolescents: Longitudinal relations among problematic internet use, cyberbullying perpetration, and meeting strangers online. *Journal of Behavioral Addictions, 5*(1), 100–107.
27. Nagy, D., Schuessler, J., & Dubinsky, A. (2016). Defining and identifying disruptive innovations. *Industrial Marketing Management, 57*, 119–126.
28. Valcke, M., De Wever, B., Van Keer, H., & Schellens, T. (2011). Long-term study of safe internet use of young children. *Computers and Education, 57*(1), 1292–1305.
29. Venkatesh, V., Thong, J. Y., & Xu, X. (2016). A unified theory of acceptance and use of technology: A synthesis and the road ahead. *Journal of the Association for Information Systems, 17*(5), 328–376.
30. Hair, J. F., Ringle, C. M., & Sarstedt, M. (2011). PLS-SEM: Indeed, a silver bullet. *Journal of Marketing Theory and Practice, 19*(2), 139–152.
31. Rahi, S. (2012). Structural equation modeling using smartPLS. *Journal of Statistical Software, 48*(3), 1–16.
32. Podsakoff, P. M., MacKenzie, S. B., & Podsakoff, N. P. (2003). Common method biases in behavioral research: A critical review of the literature and recommended remedies. *Journal of Applied Psychology, 88*(5), 879–903.
33. Hair, J., Sarstedt, M., Ringle, C. M., & Gudergan, S. P. (2017). *Advanced issues in partial least squares structural equation modeling*. SAGE Publications.

34. Cohen, J. (1988). *Statistical power analysis for the behavioral sciences* (2nd ed.). Lawrence Earlbaum Associates.
35. Ong, R. (2012). Online vigilante justice Chinese style and privacy in China. *Information and Communications Technology Law, 21*(2), 127–145.
36. Kaisara, G., & Shaun, P. (2009). e-Government in South Africa: e-service quality access and adoption factors. In *Proceedings of the 11th Annual Conference on World Wide Web Applications*. Port Elizabeth, South Africa. Retrieved January 06, 2019, from http://dk.cput.ac.za/inf_papers/26
37. Schaupp, L. C., & Carter, L. (2010). The impact of trust, risk, and optimism bias on e-file adoption. *Information Systems Frontier, 12*(3), 299–309.
38. Mbogo, M. (2010). The impact of mobile payments on the success and growth of micro-business: The case of M-Pesa in Kenya'. *The Journal of Language Technology, and Entrepreneurship in Africa, 2*(1), 182–203.
39. Fischer, R., & Derham, C. (2016). Is in-group bias culture-dependent? A meta-analysis across 18 societies. *Springer Plus, 5*(70), 1–25.

A Smart Industrial Electrical Energy Analytics and Forecasting System

Wayne Steven Okello, Jared Kelvin Nganyi, Gideon Muleme, Ramadhani Sinde, and Anael Elikana Sam

1 Introduction

For generations, energy has been a vital component of human life. The fundamental reason for this is that energy is utilized in many aspects of living, including food storage and preparation, heating and cooling, social entertainment, and transportation. Furthermore, energy is essential for a country's development, making it impossible to eliminate energy usage. Electrical energy is one of the most essential inputs in industrial production, therefore it plays an important role in both social and economic growth. In this context, energy generation is regarded to play a critical role in enhancing industrial output [1]. The industrial sector, residential sector (biomass for cooking and heating), and the transportation sector are Tanzania's key energy users. Industrial plants consume substantial amounts of electricity attributed to the operation of numerous machinery with high-power requirements in the production line. As a result, the working times of these machines in the production lines must be planned to ensure the highest level of efficiency in terms of balancing time, cost, and output.

Energy efficiency is becoming a more important aspect of several firms' business strategy, with 50% of the industrial organizations having energy management as part of their corporate strategy according to the Deloitte Resources 2020 survey report. Industrial business entities are examining their energy budgets further to uncover cost-saving measures, decarbonization, and resilience prospects. As a result, a smart system that uses data analytics and forecasts to monitor, optimize, and sustain industry assets is required. Using digital technologies such as Internet of

W. S. Okello (✉) · J. K. Nganyi · G. Muleme · R. Sinde · A. E. Sam
School of Computational and Communication Science and Engineering (CoCSE), Nelson Mandela African Institution of Science and Technology (NM-AIST), Arusha, Tanzania
e-mail: okellow@nm-aist.ac.tz; nganyij@nm-aist.ac.tz; mulemeg@nm-aist.ac.tz; ramadhani.sinde@nm-aist.ac.tz; anael.sam@nm-aist.ac.tz

J. Marx Gómez et al. (eds.), *Smart and Secure Embedded and Mobile Systems*, Progress in IS, https://doi.org/10.1007/978-3-031-56603-5_15

Things (IoT), cloud computing, and machine learning (ML), which allow ubiquitous interconnection of objects such as production machinery, lighting devices, air conditioning systems, will provide insights into energy consumption.

Forecasting energy demand is critical for manufacturing industries because it aids in the planning process, such as long-term forecasting for future expansions, mid-term forecasting for power production resource planning and tariffs, and short-term forecasting for distribution network scheduling and analysis. Controlling and lowering an organization's energy consumption is critical since it reduces costs, risks, and carbon emissions. A smart industrial electrical energy analytics and forecasting system will not only discover energy-saving opportunities, but it will also enhance response times and apply various data analysis techniques to accomplish reliable power system operation and maintenance at various levels.

2 Related Work

There are a number of related works that exist in relation to smart energy analytics as well as forecasting and some of them are described below.

Chen et al. [2] in their work propose the use of Arduino MCU and artificial intelligence to develop smart power meters with ability to perform analytics on the cloud for smart homes. It further emphasizes that demand side management can decrease electricity costs as well as carbon emissions associated with electricity in smart homes connected to a smart grid.

Alani & Osunmakinde [3] assert that there is recurring disparity between electricity demand and supply which calls for effective planning that can be based on forecasting future short-term consumption patterns to facilitate productive distribution among consumers. It goes on to propose the use of PSA-DT machine learning to predict short-term electrical energy loads with minimum predictive errors to enable efficient planning of smart grids in smart homes.

Paredes-Valverde et al. [4] highlight a growing price of energy due to various aspects that include but not limited to demand, supply as well as government regulations and users shunning away from taking time to analyze power consumption so as come up with cost-saving mechanisms. The paper presents IntelliHome, a smart home system that utilizes big data analytics, statistical techniques as well as machine learning to issue end-users with insights regarding their energy consumption behaviors to actively engage them in the energy conservation process using real-time data.

Grimaldo & Novak [5] present a tool for anticipating short-term energy demand that makes use of visual analytics and machine learning to make predictions of demand for electricity depending on end-user defined variables, i.e., weather forecasts for the next day as well as exhibit the forecast results in form of interactive visualizations.

Ahmed et al. [6] present a mutual system between homes and a transformer agent situated at the resident transformer via customer agents installed at the residence. Cloud services from IBM are used to sieve and inspect data collected at the transformer agent to predict energy consumption as well as provide distinct suggestions to customers based on their varying consumption patterns in real time.

Mosbah & El-hawary [7] propose a new methodology based on multilayer neural networks which is utilized in various topologies to increase the prediction accuracy as well as the performance of the diverse topologies analyzed to establish the most optimal architecture.

Lang et.al [8] discuss three analytics phases i.e., prescriptive, descriptive, and predictive with analysis, forecasting as well as management of the load as key application areas. It further discusses the current trends in research regarding data analytics from smart meters with main emphasis on novel machine learning techniques, big data analytics, energy systems transformation, data security as well as privacy.

Ghasemi et.al [9] developed a hybrid algorithm that forecasted the price and demand of electricity in smart grids. They outline three critical models that form this novel algorithm in which ARIMA and other machine learning models were adopted to make correlations between the price and load features. The time-varying coefficients algorithm helped in the optimization of nonlinear least square support vector machine technique in the learning stages of their work.

Olivares-Rojas J. C. et.al [10] propose a multi-tier edge-fog architecture that allows processing of data at the source rather than cloud computation. This approach used reinforcement learning algorithms. This enabled them to validate the system testing based on power quality and theft predictions as well as energy consumption forecasting in the deployment of current smart metering technologies.

From the above related work, a number of researchers have acknowledged the significance of analytics as well as forecasting in the energy sector and have thus explored various approaches in that regard. Majority of them however target households (smart homes) and this has left a gap for industrial premises, institutions as well as commercial buildings.

3 System Design

3.1 Conceptual Framework

The system was designed based on the conceptual framework in Fig. 1 where requirements were obtained from various stakeholders and scientific literature. It consists of a Data Collection Unit (DCU) for capturing electrical energy parameters, Data Terminal Unit (DTU) for processing and storage of the captured parameters,

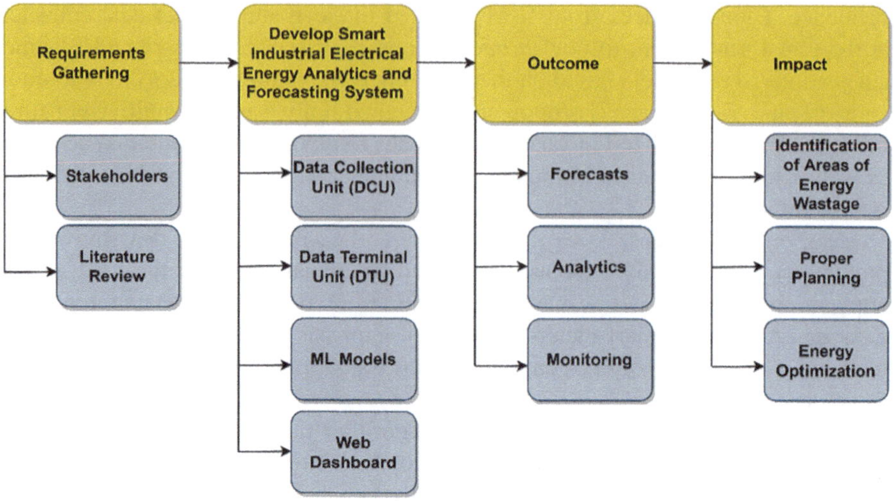

Fig. 1 Conceptual framework demonstrating the relationships between system variables

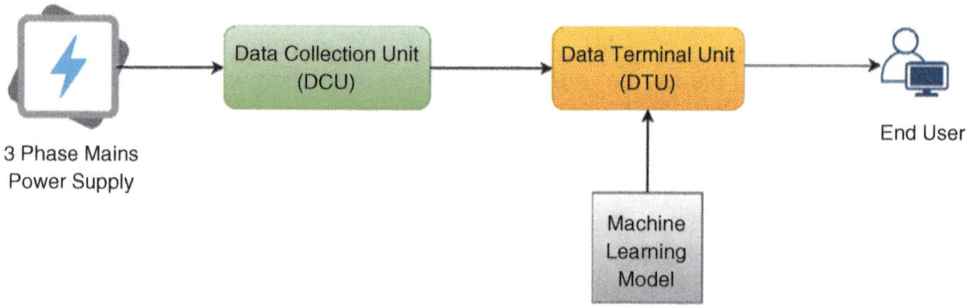

Fig. 2 General architecture demonstrating the system at the highest level of abstraction

machine learning models for forecasting future energy consumption patterns, and a web dashboard for remote monitoring and analysis of the sensed parameters.

3.2 System Architecture

The system at the highest level of abstraction consists of two electronic units, i.e. Data Collection Unit (DCU) and a Data Terminal Unit (DTU) as illustrated in Fig. 2.

The system can further be decomposed into individual components of the DCU and DTU as illustrated in Fig. 3.

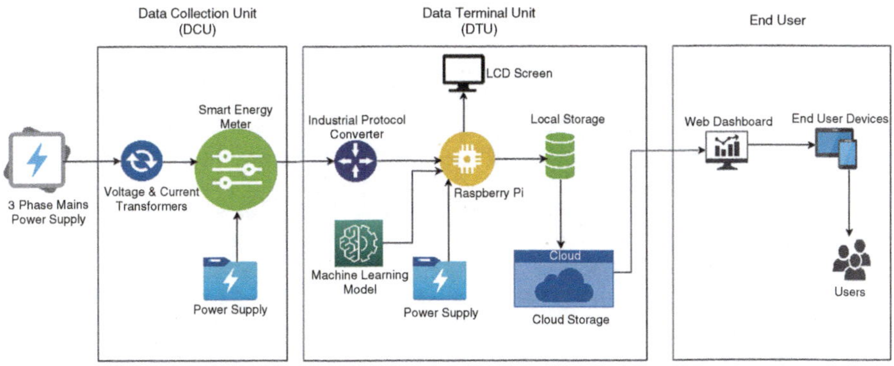

Fig. 3 Detailed architecture describing the interconnection of the individual components of the DCU, DTU, and the end-user

4 System Implementation

The system was implemented in four different phases i.e., data acquisition and calibration phase, data storage phase, forecasting/machine learning phase, and analytics phase.

4.1 Data Acquisition and Calibration

This stage entails harvesting the raw field data and making the necessary calibration to ensure the correctness of the data. The electrical energy parameters captured are current, voltage, power factor, power, energy demand (active, reactive, apparent), harmonic distortion (voltage, current), unbalance (voltage, current), and frequency.

4.1.1 Data Acquisition

Two electronic units, i.e., DCU and DTU were set up. The DCU consists of a 3-phase smart energy meter as well as voltage and current transformers while the DTU as illustrated in Fig. 4 consists of a Raspberry Pi 4 and a Modbus industrial protocol converter. The DCU was fed with 3-phase power from the CoCSE power distribution room at the Nelson Mandela African Institution of Science and Technology (NM-AIST) in the Arusha region of Tanzania. The smart energy meter was configured to acquire the necessary energy parameters. The acquired energy parameters are then transferred serially to the industrial protocol converter which in turn transfers them to the Raspberry Pi for processing and storage.

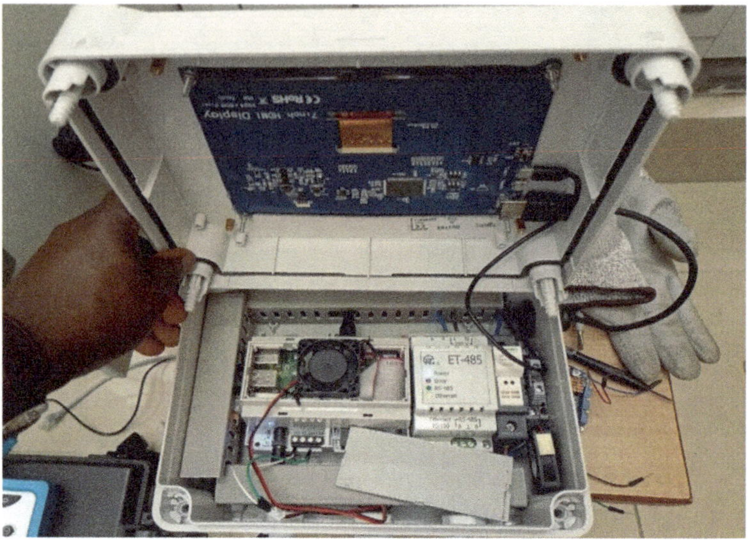

Fig. 4 DTU internal structure

4.1.2 Data Calibration

An industrial energy analyzer meter was used in calibration of parameters by comparing its values with those of developed system. This was through point-to-point checking of the individual data points from each of the sub-modules that form the entire system.

4.2 Data Storage

The required parameters are then stored locally on the Raspberry Pi in a CSV file that is later used for analysis and machine learning model development. A cron job was configured to automatically log the raw data every 5 min. It was also set up to automatically resume the data logging in the event of any interruptions such as power restarts to ensure continuity of the data collection process. The local CSV file on the Raspberry Pi was synchronized to the Google Drive cloud storage using the Rclone utility for purposes of redundancy.

4.3 Machine Learning/Forecasting

This phase involved forecasting of both short-term and medium-term future energy consumption using the dataset obtained from the data acquisition unit. The dataset was made up of a total number of 65 features and 19,823 observations. The task was accomplished in four stages, i.e., data preprocessing, exploratory data analysis, modeling, and evaluation.

4.3.1 Data Preprocessing

This stage was used to prepare the raw data from the data acquisition unit to identify any issues with the data, confirm our qualitative understanding of it, and make it appropriate for building as well as training the machine learning models. It involved data inspection, data cleaning and validation as well as data transformation.

Data Cleaning and Validation

This involved checking and handling of missing values, time series validation, data type validation as well as data range validation. The data was checked for missing data and there was found to be no missing values. It also was observed that the data was in the expected time series range. The data types of the different dataset features were explored where it was found that 1 feature was of object data type, 2 features were of datetime data type, and 62 features were of float data type. All the features were found to be in the expected standard range with no unacceptable outliers observed.

Data Transformation

New features, i.e., Unit Active Energy, Unit Reactive Energy, Unit Apparent Energy were created from the Total Active Energy, Total Reactive Energy, Total Apparent Energy features, respectively, as illustrated in Eqs. 1, 2, and 3. This is because the Total Energy features were cumulative and therefore there was need to generate new features with the respective energies consumed within a specified period.

$$\text{Unit Active Energy} = \text{Current Total Active Energy-Previous Total Active Energy} \tag{1}$$

$$\text{Unit Reactive Energy} = \text{Current Total Reactive Energy-Previous Total Reactive Energy} \tag{2}$$

$$\text{Unit Apparent Energy} = \text{Current Total Apparent Energy-Previous Total Apparent Energy} \tag{3}$$

4.3.2 Exploratory Data Analysis

This phase was used in disclosing the data limitations as well as identifying the significant features which in turn would guide on the methods to be used in modeling. More insight about the data was obtained through visualization using matplotlib library. Focus was placed on individual feature distributions as well as the relationships between different features and the target variable.

4.3.3 Modeling

The dataset was split into a train dataset and test dataset in a ratio of 0.8:0.2, respectively. The date_time and Unit Active Energy were selected as the target features. The Facebook Prophet algorithm and the Autoregressive Integrated Moving Average (ARIMA) algorithm were employed in training the models using the train dataset. ARIMA is widely used and utilizes lagged moving averages to level out time series data. Facebook Prophet provides a more automated procedure to time series forecasting since it natively handles its seasonality and trend features. In addition, it offers easier interpretability of its models as compared to other algorithms. The seasonality mode of the Facebook Prophet model was set to additive while the model growth was set to linear since no maximum achievable point was expected. The changepoint prior scale was set to 0.01 while the daily seasonality and weekly seasonality were set to true. ARIMA (1,1,2) was used as the optimal order of the ARIMA model and this was obtained using the ACF and PCFA plots.

The trained Facebook Prophet model exhibits the trend, daily and weekly seasonality as illustrated in Fig. 5;

4.3.4 Evaluation

The trained models were tested using the test dataset and the performance for each algorithm was obtained in terms of Mean Absolute Percentage Error (MAPE), Mean Squared Error (MSE), and Mean Absolute Error (MAE) as summarized in Table 1 and Fig. 6.

4.4 *Analytics*

This phase was achieved through development of a web dashboard using the plotly dash framework. The dashboard as illustrated in Fig. 7 comprises several visualizations of both near real-time raw data and the forecasted data. The visualizations

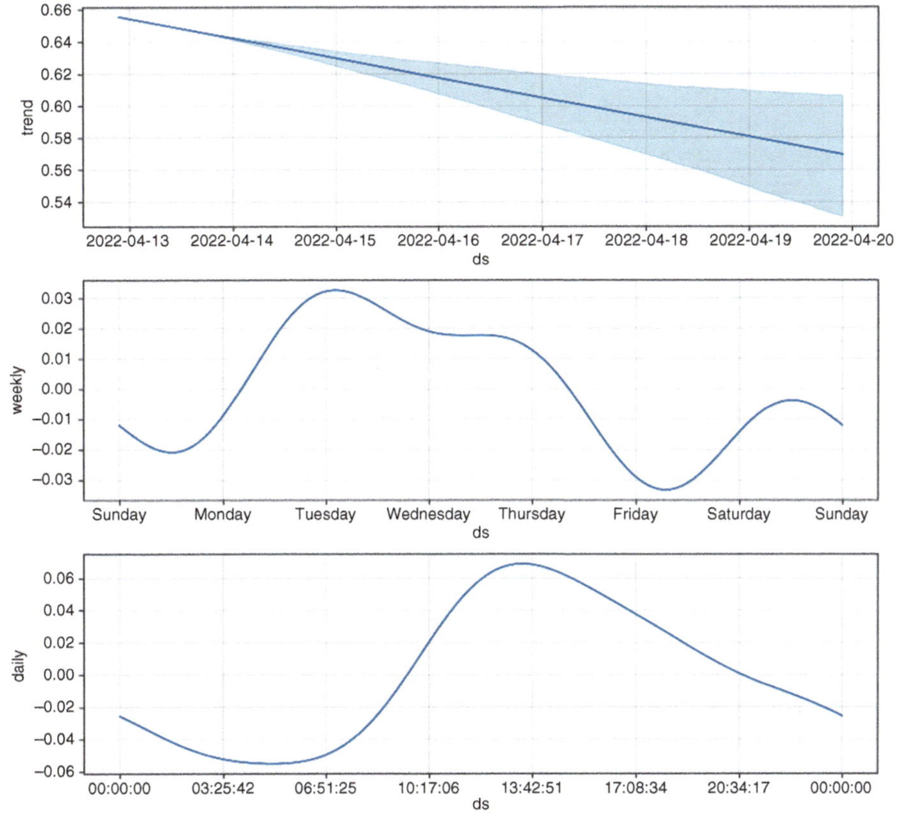

Fig. 5 Prophet trained model trend, daily and weekly seasonality

Table 1 Performance evaluation metrics of the utilized algorithms

Metric	Facebook Prophet	ARIMA
MSE	0.0361	0.0285
MAE	0.1366	0.1221
MAPE	17.72	18.86

aid in exploring data structure, detecting outliers, and gaining more insight of the current as well as forecasted energy trends which in turn can help in proper planning of production lines to ensure the highest level of efficiency in terms of balancing time, cost, and output.

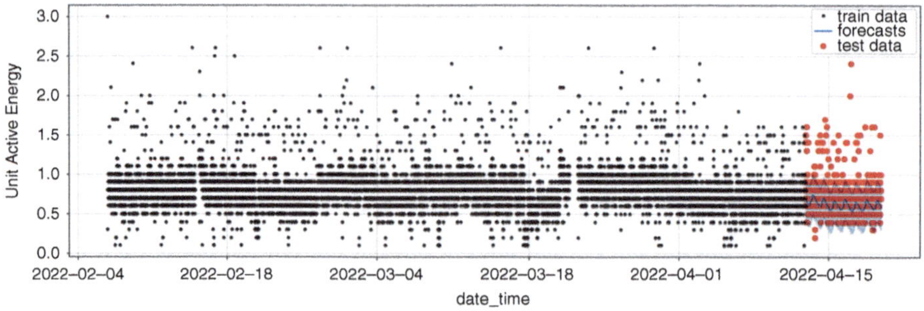

Fig. 6 Correlation between train data, test data and forecasts

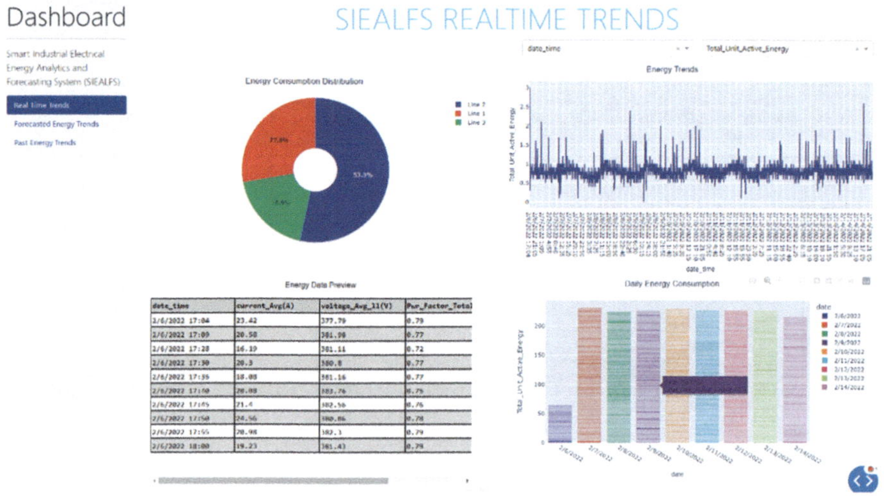

Fig. 7 System web dashboard near real-time trends page

5 Conclusion and Future Work

In this paper we have described a smart system that provides near real-time monitoring of different electrical energy parameters in an industrial setting as well as forecasts future energy consumption trends and prospective energy bill costs. This information doesn't only facilitate planning, but also identifies areas of electrical energy wastage as well as enables optimization of electrical energy utilization thus reduced costs of production. ARIMA and Facebook Prophet algorithms were utilized in developing machine learning models for forecasting energy consumption trends and exhibited an MSE of 0.0285 and 0.0361, MAE of 0.1221 and 0.1366, and MAPE of 18.86 and 17.72, respectively. In the future, we intend to employ a deep learning approach for forecasting of future energy trends as well as include an alerting module to provide notifications to system users upon detection of outliers.

References

1. Yu, Z., Liu, W., Eti, L. C. S., Dinçer, H., & Yüksel, S. (2019). The effects of electricity production on industrial development and sustainable economic growth: A VAR analysis for BRICS countries. *Sustainability, MDPI, 11*(21), 13.
2. Chen, Y. Y., Lin, Y. H., Kung, C. C., Chung, M. H., & Yen, I. H. (2019). Design and implementation of cloud analytics-assisted smart power meters considering advanced artificial intelligence as edge analytics in demand-side management for smart homes. *Sensors (Switzerland), 19*(9), 2047. https://doi.org/10.3390/s19092047
3. Alani, A. Y., & Osunmakinde, I. O. (2017). Short-term multiple forecasting of electric energy loads for sustainable demand planning in smart grids for smart homes. *Sustainability (Switzerland), 9*(11), 1972. https://doi.org/10.3390/su9111972
4. Paredes-Valverde, M. A., Alor-Hernández, G., García-Alcaráz, J. L., Salas-Zárate, M. D. P., Colombo-Mendoza, L. O., & Sánchez-Cervantes, J. L. (2020). IntelliHome: An internet of things-based system for electrical energy saving in smart home environment. *Computational Intelligence, 36*(1), 203–224. https://doi.org/10.1111/coin.12252
5. Grimaldo, A. I., & Novak, J. (2020). Combining machine learning with visual analytics for explainable forecasting of energy demand in prosumer scenarios. *Procedia Computer Science, 175*, 525–532. https://doi.org/10.1016/j.procs.2020.07.074
6. Ahmed, A., Arab, K., Bouida, Z., & Ibnkahla, M. (2018). Data communication and analytics for smart grid systems. In *IEEE international conference on communications*. IEEE. https://doi.org/10.1109/ICC.2018.8423021
7. Mosbah, H., & El-hawary, M. (2016). Hourly electricity Price forecasting for the next month using multilayer neural network. *Canadian Journal of Electrical and Computer Engineering, 39*(4), 8.
8. Lang, A., Wang, Y., Feng, C., Stai, E., & Hug, G. (2021). Data aggregation point placement for smart meters in the smart grid. *IEEE Transactions on Smart Grid, 13*(1), 14.
9. Ghasemi, A., Shayeghi, H., Moradzadeh, M., & Nooshyar, M. (2016). A novel hybrid algorithm for electricity price and load forecasting in smart grids with demand-side management. *Applied Energy, 177*, 40–59. https://doi.org/10.1016/j.apenergy.2016.05.083
10. Olivares-Rojas, J. C., Reyes-Archundia, E., Gutiérrez-Gnecchi, J. A., González-Murueta, J. W., & Cerda-Jacobo, J. (2020). A multi-tier architecture for data analytics in smart metering systems. *Simulation Modelling Practice and Theory, 102*, 102024. https://doi.org/10.1016/j.simpat.2019.102024

Multilevel Trustworthiness for Improved Process and Network Security in Critical Infrastructures and Domains

Hermann Strack, Marlies Gollnick, Sebastian Karius, Robin Kopitz, Meiko Lips, and Sandro Wefel

1 Introduction

The use of (mobile) services in IT and OT[1] for sensitive/critical applications, domains, and infrastructures in different areas like higher education (HEI) and (classified) industrial or governmental domains requires high security and trust with standards on identification and access authorization (IAM). This includes the implementation and integration of security and trust services, as well as trusted entities/roles, using methods of security by design and management. Obviously, strong authentication and access control would improve the security against different threats and vulnerabilities from outside or inside the domains or interest groups involved. This means, for example, exploiting vulnerabilities to gain access to identities, their roles, and/or other data. This also includes the misuse of user roles and administrator rights.

Embedded and mobile systems, together with appropriate processing technologies and standards, offer promising approaches here. Important new developments for these areas with embedded and mobile systems are new security standards and infrastructure like eIDAS/eID & trust services (TS) with Smart-eID. To prevent increasing threat levels (like APT), we propose new concepts and improvements for higher Levels of Assurance (LoA). These are the new concepts of mobile privacy-protected Pro-Bio-Id resp. Trustsistor network components [1].

[1] Operational Technology—cyber-physical systems to control smart factories.

H. Strack (✉) · M. Gollnick · S. Karius · R. Kopitz · M. Lips
Harz University of Applied Sciences, Wernigerode, Germany
e-mail: hstrack@hs-harz.de

S. Wefel
Martin Luther University, Halle, Germany

J. Marx Gómez et al. (eds.), *Smart and Secure Embedded and Mobile Systems*,
Progress in IS, https://doi.org/10.1007/978-3-031-56603-5_16

2 Trust and Hybrid Identities for Higher LoA in IAM Domains

We distinguish challenging needs for higher trust level (Level of Assurance—LoA) in security especially for Identification and Authorization (IAM) on the levels of securing eBusiness and eGovernment (mobile) for web-based electronic processes, on the one hand (short: ProcSec), and in network security, on the other hand (NetSec). We present new security improvements by eIDAS on the ProSec level at the COLICI project "Communication, open source, lifelong learning in educational institutions through legally compliant integration" (Chap. 5) and NetSec by the Trustsistor Concepts (Chap. 4).

The EU eIDAS regulation [2] consists of two main areas, which are eID and TS, further details, ref. [3]. Within this scope different Levels of Assurance (LoA) for the strength of authentication security according to EU eIDAS regulation (LoA: low, substantial, high) are provided. The eID online function[2] of the national identity card in Germany (notarized acc. eIDAS/eID, as first EU MS with LoA "High") offers a strong two-factor and doubled end-to-end authentication (hardware & SAML based) between the identity card at the card reader and the eID server with privacy enhancements [4]. For OZG[3] accounts of citizens in Germany, the eIDAS interoperability is being established, e.g. by the OZG user account Bund [5]. On the other hand, a high level of trust service security is achieved with qualified signatures/seals/time stamps/preservation services acc. to eIDAS standards.[4] The eID-based citizen & company account will become mandatory in Germany from 2022 in an interoperable way across the distributed/federal government structures and processes in Germany, to be acknowledged then by all public administrations (OZG—Online Access Law). The solution within project StudIES+[5] (EU CEF) is a university-based approach as an eID-university-service-account and is inspired by this German law [6, 7], interoperable with eIDAS/eID and compatible with eIDAS/TS (ETSI standards).

An eID & TS approach would be to combine eSignature and eID on "document/account" level on these eID-uni-service-accounts and this could help to bridge the difficult discussion & decision processes on common academic attributes (cross universities EU). The person could log into the account with eIDAS eID identification and could up/download documents/forms (as some use cases in Germany will need a high-level eIDAS LoA eID, e.g. because the results of the exams are legally binding) and can use then the eSignature facilities. Otherwise, the citizens accounts at the OZG infrastructures are suitable for multiple ID/eID

[2] https://www.bsi.bund.de/SharedDocs/Downloads/DE/BSI/Publikationen/TechnischeRichtlinien/TR03130/TR-03130_TR-eID-Server_Part1.html.

[3] https://www.onlinezugangsgesetz.de.

[4] https://www.etsi.org/newsroom/news/1111-2016-07-etsi-publishes-european-standards-to-support-eidas-regulation

[5] https://studies-plus.eu.

LoA levels (low to high) chosen by the citizen executing account access procedures. Obviously, by this feature there could occur a security problem. While sensitive documents might be uploaded by the citizen/owner at a high LoA authentication level, these could be downloaded by spoofed IDs at lower LoA.

To prevent this threat, we propose a labeling/tagging by the users LoA level (instead of BLP classification levels/labels) for all documents at upload to his citizen account, and an MAC-based mandatory access control according to the well-known Bell-LaPadula Model (BLP) [8]. In very sensitive cases these LoA labels could be trustworthy linked to the document by external signing/notarization additionally (by eIDAS/TS-based eNotar, [6, 7]). If needed, also multiple derived IDs of a citizen could be trustworthy linked together (and matched) by external signing/notarization additionally (by eNotar/YourCredentials, [6, 7]).

3 Improving LoA for IAM at Web Authentication Using TPM

For establishing security measurements on higher protection levels—facing the severe threat landscape and internet-based attack levels nowadays—it would be required to extend security also on client side, besides other measurements. Therefore, we are looking at additional IAM context features, to integrate those for extended authentication and authorization controls. For this extension, we follow the LoA specification.

The Web Authentication API (WebAuthn) is designed for authentication only, there is no trusted identity source, unlike eID. For authentication the higher LoAs require certificate resp. hardware-token. The WebAuthn specification satisfies those requirements. Hereby the management of the key source is handled by the browser and the operating system, whereby a TPM or hardware-token can be used. If required, the use of a TPM can be enforced [1].

Klenk et al. [9] propose a different protocol for web authentication that solves the problem of providing trusted identities. It is able to ensure that: a) the authentication is provided by a TPM module, b) the private key used for the authentication was generated by the user and c) the claimed identity belonging to the user can be confirmed.

They use OpenID to transfer the authentication and identity data between the client and the server. This is portable to any other protocol like SAML that handles the transfer of those data.

With this approach the user's ID itself can be managed self-sovereign and securely. With the growing use of TPM equipped devices, especially portable ones such as smart phones, it becomes particularly relevant. Current approaches, such as the ID Wallet or Smart-eID, also take this approach of storing derived identities on TPM-secured hardware [10, 11].

Smart-eID allows a holder of a German ID card with eID function to copy the identity information stored on the ID card to the eID-Applet secure element (smart eID), which is derived from the TPM, of a certified smartphone. After that, logging in with the smartphone is equivalent to logging in with the ID card [5].

In summary, the use of TPM attestations/attributes at IAM would enable additional higher LoA contexts, including for mandatory control policies across domain/system boundaries.

4 Improving NetSec & ProSec by Trustsistor Concepts

Currently, the needs for improved higher IAM security at NetSec and ProSec level are often solved by separated security technics level, we propose improvements here.

With current technology the use of TPM attestations/attributes at IAM would enable additional higher LoA contexts, including for mandatory control policies across domain/system boundaries. TPM-based authentication can be used for enhanced protection of workflow or system administrator roles, also in scenarios where eID is not available or necessary [9–12].

Additionally, it is important to protect workflows & trusted roles (e.g., eNotar roles as well as system administrator roles and RBAC/ABAC control schemes), entities, documents, and systems against attacks on network or systems vulnerability, especially hacking from outside and inside, or misuse of separation of duties (SOD). Important measurements are information flow protections and network segmentations based on classifications of networks, entities, and systems using firewalls and data diodes[6] [13], see Fig. 1 (inspired by privacy/BLP/MAC/MLS policies). But to protect additionally against IAM attacks (bypassing), it could be combined with different LoA levels for IAM. Therefore, also Mandatory LoA IAM attributes (cryptographically) protected/binding, e.g. by MACs, derived/based, e.g., on YourCredentials notarizations, could be securely added to protocol messages by using sub-header principles as well as on document level. This can be done in an analogous manner to IPv6[7] and would be worth exploring for enhanced and extended authentication and access control layers based on firewall, data diodes, and access control components, e.g., for improving Zero Trust[8] schemes.

Therefore, we introduce the concept of a Trustsistor TSO component that is integrated, e.g. into firewall or proxy components and reinforces trust relationships by adding trust attributes of a TSP to IP flows, e.g. between client and server as additional IAM (mandatory) access control information (MACI contexts). The notion is similar in some sense to the "transistor concept" in electrical flows. This

[6] https://ieeexplore.ieee.org/stamp/stamp.jsp?tp=&arnumber=6949883.

[7] https://www.ietf.org/blog/ipv6-internet-standard/.

[8] https://nvlpubs.nist.gov/nistpubs/SpecialPublications/NIST.SP.800-207.pdf.

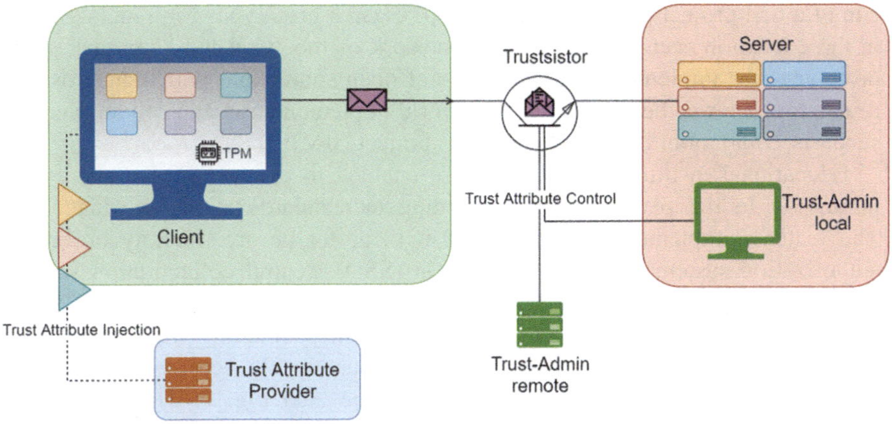

Fig. 1 Trustsistor concept. Trust attributes are injected into the TPM-secured client. The Trustsistor reinforces the trust relation between the client and the server

means, we would differentiate in a given situation between a service user SU, a service provider SP, and service access controller SPC, as well as a trust service provider TSP notarizing ACI[9] trust attributes TACI, e.g., by signatures/MACs (multilateral). Further we propose the components "Trustsistor-Injector (TSOI)" for injecting trust identifiers/labels into the IP flow on the part of the service mobile client using, e.g., IPv6 sub-headers and the "Trustsistor-Controller (TSOC)" for checking the required TACI attributes on the part of the service provider/controller according to a TACI access policy. By the way: for better multilateral system integrity security the TSOI/TSOC components should be protected by TPM. This is particularly feasible in smartphones due to the already extensive use of sandboxes and TPM-based technologies in smartphones. Based on the TSO model, secure implementation of access control policies can be done with additional TACI attributes on IP flows.

As mobile working is an increasingly widespread trend, the need for high-quality security mechanisms is growing, especially in the mobile environment. Since mobile devices are already frequently equipped with TPM modules, Trustsistor concepts can be applied here [1].

5 National Educational Platform Initiative

In Germany, an initiative to develop a National Education Platform (NBP) was launched in 2021 by the Federal Ministry of Education and Research (BMBF). The

[9] ACI: Access Control Information.

aim of a first project phase was to develop research prototypes for a meta-platform in the education sector. Within the framework of the "COLICI[10]"project, such a prototype was implemented on the basis of open source and with standards. This research phase will be pursued by real world implementation and rollout phase, all supervised and monitored by the BIRD[11] project (BMBF).

Educational institutions and users are enabled to connect secure and privacy preserving to the platform, also according to standards at the metadata level. The features implemented in the "COLICI" prototype are: identity broker and authorization system with Single Sign-On (SSO), central collaboration services, connection to user wallets, especially also to user wallets with SSI/eIDAS 2.0 functions, connectors and metadata for decentralized Identity Management Systems and Identity Providers (IDP), connections to EU service and standards (EMREX/ELMO, Europass/EDCI/VC) [14], see also Fig. 2. The security and privacy for the "COLICI" project are implemented with regard to standards and regulations, such as eIDAS/eID & TS, GDPR, and OZG.

As a special feature, the integration of SSO (Single Sign-On) takes into account the different levels of assurance (LoA) for the strength of authentication security according to the EU eIDAS Regulation (LoA: low, substantial, high). This is particularly important for cross-domain user integration and SSO. Furthermore, other additional attributes such as group membership can be transmitted.

The connection of the identity providers (IDP) of the satellite systems of the education providers takes place via the central Identity Broker. For citizens without already existing education membership, the login was connected via a state eID service provider with ID-capable login (OZG user account) in order to offer them secure identities with fully legal binding at the level of document transmission. This enables use for legally binding processes between the platform, state educational institutions and authorities, without an additional qualified electronic signature (QeS).

The applications of the Harz University of Applied Sciences connected in the COLICI platform use the online features of the German ID card to provide various services. These services are: eProsecal—provides highly secure authenticated access (LoA "high") for various university services/actors through an ID card-based logon and account process, including fully legally binding. Processes with multiple multi-user/role references (n:m) can also be mapped. Users have access to the data of all released processes via their eProsecal basic account and can also securely share them with other users and even with authorities in a legally binding manner (eID-based sharing). This results in an SSI (Self-Sovereign Identity) wallet function, without Blockchain integration, based on the properties of the eID system in Germany; eInternship—internship management/contracts between university and company; eTor/eTestate—registration/attendance management for exams and lab

[10] https://bildungsraum.de/display/PROJ/2022/09/12/Verbundprojekt%3A+Mit+Open+Source+rechtssicher+zum+lebenslangen+Lernen.

[11] https://www.uni-potsdam.de/de/multimedia/projekte/bildungsraum-digital-bird.

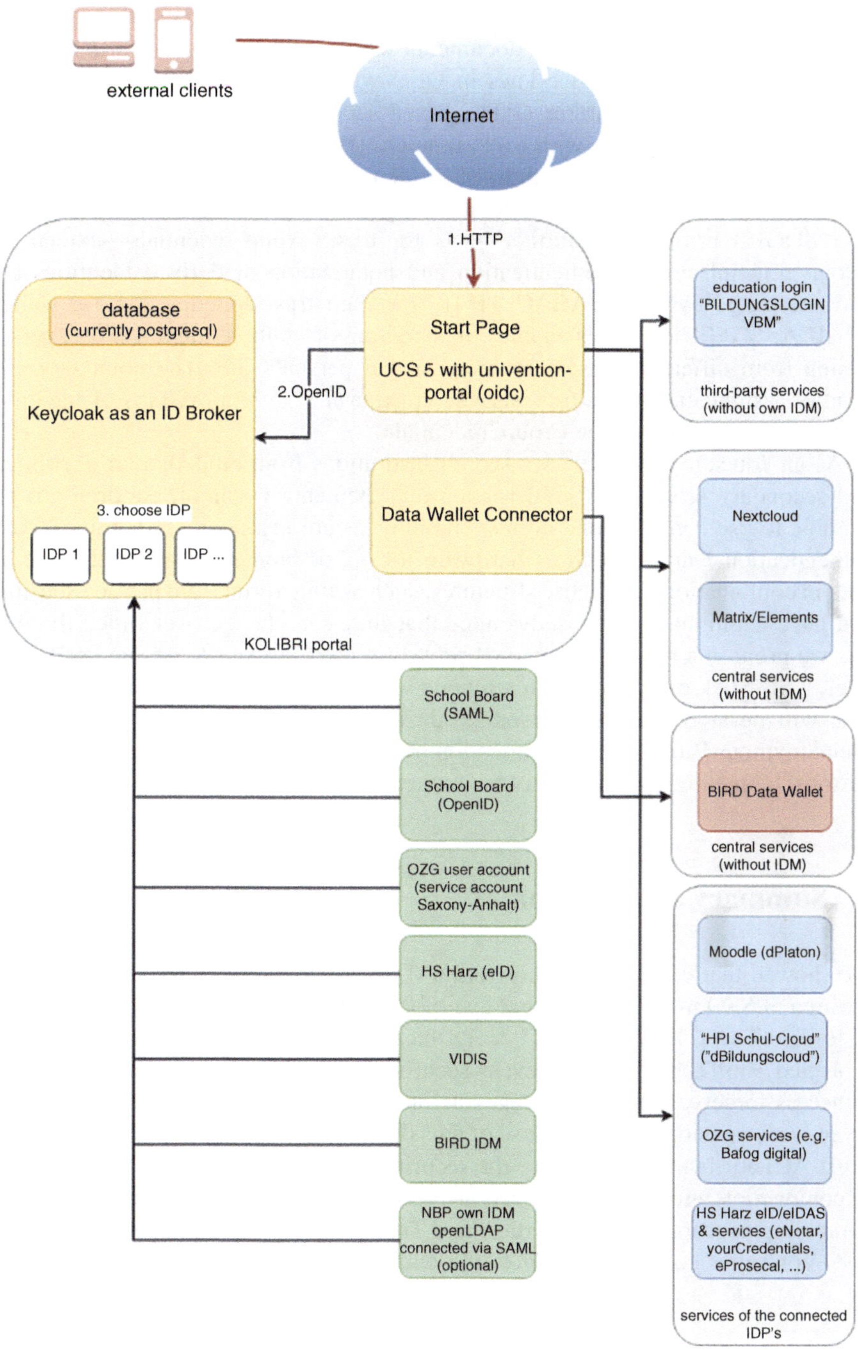

Fig. 2 COLICI NBP: Keycloak as an ID Broker and eID/OZG services as IDP

practicals; eColloquium—signed colloquium exam forms/certificates; eNotar—offers the possibility to provide documents with a qualified signature in a legally secure manner (public service laws in DE VwVfG §3a/§33, [6]). These services can be combined with further eIDAS-based services such as time-stamping and long-term storage services with over signature (BSI Standard TR ESOR,[12] eIDAS Preservation Standard). In addition, EU-wide time-dependent cybersecurity crypto requirements are covered, with the accompanying crypto algorithm management (EU SOGIS) providing a further basis for trust.; YourCredentials—extend the eNotar principle to the authentication and notarization of derived identities and attributes (e.g., by RBAC/ABAC, [15]) from their trust domains, e.g. for wallets for eIDAS 2.0/EUid.[13] This enables the handling of multiple identities of a person arising from different phases/providers in that person's life. The notarization of identity assignment by the trust service is extensible to relationships of identities such as parents and children (YourCredentials).

As an educational context we see all institutions from kindergarten to primary and secondary schools. In kindergarten and elementary school, children are not yet able to use complex, and correspondingly secure, passwords. Therefore, other authentication features such as hardware tokens or biometrics are preferable, or both in combination. Biometric structures, such as fingerprints, are privacy sensitive and have additionally the disadvantage that they can change over time. To cover this we propose a biometric personal privacy-protected security device PerBioDev (e.g., USB-Stick or protected Smartphone with fingerprint sensors). The biometric data will be stored and processed inside the PerBioDev only and translated to pseudonymous BioIDs for authentication protocol interfaces. Therefore, for privacy reasons, biometric features cannot be extracted even if the data of the IdP is leaked.

6 Summary and Outlook

We showed that eID-based authorization (LoA high) can be usefully employed in the area of SSO in the (mobile) context of Identity and Access Management (IAM) at ProSec Level, by eIDAS eID & TS means, extended additionally by privacy-protected BioID. To further prevent security vulnerabilities at NetSec level such as access forgery, spoofing, leakage, etc. at the network transmission and security layer, we have outlined how the use of data diodes and network packets marked with Trust-ACI attributes can preserve the security gained through strong authentication in conjunction with TACI notarizations at the network layer. This can be done by combining appropriate firewall rules and Trustsistor TSO injection and Trustsistor TSO controller components. Thus, the authorization defined at the IAM level is

[12] https://www.bsi.bund.de/SharedDocs/Downloads/DE/BSI/Publikationen/TechnischeRichtlinien/TR03125/BSI_TR-ESOR-LEIT.pdf.

[13] https://ec.europa.eu/commission/presscorner/detail/de/IP_21_2663.

extendable by (mandatory) Trust Attributes (also LoA high), including mandatory and multilateral trust policy enforcements also at the network level.

The research conducted within this paper was partly funded by the three EU funded projects under the umbrella of CyberSec LSA (EFRE).

References

1. Strack, H., Karius, S., Gollnick, M., Lips, M., Wefel, S., & Altschaffel, R. (2022). Preservation of (higher) trustworthiness in IAM for distributed workflows and systems based on eIDAS. In H. Roßnagel, C. H. Schunck, & S. Mödersheim (Eds.), *Open Identity Sum-mit* (pp. 125–130). Gesellschaft für Informatik e.V. https://doi.org/10.18420/OID2022_11
2. EU. (2014). Regulation (EU) No 910/2014 of the European Parliament and of the Council of 23 July 2014 on electronic identification and trust services for electronic transactions in the internal market and repealing Directive 1999/93/EC.
3. Hühnlein, D., Hühnlein, T., Hornung, G., & Strack, H. (2020). Towards universal login. In *LNI (Open Identity Summit 2020)* (pp. 193–200). https://doi.org/10.18420/ois2020_18
4. Bender, J., Kügler, D., Margraf, M., & Naumann, I. (2008). Sicherheitsmechanismen für kontaktlose Chips im deutschen elektronischen Personalausweis. In DUD.
5. BSI: Handlungsleitfaden zur Integration der Smart-eID in ein Nutzerkonto, Version 0.8, ret. (2023, July 7). https://www.personalausweisportal.de/SharedDocs/downloads/Webs/PA/DE/informationsmaterial/weiterefuehrendes-material/Handlungsleitfaden_Integration_Smart-eID_Nutzerkonto.pdf
6. Strack, H., Bacharach, G., Klinner, S., Otto, O., & Schmidt, A. (2019, EUNIS). eIDAS eID & eSignature for HEI/EDU applications - EIDAS eID & eSignature based service accounts at university environments for cross boarder/domain access. In: European Journal of Higher Education IT 2019-1. https://www.eunis.org/erai/2019-1/
7. Strack, H., Otto, O., Klinner, S., & Schmidt, A. (2019). eIDAS eID & eSignature based service accounts at university environments for cross boarder/domain access. In *Open Identity Summit* (pp. 171–176). GI LNI. https://dl.gi.de/handle/20.500.12116/20986
8. Bell, D. E., & LaPadula, L. J. (1973). Secure computer systems: Mathematical foundations MITRE technical report 2547 (vol. I).
9. Klenk, A., Kinkelin, H., Eunicke, C., & Carle, G. (2009). Preventing identity theft with electronic identity cards and the trusted platform module. In *Proceedings of the second European workshop on system security (EUROSEC '09)* (pp. 44–51). ACM. https://doi.org/10.1145/1519144.1519151
10. Fongen, A., & Mancini, F. (2013). The Integration of Trusted Platform Modules into a Tactical Identity Management System. In *MILCOM 2013–2013 IEEE Military Communications Conference* (pp. 1808–1813). https://doi.org/10.1109/MILCOM.2013.305
11. Lyle, J., & Martin, A. (2009). On the Feasibility of Remote Attestation for Web Services. In *2009 international conference on computational science and engineering* (Vol. 3, pp. 283–288). IEEE. https://doi.org/10.1109/CSE.2009.213
12. Web Authentication: *An API for Accessing Public Key Credentials*. (2022). Retrieved February 21, 2022, from https://www.w3.org/TR/webauthn-2/#sctn-attestation
13. Bhatkalkar, B. J. (2014). *Ramegowda: A Unidirectional Data-flow Model for Cloud Data Security with User Involvement during Data Transit*. In International Conference on Communication and Signal Processing, IEEE Explore. https://ieeexplore.ieee.org/stamp/stamp.jsp?tp=&arnumber=6949883

14. Mincer-Daszkiewicz, J. (2017). EMREX and EWP offering complementary digital services in the higher education area. In *Proceedings of EUNIS*.
15. Aftab, M. U., Qin, Z., Hundera, N. W., Ariyo, O., Zakria, S. N. T., & Dinh, T. V. (2019). Permission-based separation of duty in dynamic role-based access control model. *Symmetry, 11*, 669. https://doi.org/10.3390/sym11050669

A Conceptual Model of the Benefits and Concerns of Wearable Health Data Management

Lydia Izu, Brenda Scholtz, and Ifeoluwapo Fashoro

1 Introduction

Recent advancements in embedded mobile computers like wearable technologies (also known as wearables) have enormous prospects in addressing societal issues such as inadequacies in healthcare and making a significant contribution to social sustainability [1, 2]. Wearables describe a group of smart digital devices that can be worn by individuals and can detect, track, and monitor human performance, activities, and health [3, 4]. They are also important components in sustainable Smart Cities [5, 6]. One of the biggest consumers of wearables is the health sector [7–9]. The primary roles of wearables in healthcare are in diagnosis and treatment, chronic disease management, and out-of-hospital rehabilitation to alleviate shortages in healthcare [1]. Wearables can remotely collect and analyze real-time essential data for preventative health monitoring and the management of health conditions [2, 4]. Wearable health data are essential for managing and monitoring chronic medical conditions such as cancer, heart conditions, and diabetes [10, 11]. The vast and rapidly expanding amount of health data being generated, processed, and stored by wearables necessitates a focus on the data management thereof, with a particular focus on data governance and accessibility [6, 12].

Data management has become an increasingly fundamental practice considering growing technological advancements and the continuously improving capability to collect and process highly essential data [6, 13]. Data management is defined as an encompassing term describing the processes of data planning, specification, enablement, creation, acquisition, maintenance, utilization, archival, retrieval, control, and purging [14]. Hence, data management is concerned with the entire data lifecycle [15]. Data management processes involve developing a reliable infrastructure to

L. Izu (✉) · B. Scholtz · I. Fashoro
Nelson Mandela University, Gqeberha, South Africa
e-mail: brenda.scholtz@mandela.ac.za; ife.fashoro@mandela.ac.za

J. Marx Gómez et al. (eds.), *Smart and Secure Embedded and Mobile Systems*,
Progress in IS, https://doi.org/10.1007/978-3-031-56603-5_17

collect, store, access, process, disseminate, use, and discard data in varied forms [14].

In the context of wearables, data management operates as a layer between the devices and applications that generate the data and the use of the generated data for analysis and services [13]. Ensuring the proper management of wearable health data means safeguarding the data on devices, through networks, and on servers as well as providing transparency around which entities have access to the data [16]. These processes usually involve the use of third-party platforms for either permanent data storage or data analysis or both [17–20]. One concern of users is that wearable health data management architectures are lacking [21]. The concerns around the management of wearable health data have become a leading cause of restraint for users from fully embracing and appreciating the potential of wearables [4, 16]. Thus, the management of wearable health data is crucial to the sustainability of wearables in the health sector, to the quality of data generated and analyzed, and for harnessing the overall benefit of wearable health data [4, 6, 16]. While several studies have investigated data management, there is still a gap in studies investigating data management issues for health data from wearables, i.e., wearable health data management.

The purpose of this paper is to answer the research question: *What are the benefits and concerns of wearable health data management?* To answer this question, a critical literature review and a conceptual analysis approach were adopted. The structure of the paper is as follows: Section 2 specifies the research methodology. Section 3 describes the review planning strategy. Section 4 explains the review processes, while Sect. 5 reports the review findings. Section 6 concludes the paper.

2 Research Methodology

The Systematic Literature Review (SLR) process was followed to explore the benefits and concerns of wearable health data management. An SLR is a literature review methodology with a set of well-defined steps followed to aggregate and synthesize existing evidence about a given phenomenon [22]. The SLR employed in this paper followed the three phases set out in [22], which were: Planning the Review, Conducting the Review, and Reporting the Review.

3 Planning the Review

In Planning the Review, a Review Protocol was formulated that specified the research question, databases to be searched, search terms, and the inclusion and exclusion criteria used. The research question was: *What are the benefits and concerns of wearable health data management?* The databases were: ResearchGate, IEEE, Google Scholar, ACM Digital Library, and Web of Science. The search terms were wearable technologies, wearables, wearable devices, data management and wearable technologies, wearable health data, wearable health data management, data management concerns, data management benefits, wearable health data management issues, wearable health data management benefits, and wearable health data prospects. The inclusion criteria were publications written in English, publications published between 2012 and 2022, and publications that were peer-reviewed articles, conference papers or proceedings or published theses. The exclusion criteria were publications that did not meet the inclusion criteria or were duplicates.

4 Conducting the Review

The research objectives were to analyze the literature regarding wearable health data management benefits and concerns and design a conceptual model incorporating the identified concepts. In the Conducting the Review phase, the first step involved identifying existing research by interrogating the databases and search terms specified in the Review Protocol. The different search terms were used individually and in combination in some instances to generate more relevant results. During the search, synonyms such as issues and prospects were sometimes used instead of concerns and benefits, which yielded positive search results.

Database searches were conducted during March and June 2022. The search yielded 82 papers across all databases. This number was reduced to 45 papers after removing the duplicates, applying the inclusion criteria and conducting a quick screen of the titles and abstracts. The resultant papers were then assessed for quality by thoroughly reading their abstracts, discussions, and conclusions, resulting in the exclusion of a further 16 papers due to being irrelevant. The remaining 29 papers were deemed relevant and were thus included for data extraction and synthesis as the final step. During data extraction, two more papers were found to be relevant from searching the reference lists of the 29 papers through snowballing, and they also met the inclusion criteria. These papers were thus included in the next phase of Reporting the Review, thereby resulting in 31 articles.

5 Reporting the Review

Table 1 presents the findings of the SLR. The 31 analyzed papers each indicated at least one benefit or concern of wearable health data management. Only a few ($n = 10$) of these papers identified both benefits and concerns of wearable health data management. A total of 12 concepts each were identified as the benefits and concerns of wearable health data management through the review. The concepts that had the highest frequency (f) for both benefits and concerns combined were data privacy and security ($f = 21$ for concerns; $f = 4$ for benefits), data quality ($f = 11$ for concerns; $f = 7$ for benefits), and data governance ($f = 12$ for concerns;

Table 1 Benefits and concerns of wearable health data management

Benefits	Concerns
Health data privacy & security/protection [6, 8, 11, 23]	Health data privacy & security [1, 7, 8, 12, 16, 18, 20, 21, 24–36] - health data sensitivity [8, 11, 21]
Improved quality of data (and acceptance) [1, 6, 16, 23–25, 33]	Data quality - skepticism [9, 16, 18, 24, 25, 27–29, 32, 35, 36]
Health data governance [6, 16, 24, 25]	Health data governance [1, 8, 15, 16, 18, 24, 25, 29, 30, 36–38]
Health data accessibility [16, 24]	Health data accessibility [8, 16, 19, 24, 25, 28, 32, 35]
Data ownership [16, 25]	Data ownership [16, 25, 28–31, 34]
Promotes use & sustenance of wearables in health care [4, 16, 24, 26]	Inadequate use of data [17, 25, 26]
Improved data accuracy [6, 21]	Data accuracy [9, 18, 30, 35]
Strengthened data legitimacy [25]	Data legitimacy [21, 25, 27]
Creates confidence in wearable health data [8, 23, 24]	
	Health data storage [8, 17, 18, 28]
Promotes big data in healthcare [15, 23]	Digital health data explosion [23]

$f = 4$ for benefits). The two most frequently mentioned concepts relating only to concerns were data accessibility ($f = 8$) and data ownership ($f = 7$).

The **big data explosion** is the exponential growth of data on a large scale that is generated by and stored on computer systems, which becomes a challenge for data management [12, 23]. Wearable health data is a major contributor to the digital health data explosion, a data management concern [8, 23]. Vast amounts of wearable health data are collected anywhere and everywhere in real-time, resulting in the inability of these data to be easily tracked and controlled [17]. In contrast, the wide range of wearable health data can also be a major facilitating factor for big data in the healthcare industry with the appropriate data management practices [12, 15, 33].

Data privacy describes the protection of data through data anonymization and possible falsification to keep the data safe from unauthorized access, modification, or loss and to avoid harming the data owner [39–41]. The privacy concern is justified as wearables advance in the range and depth of health data collected through increasingly sophisticated software and algorithms that collect more attributes faster [11, 32]. In addition, the use of third parties for storage and analysis due to the enormous amount of data collected can result in privacy issues [19, 20, 28]. Continuously collecting personal health data and sharing it via networks with third parties increases the vulnerability of wearers to criminal abuses, such as the misuse of their health data for the adjustment of health insurance premiums and policies based on pre-existing medical conditions [28]. The process of ensuring data privacy involves setting access controls to protect information from unauthorized parties, obtaining consent from data owners when necessary, and maintaining data anonymity [11, 41, 42]. However, consent and data anonymization as privacy measures are being scrutinized due to how easily data can be de-anonymized and consent can be misinterpreted [25]. Furthermore, regarding consent, wearers believe that they are being lured into sacrificing their privacy in return for the benefits of the personalized services wearables offer [28]. Some of the researchers leading the scrutiny are championing the call for adequate data management that includes data governance strategies to define data use and access [1, 25].

Data sensitivity describes the level of value placed on data that denotes high-level data protection against unauthorized access to prevent possible harm because of unwarranted data leakage [11, 42]. Users can experience a feeling of invasiveness from data collection and a concern for data sensitivity [11, 16, 43]. Health data is considered sensitive due to the value of personal health and well-being information they contain, and the release of such information to unauthorized parties can lead to harm for the data owner [8, 11, 21, 42]. Issues such as data sensitivity and user acceptance concerns must be addressed to improve the usability and functions of health wearables for practical use [44].

Data security is the practice of protecting data and data assets from unauthorized access, disclosure, disruption, modification, inspection, recording, destruction, and theft throughout the data lifecycle using technology, processes, and training [40]. Wearable health data are sent through networks and servers for processing, analysis, and storage, which are often handled by third parties and are not adequately secured [1, 17, 26]. However, the concern is whether providers of wearables use mechanisms to protect health data on their respective devices and proposed networks for the intended use, preventing malicious attacks and profiteering from stolen data [16, 32, 39].

Data quality is determined by the extent to which data is useful for the analysis and purpose for which they were collected [39]. The large scale of collected wearable health data often involves the collaboration of more than one party in the analysis and storage, resulting in the possibility of reduced data quality from data manipulations and compromise [8, 16, 35]. The quality of wearable health data becomes a challenge when handled by several entities without strict data management [16, 24]. However, with data management, the quality of wearable health data is expected to improve, resulting in greater acceptance of wearables by consumers and health professionals in managing health and well-being [4, 16, 24].

Data governance is an overarching attribute of data management [16, 24, 45, 46]. It is, therefore, not surprising that it was one of the most frequently mentioned concepts among the identified benefits and concerns of wearable health data management in the review. Concerns relating to data governance are widely echoed [4, 5, 9]. Data governance describes the consistent standardization of data across the board to ensure the provision of all the attributes of data management, such as data quality, data privacy, data security, data accessibility, and usefulness [16, 39]. It is achieved through the development of policies and frameworks for implementing data management attributes [16, 39, 46]. The concern is, therefore, the lack of widely acceptable strategies, frameworks, or regulations that govern wearable health data [15, 24]. Since data governance is only possible when data is managed [47], there are calls for robust wearable health data management that prioritize data governance [16, 24].

Data accessibility describes the permission to access and use data within certain guidelines [25]. Data accessibility within data management borders on two dimensions: access restriction and permissions, where access is restricted for unauthorized entities and granted to authorized entities, including the data owners [40]. Wearable health data owners are increasingly concerned about access to their health data, and to whom and to what extent their data is accessible [16, 24, 28, 32]. There is also the concern of whether wearable health data are conveniently accessible and shared by consumers [8, 24, 25, 28]. Data management should define who gains access to wearable health data, how much can be accessed, and the modality for sharing [18, 23, 25].

The **data ownership** debate around wearable health data is gaining momentum in literature and has become a concern. Medhora [48] posited that, despite the existing architecture and regulations, wearers who are the data subjects should be the owners of their wearable health data. This argument is supported in [9, 28]. Similarly, it is confirmed in [34] that wearers' perceptions are that they have sole ownership of their data. However, in reality, wearers, as the perceived data owners, have limited rights and control over the sharing and use of their data, which is the bedrock of ownership [16, 25]. This lack of control raises concerns about who owns the data collected by wearables. With most wearable providers, wearers are forced to sign off control at the initial setup stage of their wearables by consenting to the terms and conditions [25]. Data management practices can define data ownership, allowing wearers more control over their data and specifying their role in the sharing and use thereof [7, 16, 25].

The **use and sustenance** of wearables in the health sector is a benefit of data management [4, 11, 16]. Raw data collected using wearables are usually not available to users or readily shared; often, only summarized information on measured attributes is shared [17]. Therefore, wearable health data are seldom effectively used [26]. Data should not be collected for the sake of collecting data; rather, wearable health data should be used as a medium to facilitate positive changes in people's lives [2, 5, 26]. This data should be processed and inferred to provide normal semantic information for the broader good [33]. Quality, flexible, and dynamic wearable health data can be a source of Big Data for health, providing more useful information and context than ever before for preventive healthcare and management [18, 49]. Data management measures can ensure that wearable health data do not remain in siloes and are used effectively [25].

The **accuracy of wearable health data** is required to be at par with or even superior to health data generated from traditional mediums [9]. However, it is often difficult for wearers to determine the accuracy of wearable health data due to the lack of transparency of wearable providers [17]. Wearers are not given access to all the collected raw data, creating doubt about the data accuracy [9, 35, 36]. More transparency in wearable health data collection and processing is required to allay accuracy concerns. Deliberate data management measures can enable transparency to ensure that wearables perform similarly or better in the accuracy of collected health data than traditional health data collection techniques [21] and create confidence in the wearables and the data they generate, leading to the harnessing of their benefits [11]. Data from wearables will not be considered legitimate without data management measures [25]. For example, health professionals have the view that the validity and reliability of wearable health data cannot be assured, especially if wearers are required to input data themselves [18, 25, 27, 28]. The suggestion is the implementation of data governance strategies that enable open data and sharing of wearable health data.

Data storage involves recording and saving data into systems and devices to be retained for future and long-term use [41]. A concern is that the vast amount of big data from wearables cannot be adequately handled with current technologies [17, 26], for example, due to limitations in memory size [17]. The data storage of wearable health data for most health wearables is collaborative and involves third parties [17, 28]. Hence, concerns are further heightened by the crucial link between the data storage architecture and the actualization of data security, privacy, quality, and accessibility [39, 40]. Storing wearable health data using remote and third-party architecture weakens wearers' privacy controls as it becomes less likely to determine the extent to which their data can be accessed [28].

6 Discussion and Conclusion

A conceptual model consists of concepts which are integrated to create an understanding of a specific problem [50]. Each concept identified in the SLR is related to either a benefit or a concern. Interestingly, similarities and overlaps between the concepts were found relating to these benefits and concerns. Figure 1 presents the conceptual model of the benefits and concerns of wearable health data management. The concepts with the highest frequency are shown in bold and italics.

Consumers using wearables to monitor and improve their health are increasingly concerned about how the data being collected and analyzed are managed. These concerns are especially expressed around the privacy, security, quality, governance, accessibility, and ownership of their health data. On the other hand, adequate data management practices toward wearable health data can be exploited to allay the concerns. Challenges arise when there is a gap in the management of wearable health data, such as the lack of adequate data governance. The opportunities lie in the proper management of wearable health data where measures are deployed to ensure that data quality and privacy are upheld and that data ownership, access, and use are defined.

This paper firstly contributes to the existing body of knowledge by amplifying the issues relating to the management of health data collected from wearables, which are major restraints to their wide utilization and adaptation in healthcare management. Secondly, it underscores the importance of data management in an era where technological advances are blurring the line between health and technology and undermining the sensitivity of health data. The paper also consolidates and

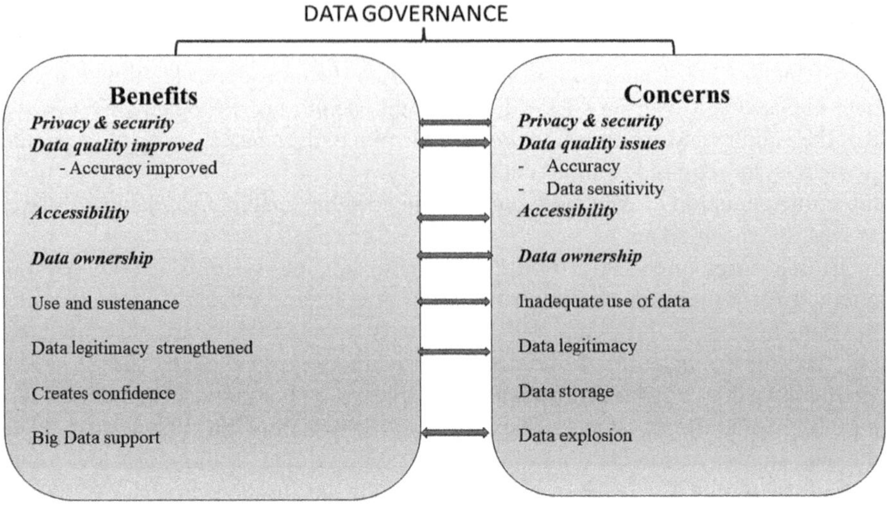

Fig. 1 Conceptual model of the benefits and concerns of wearable health data management

synthesizes the issues and concerns from various literature sources. A limitation of the paper is that it was limited to an SLR. However, efforts were made to cover most databases that contain research in the fields of Health and Computer Sciences. The research was only exploratory, but it still managed to provide a deeper understanding and scoping of the published literature on the data management of wearable health data. Future research is needed that will adopt an empirical approach by obtaining further feedback from stakeholders of wearables about the benefits and concerns they have experienced with wearable health data management.

References

1. Jiang, D., & Shi, G. (2021). Research on data security and privacy protection of wearable equipment in healthcare. *Journal of Healthcare Engineering, 6656204*, 1–7.
2. Pira, S. (2021). The social issues of smart home: A review of four European cities' experiences. *European Journal of Futures Research, 9*(3), 1–15.
3. Guk, K., Han, G., Lim, J., Jeong, K., Kang, T., Lim, E. K., & Jung, J. (2019). Evolution of wearable devices with real-time disease monitoring for personalized healthcare. *Nanomaterials, 9*(813), 1–23.
4. Peng, C., Xi, N., Hong, Z., & Hamari, J. (2022). Acceptance of wearable technology: A meta-analysis. In T. Bui (Ed.), *55th Hawaii international conference on system sciences (HICSS)* (pp. 5101–5110). HICSS.
5. Antolín, D., Medrano, N., Calvo, B., & Pérez, F. (2017). A wearable wireless sensor network for indoor smart environment monitoring in safety applications. *Sensors, 17*(2), 1–14.
6. Gharaibeh, A., Salahuddin, M. A., Hussini, S. J., Khreishah, A., Khalil, I., Guizani, M., & Al-Fuqaha, A. (2017). Smart cities: A survey on data management, security, and enabling technologies. *IEEE Communications Surveys & Tutorials, 19*(4), 2456–2501.

7. Hänsel, K., Wilde, N., Haddadi, H., & Alomainy, A. (2015). Challenges with current wearable technology in monitoring health data and providing positive behavioural support. In A. Alomainy, W. Whittow, Y. Hao, K. S. Nikita, & C. G. Parini (Eds.), *5th EAI international conference on wireless Mobile communication and healthcare* (pp. 158–161). ICST.
8. Vijayan, V., Connolly, J. P., Condell, J., McKelvey, N., & Gardiner, P. (2021). Review of wearable devices and data collection considerations for connected health. *Sensors, 21*(16), 1–31.
9. Wilson, S., & Laing, R. (2018). Wearable technologies: Present and future. In *Paper presented at the 91st world conference of the textile institute* (pp. 1–15). Textile Institute.
10. Greiwe, J., & Nyenhuis, S. M. (2020). Wearable technology and how this can be implemented into clinical practice. *Current Allergy and Asthma Reports, 20*(36), 1–10.
11. Li, C., Lin, S. H., & Chib, A. (2021). The state of wearable health technologies: A transdisciplinary literature review. *Mobile Media & Communication, 9*(2), 353–376.
12. Chen, J., Chen, Y., Du, X., Li, C., Lu, J., Zhao, S., & Zhou, X. (2013). Big data challenge: a data management perspective. *Frontiers of Computer Science, 7*(2), 157–164.
13. Abu-Elkheir, M., Hayajneh, M., & Ali, N. A. (2013). Data management for the internet of things: Design primitives and solution. *Sensors, 13*(11), 15582–15612.
14. DAMA (Ed.). (2017). *DAMA-DMBOK: Data management body of knowledge* (2nd ed.). DAMA International.
15. Maina, A. M. (2021). *Advancing big data in healthcare: A balanced approach towards reformed digital health strategies in Kenya doctoral thesis*. University of KwaZulu-Natal.
16. Arkenberg, C. (2021). *Why consumers and doctors are wary about wearable data: Consumer wearable companies are smart to watch for compliance and privacy concerns*. Deloitte Insights.
17. Arriba-Pérez, F., Caeiro-Rodríguez, M., & Santos-Gago, J. M. (2016). Collection and processing of data from wrist wearable devices in heterogeneous and multiple-user scenarios. *Sensors, 16*(9), 1–31.
18. Chong, K. P., & Woo, B. K. (2021). Emerging wearable technology applications in gastroenterology: A review of the literature. *World Journal of Gastroenterology, 27*(12), 1149–1160.
19. Aroganam, G., Manivannan, N., & Harrison, D. (2019). Review on wearable technology sensors used in consumer sports applications. *Sensors, 19*(9), 1–26.
20. Godfrey, A., Hetherington, V., Shum, H., Bonato, P., Lovell, N. H., & Stuart, S. (2018). From A to Z: Wearable technology explained. *Maturitas, 113*(1), 40–47.
21. Ometov, A., Shubina, V., Klus, L., Skibińska, J., Saafi, S., Pascacio, P., Flueratoru, L., Gaibor, D. Q., Chukhno, N., Chukhno, O., Ali, A., Channa, A., Svertoka, R., Qaim, W. B., Casanova-Marqués, R., Holcer, S., Torres-Sospedra, J., Casteleyn, S., et al. (2021). A survey on wearable technology: History, state-of-the-art and current challenges. *Computer Networks, 193*(1), 1–37.
22. Brereton, P., Kitchenham, B. A., Budgen, D., Turner, M., & Khalil, M. (2007). Lessons from applying the systematic literature review process within the software engineering domain. *Journal of Systems and Software, 80*(4), 571–583.
23. Thomason, J. (2021). Big tech, big data and the new world of digital health. *Global Health Journal, 5*(4), 165–168.
24. Aliverti, A. (2017). Wearable technology: Role in respiratory health and disease. *Breathe, 13*(2), e27–e36.
25. Kariotis, T., Ball, M. P., Tzovaras, B. G., Dennis, S., Sahama, T., Johnston, C., Almond, H., & Borda, A. (2020). Emerging health data platforms: From individual control to collective data governance. *Data & Policy, 2*(e13), 1–12.
26. Lee, J., Kim, D., Ryoo, H. Y., & Shin, B. S. (2016). Sustainable wearables: Wearable technology for enhancing the quality of human life. *Sustainability, 8*(5), 1–16.
27. Kim, B., Ghasemi, P., Stolee, P., & Lee, J. (2021). Clinicians and older adults' perceptions of the utility of patient-generated health data in caring for older adults: Exploratory mixed methods study. *JMIR Aging, 4*(4), e29788.

28. Lowens, B., Motti, V. G., & Caine, K. (2017). Wearable privacy: Skeletons in the data closet. In *2017 IEEE international conference on healthcare informatics (ICHI)* (pp. 295–304). IEEE.
29. Azodo, I., Williams, R., Sheikh, A., & Cresswell, K. (2020). Opportunities and challenges surrounding the use of data from wearable sensor devices in health care: Qualitative interview study. *Journal of Medical Internet Research, 22*(10), 1–12.
30. Jin, D., Adams, H., Cocco, A. M., Martin, W. G., & Palmer, S. (2020). Smartphones and wearable technology: Benefits and concerns in cardiology. *Medical Journal of Australia, 212*(2), 54–56.
31. Kerr, D., Butler-Henderson, K., & Sahama, T. (2019). Security, privacy, and ownership issues with the use of wearable health technologies. In *Cyber law, privacy, and security: Concepts, methodologies, tools, and applications* (pp. 1629–1644). IGI Global.
32. Honarvar, M. G., & Latifi, M. (2017). Overview of wearable electronics and smart textiles. *The Journal of The Textile Institute, 108*(4), 631–652.
33. Nahavandi, D., Alizadehsani, R., Khosravi, A., & Acharya, U. R. (2022). Application of artificial intelligence in wearable devices: Opportunities and challenges. *Computer Methods and Programs in Biomedicine, 213*(1), 1–19.
34. Zimmer, M., Kumar, P., Vitak, J., Liao, Y., & Chamberlain Kritikos, K. (2020). 'There's nothing really they can do with this information': Unpacking how users manage privacy boundaries for personal fitness information. *Information, Communication & Society, 23*(7), 1020–1037.
35. Abboushi, B., Safranek, S., Rodriguez-Feo Bermudez, E., Pratoomratana, S., Chen, Y., Poplawski, M., & Davis, R. A. (2022). Review of the use of wearables in indoor environmental quality studies and an evaluation of data accessibility from a wearable device. *Frontiers in Built Environment, 8*(787289), 1–14.
36. Iwaya, L. H., Ahmad, A., & Babar, M. A. (2020). Security and privacy for mHealth and uHealth systems: A systematic mapping study. *IEEE Access, 8*, 150081–150112.
37. Lewy, H. (2015). Wearable technologies–future challenges for implementation in healthcare services. *Healthcare Technology Letters, 2*(1), 2–5.
38. te Kulve, H., Boon, W., Konrad, K., & Schuitmaker, T. J. (2018). Influencing the direction of innovation processes: The shadow of authorities in demand articulation. *Science and Public Policy, 45*(4), 455–467.
39. Jain, P., Gyanchandani, M., & Khare, N. (2016). Big data privacy: A technological perspective and review. *Journal of Big Data, 3*(1), 1–25.
40. Mehmood, A., Natgunanathan, I., Xiang, Y., Hua, G., & Guo, S. (2016). Protection of big data privacy. *IEEE Access, 4*(1), 1821–1834.
41. Hoffman, A., & Masucci, R. (2018). *Protecting individuals' privacy and data in the artificial intelligence world. Intel's AI privacy policy white paper* (pp. 1–9). Intel Corporation.
42. Horvitz, E., & Mulligan, D. (2015). Data, privacy, and the greater good. *Science, 349*(6245), 253–255.
43. Cilliers, L. (2020). Wearable devices in healthcare: Privacy and information security issues. *Health Information Management Journal, 49*(2–3), 150–156.
44. Wu, M., & Luo, J. (2019). Wearable technology applications in healthcare: A literature review. *Online Journal of Nursing Informatics, 23*(3).
45. Ladley, J. (2019). *Data governance: How to design, deploy, and sustain an effective data governance program*. Academic Press.
46. Georgiadis, G., & Poels, G. (2021). Enterprise architecture management as a solution for addressing general data protection regulation requirements in a big data context: A systematic mapping study. *Information Systems and e-Business Management, 19*(1), 313–362.
47. Patel, U. (2022). Information technology strategy: A case for data governance. *Procedia Computer Science Journal.*
48. Medhora, R. P. (2018). Data governance in the digital age. In *Data governance in the digital age: Special report* (pp. 1–4). Centre for International Governance Innovation.

49. Schüll, N. D. (2016). Data for life: Wearable technology and the design of self-care. *BioSocieties, 11*(3), 317–333.
50. Jabareen, Y. (2009). Building a conceptual framework: Philosophy, definitions, and procedure. *International Journal of Qualitative Methods, 8*(4), 49–62.

Analysis of the Measurements of Cycle Path Surface Quality as Collected by Three Different Technologies

Jana Klemp, Jorge Marx Gómez, Johannes Schering, and Steven Soetens

1 Introduction

Cycling has a lot of advantages that can be perceived strongly in the actual crisis scenarios. According to a survey of the German Bicycle Club (Allgemeiner Deutscher Fahrrad-Club, ADFC) more and more people are switching from car to bicycle because of rising energy costs. Around 49% of the respondents announced that they now more often renounce car usage to save money and energy [1]. The state of the bicycle infrastructure and especially the surface conditions are very relevant for cycling comfort and frequent bicycle use. In contrast to motorized traffic, bicycles often do not have a comprehensive suspension. A low rolling resistance is important to avoid spending too much energy on the bike path [2]. Therefore, kerb sides, potholes, or other damages must be avoided. Because of its relevance, many studies have focused on the data-driven detection of bike path surface conditions [3, 4].

As part of this contribution, we will discuss the detection of the surface conditions with three different types of measurement technologies. The Province of Antwerp tested three different measurement technologies to analyze if the measurements of the three technologies can be transformed in a way so that they are comparable with each other. Today, a road has to be measured multiple times just because the wrong measurement device had been used. This additional expense should not be needed anymore. The overall aim is that the same street section can

J. Klemp (✉) · J. Marx Gómez · J. Schering
Department of Business Informatics (VLBA), University of Oldenburg, Oldenburg, Germany
e-mail: jana.klemp@uni-oldenburg.de; jorge.marx.gomez@uni-oldenburg.de; johannes.schering@uni-oldenburg.de

S. Soetens
Province of Antwerp, Department of Space, Heritage and Mobility, Antwerp, Belgium
e-mail: steven.soetens@provincieantwerpen.be

J. Marx Gómez et al. (eds.), *Smart and Secure Embedded and Mobile Systems*, Progress in IS, https://doi.org/10.1007/978-3-031-56603-5_18

be measured by an arbitrary technology and the taken measurements can be transformed into a standardized scale so that it is not important by which measurement technology the measurements have been collected. These measurements can, for example, then be used for a comfort score that gives information about how bicycle friendly a street section is. Another advantage is that a uniform algorithm for data processing for all devices can be implemented. Such an algorithm is, for example, for distinguishing different street types or to recognize surface anomalies. Today these algorithms are implemented for each device individually. In this paper we focus on the first part, the reliability of the measurements and analyze which of the two different forms of presentation suit better for comparing measurements. The first form of presentation plots the measurements in sequence one after the other. In the second case the measurements are plotted by using the GPS records that are stored with each measurement. The findings of this work are important for the question if it is appropriate to transform data from different devices into one scale. This is the case only when the measurements of the different devices can be visualized in a precise way on the x-axis and when the measurements are reliable.

The paper is structured as follows. First, we present related work and describe the research gap. Then, we will explain the test scenario and give a brief overview of the collected data. After that we focus on the quality of GPS measurements based on the lengths of each measured interval. In the next section we invest the reliability of each measurement technology. Then, the two forms of presentations are compared with each other. First, each device is investigated separately. Then, the presentation forms are compared when all three technologies are visualized in one diagram. The paper concludes with the results of the analyses and provides guidance on how best to visualize the measurements from the three different measurement technologies. Moreover, the conclusion outlines further research.

2 Related Work

There has been various research about measuring the surface quality. In 2018 a review of these investigations had been done regarding the use of a smartphone as a measurement device [5]. It could be proved that the surface quality can be measured [6], and surface anomalies [7–9] can be detected by using a smartphone and other measuring systems that are attached to a bicycle. However, there has been no research so far about the quality of the calculated values itself. Whereas specific applications and devices have been used for the demonstration that it is possible to measure the surface quality [6], it has not been investigated how to compare the values of different measurement technologies that all have in common to measure the surface quality. Moreover, a reasonable way to present multiple measurement tracks within one diagram has not been discussed.

Regarding the precision of GPS coordinates there is a lot of research about the precision of GPS calculated distances [10, 11]. Especially in sport research a lot of research has been done [12]. Also, the accuracy of GPS coordinates has been investigated under various conditions [13]. However, there is not much research about how precise values can be visualized when they are visualized in a graph that plots a distance that is calculated by GPS coordinates on the x-axis.

In [14] a similar study to our research has been made. However, they used smartphones and tablets. In our case the three compared technologies are very different. Instead of our research they tested the reliability of the identification of road anomalies. We focus on the reliability of the aggregated measurements.

3 Measurement Methodology

Three different mobile devices have been used on five different road sections that are located in the Province of Antwerp in Belgium. All three devices have in common that they measure the road surface conditions of bike paths by using an accelerometer. These devices are the FPP (Fietspad Profilometer, Bike Path Profilometer), a tool used by the Flemish Region, the Comfortbike (meetfiets), which has been developed by the interest group "Fietsersbond," and the device from Drivenby, which is a commercially developed tool. The device from Drivenby uses the app rRuf and the Rubix platform to process the measurements. In the case of the FPP, a scooter with a trailer detects the surface condition. The trailer integrates a laser and an acceleration sensor that measures the distance from the trailer to the surface every 3 S. The GPS location and the number of kilometers are also detected [15]. Figure 1 shows the different devices. Every device measured each road section twice. All measurements were collected on the same day (19th of July 2021).

In Table 1 the different sections are listed. The road sections are between 500 and 800 meters long and have different road surfaces of variable quality and materials: Concrete, concrete slaps, concrete tiles, and asphalt. All sections are in the Province of Antwerp. For the measurements orange marker were painted on the ground. The FPP and the device from Drivenby also started and stopped their measurements at these points. All devices record quality measurements for the road surface continuously and compute an average value for all 12.5 meters. The FPP and the device from Drivenby calculate the 12.5 meters by directly using the GPS

a b c

Fig. 1 Measuring technologies. (**a**) FPP. (**b**) Comfortbike. (**c**) Drivenby. Images by Belgian Road Research Center

Table 1 Road sections. The colors represent similar road surfaces. Images by Belgian Road Research Center, except the image of Section 3: End [16]

Section	Lengths	Surface	Start/Endpoint
Section 1 800 m	0 m–375 m 375 m–800 m	Concrete slabs/ Betonplaten Concrete tiles (Betonklinkers)	
Section 2 650 m	0 m–650 m	Concrete (Beton)	
Section 3 750 m	0 m–750 m	Asphalt (Asfalt)	
Section 4 575 m	0 m—575 m	Concrete tiles (Betonklinkers)	
Section 5 500 m	0 m–175 m 175 m–421 m 421 m–500 m	Asphalt (Asfalt) Concrete Asphalt (Asfalt)	

coordinates, whereas the Comfortbike calculates an average of the measured values every 3 S and does a postprocessing after the ride. Within this postprocessing the GPS coordinates from the start point and from the end point of the total ride are used. The test was conducted by the Belgian Road Research Center (BRRC).

In Table 2 the numbers of the measurements are listed for each trip of each device. The FPP has always recorded one measurement more than the expected number. The expected number of measurements is hereby the total length of the test section divided by 12.5-meter. This number is listed in the column "Interval sections." The measurements of the Comfortbike vary between two and four more calculated measurements.

The device from Drivenby mostly created the expected number of measurements.

4 Analysis of the GPS Interval Lengths

For each 12.5-meter calculated average the GPS coordinates have been recorded. By analyzing the lengths of these GPS tracks, the histogram of the frequency of the GPS track lengths allows us to assume that the lengths for the FPP and the device

Table 2 Overview of the test rides

					Number of measurements		
Trip	Section	Test	Length	Interval sections	FPP	Comfortbike	Drivenby
1	1	1	800 m	64	65(+1)	67 (+3)	64 (+0)
2	1	2	800 m	64	65 (+1)	68 (+4)	64 (+0)
3	2	1	650 m	52	53 (+1)	54 (+2)	50 (2 missing) (+0)
4	2	2	650 m	52	53 (+1)	55 (+3)	52 (+0)
5	3	1	750 m	60	61 (+1)	63 (+3)	60 (+0)
6	3	2	750 m	60	61 (+1)	64 (+4)	60 (+0)
7	4	1	575 m	46	47 (+1)	48 (+2)	46 (+0)
8	4	2	575 m	46	47 (+1)	48 (+2)	46 (+0)
9	5	1	500 m	40	41 (+1)	42 (+2)	39 (2 missing) (+1)
10	5	2	500 m	40	41 (+1)	42 (+2)	41 (+1)

from Drivenby have a normal distribution. The lengths of the Comfortbike have no normal distribution. From all the technologies, the device from Drivenby has the most accurate lengths that are nearly to 12.5 meter. Then follows the FPP and then the Comfortbike. All technologies have in common that the GPS tracks are mostly smaller than 12.5 meter. The H0-hypothesis, that the mean of the measurements is 12.5 meter, can be rejected for the FPP and the Drivenby measurements with at least a confidence of 95%. The 95% confidence interval for the FPP is between 12.304 and 12.356 meter, the one of Drivenby between 12.46 and 12.48 meter. The box plots for each trip of each device show that the distribution of the lengths varies between the trips. For all three devices the length of the boxes and the length of the whiskers differ a lot, whereas the median of the data of the GPS interval length is nearly the same for all trips. Additionally, the GPS interval lengths have been plotted in the sequence they have been measured. The lengths of the FPP and Comfortbike show some similarities between GPS intervals that are close to each other. The data of the device from Drivenby does not show this correlation.

5 Reliability of the Measured Values

To investigate the reliability of each individual device, every section was measured twice by each device. Obviously, since the two test rides have some variations anyway (they do not measure exactly the same line each time), some differences are expected. Some of the diagrams from the FPP are shown in Fig. 2. For Section 4 the test rides with the FPP differ the most, whereas Section 2 shows more similar graphs. The diagrams of the measurements from Drivenby show similar results as these from the FPP. The measurements of the Comforbike differ more. However, by comparing the measurements of the Comfortbike for each test ride using box plots, the test rides of the same road show similar results (see Fig. 3). For the histogram and the box plots the last measurement of a trip has been dropped.

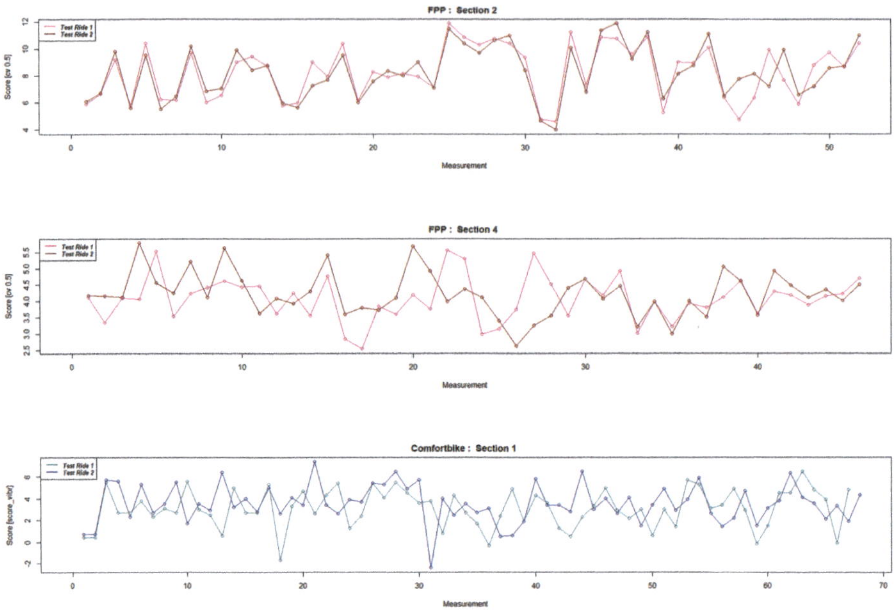

Fig. 2 Comparison of the two test rides to test the reliability. (**a**) FPP, Section 2 (red). (**b**) FPP, Section 4 (red). (**c**) Comfortbike, Section 1 (blue)

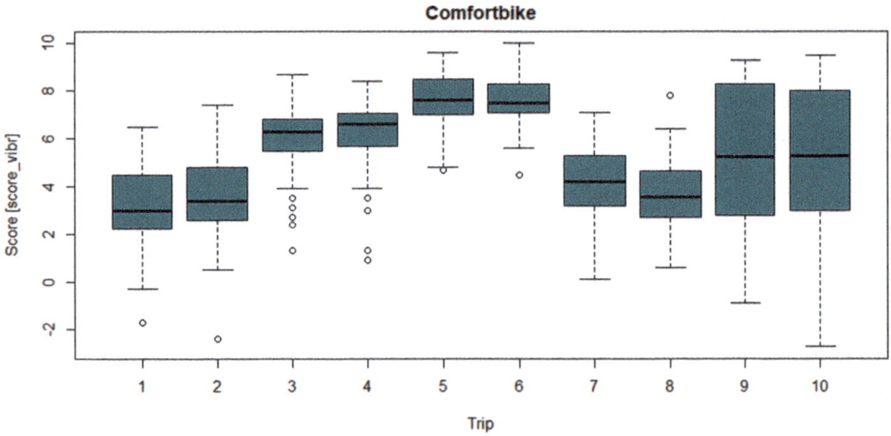

Fig. 3 Distribution of the calculated values for each test ride of the Comfortbike. Section 1: Trip 1 and 2; Section 2: Trip 2 and 3, ...

The size of the boxes of the GPS interval lengths could have an influence on the accuracy of the aggregated values. The boxes of the FPP are relatively big for Section 4. For this section the FPP has a worse reliability. The device from Drivenby has bigger boxes at Sections 4 and 1. The reliability of the measurements is for these sections also worse than for Sections 3 and 5.

6 Comparison of the Two Visualization Forms

The two test rides for a road section are visualized in two different forms of presentation. In the first way the measurements are displayed one after the other. In a second way the x-axis refers to the distance from the start point. The distances from the start point are calculated by using the GPS values that are stored with each aggregated value. Therefore, the distance between the start point and the end of the last measured section is taken together with the length of the new measured section. Doing this, the already ridden path could be computed.

The two visualizations do not differ a lot for the FPP and the device from Drivenby. For the Comfortbike the two different visualizations differ a bit more. For Section 1 sometimes the first sometimes the second plotting way leads to more similar graph sections. For Sections 2 and 3 the two test rides of the Comfortbike show more similar results, when the distance from the start point is considered. Sections 4 and 5 do not show big differences between the both plotting ways.

By plotting the data of each device in one diagram, one time using the first presentation form and one time the second (see Fig. 4), the presentation form that uses the GPS coordinates generally leads to better results. For road Sections 1 and 5

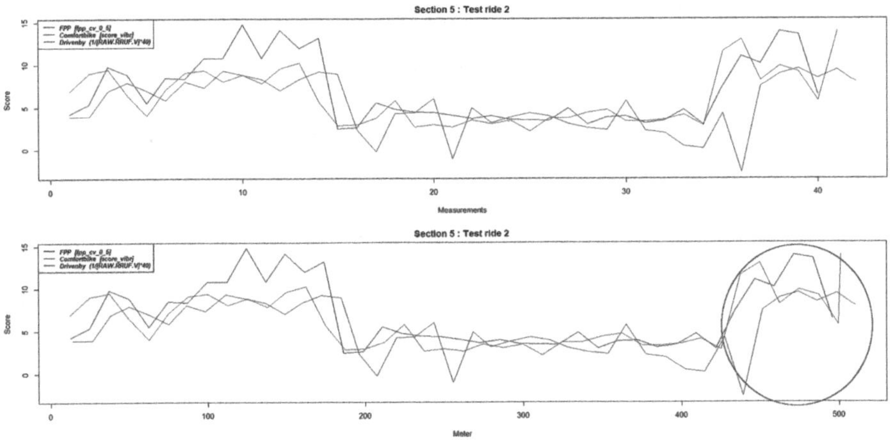

Fig. 4 Comparison of the measurements between the different devices: Section 5, Test ride 2. (**a**) Measurements in sequence. (**b**) GPS distance

this presentation form performs better for both test rides. For Sections 2 and 3 one test ride leads to better results by using this method. The values in Section 4 differ too much so that there are no clear results. Using the GPS coordinates especially gives better results for measurements that are further away from the starting point.

The evaluation has been done in such a way that the sections in the graphs have been marked where all three devices have nearly the same shape in only one of the two visualization ways. The shape is either several hundred meter long or there is a big change of the aggregated values in short distance like in Section 5.

For the research the data from the Drivenby device (1) and from the FPP (2) have been transformed, so that they can be visualized in a diagram with the other devices.

$$((1/x) * 40) \tag{1}$$

$$((1/x) * 100) \tag{2}$$

7 Conclusion

This paper describes a test with three different measurement technologies that measured five different road sections two times. These measurements have been analyzed together with the GPS coordinates that were recorded with the measurements. Regarding the reliability of the measurements most of the diagrams of the FPP and the device from Drivenby that compare the two test rides at the same section show two quite similar graphs. The reliability of the measurements for the Comfortbike exists, when the ranges and the distribution of the values are considered. The length of the GPS tracks of the FPP and the device of Drivenby have a normal distribution. All technologies have in common that the GPS tracks are mostly smaller than 12.5 meter. For all three technologies the two presentation forms are equally good when the measurements of the same technology are investigated. When the three technologies, FPP, Comfortbike, and Drivenby, should be compared, the GPS coordinates that are stored with each measurement should be used to calculate the distances from the start point. By doing this, the measurements often fit better, especially for measurements that are taken further away from the starting point.

As the measurements have been done all on the same day, it is possible that similar satellites are used for the calculation of the GPS coordinates. With different satellite constellations the results possibly could differ more. It has not been tested to ride the measurement technologies at different speeds and how are the results when the speed changes within a trip. In this test the devices were ridden in steady speed. Also, the test does not consider different weather conditions (snow, puddles). Further research can take other road surface types into account. Doing this, the characteristics of the three technologies can be further investigated. Also, this test can be done with different measurement technologies that calculate the surface roughness with something other than an accelerometer and create the 12.5-meter intervals in another way than the three technologies in this test. Interesting is also to compare the two visualization forms (plot in sequence/plot using the GPS coordinates) with longer test rides. By doing this it can be investigated whether the presentation form using the GPS coordinates works well over longer distances, too. Further, it could be investigated how far the variations of the GPS interval lengths could be an indicator for the reliability of the measurements. The code of this paper has been published and can be found in reference [17]. For data analysis R [18] has been used.

Acknowledgments The project BITS (Bicycles and Intelligent Transport Systems) is supported by the Interreg North Sea Programme (Priority 4, Promoting green transport and mobility) of the European Regional Development Fund of the European Union.

Disclaimer This paper reflects only the author's view and the Interreg North Sea Region is not responsible for any use that may be made of the information it contains.

References

1. watson: Städtetag: Wegen gestiegener Energiepreise: Viele steigen aufs Fahrrad um. Retrieved March 25, 2022, from https://www.watson.de/nachhaltigkeit/gute%20nachricht/291996777-wegen-gestiegener-energiepreise-viele-steigen-laut-adac-umfrage-aufs-fahrrad-um
2. Fenre, M. D., & Klein-Paste, A. (2021). Bicycle rolling resistance under winter conditions. *Cold Regions Science and Technology, 187*, 103282.
3. Schering, J., Janßen, C., Kessler, R., Dmitriyev, V., Marx Gómez, J., Stehno, C., Pelzner, K., Bankowsky, R., & Hentschel, R. (2021). Ecosense and its preliminary findings: Collection and analysis of bicycle sensor data. In A. Kamilaris, V. Wohlgemuth, K. Karatzas, & I. Athana-siadis (Eds.), *EnviroInfo 2020 Environmental informatics—New perspectives in Environmental information systems: Transport, sensors, recycling. Adjunct proceedings of the 34th EnviroInfo conference* (pp. 145–153). Shaker Verlag.
4. Titov, W., & Schlegel, T. (2019). Monitoring road surface conditions for bicycles–using mobile device sensor data from crowd sourcing. In *International conference on human-computer interaction* (pp. 340–356). Springer.

5. Sattar, S., Li, S., & Chapman, M. (2018). Road surface monitoring using smartphone sensors: A review. *Sensors, 18*(11), 3845.
6. Litzenberger, S., Christensen, T., Hofstätter, O., & Sabo, A. (2018). Prediction of road surface quality during cycling using smartphone accelerometer data. *Multidisciplinary Digital Publishing Institute Proceedings, 2*(6), 217.
7. Setiawan, B. D., Kryssanov, V. V., Serdült, U., Loshchilov, A., Mahmudy, W. F., & Nurwasito, H. (2020). Monitoring road surface conditions with cyclist's smartphone sensors. In *CEUR workshop proceedings, 2627* (pp. 76–82). CEUR-WS.
8. Springer, M., & Ament, C. (2020). A mobile and modular low-cost sensor system for road surface recognition using a bicycle. In *2020 IEEE international conference on multisensor fusion and integration for intelligent systems (MFI)* (pp. 360–366). IEEE.
9. Zang, K., Shen, J., Huang, H., Wan, M., & Shi, J. (2018). Assessing and mapping of road surface roughness based on gps and accelerometer sensors on bicycle-mounted smartphones. *Sensors, 18*(3), 914.
10. Palmer, M. C. (2008). Calculation of distance traveled by fishing vessels using gps positional data: A theoretical evaluation of the sources of error. *Fisheries Research, 89*(1), 57–64.
11. Ranacher, P., Brunauer, R., Trutschnig, W., Van der Spek, S., & Reich, S. (2016). Why gps makes distances bigger than they are. *International Journal of Geographical Information Science, 30*(2), 316–333.
12. Cummins, C., Orr, R., O'Connor, H., & West, C. (2013). Global positioning systems (GPS) and microtechnology sensors in team sports: A systematic review. *Sports Medicine, 43*(10), 1025–1042.
13. Merry, K., & Bettinger, P. (2019). Smartphone GPS accuracy study in an urban environment. *PLoS One, 14*(7), e0219890.
14. Astarita, V., Caruso, M. V., Danieli, G., Festa, D. C., Giofrè, V. P., Iuele, T., & Vaiana, R. (2012). A mobile application for road surface quality control: UNIquALroad. *Procedia-Social and Behavioral Sciences, 54*, 1135–1144.
15. De Swaef, A. (2019). Instruments for road agencies - fpp: Measurement of the alongside evenness of bike paths (instrumenten voor wegbeheerders—FPP: Meting van de lang-svlakheid van fietspaden).
16. Koninklijke: Photos to Augment Openstreetmap Edits. (2017). https://www.mapillary.com/app/user/koninklijke?lat=51.132525&lng=4.4021944444444&z=17&focus=photo&pKey=394314728335635&menu=tru&x=0.48905377710927 12&y=0.5034559491 5755&zoom=0. This work is licensed under CC BY-SA 4.0. Retrieved March 25, 2023, from http://creativecommons.org/licenses/by-sa/4.0/
17. Klemp, J. (2023). CyclePathSurfaceQuality: Research in cycle path surface data. https://gitlab.uni-oldenburg.de/cyclepathsurfacequality/CyclePathSurfaceQuality/-/tree/EMOS2022. R package version 0.1.0.
18. R Core Team. (2023). *R: A language and environment for statistical computing*. R Foundation for Statistical Computing. https://www.R-project.org/

Smart Energy Management System for Government Institutions: A Case of the Nelson Mandela African Institution of Science and Technology

Ateny Gabriel Aguto, Sanisse Adrielle Berinkinzo, Zacharie Niyonzima, Anael Sam, and Ramadhani Sinde

1 Introduction

Electrical energy is a secondary energy source, meaning it is produced by converting primary energy sources like coal, oil, nuclear, water, wind, and solar energy into other forms of energy. Electricity is neither renewable nor non-renewable, whereas these primary resources are either renewable or non-renewable energies. On the other hand, renewable energy sources can refill themselves at their usage rate. In contrast, non-renewable energy sources degrade over time and cannot be supplied by nature to fulfill consumption needs [1].

According to the Enerdata world energy report released in 2021, the total world electricity production in 2020 was 26,905.6 TWh, with domestic consumption of 23,176 TWh compared to 2019 energy production of 27,063.6 TWh. The difference in the downfall in 2020 is due to the Covid-19 pandemic that has engulfed the world from 2019 till today. It was found that the total electricity production had dropped by 4.5% in 2020 due to a decrease in industrial consumption. On the other hand, carbon dioxide emission was 31067.3 MtCO2 in 2020. This emitted CO2 has significantly contributed to greenhouse gas that causes dynamics in climate change. According to this report, African energy generation in 2020 is expected to be 850 TWh, with domestic consumption of 687.6 TWh [2].

Global energy demand is expected to rise 1.3% between 2020 and 2030, with CO_2 emissions falling to a few metric tons. By 2050, the world will be at zero carbon emissions [3]. According to the 2021 report, Tanzania's energy generation is 1605.86 MW (1,406,733.36 GWh), with residential premises consuming 2633 GWh and commercial and public sectors finishing 1311 GWh [4]. This energy consumed

A. G. Aguto · S. A. Berinkinzo (✉) · Z. Niyonzima · A. Sam · R. Sinde
School of Computational and Communication Science and Engineering, The Nelson Mandela African Institution of Science and Technology, Arusha, Tanzania
e-mail: berinkinzos@nm-aist.ac.tz

J. Marx Gómez et al. (eds.), *Smart and Secure Embedded and Mobile Systems*,
Progress in IS, https://doi.org/10.1007/978-3-031-56603-5_19

by the residential, commercial, and public sectors is a massive amount of energy that needs to be managed to avoid waste of energy through heating, lighting, and air-conditioning in the case of the high institution of learning.

The decrease of electricity consumption, energy costs resulting from production, and CO2 emissions is one of the main goals of the smart energy management system. It might identify inefficient areas and provide ways to save electricity usage by evaluating and tracking energy usage patterns. This not only aids in lowering energy expenses, but it also reduces the CO2 emissions linked to energy production. Implementing such a system, sustainable habits may be promoted and overall energy efficiency can be increased [5].

For the case of NM-AIST, the metering system is only read using the Global Position System (GPS), which does not give the technician on the ground a chance to evaluate how much energy is consumed by each section and equipment per month. Also, the electrification system of the NM-AIST is so analog that all the equipment is always turned ON and OFF manually. Such a system always leads to power wastage and high energy consumption. Sometimes, most security lights do light during the day, when they were supposed to light at night. Some university employees forget and leave their lights, fans, and air conditioners on the whole night without any necessary use. Due to this poor energy management, the monthly electricity bill of NM-AIST is around 23,000,000 Tshs per month [6]. This monthly bill is so huge in such a way that it affects the budget of other sectors such as research and development.

The main objective of this study was to develop a Smart Energy Management System for Government Institutions: A Case of the Nelson Mandela African Institution of Science and Technology to minimize energy and costs.

2 Related Works

Different researchers have developed various systems to reduce energy consumption and save money.

Smart energy monitoring and management system for industrial applications identified the energy consumption of individual machines with the help of a graphical user interface and a schedule of operations [7]. The results showed that this system is an opportunity for energy-intensive sectors to improve the ecological profile, increase energy cost savings, and improve energy. However, the system was not efficient.

An intelligent energy management system that aims to replace the scenario of a complete power failure in an area with a partial load shedding, in a controlled manner according to the consumer's preference was deployed with a reliable ZigBee communication for the home network [8]. An IoT environment has also been developed for analysis and data storage. The data, such as an appliance's daily and monthly power usage, were viewed via the graphical user interface and the energy management system.

"Smart Institutions" refers to higher education institutions in India that has implemented an energy management system to control and minimize the increase in electricity bills [9]. This system was based on the game theory and timing formulation results. It was concluded that the current model's performance was efficient and practical while promising a possible energy-saving system. However, they did not host the data on the cloud, it was not tested or monitored and controlled for the real-life experiment.

An intelligent IoT-based energy management system using an Entrack software for data collection and analysis was developed. The result showed that the presented Smart Energy Management System helps consumers to efficiently, easily, reliably, and accurately track their energy consumption, helping them to manage unwanted energy consumption, resulting in energy savings [10]. As a limitation, the proposed system did not handle smart energy meters based on the Internet of Things to exchange energy use and quality with power grids, allowing them to improve their performance and cost.

Therefore, a smart energy management system is essential and useful for an institution to reduce energy consumption, cost, and electricity bills in controlling and monitoring appliances such as lights, fans, and air conditioners. The system was designed, developed, and tested in a real-life environment. Low-cost, efficient components with simple language have been employed to ensure an efficient system. The system allowed the user to monitor the metering and some appliances via a website and a mobile application by using a Wireless Sensor Network, Wi-Fi, Motion Sensor to detect the presence of a human in the classes or offices and a Global System for Mobile Communications (GSM) as a backup to receive data from those devices if there is an internet failure. In addition, this system can be deployed to home, business area, and non-government institutions.

3 Materials and Methods

3.1 System Development Approach

The design science research methodology (DSRM), which comprises three stages, problem identification, solution design, and assessment and validation was employed in this work. The outcome technique of DSRM, which enables methods for evaluation and iteration inside the study, was the basis for choosing it. On the other hand, DSRM improves the interfaces' functional performance.

3.2 Case Study and Data Analysis

This study was carried out at the Nelson Mandela African Institution of Science and Technology (NM-AIST) in Arusha. The institution is divided into two zones: residential and administrative zones. The scope of this study was focused on the administration zone, i.e., the administration offices, classes, laboratories, and libraries because most of the energy consumed is from the administration area.

The collected data from the Estate and administration of NM-AIST was from December 2018 to 2021. The data were analyzed, and we realized that there is more energy consumption in the administration zone. Still, it was impossible to see an area that consumed more energy because NM-AIST uses only 1 m for the whole area. It is challenging to know energy consumption from different areas such as laboratories, libraries, and classes.

3.3 Hardware Integration

The developed system was designed with four nodes and the gateway, as shown in Figs. 1, 2, 3, and 4. The four nodes are from the admin block, cafeteria, CoCSE lab, and LISBE lab, which send data to the gateway through wireless sensor network (WSN) technologies, then from the gateway to the cloud via Wi-Fi. Every node has a PZEM 004 T module which measures voltage, current, energy, and frequency, a liquid crystal display (LCD) that displays the status, a DS3231 timer for counting time, a passive infrared sensor (PIR) that detects motion, an esp32 microcontroller within Wi-Fi, a buzzer for warning, a relay, a light-dependent resistor (LDR) to determine the intensity of light and a ZigBee module. Indeed, when the gateway has received the data from all the nodes, it hosts them on the cloud. The user visualizes the appliances' status in real-time through a web dashboard and mobile application. Furthermore, the user receives short message service (SMS) by the global system for mobile communication (GSM) technology on the phone in real-time, even when there is a lack of internet.

4 Results and Discussion

4.1 Results

4.1.1 System Requirements

4.1.2 System Architecture

The energy nodes collect energy consumption from various appliances and different sections of the administration zone (Tables 1 and 2). The gateway receives these data (energy consumption) via a wireless sensor network and relays them to the

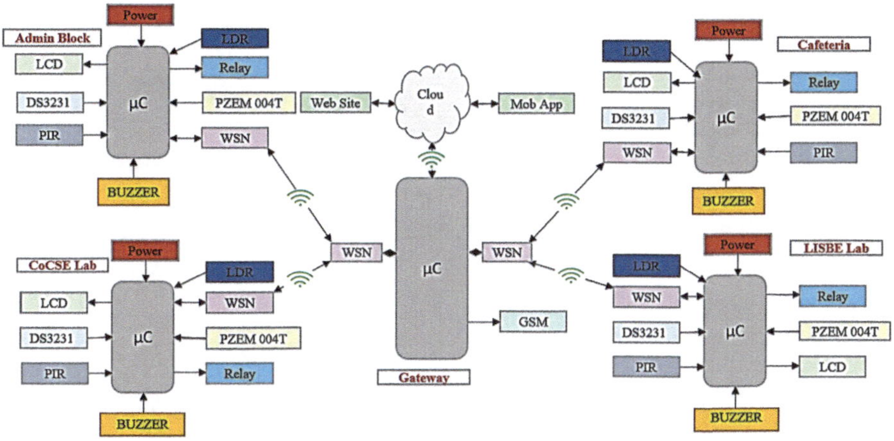

Fig. 1 Block diagram

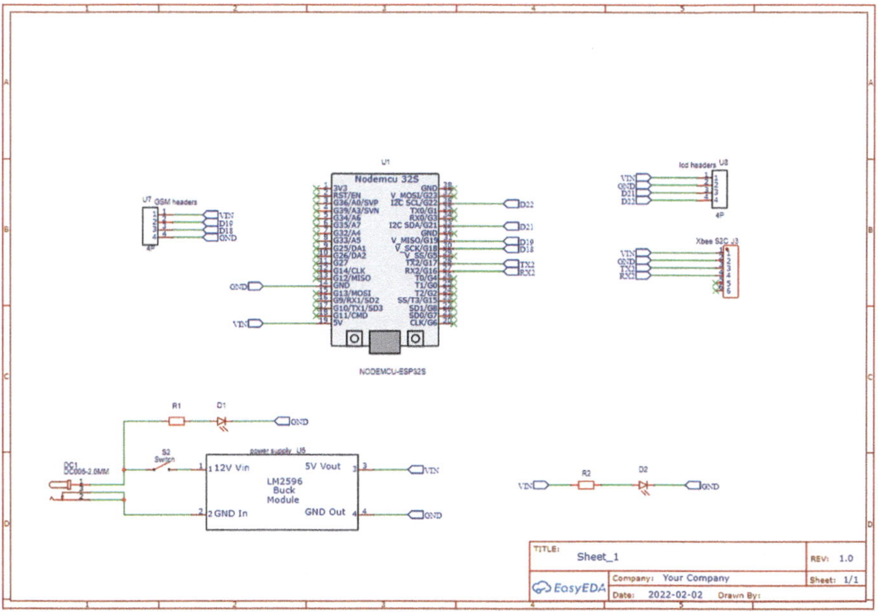

Fig. 2 Gateway schematic

cloud, where they have been stored on the server. The user, through an SMS and a web dashboard, can access the system and be able to control and monitor appliances online. Figure 4 shows the essential architecture of the proposed SEMS.

Table 1 and 2 illustrate the functional and non-functional requirements. These requirements were gathered to describe what the system should do and how it must

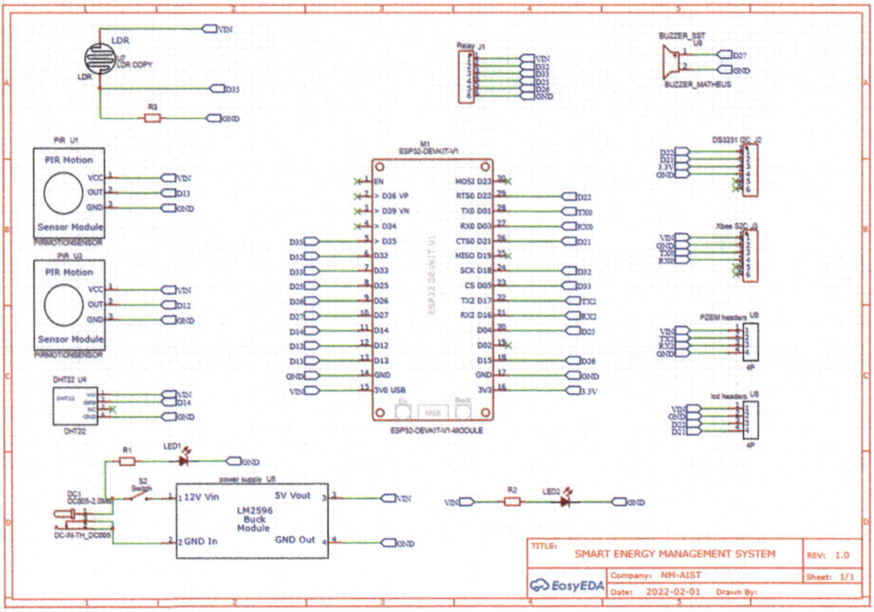

Fig. 3 Node schematic

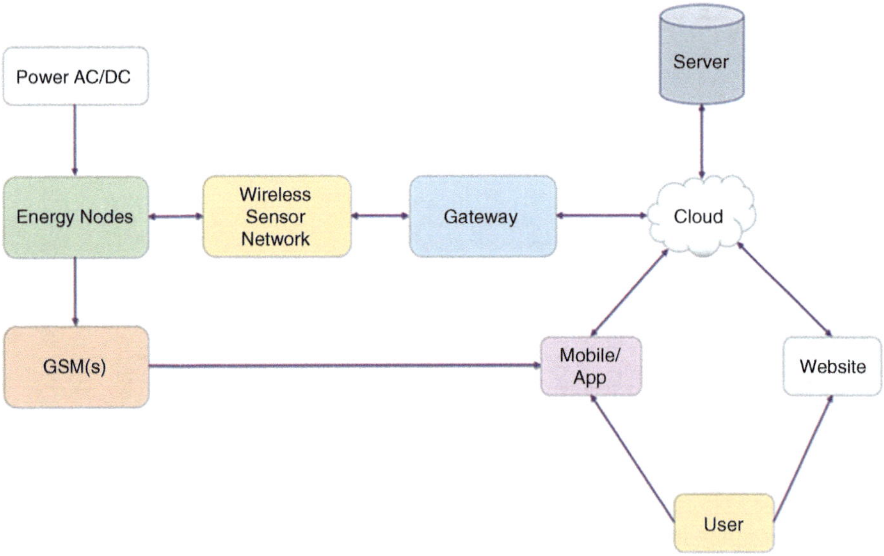

Fig. 4 Conceptual framework

Table 1 Functional requirements of the developed system

SN	Requirement	Description
1	Sign in	The system should allow the user to log in
2	Energy measurement	The system should measure the energy consumption from the appliances in all nodes
4	Link to the cloud	The system should be linked to the cloud
5	User interface	The system should allow the user to see the appliances' status in real-time (power consumption, energy, voltage, current, and frequency).
6	Mobile app	The system should be accessible by the user in a mobile application.
7	User's control	The system should allow the user to switch off/on the appliances (fan, lights, and air conditioner)
8	Notification	The system should send messages to the user via GSM

Table 2 Non-functional requirements

SN	Requirements	Description
1	Usability	The system should have a user-friendly interface
2	Confidentiality	The data in the system should be confidential by being accessed by who is concerned
3	Security	The user admin should be able to log in, see the status of all appliances, and give access to the other preferred users. The system should be secured from IoT environment.
4	Maintainability	The system should be easy to maintain with available devices on the market.
5	Performance	The system should be able to minimize power consumption.
6	Operability	The system uses Blynk, an Internet of Things platform for IOS or Android smartphones, which is easy to be accessed. The system is written in Arduino IDE

perform specific tasks based on user's and technical perspectives. Additionally, these requirements are essential for developing a successful system because they guarantee that the system will satisfy user needs, prevent costly rework and delays, and enhance cooperation among stockholders.

4.1.3 System Development

The following figure is the hardware prototype of the smart energy management system. Figure 5 shows one energy node of the system.

Figure 6 shows the Blynk environment of the web dashboard for an administrative unit. The administrator can see the status from all four nodes (Admin block, LISBE lab, CoCSE lab, and cafeteria). Figure 7 shows the web dashboard where the user can visualize the status of the appliance's parameters, such as voltage, energy,

Fig. 5 Hardware prototype

frequency, current, light intensity temperature, and power consumption. Moreover, the user can monitor and control the appliances on that web dashboard.

Figure 8 shows the mobile application's interface of LISBE and MEWES LAB where the user can also monitor, visualize data from devices, and control the appliances. It shows also the system has been offline. Figure 9 shows the SMS received from the system of the total power and energy.

4.2 Discussion

Due to the growing demand for efficient and sustainable utilization of energy, SEMS got a lot of attention in recent years. In order to optimize energy usage across a variety of domains, including residential, commercial, industrial, and governmental institutions, SEMS is a technology-driven method that combines cutting-edge algorithms, data analytics, and intelligent sensors [11].

As illustrated on the web dashboard in Figs. 6 and 7, the study's findings demonstrated that the nodes of each area, such as the administrative zone, CoCSE lab, and LISBE/MEWES lab, provided the status in real-time, the power consumption, current, voltage, and frequency. Using a website and a mobile application, the smart system gave the ability to the users to turn on and off various appliances such as lights, fans, and air conditioners as shown in Fig. 8. Then, as illustrated in Fig. 9, the GSM can send an SMS. Even if the internet is down, the user can still be informed about the status of the equipment.

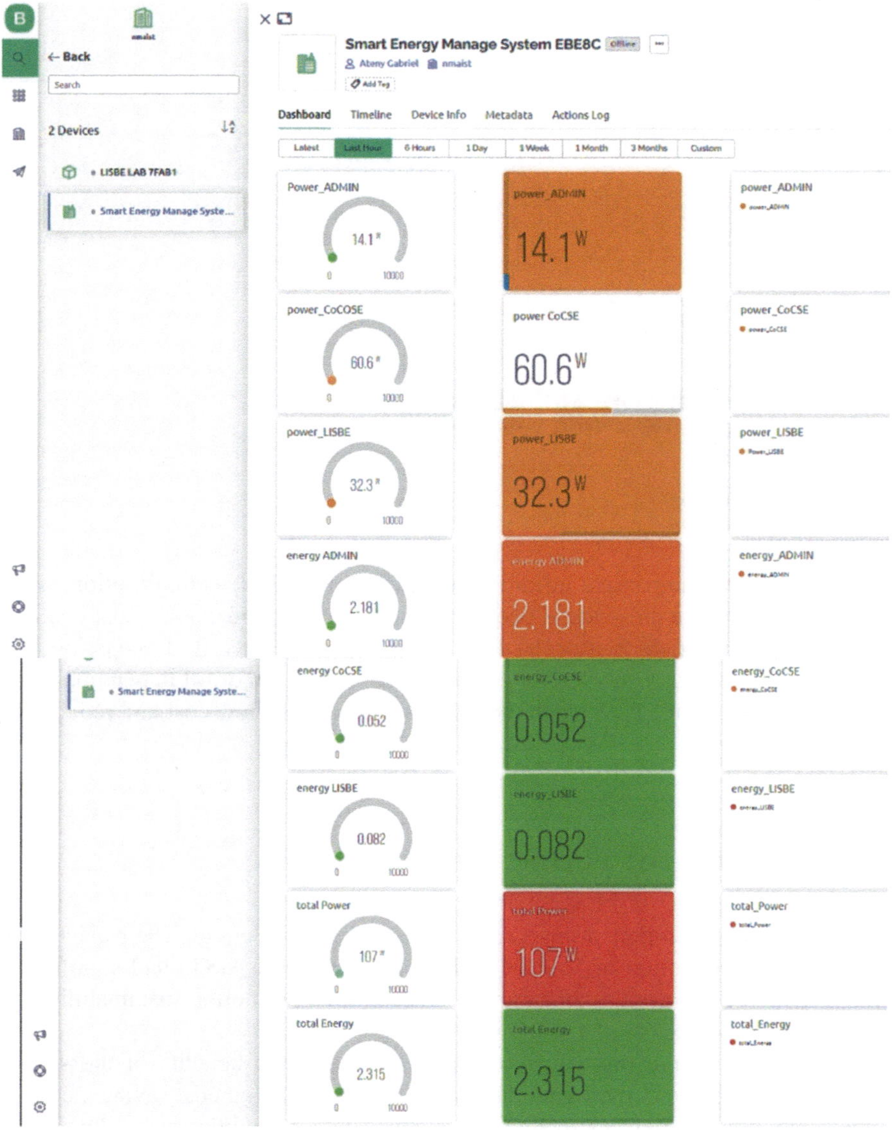

Fig. 6 Administrator interface

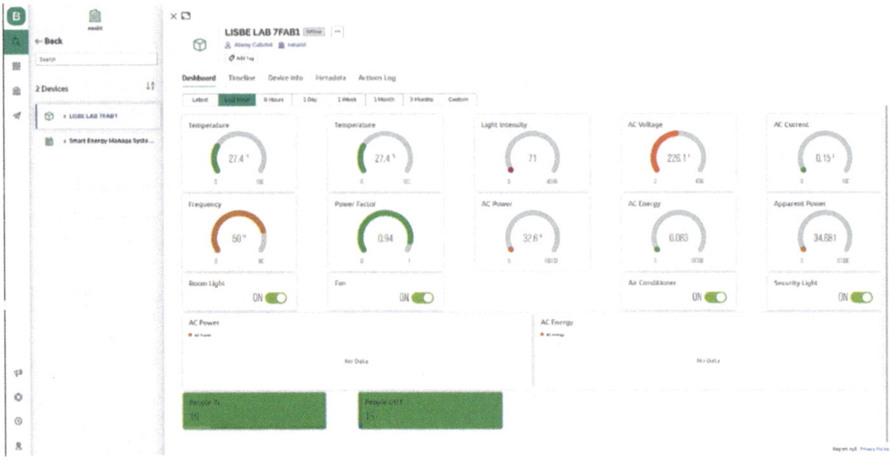

Fig. 7 Web dashboard

Furthermore, the passive infrared sensor (PIR) aids in detecting motion, which helps to identify the presence of people within the offices and classrooms; while the light-dependent resistor sensor (LDR) measures light intensity. Both scenarios allow the user admin to choose whether to keep all appliances on or off depending on the number of occupants. As a result, the SEMS was reliable, low cost and reduced the energy wastage.

5 Conclusion and Further Works

In conclusion, developing a smart energy management system for The Nelson Mandela African Institution of Science and Technology (NM-AIST) had significantly more advantages for optimizing energy consumption, promoting sustainability, and extending cost-effectiveness of the institution.

The findings from this paper highlight the numerous benefits of the system, including reduced energy waste, the potential for substantial cost savings, controlling some of the appliances such as lights, fans, and air conditioners, and generated real-time live data that can be visualized online via a web dashboard and mobile application. Also, the system was able to send a message via GSM when there is a failure of the internet. Furthermore, the system was developed not to meet only the predefined institution, but it could be used for all high institutions, industries.

For future works, there is a need to interface the camera with the PIR sensor to avoid the instability caused by the sensor operation and to integrate machine learning for energy consumption prediction.

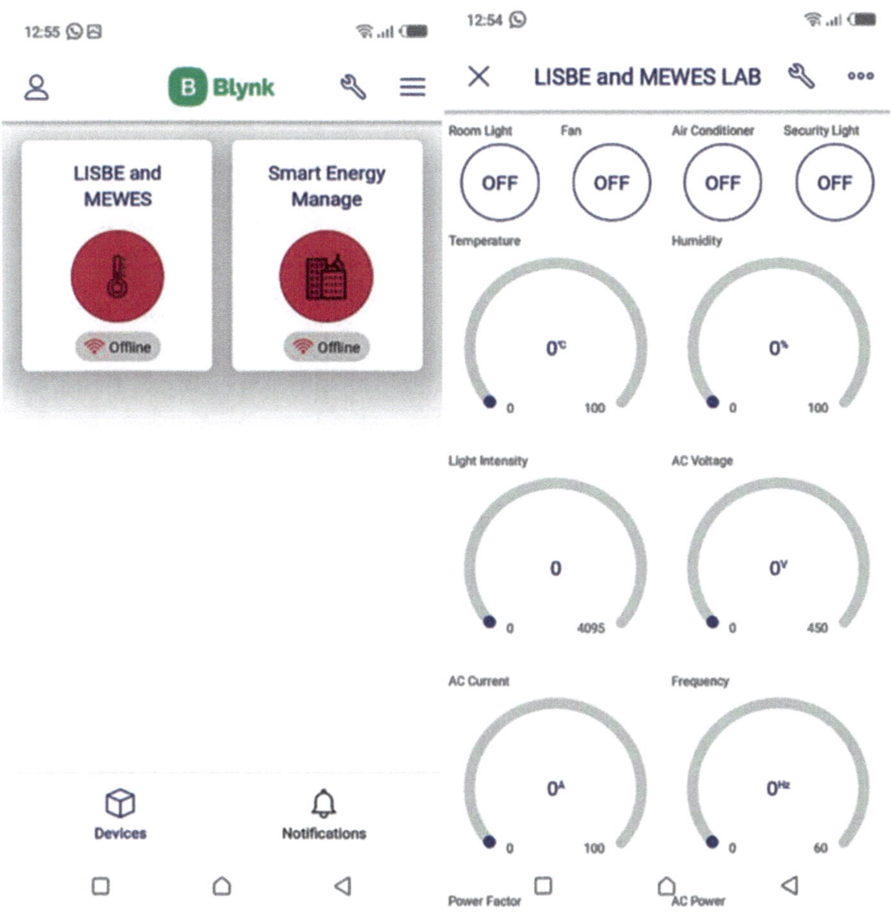

Fig. 8 Mobile application

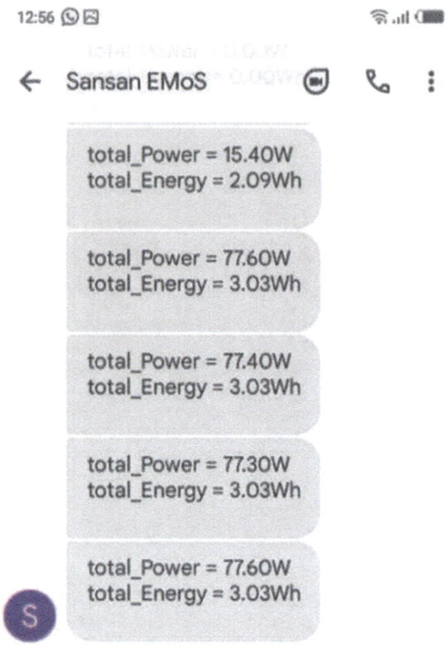

Fig. 9 SMS from GSM

References

1. Pavana, A. T. Pradeepthi. (2017). Multi are load frenquency control of power system involving renewable and non-renewable energy sources. *International Conference on innovations in Power and Advenced Computing Technologies,* pp. 1–5.
2. IEA. (2021). *Global energy review:C02 emissions in 2021*. International Energy Agency.
3. IEA. (2021). *Net zero by 2050: A roadmap for the global energy sector*. International Energy Agency.
4. M. O. F. Affairs-Netherlands. (2018). *Final energy report Tanzania*. Netherlands Enterprise Agency.
5. Marinakis, V., & Doukas, H. (2018). An advanced IoT-based system for intelligent energy management in buildings. *MDPI Sensors, 18*(2), 610.
6. N. A. O. Tanzania. (2019). *Report of the controller and auditor general on the consolidated and separate financial statements of Tanzania Electric Supply Company Limited (TANESCO)*. National Audit Office.
7. Collins, K., Mallick, M., Volpe, G., & Morsi, W. G. (2012). Smart energy monitoring and management system for industrial applications. In *2012 IEEE Electrical Power and Energy Conference* (pp. 92–97). IEEE.
8. Prakash Pawar, P. V. K. (2019). Design and development of advanced smart energy management system integrated with IoT framework in smart grid environment. *Journal Energy Storage -ELSERVIER, 25*, 100846. https://doi.org/10.1016/j.est.2019.100846
9. Surya, P., Gunalan, K., & Sai Sachin, G. (2018). *Smart institutions using energy management system* (pp. 459–464). IEEE.

10. Mehmood, Y., Ahmad, F., Yaqoob, I., Adnane, A., Imran, M., & Guizani, S. (2017). Internet-of-things-based smart cities: Recent advances and challenges. *IEEE Communications Magazine, 55*(9), 16–24.
11. Tanzania Electric Supply Company Limited. (2019). *Electricity bill*. Tanzania Electric Supply Company Limited.

Development of the Web-based Data-driven University Information Management System (UIMS) for the Inter-University Council for East Africa (IUCEA)

Abel Nshimiye, Mussa Dida Ally, Silas Steven Mirau, and Ben Ruhinda

1 Introduction

The conviction that education is one of the most powerful and proven engines for sustainable development is reaffirmed by achieving inclusive and high-quality education for all. The purpose of education is to achieve the success of a society which we can define as measuring how successfully the community meets the needs of its members [1].

The EAC is an African region that brings Burundi, Kenya, Rwanda, South Sudan, Tanzania, and Uganda into variant modes of economic partnership. The eventual dream is to achieve a political alliance [2]. The EAC, as a union of Uganda, Kenya, and Tanzania, was established in 1967. The partnership did not take long since it collapsed in 1977, but after a few years, in 1999, it was re-established. Burundi and Rwanda joined the community in 2007, and South Sudan followed in 2016 [3].

EAC aims to provide elite education to United Nations Member States. The EAC member states signed the treaty to expressly pursue deliberate steps to encourage collaboration in education and training in the community in a cooperative effort to foster the development of higher education. In addition, the agreement concerns harmonizing education and training systems for comparability and compatibility among partner nations [4]. The contribution to the development of higher education, professional and affordable training, elimination of equitable gender and wealth gaps, and achieving universal access to high-quality higher education is provided by EAC through the IUCEA in the region.

A. Nshimiye (✉)
Princeton University, Princeton, NJ, USA
e-mail: nshimiyea@nm-aist.ac.tz

M. D. Ally · S. S. Mirau · B. Ruhinda
Springer Heidelberg, Heidelberg, Germany

J. Marx Gómez et al. (eds.), *Smart and Secure Embedded and Mobile Systems*,
Progress in IS, https://doi.org/10.1007/978-3-031-56603-5_20

Furthermore, the IUCEA must develop a tool to harmonize the education and training system in the EAC region. According to [5], the tool will be a framework that will stipulate the easy mobility of learners and labor in the community, which will be called the East African Community University High Education Information System (EACHEIS). The final report on the EACHEIS submitted to the IUCEA by individual consultant Prof. Venansius BARYAMUREEBA in July 2020 presents that the EACHEIS shall integrate four modules. (a) EAC Academic Programs Information Management System (EACAPIMS); will be used by universities and university colleges to submit curricula for review or approval before being operational and publishing approved curricula. (b) EAC Universities Information Management System (EACUIMS) manages information for accredited or licensed Universities and University Colleges. (c) The EAC Human Capital Information Management System (EACHCIMS) should derive its information from the National Human Capital Information Management Systems. (d) EAC Research Information Management System (EACRIMS) should derive its information from the National Research Information Management Systems.

This paper aims to present the development of the web-based data-driven University Information Management System (UIMS) for the IUCEA, the second module of the EAC HEIS. First, the project's background, the objective has been explained. Then, related work, technology, and method used to integrate the system are described in the following session.

2 Related Work

The study made by [6] examines the influence of policy environments, system design, and leadership on the performance of state higher education systems, using case studies of seven large and diverse state higher education systems: California, Florida, Georgia, Illinois, Michigan, New York, and Texas, starting by an overview of the evolution of state higher education governance structures. This study illustrates the differences in system design and policy environments among states. The study presents the state context, characteristics, and history of higher education; the creation of the higher education-state government interface; and work processes, including information management, the budget process, program planning and review, and system articulation. This study has reported that the difference between the performance observed across the seven systems is related to system design and policy environments. The lack of direct communication between the system and universities is the main problem with the system's functionality. As a result, the system got different information which was supposed to do the same thing.

The study by [7] at seven UK higher education institutions focuses on knowledge management. Even the complexity of Higher Education Institutions within the United Kingdom has insite the universities in today's knowledge economy with a dichotomy of priorities that aims to provide quality teaching and research activity.

However, this study does not involve the use of ICT in the knowledge management process, which wastes time. Furthermore, the lack of ICT in the process causes hard work in evaluating the process since the records are not well-tracked.

Gulf Cooperation Council (GCC) nations have integrated ICT into their education systems, according to research by [7]. ICT-based education has been a driver for developing national innovation systems (NIS) and RDI capacities. The study shows that the GCC countries have the institutional capacity in ICT, which is not used for knowledge development because of limitations imposed by the cultural contexts for education in the Gulf. Finally, this study recommends ways GCC teachers can use ICT to create national innovation systems and research capacity.

3 Method

3.1 Web Technology

In short, called web technologies, the world wide web technologies refer to how computers or devices communicate using markup languages. It is communication across the web and creating, delivering, or managing web content using a HyperText Markup Language (HTML) [8].

When we talk about web technology, we have two types of computers called Server or Backend and Client or Frontend, which must communicate through the Internet, as demonstrated in Fig. 1. The backend is the part that runs on a web server and is responsible for data processing and validating business rules. The front end is the part loaded inside a web browser on a client machine; it is the part the user sees and interacts with it. At the same time, HyperText Transfer Protocol (HTTP) defines data exchange, basically how clients and servers communicate, which involves the client sending an HTTP request to the server and receiving an HTTP response [9].

To build the backend for the website, we need to decide how we will respond to clients. One option is to generate the requested page on the server and return it to

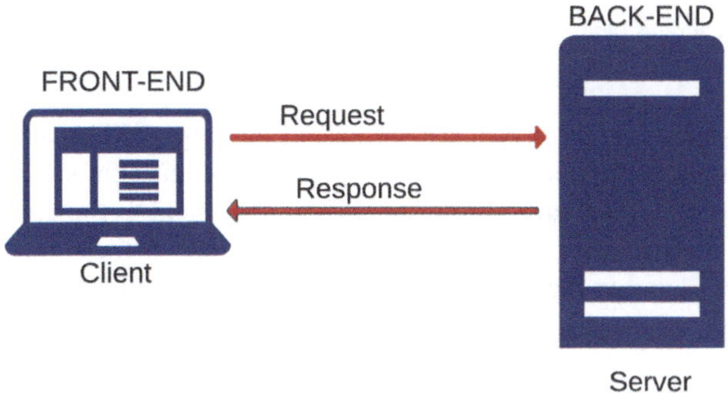

Fig. 1 General concept of web technology [10]

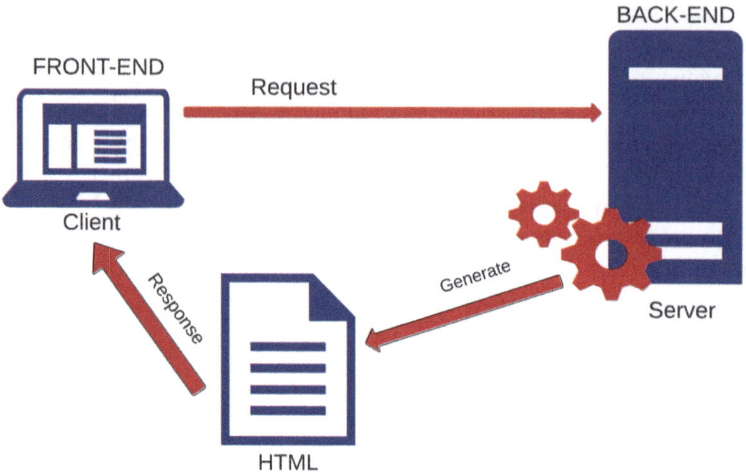

Fig. 2 First approach of responding to the client by generating an HTML file

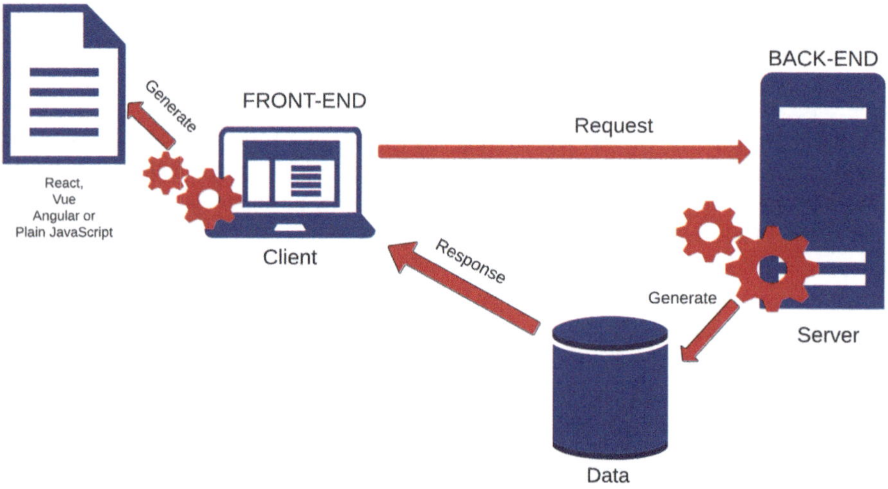

Fig. 3 Server generates data, and the client generates a file to present data [10]

the client (Fig. 2). We use HyperText Markup Language (HTML) for that. HTML is a simple language for representing web pages and their content. Technically, the server generates the page and returns an HTML document to the client.

The other option is to return only the data needed on the requested page and have the client generate the page. Instead of putting a complete page or a complete HTML document in an HTTP response, we only return the data as shown in Fig. 3.

This approach frees up the server, enables it to serve more clients, and makes it more scalable. The server becomes a gateway to the data. On the server, we can provide endpoints the client can talk to get or save various pieces of data. Together,

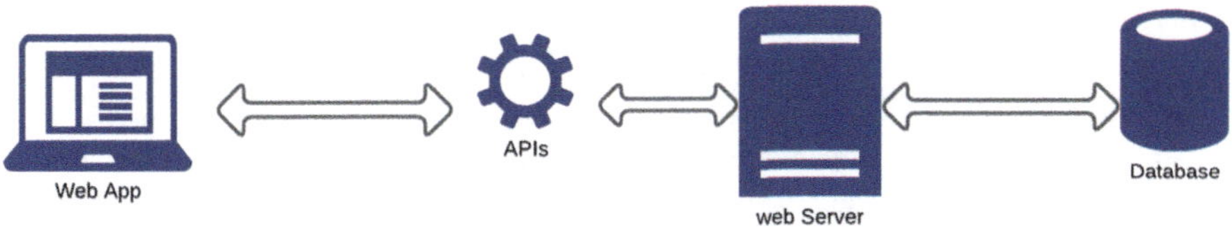

Fig. 4 Illustration of the web APIs programming [10]

these endpoints represent the clients' interface to talk to the server. In technical terms, the server serves the client with an Application Programming Interface (API).

This approach has been used to develop this project; react generates web pages on the client-side (Frontend), and the server-side (Backend) has been developed using the Django REST framework.

3.1.1 Web APIs

An application Programming Interface (API) is an interface for software, a point where two programs may meet and interact (Fig. 4). API is often used to name the whole software product, including the API and its implementation [11].

3.2 Requirements Analysis

The requirement engineering process describes the next stage: requirement analysis, after requirements elicitation or gathering. Both functional and non-functional requirements have been analyzed to understand the need for the proposed system.

3.2.1 Non-Functional Requirements

Non-functional requirements set the criteria and define the performance attribute of the system according to how the system has to function; it defines how the system is supposed to be [12]. Finally, Table 1 describes all quality attributes the developed system will have.

3.3 Agile Software Development

During the development of this project, we used agile development methodology for a continuous iteration of the development and testing of the variable prototype. There will be a continuous improvement at each system stage [13]. Among the

Table 1 Non-functional requirements of the proposed system [10]

No	Requirements	Description
1	Security	The system should permit only authenticated universities to access and modify information submitted by these universities. Each university should view and modify the information concerning their universities.
2	Robustness	The system has been developed to reduce the impact of operational mistakes, hardware errors, and erroneous input data.
3	Testability	The system has been developed upon different frameworks, which accept the modularity and structuredness approach. Therefore, the testability of the developed system depends on it.
4	Usability	The proposed system should be usable to IUCEA and let the institution automate many actions in high education. In addition, IUCEA should enjoy the easy way to operate the system should bring.
6	Reusability	The proposed system should fulfill all functions defined in the final report about the high education information system.
7	Performance	The system will support numerous statuses concurrently and handle different users without disappointment.
8	Maintainability	The system shall be suitable for debugging, the extension of functionality, and modification. In addition, the proposed system should allow the integration of new technology and easily update the functionality.
9	Extensibility	The system shall allow required modifications at the appropriate locations to be made without undesirable side effects.

different approaches of agile software development such as scrum, crystal methods, adaptive software development, extreme programming, and learn development [14].

3.3.1 SCRUM Agile Methodology

During the development of this project, we used the SCRUM agile methodology (Fig. 5) approach to have good time management since this methodology evaluates the progress of the project day by day.

3.4 Architectural Design

3.4.1 Conceptual Design

Conceptual Design is defined by [15] as an umbrella term for all non-aesthetic design management displaces. Figure 6 presents an initial phase of the design process, which articulates the general lines of software function and structure.

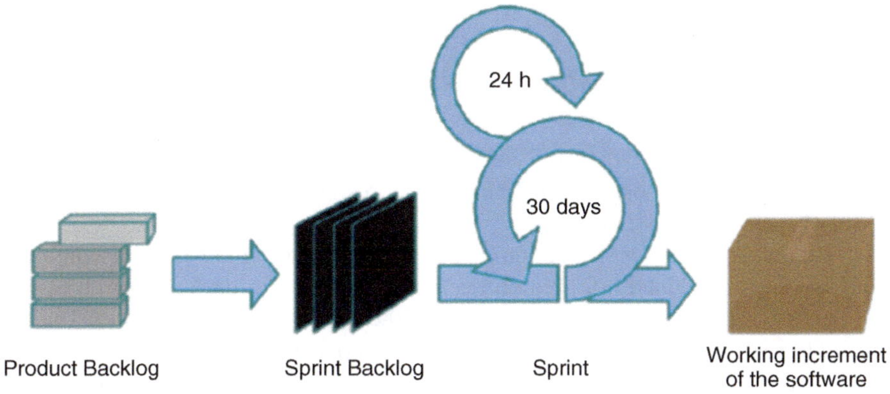

Fig. 5 Diagram of scrum agile method [14]

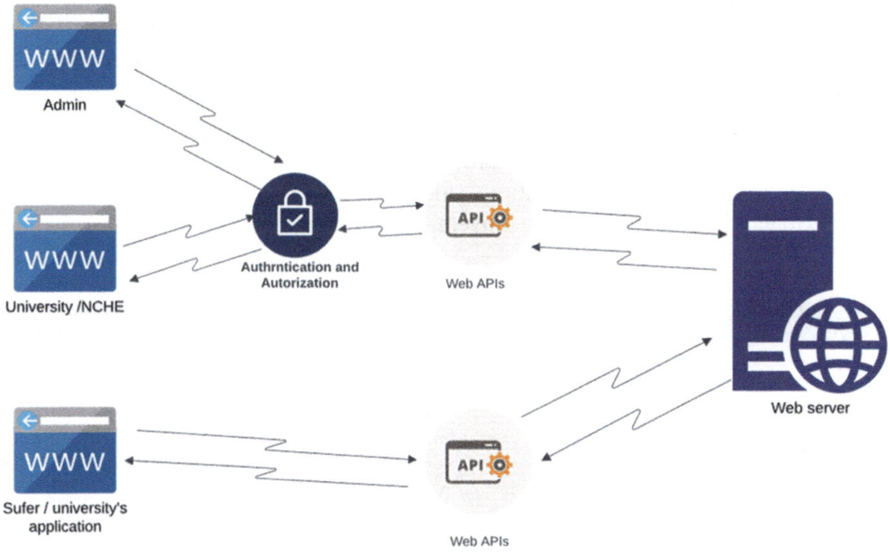

Fig. 6 Conceptual diagram [10]

The proposed web-based university information management system will manage four types of users: the overall admin, Universities, the National Commission for High Education (NCHE), and Surfer. All those users will be able to access the information of universities concerning academic life cycle, human resources, assets, and finance through the role-based access control (RBAC) model.

4 Results

4.1 *Public Dashboard Design Section*

The public dashboard displays information subdivided into three submodules: academic life cycle, cost of study, and human resources. Figure 7 shows the home page of the shared dashboard.

The academic life cycle section displays enrollment, graduation, discontinued, and schools abandoned information per academic year for each state and, overall, by gender, nationality, and thematic area of the East African community. The cost of study section displays statistical information concerning the cost of the study in EAC's state. The last displays statistical information concerning human resources by gender, specification area, and group age.

4.1.1 University Application Portal Design Section

The Status of high education report reported that IUCEA works with a hundred and thirty-three (133) institutions in EAC. On the other hand, within EAC, there are more than that reason we design a portal to help universities apply for being among all degree-awarding higher education. This portal will receive all information about universities. Figure 8 presents the universities application portal.

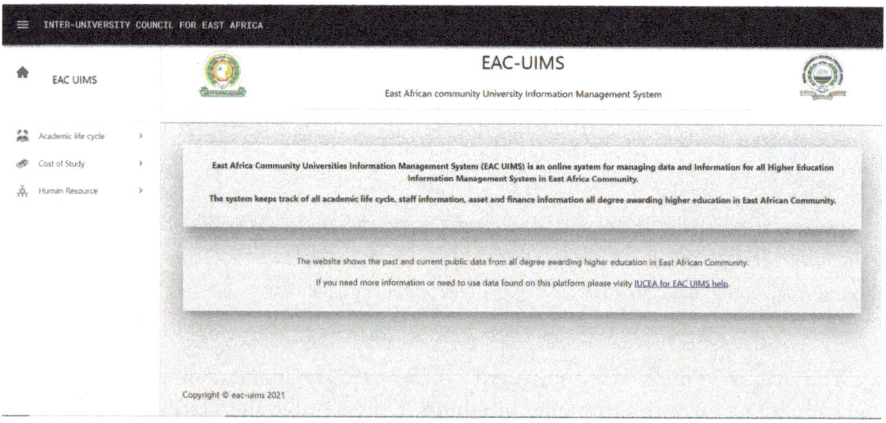

Fig. 7 Home page of the public dashboard [10]

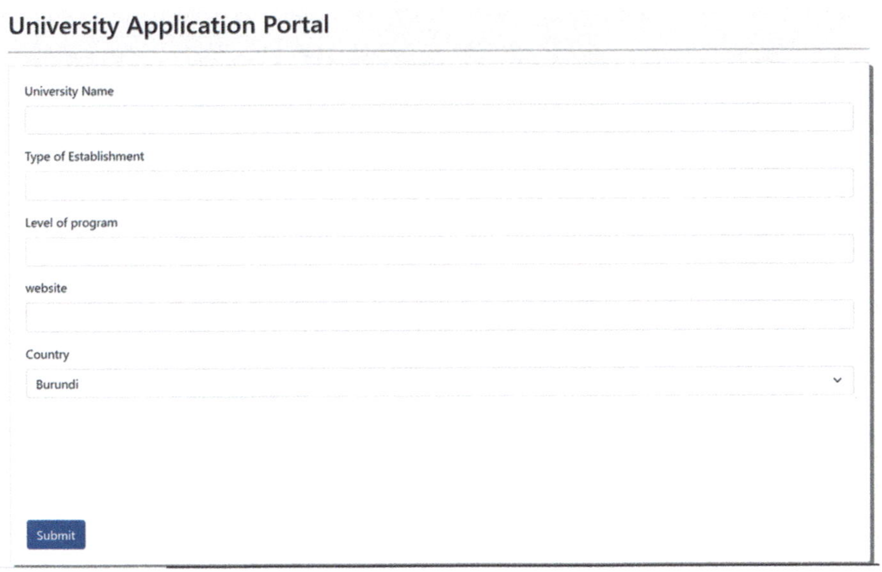

Fig. 8 University application portal

4.1.2 University Portal Design Section

All degree-awarding high education should feed the system by submitting information about assets, academic life cycle, finance, and human resource. Of course, that information can also come from Nation Commission High Education (NCHE) Systems within each country. The proposed portal has been designed assuming all information comes directly from universities. Otherwise, many propositions have been given of how the system will get valid data.

All universities must be known before submitting the information starting with the university login page. Figure 9 shows the login page of the universities.

4.1.3 User Acceptance Testing Result

User acceptance testing involves testing the developed system with dummy data to inspect that the system meets the requirements defined by the final report about EACHEIS. Under this, different levels of management had to test the developed system to determine whether or not the developed system was ready to be accepted for use and deployed in the client's environment. The respondents found the system impressive and could yield positive results. In addition, the system offered outstanding contributions such as a better management information system and better decision-making support.

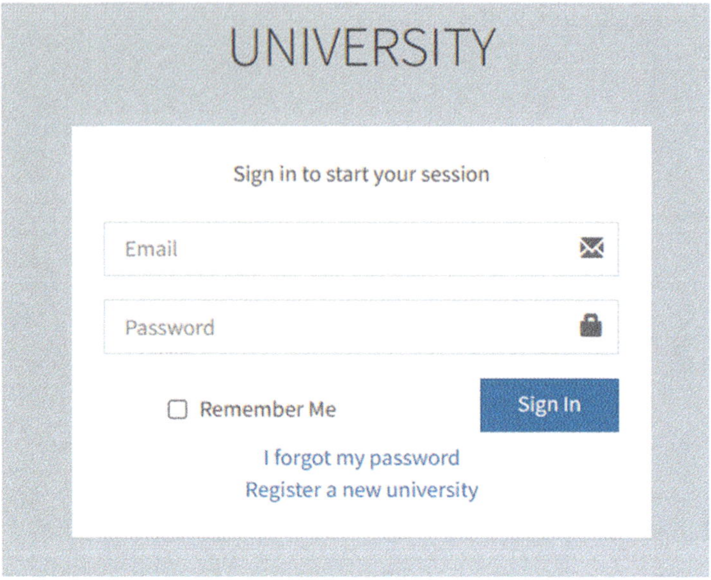

Fig. 9 University login portal

The higher education experts of the IUCEA were clustered into 3 (three) clusters, i.e., All Staff, the ICT team, and the Quality assurance team. The purpose of this clustering was to collect domain-specific data. For this study, we got fifteen (15) responses from who are the staff of IUCEA and are fully involved in the harmonization of education and training systems in East Africa. At the time of data collection, the Quality Assurance Unit had one (01) female, the ICT unit had two (02) members, and 12 respondents filled out the questionnaire for all staff, 41.7% male and 58.3% female.

Table 2 contains user acceptance testing results from different users on the public dashboard interface, which helps the surfer know extra information about universities in the EAC region.

4.2 Discussion

The developed UIMS has fulfilled all requirements reported by Prof. Venansis BARYAMUREEBA within the final report on the Status of the EACHEIS. The system is suitable to support higher education within the EAC region. Its suitability is the required goal for higher education, where IUCEA will use information about higher education from the EAC region. The system is the continuous development of EAC HEIS, which will help the IUCEA support higher education activities in the EAC region. The EAC HEIS as one stops live repository for information and

Table 2 User acceptance testing results for the public dashboard [10]

	Respondents			
	Strong agree (%)	Agree (%)	Disagree (%)	Not sure (%)
The web application is easy to use	75	25	0	0
The appearance of the web application is user friendly	100	0	0	0
The interfaces are well organized	75	25	0	0
The purpose of the system is well implemented.	70	30	0	0
The system is comfortable to use.	65	30	0	5

data will allow IUCEA to generate regional reports for partner states and member universities of higher education status and dynamics. Moreover, EAC UIMS, as a second module, has successfully been developed to produce public and private data visualization reports.

However, EAC and IUCEA should establish a legal framework before the developed system operates within EAC's state. As reported, EAC should implement the EAC access to information and data law, and IUCEA should implement the IUCEA policy framework and EAC regional policy for higher education information and data management.

5 Conclusion

The project aimed to improve higher education in the EAC region by designing the second module of EACHEIS called EAC UIMS. Since EAC PIMS has been designed as the first module to deal with higher education programs in the EAC region, the EAC UIMS has been designed to manage the academic life cycle, finance, assets, and human resource within the universities in EAC region.

However, data needed by the developed system will come from NCHE and universities. The NCHE will help validate data from national universities, and all degrees awarding high education will share data needed by the system that are not in the NCHE databases. During the development, we did not contact a survey to learn more about the different data-managed systems of different NCHEs. Therefore, we assumed that all data needed by the system would come directly from all degree-awarding high education.

The developed system will help IUCEA manage higher education in the EAC region and all users to know the universities' public information. Considering the system's data where the universities upload information about academic, finance, and human resource, the system allowed the public to visualize the academic life cycle, the cost of the study, and staff information statistically.

References

1. Bass, B. M. (1997). Does the transactional - transformational leadership paradigm transcend organizational and National Boundaries? *The American Psychologist, 52*(2), 130. https://doi.org/10.1037/0003-066X.52.2.130
2. Baariu, S. N., Mulaku, G. C., & Siriba, D. N. (2019). State of cartographic services among the east African community member states. *Journal of Geographic Information System, 11*(01), 56. https://doi.org/10.4236/jgis.2019.111005
3. The Eac Common Market. (2017). In *East African Community Law*
4. O'leary, Z. (2017). *The essential guide to doing your research project*. Sage.
5. Ng'ingo, G. A. (2019). *Assessment of the implementation of EAC common market protocol on free movement of labor in Tanzania*. Mzumbe University.
6. Richardson, R. C., Jr., Bracco, K. R., Callan, P. M., & Finney, J. E. (1998). *Designing state higher education Systems for a new Century. Series on Higher Education*. ERIC.
7. Wiseman, A. W., & Anderson, E. (2012). ICT-integrated education and national innovation systems in the Gulf cooperation council (GCC) countries. *Computers in Education, 59*(2), 607–618. https://doi.org/10.1016/j.compedu.2012.02.006
8. Berners-Lee, T., Cailliau, R., Luotonen, A., Nielsen, H. F., & Secret, A. (1994). The world-wide web. *Communications of the ACM, 37*(8), 76–82.
9. Preist, C. (2004). A conceptual architecture for semantic web services. In *International Semantic Web Conference*, pp. 395–409.
10. Nshimiye, A. (2022). Development of the web-based data-driven university information management system (UIMS) for inter-university council for East Africa.
11. Robillard, M. P. (2009). What makes APIs hard to learn? Answers from developers. *IEEE Software, 26*(6), 27–34.
12. Chung, L., Nixon, B. A., Yu, E., & Mylopoulos, J. (2012). *Non-functional requirements in software engineering* (Vol. 5). Springer Science & Business Media.
13. Abrahamsson, P., Salo, O., Ronkainen, J., & Warsta, J., (2017). Agile software development methods: Review and analysis. CoRR, abs/1709.08439.
14. Way, T., Chandrasekhar, S., & Murthy, A. (2009). The agile research Penultimatum. In *Software Engineering Research and Practice* (pp. 530–536).
15. Andreasen, M. M., Hansen, C. T., & Cash, P. (2015). *Conceptual design*. Cham Springer International Publishing.

An Expert System Model for Animal Welfare for Bovine Cattle Dehydration Risk Detection Using Precision Livestock Farming

Silvia Molina, Emilio Luque, and Dolores Rexachs

1 Introduction

The Internet of Things (IoT) is part of the Internet of the future [1], the future of the Internet will consist of heterogeneously connected devices that will further extend the borders of the world with physical entities and virtual components. Actually, the IoT is present in the urban big areas and it is extending to rural areas increasingly, they combined with Artificial Intelligence (AI), particularly, expert systems [2] help to improve the people's quality of life as well as they help to improve the efficiency, productivity, and security of many businesses.

In the agricultural production field, mainly in bovine cattle production, there is interest in improving livestock practices regarding sustainability, animal welfare (AW), social and economic impacts. The IoT is increasingly contributing to these interests.

Furthermore, it is observed that one of the essential factors that substantially enriches this interest is the set of knowledge emerging from the multidisciplinarity of sciences, computer science being an important field for this purpose. The Precision Livestock Farming (PLF) is an example of this.

The PLF is new paradigm that is increasingly applied to rural areas, it is another alternative or a complementary way for traditionally managing a farm. The PLF

S. Molina (✉)
Computational Intelligence Research and Development Lab., University, National of San Luis, San Luis, Argentina

Fac. of Informatics, University National of La Plata, La Plata, Argentina
e-mail: smolina@unsl.edu.ar

E. Luque · D. Rexachs
Computer Architecture and Operating Systems Department, University, Autonoma of Barcelona, Barcelona, Spain
e-mail: emilio.luque@uab.es; dolores.rexachs@uab.es

J. Marx Gómez et al. (eds.), *Smart and Secure Embedded and Mobile Systems*, Progress in IS, https://doi.org/10.1007/978-3-031-56603-5_21

combines basically the agricultural sciences with information and communication technologies as IoT such as: the geolocation and sensors [3, 4].

The use of PLF has shown that it favors the increase in production and AW, reduces investment costs, and allows timely resolution of problems [5].

From the National Institute of Agricultural Technology of Argentina (INTA) [6], they understand the PLF, in a broad sense, as the process of collecting information, automating procedures, robotization and miniaturization of technology to obtain data, in order to generate greater efficiency, time savings in processes, sustainable management of resources, improvements in competitiveness, cost reduction, and enhancement of the added value and quality of products.

[7] denotes that the aim of PLF is to manage individual animals by continuous real-time monitoring of health, welfare, production or reproduction, and environmental impact. This would allow farms with large numbers of animals, large-scale producers, to improve their management and know their animals in a similar way to the knowledge that small producers can have [8].

The devices of PLF such as sensors, monitoring devices, and electronic caravans can be placed on different cattle environment places, e.g. in drinkers, stalls and pens, inclusive they can be placed on the animal's own body, such as in ears, neck, even inside body. This way, it's possible to gather animal state information such as: if the animal is at rest or in motion, if it is in heat and its position; and its environment, e.g. if the drinkers have water, the temperature and humidity of the place, if there are animals in a certain place. Next, this information can be processed through some analysis service in some cloud computing platform, inclusive an expert system to later be used in decision making.

The AW [9, 10] refers to how an animal copes with conditions in its environment.

An animal is in good welfare conditions if it is healthy, comfortable, well fed, safe, able to express its innate forms of behavior and if it does not suffer from unpleasant sensations of pain, fear, or restlessness.

Producers and consumers consider that AW is an aspect that has a positive impact on the quality of products, which is why certification is increasingly sought as proof of quality [11].

Promoting AW implies adopting good management practices, preserving health through veterinary controls and zootechnical practices, maintaining adequate facilities, guaranteeing biosecurity, among other aspects.

More specifically, one of the basic premises on which the AW is based is that the five freedoms of animals must be respected [9, 12, 13], that is: (1) freedom from hunger, thirst, and malnutrition, (2) free from fear and sustained stress, (3) free from discomfort, (4) free from pain, injury, and/or sickness, and (5) free to manifest natural behavior, contributing to the welfare of the animal and thus to the maximizing your productivity.

Regarding water, animals must have access to a supply of water that is chemically and bacteriologically suitable for animal consumption in sufficient and adequate quantity so as not to suffer from thirst for a long time [14].

Monitoring the hydration of the animals is essential, since the lack of it can make the animal sick, causing dehydration, which in severe cases can cause death.

In the particular case in rural areas dedicated to extensive cattle production, provision of water is sought through dams and/or drinking fountains, which may be distributed in distant areas with difficult access and control such as forest areas. Animals instinctively turn to water, both to cool off and to drink. It may happen that for some eventuality, the animal cannot reach the water sources provided, such as due to a health problem that prevents its mobility, or may happen that the accesses to water provided are insufficient and are not covering the needs of the animal optimally.

Sometimes just water is not enough for the animal to be hydrated, it can happen that with certain climatic conditions, they suffer abundant loss of minerals through the elimination of liquids that can be irreparable.

Depending on the type of management of the cattle in a particular establishment, its infrastructure, the type of farm and the number of animals to observe, the detection of cases of dehydration in time or other conditions that are affecting the AW maybe inefficient, due to how complex it can be, including costly logistics activities that require a significant amount of time and personnel. For example, the animals's control activities, in areas with abundant mountains or with hills or dunes and without roads for vehicles, it is necessary means to use horses for put together gather the animals.

The PLF can be a complementary means and support to the current observation methods, for the people responsible for the care of the animals, for the detection of dehydration risk indicators, in early phases, allowing to create alerts and decision-making aids to act and avoid serious dehydration problems.

The objective of this work is to contribute to AW and consequently to improve bovine production, proposing a model of an expert system based on rules for bovine cattle dehydration risk detection using PLF considering farms dedicated to breeding, in an extensive livestock production system.

This model considers indicators of the physical condition of each animal and of the infrastructure of its environment, furthermore of the farm weather condition measurements that can be measured or sensed through the use of PLF. These measurements or data can be used directly or indirectly in the model through partial results of analysis services and monitoring ecosystem services provided in a Cloud Computing platform. The rest of this article is organized as follows: Sect. 2 describes aspects of behavior of bovine cattle in relation to water, questions are raised that, depending on the characteristics of the farm and its group of animals, accept diverse answers, in Sect. 3 are described aspects of dehydration in bovine cattle, symptoms and levels of dehydration; Sect. 4 describes the proposed model. Finally, the conclusions and future work are presented in Sect. 5.

2 Behavior of Bovine Cattle in Relation to Water

The behavior of bovine cattle, being herd animals, can be observed at the individual level or at the group level.

Bovine ethology is the science that is responsible for studying the behavior or spontaneous behavior of the bovine species and that today is applied through management techniques in livestock, due to the great utility it provides to the producer.

In addition to experts such as ethologists, veterinarians, nutritionists, and biologists, producers and animal care personnel are experts to consider due to their acquired experience, mostly through direct observation of cattle from a particular rural farm, providing knowledge that cannot be obtained directly through sensors.

Animals instinctively turn to water both to cool off and to drink, so water is an ally to prevent stress caused by excess heat. Dehydration due to lack of water can occur due to a failure in infrastructure, human or a health condition that prevents the animal from hydrating.

For to building the expert system, the system's designer keeps in mind the animal's need observed by those who daily care for livestock, that is from direct experience, needs such as: Number of days that they can go without drinking water, number of liters of water they usually drink per day which depends on many factors [14], this may vary depending on the breed of the animal, its age, its category: if it's cow, bull, or calf and its condition such as: if it's a cow with calves or if it's in heat; the natural environment where it lives; including the distribution of the infrastructure in the different grazing places and the weather conditions and its diet. Therefore, the observations serve to tune or adjust the expert system to a particular farm.

For example, in Argentina four different livestock regions are distinguished in terms of geographical characteristics and agricultural activities that are carried out, each of these with its own characteristics. Therefore, knowledge of the answers to these questions for a particular area is very important. San Luis is in the Argentine livestock region called Cuyo, according to the results of the agricultural census [15] and is characterized by contributing 5% of the national cattle related to breeding activity.

In the case of farms in the northern areas of San Luis, in the Department of Belgrano, in the town of Vizcacheras, an animal can spend up to 2 days without drinking water. One calf of cow, generally when it is very small, it can spend even more time without drinking water, since it hydrates through its mother's milk, which goes alone to drink water leaving his calf in the field. This is an area with bushes and trees, with a temperate semi-dry climate of the plains [16], characterized by low rainfall, these are less than 300 mm per year and predominate in the summer months, being in the decrease in recent years. It has very hot summers, reaching 45 degrees on extremely hot days and cold winters.

Although the calculation of water consumption is very complex due to the large number of factors that affect it, nutritionists have developed formulas to calculate it [14]. Today with technologies such as the Intraruminal Bolus it is possible to measure the water consumption of an animal [17].

With the use of PLF technology, particularly IoT, it is possible to have measurements of each one of the animals and thus its history can be obtained over time, as well as generate calculations to obtain measurements of the entire group and from these generate new knowledge through the expert system.

3 Aspects of Dehydration in Bovine Cattle

Dehydration is a deficit of body water and electrolytes due to decreased fluid intake i.e. loss of appetite or increased water loss.

For cattle to be hydrated, sometimes water alone is not enough, it may happen that animals suffer abundant loss of minerals through the elimination of liquids that may be irreparable, for example in certain unstable climatic conditions of temperature and humidity.

Dehydration due to fluid loss usually affects the amount of H2O that the animal has and the hydroelectrolytic balance, that is, the adequate amount of essential minerals for the correct functioning of the organism, such as: sodium, potassium, and magnesium, in addition to chloride, phosphate, and calcium.

The lack of certain infrastructure requirements or failures can prevent the animal from ingesting water on time, making the animal thirsty and in extreme cases enter a state of dehydration. For example, depending on the season of the year and the climate, it may happen that the distance an animal must travel between the grazing area and the watering place causes the animal not to go to drink water every day and does so when it feels a greater need for water when it starts to feel thirsty.

In the Subsect. 3.1 some symptoms that the bibliography mentions regarding dehydration are presented, next in the Sect. 3.2 the possible levels of dehydration are shown.

3.1 Symptoms to Detect Dehydration

At first, when the animal begins to show dehydration, they become somewhat surly or restless. However, they quickly go into inactivity, to save resources in their body and there comes a time when they do not move, neither to eat nor to drink, despite the fact that they need it.

Below some symptoms are enumerate that serve as a warning that animals may be suffering from a lack of sufficient amount of fluid in their body, that is than they are in risk dehydration: (a) Dryness in the mucous membranes or cracks in the nose is a symptom of fluid loss; (b) Regarding respiratory activity: if the animal is panting, it may be suffering from heat stroke; (c) Regarding its movement: the animal can go through a state of irritability followed by inactivity; (d) Regarding the eyes: if the animal's eyes are sunken or dull; (e) If when pinching the skin of the animal it does not have enough water, it is possible that the skin takes time to return to its initial position due to dryness; (f) Regarding weight, the loss of liquid is quickly manifested both in the volume and in the mass of the animal.

3.2 Dehydration Levels

Depending on the weight loss percentages of the animal, different levels of dehydration can be diagnosed [18]:

1. *Mild Dehydration*: If the loss of water or decrease in the weight of the animal is less than 5%. Symptoms of diarrhea, warm mucous membranes, oliguria, i.e. decreased urine output, and the hematocrit level is between 37% and 42%.
2. *Moderate Dehydration*: If the loss of water or decrease in the weight of the animal is between 5–10%. Sunken eyes can be seen, a persistent skin fold between 2 and 4 s, a marked oliguria, depression, and hematocrit level increases from 42 to 50%.
3. *Serious Dehydration*: If the loss of water or decrease in the weight of the animal is greater than 10%. With losses greater than 15%, a situation of hypovolemic shock can be triggered. When it is between 8 and 10%, the eyes are even more sunken, the skin fold persists for 6 to 10 s, the mucous membranes are dry and sticky, there are depression, anorexia, and anuria, i.e. much less urine excretion. If it reaches 10 or 12%, it is called very severe. The eyes remain pitted and the cornea dry, the skin fold persists for up to 45 s, the mucous membranes are dry, the anuria is much greater, and the cows no longer get up.

The model proposed and presented in the next section considers those animal symptoms mentioned that can be measured through PLF technologies, such as sensors.

In addition, measurements of the weather conditions and the state of the surrounding infrastructure, also provided by PLF, are considered.

4 Dehydration Risk Detection Expert System Model

This section presents the rule-based expert system model for the detection of dehydration risk in bovine cattle: The Dehydration Expert System (DES) whose architecture is shown in Fig. 1.

We considered a rule-based model because it adapts our case of studies, we consider it adequate to include both knowledge and experience of the different experts, as mentioned in Sect. 2, such as ethologists, veterinarians, nutritionists, and biologists, but mainly, the knowledge referring to a particular farm granted by producers and animal care personnel. Both the knowledge and the data stored in a Data Base are used by the inference engine through the rules.

The DES inputs, knowledge and data, are provided by experts and PLF technology, respectively. Regarding the data generated with PLF technology, to obtain it, IoT technologies such as sensor networks and devices with GPS are mainly used, in addition to some data analysis service to perform some intermediate calculation from PLF as in [17]. Regarding knowledge, this is obtained from information

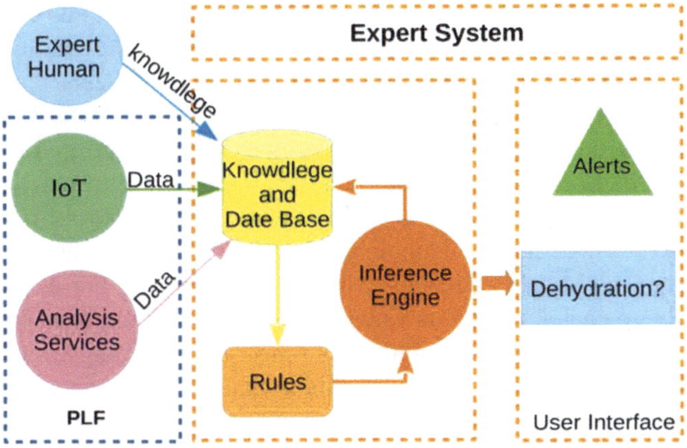

Fig. 1 Bovine dehydration risk detection experts system model

Table 1 Variables (Var) of the DES and its type (T) associated with the animal (A), associated one group of animals (G), at the infrastructure (I) and the weather conditions (M). In addition, the possible PLF technologies to be used are shown, we denote WS by Weather Station, GPS-C for Caravana with Global Positioning System, IB for Intraruminal Bolus, and ME for Ecosystem Monitoring

Var	T	Description	PLF technology
t_e	M	Environmental temperature	WS [19], Sensors [20]
h_e	M	Humidity	WS [19], Sensors [20]
d_w	I	Amount of water in the drinker	ME [17]
t_{dw}	I	Drinker water temperature	Sensors [20]
lp_w	I	Drinker water purity level	Sensors [20]
w	A	Body weight	Electronics Scales [21]
t_c	A	Body temperature	GPS-C [3], Sensors [22]
l_w	A	Liters of water consumed	GPS-C and IB [17]
km_w	A	Kilometers walked	GPS-C and IB [17]
t_w	A	Moving time	GPS-C and IB [17]
n_w	A	Number of times you drink water per day	GPS-C plus sensors for water [3, 20]
a_{ig}	G	Existence of isolated animals	GPS-C [3, 23]
v_a	G	Average entry speed of drinking group	GPS-C [3, 23]

provided by experts and refers to the range of possible values for each variable, those considered normal. The relationship between these variables can be expressed through rules.

Table 1 shows the variables (attributes) of the DES associated with the different types of data, being denoted with: M meteorological conditions variables, I Infrastructure variables, A variables for individual animal, and G variables for a group of animals. In addition, it shows possible ways of obtaining data with PLF technologies: Sensors, Electronics Scales, Weather Station (WS), Caravana with Global Positioning System (GPS-C), Intraruminal bolus (IB), and Ecosystem

Monitoring (ME). As can be seen with these sensed data, the aim is to determine if the animal has drunk enough, on time, and has not suffered fluid losses that indicate a risk of dehydration, bearing in mind aspects mentioned in Sects. 2 and 3.

The Inference Engine feeds back new knowledge to the Data Base in addition to answering the question: Is there a risk of dehydration? and giving warnings or alerts through the User Interface. The Data Base contains current and historical data on each one of the animals, these are Multi-Individuals and Multi-temporary data, in addition to storing relevant data on weather conditions and the infrastructure of the farm, these are Multi-entities and Multi-temporary data. For example, the data corresponding to each cow and its values in relation to time are of interest because it can even change inclusive its state over time, such as going from the pregnant state to cow with calf and this influences their values related to water consumption considered normal, generally cows when they are with calves they need to ingest more water because their body needs to produce milk.

The rules are determined in relation to a dehydration risk state detection protocol, through which the measurable aspects are described (in correspondence with the variables shown in Table 1). This protocol reviews aspects: the environment where cattle live (state of infrastructure, weather conditions), the state of the animal and its individual and group behavior. These revisions are described below:

- *Review of environmental conditions and the state of the water infrastructure.* The ambient temperature (t_e) and humidity (h_e) values are controlled in order to detect extreme heat situations, in addition to reviewing the availability of drinking water, the state of the watering places (drinking fountains, dams, etc.) is controlled through the control of its temperature, quantity, and level of purity (d_w, t_{dw} y lp_w).
- *Review of individual animal behavior.* The amount of water that an animal has taken per day (l_w), the frequency with which it drinks water, and when was the last time it drank water is controlled. Control of weight loss (w) in relation to the amount of urine that is estimated to be produced per day. Control of animal movement (km_w,t_w).
- *Review of the group behavior of animals.* Control of the average speed of the group (v_a) and the detection of isolated animals (a_{ig}).

5 Conclusions

We present a proposal for a rule-based expert system model, oriented to detect the bovine's dehydration risk in cattle farm with extensive production systems, combining the knowledge of human expert and PLF technology.

Using PLF technology, particularly IoT, it is possible to have measurements of each one of the animals and thus its history can be obtained over time, as well as generate calculations to obtain measurements of the entire group.

As future work, for the generation of knowledge, it is proposed to review known alternative techniques or combinations of these that best adjust to the reality of the field for the detection of risk situations in relation to the lack of water, to contribute to the preservation of AW.

Acknowledgments The first author acknowledges the continuous support of Universidad Nacional de San Luis through the Research Project PROICO 03-1018 and the Dept. of Informatics of this university.

The authors thank the Agencia Estatal de Investigación (AEI) Spain and the Fondo.

Europeo de Desarrollo Regional (FEDER) UE under contract PID2020-112496GB-I00.

References

1. Li, S., Xu, L. D., & Zhao, S. (2015). The internet of things: A survey. *Information Systems Frontiers, 17*, 243–259.
2. Gutiérrez, J. M. (2008). Sistemas Expertos Basados en Reglas. Tech. Rep. 1–12, Universidad de Cantabria. Dpto. de Matemática Aplicada.
3. Ormaechea, S. G., Peri, P. L., Cipriotti, P. A., Anchorena, J. A., & Huertas, L. (2012). Uso de collares GPS para Evaluar la Preferencia de Ovinos por Diferentes Ambientes en Patagonia Sur. II Congreso Nacional de Sistemas Silvopastoriles. Area 4: SSP a Escalas de Paisaje y Región.
4. Gorandi, E., Moltoni, A. F., & Clemares, N. (2016). Desarrollo y Evaluación de un Sistema de Monitoreo Animal Georreferenciado para Ganadería de Precisión, 3022–3027.
5. Ganadería de Precisión. (2018). Tech. Rep. 023, INCYTU, México.
6. Tallarico, G. A. (2021). ¿Qué es la ganadería de precisión?. Retrieved November 2022, from
7. Berckmans, D. (2017). General introduction to precision livestock farming. *Animal Frontiers, 7*, 6–11.
8. Werkheiser, I. (2018). *Precision livestock farming and Farmers' duties to livestock*. Springer Science+Business Media B.V., part of Springer Nature.
9. del Valle, M. P., Vicari, C., Faravelli, M. F., Glauber, C., & Winter, N. (2015). Manual de Bienestar Animal. In *Un Enfoque Práctico para el Buen Manejo de Especies Domésticas Durante su Tenencia, Producción, Concentración, Transporte y Faena. Versión 1, Winter edn.* SENASA, Nicolás.
10. Bousfield, B., & Brown, R. (2010). In B. Bousfield, R. Brown, M. Chow, & L. T. Ng (Eds.), *Animal welfare* (Vol. 1). *Agriculture, Fisheries and Conservation Department.*
11. Humane Farm Animal Care.(2018). PO Box 82, Middleburg VA 2018. *Normas de Bienestar Animal*, 21v2 edn. Friedrich, N. O. Bienestar Animal. Tech. Rep., Sitio Argentino de Producción Animal. www.produccion-animal.com.ar
12. Friedrich, N. O. (n.d.). *Bienestar Animal.* Tech. Rep., Sitio Argentino de Producción Animal. www.produccion-animal.com.ar
13. Animal Humane Society. (2022). The five freedoms for animals. Retrieved November 2022, from https://www.animalhumanesociety.org/health/five-freedoms-animals
14. González Martín, J. V. (2014). ¿Cuánta agua necesitan mis vacas? *Frisona Española.*
15. ValorCarne Información para la Nueva Ganadería. (2019). Censo agropecuario: El nuevo mapa ganadero nacional. Retrieved November 2022, from https://www.valorcarne.com.ar/censo-agropecuario-el-nuevo-mapa-ganadero-nacional/
16. GeoSL. (2022). Clima. Retrieved November 2022, from https://geo.ulp.edu.ar/Articulo/398/Clima
17. CARAVAN TECH. (2022). Ecosistema IoT Caravan Tech. Retrieved November 2022, from https://www.caravantechs.com/ecosistema/

18. CONtextoganadero. (2017). Estos son los Grados de Deshidratación en Bovinos. Retrieved November 2022, from https://www.contextoganadero.com/ganaderia-sostenible/estos-son-los-grados-de-deshidratacion-en-bovinos
19. Proyect Hub. (2022). IoT weather station using Arduino. Retrieved November 2022, from https://create.arduino.cc/projecthub/RucksikaaR/iot-weather-station-using-arduino-163911. https://lainholding.com/calidad-del-agua-iot/
20. Control IoT de la Calidad del Agua. (2022). Retrieved November 2022, from https://lainholding.com/calidad-del-agua-iot/
21. Vaca, C. (2021). Cómo es y Cómo Funciona la Balanza Inteligente para Bovino. Desarrollada por el INTA. Retrieved November 2022, from https://agrovedad.com.ar/2021/04/como-es-y-como-funciona-la-balanza-inteligente-para-bovinos-desarrollada-por-el-inta
22. Portal Veterinaria. (2009). El diario digital de los veterinarios. Nuevo Sensor de Vacas para Detectar Enfermedades. Retrieved November 2022, from https://www.portalveterinaria.com/actualidad-veterinaria/actualidad/100/nuevo-sensor-en-oreja-de-vacas-para-detectar-enfermedades.html
23. Ormaechea, S. G., Peri, P. L. & Ceccaldi, E. (2012). Uso Espacial de Vacunos Bajo Dos Tipos de Manejo Ganadero en Establecimientos con Bosque de Ñire (Nothofagus Antárctica). *II Congreso Nacional de Sistemas Silvopastoriles. Area 1: SSP a Escalas de Paisaje y Región.*

A Brief Introduction into (De-)Coupling Lifecycles in Net-Centric Systems-of-Systems

Johann Schütz and Jorge Marx Gómez

1 Introduction

The future viability of all artificially engineered systems is significantly influenced by their ability to evolve—their evolvability. Evolvability itself can be regarded as the long-term ability of an architecture of a given system (−of-interest) to adapt to change over time. How time and cost intensive such adaptations are, however, is significantly determined by the overall architecture or design of the respective system.

As historically isolated grown infrastructures coalesce within emerging domains/sectors such as the *Fourth Industrial Revolution*, *Internet of Things,* or *Smart Grids* into collaborative *Systems-of-Systems* (SoS), new higher-level structures with their own architecture are created. However, as the fundamental system concepts of holism and interaction theory suggest, these structures are governed by new paradigms [1, 2] that are not addressed by the traditional *Systems Engineering* (SE) approaches.

1.1 Motivation

From an SE perspective, an SoS is defined as a synergetic integration of several (managerial and operational) independent systems with the objective to realize

J. Schütz (✉)
OFFIS, Oldenburg, Germany
e-mail: johann.schuetz@offis.de

J. Marx Gómez
Carl von Ossietzky—Universität Oldenburg, Oldenburg, Germany

J. Marx Gómez et al. (eds.), *Smart and Secure Embedded and Mobile Systems*,
Progress in IS, https://doi.org/10.1007/978-3-031-56603-5_22

unique joint mission capabilities that none of the *Constituent Systems* (CS) could accomplish on its own [3]. Organizations or enterprises that participate in such an SoS—as so-called CS—or intend to do so in the future, need to embed their respective systems into these higher-level structures. Such an integration, however, changes the engineering paradigms. As systems within an SoS environment no longer operate in isolation, the CS have to meet their own requirements as well as the requirements of the SoS as a whole. However, as these kinds of systems (of systems) are characterized by an immense co-development, co-evolution as well as co-innovation, this requires a common point of reference. If the manifold solutions of the heterogeneous CS are developed in parallel and not viewed from a holistic point of view, innovations emerge locally and uncoordinated resulting in an unmasterable complexity of the overall architecture—unwanted dependencies with a multitude of undesirable side effects for both the SoS and the CS are the inevitable consequence. In consistence to Lehman's *Laws of Software and System Evolution* [4], the steadily increasing complexity will result in unbalanced productivity growth. If not adequately managed, the further evolution will be dominated by the cost and, therefore, lead to significantly higher costs in *CAPEX* and *OPEX*.

1.2 Problem Statement

Such strategical cost considerations are well-known and commonplace business decisions in the domain of *Software Engineering* (SwE). If such costs could have been prevented, these additional costs are classified as so-called *Technical Debt* (TD). TD commonly consists of design or implementation constructs that are expedient in the short term but that set up a technical context that can make future changes more costly or impossible [5]. However, while the traditional SwE can resort to a comprehensive knowledge base consisting of inter alia design and architecture patterns, design principles (e.g., SOLID principles for object-oriented software code) and best practices, these have yet to be explored for the SoSE [6–8].

Nevertheless, in general, interoperability has been identified as a key driver for the control and evolution of net-centric SoS [9, 10]. Vice versa, if interoperability is not sufficiently mature, it will constrain the evolvability of the overall SoS and lead to an accumulation of TD. Correspondingly, this contribution deals with the question: "*In what way does insufficient interoperability maturity lead to the coupling of CS within an SoS environment and how to overcome it.*"

1.3 Objective and Methodology

The main objective of this contribution is to assist the CS in their design decisions regarding interoperability and the potential impact on the evolvability, as well as on the avoidable dependencies by providing an appropriate methodology. At the same time, this contribution aims to sustain the complexity of the overarching SoS on a manageable degree. Considering the presented issue and the overall objective, this work follows the Design Science methodology that provides an appropriate framework, which in essence unites the scientific rigor with the practical relevance. While the practical relevance has already been presented and motivated, the scientific rigor is ensured by the inclusion of the state-of-the-art from various domains.

1.4 Related Work

Leveraging the concept of TD to the SoS level and scope is not a fundamentally novel approach and was first introduced in [11], which combines two research areas: TD and *SoS Engineering* (SoSE).

Within the combined areas of TD and SoSE, there are currently two distinct research directions. The first—based on the work of Schuetz and Marx Gómez in [11] —examines to which extent an SoS or more precisely its architecture can exhibit TD, what its distinctive traits are, and how this can be adequately addressed from a Systems (−of-Systems) Engineering point of view, with a focus on the evolvability of the SoS as a whole. While the second research direction—based on the work of Cadavid et al. in [12] —examines TD within the context of the interplay between SwE and SE during SoS architecting, with a focus on the evolvability of the underlying software systems from a CS point of view. Both research directions deal with different system levels, whereby the reductionistic assumptions of the CS perspective cannot be appropriately applied to the unique characteristics of an SoS and vice versa [8]. Thus, due to the focus on the evolvability of the SoS as a whole, this contribution adapts the SoS level perspective of Schuetz and Marx Gómez from [11].

Additionally, it has to be recognized that other domains are also exploring the impact of an insufficient interoperability in SoS. In particular, the results and findings of the *GridWise® Architecture Council* (GWAC) in [10, 13] are crucial. As these have been adopted in various domains later on with, e.g. the *Smart Grid Architecture Model* (SGAM) in 2012, the *Reference Architectural Model Industrie 4.0* (RAMI 4.0) in 2016 or the *Maritime Architecture Framework* (MAF) in 2017 [14, 15], these findings as well as the resulting models and/or frameworks have been taken into account as a key concept.

1.5 Organization

This paper is organized in five chapters. While the first section introduced and motivated the problems arising from tightly coupled systems in an SoS environment, Sect. 2 introduces the unique traits of tightly coupled systems in an SoS environment and in which way it affects the evolvability of the SoS. Then, Sect. 3 takes a more in-depth look into interoperability characteristics and, thus, into the higher-level interoperability requirements within the scope of SoSE. Subsequently, Sect. 4 provides a brief example of how different domains try to address these characteristics and associated requirements. Finally, Sect. 5 concludes this contribution.

2 The Lack of Interoperability as a Key Driver for Technical Debt in Systems-of-Systems

In order to ensure a manageable degree of complexity, interoperability—as the fundamental enabler of net-centric SoS—is considered as the key concept for the control and evolution [9]. Within the scope of the "traditional" Software and Systems Engineering, interfaces are (mostly) negotiated and implemented individually between the partners as required, resulting in a system landscape dominated by proprietary solutions based on their individual requirements [16]. Proprietary solutions, however, may work fine for their specific requirements, but prevent the (seamless) integration of additional systems, which necessitates individual integration and maintenance efforts and increases the overall complexity of the SoS [17]. Analogous to the concept of TD, proprietary solutions are coupling the lifecycles of the interacting systems by dependencies tightly, resulting in problems for the SoS as well as the CS. Proprietary solutions are leading to the trait, that new components or changing communication or business partners cannot be connected or exchanged without additional manual integration efforts, since a so-called *vendor lock-in* is created. Vendor-independent interoperability between the CS becomes inconceivable—the entrepreneurial risk increases, while the investment security decreases. [16]

As SoS are subject to a so-called *path dependency*, vendor lock-ins become particularly problematic. In systems that are path dependent, design decisions cannot be reversed easily, as the independence of the CS implies that these systems are typically not designed to optimize for SoS objectives [6]. Accordingly, the *Department of Defense (DoD) of the United States of America*, for example, recognized the cross-system interdependencies and the resulting political and cost considerations on technical issues as the most challenging aspect of SoSE [18].

As depicted in Fig. 1, due to the interdependencies between the CS, internal technical decisions of one CS may affect one or more directly or indirectly coupled other CS with the result that changes can only be made in collaboration. However, as each CS is represented by managerial and operational independent organizations with individual intrinsic interests and business objectives and the additional lack of a central authority over the CS, the diverse individual interests can rarely be aligned [6]. The different domains and heterogeneous systems along their respective value chains as well as the different levels of their automation chains of the different CS are characterized by diverging requirements, understanding of the problem and,

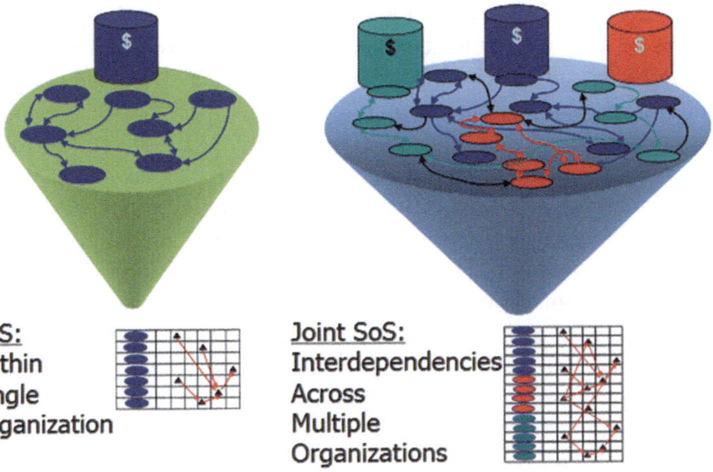

Fig. 1 Political and cost considerations on technical issues [18]

therefore, preferred solutions [19]. As a result, the interdependent CS rarely have an incentive to support changes.

3 (De-)Coupling Lifecycles in Systems-of-Systems Environments

Based on the *Open Systems Interconnection* (OSI) reference model, interoperability is traditionally considered as a mainly technical issue [20]. However, since the OSI reference model was officially introduced in 1983, the main issue at that time and, consequentially, the focus at that time was on technical connectivity and data transmission. In order to highlight the problems and associated challenges for SoS beyond the technical interoperability, the GWAC developed the so-called GWAC-Stack as a key component of the so-called *Interoperability Context-Setting Framework*. The GWAC-Stack extends the technical view of the OSI-Model and differentiates between three levels or views of interoperability "*Technical,*" "*Informational,*" and "*Organizational*" [13]. Within the scope of an SoSE, interoperability is the ability to exchange information (technical), to understand and interpret the information right (informational), and integrate them purposefully into the business functions and processes in compliance with the legal requirements of (e.g.) cross-border collaborations (organizational).

Coupling in general refers to an interdependence between (the lifecycles of) interacting elements/components. In this context, dependencies can arise in a wide variety of ways and can be both uni-directional and bi-directional. If systems are tightly coupled, one element cannot be changed without a direct or indirect effect on the coupled elements. On the other hand, elements that are loosely coupled can be changed without notice or at least be reduced to a minimum—saving a time-consuming re-engineering or—factoring. Unintended dependencies create an unnecessary design and architectural complexity—the accumulation of TD is the result. Within the SwE discipline the SOLID principles, for example, provide guidance on how to prevent different kinds of unwanted dependencies from a programming style perspective [21]. For example, the so-called *Dependency Inversion Principle* or P*attern* formulates a specific methodology for loosely coupling software modules [21]. Within the discipline of SoSE, on the other hand, such principles do not yet exist, although the consequential problems are already observable. The various independently developed solutions in the context of the *Fourth Industrial Revolution*, *Internet of Things*, or *Smart Grids* still lack an adequate level of interoperability beyond the technical level.

As most emerging SoS will have to cope with the integration of an unpredictable amount of heterogeneous systems from different domains [7], the ability for a so-called *seamless integration* and plug-and-play mechanisms will become indispensable. In an SoS it would be logistically impossible to coordinate between all CS with regard to their respective interfaces, as this would lead (in a hypothetical worst-case scenario) to a (design and development) complexity of N x M interfaces and a systems landscape characterized by proprietary solutions [17]. As Fig. 2 illustrates, the so-called "*Distance to Integrate*" decreases with the degree of standardization. Reducing the distance to integrate has a direct (positive) impact on the integration costs, as it creates well-defined integration points that enable a composability of CS with a reasonable amount of effort [13].

1. Absence of standards: The use of proprietary solutions or the absence of standards represents the greatest integration effort, as these usually result in complete individual integrations.
2. Mapping: The integration efforts can be reduced by the use of suitable middleware technologies, such as an *Enterprise Service Bus* (ESB). ESBs allow the mapping of incompatible data models and communication protocols—with a corresponding configuration effort.

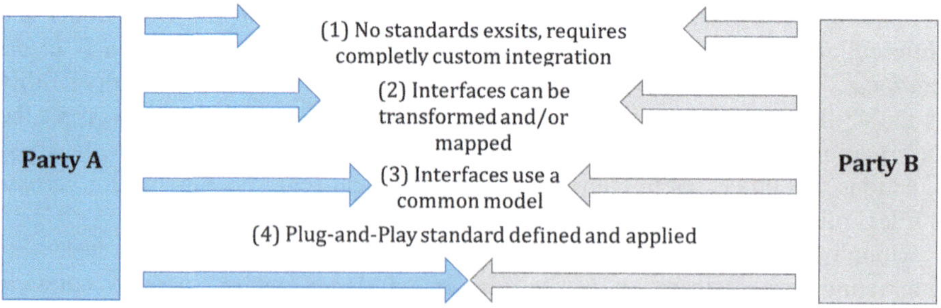

Fig. 2 Distance to integrate [13]

3. Shared models: The application of standardized information models reduces the configuration effort and the susceptibility to errors, since time-consuming, manual mapping, or the interface analysis required for this can be reduced to a minimum.
4. Plug-and-play: A *plug-and-play mechanism* with a correspondingly high quality of (well-defined) interfaces, the costs of integration, and possible sources of errors can be sustainably reduced or completely avoided.

In essence, these four stages can be understood as maturity levels for the degree to which extent standards are applied to realize interoperability in SoS environments.

Although Fig. 2 already differentiates between four interoperability maturity levels, the one-dimensional view of the "*distance to integrate*" alone is not sufficient to prevent vendor lock-ins completely. As standards are defined as "*something considered by an authority or by general consent as a basis of comparison; an approved model,* these are subject to a certain degree of "locality" that has to be considered as a secondary dimension of the maturity. For instance, an agreement or general consent can be reached at the project level as a (local) consortial standard, at the country level as a national standard, or at the international level as a global standard. Thus, a consortial standard does not necessarily have to be compliant to a national standard and a national standard does not have to be compliant to an international standard and vice versa. Although these three levels of locality are only intended to serve as examples, in general applies: while locality couples, globality decouples. If both dimensions are considered, a two-dimensional matrix can be derived as depicted in Fig. 3 as a simplified reference for the "*Degree of Coupling in SoS Environments.*"

Note: Beyond these two dimensions, the way how standards are governed is considered as an important aspect [17]. To this end, the GWAC, for example, distinguishes between five maturity levels for the governance of standards by their "Management," "Documentation," "Integration," and "Testing" [10]. Each aspect addresses different (potential) issues associated with standards and interoperability. However, although the relevance of the governance and its aspects has to be acknowledged, as these governance aspects correlate to the "*degree of coupling*"

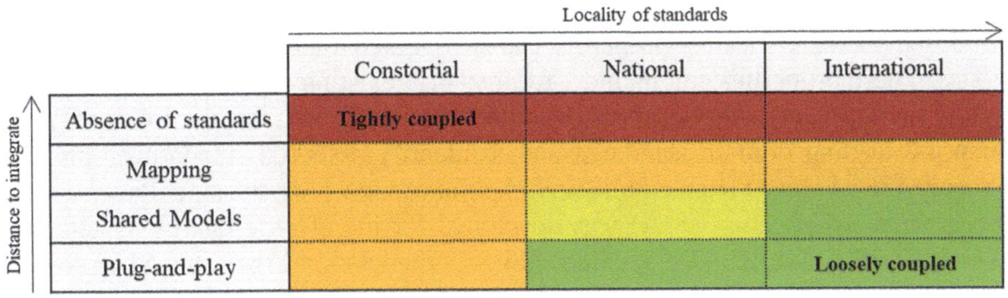

Fig. 3 Degree of coupling in SoS environments

based on both dimensions ("*distance to integrate*" and "*locality of standards*") these are not highlighted in depth.

4 Facilitating Reference Designation Systems

As interoperability is a challenging issue in all *Information Technology* (IT)-supported domains, since most legacy IT and *Operational Technology* (OT) systems were originally developed as isolated stand-alone solutions, which now need to be integrated to a larger SoS, it has been identified as a core success factor for sustainable SoS. Consequently, different domains are exploring approaches to facilitate interoperability on a domain-wide basis. In this context, the so-called *Reference Designation Systems* (RDS) have been identified as a best practice by both industry and research [14].

A reference designation provides an "*identifier of a specific object formed with respect to the system of which the object is a constituent, based on one or more aspects of that system*" and *serves* the unambiguous and exact identification and classification of technical objects within a given domain or area [22]. As presented by Uslar and Engel [14], RDS in general defines a baseplane that connects all sub-domains of a given value chain (of a given domain) with their respective automation chains, strictly following structuring principles and application rules [22]. For example, the value chain of the electric energy domain is subdivided into "*Bulk generation,*" "*Transmission,*" "*Distribution,*" "*Distributed Energy Resources,*" and "*Customer Premises.*" As each of these sub-domains were never designed to be integrated, these are characterized by individual requirements and needs along their respective automation chains (so-called zones) in "*Process,*" "*Field,*" "*Station,*" "*Operation,*" "*Enterprise,*" and "*Market.*" The baseplane, i.e. the combination of the (sub-)domains and zones that constitute the core of most RDS, enables the creation of a domain-wide point of reference for all participating CS. Following the example of the electric energy domain with its RDS (in general referred to as the SGAM) as a successful archetype, a variety of deviates have already been developed and successfully deployed in various domains. For example, in the *Fourth Industrial Revolution* with the RAMI 4.0 or the maritime sector MAF [14].

Based on the RDS, clear properties can be assigned to the respective domains and zones. These properties can include, for instance, existing regulatory requirements, safety requirements, and/or prevailing standards. Thus, with the aim to identify and map the leading domain standards and to identify potential standardization gaps that need to be closed from a holistic SoS point of view [14], the so-called *Seamless Integration Architecture* (SIA) was developed for the electric energy system as a part of the IEC TR 62357-1 standard [23]. As depicted in Fig. 4, the SIA provides "*a clear and comprehensive map of all standards which are contributing to support interactions within the energy system*" [23].

The SIA and its underlying RDS, i.e. the SGAM, allow a distinct contextualization of the role and functions of each CS as a part of the electric energy

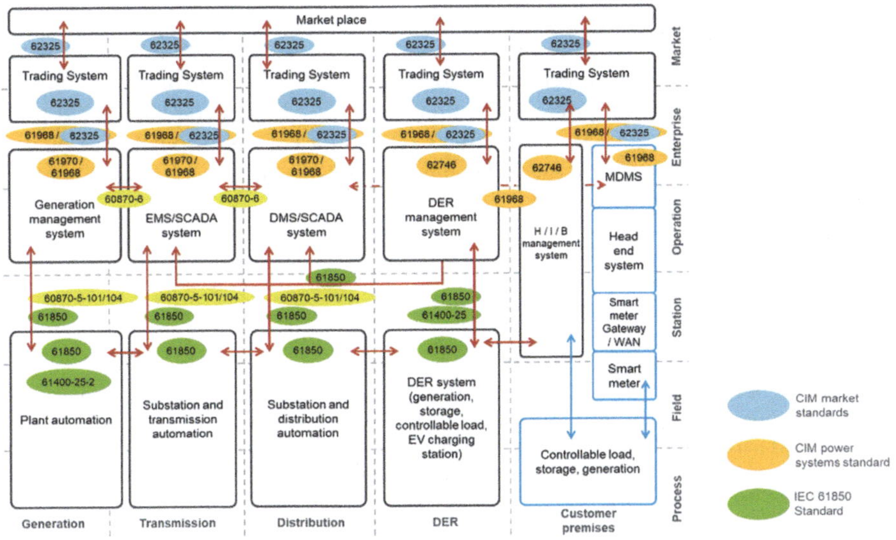

Fig. 4 Seamless integration architecture of the electric energy domain [23]

domain as an SoS; hence, allowing an easy identification and shared understanding in which way every CS should be embedded within the higher-level structures of the SoS [24]. If, for example, a CS wants to participate in the energy market in the role of a *Distribution System Operator* (DSO), the CS (or more its owner) can easily determine the adequate standard for its respective role in the energy system based on the classification (domain: distribution; zone: market): the *IEC 62325—Common Information Model (CIM) for Energy Markets* as an internationally established standard. Thus, preventing an unnecessary tight coupling by identifying and implementing globally established standards instead of proprietary solutions.

5 Conclusion

While "local" technical systems have clearly defined system boundaries (in scope and context), areas of responsibility and stakeholders, more modern systems have to deal with additional layers of socio-technical, −political and -economical complexity, blurred system boundaries, interoperability, and the resulting mutual interdependencies. In order to fully grasp the cross-system requirements, a holistic SoS perspective is required. This contribution gave a brief introduction on tight coupling in SoS and how it can be addressed by facilitating RDS as a domain-wide point of reference.

With a holistic perspective on joint interoperability and standardization requirements, sustainable SoS can be realized. Thus, future systems could be integrated in a cost-effective way or existing components could be exchanged with ease due to an appropriate maturity of the underlying standards. Proprietary solutions would not have to be planned, developed, and maintained in a cost-intensive manner, specialized experts for proprietary solutions no longer have to be bound and it can be profited from collective learning effects on the market. Additionally, decoupling also fosters the techno-economic independence, as the effects of arbitrary behavior become encapsulated.

References

1. Haberfellner, R., de Weck, O., Fricke, E., & Vössner, S. (2019). *Systems engineering - fundamentals and application* (p. 458). Springer Nature Switzerland.
2. von Bertalanffy, L. (1968). General system theory: Foundations, development, applications. In *International library of systems theory and philosophy*. G. Braziller.
3. ISO/IEC/IEEE 21839:2019. (2019). Systems and Software Engineering—System of Systems (SoS) considerations in life cycle stages of a system.
4. Lehman, M. M. (1980). Programs, life cycles, and laws of software evolution. *Proceedings of the IEEE, 68*(9), 1060–1076.
5. Avgeriou, P., Kruchten, P., Ozkaya, O., & Seaman, C. B. (2016). Managing technical debt in Software Engineering (Dagstuhl Seminar 16162). In P. Avgeriou, P. Kruchten, I. Ozkaya, & C. Seaman (Eds.), *Dagstuhl reports 6.4* (pp. 110–138).
6. Dahmann, J. S. (2014). System of systems pain points. *INCOSE International Symposium, 24*(1), 108–121.
7. Northrop, L., et al. (2006). *Ultra-large-scale systems: The software challenge of the future*. Software Engineering Institute, Carnegie Mellon University.
8. Sillitto, H. G. (2010). Design principles for ultra-large-scale (ULS) systems. *INCOSE International Symposium, 20*, 63–82.
9. Billaud, S., Daclin, N., & Chapurlat, V. (2015). Interoperability as a key concept for the control and evolution of the system of systems (SoS). In *Enterprise interoperability* (pp. 53–63).
10. GridWise Architecture Council. (2008). Smart grid interoperability maturity model beta version.
11. Schütz J., & Marx Gómez J.. (2020). Towards collaborative technical debt management in Systems of Systems. In: Proceedings of the 3rd International Conference on Technical Debt. TechDebt '20. Seoul, Republic of Korea: Association for Computing Machinery, pp. 87–91.
12. Cadavid, H., Andrikopoulos, V., & Avgeriou, P. (2020). *Architecting systems of systems: A tertiary study* (Vol. 118). Information and Software Technology.
13. GridWise Architecture Council. (2008). GridWise® Interoperability context-setting framework. version 1.1.
14. Uslar M., Engel D. (2015). Towards generic domain reference designation: How to learn from smart grid interoperability. D-A-Ch Energieinformatik Karlsruhe.
15. Weinert, B., Uslar M., & Hahn A. (2017). System-of-systems: How the maritime domain can learn from the Smart Grid. 2017 International Symposium ELMAR, Zadar, Croatia, pp. 229–232.
16. Schütz J., Uslar M., & Clausen M. (2022, May). ‚Digitalisierung. Synthesebericht 3 des SINTEG Förderprogramms, Studie im Auftrag des BMWK, Berlin". Berlin.
17. Schütz, J., Uslar, M., & Meister, J. (2021). A case study research on interoperability improvement in smart grids: State-of-the-art and further opportunities. *Open Research Europe, 1*, 33.

18. Office of the Deputy under Secretary of defense for acquisition, technology; systems, and software engineering: "Systems engineering guide for Systems of Systems", Version 1.0. (2008). ODUSD.
19. Boardman, J., & Sauser, B.. (2006). System of systems - The meaning of IEEE/SMC International Conference on System of Systems Engineering, p. 6.
20. ISO/IEC 7498–1:1994. (1994). Information technology—Open Systems Interconnection—Basic reference model: The basic model.
21. Martin, R. C. (2017). *Clean architecture: A craftsman's guide to software structure and design* (1st. ed.). Prentice Hall Press.
22. IEC 81346–1:2022. (2022). Industrial systems, installations and equipment and industrial products - Structuring principles and reference designations - Part 1: Basic rules.
23. IEC TR 62357–1:2016. (2016). Power systems management and associated information exchange - Part 1: Reference architecture.
24. Schütz J., Clausen M., Uslar M., & Marx Gómez J. (2021, September). IEC 62559–2 use case template-based smart grid architecture analytics, CIRED 2021 workshop proceedings.

Smart System for Monitoring and Controlling Oxygen Gas Level in High Purity Germanium Detector Room

Yvonne Uwamahoro, Devotha G. Nyambo, Anael Sam, and John Ben Ngatunga

1 Introduction

Due to the danger imposed by nitrogen gas on human life when it exceeds its safe level of 78% by volume in air, this project is necessary to avert the loss of human lives in Tanzania Atomic Energy Commission and beyond. Around the World, inhaling oxygen-deficient air results in deaths; though the number of deaths varies from year to year and location to location, nitrogen gas displaces oxygen in the air reducing the percentage of oxygen to below 21% by volume [1]. Due to the massive liquid-to-gas expansion that occurs during evaporation, liquid nitrogen is capable of displacing enough oxygen to create an oxygen-deficient environment in a small or inadequately ventilated room, posing a danger of asphyxiation [2]. Because the human brain requires an ongoing flow of oxygen to stay active; without it, the brain cannot operate correctly, which can eventually lead to death [3]. The only gas that sustains life is oxygen. Approximately 21% of oxygen by volume in the air is typically considered safe to breathe [4]. The atmosphere becomes dangerous if oxygen concentration falls below 19.5% [5]. When the oxygen concentration falls only a little below average, focus, thinking, and decision-making are all hampered. These side effects are undetectable to the person who is affected. If the oxygen concentration in the air declines or the attention of other gases rises, a condition where asphyxiation is a severe risk arises quickly [6]. High Purity Germanium Detector is an exceptional device used to detect inner and outer contamination of various radioactive gamma emitters of a person. This device plays an essential

Y. Uwamahoro (✉) · D. G. Nyambo · A. Sam
School of Computational and Communication Science and Engineering, Nelson Mandela African Institution of Science and Technology, Arusha, Tanzania
e-mail: uwamahoroy@nm-aist.ac.tz

J. B. Ngatunga
Tanzania Atomic Energy Commission, Arusha, Tanzania

J. Marx Gómez et al. (eds.), *Smart and Secure Embedded and Mobile Systems*, Progress in IS, https://doi.org/10.1007/978-3-031-56603-5_23

role in nuclear safety. It enables the performance of quantitative and qualitative radioactivity analyses and specifies the contaminated spots of a human body (head, lungs, or legs) [7]. Liquid nitrogen is employed for chilling the High Purity Germanium Detector to its working temperature [8]. However, if liquid nitrogen is not handled correctly, it can be harmful. Liquid nitrogen, which is colorless, odorless, and tasteless, can inflict frostbite or cryogenic burns, and if used or spilled in a confined place, it can kill a person [9]. A person cannot breathe if there is insufficient oxygen in the room. Therefore, it is preferable to be alert than to assume that nothing will happen if liquid nitrogen is accidentally spilled in a confined location [10].

As one of the safety measures for the radioactive mining workers, Tanzania Atomic Energy Commission has installed a full-body scan device in one of the rooms, which uses liquid nitrogen to keep it cool. However, every time liquid nitrogen is refilled, it pours and evaporates in the room. When nitrogen evaporates, it becomes a gas form that is impossible for a human being to see because it is colorless, odorless, and tasteless [11]. Therefore, to create a safe and healthy environment for both the workers and the clients in the full scan room, there is a great need to install a system that can monitor, control, and provide information on the level of oxygen in the room before entering both locally and remotely and when the level of oxygen gas is low, to alert the workers and switch on the exhaust fan automatically.

The Blynk Application is used to display detected data with the help of Internet connectivity provided by Global System for Mobile Communication. Currently, no system can detect the oxygen level in the room at Tanzania Atomic Energy Commission. Therefore, for fear of danger of air impurity, workers open the door and windows because they do not know the oxygen level in the room. An intelligent system for monitoring and controlling oxygen levels in the High Purity Germanium Detector room is proposed to solve the abovementioned problem; the system stores the data locally using SD card in case of connection failure, and it will upload all the waiting data lists when the connection is re-established.

The developed system will not only be used at Tanzania Atomic Energy Commission as an experiment, but will also contribute to science worldwide. It is to solve current identified problems and more that will come. Therefore, the system is designed and developed to solve real-life existing issues. The cost of the system is lesser than the use of coloring substances. It is developed once to provide intended solutions for it is lifetime, making it cheaper. Technically, it has no moving parts, which may require replacement due to wear and tear.

2 Related Works

Due to the apparent significant adverse effects of air pollution on public health, air quality monitoring is becoming highly relevant. For example, the Bangladesh study underscored the importance of monitoring methane gas, which can cause asphyxiation at excessively high levels and displace oxygen in the blood, resulting in unconsciousness or death. Data collected by sensors were stored in the cloud, and the system was able to alert the workers and allow users to track the surrounding air quality of their homes, office, or industries from anywhere. However, the system was not easy to be monitored and controlled remotely even though the system lacked the functionality of notifying workers through SMS [12].

Harmful gases like carbon monoxide, methane, and alcohol are hazardous to humans and the environment in general; humans must take measures to ensure a safe and healthy environment; that is why, MQ-135 is being used to detect other harmful gases in the room. Toxic gas detection systems were developed that employ the Global System for Mobile Communication (GSM) module to generate Short Message Service (SMS) notifications to users and a buzzer to alert them [13]. However, this system lacks Internet of Things technology on it because the way of alerting workers was done locally using buzzer and SMS, which are not enough. The Internet of Things technology system can be monitored or controlled remotely.

Furthermore, human beings need to be in an environment that facilitates their living condition because without a good environment, fresh air is available. Several problems can put people's lives in danger [14]. One of the essential measures to be taken seriously by a human is air quality. Air quality has to be monitored because it directly influences human health. It threatens life safety and human productivity and causes discomfort in the ecosystem of urbanization [15]. To effectively control the negative impact of primary air pollutants such as nitrogen and other gases, there is a need to develop a system to monitor and regulate air quality accurately. Both people's health and the environment can be harmed by pollutants and cause other damage according to the level and location. Several devoted researchers have put great efforts into addressing issues related to research on systems that monitor air quality indoors. It is made known that there is a need to come up with new methodologies and modern techniques for monitoring air quality in real-time to save human lives [16].

Environmental contamination has substantially hindered human life in the growing society. Most indoor air quality measures are beyond the threshold of health. Therefore it is difficult to maintain a productive and stable environment. The system developed by [15] provided real-time monitoring of indoor air quality parameters and alerted workers through a subscribed mobile phone. However, the easy way of minimizing the concentration of harmful gases in the room was to open doors and windows to increase indoor air quality significantly.

The effect of domestic and commercial cooking fuel on human health increases daily. According to research conducted in India by [17], it shows that every year people lose their lives due to inhaling unsafe air. Therefore, to monitor the concentration of harmful gases in the indoor atmosphere, the system was developed to take up appropriate steps in case gases increase. The system is used for domestic air monitoring purposes in homes or personal indoor spaces to measure the quality of air. However, the way of removing air impurity inside the room was to open doors and windows, the Internet was required to send messages to the user, and it was not able to control the system remotely. Gas leakage is a mutual issue in households and manufacturing environments. Its very existence is threatening if it is not detected and controlled right away. The system is designed [18] for detection of methane, butane, liquid petroleum gas leak, and methane outflow and alert authorized people via short message service and sound alarm. However, the system lacks the functionality of removing harmful gases from the room.

The system developed by [19] was Arduino-based real-time air quality monitoring. This system was able to monitor air quality using MQ-135 sensor and display it locally using LCD display. This system needs to be upgraded to a level that it can alert workers through buzzer, remotely monitoring and controlling and saving the processed data in the cloud for making decision.

There is a need to develop the smart system for monitoring and controlling oxygen level in High Purity Germanium Detector Room at Tanzania Atomic Energy Commission to tackle with the addressed challenges by existing systems. The developed system is able to continuously monitor and control the levels of oxygen, air quality, and temperature both locally and remotely, it can alert workers using a buzzer and send a short message service to the subscribed phone numbers, and automatically switch on the exhaust fan to expel concentrated air and bring fresh air from outside.

3 Material and Methods

This study was conducted at Tanzania Atomic Energy Commission located in Arusha district, Njiro subward. The Tanzania Atomic Energy Commission is the government regulatory organization in charge of all atomic energy affairs in Tanzania. It was formed by the Atomic Energy Act No. 7 of 2003. Tanzania Atomic Energy Commission was established with responsibilities; control of the uses of ionizing and non-ionizing radiation sources, as well as the promotion of safe and peaceful usage of atomic energy and nuclear technology [20].

Tanzania Atomic Energy Commission has many departments, and the developed project is under the Department of Technical Support and Radiation Protection. The reason for choosing this project under the Technical Support and Radiation Protection department was the presence of two rooms and one named a food and environment monitoring laboratory. The food and environment monitoring laboratory room is equipped with a system which can detect excessive air impurity and the workers do not have to be afraid as they carry on their daily duties in the room. The existing system in this room can detect excessive air impurity and alert workers, but it can neither automatically expel the excessive air impurity from the room nor send information about the level of oxygen remotely. This system still needs to be upgraded to a level where it can be able to expel excess air impurity from the room without human intervention and provide information about the level of oxygen remotely. However, in the other room, named the High Purity Detector Room, there is no installed system. Activities in this room are performed under fear of the unknown.

3.1 System Development Approach

In the project, we used V-Model, which works effectively for small projects where the requirements are clear [21]. It was easy to check every step before proceeding to the next level of development, which led to the development of an error-free and good-quality system. The V-Model is a Software Development Life Cycle where the execution of processes happens sequentially in a V shape [22]. V-Model is simple, easy to understand, and use. It is the right model for carrying out a project with straightforward specified unchanging requirements.

3.2 System Design

During the development of the system, the system was designed with four distinct parts known as the sensing part, the data processing part, the notification or alerting part, and the controlling part.

3.2.1 Sensing Part

This part comprises gas sensor (O2) which senses oxygen, MQ-135 senses the presence of other gases that can cause air impurity, and the DHT22 Sensor senses temperature in the room. A gas sensor (O2) is a kind of Sensor used to detect the oxygen concentration in the room. The purpose of using a gas Sensor (O2) is to ensure that the oxygen level in the room is monitored to prevent injuries and deaths caused by insufficient oxygen. MQ-135 is used to sense the presence of other gases that can cause air impurities in the room. An increase in temperature in the room makes liquid nitrogen evaporate; that is why the DHT22 Sensor is used to monitor the temperature in the room and report to the ESP32 for the procession.

3.2.2 Data Processing Part

In this part, the ESP32 microcontroller is used as the brain of the system to control all the processes. It operates at 3.0 V–3.6 V of voltage, and the CPU clock frequency is adjustable from 80 MHz to 240 MHz. Once the data from the sensors are received by the ESP32 microcontroller, it processes and analyzes the data. After data analysis, the microcontroller compares the sensed values to the threshold values of each data that is programmed in the microcontroller. The use of the ESP32 microcontroller with Arduino IDE provides a suitable platform for implementing the project, which is an embedded control system where hardware is controlled by software.

3.2.3 Notification and Controlling Part

This part consists of a Buzzer, LCD, Relay, and GSM module; when the sensed values exceed the threshold value, the microcontroller sends the signal to a Buzzer to alert the workers. This part also helps workers to access information about air quality, temperature, and oxygen levels in the room, both locally and remotely. Locally it provides information on the levels of air quality, oxygen, and temperature on LCD and Buzzer. The microcontroller sends information to the GSM to alert workers through the subscribed phone numbers in the form of SMS. Blynk App is also used. Through Wi-Fi integrated with the ESP32, data are stored on the Blynk App server. These data are about air quality, oxygen, and temperature levels in the room. From the Blynk App server, workers can access the information remotely before entering the room. The relay switches on the exhaust fan automatically once air impurity is detected to remove air impurity from the room. The exhaust fan will expel the concentrated air impurity and replace it with fresh air from outside. Figure 1 below shows block diagram.

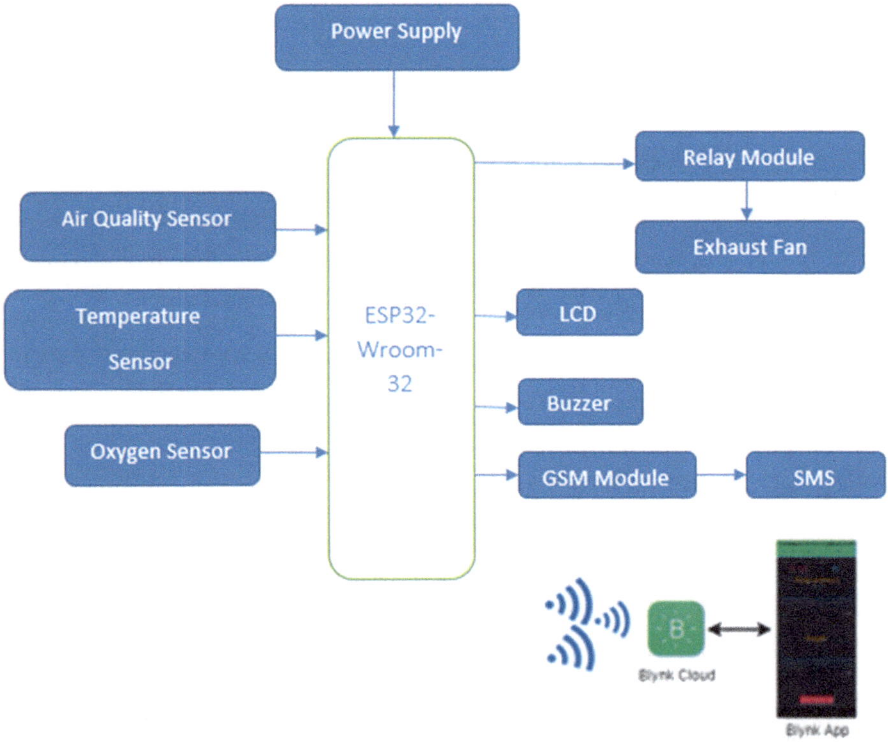

Fig. 1 Block diagram of the developed system

3.3 The Functionality of the Developed System

When the system was switched on, the oxygen sensor started to sense the concentration of oxygen gas, MQ-135 sensor started to sense the air quality concentration, and DHT22 sensor continuously monitored the temperature in the room. Immediate actions such as the beeping of a buzzer and automatic switching on of the exhaust fan were carried out when there was air impurity in the room or the oxygen level was low. As a result, this triggers the system to send SMS to the subscribed phone numbers. The complete flowchart of how the system works is shown in Fig. 2 below.

4 Results and Discussion

The experimental results obtained from the developed system are shown below. The developed smart system for monitoring and controlling oxygen levels is able to perform its function at a significant level (Figs. 3 and 4). When the system is turned on, it monitors the levels of oxygen, air quality, and temperature. Locally, the monitored levels of oxygen, air quality, and temperature in the room were successfully displayed on the LCD as shown in Fig. 5. The same results displayed on the LCD were automatically uploaded to the Blynk App at the same time so that workers may access the room's oxygen, air quality, and temperature levels remotely wherever they are as shown in Figs. 6 and 7. The information about the data saved on the Blynk cloud server can be stored for up to a year without being destroyed and viewed at any time. Figure 3 shows the system testing and each component was tested. Also Fig. 4 shows the system at off state, here nothing was displayed because the system was off.

With the help of the Blynk App as shown in Figs. 6 and 7, the levels of oxygen, air quality, and temperature were displayed successfully. In safe mode, air quality is represented by 0 with black-red color, whereas when it is in the unsafe mode, it is represented by 1 with red color. In safe mode means that the level of oxygen in the room is above 19.5% by volume, while unsafe mode means that the level of oxygen in the room is below 19.5% by volume.

GSM successfully sent a short messaging service to the subscribed phone number containing the status of oxygen and temperature in the room. The temperature must be less than or equal to 20 °C. In case the temperature was greater than 20 °C, a short messaging service was sent to the workers. A short messaging service also was sent to the subscribed phone number when the level of oxygen in the room was below 19.5% by volume. Figure 8 shows how the system was able to alert the workers by sending a short message service to subscribed users.

The results obtained from the developed system showed that the system met the user requirements because, by the time of testing, there was no need to open door and widows for fear of unknown. The levels of oxygen, temperature, and air quality were monitored and controlled locally and remotely. There is a possibility to add a

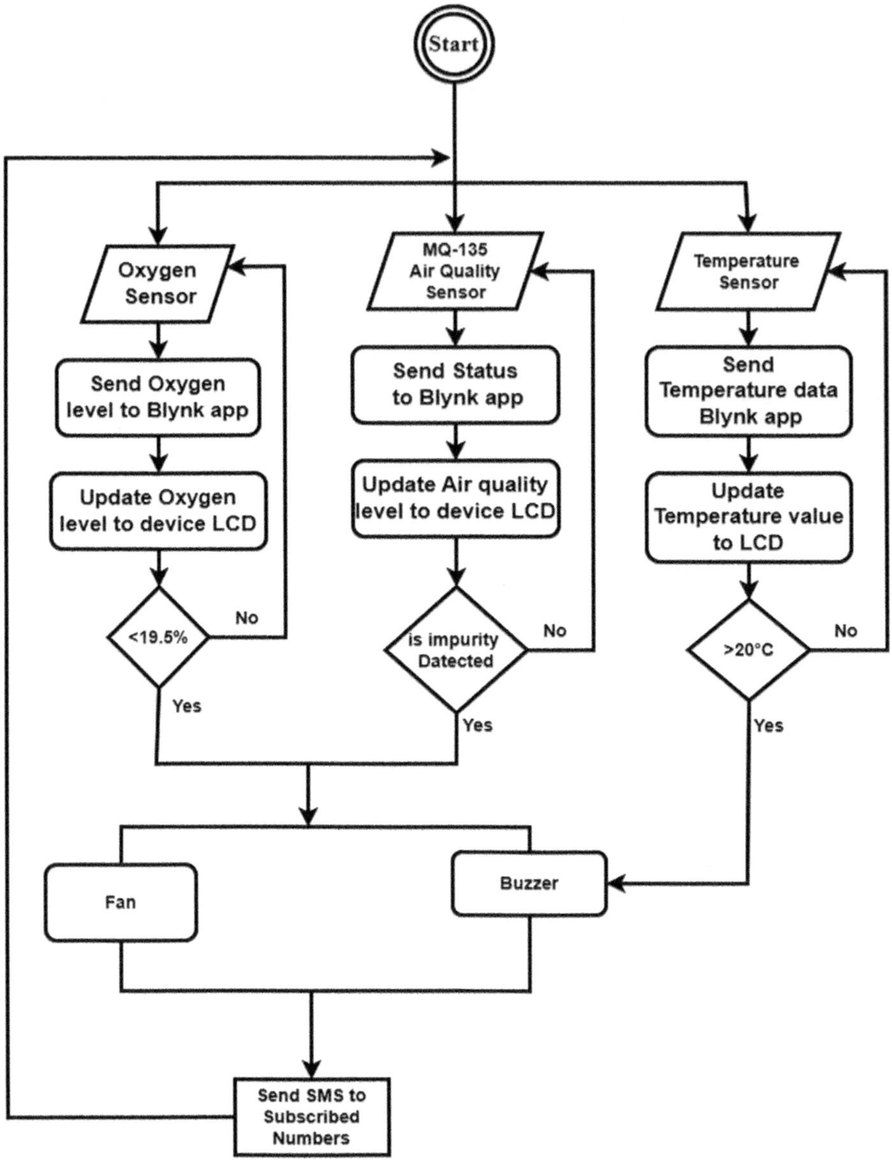

Fig. 2 Flowchart of the developed system

substance to the fluids that in case of contact with oxygen or leakage from a leak leaves a colored mark to warn of danger similar to the marking of fuels to identify. However, this would not give timely and accurate information about the levels of impurity and temperature. Moreover, it cannot provide remote information to the personal which would make the personal only to guess and still live under fear

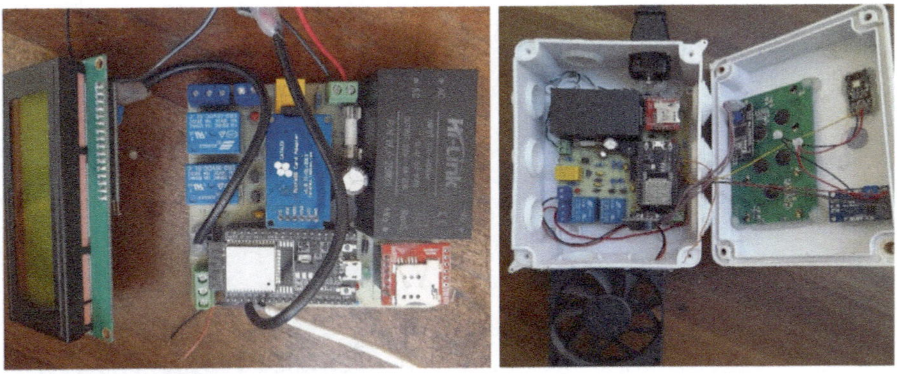

Fig. 3 Testing each component and integration system

Fig. 4 System at off state

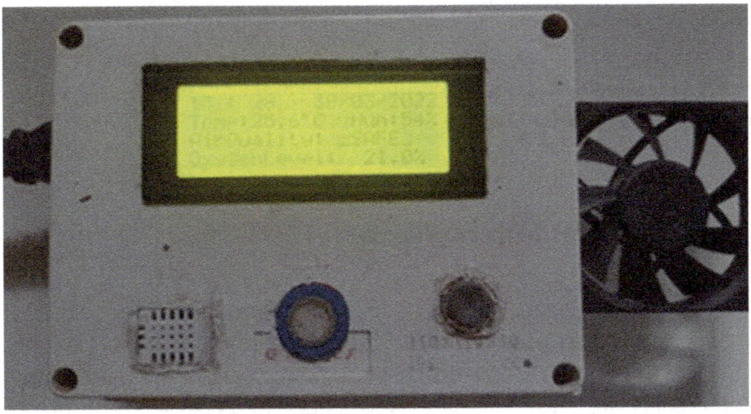

Fig. 5 System displaying oxygen, temperature, and air quality

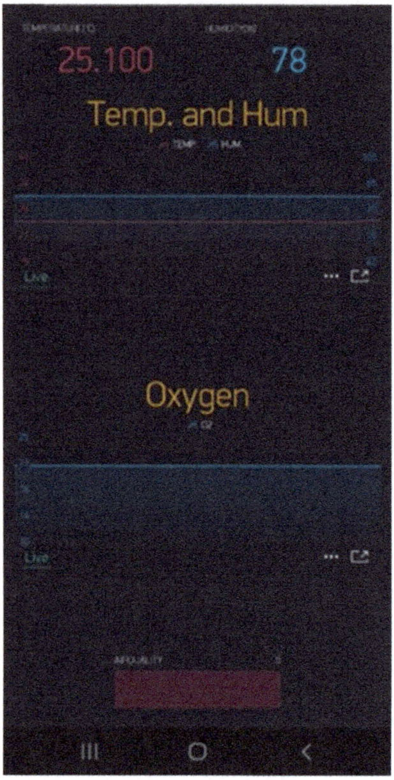

Fig. 6 Complete system testing using Blynk App in safe mode

of unknown. The system uses both GSM and Wi-Fi connections. The system is designed to be located inside the room where leakage is suspected. The system has the ability to pass information globally as long as it is connected through Wi-Fi without changes, but GSM requires changes in the number and country code locally. I have no ability to store the data for the room for the purpose of record keeping. Below are tables that show functional and non-functional requirements validation results. Table 1 shows functional requirements validation results and Table 2 shows non-functional requirements validation results.

5 Conclusion and Future Work

We developed a system to monitor and control the level of oxygen in the High Purity Germanium Detector Room at Tanzania Atomic Energy Commission. In the project, we used V-Model, which works effectively for small projects where the requirements are clear. It was easy to check every step before proceeding to the next level of development, which led to the development of an error-free and good-quality system. I can ensure you that the prototype is error-free because by

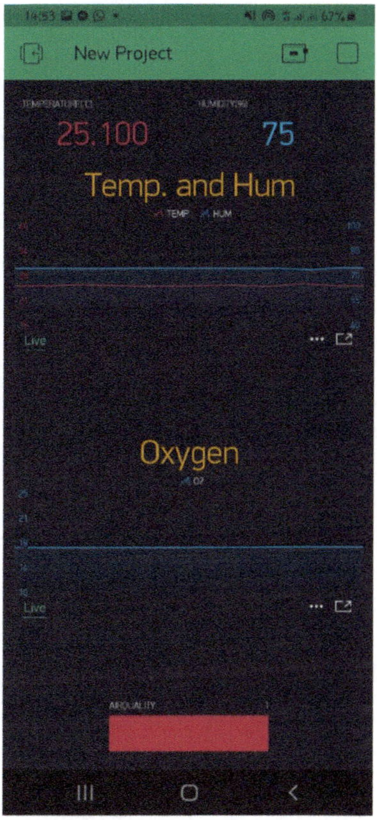

Fig. 7 Blynk app with the result in unsafe mode

carrying out tests for several times, in different environments and by different people while paying keen attention to the results. The aim of the proposed solution was successfully achieved. The developed system provides a better solution compared to the existing system because it can monitor and control the level of oxygen, to reduce the negative effects of oxygen deficiency in the High Purity Germanium Detector Room at Tanzania Atomic Energy Commission. It can help workers to take precautionary measures in case the system alerts them of any air impurity in the room. Moreover, the system can both provide an alarm and remove the oxygen-deficient air from the room by the use of an automated exhaust fan; also, it can help the workers to keep safe from the effect of leaking liquid nitrogen.

Through the results obtained from the developed system, it is true that the required functionalities for the proposed system to monitor and control oxygen level have been satisfactorily met. Every activity carried out by human beings must protect their lives. The human brain requires an ongoing flow of oxygen to stay active; without it, the brain cannot operate correctly, which eventually could lead to death. The developed system is strongly recommended for use to solve the identified issue at Tanzania Atomic Energy Commission because it will

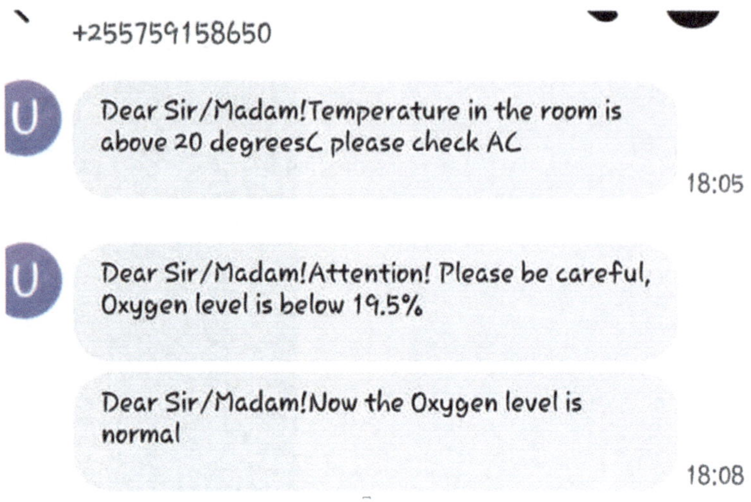

Fig. 8 Showing the results through SMS

Table 1 Functional requirements validation results

Requirements	Description	Score
Powered with DC or AC	The system should be powered with DC or AC	Pass
Detect the level of oxygen	The system should be able to detect oxygen level in the room	Pass
Detect air quality	The system should be able to detect air quality in the room	Pass
Detect temperature	The system should be able to detect the temperature in the room	Pass
Alert workers	The system should be able to alert through the buzzer	Pass
Send message	The system should be able to send short message service	Pass
Availability	The system should be available every time	Pass

Table 2 Non-functional requirements validation results

Requirements	Description	Score
Update data on SD card	The system should be able to update data on SD card	Pass
User friendly	The system should be user friendly	Pass
Acceptable and usable	The system should be acceptable and usable	Pass
Security	The system should be secured	Pass

effectively improve monitoring and controlling oxygen deficiency in the High Purity Germanium Detector Room.

There is a need to develop a customized app for the system instead of using the Blynk App. The system data should be directly stored in the cloud so that it can be accessed not only on mobile phones but also on any device which is connected to the internet. Also cooling system should be added so that it could be used in case there is a failure of exhaust fan.

References

1. Mahanth, D., & Karishma, S. (2017). Automated indoor air quality monitor and control. *International Journal of Computers and Applications, 159*(6), 33–38. https://doi.org/10.5120/ijca2017912968
2. Nitrogen, I. (n.d.). Hudson valley community college liquid nitrogen safety guidelines.
3. T̈r, F. Ç., & Aksay, E. (2012). "Asphyxia due to accidental nitrogen gas inhalation: A case report," Hong Kong. *The Journal of Emergency Medicine, 19*(1), 46–48. https://doi.org/10.1177/102490791201900108
4. Nitrogen, L. (2014). Report | liquid nitrogen.
5. Yanisko, P., & Croll, D. (2012). Use nitrogen safely. *Chemical Engineering Progress, 108*(3), 44–48.
6. AIGA. (2008). *Hazards of inert gases and oxygen depletion.* Asia Industrial Gases Assoc.
7. Dararutana, C., & Abdullah, N. (2021). Calibration of whole body counter for assessment of internal dose in the human body. *Journal of Physics Conference Series, 1719*(1). https://doi.org/10.1088/1742-6596/1719/1/012044
8. Cryogen, G. (2008, February). Awareness of oxygen depletion, pp. 12–13.
9. Wallace, S. J. (2004, June 7). Hazards of nitrogen asphyxiation.
10. Headlines, M., Safely, W., & Lifestyle, Y. H. (2014). How dangerous is liquid nitrogen ? Drivers are reminded to adjust the headrest, *11*(6), 9–11.
11. Introduction, G.. (2018). Cryogenic liquid/solid safety, pp. 1–9.
12. Ahmed, M. M., Banu, S., & Paul, B. (2018). Real-time air quality monitoring system for Bangladesh's perspective based on Internet of Things. 3rd Int. Conf. Electr. Inf. Commun. Technol. EICT 2017, vol. 2018-January, no. December, pp. 1–5. https://doi.org/10.1109/EICT.2017.8275161.
13. Siddharthan, T. (2016). Detection of Toxic Gases using Arduino and GSM Network. *International Journal of Engineering Research & Technology, 4*(24), 1–4.
14. Mir, A., & Khachane, A. (2018). Sensing harmful gases in industries using IOT and WSN. Proc. – 2018 4th Int. Conf. Comput. Commun. Control Autom. ICCUBEA 2018, pp. 1–3. https://doi.org/10.1109/ICCUBEA.2018.8697380.
15. Jayasree, B., Subash, T., Priyadharsan, V., Priya, N., & Students, U. G. (2021). Implementation and measurement of IOT based indoor air quality monitoring system. *International Journal for Scientific and Development Research, 6*(4), 372–376. www.ijsdr.org
16. Kim, J. Y., Chu, C. H., & Shin, S. M. (2014). ISSAQ: An integrated sensing systems for real-time indoor air quality monitoring. *IEEE Sensors Journal, 14*(12), 4230–4244. https://doi.org/10.1109/JSEN.2014.2359832
17. Gupta, K., Gokul Krishna, G., & Anjali, T., (2020). An IoT based system for domestic air quality monitoring and cooking gas leak detection for a safer home. Proc. 2020 IEEE Int. Conf. Commun. Signal Process. ICCSP 2020, pp. 705–709, https://doi.org/10.1109/ICCSP48568.2020.9182051.
18. Paculanan, R. S., & Carino, I. (2019). F10420486C219, no. 6, pp. 221–225.

19. Al Ahasan, A., Roy, S., Saim, A. H. M., Akter, R., & Hossain, Z., (2018, July). Arduino-based real time air quality and pollution monitoring system. https://doi.org/10.21276/ijircst.2018.6.4.8.
20. Plan, S. E. (2018). Tanzania atomic energy commission communication and stakeholder engagement plan.
21. Stephen, O., & Oriaku, K. (2014). Software development methodologies: Agile model vs V-model. *International Journal of Engineering Technology and Research, 2*(11), 108–113. https://www.erpublication.org/admin/vol_issue1/upload Image/IJETR022742.pdf
22. W3schools. (2016). SDLC – V-Model, W3schools, p. https://www.w3schools.in/sdlc-tutorial/v-model/, 2016, https://www.w3schools.in/sdlc-tutorial/v-model/%0Ahttp://www.tutorialspoint.com/sdlc/sdlc_v_model.ht.

Development of an Arithmetic Video Game and Console for Standard I and II Pupils in Tanzania

Winny Tuitoek Bundotich, Luciana Nyaoke Murimi, Alvareze Ntafatiro, Kisangiri Michael, and Devotha Nyambo

1 Introduction

Games in education are an essential part of learning that instructors use to provide a more exciting and interactive way of teaching their learners. Gaming activities have helped learners understand complex concepts in an exciting and non-monotonous way by promoting mighty memory, class competition, minor stress, peer positivity, controlled competitiveness, friendly fun, new knowledge, more motivation, and careful attention, among others [1].

With the growth of technology, game-based learning has since taken the digitized path and adopted new technologies, with computer games being the most famous. Classroom learning has drifted toward the digital learning paradigm, which has adopted digital games as a learning method. Computer games in classrooms have a wide range of advantages and have been adopted and considered to enhance learners' engagement, collaboration, and interaction skills. Games also improve audio-visual skills, enabling them to apply gaming values to real-world situations [2]. Most digital games in the classroom are played on Personal Computers, even if people purchase them for other purposes [3]. However, other game platforms such as hand-held game consoles and mobile systems have been experimented with in classrooms in many places.

Several existing educational video games suit personal computers. However, most learners use video games for entertainment purposes [4]. Therefore, most game developers lean more toward entertainment games. 69% of children 6–11 years old like to play video games [5]. Nintendo has developed educative games; however, these games do not fit the Tanzanian curriculum for primary education. Tanzania

W. T. Bundotich (✉) · L. N. Murimi · A. Ntafatiro · K. Michael · D. Nyambo
The Nelson Mandela African Institution of Science and Technology, Arusha, Tanzania
e-mail: bundotichw@nm-aist.ac.tz

J. Marx Gómez et al. (eds.), *Smart and Secure Embedded and Mobile Systems*,
Progress in IS, https://doi.org/10.1007/978-3-031-56603-5_24

basic education curriculum uses both English and Kiswahili as the primary language of instruction, whereas the games developed by Nintendo use English only [6], this creates bias toward the schools that use only Kiswahili as the language of instruction. Furthermore, personal computers are high power consumption devices and expensive; hence, purchasing them for children's video games in the classroom wastes the more extensive computing power and resources that institutions can utilize for other complex activities. Therefore, the main objective of this project was to develop a learning video game and console that enhances arithmetic competency for Tanzania's standard I and II learners.

2 Materials and Methods

2.1 System Requirements Identification

We used the exploratory sequential mixed methods design. The system requirements were gathered from both secondary and primary data sources. Qualitative (interviews, focus group discussions, and observations) and quantitative (questionnaires) research methods were used. Existing documents on game-based learning were reviewed and analyzed. Challenges and gaps in the existing solutions were identified and used in refining the system requirements. Interviews, observations, and focus group discussions with the relevant stakeholders including the curriculum developers, teachers, learners, and parents were also carried out. This study was conducted in Arusha region specifically: Arumeru, Ngorongoro, Monduli, Karatu, Arusha, and Longido districts.

From the data gathered, it was evident that there was a need for the development of a learning video game that can be integrated into classroom learning. The results also demonstrated a need for a game that specifically covers counting objects, number recognition, number relationships, and number operations to be used in standards I and II. The teachers and curriculum developers suggested these concepts as the core concepts to be learned at this level. The requirements gathered from all these sources were then analyzed, verified, validated, and documented.

Ethical consideration. Approval to conduct the project from NM-AIST was obtained before data was collected from the selected curriculum developers, teachers, and parents. As for the children involved, the exercises were carried out under the supervision and consent of a trusted adult. Permission was also requested from the primary education officer in charge of Arusha region who granted us consent to carry out the project in the region's primary schools and education offices. Participation of the respondents during observation, filling of questionnaires, interviews, and focus group discussion was voluntary and all the participants were informed of their rights, the type of data collected, and how the data was to be used. Ethical interpretation and reporting of results was observed. No personal and identifying information was included.

2.2 Software Development

The game described below was named Math Bubbles. Math bubbles game falls under the Educational game's genre. It has been designed to be both educating and entertaining to the learner. The game is available to be played on a console. The target audience for the game are learners in standards I and II; hence, using a lightweight console with a simple interface was necessary so as to make it easier for the children to interact with the game and promote a high level of immersion.

The game is divided into two main levels: Standard 1 consisting of level 1 and level 2 and Standard 2 consisting of level 1, level 2, and level 3. Standard 1 covered identifying missing numbers and counting objects whereas standard 2 covered addition, subtraction, and multiplication. The game is aimed at helping learners be competent in the following areas as per the Tanzania Basic Syllabus for Standard I and II [7]. At Standard 1 level, the pupil learns and is able to recognize numbers, fill numbers in sequential order, and count objects. At standard II level, the pupil learns and is able to recognize numbers and perform number operations limited to addition, subtraction, and multiplication.

Each of the levels had a different game setting so as to avoid monotony, bringing in variety to keep the learners interested and excited about the different levels. Simplicity was at the core of each setting, presenting an environment that the learners could easily identify with, interact with, and at the same time find attractive enough to keep the learners interested and entertained.

Standard 1 Level 1 was about identifying the missing number in this level, the setting is the playing ground. This setting was designed because it was very familiar to the children. They were able to identify the playing ground, the balls, and the boy sprite. A sequence of numbers is provided with one missing number. The sequence of numbers is generated at random and ranges between one (1) and nine (9) in line with the Tanzania curriculum for basic education. The numbers are either in ascending or descending order, and the player is expected to identify the missing number. After identifying the missing number, the player should move the boy sprite to kick the ball with the missing number (Figs. 1, 2, 3, 4, 5, 6, 7). If the player kicks the ball with the right answer, the player gains five (5) more points, and the setting is reset. Else if the player kicks the ball with the wrong answer, no points are earned, and the setting is also reset (see Fig. 8).

Standard 1 Level 2: Counting Object. In this level, the setting is a garden field. This setting was chosen because it is also very familiar to the children. The children were able to identify the field, the footballs, bubbles, and the bee sprite. A random number n, ranging between one (1) and nine (9), was generated. And n number of footballs drawn. The player is expected to count the number of footballs drawn. After counting, the player should move the bee sprite till they pop the bubble with the number n, which is the total number of footballs drawn on the screen. If the player pops the bubble with the right answer, the player gains five (5) more points, and the setting is reset. Else if the player pops the bubble with the wrong answer, no points are earned, and the setting is also reset (see Fig. 5).

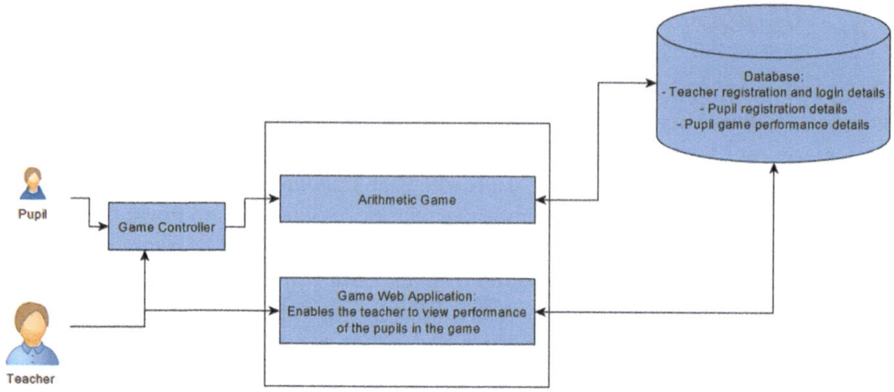

Fig. 1 System architecture overview

Standard 2: level 1(Addition), level 2(Subtraction), level 3(Multiplication). In this level, the setting is underwater: This setting was chosen to bring an element of fantasy into the game. The children were able to identify the underwater scene, fish sprite, and bubbles used in this setting. Two random numbers, a and b, were chosen. In the addition level, the numbers a and b were each ranging between 0 and 100; in the subtraction level, the numbers a and b were each ranging between 0 and 100, whereas, in the multiplication level, the numbers a and b were ranging between 0 and 10. These ranges were identified following the Tanzania Basic Syllabus for Standard II [8], whereby the learners are expected to: add numbers to obtain a sum not exceeding 1000, subtract numbers less than 1000, and multiply numbers to obtain a product not exceeding 1000. After adding, subtracting, or multiplying the numbers and getting their result, the player should move the fish sprite to pop the bubble with the right answer. If the player pops the bubble with the right answer, the player gains five (5) more points, and the setting is reset. Else if the player pops the bubble with the wrong answer, no points are earned, and the setting is also reset (see Fig. 6).

Game Rules and Mechanics. The overall rule that applies at all levels is to avoid bubbles or balls with the wrong answers. To gain points in the game, the player must move the sprite or character at that level to hit the ball or pop the bubble with the right answer. Using the LEFT, RIGHT, UP, and DOWN buttons of the console, the player should move the sprite either up, down, forward, or backward as they navigate to the right answer while avoiding all the other balls or bubbles with the wrong answers.

Incentive System Mechanism. After popping the bubble with the right answer or kicking the ball with the right answer, the player gains five (5) points. The total points gathered once the game is over are sent over to a MySQL database from which the students can then be ranked on the web app scoreboard, with the highest-ranking child at the top of the scoreboard (see Fig. 7).

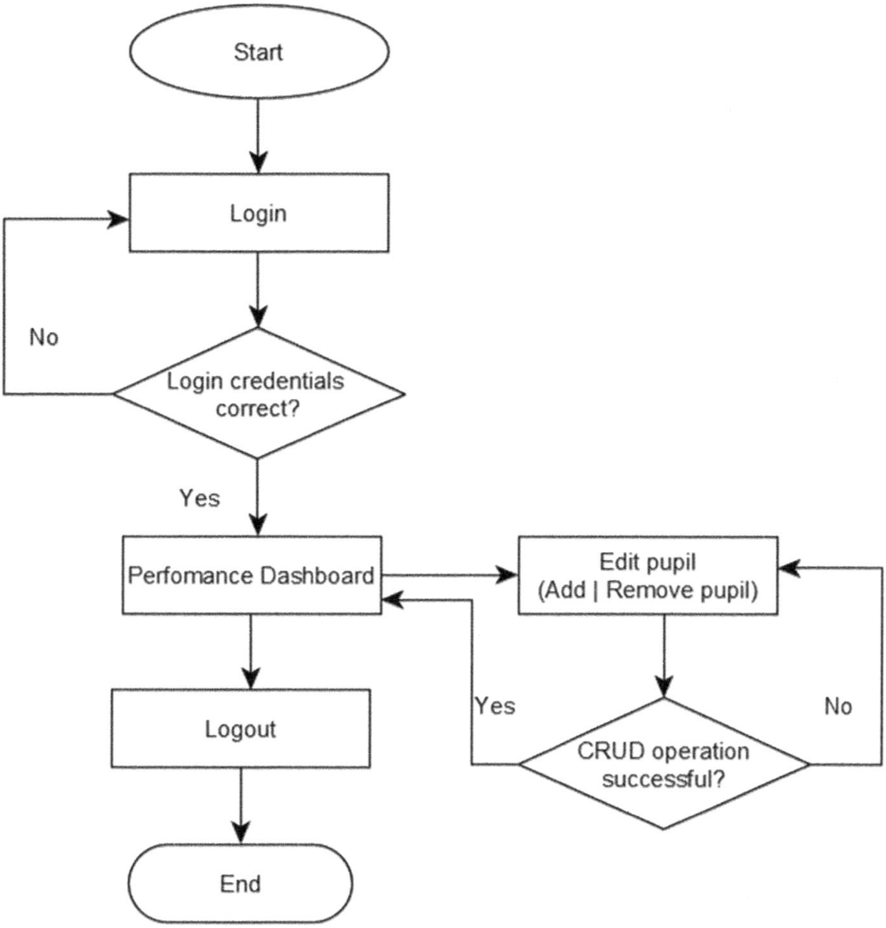

Fig. 2 Web application flow chart

Pupil Performance assessment. The game connects to a MySQL database. The teacher can sign in a student such that after the game is over, the pupil's scores are sent to the database so as to keep track of the pupil performance. Through a web application, the teacher can then access a summarized performance of the learners and can therefore determine the learning progress of individual learners in the different game levels.

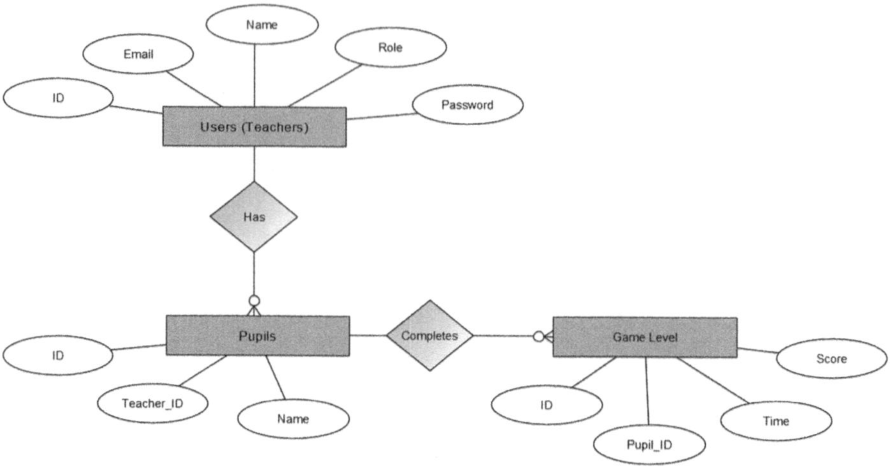

Fig. 3 Entity relationship diagram

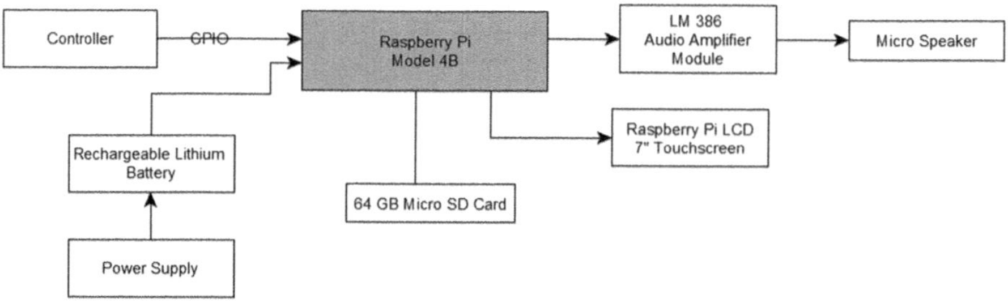

Fig. 4 Hardware design

2.3 *Software Development*

From the requirements identified the game system was then designed. The system architecture overview is presented (see Fig. 1). Extreme programming (XP) agile software development life cycle was used in the development of the game Math Bubbles. The game was planned, developed, and tested in incremental iterations.

The system has two primary users, the pupil, who plays the arithmetic game and the teacher, who guides the pupil. By using the game controller, the pupil is able to interact with the game; and using the game controller also, the teacher is able to guide the pupil through the game. In order to view and track the performance of the learners, the teacher registers and logs into the web application where he or she is presented with a summarized performance of his or her learners in the game. A MySQL Database is used to store the teacher's registration and login details, the learners' registration details, and the pupil's game performance details at the different game levels.

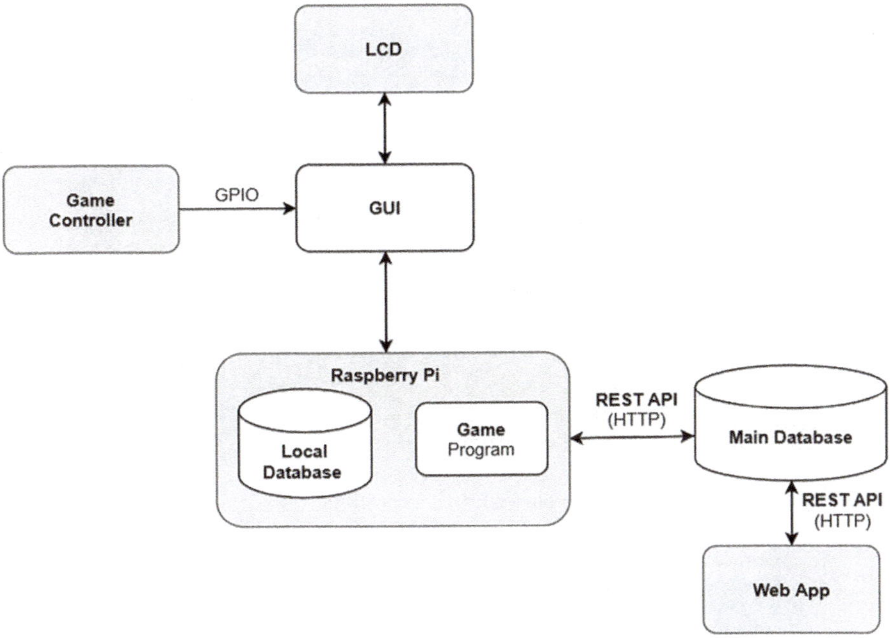

Fig. 5 System communication architecture

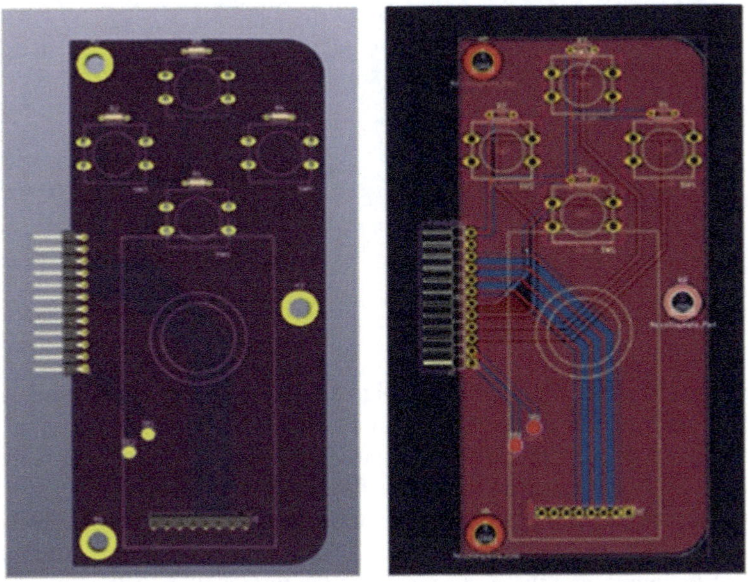

Fig. 6 PCB boards design

Fig. 7 Standard I level 2 (counting objects)

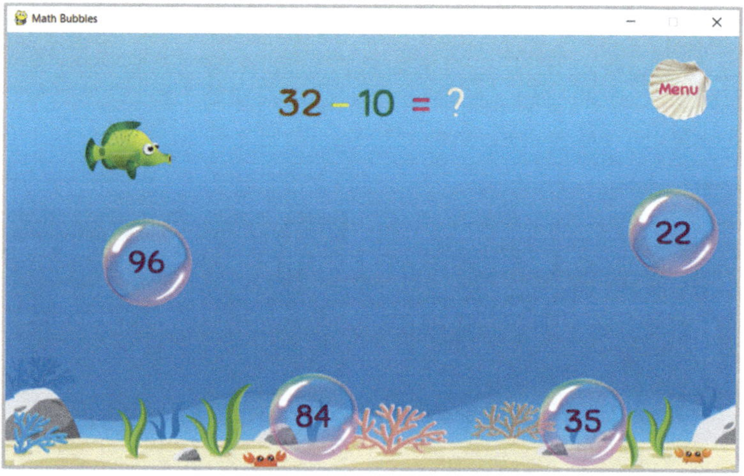

Fig. 8 Standard II level 2 (subtraction)

Web Application Design. A simple, easy-to-use web application was also designed. Through the web application, the teacher can register and log in, register his or her learners, view student performance, and edit student details. A flow chart representing the web application process flow is shown (see Fig. 2).

Database Design. In the game system development, a MYSQL database was used to store registration and login details of the user (teacher), the registration details of the pupil, and the performance of the pupils at the different game levels (see Fig. 3)

The user's table stored the teacher's registration and login details. Each teacher can have many pupils, and therefore the Teacher_ID was the foreign key to link the two tables. The only pupil information required was the pupil name, and on successful registration, the pupil was assigned a unique ID. A pupil can complete various game levels, and upon completion, the score is recorded alongside the timestamp of completion. The pupil_ID was the foreign key to link the two tables.

Software Development Tools. Python language was used to develop the game. Among the reasons that lead to this choice include the fact that python is an excellent cross-platform language, running smoothly on various platforms making it suitable for the development of the game. Pygame library was used as the main game development library. Pygame includes several modules with functions for drawing graphics, playing sounds, handling mouse inputs, all of which were essential for game development. Moreover, Pygame is portable across different platforms and devices, making it suitable for the Arithmetic Video Game and Console, which runs on Raspberry Pi 4.

The web application used by the teacher to track the performance of the learners was implemented using HTML, CSS, and JavaScript for the front end and PHP for the backend; MySQL database was also used to store the teacher's registration and login details and the students' registration and performance details. An object-oriented approach was used in the design and implementation of the game. This approach allowed for modularization of the code, enabling reusability and easy maintenance.

2.4 Hardware Design

The system's hardware design comprises a game controller to provide the inputs to a video game and a console that outputs the video signal to display a video game. The game console is based on the Raspberry Pi 4 model B. The Raspberry Pi is a low-cost, compact, high-performing, single-board microcontroller that lets you build hardware projects with some code running on the microcontroller. Raspberry Pi is attached to LCD 7″ with Touchscreen and a rechargeable lithium battery to power the game console unit, this is to avoid the use of direct power when using the game console as it is designed to be used by children. A 64GB microSD card was used for storage. This is because it provided enough memory to store the Raspbian operating system, GPIOzero library, XAMPP server, the game, and the game assets (see Fig. 4). The system communication architecture is illustrated (see Fig. 5).

A game controller was developed using push-buttons and a digital five directional joystick. It is interfaced with Raspberry Pi via the GPIO pins. The controller is comprised of eight push-buttons and a joystick for interacting with the game. Four of the push-buttons were used for sprite movement in up, down, left, and right directions. The other four were used for quit, cancel, menu, and select options. The joystick provided an alternative movement control input option. The pupil who is the player controls the game through the game controller (see Fig. 4).

LM386 audio amplifier module was used to amplify the game sound features and micro speaker was used as the sound output. The selection of these speakers and an amplifier was due to their low power consumption, small size and lightweight, which was a desired feature of the entire game console. The PCB etching was done using toner transfer and ferric chloride and the outer casing was made of polylactic acid (PLA) standard 1.75 mm (see Fig. 6).

3 Results and Discussions

3.1 Game Screenshots

A few screenshots from the game are as shown in figures below: (see Figs. 7, 8, 9, 10).

3.2 Expert Assessment

Two curriculum development experts, one psychologist, and five teachers interacted with the game and console. Afterward, they evaluated the game based on a 5-point Likert scale (strongly agree, disagree, neutral, agree, strongly agree). The evaluation assessed whether the game and console met the requirements on syllabus matching, level of immersion, motivation, and learning outcome. All the eight respondents awarded five (5) points for syllabus matching, level of immersion, motivation, and learning outcome; and one respondent out of the 8 awarded the game and console

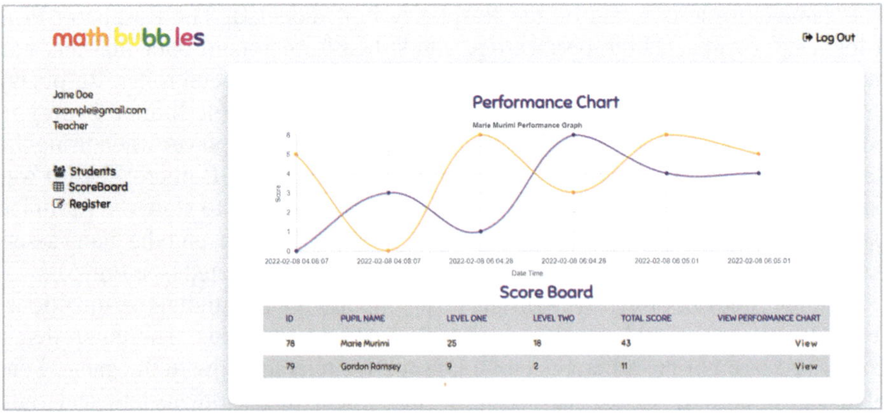

Fig. 9 Application score board showing learners' performance in the various game levels

Fig. 10 Game console: Standard I level 1 (identifying missing numbers)

four (4) points for the incentive system used. These responses confirm the game's high performance and effectiveness.

3.3 Usability and Effectiveness Testing

At this stage, the system's usability was assessed basing on the system's status visibility, compatibility, consistency, and visibility of elements. Fifteen (15) standard I and II learners played the game under observation in two phases. In the first phase, learners played with the help of their teachers, while in the second phase, they played on their own. In each of the phases, the children played only their levels. Tremendous improvement was witnessed in the second phase. The more the learners played the same game level, performances were seen to improve, and they could navigate through the game levels with ease. This was a desired result as this means that the player could understand the game concept and mechanics. The learners showed more interest and enjoyment as they played through.

4 Conclusion and Recommendations

The project was aimed at developing an affordable arithmetic learning video game and console that could be integrated into classroom learning. The video game and console was to fit the curriculum and cultural context of Tanzania. It was desired that the game be available in both English and Kiswahili which are widely used as the language of instruction in private and public schools, respectively.

This project achieved a prototype demonstrating the viability of a digital game-based learning system in Tanzania. Due to funds and time constraints some features such as games based on other subjects such as Science, English, and Kiswahili were not included in the first version of the game. Upon further improvements, more features and subjects can be included. Further work to include machine learning and artificial intelligence to improve the game mechanics, user learning, and gaming experience should also be researched. This includes image processing to collect feedback on the users' experience.

We recommend that this project be integrated into classroom learning activities. Mass production of the game console and video game will also cut down on the cost of production making it much more affordable.

References

1. Gozcu, E., & Caganaga, C. K. (2016). The importance of using games in EFL classrooms. *Cypriot Journal of Educational Sciences, 11*(3), 126–135.
2. Zirawaga, V. S., Olusanya, A. I., & Maduku, T. (2017). Gaming in education: Using games as a support tool to teach history. *Journal of Education and Practice, 8*(15), 55–64.
3. Pakhrani, J., Varghese, A., & Vyas, S. (2020). Comparative study of PC and gaming console for video games.
4. Adžić, S., Al-Mansour, J., Naqvi, H., & Stambolić, S. (2021). The impact of video games on students' educational outcomes. *Entertainment Computing, 38*, 100412.
5. Picton, I., Clark, C., & Judge, T. (2020). *Video game playing and literacy: A survey of young people aged 11 to 16. A National Literacy Trust Research Report*. National Literacy Trust.
6. McAleese, J. R. (2021). *Video game archive: Nintendo 64 [PhD Thesis]*. Worcester Polytechnic Institute.
7. Curriculum for Basic Education Standard I and II. (2015). The united republic of Tanzania ministry of education, science and technology.
8. Basic Education Syllabus for Standard II. (2016). The united republic of Tanzania ministry of education, science and technology.

Definition of the Data Value Chain

Dirk Bendlin, Jorge Marx Gómez, and Moritz Werther Häckell

1 Introduction

"Data is the new oil!" [1]. This expression, which has been adopted by other authors [2, 3], describes the abstract relationship between data and the value created from it. In this context, data has been compared to crude oil and the complex process of refining it into various end products. Similar to how crude oil is not suitable for automobiles, not all data processing algorithms are appropriate for all applications. The DVC assists in determining the optimal data management and analysis method with respect to the use case.

Three main components are necessary for the application of data science in decision-making, namely application knowledge, high-quality and analyzable data [4], and methodological expertise [15]. Data can be described as "big data" if it is characterized by high quantity, variety, and velocity of the data production [5]. According to [2], classical analytical applications can be found in business intelligence (BI) and data science (DS). BI and DS represent the interface between data analysis and decision-makers in their domain. In addition to the statistics that are mainly used in BI, DS applications are realized through various advanced analytic methods such as artificial intelligence and subcategories such as machine learning or deep learning [2]. The process of creating value from data needs to be defined in order to understand the value that BI or DS applications can provide to decision-makers. Depending on the use case, BI analysis may be sufficient and replace more complex DS analysis. The objective of this paper is to identify different views regarding data value chains (DVCs) based on a literature review. For this paper the term DVC should be understood as the process of creating value from

D. Bendlin (✉) · J. Marx Gómez · M. W. Häckell
Carl von Ossietzky Universität Oldenburg, Oldenburg, Germany
e-mail: dirk.bendlin@uni-oldenburg.de; jorge.marx.gomez@uni-oldenburg.de; moritz.haeckell@ramboll.com

J. Marx Gómez et al. (eds.), *Smart and Secure Embedded and Mobile Systems*, Progress in IS, https://doi.org/10.1007/978-3-031-56603-5_25

data for an organization, from the acquisition over the management and analysis of data to the decision. After identifying different approaches for defining DVCs, the goal is to derive a commonly understood definition of the term. This will help data scientists and decision-makers from organization to find common ground for their data management strategy.

2 Definition of a Data Value Chain

The basis for data-driven decisions is a representation of the real world through data. Data processing and analysis shape this data into contextualized information, knowledge, or wisdom [6]. As the final stage, wisdom indicates when and why knowledge should be used [7]. To summarize these relationships, [8] developed the DIKW (data, information, knowledge, wisdom) pyramid as a model of thinking. In many cases, this concept represents a simplified four-level pyramid that excludes the real world as a data provider [6, 7, 9]. Because this paper considers the entire DVC, a five-stage representation that includes the real world has been chosen for evaluation [6]. One criticism of the DIKW pyramid is oversimplification of the hierarchy levels and their interrelationships [9]. To define the interrelationships more clearly, the DIKW pyramid has been expanded to include core questions and objectives from the analytical maturity model according to [10] (Fig. 1). This expansion allows the levels of the pyramid to be combined with the objectives of analytics. Analytic maturity ranges from a descriptive view of data to diagnostic evaluation, predictive forecasting, or even workflow automation [11].

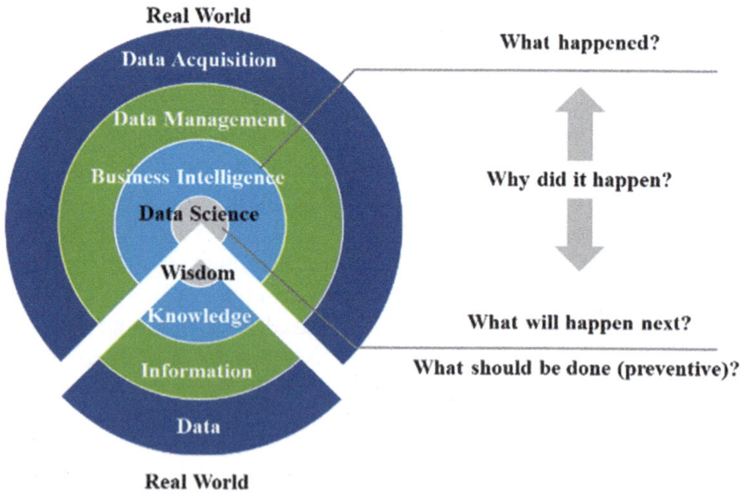

Fig. 1 Prerequisites for the implementation of data science

To assess data in a tangible and understandable way for users and decision-makers, data analysis is required, which creates data products. A data product is a product of data analysis that creates added value for a company [3]. For this work, a data product is defined as at least one definitive and clearly business-relevant question to be answered by data analysis. For this purpose, the interpretation of all parts of the DVC must be clearly and comprehensibly defined (decision boundaries). Decisions should be based on distinct key performance indicators (KPIs). The data sources and the processing of the KPIs should also be defined as clearly as possible.

Various approaches in theoretical and empirical studies have addressed the question of how data analysis can be successfully implemented in companies. A subset of four data mining processes (KDD,[1] CRISP-DM,[2] FMDS,[3] and TDSP[4]) have been summarized by [12]. The processes presented, excluding KDD, have in common that they consist of iterative phases of problem definition, data collection, data modelling, and product development. According to [12], the KDD process was used in only 7.5% of the projects studied. In addition to the processes already presented, alternatives such as the Sample, Explore, Modify, Model, and Assess (SEMMA) process exist. Originally, SEMMA was developed by the SAS[5] Institute and is therefore linked to the SAS Enterprise Miner software. Due to this limited application, SEMMA is not discussed further here [13].

CRISP-DM has become established across industries worldwide and is by far the most widely used method for data mining projects (42% in 2014) according to [12]. The CRISP-DM process was introduced in 1996 by SPSS, Teradata, NCR, Daimler, and OHRA [12]. It is a cycle consisting of six phases; the order is not fixed and can be adjusted flexibly according to the needs of the project [14]. CRISP-DM has a logical and intuitive structure and provides a high level of quality and efficiency, even for the most challenging projects [12]. The model provides a detailed overview of the typical phases of a project and the tasks in each phase, as well as explanations of the relationships between tasks [14]. Numerous studies have examined this method. One factor that is critical to project success is that CRISP-DM can be performed independently from the chosen analysis method [12, 13]. The six phases of CRISP-DM include business understanding, data understanding, data preparation, modelling, evaluation, and deployment. The CRISP-DM process places a high emphasis on the data-analytic aspects of a DVC. Other process models focus more on the business understanding and business value of data science. CRISP-DM can be used as a framework for surveys [15]. However, even after successful implementation of CRISP-DM to support data analysis, the question arises as to how more efficient decisions were made and how much potential for optimization remains. There is also the question of how easily CRISP-DM can be used to

[1] Knowledge Discovery in Database.

[2] CRoss-Industry Standard Process for Data Mining.

[3] Foundational Methodology for Data Science.

[4] Team Data Science Process.

[5] Statistical Analysis System.

communicate with various stakeholders [15]. This aspect has been highlighted as particularly challenging by the original developers of CRISP-DM [15].

3 Comparison of Existing Models

This work is related to the topic of information systems (IS). According to [16], IS positions itself along two main research fields: design science and behavioral science:

1. Behavioral science is concerned with the creation of theories to explain human or organizational behavior [16, 17].
2. Design science is concerned with expanding human or organizational boundaries [17].

Because a DVC allows individuals and organizations to expand their boundaries, this work can also be classified as related to design science. The design science research methodology (DSRM) model, defined by [18] has been chosen to describe how the definition has been derived as shown in Fig. 2.

The business model canvas (BMC) is an established way to study the value chain of (data) products [6, 19, 20]. The BMC is divided into nine elements: The value proposition (VP, in the center), the infrastructure consisting of key activities (KA), key partners (KP), and key resources (KR), and the customer interface consisting of the customer relationship (CR), the customer segment (CS), and the channels (CH) [20]. These elements are accommodated by the cost structure (C$) and the revenue stream (R$) [20]. The BMC is focused on the VP of any product and thus can be used for data products. However, extensions of the model have been developed, focusing more deeply on particular aspects of the DVC. [21] identified nine different tools, which they mapped to 12 elements (business case, data collection, data source, data quality, data integration, methods, skills, software, model quality, costs and

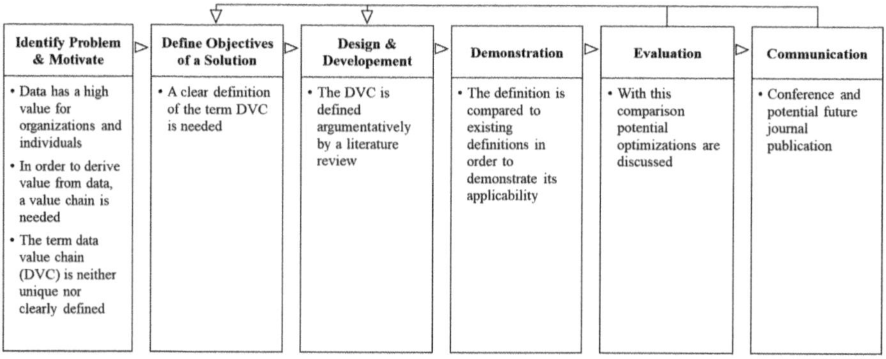

Fig. 2 Methodology chosen for this work

revenue, value added, and stakeholders). As a result, [21] created their own canvas model, the data science canvas. [22] identified nine tools as well, of which five were not included by [21]. Thus, these two reviews together identified 14 distinct tools. [22] categorized their tools into five different elements (data source, analytics methods, user wishes, user benefits, data product) to compare them and create an extended model, which is the data product canvas. An alternative model has been developed by [23] and [24], they aim to develop DVCs for big data projects. In order to obtain an overview of further models, a detailed literature review was performed following the process suggested by [25]; thus, a search algorithm was defined and used to screen various online sources as defined by [26]. In the next steps, the sources were clustered into "A" and "B" sources as outlined by [27]. Out of the 27 "A" sources that were found, only 21 were publicly available; these 21 sources have been used as the basis for this report (see Table 1).

The most relevant models identified by this work are summarized and compared in Table 2. Some models, such as the "IoT-enabled product visual analytics value chain" by [28] or the data value chain from [29], are limited to specific use cases, such as predictive maintenance, and thus have not been included in the final model.

The models of [24, 23] have been referenced by different researchers, including [31, 33, 34, 28]. Another work by [9] only refers to [23]. Thus, both models appear to be applicable in a broader sense as comparable models such as [28] or more simplified models such as those used by [30] or [32]. The review of [33] also presents a systematization which can help to distinguish the two main approaches, the Data value chain (for Big Data) [23] and the Big Data Value chain [24]. Similar approaches can also be found, such as that of [35], which is limited to information-intensive services such as fitness tracking or car infotainment, for example. Other reports, such as [11], only define the term DVC.

As a result, the DVC can be schematically illustrated as shown in Fig. 3. Data-driven decisions can be supported if data is understood as an important resource for a DVC. Five main components of this value chain form the basis for data-driven decisions (Fig. 3 Parts of the DVC). First, sufficient data acquisition provides the foundation for decisions. Second, data governance ensures that processes are

Table 1 Results of the literature review

Library	Total [All]	Relevant [B]	Relevant [A]	Search algorithm
IEEE Xplore including IET	34	17	3	"Data value chain"
ACM digital library	28	3	1	"Data value chain"
Springer link	201	34	12	All: "Data value chain" Within computer science
Science direct	144	23	8	"Data value chain"
AISeL[a]	51	17	3	"Data value chain"
Wiley online library	47	8	0	"Data value chain"
Total	505	102	27	–

[a]Association for Information Systems (AIS) eLibrary

Table 2 Comparison of data value chain models

CRISP-DM	BMC	Data value chain (for Big Data) [23]	Big Data Value chain [24]	Covered in DVC under
• Business understanding	• Key activities • Key partners • Customer relationship Customer segments	• N/A	• N/A	• Decision
• Data understanding	• Key resources • Key activities • Key partners	• Data discovery: • Collect and annotate	• Data acquisition	• Data acquisition
• Data preparation	• Key resources • Key activities • Key partners	• Data discovery: • Prepare • Organize • Data integration	• Data storage • Data curation	• Data governance • Data management
• Modelling	• Key resources • Key activities • Key partners	• Data exploitation: • Analyze • Visualize	• Data analysis	• Data analysis
• Evaluation	• Value proposition • Cost structure • Revenue streams	• N/A	• N/A	• Data analysis
• Deployment	• Channels	• Data exploitation: • Make decisions	• Data usage	• Decision

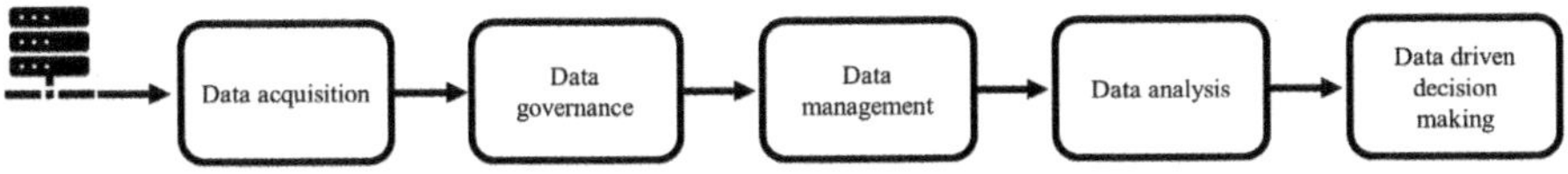

Fig. 3 Parts of the DVC

followed and that roles are established to pursue high data quality. Third, data management ensures that the data is accessible. Fourth, potential data analyses can be performed. The data analysis must generate data products that, in the fifth step, add value to organizations decisions in time. Improved data utilization can thus lead to a better basis for planning and can help avoid or reduce additional costs or other project risks.

The resulting DVC model is generic and can be extended to suit individual needs. As this review demonstrates, there are several approaches to describe or examine value creation with data. For this reason, solutions should always be adaptable to the goal of the evaluation and the target groups involved (e.g., data scientists and decision-makers). A common understanding of DVC can help companies discuss and identify potential areas of improvement along the DVC.

4 Summary and Outlook

The value of data has been compared to the value of oil in today's world. In this sense, data can be seen as a lubricant for future industrial developments. However, like oil, the value of raw data can only be fully exploited through a complex process of refinement. Exploring how value can be created from data is currently attracting considerable interest from researchers and users alike. This has been reflected in the variety of approaches that have been developed to better integrate data analytics into a value-creation process. CRISP-DM places a stronger focus on data-analytics aspects; business understanding is seen as more subordinate. To address this gap, many canvas models that focus heavily on either data analytics or business understanding have been developed. The existing approaches to defining a DVC assume generality without providing sufficient evidence to support this statement. Based on the large number of different approaches, it is difficult to imagine that there is a universal solution. A universal approach to DVC can therefore only function if the value chain can be extended to meet individual needs. In addition it must be ensured that data products provide added value for users and decision-makers.

Our approach to define the DVC and compare it to existing models represents a small contribution to better simplify existing approaches and to understand the need for extensible models which can be customized to the research goal at hand. In addition, it may further stimulate discussion in the research community.

References

1. Humby, C. (2006). Data is the new oil. Retrieved February 28, 2022, from https://ana.blogs.com/maestros/2006/11/data_is_the_new.html
2. Kordon, A. K. (2020). *Applying data science. How to create value with artificial intelligence*. Springer International Publishing; Springer.
3. Stockinger, K., Stadelmann, T., & Ruckstuhl, A. (2016). Data Scientist als Beruf. In D. Fasel & A. Meier (Eds.), *Big data, vol. 16. Edition HMD* (pp. 59–81). Springer Fachmedien Wiesbaden.
4. Kenett, R., & Redman, T. C. (2019). *The real work of data science. Turning data into information, better decisions, and stronger organizations*. Wiley.
5. Cielen, D., Meysman, A., & Ali, M. (2016). *Introducing data science. Big data, machine learning, and more, using python tools*. Manning Publications.
6. Haneke, U. (Ed.). (2019). *Data science. Grundlagen, Architekturen und Anwendungen, 1st ed. Edition TDWI*. dpunkt.verlag.
7. Jifa, G., & Lingling, Z. (2014). Data, DIKW, Big Data and Data Science. *Procedia Computer Science, 31*, 814–821. https://doi.org/10.1016/j.procs.2014.05.332
8. Ackoff, R. (1989). From data to wisdom. *Journal of Applied Systems Analysis, 1*(16), 3–9.
9. Bernstein, J. H. (2009). The data-information-knowledge-wisdom hierarchy and its antithesis. *NASKO, 2*(1), 68–75. https://doi.org/10.7152/nasko.v2i1.12806
10. Taylor, D. (2013). Predictive analysis enables operational insights. Retrieved February 22, 2021, from https://blogs.sap.com/2013/03/05/predictive-analysis-enables-operational-insights/
11. Gross, D., & Thomsen, C. (2016). Opitz consulting: Advanced analytics - die konsequente Antwort auf big data. *Predictive & Advanced Analytics*, 1–5.
12. Foroughi, F., & Luksch, P. (2018). Data science methodology for cybersecurity projects, pp. 1–14. https://doi.org/10.5121/csit.2018.80401.
13. Azevedo, A., & Santos, M. F. (n.d.). KDD, semma and crisp-dm: A parallel overview.
14. IBM: IBM SPSS Modeler CRISP-DM Guide. (2016). Retrieved June 4, 2023, from https://www.ibm.com/docs/it/SS3RA7_18.3.0/pdf/ModelerCRISPDM.pdf
15. Wyss, M. (2019). Aufbau eines starken Data Science-Teams von Grund auf. Retrieved July 12, 2021, from https://www.inwt-statistics.de/blog-artikel-lesen/aufbau-eines-starken-data-science-teams-von-grund-auf.html
16. Wirth, R., & Hipp, J. (2000). CRISP-DM: Towards a standard process model for data mining. In: Proceedings of the fourth international conference on the Practical application of knowledge discovery and data mining, New York, New York, 27–31.08.1998. 5133.
17. Hevner, A. R., March, S. T., Park, J., & Ram, S. (2004). Design science in information systems research. *MIS Quarterly, 28*(1), 75–105.
18. Peffers, K., Tuunanen, T., Rothenberger, M. A., & Chatterjee, S. (2007). A design science research methodology for information systems research. *JMIS, 24*(3), 45–77. https://doi.org/10.2753/MIS0742-1222240302
19. Kruse, F., Dmitriyev, V., & Marx Gómez, J. (2018). Building a connection between decision maker and data-driven decision process. *Archives of Data Science, Series A, 4*(1). https://doi.org/10.5445/KSP/1000085951/03
20. Osterwalder, A., Pigneur, Y., Bernarda, G., & Smith, A. (2014). *Value proposition design. How to create products and services customers want. Strategyzer series*. John Wiley & Sons.
21. Neifer, T., Lawo, D., & Esan, M. (2021). Data science canvas: Evaluation of a tool to manage data science projects. In: Proceedings of the 54th Hawaii International Conference on System Sciences. Hawaii International Conference on System Sciences (HICSS), Honolulu, Hawaii, pp. 5399–5409.
22. Fruhwirth, M., Breitfuss, G., & Pammer-Schindler, V. (2020). The data product canvas: A visual collaborative tool for designing data-driven business models. In A. Pucihar, M. Kljajić Borštnar, R. Bons, H. Cripps, A. Sheombar, D. Vidmar, A. Baggia, E. Jereb, D. Kofjač, G. Lenart, M. Marolt, M. Urh, & B. Werber (Eds.), *33rd bled eConference enabling technology for*

a sustainable society. June 28–29, 2020, online: Conference proceedings (1st ed.). University Press; Faculty of Organizational Sciences.
23. Miller, H. G., & Mork, P. (2013). From data to decisions: A value chain for big data. *IT Professional, 15*(1), 57–59. https://doi.org/10.1109/MITP.2013.11
24. Cavanillas, J. M., Curry, E., & Wahlster, W. (Eds.). (2016). *New horizons for a data-driven economy. A roadmap for usage and exploitation of big data in Europe* (1st ed.). Springer International Publishing.
25. Hay, L., Duffy, A. H. B., McTeague, C., Pidgeon, L. M., Vuletic, T., & Grealy, M. (2017). A systematic review of protocol studies on conceptual design cognition: Design as search and exploration. *Design Science, 3*, 1–36. https://doi.org/10.1017/dsj.2017.11
26. Kuhrmann, M., Fernández, D. M., & Daneva, M. (2017). On the pragmatic design of literature studies in software engineering: An experience-based guideline. *Empirical Software Engineering, 22*(6), 2852–2891. https://doi.org/10.1007/s10664-016-9492-y
27. Prexl, L. (2019). *Mit digitalen Quellen arbeiten* (3rd ed.). UTB GmbH; Schöningh.
28. Faroukhi, A. Z., El Alaoui, I., Gahi, Y., & Amine, A. (2020). Big data monetization throughout big data value chain: A comprehensive review. *Journal of Big Data, 7*(1), 1–22. https://doi.org/10.1186/s40537-019-0281-5
29. Åkerman, M., Lundgren, C., Bärring, M., Folkesson, M., Berggren, V., Stahre, J., Engström, U., & Friis, M. (2018). Challenges building a data value chain to enable data-driven decisions: A predictive maintenance case in 5G-enabled manufacturing. *Procedia Manufacturing, 17*, 411–418. https://doi.org/10.1016/j.promfg.2018.10.064
30. Mörth, O., Emmanouilidis, C., Hafner, N., & Schadler, M. (2020). Cyber-physical systems for performance monitoring in production intralogistics. *Computers & Industrial Engineering, 142*, 106333–106343. https://doi.org/10.1016/j.cie.2020.106333
31. Dinter, B., & Kollwitz, C. (2016). Towards a framework for open data related innovation contests. In: Association for information systems 2016—Proceedings of the Pre-ICIS SIGDSA/, pp. 1–9.
32. Beyan, O. D., Handschuh, S., Koumpis, A., Fragidis, G., & Decker, S. (2016). A framework for applying data integration and curation pipelines to support integration of migrants and refugees in Europe. *IFIP Advances in Information and Communication Technology, 480*, 588–596.
33. Straßburg, S., & Beckmann, H. (2022). Datenwirtschaft und Datenwertschöpfungsketten—Eine systematische Übersicht.
34. Kaiser, C., Stocker, A., Viscusi, G., Fellmann, M., & Richter, A. (2021). Conceptualising value creation in data-driven services: The case of vehicle data. *International Journal of Information Management, 59*, 102335–102350. https://doi.org/10.1016/j.ijinfomgt.2021.102335
35. Lim, C., Kim, K.-H., Kim, M.-J., Heo, J.-Y., Kim, K.-J., & Maglio, P. P. (2018). From data to value: A nine-factor framework for data-based value creation in information-intensive services. *International Journal of Information Management, 39*, 121–135. https://doi.org/10.1016/j.ijinfomgt.2017.12.007

Analysis of Bicycle Use in German Cities Based on Smartphone App-Generated Data

Firdaous Hebbal, Johannes Schering, Jorge Marx Gómez, and Jana Klemp

1 Introduction

Rising fuel and energy prices [1], environmental pollution [2], health protection [3], and many other common known reasons have strengthened the interest in cycling in the past few years. During the Corona pandemic, many people preferred to use individual means of transport which means the car or the bike instead of public transport [4]. The bicycle shows itself as a means of transport with great potential to meet these challenges because it can facilitate our mobility in many ways. As a consequence of the mentioned advantages, more than 80% of the people in Germany use the bicycle and 55% consider it as an indispensable means of transport [5]. In order to enable safe, reliable, and comfortable cycling whenever possible, there is a need to invest in the bicycle traffic infrastructure. More and more cycling datasets are becoming available that can support stakeholders in decision-making. So far, data-centric cycling approaches are based to a large scale on information generated by smartphones or bike computers. We can find many cycling smartphone applications that are used in different places, such as "Strava" [6] which is an app for athletes to track their training [7]. "Komoot" [8] and "Bike Citizens" [9] are apps that are used to plan bike tours, but the significance of these applications and their relevance is not yet clear. We know from the literature that these applications are often used by younger, male, and sportive cyclists [10]. The "Company Bike Challenge" [11] which is promoting the use of another bike app was implemented with a special focus on commuters and employees in the context of business mobility. The campaign tried in 2021 to motivate this target group to ride the bicycle more often supported by another smartphone app. The Ciclogreen application and its

F. Hebbal (✉) · J. Schering · J. Marx Gómez · J. Klemp
Department of Business Informatics VLBA, University of Oldenburg, Oldenburg, Germany
e-mail: firdaous.hebbal@uni-oldenburg.de; johannes.schering@uni-oldenburg.de; jorge.marx.gomez@uni-oldenburg.de; jana.klemp@uni-oldenburg.de

J. Marx Gómez et al. (eds.), *Smart and Secure Embedded and Mobile Systems*, Progress in IS, https://doi.org/10.1007/978-3-031-56603-5_26

related gamification approach enable app users to win prizes for cycled kilometers. Users can receive the so-called "Ciclos" points, which can be exchanged for gifts or discount codes at local dealers [12].

The main goal of this contribution is to present the preliminary results of the data analysis part. We want to discuss how and to what degree the different cities that were part of the data collection can be compared. After the introduction, we will briefly introduce the Company Bicycle Challenge and its related working processes. In the main chapter, we are going to describe how the smartphone app data was processed. Section 3.2 compares the collected data from different cities in the geographical and temporal dimensions. Durations, distances, and speed levels are compared among different cities. The trips were visualized on a map according to the speed levels. To evaluate the bicycle friendliness of the cities, these were compared regarding the number of braking processes and average waiting time. The conclusion summarizes the results.

2 Company Bike Challenge

The Company Bike Challenge which is very similar to the "Bike to work" campaign in Switzerland [13]—employees may win prizes if they commute to work by bike for more than 50 percent of their working days—was part of the European research project BITS [14] and took place between the end of May and the beginning of July 2021. As we can conclude from the naming, the focus was on companies, their employees, and their daily way to work. The research question behind this challenge was to check whether and to what degree an app-based gamification approach can nudge people to cycle more often.

The employees of the participating companies had the opportunity to download the app from the Spanish provider Ciclogreen [15]. The app anonymously recorded the cycled distance, the number of kilometers, and the average speed. The employees had access to a user interface to look up their own statistics and their collected points, so-called "Ciclos." Around 16 companies from all over Germany have supported the challenge. Among these 13 companies participated actively with their employees, the most active employer which is located near Dresden (Saxony) contributed more than 16.000 kilometers. Figure 1 visualizes how the data collection and processing process as part of the Company Bicycle Challenge worked. As part of the European research project BITS the company Baron Mobility Service provided the Ciclogreen app to its bike leasing customers. The employers made aware their employees of the project and its benefits. Besides the employees, all other interested people are able to download and to use the app. The gathered app data about cycling behavior was provided to the University of Oldenburg by the app provider Ciclogreen. Personal user information was not submitted.

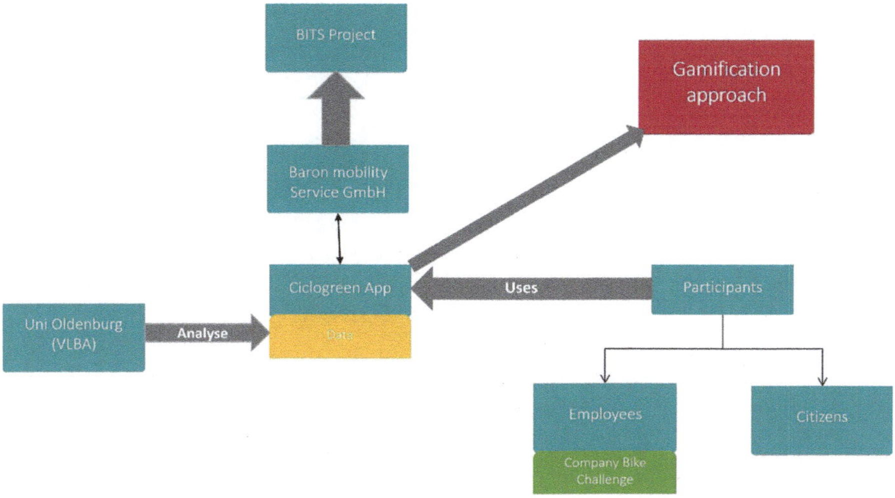

Fig. 1 Process of data collection and processing as part of the Company Bicycle Challenge

3 Characteristics of the Datasets

3.1 Data Processing

The Company Bike Challenge was running from the 24th of May till the fourth of July 2021. The whole dataset belongs to that timeframe. The initial dataset contains around 4.419 different trips. About 34 trips among these were considered as short trips (distance less than 400 meters), one trip was considered as not important (duration less than 1 min), and 26 trips were identified as fast trips (average speed higher than 35 km/h), and 204 were identified as slow trips (average speed less than 5 km/h). At more than 25.620 rows (steps) the speed level was higher than 48 km/h. These were left out in the analysis which led to a remaining dataset of 4.173 trips which consists of about 3.864.254 rows. For the comparison of different cities regarding bike use, cities with more than 50 trips during the Company Bike Challenge were considered in the data analysis. This final dataset consists of 2.675 bike trips.

3.2 Data Analysis

a) Geographical distribution of the trips.

The raw data includes the GPS coordinates, a trip ID, and a timestamp. Based on this information the durations, distances, and speed levels were calculated city

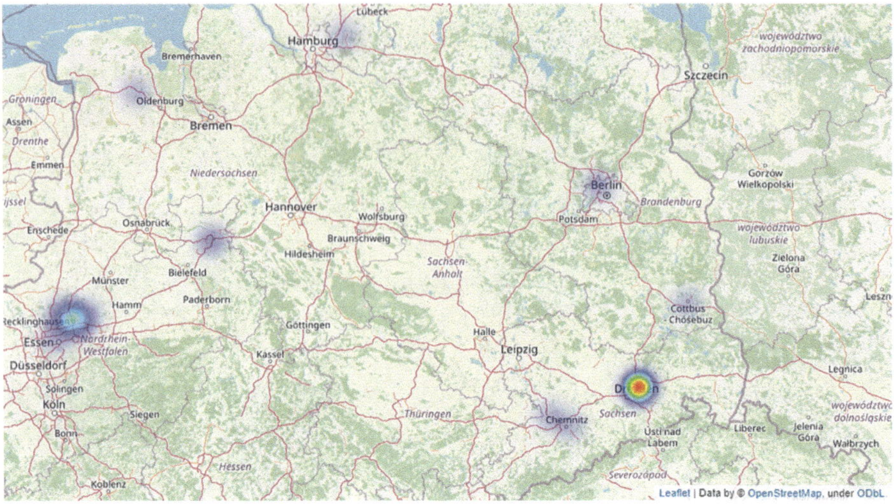

Fig. 2 Spatial distribution of the bike trips as heatmap

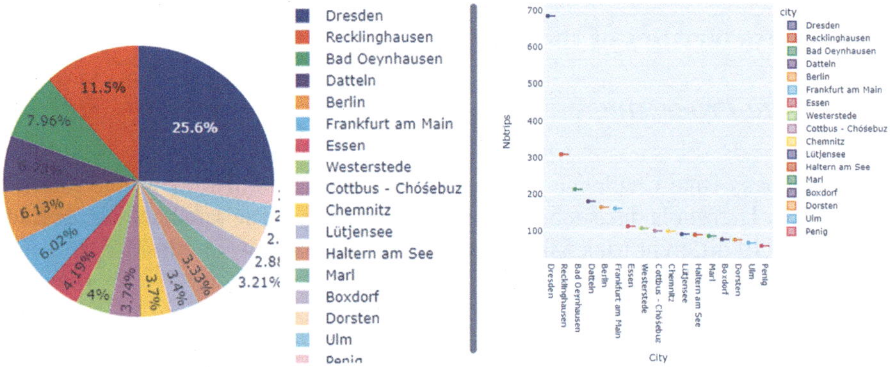

Fig. 3 Distribution of the trips per city: pie chart (left, in percent), violin plot (right, in total numbers)

by city. Figure 2 shows a heatmap where most of the bike trips were made. The most visible hotspot is Dresden in the Eastern part of Germany. Recklinghausen, Bad Oeynhausen, Frankfurt, and Berlin are other cities with an increased number of bike trips.

Figure 3 shows more in detail the distribution of the trips by city. One-fourth and more than 600 of the bike trips were made in Dresden. Recklinghausen follows with 11.5 percent and more than 300 trips. With the exception of Bad Oeynhausen (third place), all other cities and villages have less than 200 bicycle trips during the Company Bike Challenge.

b) Temporal distribution of the trips.

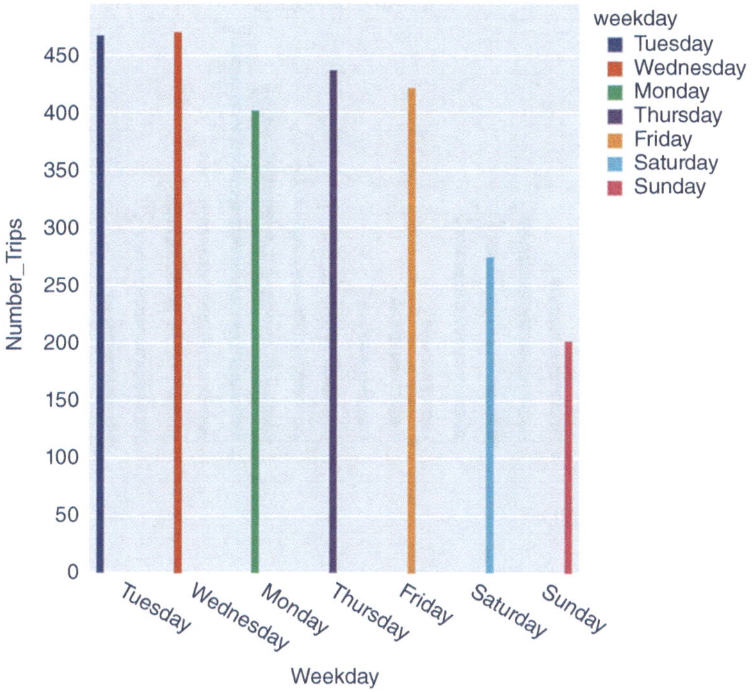

Fig. 4 Number of trips per day

The temporal dimension gives an overview of when the bicycle app was used. Figures 4 and 5 show the temporal distribution of the bike trips. The majority of the bike trips were detected at working days. The number of weekend trips is less (Fig. 4). The hourly distribution in Fig. 5 shows when the bicycle app is used over the day. The highest number of bike trips were registered in the afternoon hours between 2 and 4 pm. Almost 400 trips were detected in the morning peak hours (7–9 am).

c) Durations, distances, and speed levels in different cities.

The Company Bicycle Challenge was conducted at companies all over Germany, as described in the second section of this chapter. The different cities that were part of the data collection can be compared regarding (a) speed levels, (b) durations, and (c) distances (Fig. 6). The average duration and distance are about 36 min and 9.5 kilometers, what is presented by the horizontal line in the plot. Datteln, Frankfurt, or Chemnitz shows much longer trips with around 15 kilometers on average. In contrast, Berlin trips tend to be very short (less than four kilometers per trip). The average speed level per trip is about 16 km/h. Trips in Penig and Bad Oeynhausen tend to be faster. Duration and distances tend to be longer on Sundays.

d) Categorization of speed levels.

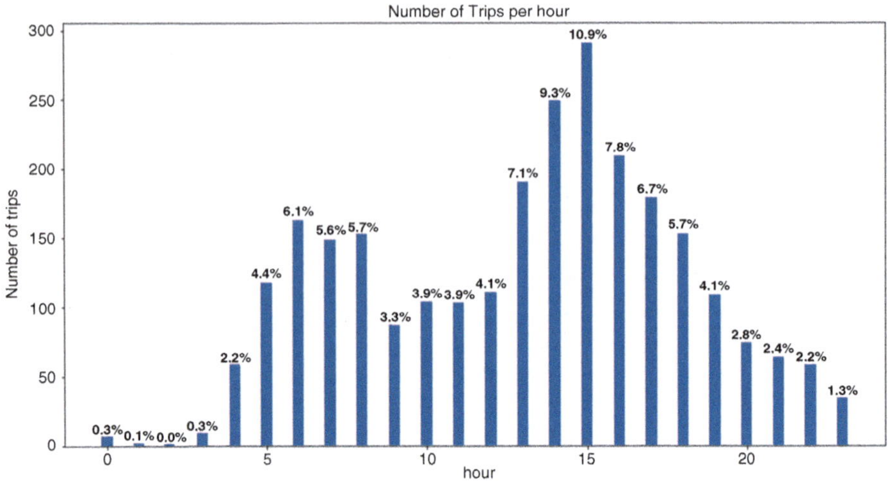

Fig. 5 Number of trips per hour

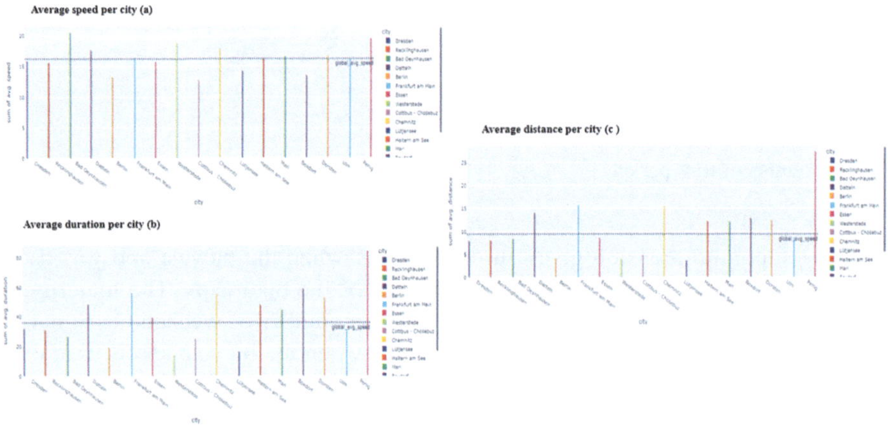

Fig. 6 Comparison of the average speed levels (a), durations (b), and distances (c)

The speed levels can be divided into different categories. The diagram in Fig. 7 represents how the trips are distributed per city. In general, there are three speed categories: Slow (5–10 km/h), medium (10–20 km/h), and fast (20–35 km/h). The overwhelming majority of the bike trips belong to the medium speed level. In contrast to other cities, Bad Oeynhausen shows more trips with fast than medium speed levels.

The bike trips were also visualized on a map according to the speed levels. It is confirmed that most of the trips belong to medium speed levels. Fast trips can be registered outside the city (e.g., at rural roads). Slow trips can be mainly detected in the inner city. Figure 8 shows the bike trips per category for the Dresden area. The

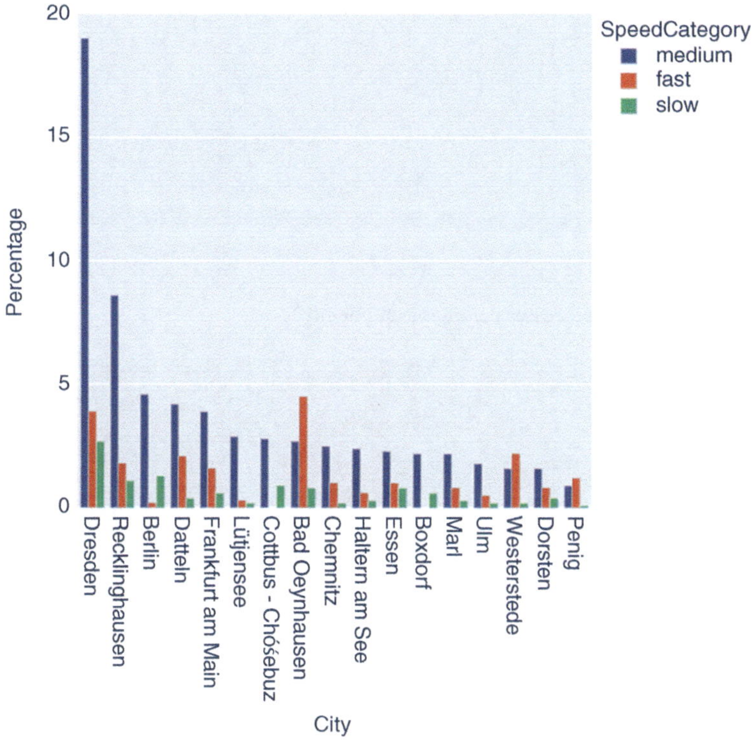

Fig. 7 Distribution of the trips per speed category per city

Fig. 8 Trips classification according to speed categories in Dresden (Saxony)

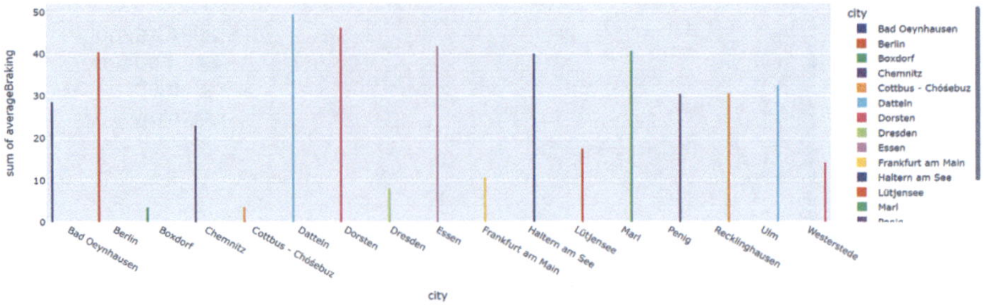

Fig. 9 Average braking processes per kilometer per city

Fig. 10 Heatmap of braking processes in Dresden (Saxony)

green lines represent slow, the orange lines medium, and the red lines fast speed levels.

e) Braking processes and waiting time.

The braking processes were also analyzed. Figure 9 shows the average braking processes per kilometer in each city. Cottbus and Boxdorf have the smallest average braking process (about three braking processes/km). The cities of Datteln, Dorsten, Essen, Marl, and Haltern am See. All of these North Rhine-Westphalia locations are very nearby to each other. Berlin also shows many braking processes per kilometer.

The braking processes were also visualized on a georeferenced map for each city. Figure 10 shows the braking processes as a heatmap for Dresden. The dark areas (orange/red) are where many braking processes took place. The hotspots are located at the main roads.

The cities can also be compared according to waiting time. Similar to the braking processes, waiting time hotspots were visualized on a map for each city. The employees and other app users mainly waited at intersections or near the company location. The DRK-Blutspendedienst Nord-Ost (Blood Donation Center of the

Fig. 11 Waiting time hotspots in Dresden (Saxony)

German Red Cross in North-East Germany) gathered 16.504 kilometers during the Company Bicycle Challenge and was awarded as the company with the highest number of cycled kilometers [16]. The website also provides a general information about the number of participants (312), the cycled kilometers (62.885 km), and the amount of CO_2 savings (15.490 kg). Figure 11 shows the waiting times as a heatmap for Dresden. The company location is one of the hotspots. Waiting times also often occur at inner city intersections.

4 Conclusion

The Company Bicycle Challenge aimed to motivate commuters to cycle to work more often by a gamification approach. The smartphone app collects cycling data that can support the understanding of how the bicycle is used in different cities. The results show that some companies and employees were very engaged in cycling (and the use of the app), others less. The cities of Dresden, Bad Oeynhausen, and Recklinghausen in Germany have the highest number of trips. Several companies and their employees were engaged in collecting kilometers. Most of the trips are registered on working days in the afternoon, which underlines that the results may reflect reality. However, it can be assumed that the share of leisure trips is relatively high. For instance, in Penig (Saxony), very long trips can be registered. No substantial differences in speed levels can be detected among different cities. Most trips reach an average speed level between 10–20 km/h, which can be described as normal bicycle speed (depending on the bicycle type). Trips outside the cities tend to be faster. Here we find a smaller number of pedestrians and intersections. Some cities in North Rhine-Westphalia and Berlin show an increased number of braking processes per kilometer what could be an additional information about the cycling quality in these cities. Waiting times often occur at inner city intersections. The preliminary results that are presented in this contribution will be expanded in the future. For instance, the bicycle app data can be combined with other cycling data sources to learn how representative the data collection by the smartphone is compared to stationary measurement systems (stationary bike counters, etc.) and whether the traffic safety situation is well reflected (e.g., comparison to bike accidents). These results will be discussed in further publications.

Acknowledgments The project BITS (Bicycles and Intelligent Transport Systems) is supported by the Interreg North Sea Program (Priority 4, Promoting green transport and mobility) of the European Regional Development Fund of the European Union.

Disclaimer This paper reflects only the author's view, and the Interreg North Sea Region is not responsible for any use that may be made of the information it contains.

References

1. Kisling, T. (2022). Benzinpreise: Das Fahrrad wird beliebter—die Bahn nicht. Retrieved August 20, 2022, from https://www.waz.de/politik/auto-tankenbenzin-preise-fahrrad-bahn-9-euro-ticket-id235221471.html
2. Umweltbundesamt: Radverkehr. (2022). Retrieved August 20, 2022, from https://www.umweltbundesamt.de/themen/verkehr-laerm/nachhaltige-mobilitaet/radverkehr#vorteile-des-fahrradfahrens
3. Green, S., Sakuls, P., & Levitt, S. (2021). Cycling for health: Improving health and mitigating the climate crisis. *Canadian Family Physician, 67*(10), 739–742.
4. Anke, J., Francke, A., Schaefer, L.-M., & Petzoldt, T. (2021). Impact of SARS-CoV-2 on the mobility behaviour in Germany. *European Transport Research Review, 13*(10). https://doi.org/10.1186/s12544-021-00469-3
5. German Federal Ministry of Digital and Transport: Radverkehr. (2022). Retrieved August 20, 2022, from https://www.bmvi.de/DE/Themen/Mobilitaet/Fahrradverkehr/fahrradverkehr.html

6. Strava. (2022). Retrieved August 20, 2022, from www.strava.com
7. Hall, C. (2022). Was ist Strava, wie funktioniert es und lohnt es sich zu bezahlen?. Retrieved August 20, 2022, from https://www.pocket-lint.com/de-de/software/news/154854-was-ist-strava-und-wie-funktioniert-es
8. Komoot. (2022). Retrieved August 20, 2022, from www.komoot.de
9. Bike Citizens. (2022). Retrieved August 20, 2022, from www.bikecitizens.net
10. Garber, M. D., Watkins, K. E., & Kramer, M. R. (2019). Comparing bicyclists who use smartphone apps to record rides with those who do not: Implications for representativeness and selection bias. *Journal of Transport and Health, 15*, 100661. https://doi.org/10.1016/j.jth.2019.100661
11. Oldenburger Fahrrad Challenge. (2022). Retrieved August 20, 2022, from https://www.ol-fahrradchallenge.com/
12. European Innovation Council: Ciclogreen. (2022). Retrieved August 20, 2022, from https://eic.eismea.eu/challenges/solution/ciclogreen
13. Bike to Work. (2022). Retrieved August 20, 2022, from https://www.biketowork.ch/
14. Bicycles and ITS (BITS). (2022). Retrieved August 20, 2022, from https://northsearegion.eu/bits/
15. Ciclogreen. (2022). Retrieved August 20, 2022, from www.ciclogreen.com/?lan=en
16. Dienstradchallenge: Firmenranking (company ranking). (2022). Retrieved August 20, 2022, from https://www.dienstradchallenge.com/

An Investigation on Internet of Things (IoT) Technology in Smart Homes

Carmel Nkeshimana, Tumusiime Kwiringira, Amuki Joseph Kesi, and Ramadhani Sinde

1 Introduction

The term "Internet of Things" or "IoT" refers to the billions of physical devices (referred to as "things") that are embedded with sensors, software, and other technologies and are connected to the Internet to exchange data with other devices and systems. The "thing" in the term "Internet of Things" can be an automobile that has built-in sensors to alert a driver when the tire pressure is low, an animal with a bio-chip corresponder, a person with a heart monitor implant, or any other object that can be assigned an internet protocol (IP) address or a unique identifier and can transfer data over a network. The phrase "Internet of Things" was first coined by Kevin Ashton, the co-founder of the Auto-ID Center at the Massachusetts Institute of Technology (M.I.T) in his presentation titled "The Internet of Things" in 1999 to describe a system where the Internet is connected to the physical world via ubiquitous sensors. An IoT ecosystem comprises internet-enabled smart devices that use embedded systems and communication hardware such as sensors and processors to collect, manipulate, and send data they receive from their environments. The data can be sent to the cloud or analyzed locally and these devices often communicate with other related devices and respond to information received from each other using various technologies such as ROR, BAN AVISPA, J48 Machine Learning Algorithm, and Weka API, NFDA, Edge Computing Paradigm, Fuzzy logic, KNX Technology, Scheffe's Regression Analysis, REST API, RF energy, OCTAVE, 3D substitution box, PUF, CNN, TAM, Zi Wi, PLS-SEM, and Reinforcement Learning. They often do this without human intervention as they (humans) only stop at setting them up, giving them instructions, and accessing data. A smart house could be

C. Nkeshimana (✉) · T. Kwiringira · A. J. Kesi · R. Sinde
The Nelson Mandela African Institution of Science and Technology, Arusha, Tanzania
e-mail: nkeshimanac@nm-aist.ac.tz

J. Marx Gómez et al. (eds.), *Smart and Secure Embedded and Mobile Systems*, Progress in IS, https://doi.org/10.1007/978-3-031-56603-5_27

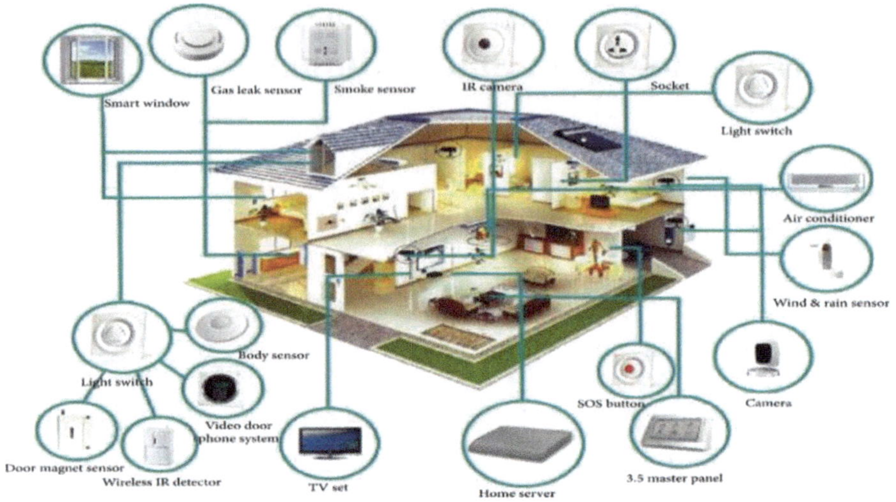

Fig. 1 A typical IoT-based smart house

based on a platform or a smart home hub such as the Amazon Echo, Google Home, Apple's home kit, and Samsung SmartThings Hub to control smart devices and appliances which can include lighting, heating, air conditioning, media, security systems, camera systems, etc. as shown in Fig. 1.

2 Problem Statement

The use of various IoT technologies to connect different things to the internet in smart houses brings a lot of privacy and security concerns regarding the authenticity, integrity, and confidentiality of the data captured, collected, and exchanged over the network as well as high energy consumption rate by the different devices. These problems make smart houses extremely susceptible to various types of security threats or attacks and insecure and also affect their performance. Therefore, it is essential to assess the potential security risks in order to improve the security status of smart houses and also the energy consumption rate of the various things connected to the Internet.

3 Challenges of Using IoT in Smart Houses

The Internet of Things (IoT) in smart houses faces a lot of challenges and these include but are not limited to the following: Reliability; the distributed nature of IoT devices makes it difficult to ensure their dependability. Various conditions such as natural disasters, cloud service interruptions, and power outages may make IoT devices inactive and easy to breach when power is off or cause system failures which greatly impact their functionality. Privacy; IoT devices that are connected to the internet are susceptible to external attacks and these collect and send private data over open networks that are not encrypted making it easily accessible to hackers. Internet availability; can be a challenge for many IoT devices, especially if they are widely distributed in remote areas or if the bandwidth is very limited. Insufficient testing & Outdated products; the IoT industry is currently flooded with a large number of manufacturers and due to competition, they tend to rush to launch their products and software without sufficient testing. Most manufacturers do not provide timely updates, and their IoT devices are not normally updated, which can make them susceptible to data theft. As new weaknesses are identified to maintain security, IoT devices should be thoroughly tested and updated. Lack of technical know-how; IoT technologies have been around for some time and it's a fast-growing industry but unfortunately, most people do not know much about it. One of the biggest security threats associated with this technology is the lack of technical knowledge of users about its capabilities, which poses a threat to all users. Energy consumption; is also a big problem in the IoT industry as IoT devices need a lot of energy to collect, process, and communicate information. If the grid-separated things depend on battery power, a replacement can be a problem.

4 Related Works

This section describes the previous works that different researchers have done in developing and implementing improved smart home systems with the main focus on how to reduce energy consumption, mitigate security flaws, and predict smart homes' usage patterns. The authors in [1] examined the protocol developed by Xiang and Zheng and they emphasized its limitations as it is insecure, unable to perform mutual authentication, and is susceptible to attacks. Using the ROR model and BAN logic, they developed a lightweight secure authentication protocol for IoT-based smart homes to address vulnerabilities in the Xiang and Zheng protocol. However, there are still problems with their protocol as it has not been fully developed and has not been implemented in a real environment. In [2], researchers used machine learning algorithms to learn the behavior and energy usage patterns and rank homes by energy usage. They also proposed a smart home energy management system for home IoT devices that is based on big data and machine learning called HEMS-IoT to monitor energy consumption patterns for home comfort, security, and energy savings. The proposed system only supports Android OS and does not give custom power-saving recommendations due to some limitations.

Researchers in [3] presented a traffic monitoring and capturing mechanism that is used to monitor smart-home activity holistically and it also enables the ex-traction of significant data from traffic captures of multiple IoT protocols. The proposed model was only limited to a single data set and subjected to a few scenarios. A cost-effective integrated system for smart homes based on IoT and Edge-Computing paradigm was proposed in [4] which is a cheap IoT integrated system for smart homes that controls home appliances remotely ensuring security and safety using edge-computing paradigm to store sensitive data in a local cloud to preserve the customer's privacy. However, the system does not support built-in vision-enabled technologies for processing different kinds of multimedia data such as images and surveillance video. In [5], researchers used fuzzy logic to simulate a smart home model for the safe and robust mobility of visually impaired people. The system allowed users to move with ease while avoiding obstacles. However, it is limited to simulation only and does not take into account the integration of additional functionalities such as vibration of signals.

In [6], authors used KNX technology to implement a standard with home automation ontology and provide a Living Lab gateway to enable users to leverage any IoT device from their smart home. Their research suggested mitigation technology fragmentation and improving access to diverse operations in heterogeneous device ecosystems. The Living Lab Gateway was not benchmarked with other similar technologies for performance comparison.

A platform based on IoT and cloud technologies to enable users to use a mobile application to monitor and control their wireless devices in the home remotely was proposed by [7]. Their system can collect and store e-switch data for further processing and analysis, but there was no tool to convert home automation devices to smart devices. An element of AI is missing to allow devices to make their own decisions based on the residents' habits.

Researchers in [8] investigated SYN flood attacks & HTTP Get flood attacks by behavior when IoT devices and the entire smart homes were victims of DDoS attacks. They presented experimental results for single-scenario attacks performed and demonstrated the response of real IoT device sensors against such attacks. Their work did not give a detailed study on the case of cloud communication between IoT sensors and personal assistant systems and no strong framework against DDoS attacks was proposed. Authors in [9] proposed a system to provide important information to build effective services and identify appropriate target users using Regression analysis. But their study failed to present the correlation between demographic factors and their scope did not include services. The importance of simulation was shown by [10] when they used Cisco packet tracer 8.0 to show how to use simulation tools effectively in the building of IoT supported home intelligent control systems but the analysis of network traffic and bandwidth consumption was not examined. Researchers in [11] designed an energy-efficient IoT platform system for reducing energy consumption using RF energy but their scheme has a high-power consumption and node failure.

In [12] they proposed an IoT-based smart home environment system to protect against various failures but their methods were not consistently applied to the security of the entire vulnerability. Those in [13] tackled 15 security risks from within and outside of IoT-based smart houses and they proposed some countermeasures using the OCTAVE method, but a platform for the realization and evaluation of security threats in IoT-based smart homes was not included. The researchers [14] demonstrated a concept to help in financial transactions and smart-home recognition by voice commands using PUF, but their scheme doesn't evaluate experimentally and doesn't provide better results for the trusted IoT device with PUF. A design of a multi-purpose Android OS mobile application for remotely controlling a smart home was proposed by [15] and they used a machine learning algorithm, a convolutional neural network (CNN) but they failed to build a model to classify extended family members and their friends. Researchers in [16] used the technology acceptance model (TAM) in their proposed smart home IoT system to minimize energy consumption and production using a small sample size. Zi-Wi protocol was demonstrated by [17] when they demonstrated the usability of ZigBee and Wi-Fi for computing in home automation systems (HAS) but they found that Zi-Wi increases power consumption measurements.

The other researchers in [18] demonstrated using PLS-SEM interconnectivity and reliability which are required in the implementation, development, and adoption of smart home systems but they didn't take into consideration a significant variation between existing and potential smart home service users. While those in [19] designed a system using RSSI which combines sensor technology and smart home design, however they selected a lower threshold which affects the complex home environment. Using reinforcement learning (RL) in [20] they were able to reduce power consumption while meeting the quality requirements of all relevant applications, resulting in reduced computing power and failure to meet overall context-aware performance goals.

We have carefully handled the overview of merits and demerits as shown in Table 1 based on our demonstration, showing our thorough comprehension and application of related works.

5 Recommendations of the Proposed Projects in the Global Context

Based on the review conducted on the various papers published by different researchers, it has been observed that they mostly recommended the implementation of security and privacy features as key requirements in future systems because the IoT systems discussed in the papers above did not fully address the issues of security and privacy clearly, there is still a gap. We, therefore, propose the following ways to solve IoT vulnerabilities if these systems were to be implemented globally, these include: Avoiding universal plug-and-play devices/features. The majority of the IoT devices have these plug-and-play features that allow them to communicate with each other without configuration. Although this provides convenience to the smart homeowners, these devices use local area networks for connectivity, and these networks are extremely vulnerable to external attacks and are easily accessible by anyone connected to the internet. IoT devices need to be updated regularly; as

Table 1 The description of merits & demerits of the related works

Sn	Author name	Method	Contribution	Objective	Demerits/limitations
1	JiHyeon Oh et al. [1]	ROR, BAN, AVISPA	Developed a secure lightweight authentication protocol for IoT-based smart homes to deal with the security flaws of the protocol developed by Xiang and Zheng.	To examine a protocol developed by Xiang and Zheng and point out its flaws such as its inability to provide secure, mutual authentication, and vulnerability to attacks.	The suggested protocol still containsflaws, as it was not fully developed and wasn't implemented in an actual environment.
2	Isaac Machorro-Cano et al. [2]	J48 ML algorithm & Weka API	It proposed a home energy management system for IoT devices In homes (HEMS-IoT) to monitor energy consumption patterns.	To develop a smart home managementsystem for energy consumptionbased on big data and machine Learning.	The system only supports android OS, it does not generate customized energy-saving recommendations.
3	Morios Anagnos-topoulos et al. [3]	NFDA	It enables the extraction of significant data from traffic captures of multiple IoT protocols.	To develop a model/mechanism that is capable of monitoring smart-home activities.	The proposed model was only limitedto a single data set and subjectedto a few scenarios.
4	Hikmat Yar et al. [4]	Edge computing paradigm	Energy usage, processing, and response time were improved.	To develop a cheap IoT integrated system for smart homes that controlshome appliances remotely.	The system does not support built-in vision-enabled technologies to process different kinds of multimedia data such as images and video.
5	Shahzadi Tayyaba et al. [5]	Fuzzy logic	Proposed a smart house model for visually-impaired people's safe and reliable mobility, which aids in navigation and obstacle avoidance.	To create a model for smart houses that uses IoT devices to help visually-impaired people navigate more comfortably.	There was no consideration for Extra vibrational signals, electronics, or IoT device integration because it was merely a simulation.

6	Ezequiel Simeoni et al [6]	KNX Technology	It reduces technology fragmentation and improves device manipulation accessibility for heterogeneous devices.	To build and implement a secure and scalable smart home gateway to bridge technology fragmentation.	For performance comparison, the Living lab gateway was not benchmarked with other similar technologies.
7	Fabian Garcia-Vazquez et al. [7]	Cloud technology	The system is capable of collecting and storing e-switch data used for further processing and Analysis.	To design and develop a mobile application to monitor and control wireless devices in a smart home.	The system is missing tools needed to turn home automation devices into smart gadgets. There isn't enough AI in the system to allow devices to make their own judgments
8	Ladislav Huraj et al. [8]	SYN & HTTP (flood attacks)	It shows the response of IoT device sensors when they are subjected to distributed denial of service attacks.	To investigate how IoT devices and the entire smart home will behave if they become victims of a distributed denial-of-service attacks.	There was no robust mechanism for defending against DDoS attacks proposed.
9	Soojung Chang et al [9].	Scheffe's Regression analysis	All findings are useful to service providers and related enterprises such as IT, engineering, and architecture, to build effective services and identify appropriate target users.	To learn more about user views on the relationship between smart home service choice and adoption.	The association between demographic parameters was not taken into account and the scope did not include all of the services that make up the home market.
10	Erdal Ozdogan et al. [10]	REST API	Used sample situations to demonstrate The value of utilizing Cisco Packet tracer 8.0 simulation software.	To discuss how to use simulation tools effectively in the development of IoT home control systems.	Network traffic and bandwidth consumption was not examined.

(continued)

Table 1 (continued)

Sn	Author name	Method	Contribution	Objective	Demerits/limitations
11	Nermeen A. Eltresy et al. [11]	RF energy	Proposed an IoT platform for smart homes that are powered by electromagnetic energy harvesting	To develop an energy-efficient Internet of things system to reduce the overall energy consumption.	The proposed scenario has high power consumption and sensor node failure.
12	Ziaur Rahman et al. [12].	3-dimensional S-box (substitution Box)	Uses a 3-dimensional key generation to increase the difficulty of key generation and reduce the probability of keys being broken.	To evaluate whether the suggested approach is secure against a range of faults, an IoT-based smart-home environment was created.	The proposed solution is not always appropriate for securing against various vulnerabilities.
13	Bako Ali et al. [13]	OCTAVE	Identifying 15 security dangers that originate from both within and outside of the smart home as well as potential solutions.	To identify security dangers to residents and provide ways to mitigate the identified hazards.	The proposed solution lacks a framework for identifying and assessing security concerns in IoT- based smart homes.
14	Victor Takashi Hayashi et al. [14]	PUF	Developed a smart home authentication system that uses voice recognition commands	To develop a device for hands-free scenarios, integrated with smart home behavior for continuous authentication.	This scenario doesn't use obfuscation, key splitting, or secure multi-party computing procedures.
15	Olutosin Taiwo et al. [15]	CNN (convolution neural network)	Designed and developed a multi-purpose android-mobile application for controlling and monitoring the smart home.	To develop a mobile application for smart home automation with machine learning capabilities.	The model failed to classify extended family members and friends.

16	Adrian Micu et al. [16]	Technology acceptance model (TAM)	Energy consumption of IoT devices was reduced.	To develop a smart home IoT system that minimizes energy consumption.	The sample data used was limited.
17	Ván Froiz-Míguez et al. [17]	Zi-Wi	Demonstrates the advantages of using Zi-Wi, a low-cost IoT fog computing home automation system (HAS).	To show that Zi-Wi can provide a low-cost and adaptable home automation system (HAS).	The use of Zi-Wi increases the amount of energy consumed.
18	Heetae Yang et al. [18]	PLS-SEM	It indicates that interconnection and reliability, as well as the right level of automation, are essential to deliver valuable insights regarding smart home service adaptation.	To examine the elements of smart homes services that present customers want, as well as experimentally assessing the relationship between important aspects and adaptation behavior.	Existing and potential smart home service users may have a considerable difference in the influence of antecedents on behavioral intention
19	Ruili Zheng [19]	RSSI	Design of a sensor-enabled smart home system.	To study a smart home automation system based on wireless sensor network positioning.	It chooses the lowest threshold that has an impact on the home’s complex surroundings.
20	Metin Ozturk et al. [20]	Reinforcement learning (RL)	It reduces computing power while meeting the quality requirements of all related applications.	To create a framework that maximizes the IoT network’s connectivity and processing speed.	There are predictable scenarios that could result in lower computing costs or energy usage.

mentioned in Sect. 3 above about the lack of updates as one of the IoT security issues, smart homeowners need to set up or implement automatic updates to get official updates by device manufacturers. This will install the required security patches in the IoT devices and prevent hackers from breaking into them as well as increase the security level of the smart houses. Authentication of access, using frequently changed passwords; we encourage additional levels of security while accessing these IoT devices by using not-easy-to remember passwords on internet accounts and recommend each IoT device to have a unique password that is complex, tough to crack with occasional modification. Cloud Technology, most of these devices have their own cloud storage space but it is highly susceptible to external attacks. For this reason, users of these systems are advised to always thoroughly review the data protection measures that come with their cloud accounts and store or back up files and data locally whenever possible. Use multiple networks; The approach of creating additional restricted networks can also be used for home IoT devices to prevent unauthorized access to personal data.

Other factors for IoT-based implementation in smart houses are: Internet availability, most countries in the world still face internet connectivity challenges. Electricity fluctuations; for IoT-based systems to perform effectively, they need 24/7 round-the-clock availability of electrical power which is not consistently available in the most parts of the world. This could be solved by using onboard batteries or even using solar power. Cost of the system; before implementing such systems, their cost should be considered because the majority of the people are poor with little or no knowledge at all of how these systems operate.

6 Conclusion and Future Research

Smart homeowners are now able to remotely monitor and control their smart houses and surroundings regardless of where they're in the world all because of IoT technologies. In the past few years, prominent companies like Google, Amazon, Apple, Samsung, Xiaomi, LG, etc. have brought to the market several IoT smart home devices that have already been implemented, tested, and applied for automated control and monitoring of homes. However, we've noticed that a lot of challenges stipulated in Sect. 3 still exist while in Sect. 4, several researchers.

proposed and presented different approaches to mitigate these challenges such as ROR, BAN AVISPA, Scheffe's Regression Analysis, REST API, OCTAVE, 3D substitution box, RF energy, PUF, CNN, TAM, Zi Wi, PLS-SEM, Reinforcement Learning, etc. with different levels of performance, reliability, and dependability. Having analyzed all the different proposed works from the above-mentioned researchers, we also realized that technologies such as machine learning/deep learning were not fully utilized in building predictive smart house automation systems. We, therefore, propose a machine learning IoT-based home automation system that is capable of remote monitoring and controlling all electrical appliances, monitoring all home environmental conditions, detecting and reporting intruder movements in the home, and the data collected can then be stored on the cloud, which can be accessed and used for predicting home user patterns using machine learning algorithms.

References

1. Oh, J., Yu, S., Lee, J., Son, S., Kim, M., & Park, Y. (2021). A secure and lightweight authentication protocol for IoT-based smart homes. *Sensors, 21*(4), 1–24. https://doi.org/10.3390/s21041488
2. Machorro-Cano, I., Alor-Hernández, G., Paredes-Valverde, M. A., Rodríguez-Mazahua, L., Sánchez-Cervantes, J. L., & Olmedo-Aguirre, J. O. (2020). HEMS-IoT: A big data and machine learning-based smart home system for energy saving. *Energies (Basel), 13*(5), 1097. https://doi.org/10.3390/en13051097
3. Anagnostopoulos, M., Spathoulas, G., Viaño, B., & Augusto-Gonzalez, J. (2020). Tracing your smart-home devices conversations: A real world IoT traffic data-set. *Sensors (Switzer-land), 20*(22), 1–28. https://doi.org/10.3390/s20226600
4. Yar, H., Imran, A. S., Khan, Z. A., Sajjad, M., & Kastrati, Z. (2021). Towards smart home automation using IoT-enabled edge-computing paradigm. *Sensors, 21*(14), 4932. https://doi.org/10.3390/s21144932
5. Tayyaba, S., Ashraf, M. W., Alquthami, T., Ahmad, Z., & Manzoor, S. (2020). Fuzzy-based approach using IoT devices for smart home to assist blind people for navigation. *Sensors (Switzerland), 20*(13), 1–13. https://doi.org/10.3390/s20133674
6. Simeoni, E., et al. (2021). A secure and scalable smart home gateway to bridge technology fragmentation. *Sensors, 21*(11), 3587. https://doi.org/10.3390/s21113587
7. García-Vázquez, F., Guerrero-Osuna, H. A., Ornelas-Vargas, G., Carrasco-Navarro, R., Luque-Vega, L. F., & Lopez-Neri, E. (2021). Design and implementation of the e-switch for a smart home. *Sensors, 21*(11), 3811. https://doi.org/10.3390/s21113811
8. Huraj, L., Šimon, M., & Horák, T. (2020). Resistance of IoT sensors against DDOS attack in smart home environment. *Sensors (Switzerland), 20*(18), 1–23. https://doi.org/10.3390/s20185298
9. Chang, S., & Nam, K. (2021). Smart home adoption: The impact of user characteristics and differences in perception of benefits. *Buildings, 11*(9), 393. https://doi.org/10.3390/buildings11090393
10. Özdoğan, E., & Daş, R. (2021). IoT based a smart home automation system design: Simulation case. *Balkan Journal of Electrical and Computer Engineering, 9*(3), 297–303. https://doi.org/10.17694/bajece.918826
11. Eltresy, N. A., et al. (2020). Smart home IoT system by using RF energy harvesting. *Journal of Sensors. Hindawi Limited, 2020*, 1–14. https://doi.org/10.1155/2020/8828479
12. Rahman, Z., Yi, X., Billah, M., Sumi, M., & Anwar, A. (2022). Enhancing AES Using Chaos and Logistic Map-Based Key Generation Technique for Securing IoT-Based Smart Home. *Electronics (Basel), 11*(7), 1083. https://doi.org/10.3390/electronics11071083
13. Ali, B., & Awad, A. I. (2018). Cyber and physical security vulnerability assessment for IoT-based smart homes. *Sensors (Switzerland), 18*(3), 817. https://doi.org/10.3390/s18030817
14. Hayashi, V. T., & Ruggiero, W. V. (2022). Hands-Free Authentication for Virtual Assistants with Trusted IoT Device and Machine Learning. *Sensors, 22*(4), 1325. https://doi.org/10.3390/s22041325
15. Taiwo, O., Ezugwu, A. E., Oyelade, O. N., & Almutairi, M. S. (2022). Enhanced intelligent smart home control and security system based on deep learning model. *Wireless Communications and Mobile Computing, 2022*, 1–22. https://doi.org/10.1155/2022/9307961

16. Micu, A., Micu, A. E., Geru, M., Capatina, A., & Muntean, M. C. (2021). The challenge for energy saving in smart homes: Exploring the interest for IoT devices acquisition in Romania. *Energies (Basel), 14*(22), 7589. https://doi.org/10.3390/en14227589
17. Froiz-Míguez, I., Fernández-Caramés, T. M., Fraga-Lamas, P., & Castedo, L. (2018). Design, implementation and practical evaluation of an IoT home automation system for fog computing applications based on MQTT and Zig Bee-WiFi sensor nodes. *Sensors (Switzerland), 18*(8), 2660. https://doi.org/10.3390/s18082660
18. Yang, H., Lee, W., & Lee, H. (2018). IoT smart home adoption: The importance of proper level automation. *Journal of Sensors, 2018*, 1–11. https://doi.org/10.1155/2018/6464036
19. Zheng, R. (2022). Indoor smart design algorithm based on smart home sensor. *Journal of Sensors, 2022*, 1–10. https://doi.org/10.1155/2022/2251046
20. Ozturk, M., Jaber, M., & Imran, M. A. (2018). Energy-aware smart connectivity for IoT networks: Enabling smart ports. *Wireless Communications and Mobile Computing, 2018*, 1–11. https://doi.org/10.1155/2018/5379326

The Role of Mobile Application to Control the Existing Customer Needs, Pains, and Gains in the Municipal Solid Waste Collection Systems

Stanley Manyonyi, Silas Mirau, Mussa Ally, and Kuchibanda Kizito

1 Introduction

Waste management is a growing global and environmental critical issue in developed and developing countries that inhibits human and government activities. This critical issue is due to the increase of urbanization, rural–urban migration, rising living standards, and rapid development. These triggers are associated with population growth, which has resulted in increased solid and liquid waste generation by industrial, domestic, and other activities [1, 2], and often waste treatment is entrusted to the government or administrative authorities [3]. Also, weak government policies, a shortage of resources and a lack of awareness or willingness among stakeholders, low stakeholder environmental knowledge, and the reluctance to accept new technologies have all been obstacles and challenging to a better and improved solid waste collection system [4–6]. Proper mechanisms for collecting solid waste data in municipal solid waste collection systems are required.

Although solid waste collection services were provided free by the government of Tanzania, since the country's transformation to free market economics in the early 1990s, solid waste collection services have increasingly been publicly owned and outsourced to the private sector. Approximately 12.1–17.4 million tons of municipal solid waste were reported to increase in the country each year (0.66–0.95 kg per capita per day). Waste generation in Tanzania is increasing at 5% per year. Households, businesses, and commercial locations, institutions, markets, and street sweeping are among the main sources of solid waste [7].

S. Manyonyi (✉) · S. Mirau · M. Ally
School of Computational Communications and Engineering, The Nelson Mandela African Institution of Science and Technology, Arusha, Tanzania
e-mail: manyonyis@nm-aist.ac.tz

K. Kizito
Department of Sanitation and Environment, Shinyanga Municipal Council, Shinyanga, Tanzania

J. Marx Gómez et al. (eds.), *Smart and Secure Embedded and Mobile Systems*,
Progress in IS, https://doi.org/10.1007/978-3-031-56603-5_28

In addition, residents in municipality areas are little aware of improved solid waste management in their community for the circular economy and to influence them to adopt a favorable attitude toward participation in controlling the increase in solid waste [8]. Despite municipal regulations and bylaws that offer awareness, punishment, and penalties for noncompliance with solid waste management, efforts to promote friendly solid waste collection system have been unsuccessful. This is likely due to the incapacity to access opportunities and the lack of a mobile tool to spread awareness [9].

The advantages of effective and efficient solid waste collection system are vast; it can rescue entire communities from poverty and improve the economy of a country. Besides environmental benefits, empowering citizens to take responsibility for their own waste disposal is an investment for the future. An understanding of how to effectively collect, treat, dispose of, or reuse solid waste is needed to undertake initiatives to improve the situation [10]. However, in most municipalities, the lack of the reliable mobile framework for collecting and presenting solid waste data negates the commitment of controlling pains, gains, and needs for customers who seek the solid waste collection service, such as a quick booking of waste collection service by selecting the desired waste collector on the list of waste collectors.

Mobile app technologies are dynamic these days, and the variety of applications being developed is rapidly growing and simple and inexpensive to adopt [11] with limited functions designed to operate on mobile devices which are movable, simple to use, and accessible from any location such as smartphones and tablets [12, 13]. Mobile apps have been employed and proven to succeed in a variety of areas all over the world, including distant collection of data, training, support, and awareness campaigns [14].

This chapter examines the current process of solid waste data collection in Shinyanga Municipal Council and then proposes the appropriate mobile app technology in solid waste collection system for effective data collection and reporting, which are critical in controlling customer pains, gains, and needs.

2 Overview of Solid Waste Collection System

Data from this study were collected from ten wards, namely, Ibadakuli, Ibinzamata, Kambarage, Kitangili, Lubaga, Mjini, Chamaguha, Ndala, Ndembezi, and Ngokolo, in Shinyanga Municipal Council. The listed wards were chosen based on the prevalence of solid waste collection, such as wards with a solid waste collection schedule, qualified to be mixed or urban, high and medium solid waste generation, and high percentage of populations. The multistage sampling process was performed by choosing ten wards using simple random sampling. To achieve the objective of this study, questionnaires, interviews, and observation checklist were used to gather primary data. The focus of the study was on (1) households to assess the access of solid waste collection service, (2) the willingness of waste generators to pay for the service, (3) municipal officials to manage revenue and complaints, and (4) the

Fig. 1 Public bin positioned at Kitangiri ward

participation of political leaders to offer cooperation to the solid waste collection system.

Data collected were demographic characteristics, awareness and attitude, barriers, and the desired future for solid waste management. These data revealed that there are various methods for collecting municipal solid waste in the Shinyanga Municipal Council. These methods are self-solid waste collection, public bin collection (Fig. 1), and house-to-house collection used by contracted waste collectors with wood-made wheelbarrows, three-wheeled motorcycles, and solid waste cars to visit each house to collect solid waste and transfer it to dumping sites, and the customer is usually charged monthly.

2.1 *Sociodemographic Characteristics*

A total of 63 people responded to questionnaires and interview questions from ten wards. Table 1 shows sociodemographic characteristics where 84.12% identified as participants with an income of more than TZS 50000 monthly, and the majority, 57.14%, were in the self-employment system. These two characteristics, income and employment status, indicate that two-thirds of the respondents can afford to pay the solid waste service fee monthly because it costs at least 5000 Tanzania shillings per month per household. The percentage of those who had completed their college education was 46.03%, and 7.94% were above 60 years. The findings reveal that more than two-thirds of the respondents were those who are still energetic to learn and can have a good attitude toward using proposed mobile systems. The majority of the respondents (84.12%) in this study have a residence for more than 5 years where

Table 1 Sociodemographic characteristics of the participants

Characteristics	Frequency (n = 63)	Percentage (%)
Gender (sex)		
Male	35	55.56
Female	28	44.44
Age in years		
21–40	36	57.14
41–60	22	34.92
Above 60	5	7.94
Level of education		
Primary education	10	15.87
Secondary education	24	38.10
College education	29	46.03
Employment status		
Self-employed	36	57.14
Employed for wages	25	39.68
Retired	2	3.17
Monthly income status in Tanzania shillings		
0–50,000	10	15.87
50,001–100,000	15	23.81
100,001–150,000	2	3.17
150,001–200,000	4	6.36
More than 200,000	32	50.79
Duration of households in years		
0–4	10	15.87
5–10	25	39.68
Above 10	28	44.45
Household occupants		
1	6	9.53
2–4	43	68.25
More than 4	14	22.22

the population in the participating households has more than two occupants, which equals 90.47%. These results show that, rather than implementing manual processes that promote mistrust among residents without the characteristics of migrating their households away from Shinyanga Municipality, a mobile-based system is needed for them to develop a feasible solution for solid waste collection. This means they are not migratory residents, so they are residents who will continue using the mobile-based system for a long time.

2.2 Practice in Solid Waste Collection

Based on this study, 49.21% of lifestyle-related activities that generate solid waste are cooking and eating habits, daily inside and outside cleaning routine with the composition of food, papers, plastics, glass, electrical and electronic waste, and food-related formal and informal business activities such as selling food, vegetables, and fruits (Table 2). These statistics show that everyday waste generation does not match the pace of waste collection, as two-thirds of respondents do not receive daily waste collection services. Only 3.17% of the respondents were very satisfied with the service and the majority of the respondents (92.06%) will pay the waste collection fee (Table 3). The findings show a positive correlation between education level and willingness to pay for better solid waste collection services. Therefore, as individual education advances, the willingness to pay for better solid waste collection services increases [3]. So, the proposed mobile app is the right tool to motivate waste collectors to deliver the service daily on time.

Solid waste is most commonly transported from the collection point to the dump site by placing outside the place the collection sacs such as boxes, plastic bags, and plastic buckets, which are carried over the head to the dump site, while 9.52% of the respondents have waste pit at home where the method used to dispose of

Table 2 Practice of participants in solid waste management

Practice	Frequency (n = 63)	Percentage
Availability of a solid waste collection service		
Yes	36	57.14
No	27	42.86
Lifestyle-related activities that generate solid waste		
Cooking and eating habits	31	49.21
Daily indoor and outdoor cleaning routine	21	33.33
Food-related informal business activities such as selling food, vegetables, and fruits	11	17.46

Table 3 Percentage of respondents broken down by willingness to pay the waste collection fee and satisfaction status with the waste collection service vs. level of education

Level of education	Willingness to pay for the service	Satisfaction status with the waste collection service			
		Not satisfied	Less satisfied	Very satisfied	Total
College education	No	3.17			3.17
	Yes	19.05	20.63	3.17	42.86
Secondary education	No	1.59	1.59		3.17
	Yes	11.11	1.59		12.70
Primary education	No	1.59			1.59
	Yes	30.16	6.35		36.51
Total		66.67	30.16	3.17	100

Table 4 Percentage of respondents broken down by points of solid waste collection and methods of disposing solid waste

Points of solid waste collection	Methods of disposing solid waste	Percentage
Carrying to the collection point	Illegal dumping	9.52
	Open dumping	23.81
Placing outside	Boxes	7.94
	Plastic bags	33.33
	Plastic buckets	14.29
	Give to recycling	1.59
Home waste pit	Burning	4.76
	Burying	4.76

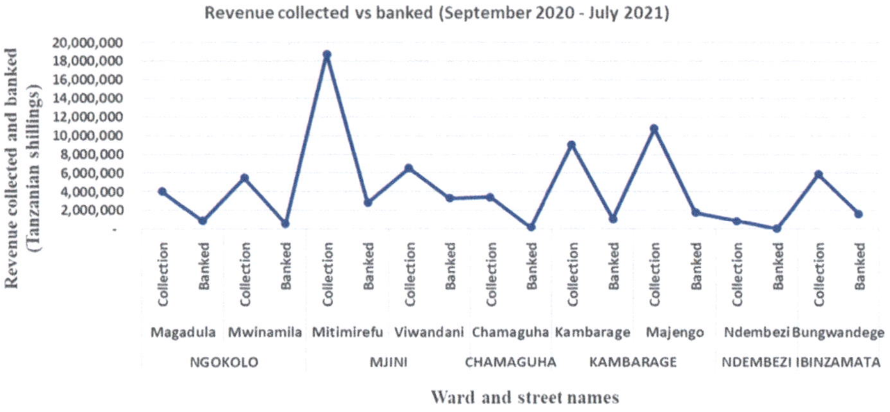

Fig. 2 Revenue collected vs, banked by 6 solid waste collection groups

their generated solid waste includes burying and burning (Table 4). Only 19% of the total revenue collected from this revenue source was deposited in the council account (Fig. 2). This indicates that there are other expenditures being made outside the corrected system and creates unnecessary defaults. The percentage of the respondents sending complaints about the solid waste collection service to the authority by a telephone call was 6.35% (Fig. 3). These findings reveal that a large population wastes time to submit a complaint to the municipal office or fails to arrive at the municipal office due to the physical distance to reach the officials responsible for resolving the complaint. The study finds there is a need of using a mobile-based system which can help anyone to send the complaints anywhere and anytime. The irregular solid waste collection service, the low frequency of the service, and improper waste collection are the main reasons for dissatisfaction felt by 66.67% of the respondents (Table 3).

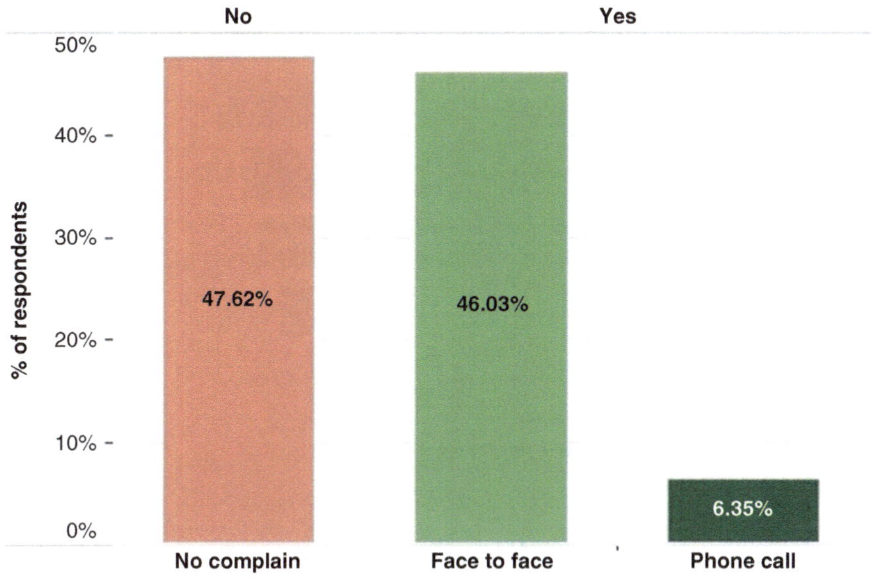

Fig. 3 Percentage of respondents of sending complaints and methods used to send complaints about solid waste to the authority

3 Desire Expected in the Collection of Solid Waste

The majority of respondents (57.14%) to the questionnaires and interview indicated the desire to have solid waste collectors capable of arriving on time. In addition, 12.70% of the people who participated in the survey in this study showed interest in obtaining the service of waste collection from professional solid waste collectors. While 9.52% of the respondents needed a friendly and easy payment system, 7.94% indicated that the system needed to allow customers to view current and updated solid waste information (Fig. 4). Also, the findings in Table 1 reveal that municipal residents do the jobs that create income for them. This indicates that the challenge in the solid waste collection system is not about the lack of money to pay for services. So, if citizens are educated on solid waste management, they can afford to pay for services. The proposed mobile-based system will be a tool for educating and informing the community on various benefits of collecting solid wastes.

4 Requirements for the Proposed Mobile-Based System

Two categories of requirements for the proposed mobile-based system are functional requirements that specify what the mobile application can perform and nonfunctional requirements that describe the quality attributes of the application to address a variety of challenges, as summarized in Tables 5 and 6.

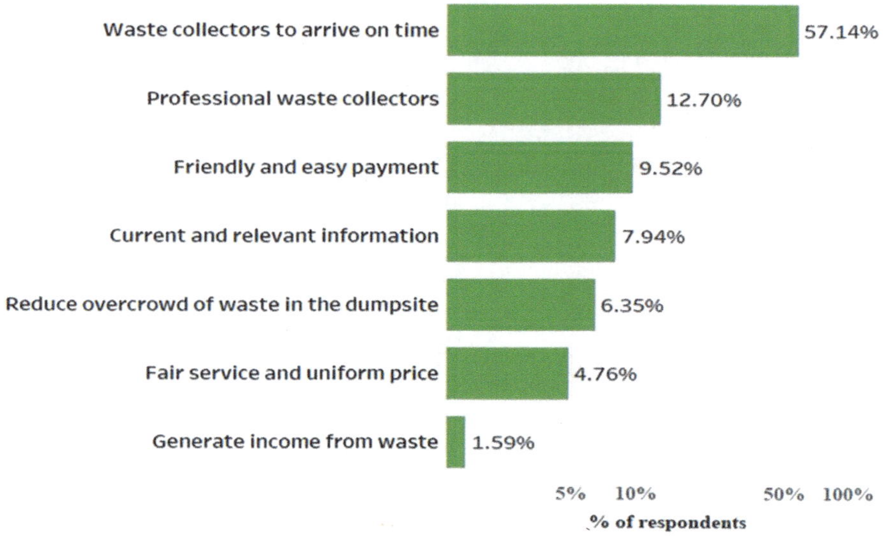

Fig. 4 Percentage of respondents for each desire expected in solid waste collection

Table 5 User roles and system functionalities

User	Roles
Municipal official	Manage users (update payment status, send payment alert, and delete)
	Manages waste collectors (approve, reject, and delete)
	Manage complaints
	Manage news for visualization (adding news, deleting old news)
	View revenue collection and distribution reports (council, wards, street, and collectors)
	View usage reports (total customers, total collectors, and waste collected)
Waste collectors	View service requests from the users (new, pending, and completed)
	Create bills
	Send complaints
	View individual revenue allocation (collect solid waste)
User	View list of waste collectors
	Send a service request
	Send complaints
	View payment history
	View request status (new, pending, and complete)
	Pay for service
	Receive notification (payment short message alert)
	Visualize news (solid waste information)
	Live chat through the official municipal WhatsApp number

Table 6 System non-functionalities

Nonfunctional requirement	Description
Business requirement	Approval of workflows and authorization levels of the system
Administrative function	The ability of the system to perform basic tasks like reporting
Operation function	The ability of the system to operate on the handset which includes the operating system and hardware parameters
Performance function	The ability of the system to perform the quantity of valuable tasks in a specific time
Security function	The ability of the system to secure the data and privacy of the users
Maintenance function	The ability of the system to be useful and easy to support and technical assistance, which does not hinder the availability of other services
User-friendly function	The ability of the system to be easy to learn, use, and understandable

4.1 The Data Flow of the Proposed Mobile System

Based on the needs of customers, we designed the entity relationship diagrams (Fig. 5) and data flow diagram in which entities, attributes, and relationship were described for the purpose of quickly database design. Customers must connect the interfaces of the developed mobile application to the remote database. The mobile application allows the input of user information which then can be transferred through the application interface to the server for storage. The mobile application receives, processes, and transmits information to the server and can retrieve the information from the server to the interface of the mobile application.

In Fig. 6, the developed mobile application interfaces display the user-friendly and interactive links for managing solid waste collectors, news, submitting complaints, and viewing various reports.

5 Evaluation of the Mobile App Modules

Solid waste generators, waste collectors, and municipal officers from Mitimirefu and Viwandani streets in the Mjini ward were used in the validation process to see if the mobile-based system is reliable and satisfies their essential business requirements. To evaluate their effectiveness and other performance characteristics, including availability, scalability, user friendliness, consistency, navigation, feedback, performance, and security, they could install the mobile system on their Android phones. The mobile-based system was readily accepted by respondents. They recommended that it should be implemented in real-life settings because it would encourage several local government authorities to adopt an electronic solid waste collection system. They added that the mobile app would discourage the

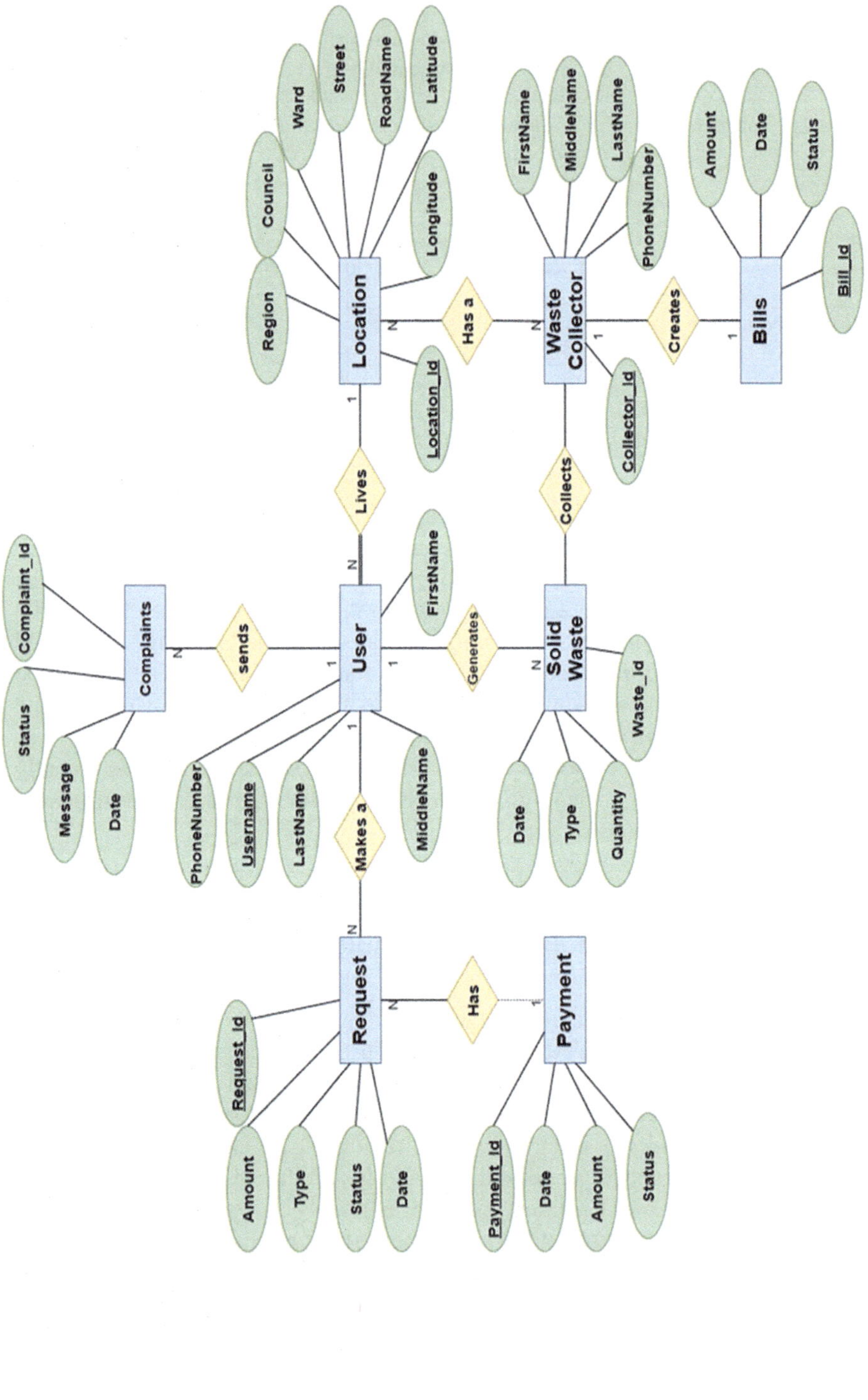

Fig. 5 Entity relation diagram for solid waste collection

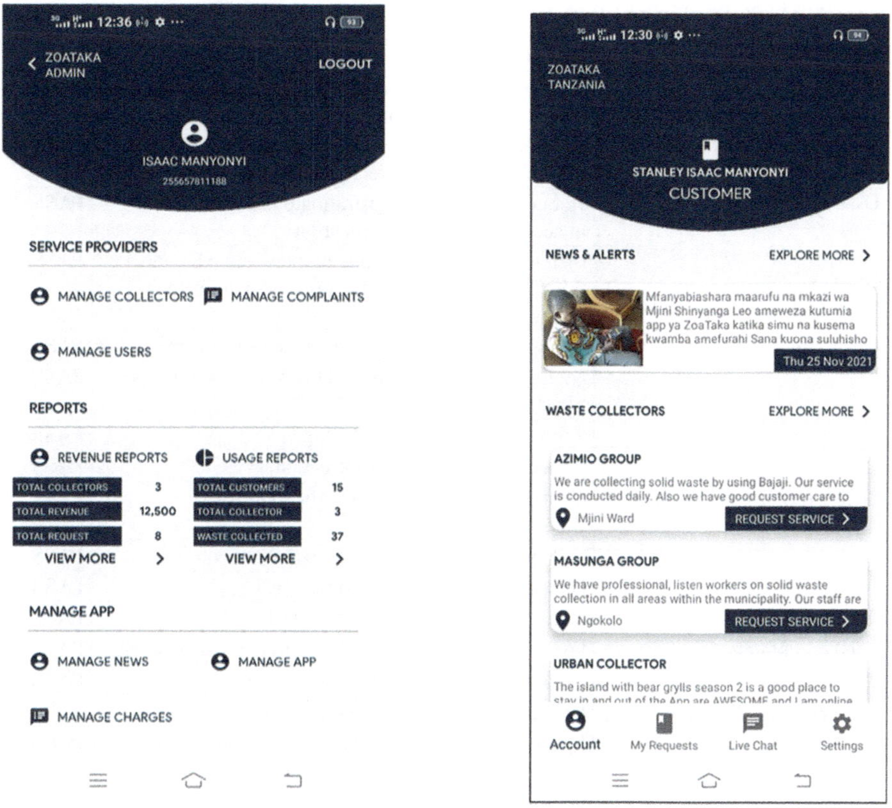

Fig. 6 Mobile app admin and customer interfaces

use of cash payments for the service, will increase revenue collection, improve customer satisfaction, and keep the environment clean. The mobile app customers were classified according to the expected functions they would require from the mobile application (Table 7).

6 Discussion and Recommendations

According to the results, most respondents relied on direct personal contacts with waste collectors and government officials, either by visiting them or by telephone, to share information about waste collection services. To minimize the challenge of finding waste collectors and municipal employees in their workplace, our mobile app has considered this by setting up the features to accommodate their needs to facilitate communication and solving challenges promptly electronically. Numerous previous studies have shown similar results, which these findings support by show-

Table 7 Mobile application testing for the key modules

Function of the mobile app	Description	Results
User verification	The user can enter the valid phone number and enable to register after receiving verification codes	PASS
	The mobile app displays error notifications when certain details are incorrectly entered	PASS
User login	After completing the registration process, the user can access the mobile application	PASS
	When the credentials (phone number and password) are incorrect, the application prevents you from logging in	PASS
News and notification alerts	The app displays the most recent news and alerts	PASS
	The user may access and read the most recent news and alerts	PASS
	The user can add news and images	PASS
	The user can delete old information	PASS
Send a request for service	The user can send the request for solid waste collection service	PASS
	The app can display the list of waste collectors	PASS
	The user can access the request status	PASS
	The user can accept or reject the bill	PASS
Send complaints	The user can send the complaints to the management	PASS
	The app can display the complaints status	PASS
Payment	The user can view the payment history	PASS
	The app can display the allocation of funds from revenue collections	PASS
User logout	The user can log out	PASS
Admin access	The app can provide a list of waste collectors	
	The app can display the status of applying solid waste collectors	PASS
	The user can approve the application of waste collectors	PASS
	The user can reject the application of waste collectors	PASS
	The user can delete the account of the waste collector	PASS

ing that mobile technologies enable citizens to collect and share data to promote community action, which ultimately results in beneficial societal transformation [5]. Communities can transform due to the availability of infrastructure that enables them to submit their views and receive timely feedback.

The following are advantages of utilizing our mobile app for different user subgroups:

(i) The municipal residents: A mobile app will enable them to submit request for a waste collection service once their solid waste cans are full, communicate their emotions about the service, and receive various information related to solid waste management to increase their knowledge of environmental protection and to simplify the payment process for solid waste collection services.

(ii) Waste collectors: Their work of collecting solid waste will be simplified because the mobile app will enable them to view and manage the status of requests from the residents on time and anywhere. It will also help them plan alternative preparations early to minimize delays and running costs in waste collection.

(iii) Municipal officers: By using the mobile application, their activity on waste management process such as management of solid waste collectors, complaints, customers, revenue, and usage will go more smoothly because the management reports will be well arranged using the mobile application.

(iv) Political leaders (municipal councilors and local government chairpersons): By requesting the revenue distribution reports from the municipal officials responsible for waste management, the mobile system will assist political leaders to cooperate with both the parties they lead (citizens and municipal authority) in managing the solid waste collection service because the system will display transparently the information on revenue collection, revenue distributions, and the status of complaints. It will promote accountability for all parties, from the street level to the municipal authority.

7 Conclusion

Using the findings of the Shinyanga Municipal Council, this study aimed to propose a mobile app for solid waste collection with the specific objectives of controlling the existing customer needs, pains, and gains in the municipal solid waste collection system. Our study found that most municipal residents have used a smartphone before and know how to use it, that few people need help using it, and good cellular networks are among the main benefits that encourage the development of a mobile app for solid waste collection. Other problems, such as the need for assistance, were viewed by the participants in our study as balanced in terms of the benefits that a mobile app solution can provide. This served as the foundation for the development of a mobile application for solid waste collection. The findings of this study are expected to contribute to using the mobile application to control the pains, needs, and gains of municipal residents in the solid waste collection system. Most of the participants in this study agreed that a mobile application for the delivery of solid waste information is necessary. Both solid waste generators and collectors and municipal health and sanitation practitioners indicated that a mobile application is needed to share solid waste information among them and that they will utilize it and recommend it to others. While there are many mentioned advantages of using mobile app, there are also drawbacks that the older people may be excluded from having to use a mobile app. This study is encouraging other scholars to use these findings to develop all technical aspects of backend, security, and cost to implement both mobile app and backend.

References

1. Moh, Y., & Abd-Manaf, L. (2017). Solid waste management transformation and future challenges of source separation and recycling practice in Malaysia. *Resources, Conservation and Recycling, 116*, 1–14.
2. Nyampundu, K., Mwegoha, W. J. S., & Millanzi, W. C. (2020). Sustainable solid waste management measures in Tanzania: An exploratory descriptive case study among vendors at Majengo market in Dodoma City. *BMC Public Health, 20*(1), 1–16.
3. Patnaik, M. L. P., & Mishra, B. B. (2021). Factors that affect the willingness of residents to pay for solid waste in Bhubaneswar. *International Journal of Research Science and Management, 8*(8), 32–38.
4. Kumar, S., Smith, S. R., Fowler, G., Velis, C., Kumar, S. J., Arya, S., Rena, K. R., & Cheeseman, C. (2017). Challenges and opportunities associated with waste management in India. *Royal Society Open Science, 4*(3), 160764.
5. Nagendra, B., Lakshmisha, A., & Agarwal, P. (2019). Mobile application in municipal waste tracking: A pilot study of "PAC waste tracker" in Bangalore city, India. *Journal of Material Cycles and Waste Management, 21*(3), 705–712.
6. Shekdar, A. V. (2009). Sustainable solid waste management: An integrated approach for Asian countries. *Waste Management, 29*(4), 1438–1448.
7. Biswas, A., & Singh, S. G. (2021). *Tanzania: An assessment of the solid-waste-management ecosystem*. Centre for Science and Environment.
8. Ezeudu, O. B., & Ezeudu, T. S. (2019). Implementation of circular economy principles in industrial solid waste management: Case studies from a developing economy (Nigeria). *Recycling, 4*(4), 1–18.
9. Ballaran, P. M., Corpuz, C. B. A., Paras, L. A. R., Fabito, B. S., & Rivera, E. R. (2019). Perazuhan: A Mobile application for solid waste micro-management framework. *Student Conference on Research and Development, 2019*(9003), 17–20.
10. Ahsan, A., Alamgir, M., El-Sergany, M. M., Shams, S., Rowshon, M. K., & Daud, N. N. N. (2014). Assessment of municipal solid waste management system in a developing country. *Chinese Journal of Engineering, 2014*, 1–11.
11. Leo, J., & Michael, K. (2019). The role of GIS, Mobile app and satellite technologies to enhance data collection process: A case of environmental factors and epidemics linkages. In *Smart Cities/Smart Regions–Technische, wirtschaftliche und gesellschaftliche Innovationen* (pp. 417–428). Springer Vieweg.
12. Islam, R., & Mazumder, T. (2010). Mobile application and its global impact. *International Journal of Engineering & Technology, 10*(06), 72–78.
13. Techopedia. (2022). Retrieved September 14, 2022, from https://www.techopedia.com/definition/2953/mobile-application
14. Nasi, G., Cucciniello, M., & Guerrazzi, C. (2015). The role of mobile technologies in health care processes: The case of cancer supportive care. *Journal of Medical Internet Research, 17*(2), 1–14.

DLT Architecture Proposal for IoT Applications Based on Data Streams

Francisco Moya, Luis Martínez, Fco Javier Estrella, Jorge Marx Gómez, and Rafael A. Espin

1 Introduction

Internet **o**f **T**hings (**IoT**) has been defined from different viewpoints, but in general, it is related with a wide heterogeneity of devices and sensors, as well as computer-based solutions. Different definitions have been provided in the literature [1–3]; some of them focus on its characteristics [4], others in the typology of communication [5], and others based on the type of applications that can build.

In spite of advantages and features that empower IoT technology, it should be noted out that IoT devices in general suffer from security problems [6], which make hard the use of IoT solutions in multiple real-world problems. To mostly solve this type of problem, in the literature [7, 8] has emerged a trend that explores the use of **d**istributed **l**edger **t**echnology (**DLT**). Such a trend focuses on the promise of resistance to information tampering and resilience to single points of failure.

In this contribution, we will look more deeply into the applicability of DLTs to a real-world sensor-based scenario where data are received by data streams, with special emphasis on securing the collecting, storing, and publishing of sensor-based data streams. Our proposal is a DLT architecture for IoT applications based on

F. Moya (✉) · L. Martínez · F. J. Estrella
Universidad de Jaén, Jaén, Spain
e-mail: fpmoya@ujaen.es; martin@ujaen.es; estrella@ujaen.es

J. Marx Gómez
Carl von Ossietzky Universität Oldenburg, Oldenburg, Germany

R. A. Espin
Autonomous University of Coahuila, Coahuila, Mexico

J. Marx Gómez et al. (eds.), *Smart and Secure Embedded and Mobile Systems*,
Progress in IS, https://doi.org/10.1007/978-3-031-56603-5_29

continuous data streams. It will allow us to pair sensor-based devices, listen to their data streams, and publish them on a DLT infrastructure (**DLTI**).[1]

The structure of this contribution is as follows. The background concepts used, like IoT or DLT, are reviewed in Sect. 2. The advantages and drawbacks of employing DLTs in this scenario are discussed in Sect. 3. Our proposed architecture is presented in Sect. 4 which also examines each service in detail and provides justifications for its design choices. Conclusions and future research are presented in Sect. 5 at the end.

2 Background

Some fundamental concepts necessary for our proposal are revised here, mainly IoT and DLT basics and some related works about how DLT can solve some problems on IoT applications.

2.1 IoT

IoT is a powerful ubiquitous technology but suffers from many security issues [6] that make it challenging to employ in practical environments. IoT solutions are related to different aspects of human life. Atzori et al. categorized them as follows [9]: (i) transport, (ii) smart environments, (iii) social and personal applications, and (iv) healthcare.

IoT solutions are impacted and occasionally constrained by the following facts:

- **Massive amount of data/nodes**. IoT equipment is widely used and is constantly growing. Each device produces lots of data throughout its lifetime.
- **Decentralization**. Since so many nodes can coexist in an IoT network and interact with one another [10].
- **Unstable and unexpected connections**. IoT solutions frequently present this type of connections because of the volume and diversity of devices.

The characteristics of IoT-based solutions and their equipment can cause many technological vulnerabilities to emerge, which could then lead to potential attacks on such applications. Wang et al. categorized such attacks [6]: (i) end devices, (ii) communication channels, (iii) network protocols, (iv) sensors, (v) denial of service, and (vi) software.

Several authors [3, 11] are analyzing DLTs in this context to deal with them.

[1] The acronym DLTI refers to the deployment of an infrastructure using DLT technology.

2.2 DLT

DLT can be defined as a system that processes, validates, or authenticates information transactions using transactional databases that are present across multiple locations or between several users, with or without the support of a central authority. Some authors have outlined its primary characteristics [2]:

- **Shared copy**. A shared set of records, usually called **ledger**, which are kept by several entities.
- **Network participation design**.
  - **Permissioned**. Participation requires authorization in advance.
  - **Permissionless**. Participation is not subject to prior approval.
- **Consensus**. All entities reach a consensus before the ledger update.
- **Inmutability**. Past records cannot be changed by an entity.
- **Independent validation**. Everybody can check the integrity of the ledger.
- **Tamper detection attribution**. Non-consensual alterations are detectable by each entity.

One of the harder parts of a distributed system is reaching consensus. It involves reaching a consensus among several nodes and creating fault-tolerant systems. The decision's outcome is regarded as final and cannot be changed. Different consensus algorithms for DLT have been published in the literature over the years, and today we can discover various taxonomies depending on the algorithmic characteristics [12]; however, the most of them ask for proof to verify their authenticity.

3 Study of Scenario Applicability

Before introducing our architectural proposal, this section provides an analysis of the impact of publishing information on a DLTI as well as the adaptation of a DLT to a streaming sensor-based scenario.

3.1 DLTI's Impact on Data Storage

The ability to store data on a DLTI facilitates the creation of solutions with properties like:

1. Resistance to data tampering and/or deletion.
2. Resistance to write timestamp manipulation.
3. Resistance to provider identity spoof.
4. Resilience to single points of failure.

A distributed ledger that is modified via a decentralized consensus process is used to acquire characteristics (1) and (2). Asymmetric cryptographic tools, such as digital signatures, are also used to acquire characteristics (3) and (4).

3.2 DLTI Selection for an IoT Scenario

The analysis of the most appropriate DLTI for IoT applications is focused on the features of our proposal with the aim of strengthening them and the potential solutions that could be created with it.

The more critical point in the DLT selection is related to the network participation design, permissioned versus permissionless [13]. In general, a permissioned DLT, where the ledger is modified by a small group of authorized participants who reach consensus in a non-competitive manner, makes it possible to lower operational costs, improve the performance of the ledger, reduce the computational load on the nodes, and add more control over information access. Hyperledger Fabric[2] and Quorum[3] can be highlighted as permissioned DLTs. A permissionless DLT, on the other hand, makes it easier to verify data for all types of entities and allows third-party users to create their applications using this data. Bitcoin[4] and Ethereum[5] can be highlighted as permissionless DLTs.

Furthermore, we believe that a permissionless DLT would enable the conceptualization of a greater variety of applications, which is why our proposal focuses on these DLTs. Another key point is related to the transaction fee; it is usually used as a mechanism to support networks and nodes or as SPAM control. Taking into consideration the IoT use cases we should focus only on the SPAM control objective to allow IoT real-world applications. With these 2 premises, we have to discard thousands of DLT proposals, and, in particular, our architectural proposal employs IOTA [11] as DLT base. Among permissionless DLTs, IOTA is a DAG-based DLT that provides several uncommon characteristics:

- **Feeless for writing commissions**. To publish, users don't need to own any tokens.
- **Low write latency**. Due to the lack of blocks in IOTA, the infrastructure has a high write throughput.
- **Libraries**. Some libraries with particular relevance to the development of our platform are available in the IOTA ecosystem, in particular **Identity** [1], a framework for the **S**elf-**S**overeign **I**dentity (**SSI**), and **Streams** [14], a framework for building encrypted or unencrypted communication channels.
- **Smart contracts.** Recently added through the **IOTA** **S**mart **C**ontract **P**rotocol (**ISCP** [15]).

---

[2] https://www.hyperledger.org/use/fabric/.

[3] https://consensys.net/quorum/.

[4] https://bitcoin.org/.

[5] https://ethereum.org/.

IOTA is distinguished by these properties in terms of effectiveness and performance, making it a very good DLT for our platform. However, its use raises two major problems:

1. Its ledger quickly grows in size since it is feeless. This is addressed by performing a procedure of taking a balance snapshot and creating a fresh ledger regularly. A **Permanode** [16] is necessary to obtain historical data.
2. IOTA requires PoW for each transaction as a SPAM protection measure. If the publishing device's computing capabilities are constrained, it should assign the PoW to a different party.

4 DLT Architecture Proposal for IOT Applications

Our proposal is a platform that consists of services for gathering data streams from sensor-based devices and posting them to IOTA. Although it should be highlighted that there are still open lines of study focused on the use of SSI and homomorphic computing to secure the solutions and assist the analysis of the recorded data, this contribution only focuses on its interface layers of data collecting/gathering and publication.

4.1 General Architecture Overview

The functionality is divided into five services, whose interconnections and primary functions are shown in Fig. 1, to maximize the platform's flexibility to adapt to the environments in which it is deployed as well as to the characteristics of IoT devices, among which low computational capacity and criticality of information prevail.

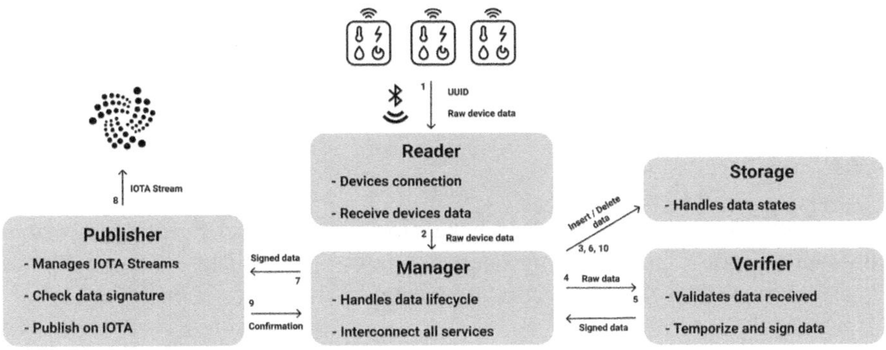

Fig. 1 DLT architecture proposal for IoT

The following technical decisions have been addressed:

- Each service was created using the programming language that best suited the functionality that will be offered.
- **LibP2P**[6] handles the communication between the different services.

4.2 Services

Here is a description of the services represented in the architecture in Fig. 1.

4.2.1 Reader

It serves as the system's gateway and is in charge of controlling the communication with senders and receiving their data. It has been created in Rust to reduce its computing requirements and enable it to operate on IoT gateways installed on inexpensive single-board processors.

4.2.2 Manager

When a Reader instance notifies this service with new data, this service starts managing the data's life cycle from capture to publication. Node.js was utilized as the programming language to make development easier.

4.2.3 Storage

This service enables information modeling and managing a data's state within an operational flow. The service has been created using Node.js to maximize flexibility in handling various data typologies and potentially replace the underlying database engine. The database engine employed in this implementation is LevelJS.[7]

4.2.4 Verifier

As a result of its execution, this service generates a signed message that timestamps the data's capture, implementing heuristics to verify the data's integrity. It was created with Node.js to make it easier to create new heuristics in the future.

---

[6] https://libp2p.io/.

[7] https://leveljs.org/.

4.2.5 Publisher

The messages produced by the Verifier component are published on the IOTA [16] streams under the management of this service. This service was created in Rust to maximize its computational efficiency because it will have to deal with the PoW that IOTA requires for transactions.

4.3 Data Flow

Here different stages (see Fig. 1) of the platform's ideal data flow are shown in detail. For the sake of clarity, steps like creating and managing private keys have been left out.

1. **Pairing**. The sensor-based devices are registered in Reader. They will begin transferring data once they are verified as authorized senders.
2. **Data reception**. When data is received, Reader notifies the Manager.
3. **Processing data**. Manager asks Storage to model the data and receives a JSON document as a result. This data is saved internally by Storage, which changes its status to "Captured."
4. **Verification**. A signed JSON document is generated after Manager asks Verifier to verify and sign this document.
5. **Status update: Verified**. Storage updates the status once Manager notifies it of the data verification.
6. **Publishing of data**. Manager asks Publisher for publishing and, as a consequence, gets IOTA's confirmation of publication.
7. **Status update: Published**. Storage removes the data from the database when Manager notifies Storage of the publishing.

5 Conclusions and Future Work

This contribution describes the information capture and publication interface levels of a DLT architectural platform for IoT applications. The scenario has been studied in order to modify its design for use with sensor-based devices.

Our proposal is a platform that is still in development, so at this time, aspects like information encryption, access control, query resolution, or the ability to generate analytical information from the available information have only been briefly discussed. Future research will be required to conduct a more thorough analysis of each of these aspects.

References

1. Correcting the IoT History. (2022). Retrieved October 31, 2022, from http://www.chetansharma.com/correcting-the-iot-history/
2. Raji, R. (1994). Smart networks for control. *IEEE Spectrum, 31*(6), 49–55. https://doi.org/10.1109/6.284793
3. Rose, K., Eldridge, S., & Chapin, L. (2015). The internet of things: An overview. *The internet society (ISOC), 80*, 1–50.
4. Rauchs, M., Glidden, A., Gordon, B., Pieters, G., Recanatini, M., Rostand, F., Vagneur, K., & Zhang, B. (2018). Distributed ledger technology systems: A conceptual framework. *SSRN Electronic Journal*. https://doi.org/10.2139/ssrn.3230013
5. Popov, S. (2018). Iota whitepaper v1.4.3. *New Yorker, 81*(8), 1–28.
6. Voulgaris, S., Fotiou, N., Siris, V. A., Polyzos, G. C., Jaatinen, M., & Oikonomidis, Y. (2019). Blockchain technology for intelligent environments. *Future Internet, 11*(10), 213. https://doi.org/10.3390/fi11100213
7. Atzori, L., Iera, A., & Morabito, G. (2010). The internet of things: A survey. *Computer Networks, 54*(15), 2787–2805. https://doi.org/10.1016/j.comnet.2010.05.010
8. Vermesan, O., Friess, P., Guillemin, P., Gusmeroli, S., Sundmaeker, H., Bassi, A., Jubert, I., Mazura, M., Harrison, M., Eisenhauer, M., Doody, P. (2009). Internet of things strategic research roadmap.
9. Iota Streams. (2022). Retrieved October 31, 2022, from https://wiki.iota.org/shimmer/smart-contracts/overview
10. Sengupta, J., Ruj, S., & Bit, S. D. (2020). A comprehensive survey on attacks, security issues and blockchain solutions for IoT and IIoT. *Journal of Network and Computer Applications, 149*, 102481. https://doi.org/10.1016/j.jnca.2019.102481
11. Lashkari, B., & Musilek, P. (2021). A comprehensive review of blockchain consensus mechanisms. *IEEE Access, 9*, 43620–43652. https://doi.org/10.1109/ACCESS.2021.3065880
12. Du, Y., Wang, Z., & Leung, V. C. M. (2021). Blockchain-enabled edge intelligence for iot: Background, emerging trends and open issues. *Future Internet, 13*(2), 48. https://doi.org/10.3390/fi13020048
13. Wang, X., Zha, X., Ni, W., Liu, R. P., Guo, Y. J., Niu, X., & Zheng, K. (2019). Survey on blockchain for internet of things. *Computer Communications, 136*, 10–29.
14. Iota Identity. (2022). Retrieved October 31, 2022, from https://www.iota.org/solutions/digital-identity
15. Iota Streams. (2022) Retrieved October 31, 2022, from https://www.iota.org/solutions/streams
16. The Complete Reference for IoTa. (2022). Retrieved October 31, 2022, from https://wiki.iota.org/

Mobile-Based Application for e-Services and e- Payments: A Study Case of Habari Node Public Limited Company in Arusha, Tanzania

Umuhoza Ritha, Anael Sam, and Devotha G. Nyambo

1 Introduction

There have been significant advancements in information communication and technology (ICT) worldwide. The devices and tools used to access data 10 years back are no longer the same as they are now. ICT has revolutionized the way individuals work and allowed the business to reach out to new markets and consumers [1]. People are forced to adopt new technologies in the ICT industry in order to fit well in the Fourth Industrial Revolution. As a result, numerous websites and blogs were created to assist users in accessing information. Many of the installed websites are not mobile based, making it difficult for consumers to navigate when their only alternative is to use a mobile device. With the rise in the number of mobile devices users, different companies and institutions that were previously relying on their websites or blogs to reach users/customers began to consider implementing mobile-based applications that can be downloaded from the Google Play Store for Android smartphone users or the Apple App Store for iPhone users. Also, we must remember that the number of devices connected to the Internet increases daily as an Internet connection becomes affordable and reachable.

In Fig. 1, the projection made by the GSMA Intelligence displays how in 2025, 7.5 billion smartphones will be connected to the Internet. When we consider the growth in smartphone connectivity (see Fig. 1), the number of devices connected to the Internet increases daily. To reach more people, companies and organizations should develop different mobile applications to allow them to sell goods and

U. Ritha (✉)
Nelson Mandela African Institution of Science and Technology University, Arusha, Tanzania
e-mail: rithau@nm-aist.ac.tz

A. Sam · D. G. Nyambo
School of Computational and Communication Sciences and Technology, Arusha, Tanzania
e-mail: anael.sam@nm-aist.ac.tz; devotha.nyambo@nm-aist.ac.tz

J. Marx Gómez et al. (eds.), *Smart and Secure Embedded and Mobile Systems*,
Progress in IS, https://doi.org/10.1007/978-3-031-56603-5_30

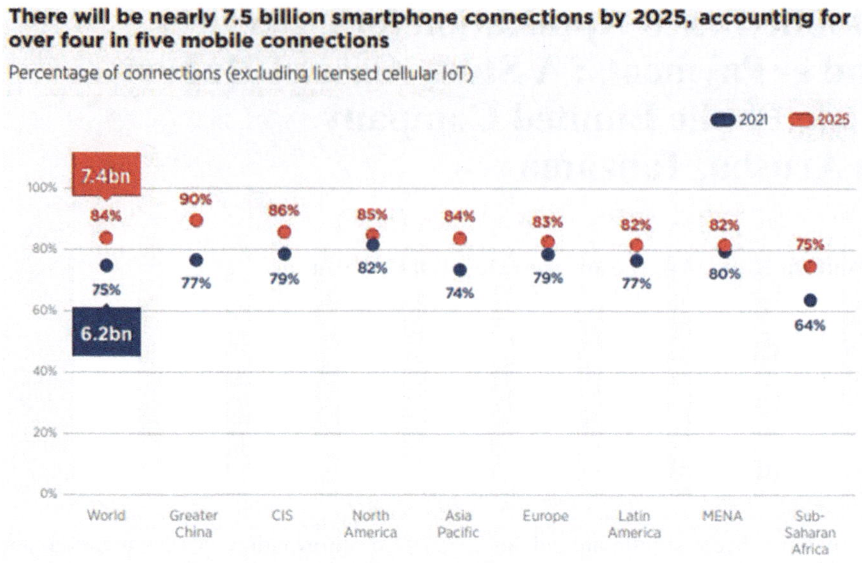

Fig. 1 Smartphones connectivity growth [2]

services and share company information through their mobile devices. In addition, some mobile-based applications can be used without an Internet connection. However, others still need an Internet connection to allow the accessibility of data stored on cloud servers. Currently, Habari Node PLC is using a website platform as a source of information about services provided to the customer and additional helpful content about the company. However, the company has two problems related to customer service attainability and payments. The first problem is that the website is not mobile based. When a customer tries to view the website on his phone, the website's size is not compatible with the mobile device screen, and as a result, not all website content can be viewed by the user. Secondly, the service payment procedures make it a challenge to the customer. This process involves the customer coming to the company to collect the invoice and deposit the money to the provided company's financial accounts.

In this case, a mobile-based application for e-service and e-payments is implemented to be a solution for clients and Habari Node PLC since it lays out all of Habari Node's services to the client through the mobile application. Additionally, the consumer can complete payment transactions without moving from one location to another. Instead, the client is able to carry out all these actions while sitting in one spot and accessing the mobile application through his mobile device.

2 Literature Review

I have reviewed several papers by using a scoping review to find the gaps in those papers and find the solution for the proposed mobile application which will be a solution to the adoption of e-services and e-payments in the current society. The papers show how e-services and e-payments helped in the rising of the African economy as well as making life easy. A lot of writers did research on the use of e-services or digital services. It was found that in the USA and South Africa that mobile-based payment services give a portable and secure solution to users. In addition, users found benefits in accessing different services like health, education, etc., through the mobile application payment systems [3]. Even though the adoption of mobile services payment applications threatened traditional banking and foreign exchange bank laws, this adoption contributed to the gross domestic product growth [4]. During the literature review of this study, different e-payment methods were reviewed and research was done which brought some challenges in the usage of those systems.

2.1 e-Payment Methods and Their Limitation Found During the Research

e-Payment gateway is one of the e-payment software services that connect the service provider networks with the retailer, and it allows the customers to make payments through these. When the customer makes a request to the merchant to pay for a service or good, the merchant will use the application on his terminal to send the payment request to the e-payment provider; at the end, the e- payment will send the request to the service provider to be paid. But still, managing the security of the user's payment information is problematic because it is mainly attacked by hackers who want to get unauthorized access [5].

Internet banking was reviewed as the safest type among the types of e-payments [5]; it involves online banking where you can pay for any product or service of your choice by using the money stored in your bank account. This does not require the use of a credit or debit card to perform the payment through Internet banking; you must provide your bank user id as well as the password to finish the process. The bank provides a mobile application for the user to access Internet banking purposes, or the user can access it through the bank website. Though this is considered a perfect e-payment system, the challenge with this method is that you can't integrate it into your e-commerce system for payment purposes.

The e-check also was reviewed [5]; it is done by the purchaser entering the bank routing number and the account number of company or merchant in the online purchasing or order form; the details will be then forwarded to the person who is in charge of processing the completion of the transaction and will deposit the full or net amount to the merchant bank account. The challenge with this e-payment method is that sometimes the purchaser writes a wrong e-check to the merchant, which may cause a significant loss.

The e-wallet is a prepared account that stores the user's financial details for future payments; this type of payment includes PayPal, Apple Pay, and Google Pay. It allows the customer to perform prepayments and bank transfers in order to cover online payments. PayPal has more than 200 million active users because it works on all devices which have Internet access. The process starts with the customer opening a bank account and installing an e-wallet application on his gadget. The e-wallet permits the purchaser to pay the merchant, send money to other wallets with the same banks or different ones, receive money from different e-wallet accounts as well, perform cash in and cash out, and also help the customer to pay his bills [5].

Unified Payment Interface (UPI) is a payment method that is used in India. To use it, the user must do bank account registration, have a smartphone connected to Wi-Fi or Internet connection, and lastly, and should have the UPI app of the bank on his mobile device. Then, the user creates the virtual payment address (VPA) to make transactions [6]. The limitation with this kind of payment is that the sender and the receiver of money should hold a VPA to make any transfer.

Bitcoin—Satoshi Nakamoto brought this idea in 2008—allows the user to send and receive payments immediately without any involvement of the financial institutions, government, or any other third party to participate in that transaction. Transactions that are done by using bitcoin are not controlled by the government though there are some rules and regulations to follow if you want to use Bitcoin. Bitcoin has high usage because of its transparency and is not supervised by any institution. However, it is not supported by many governments to be used in their countries because it cannot be regulated and supervised by the central banks, which makes its usability not grow as intended [7].

P2P-Paid is a wireless mobile payment method that allows the user to perform payments on mobile phones through the wireless Bluetooth connection or perform any related operations over the server. This was developed in 2004 as a research system prototype at the University of San Jose State [8]. The limitation of this work was that the author needed to specify at which distance the Bluetooth network could work since the highest power device can only work at 100 meters distance [9].This distance will be between the server and the device owner. Therefore, it always requires the user to be within distance to stay connected without interruption.

Smart cards-based electronic payment systems are plastic sized cards with memory chips, and in some cases, they are made with a microprocessor embedded to increase the storage capacity. In addition, some smart cards allow the user to enter the PIN (personal identification number) as a kind of security or even use the encrypted key related to a secret key in the user's processor. This card was taken as a highly secured card because it permanently anonymizes transactions of the user, but the only limitation it has is the transfer of money depending on how much money is saved on the smartphone to be used [10].

3 Methods

3.1 Area of Study

In this chapter, the study area is based on the e-services and e-payments systems, whether mobile-based or web-based. There are multiple services that can be accessed by customers through the mobile app or website. Among them, we can say e-health services, e-government services, e-taxes services, e-commerce services, etc. Not all the listed services are free, which means there is a specific price you have to pay in order to access them, that is where e-payment comes in. e-Payment allows the payment of the service or product without the need to move from one place to another, the payments are made through the payment system, and the customer will be able to access the service he paid for. This study was carried out at Habari Node PLC, Arusha. It involved the development of a mobile-based application for e-services and e-payments for Habari Node PLC customers and potential customers.

3.2 System Development Approach

Agile development methodology will be used to implement the proposed system because it allows delivery of a working software increment and welcomes changes in the requirements even late in the development for the customer's advantage. Since e-services and e-payments mobile application is going to be mainly used by customers, I used the Extreme Programming language model (see Fig. 2) to deliver the final product increment.

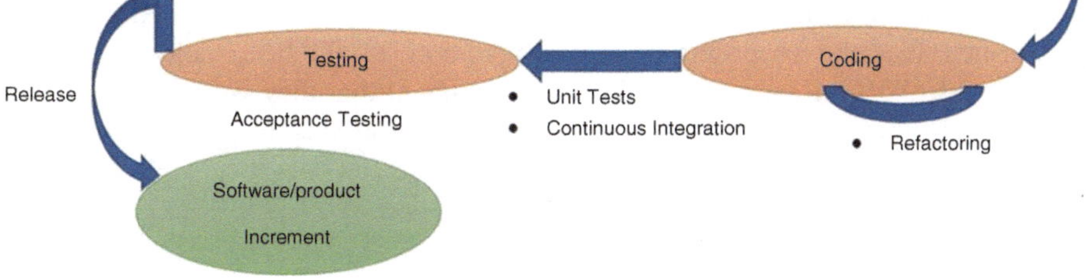

Fig. 2 Extreme programming model

This model was chosen because it allows the requirements to be removed and added or changed throughout the development process according to the customer's need services payments and also shared with me the challenges the customers complain about.

3.3 Data Collection

The requirements gathering process from Habari Node PLC customers was needed to develop the above mobile application. The gathered data are going to be used during the implementation of the mobile application because this application will be for customer's use. There are two methods that were used during data collection:

3.4 Qualitative Method

This method was carried out by conducting interviews and observation. I did an interview with the Habari Node CRM officer, where she shared with me the procedures that customers undergo, from registration to service attainability. From there, I managed to get some of the customer's complaints, which can be solved by the mobile-based e-services and e-payments application. Also, I managed to interview the Finance Manager, who elaborated on the procedures for them.

3.5 Quantitative Method

This method was carried out by distributing questionnaires to Habari Node customers. Habari Node has about 2500 customers; the data sampling showed that the survey has to be done for about 300 customers. Two hundred seventeen (217) customers replied to the questionnaire. The purpose of this survey was to find customers' challenges in accessing Habari Node services and performing payments for those services and also if the proposed mobile application will solve the stated challenges. The collected data state that 87.2% of the responded customers confirmed that the proposed mobile application would be a solution to their challenges, 9.3% of the responded customers stated that they would confirm after using the proposed mobile application, and the remaining percentage responded "no."

4 Results and Discussion

4.1 *Requirements of the Proposed Mobile Application*

After the data collection phase, data analysis was carried out, and the collected data were classified into functional and non-functional requirements as shown in Table 1, to start developing the proposed mobile application.

Table 1 Proposed system functional and non-functional requirements

Functional requirements	Non-functional requirements
1. A new user must be able to register with his username, phone number, email, and password and log in with the confirmed username and password	1. Maintainability—The mobile application should provide support/modification or reconfiguration at a particular time or when required
2. The phone number verification must be carried out each time the user logs in after he has logged out of the mobile app	2. Performance—The system should respond to user queries as expected and be able to handle multiple users as well as multiple queries
3. After user registration and login for the first time, the next login will only require the phone number verification for security purposes because multiple users can have the same usernames, and even passwords are more likely to be hacked nowadays	3. Security—The system should allow users to be authenticated with phone verification each time they access the mobile application. There should not be a user's pin system capturing while performing payment
4. The application must allow the user to update his account details when needed	4. Usability—The system must be simple to use for any user
5. The user should be able to get new offers, or any other information related to the Habari node or his account through the notification symbol in the menu	5. Compatibility—The mobile application must be able to function on a mobile device with an android OS Or IOS
6. The user should be able to view Habari node services and subscribe to any of his choices	
7. The subscribed services must be moved to my subscriptions so that the payment process can be carried out	
8. The payments must be carried out through mobile money like Mpesa, Halopesa, Tigo Pesa, Airtel money, Master cards, or visa cards. It will depend on the customer's choice	

(continued)

Table 1 (continued)

Functional requirements	Non-functional requirements
10. Hover technique will be used to automate the existing USSD sessions in the application's background, and the user will be asked just to put in the pin to con firm the payment. This technique prevents the customer from typing the USSD code	
11. A payment receipt must be sent to the customer's email after the transaction	
12. The customer should be able to send feedback to Habari node and get the message confirming the payment	
13. The customer must be able to contact Habari Node employees through calls, email, WhatsApp, Facebook, etc. directly from the application	
14. Once the phone number verification is attempted and failed three times, the user account will be locked, and the user has to contact Habari Node for further actions	
15. Once the system is idle for a specific time, the user must be logged out of the application	
16. The user account will be locked after two attempts of entering the wrong mobile money pin during service payment	
17. Each account should be registered under a different phone number	

4.2 Design of the System

Functional and non-functional requirements helped me design different designs for the proposed system. System designs help to understand how the system will function, the processes, and the users of the proposed system. We have the conceptual and use case diagrams among the architectural designs included in this chapter.

4.2.1 Conceptual Diagram

The conceptual diagram (see Fig. 3) will give an overview of the system processes. The mobile-based application for e-services and e-payments will have three kinds of users: the system admins, the customer, and Habari node Employees. All the users will be authenticated before accessing this mobile application though users will have different privileges. The system admin will be able to make any changes on the system in the back end when needed. The customer, as well as the Habari Node employee, will just view the services, perform payments, give feedback, and perform other multiple operations he is authorized to perform.

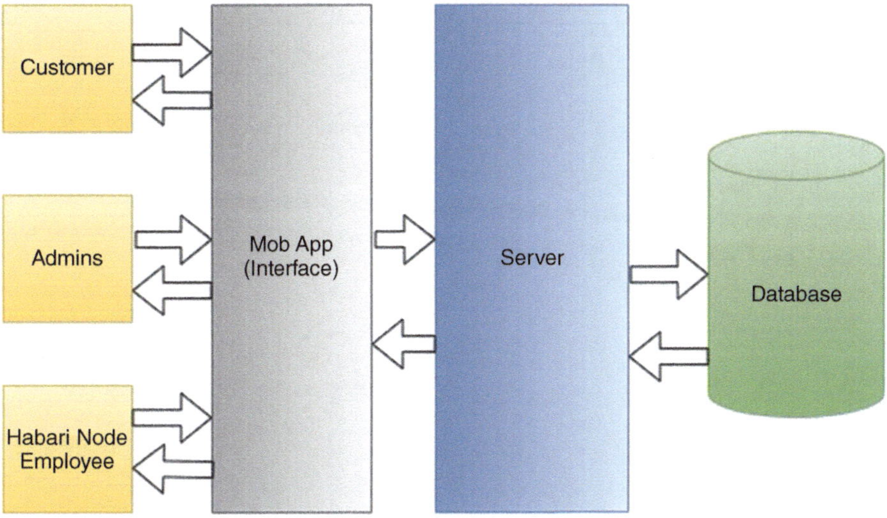

Fig. 3 Conceptual diagram of the proposed system

4.2.2 Use Case Diagram

The use case diagram (see Fig. 4) shows what the system will do, which means all the functionalities of the system will be summarized in the use case diagram. By the use of symbols and connecting lines, the actors will be linked to the functionalities they will be able to perform on the system, and the actor can have one or more than one functionality.

4.3 Developed Mobile-Based Application for e-Services and e-Payments

According to the data collection, we came up with customer requirements, and the system was developed to fulfill the customer's needs. The developed mobile application has the registration interface, home interface, etc.

4.3.1 Registration and Phone Number Verification Interface

The registration interface (see Fig. 5) shows the page the customer or any other user will use to register with the mobile application. The user will have to enter his name, location address, and email. After that the user will be required to enter the phone number (see Fig. 6) and the user must choose the country code. After entering the phone number, a one-time password will be sent through the message for

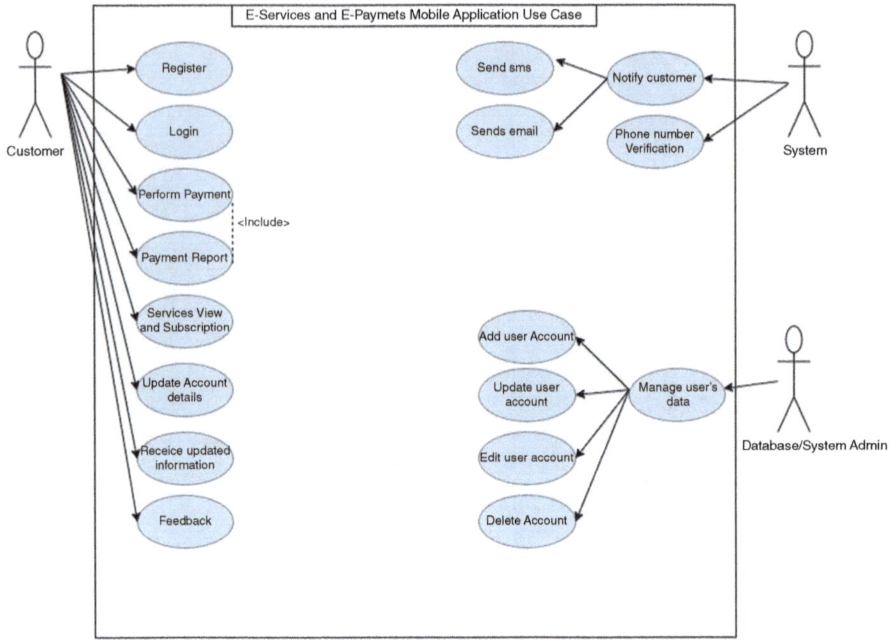

Fig. 4 e-services and e-payments mobile application use case diagram

verification for security purposes. The phone number verification will be required each time the user logs out from the system. Once the one-time password (OTP) entered fails three times, the system will warn the user against entering the wrong OTP and be locked from proceeding with any subsequent action.

4.3.2 Home Page, Subscription List, Payment, and Payment Options Interfaces

After the user has registered and verified the phone number correctly, the homepage interface will be displayed (see Fig. 7) with multiple services that Habari Node offers. The user will choose the service of his choice, and immediately that service will be added to the subscription list (see Fig. 8) from My Subscriptions. Once the user clicks on the subscribe now button, the payment page will be displayed (see Fig. 9), and the user will choose to pay either through mobile money or by using a credit or visa card. Fig. 10 shows different mobile money service providers the user can choose to perform the digital payment. The user will not be asked to run

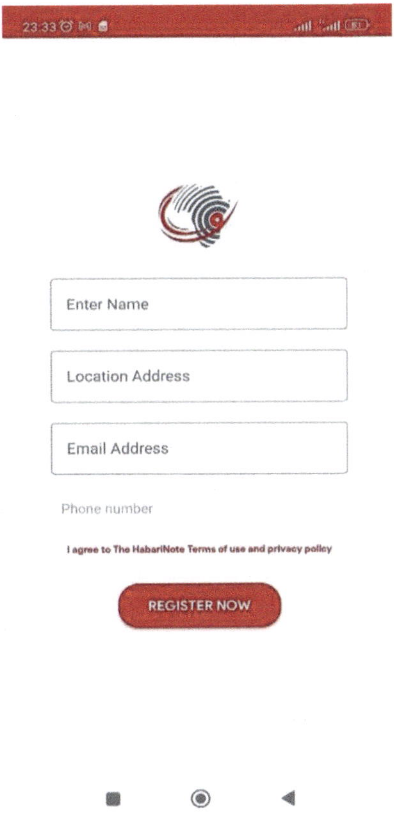

Fig. 5 User registration interface

any USSD code; after selecting the mobile money to pay with, he will be asked to enter his mobile money pin, which for security purposes will not be captured by the system. Once the payment is made, a payment receipt will be sent to the user's email confirming the payment of that particular service.

5 Conclusion and Recommendation

Mobile devices have been advanced and can perform many tasks a personal computer can carry out. For that reason, using a mobile device gives a person information about any service he wishes to know. Multiple Internet service providers have mobile money services which allow the customer to send, pay, or receive money without moving from one place to another; it can be a tangible product or an intangible service. This technology allows people to perform any transaction on the Internet without needing a third party; only the device needs to be connected to the Internet connection. Though multiple countries fear using electronic payment

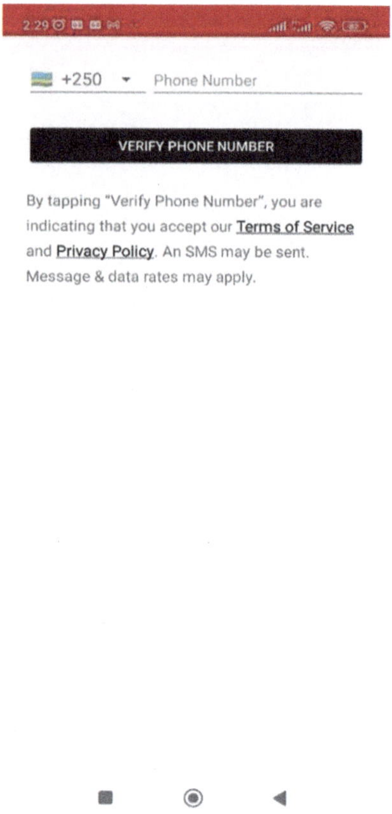

Fig. 6 Phone number verification interface

due to different experiences of fraud, multiple security solutions were developed and used to avoid that Internet fraud. This study advises the implementation of different mobile applications which can be used in e-commerce and e-payment to make the purchasing process simple and fast. Mobile subscribers will grow to more than 5 million in 2025 [2], and as the number of mobile device owners increases, the number of connected devices increases. This brings good opportunities to business owners and companies using mobile applications to sell or advertise their goods and services. With the advance of the ICT, many selling transactions expect logistics to be done through a mobile application. This will help small businesses to grow, and it will also avoid inequity and fights for customers at markets; also, the customers will have more information about the goods or services and pay by choice without any convincing, which is unnecessary. As it was found that security is at high risk while using electronic payment, different measures and techniques must be developed by the researchers to make the e-payment or e-commerce a safe process for everyone.

Fig. 7 Home page of the developed mobile app

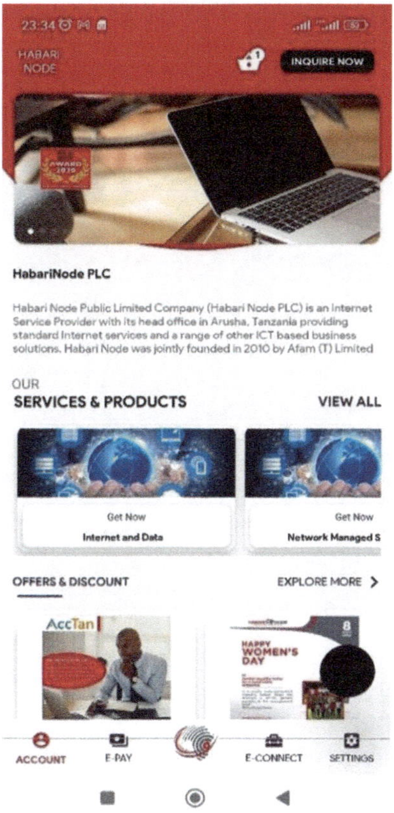

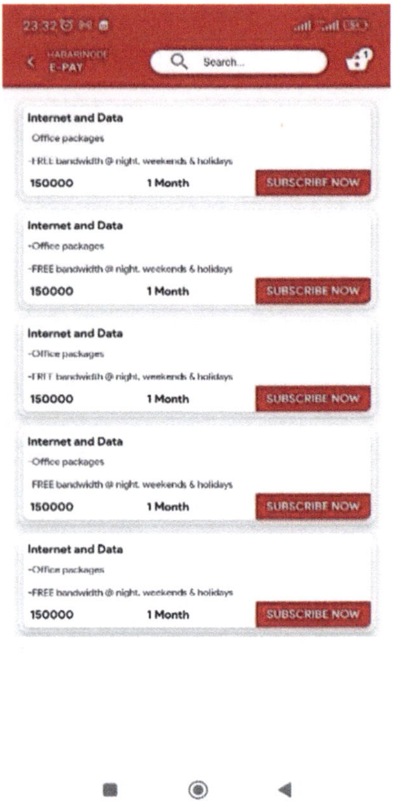

Fig. 8 Services subscription list

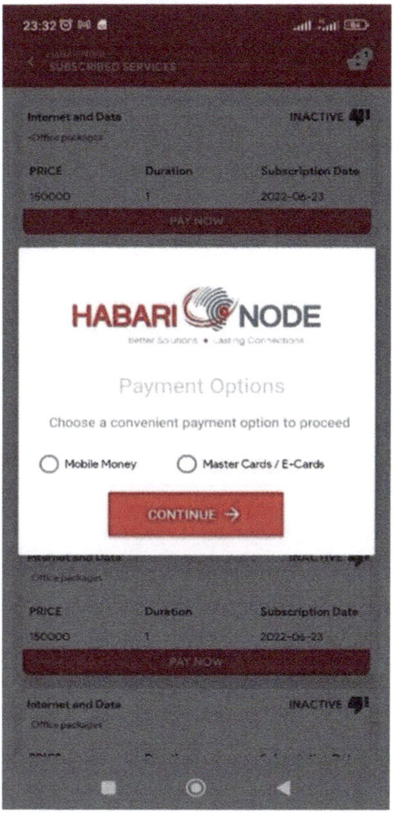

Fig. 9 Payment interface

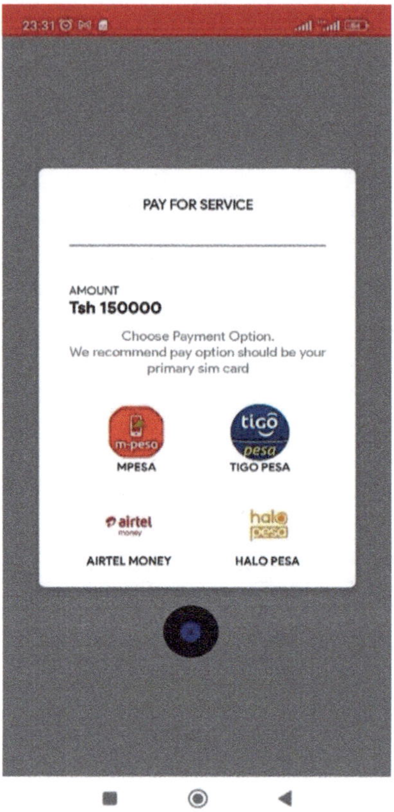

Fig. 10 Payment options interface

References

1. Ismail, M. H., Khater, M., & Zaki, M. (2018, January). Digital business transformation and strategy: What do we know so far? *ResearchGate*
2. Okeleke, K., & Suardi, S. (2022, March). The mobile economy 2022. Retrieved March 31, 2022, from https://data.gsmaintelligence.com/research/research/research-2022/the-mobile-economy-2022
3. Danaiata, D., Margea, C., Hurbean, L., & Artene, A. S. (2014). Electronic Services for Business Environment. *Procedia -Social and Behavioral Sciences, 124*, 351–360.
4. Glajchen, D.. (2011). A comparative analysis of mobile phone-based payment services in the United States and South Africa. *Dissertation Abstracts International Section A: Humanities and Social Sciences.*
5. Nasr, M. F. M. M. N. M. H. (2016). e-Payment systems risks, opportunities and challenges for. *International Journal of Intelligent Computing and Information Science, 20*(1), 16–27.
6. Sujith, T. S., & Julie, C. D. (2017). Opportunities and challenges of E- payment system in India. *International Journal of Scientific Research and Management (IJSRM), 5*(09), 6935–6943.
7. Nadeem, M. A., Liu, Z., Pitafi, A. H., Younis, A., & Yi, X. (2021). Investigating the adoption factors of cryptocurrencies—A case of bitcoin: Empirical evidence from China. *SAGE Open, 11*(1), 2.
8. Cai, J., Patel, K., Shim, S., & Gao, J. (2005). *A wireless payment system, Proceedings of the Second International Conference on Embedded software and systems*. IEEE.
9. Dahiya, M. (2017). A short range wireless network: Bluetooth. *International Journal of Advanced Research in Computer Science, 8*, 37.
10. Sumanjeet, D. (2009). *Emergence of payment systems in the age of electronic commerce: The state of art. IEEE.*

Embracing Sustainable Tourism Development through Information Communication Technology (ICT) in Tanzania

Analysis Using Selected Tour Operators in Dar es Salaam

Nassor Sadick and Juma James Masele

1 Introduction

Tourism is an important sector and has been acknowledged to have high potential for growth in the world economy [1, 2]. The sector offers huge opportunities for income generation to the government through foreign currencies from tourists' arrivals, taxation from the tourist companies, and business establishments liable for tax payments. It is therefore considered one of the principal exports for 83% of developing countries and the least developed countries (LDCs). It is also a source of income generation for the individuals and small business undertakings through sales of several tourism goods and services [3]. It is growing rapidly and is the most significant source of foreign exchange after petroleum, fostering economic development through its significant contributions toward the gross domestic product (GDP) [4]. With that, countries endowed with attractive tourist areas such as reserves, parks, mountains, cultural heritages sites, water bodies, and several others, both natural and man-made features, have greatly invested in the sector to ensure that the sector keeps on flourishing and has a high level of sustainability [5].

Worldwide, efforts to ensure that tourism growth is sustainable economically, socially, and environmentally are apparent. Sustainable tourism development (STD) is considered essential if nations have to guarantee positive tourism impact on the gross domestic product (GDP) contribution; foster the preservation of the environment, recreation, and sites for further tourist visits while fostering environmental protection and sustainability; and ensure that the growth is socially sustainable [6]. With that, where tourism business fulfills what sustainable development agenda calls

N. Sadick · J. J. Masele (✉)
Alpha Digital Systems Limited, Dar es Salaam, Tanzania
e-mail: masele@udsm.ac.tz

J. Marx Gómez et al. (eds.), *Smart and Secure Embedded and Mobile Systems*,
Progress in IS, https://doi.org/10.1007/978-3-031-56603-5_31

for, the undertaking has significance for the economy, with a positive impact on the environment, its natural resources and ecosystems, and human well-being [7].

The World Travel and Tourism Council (WTTC) held in 2002 encouraged companies to set up systems and procedures to incorporate sustainable development issues into core management functions as well as identify actions needed to bring about sustainable tourism. However, according to Ali and Frew [8], researchers in the fields relevant to sustainability have been far from idle; sustainable tourism research enjoys a rather limited corpus of knowledge with much of the work adopting traditional approaches.

Information and communication technology (ICT) is not new to tourism but rather can be argued that its applications to sustainable development are new [8]. It is just recent that researches in ICT and related areas have turned their attention to sustainability issues and give consideration to how technologies may bring about a step change in practice. Thus, although there are currently plenty of sophisticated ICT facilities considered sufficient to foster sustainable tourism development [9], understanding the relationship between ICT and sustainable tourism development is of vital significance if the tourism sector is to take full advantage of ICT for its growth and prosperity [8]).

As technology advances, emphasis has been placed on the use and application of ICT to facilitate access for as many as possible individual tourists through electronic facilities such as e-mails, websites, social media, and several others [10]. ICT has a global reach facilitating access for as many as possible individual tourists using electronic facilities such as e-mails, websites, social media, and several others [10]. It also has been useful in facilitating easy pattern of communication of reliable information since the use of facilities enables the generation of adequate facts among tourists on different destinations for one to decide the place to visit [11, 12]. It is considered a better candidate to sustain nations' tourism business given its ability to link sellers and buyers for a business deal ubiquitously in a coordinated fashion [13, 14]. In doing so, ICT offers a firm with wider reach, thus increasing the income to be received at the end.

Besides, ICT is acknowledged to have huge importance in fostering a greener, low-carbon emission economy while both technology and innovation based on ICT are the main forces for ensuring sustainability [15]. This is evident due to the fact that duties and activities in most cases are performed electronically which is friendly to the environment and the ecosystems, thus preserving the tourist attractions [5]. ICT application is also useful in fostering sustainable tourism by minimizing traveling through precise tourist location which ensures a positive impact on the environment, the economy, and society at large [7].

According to Ali and Frew [8], ICT can stand as an instrumental tool for local community participation to matters pertaining to tourism management through awareness creation on plans, opportunities, and ongoing challenges including managing destinations and handling the tourists. With ICT enabled by the Internet and the Web 2.0, these actors can be easily connected to socially, economically, and environmentally share information among themselves but also with other tourism stakeholders such as customers, suppliers, and the government. Moreover, conditions of the practice tend to be further stable and advancing in terms of surroundings that they are well improved and monitored by the relevant authorities to keep on attracting as many tourists as possible (Lu & Lu, [12]).

Tanzania in particular is a home for large tourist attractions with 38% of the land reserved for tourist activities to be undertaken. The country has about 17 national parks, 29 game reserves, marine parks, and 40 controlled conservation areas including the famous Ngorongoro crater (URT, [16]). The sector is highly useful in the country since 17.5% of the country's gross domestic product (GDP) is generated from the sector. The government on the other hand values the sector including highly promoting it to ensure that its growth fosters sustainable development and stability (URT, [16]). However, although several measures have been taken in ensuring promotion of tourism using both traditional and ICT, emphasis on the role ICT for tourism sustainability promotion is still considered low [9].

Accordingly, ICT is not only a media for information sharing but also a tool to ease the operations in the sector, thus enhancing both efficiency and effectiveness of services provision. It aids in resource use minimization including minimizing use of space, equipment, energy, transportation, and water, thus favoring reduction in firms' operational costs. Facilities such as global positioning system (GPS), Local Based Systems (LBS), Intelligent Transport Systems (ITS), and others of that kind for example enable easy provision of location information within the destination that would enhance tourists' satisfaction (Ali & Frew, [8]). It is also instrumental in optimization of production and supply chain processes or environmental information systems, large-scale simulation, and real-time control. Studies (e.g., [17]) reveal that ICT helps to come up with better decisions with respect to resource and energy consumption. ICTs can facilitate the monitoring in real-time energy and other resources consumption or depletion, helping managers surf through large volumes of data to identify patterns and trends which could validate the impacts of their decisions [17].

Although various studies have been performed in tourism practices in Tanzania (such as [18], their focus is only related to assessment of ICT adoption, opportunities, and challenges for tourism in East Africa including Tanzania. Yet, studies on ICT's role in tourism sustainability are scant and inconclusive, a gap which this study entailed to fill. The study was therefore performed to assess the role of ICT on sustainable tourism development in Tanzania.

2 Literature Review

This study is guided by the task-technology fit (TTF) theory. The theory explains the possible fit between the technology available and the task as goal to be attained [19]. TTF theory holds that IT is more likely to have a positive impact on individual performance and be used if the capabilities of the IT match the tasks that the user must perform [20]. This is influenced by the fact that the use and application of any technology is not only useful but also ease to use and user friendly [21, 22] for sustaining tourism business [13, 14]. At one point UNCTAD termed ICT and tourism as natural partners due to the potential of ICT applications in sustainable tourism.

With ICT it can be easy to efficiently disseminate and share information regarding expected tourism business ethical adherence by the tour operators, the local community, and the tourists. This is because, according to study by Apollo [23] in the European context using comparative approach in the region, tourism ethics was identified as a key to development, prosperity, and well-being in the tourism sector to facilitate sustainability. Impliedly, well deployment of ICT facilities guarantees information management and flow to the stakeholders, community participation, and efficient resource usage which foster tourism sustainability. However, there are scant studies that have been conducted in Tanzanian tourism context: a gap to be filled by this study.

The study by Arts et al. [24] which examined digital technology and its potential to facilitate nature conservation indicated that digital technology applications have changed significantly the pattern of conservation in different manners including enabling to capture and store and share data on people in the area, data on nature, communication, and experience, and participatory governance. Thus, it also has a significant effect on community participation as well as efficient resource use including energy, equipment, and data/ information. This is of significant impact for sustainable tourism development and promotion. In that case, this entails a gap to be filled in the Tanzanian context since available studies lack focus on ICT use related to sustainable tourism development. It is from this background this study was formulated to assess the role of ICT for sustainable tourism development.

This study seeks to test the hypothesized relationship between the independent variables and the dependent variables presented in the study's conceptual model in Fig. 1.

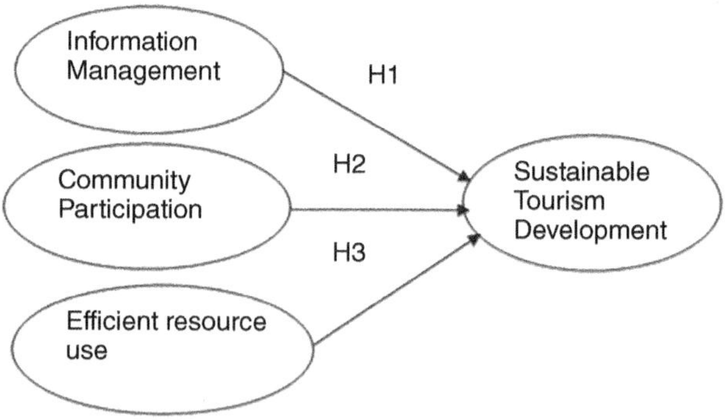

Fig. 1 Conceptual framework

2.1 Model Description and Hypotheses Formulation

The main study assumption as presented in the conceptual model in Fig. 1 and explained in Table 1 is that ICT positively influences sustainable tourism development in Tanzania through ensuring effective information management, community participation, and efficient resource use.

Information management refers to the application of management techniques to collect information, communicate it within and outside the organization, and process it to enable managers to make quicker and better decisions. In a study conducted by Ali and Frew [33], destination managers ranked information management as the most important area of applying ICT for sustainable tourism. This is because, tourism is an information-intensive industry and managing this information is crucial to the success of the industry [34]. Through better information management, destination managers can better plan and manage tourism business. In fact, one of the most important determining elements of satisfaction is receiving accurate and comprehensive tourist information [35].

According to Schwalbe [25], ICT use promises smooth information management through enhanced quality information provision, accessibility to information, utility of the information, safe storage pattern of the information, and the pattern of information disposal. According to a number of studies (such as [26, 36, 37]), information management tools are necessary for these professionals to navigate through the vast amounts of data and information available to retrieve valuable information useful for fostering sus tainable tourism development. In tourism, for example, the ICT tools are diverse to include computer simulation systems; destination management systems (DMS); economic impact analysis software; environmental management information systems (EMIS); geographical information systems (GIS); Global Positioning Systems (GPS); tourism information systems; and information management of weather, climate, and oceanic changes; and others [38]. These all hold promise for sustainable tourism development. This study hypothesizes that:

H1: Information management positively influences sustainable tourism development in Tanzania.

Community participation is a tool to facilitate host population to feel having control in their surrounding tourism development decisions an aspect that is critical for sustainable tourism development [38]. It should also be not ed. that sustainable tourism development is a multifaceted agenda that requires a close involvement of diverse stakeholders including the government and its agencies, local community, the tourists, and linked business sectors such as hotels, transportations, the tour operators, and many others. Involvement of community members including important decisions made is important in order to actively participate in the tourism sector development agenda. According to Bracht [28], the amount and duration of time devoted to goal activities by the member of the community, degree of local ownership perceived and/or achieved within the community, and representativeness of member and group leaders in the community is important for sustainable tourism development. Unlike the technologies of the twentieth century such as

Table 1 Measurements of variables

Construct	Definition	Item indicators/Statements	Citations
Information management	. . . the practice in an organization activity whereas there is gath ering of in formation and collection from one or more sources and its distribution to those who need it	• Quality of information shared fosters sustainable tourism • Accessibility of reliable information influences sustainable tourism development. • Utility in information assists in sufficient tourism development. • Safe storage of relevant information is essential in facilitating tourism development. • Disposal of unwanted and irrelevant information may have positive outcome on sustainable tourism development.	[25, 26]
Community participation	. . . a social process in which groups with shared needs living in a "certain geographical area" actively identify needs, make decisions, and set up mechanisms to achieve solutions	• Efficient communication, coordination, and feedback provision to the community. • Opportunities and levels of.Involvements in decision making • Amount and duration of time devoted to goal activities. • Degree of local ownership perceived and/or achieved. • Representativeness of member and leader groups. • Satisfaction with the process of participation and long-term goals.	[27, 28]

Efficient resource use	. . . reduction of amount of resource (e.g., equipment, energy, water, space, transportation, and waste) used in accomplishing a certain organization task	• Energy use minimization. • Reducing amount of transportation. • ICT waste minimization. • Equipment (hardware and software) use minimization. • Space use minimization. • General operational costs minimization.	Bytheway [17]
Sustainable tourism development	. . . the practice of tourism which ensures positive outcomes von society, the environment, and the economy	• Volume and spread of tourism. • Visitors' satisfaction. • Tourism enterprise performance as well as satisfaction. • Community reaction, and socio-cultural improvement. • Environment impact.	[29–32]

television, radio, magazines, billboards, and others, ICT has come as a panacea to achieve ubiquitous involvement of important stakeholders for sustainable tourism development. Enabled with the emergency of the Internet and tools like Web 2.0, ICT (e.g., use of tools like groupware) is considered an enabler for stakeholders to communicate, coordinate, and collaborate through means like social media, Instagram, short messages, and video conferencing even using their smart phones [39, 40]. These features, in turn, enhance community involvement and awareness creation on matters affecting environment and on the way to maximize local economic benefits. For this sake, ICT is a tool for effective sustainable tourism planning and decision making. This study therefore had its second hypothesis as.

H2: Community participation through ICT positively influences sustainable tourism development in Tanzania.

The third variable was "Efficient resource use"—defined as the sum total of all the reduction of amount of resource (e.g., equipment, energy, water, space, transportation, and waste) used in accomplishing a certain task. According to Bytheway, if sustainability is to be achieved then transformation should include reduction strategies across four areas: carbon emission, space utilization, transport, and material. These are made possible using ICT [41]. A few examples include (1) reducing carbon emission by saving energy costs, making the business less dependent on energy cost fluctuations, and reducing carbon footprint thereby combating climate change; (2) reducing space usage, thereby requiring less office space and reducing managed floor space needs in data centers including related power and cooling costs, (3) reducing the amount of transport, thereby enabling the workforce to work from any location (office or home) by instituting required unified communications and collaborations tools and improving connectivity with business customers; (4) reducing the use of equipment and material by virtualizing infrastructure, hence lowering costs and improving business agility; and (5) reduced energy consumption, thereby saving costs for paying energy bills, and the money saved can be allocated to other strategic business endeavors (([41]). In so doing, it improves both firm's economic gains and the environment welfare, resulting in eco-sustainable development [42].

In addition to that, efficient energy use is influenced by structure which implies the type of activities taking place in the area and their linkage in other sectors ([26]). Studies (such as [42, 43] have argued that activities such as destination selection, booking, payment, pre-delivery support activities, transfer arrangements from/to the airport, and so forth all involve some form of ICT, hence reducing to a great extent the amount of commuting. Consequently, it brings efficient resource use and emissions. This study therefore hypothesizes that:

H3: Efficient resources use through ICT positively influences sustainable tourism development in Tanzania.

3 Methodology

This study was conducted in Dar es Salaam where the majority of the tour operators have either headquarters or sub-offices upcountry [44]. The operators were considered appropriate unit of analysis since they are direct practitioners in the business. The study adopted a positivist approach because the researcher sought to measure and observe objective reality through structured questionnaire. Data obtained from a five-point Likert scale questionnaire from strongly agree to strongly disagree collected from 90 tour operators from registered tour companies in Dar es Salaam (randomly selected from management and operational cadres) was subjected to a multiple regression analysis. The regression model is presented as.

The regression equation model is presented as: $STD = \beta o + \beta 1IM + \beta 2CP + \beta 3ERU + e$

Where

STD = Sustainable tourism development

βo = Constant factor

$\beta 1, \beta 2, \beta 3$ = Factor coefficient

IM = Information management

CP = Community participation

ERU = Efficient resource use

e = Error term.

Both validity and reliability were tested to ensure accuracy of the study variables. Validity was done specifically through the pre-testing of the questionnaire as the research tool. Apart from that the questions used were extracted from the literature and subjected to little contextualization. After a pilot test, all study variables were specifically subjected to Cronbach's alpha test. The test proved that the instrument was reliable as it had a Cronbach's alpha value greater than or equal to 0.7.

4 Analysis of Results

4.1 Respondents' Demographic Profile

The demographic profile of respondents as presented in Table 2 indicates 66 (73%) males and 24 (27%) females. Age wise, 9 (10%) were aged from 21 to 30 years, 54 (60.3%) were aged 31–40 years, and 27(30%) were aged 41–50 years. Education level of respondents indicates that 10 (11%) had secondary education, 19 (21%) had certificate education level, 30 (33%) had diploma education, 26 (29%) had first degree, and 6 (6.3%) had master's degree.

Table 2 Demographic profile of respondents

Attribute	Details	Frequency	Percent (%)
Gender	Male	66	73
	Female	24	27
	Total	***90***	***100***
Age	21–30	9	10
	31–40	54	60
	41–50	27	30
	Total	***90***	***100***
Education level	Secondary education	10	11
	Certificate	19	21
	Diploma	30	33
	Bachelor's degree	26	29
	Master's	6	7
	Total	***90***	***100***

4.2 Inferential Statistics Analysis

For inferential statistics analysis, a multiple regression analysis was used to describe the hypothesized relationship between the independent variables and dependent variable. Findings in Table 3 show the overall contribution of all independent variables to the dependent variable through the respective value of R2. The prediction power of the hypothesized independent variables information management, community participation, and efficient resource to sustainable tourism development in Tanzania is by 37.7%, meaning that 62.3% of its variance is explained by other factors. The results indicate that the ICT's role in sustainable tourism development in Tanzania at the moment through enabling information management, community participation, and efficient resource use is still limited, and it implies that it may support other factors besides ICT.

The analysis of variance (ANOVA) indicated that the regression model was significant and a good fit for the data. The F value of 11.925 and $p < 0.000$ (see Table 3) was obtained (see also [45]). This implies that the independent variables were significant in predicting the dependent variable.

The analysis further indicates that all hypothesized independent variables (information management, community participation, and efficient resource use) had a positive influence on sustainable tourism development. Results on multiple regression analysis (Table 3) showing the contribution of each independent variable on the dependent variable indicates that the two independent variables, information management and efficient resource use, are positive and statistically significant for sustainable tourism development at $\beta = 61.0\%$, $t = 5.743$, and $p = 0.000$ and $\beta = 27.3\%$, $t = 2.580$, and $p = 0.012$, respectively. However, community participation on the other hand although was found positive, its influence had an

Table 3 Multiple regression table Coefficients[a]

Model	Unstandardized coefficients		Stan dardized coefficients	t	Sig.	95.0% confidence interval for B		Collinearity statistics	
	B	Std. error	Beta			Lower Bound	Upper bound	Tolerance	VIF
(Constant)	1.242	0.228		5.448	0.000	0.786	1.698		
Information management	0.528	0.092	0.610	5.743	0.000	0.344	0.712	0.935	1.070
Community participation	0.037	0.076	0.050	0.479	0.634	0.116	0.189	0.980	1.020
Efficient resource use	0.245	0.095	0.273	2.580	0.012	0.436	0.055	0.943	1.061
R-square (R^2) = 0.377; adjusted R-square (Adj. R^2) = 0.346; F = 11.925; Durbin–Watson = 1.964									

[a]Dependent variable: sustainable tourism development

insignificant effect on sustainable tourism development since $p > 0.05$. $\beta = 5.0\%$, $t = 0.479$, and $p = 0.634$.

This implies that when information management facilitated by ICT goes up by one standard deviation, sustainable tourism development goes up by 61%. When efficient resource use goes up one standard deviation, sustainable tourism development goes up by 27.3%. At the same time as community participation goes up by one standard deviation, sustainable tourism development goes up by 5%. The multicollinearity error value of VIF less than 5 on all study predicting variables implies that sustainable tourism development in Tanzania by means of ICT is significantly influenced by information management and efficient resource use.

5 Discussion

The study findings showed that information management as the independent variable is positive with significant effect statistically on sustainable tourism development with $p < 0.05$. This implies that sustainable tourism development in Tanzania through ICT is significantly facilitated by information management. This is further acknowledged by Anderson [9] stating that sustainable tourism is likely to be attained in Tanzania where there is proper information communication technology (ICT) to support information management. Where there is sufficient information management to a great scale travelers from different destinations are ensured of getting quality information which is useful in decision-making prior to tourism practices in the area.

In addition to that, Okello and Novelli [18] also suggest that tourism in the region of East Africa including Tanzania for some time has been difficult to reach sustainability since the facilities pertaining to information communication technologies have been very poor and inadequate. This has been a setback because once they are well improved and assured of their functionality they are useful in fostering sustainable tourism since they foster accessibility to adequate and reliable information for the tourists from all over the globe in the country. Yet, unlike the past studies [9, 18] which focus on the tourism sector's ICT adoption, opportunities, and challenges, this study of its own kind focuses on the role of ICT in sustainable tourism development in Tanzania, thus adding to a body of literature an important contribution to the sustainable tourism development knowledge.

Apart from that, study results have also indicated that community participation as the predicting variable is also positive but with insignificant effect statistically on sustainable tourism development with $p > 0.05$. This implies that the influence of community participation through ICT on sustainable tourism development though positive is insignificant. This is also acknowledged by Arts et al. [24] who argue that sustainable tourism development based on ICT efforts is lowly fostered through effective community participation among the public within and outside the borders. The argument is also supported by Ali and Frew [33] who in their study on "Technology innovation and applications in sustainable destination development" found that community participation is the least important area identified by Destination Management Officers (DMOs). Yet, the influence was revealed to be positive.

This is certain because the ICT facilities foster quick spread of information with frequent feedbacks among people and groups on the attractions and several other remedies that may foster tourism development, but they may be far from them as far as interest is concerned. Also, Ali and Frew [8] provide that in an area with effective ICT facilities usually the tourism sector is likely to be boosted because information as well as several opportunities are likely to be quickly shared and disseminated which creates attraction and ensures sustainability in practice. However, unlike the available studies [8, 24], the focus of this study was on the contribution of ICT on sustainable tourism development in Tanzania marking an important contribution to sustainable tourism development knowledge.

The study also shows that the influence of efficient resource use through ICT as the third predicting variable on sustainable tourism development is positive and statistically significant where $p < 0.05$. The implication of the findings is that sustainable tourism development in Tanzania is fostered through efficient resource utilization through ICT. This is supported by Anderson [9] stating that the in vestment in ICT in tourism development is essential to foster its sustainability since it reduces several transport concerns for verification and other remedies for the reason that the facilities tend to provide information which is certain and valid by all standards.

According to Bytheway, sustainability will be achieved because of reduction across four areas: carbon emission, space utilization, transport, and material. Moreover, Arts et al. [24] suggest that ICT use and application in tourism is highly essential as it ensures the actual minimization of digital space and other costs in advertising since the flow of information between people and across nations is large and massive which is useful in ensuring sustainable tourism development attainment. However, unlike the available studies, the focus of this study was on the role of ICT toward sustainable tourism development marking an important knowledge contribution to the literature.

6 Conclusion

It is certain that sustainable tourism development in Tanzania is facilitated by ICT use, through enhanced information management, community participation, and efficient resource use. This is attributed by the fact that all the hypothesized variables were revealed to have positive and significant effect on sustainable tourism development. With the exception of community participation, whose influence was revealed to be insignificant, the two variables—information management and efficient resource use—each had significant influences. This reveals that ICT is an important component to boost the tourism industry in a sustainable manner.

7 Recommendations

From the findings, the study recommends that it is important for the tour operators to resort to the use and applications of the effective and efficient ICT facilities in promoting tourism and all its endeavors. This is important to foster adequate and sufficient information management, communities' participation, and the efficient use of resources which in turn foster sustainable tourism development, the deed that promotes sustainability in the sector. The study also recommends that it is important for the government and stakeholders to encourage through supportive policies and regulation on the use and applications of the ICTs facilities among tour companies that will enable to actively engage in the sustainable tourism management practice and constitute significant generation as far as income is concerned.

Acknowledgments The authors thank the tour operators who participated in answering the questionnaire on this study. The authors would also like to thank the reviewers for the useful and helpful comments on our manuscript that helped to improve it.

References

1. Naude, W., & Saayman, A. (2005). The determinants of tourism arrivals in Africa: A panel data regression analysis. *Tourism Economics, 11*(3), 365–391.
2. Sugar, R. (2016). *More tourists visited NYC in 2016 than ever before*. Vox Media.
3. Garlick, S. (2002). Revealing the unseen: Tourism, art and photography. *Cultural Studies, 16*(2), 289–305.
4. Purdie, H. (2013). Glacier retreat and tourism: Insights from New Zealand. *Mountain Research and Development, 33*(4), 463–472.
5. Ritchie, J. R. B., Amaya, M., Carlos, M., & Frechtling, D. C. (2011). Impacts of the world recession and economic crisis on tourism: North America. *Journal of Travel Research, 49*(1), 5–15.
6. Peeters, P., & Dubois, G. (2010). Tourism travel under climate change mitigation constraints. *Journal of Transport Geography, 18*(3), 447–457.
7. Gossling, S., Hall, M., Peeters, P., & Scott, D. (2010). The future of tourism: Can tourism growth and climate policy be reconciled? A mitigation perspective. *Tourism Recreation Research, 35*(2), 119–130.
8. Ali, A., & Frew, A. J. (2014a). Technology innovation and applications in sustainable destination development. *Information Technology & Tourism, 14*(4), 265–290.
9. Anderson, W. (2015). *Human resource needs and skills gaps in the tourism and hospitality sector in Tanzania*. BRN Reviews; University of Dar es Salaam Press Release.
10. Urry, J. (2003). Social networks, travel and talk. *British Journal of Sociology, 54*(2), 155–175.
11. Lew, A. A. (2011). Long tail tourism: New geographies for marketing niche tourism products. *Journal of Travel & Tourism Marketing, 25*(3–4), 409–419.
12. Lu, J., & Lu, Z. (2004). Development, distribution and evaluation of online tourism services in China. *Electronic Commerce Research, 4*(3), 221–239.
13. Ide, A. (2021). Tourism and ICT solutions in the COVID-19 era: A comparison between Japan and Sweden. *The Review of Socionetwork Strategies, 15*(1), 95–211.
14. Masele, J. J., Mrisha, H., Warren, T., & E. (2023). E-commerce service quality influence on domestic tourists' satisfaction in Tanzania: A pursuit to sustaining tourism growth amid COVID-19 pandemic. *International Journal of Digital Culture and Electronic Tourism, 4*(2), 171–188.

15. Scheel, C., & Vazquez, M. (2011). The role of innovation and technology in industrial ecology systems for the sustainable development of emerging regions. *Journal of Sustainable Development, 4*(6), 197–210.
16. United Republic of Tanzania. (2015). *Protected area highlights for Tanzania*. Government Handbook.
17. Córdoba-Pachón, J. R., & Marx Gómez, J. (2013). IT goes green: Systemic approaches to IT policy making, design, evaluation and management. *International Journal of Information Technologies and Systems Approach (IJITSA), 6*(1), i–iii. IGI Global Publisher.
18. Okello, M. M., & Novelli, M. (2014). Tourism in the East African Community (EAC): Challenges, opportunities, and ways forward. *Tourism and Hospitality Research, 14*, 1–2. https://doi.org/10.1177/1467358414529580
19. Franklin, U. (1999). *The real world of technology (revised ed.)*. House of Anansi.
20. Goodhue, D. L., & Thompson, R. L. (1995). Task-technology fit and individual performance. *MIS Quarterly, 19*(2), 213–236.
21. Arthur, W. B. (2009). *The nature of technology*. Free Press.
22. Rahimi, B., Nadri, H., Lotf, N. A. H., & Timpka, T. (2018). A systematic review of the technology acceptance model in health informatics. *Applied Clinical Informatics, 9*(3), 604–634.
23. Apollo, S. (2018). Revealing the unseen: Tourism, art and photography. *Cultural Studies, 16*(2), 289–305.
24. Arts, H., Costa, P., & McCollough, F. (2015). Managing tourism carrying capacity of art cities. *The Tourist Review, 46*(4), 8–11.
25. Schwalbe, K. (2013). *Information technology Project Management*. Course Technology.
26. Phylipsen, G. J. M. (2010). *Energy efficiency indicators: Best practice and potential use in developing country policymaking*. Phylipsen Climate Change Consulting.
27. Bichmann, W., Rifkin, S. B., & Shrestha, M. (1989). Towards the measurement of community participation. *World Health Forum, 10*(3–4), 467–472.
28. Bracht, N. (1990). *Health promotion at the community level* (p. 320). Sage.
29. Meyboom, J. (1993). Canada's approach to sustainable tourism, Proceedings - 23rd Travel and Tourism Research Association Canada Conference, Whistler, BC, June 13–16, 192–195.
30. WTO. (2001). *A survey of sustainable development: Social and economic dimensions* (Volume 6 in the series frontier issues in economic thought). Island Press.
31. WTO. (2004). *Indicators of sustainable development for tourism destinations: A guidebook*. World Trade Organization.
32. Blackstock, K. L., McCrum, G., Scott, A., & White, V. V. (2006). *A framework for developing indicators of sustainable tourism*. Macaulay Institute.
33. Ali, A., & Frew, A. J. (2014b). ICT for sustainable tourism: A challenging relationship? *Information Technology and Tourism, 14*(4), 261–264.
34. Werthner, H., & Klein, S. (1999). *Information technology and tourism: A challenging relation*. Springer Verlag. https://doi.org/10.1007/978-3-7091-6363-4
35. Buhalis, D., & O'Connor, P. (2006). Information communication technology revolution- izing tourism. *Tourism Recreation Research, 30*(3), 7–16.
36. Joshi, A., Meza, J., Costa, S., Perin, D. M. P., Trout, K., & Atul, R. (2013). The role of information and communication technology in community outreach, academic and research collaboration, and education and support services (IT-CARES). *Perspectives in Health Information Management, 10*(Fall), 1g. eCollection 2013.
37. Subashini, R., Rita, S., & Vivek, M. (2011). The role of ICTs in knowledge management (KM) for organizational effectiveness. International Conference on Computing and Communication Systems. In ObCom 2011, Global Trends in Information Systems and Software Applications, 542–549.
38. Ali, A., & Frew, J. A. (2010). ICT and its role in sustainable tourism development. In U. Gretzel, R. Law, & M. Fuchs (Eds.), *Information and communication technologies in tourism 2010. Lugano, February 10–12 2010* (pp. 479–491). Springer.

39. Baccarella, C. V., Wagner, T. F., Kietzmann, J. H., & McCarthy, I. P. (2018). Social media? It's serious! Understanding the dark side of social media. *European Management Journal, 36*(4), 431–438.
40. Laudon, K., & Traver, C. (2006). *E-commerce: Business, technology, society* (3rd ed.). Prentice Hall.
41. Atos Origin. (2010). Making the case for green IT: Driving sustainability and having a positive business impact at the same time. In Green IT Fact sheet.
42. Masele, J. J. (2011). Towards sustainable tourism: Utilizing e-commerce applications for minimizing impacts of climate change. *Information Technologies in Environmental Engineering Environmental Science and Engineering, 3*(4), 445–459. SpringerLink.
43. Padayachee, K. (2008). *Utilizing E-commerce and M-commerce applications to address the effect of global warming*. E-leader.
44. Elly, T. (2010). The Nexus between information systems use and firms' competitive advantage: A study of small and medium tourism enterprises in Tanzania. PhD (Business Administration) Thesis. University of Dar es Salaam. September, 2010.
45. Babin, B. J., & Anderson, R. E. (2014). *Multivariate data analysis*. In Joseph F. Hair Jr., & William C. Black (eds.), (7th ed.).

Design and Implementation of a Closed-Loop Traffic Control System with Speed Control Influence on Proximity Vehicles and Overriding Capabilities

Daniel Mkongo and Zeeshan Ahmed Khan

1 Introduction

An open-loop control system is a system that operates without feedback, meaning it does not take any external parameters or phenomenon into account during its operation. The existing traffic control system is an open-loop control system as it does not take traffic density into consideration; instead, it operates by continuously allowing and stopping vehicles by turning colored lights on and off at preset time intervals and sequences, which are set during traffic light installations.

The open-loop light-based traffic control system is the most common traffic control mechanism which has been adapted worldwide as the standard for traffic management since it was first introduced in 1868. It is clear now that after more than 150 years since traffic lights were introduced, there have been major technological advancements and improvements in industrial automation which have made land vehicles more accessible and by far the most widely used mode of transportation today. An unprecedented increase in land transportation vehicles has made it difficult for the open-loop light-based traffic control system to cope up with ever-increasing traffic densities due to its inability to intelligently identify and control traffic congestion. This calls for a major traffic management system overhaul.

In order to combat the setbacks faced by the open-loop light-based traffic control system, it is of high importance to construct an intelligent system that is aware of its surroundings. For a system to be intelligent, it needs to make smart decisions based on faced situations just like how an intelligent human being would, and for a system

D. Mkongo
Arusha Technical College (ATC), Arusha, Tanzania

Z. A. Khan (✉)
Nelson Mandela African Institute of Science and Technology (NM-AIST), Arusha, Tanzania
e-mail: zeeshan.khan@nm-aist.ac.tz

J. Marx Gómez et al. (eds.), *Smart and Secure Embedded and Mobile Systems*,
Progress in IS, https://doi.org/10.1007/978-3-031-56603-5_32

to recognize and understand situations, it needs sufficient feedback/data about the faced situation.

A closed-loop control system is a system that regulates itself to maintain or archive a desired state. The regulation is done by taking into account feedback from the controlled phenomena and adjusting controlled parameters until the feedback is at an acceptable state.

The proposed system is a closed-loop system as it generates sequences and time intervals based on pedestrian presence, traffic density on respective lanes, and overriding signals given by an operator from a computer software. The proposed system is also capable of influencing vehicle speeds by allowing an operator to set speed limits through a computer software, which are then broadcasted via a radio transmitter to all vehicles in the proximity of the radio signal, and cause the vehicles to mechanically limit their speed, therefore archiving emphasis of speed limits and safety.

2 Literature Review

The development of intelligent traffic control systems is a hot research topic with numerous researchers proposing various methods and techniques that could solve this century-long predicament. A lot of research has been put into the development of intelligent traffic control systems with various methods being put into action from using mathematical models to estimate optimal delay times for red, green, and yellow lights at different times of the day to using proximity sensors to detect incoming vehicles, the use of computer vision techniques to count the number of vehicles on respective sides of the roads and traffic violations, and the use of deep neural networks.

2.1 Marcin Lewandowski, Et al., Road Traffic Monitoring System Based on Mobile Devices and Bluetooth Low-Energy Beacons

The authors propose a system for monitoring road traffic which is based on mobile devices and Bluetooth beacons with low-energy consumption (Marcin et al., [1]). The vehicle detection offered by their proposed system uses mobile devices installed on the sides of the road to measure the strength of the RSSI signal when receiving radio frequency frames that are emitted by Bluetooth beacons on the other side of the road. Bluetooth beacons are installed along the road at different heights in order to identify and classify the type of vehicles traveling on the road (cars or trucks).

2.2 *Ninad Lanke Et al., Smart Traffic Management*

Ninad and Koul [2] proposed a system that uses radio frequency identification devices (RFID) to gather information about and count vehicles passing by an RFID receiver. In this system, there will be an RFID tag that would store all the information regarding the vehicle such as the vehicle number, etc.; these tags will be placed in a vehicle to automatically identify and count each vehicle uniquely as it passes through an RFID reader, and therefore helping in detection of traffic congestion.

2.3 *Shubhangi Sanjay Bhargave Et al., Automatic Vehicle Speed Control System*

Shubhangi et al. [3] proposed a system to automatically reduce vehicle speed to the allowed speed in low-speed zones. This system uses a microcontroller which will be interfaced with an IR receiver that communicates with an IR transmitter to detect if the vehicle is in a low-speed zone, and if it is, a control signal will be generated and sent to the vehicle's control system which will then activate the speed control mechanism in the vehicle causing the speed of the vehicle to be reduced to the required speed for that zone.

2.4 *Amulya A M Et al., Intelligent Vehicle Speed Controller*

Amulya and Karuna [4] focused on reducing land vehicle accidents due to over-speeding in speed-restricted zones, by limiting vehicle speed, automatically. The chapter proposes the use of radio frequency (RF) transmitter and receiver modules to let the vehicle know when it is in a speed-restricted zone and then taking action to automatically control the vehicle's speed. When the vehicle enters a speed-restricted area it will receive an RF signal which is transmitted from a programmed RF transmitter; upon reception of the signal a microcontroller will decode the signal and alert the driver through an LCD display, urging the driver to reduce the speed of the vehicle manually; however, if the driver does not slow down the vehicle, then the microcontroller will take the initiative in automatically controlling and reducing the speed of the vehicle as per the received signal.

2.5 Nang Hom Kham and Chaw Myat New, Implementation of Modern Traffic Light Control System

Nang Hom Kham and Chaw Myat New ([5]) proposed a system that provides traffic control of a six-way and four-way junction of modern traffic lights that has been implemented with arrowed signals for each direction. The arrowed signals of red, yellow, and green light are displayed with LEDs. There are two modes of traffic light sequence in this system: one is the normal sequence and the other is the emergency sequence. The emergency mode is used when important vehicles such as ambulances, fire brigade, police cars, and VIP are present; the emergency mode is set by pushing switches. In the normal mode, the delay for junctions that have high traffic is set to be longer than the delay for the junctions that have low traffic.

2.6 K. Vidhya and A. B. Banu, Density-Based Traffic Signal System

K. Vidhya and A. B. Banu [6] proposed a system which uses a single board computer (Raspberry pi in this case) as a controller, to generate traffic light sequences and delays based on traffic density. The sequence and delays change automatically depending on traffic density on different sides of the road at a junction. The system employs cameras and computer vision techniques such as converting an RGB image to grayscale and threshold and contour detection in order to detect the number of vehicles present on respective sides of the road. Once the determination of the number of vehicles on all sides of the road is done, the side with the highest traffic density is determined.

2.7 Literature Review Conclusion

The above study gives some insight about various possible solutions to some traffic problems, but we have yet to find a system that collectively solves all these traffic issues in a unified and smart manner like the proposed system.

3 Statement of Problem

Traffic congestion and accidents are major problems in land transportation systems, and because of the ever-growing number of land transport vehicles, these problems will continue to increase and get worse if proper actions are not taken.

Poor traffic management leads to unnecessary time consumption, fuel wastage, increased air pollution, time wastage, and accidents and drives up stress. This is because the existing system is not intelligent. It has been observed that the existing traffic control system often allows lanes with no vehicles while stopping lanes with heavy traffic.

Drivers tend to ignore important traffic signs such as speed limits, which is a major cause of accidents; in 2020 alone overspeeding caused 29% of all road accidents, killing more than 11,000 people, an average of over 30 people in 1 day.

In countries such as Tanzania it has been observed that sometimes traffic becomes so congested that a traffic personnel has to be physically present in order to override the normal traffic control system as it becomes useless in such situations; also during events like presidential escorts and evacuation emergencies, a number of traffic personnel have to be physically present in the proximity of the traffic lights, in order to override the traffic control systems.

The existing system does not take pedestrian presence into consideration; hence, valuable time is often lost when pedestrians are allowed to cross when there are no pedestrians or when pedestrians are trying to cross but the traffic control system is unaware of their presence.

The main objective is to design and fabricate a prototype to showcase a system that will combat all the problems discussed above.

4 Research and Development

Under normal conditions, with no traffic congestion detected, the proposed system operates as a normal open-loop traffic control system but changes its behavior when a signal is sent from any of the sources (sensors, buttons, software) to the controller.

Proximity sensors are placed at a relatively large distance away from the traffic lights so that if a vehicle is sensed by the sensors continuously for some time (say 10 s) the controller will detect that the vehicle has stopped due to traffic jam and that the lane from which the vehicle is sensed should be prioritized; therefore, the controller will prioritize that side by giving it more time (green light) compared to other lanes/sides and also by stopping other lanes often, until the traffic jam is depreciated.

The system also takes pedestrians into consideration by employing a button, which when pressed will prioritize pedestrian crossing by allowing pedestrians to cross earlier than they would have, if their presence was not sensed.

In order to prevent overspeeding an operator can use computer software to set and broadcast the speed limit via a radio transmitter to all vehicles in the radio transmitter's range. Upon reception of the speed limit signal, the vehicles in the proximity will be limited to the set speed limit automatically while they are in the broadcast range. The speed control mechanism in electric vehicles can be done by adjusting the voltage and frequency that the motor is running at. In petrol vehicles, speed can be limited by controlling the opening of the throttle valve (larger opening = more fuel and air mixture = more power = more speed); therefore, through collection of data and calibration we can find the correspondence between vehicle speed and throttle opening which will make it possible to limit petrol vehicles to any set speed. As for this chapter, a demo version of an electric vehicle equipped with a radio receiver is used to demonstrate how speed can be influenced remotely.

The computer software communicates with the microcontroller via serial communication. The software receives light states and traffic video feed from the microcontroller and remote camera, respectively, and displays it to the operator; this enables the operator to get visual feedback and helps authorized personnel to set various system parameters including maximum vehicle speed near the traffic lights and zebra crossing and delay intervals for each side (setting priorities) and also gives them the ability to override the traffic lights from the software, thereby eradicating the need for them to be physically present on the road. Figure 1 shows the connectivity and flow of information of the system's constituents explained above.

The prototype is developed and tested to perform traffic optimization at a junction, but the idea and functionality can be replicated and installed wherever there is conventional traffic light system already.

The prototype has been tested using toy cars which were strategically placed on the demo road to simulate real traffic conditions; through visual observation and logical analysis the system has been observed to intelligently react to different traffic conditions, which clearly shows that the system can drastically improve traffic experience when compared to the conventional traffic light system.

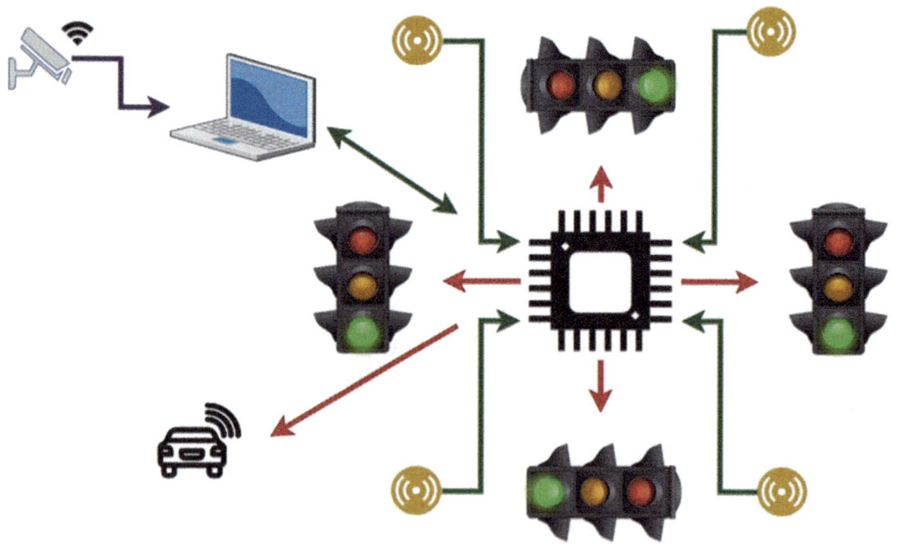

Fig. 1 Flow of information in the proposed system

The prototype's development is divided into two parts.

1. Traffic control system.
2. Vehicle Demo

4.1 *Traffic Control System*

This section discusses the architecture and design of a closed-loop traffic control system. At the heart of the system is a microcontroller which acts as the brain of the system; the microcontroller is programmed to drive traffic lights normally as an open-loop traffic control system whenever traffic conditions are balanced (traffic congestion on all sides, or no traffic congestion on any side); however when an imbalance is sensed by the sensors, the microcontroller will try to eradicate the imbalance by assigning more time to lanes with heavy traffic while also allowing less congested lanes often in between longer delays, in order to archive a seamless transport experience even in heavy traffic situations. The system also employs buttons which are used to signify pedestrian presence in order to prioritize pedestrian crossing; not only that but the traffic control system also has a computer software which enables an authorized operator to view and change traffic light states, view video feed, and set speed limits which will be sent to the vehicles via radio waves. The architecture and individual component functions are shown below (Figs. 2, 3, 4).

Microcontroller. A microcontroller is a compact integrated circuit designed to govern a specific operation in an embedded system. A typical microcontroller includes a processor, memory, and input/output (I/O) peripherals on a single chip.

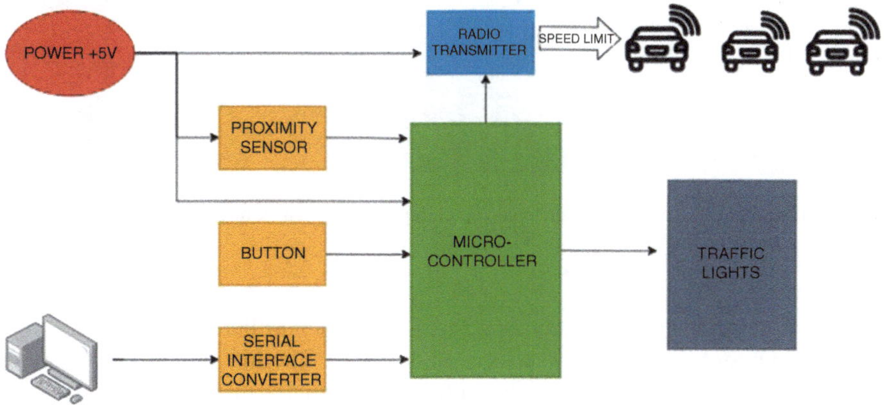

Fig. 2 Closed-loop traffic control system block diagram, which shows connectivity of constituent components and information flow in the proposed system

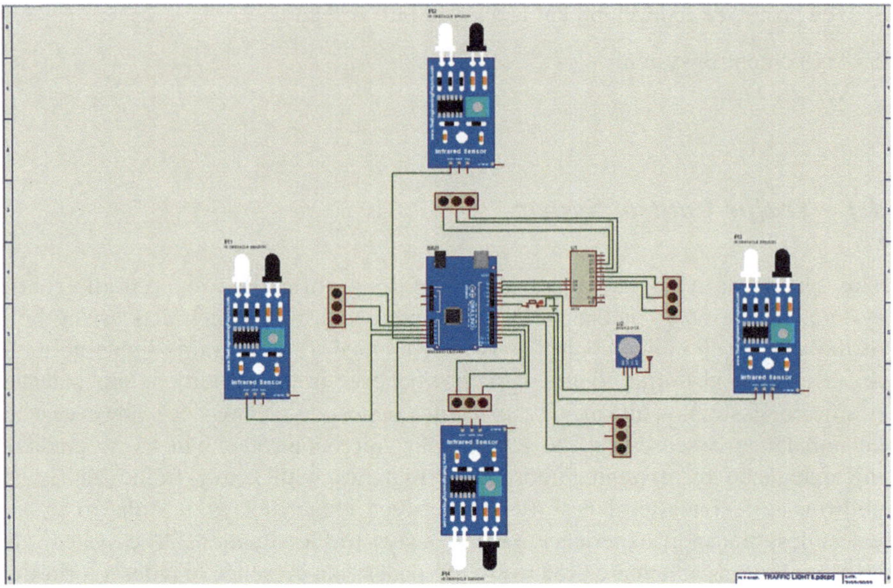

Fig. 3 Closed-loop traffic control system circuit

Fig. 4 Complete closed-loop traffic control system with speed control influence on proximity vehicles and overriding capabilities

In this system, we use the atmega328p avr microcontroller which is incorporated in an Arduino development board shown in Fig. 5. The function of the microcontroller in this system is to execute logic to sequentially turn LEDs on and off at set intervals as well as receive signals from signal sources, and act accordingly in order to prioritize lanes with heavier traffic. Signal sources are sensors, buttons, and overriding signals from the software via serial communication. To make this

Fig. 5 Arduino Uno

Fig. 6 IR sensor. **Note:** Other proximity sensors such as RADAR or ultrasonic sensors may be used to achieve a more robust sensing mechanism

possible, the microcontroller is connected to LEDs, and signal sources as shown in Fig. 3, and the flow of information between the microcontroller and the signal sources can be shown in Fig. 2. Figure 4 shows the layout of the prototype.

Proximity sensors. A proximity sensor is a sensor able to detect the presence of nearby objects without any physical contact. A proximity sensor often emits an electromagnetic field or a beam of electromagnetic radiation and looks for changes in the field or return signal.

The system uses proximity sensors to detect vehicle presence in a non-contact manner. The type of proximity sensor chosen for this particular task is the inferred sensor (IR), which is calibrated to operate at desired light conditions. The inferred (IR) sensor gives a high digital signal to the microcontroller whenever it senses an obstacle. The microcontroller will analyze if the sensor has sensed a stopped vehicle, by considering how long the sensor sends a high digital signal. Figure 6 shows an image of an IR obstacle sensor.

Fig. 7 Red, yellow, and green LEDs

Light emitting diodes (LED). Light emitting diodes are semiconductor diodes which glow when a voltage is applied.

LEDs can glow in many different colors and brightness; for this particular project, we use green, red, and yellow LEDs to indicate GO, STOP, and WAIT conditions, respectively. These LEDs are driven by the microcontroller to turn on and off at set intervals. Figure 7 shows a traffic light module made by using red, yellow, and green LEDs.

Shift register. A shift register is a type of digital circuit using a cascade of flip-flops where the output of one flip-flop is connected to the input of the next. They share a single clock signal, which causes the data stored in the system to shift from one location to the next.

Due to the limitations of GPIOs on the atmega328p, we use a shift register to drive some LEDs. Figure 8 shows an image of the SN74HC59N shift register.

Buttons. A button is a physical device that can be used to provide digital input to a system.

In the prototype, we use a button which can be pressed by a pedestrian to indicate that they want to cross the road. The event of pressing the button will send a signal to a microcontroller, and the microcontroller will gently set a traffic light configuration that will allow pedestrians to cross the road earlier. Figure 9 shows push buttons and how they are placed in the prototype.

Resistors. Resistors are devices which provide resistance to the flow of electric current. Resistors can be used as current limiting devices.

We use resistors to limit the current flowing to the LEDs, in order to protect them from damage and obtain the right level of brightness.

Radio transmitter. A radio transmitter is a device which can transmit data over radio waves.

Fig. 8 Shift register

Fig. 9 Push buttons

We use radio transmitters to broadcast speed control signals to all vehicles in the proximity of the radio transmitter's range. Once the vehicle receives these speed control signals, then the vehicle's speed control system will make sure that the driver cannot exceed the set speed limit. Figure 10 shows a 433 MHZ radio transmitter module with 10 m of range.

Computer software. From the software, an operator can see traffic light states as they appear on the road, remotely view a live video stream of the road from a remote camera, override traffic light states by selecting which lights should turn on/off and for what duration, and also set and broadcast maximum vehicle speed for zones which are in the transmission range of the radio transmitter.

The functionality and capabilities of the software effectively eradicate the need for physical presence of traffic personal on traffic light premises.

Fig. 10 433MHZ radio transmitter module

Fig. 11 Computer software which removes the need for traffic personnel to be physically present in order to override traffic lights

To archive such level of control and functionality, the software communicates with the microcontroller via serial communication, which allows the operator to send commands to and receive logs and traffic states from the microcontroller (Fig. 11).

Figure 12 shows a traffic officer using his hands and a hand-held traffic light to override the traffic light system. Figure 11 shows the computer software which can

Fig. 12 Traffic personnel physically present in order to override traffic

be used to remove the need for traffic personnel to be physically present on the road in order to perform traffic light overriding.

4.2 Vehicle Demo

This section discusses the architecture and design of a demo vehicle prototype that demonstrates how vehicle speeds can be controlled remotely. At the heart of the system there is a microcontroller which is used to control an actuator based on user's input (joystick) as well as a remotely received signal from a radio receiver. This is analogous to how a vehicle can receive a radio signal carrying speed limit information and be able to mechanically limit the vehicle's speed to the speed limit received. This demo vehicle model is closer in functionality to electric vehicles; however, possible methods to achieve similar speed control functionality in petrol vehicles will be briefly discussed. The architecture and individual component functions are shown below. Figures 13, 14, and 15 show the block diagram, the schematic, and a picture of the vehicle demo circuit, respectively.

Microcontroller. In the vehicle's circuit, we use an Arduino Uno which contains an atmega328p microcontroller at its heart. The function of the microcontroller in this system is to be able to analyze received speed control signals and limit the

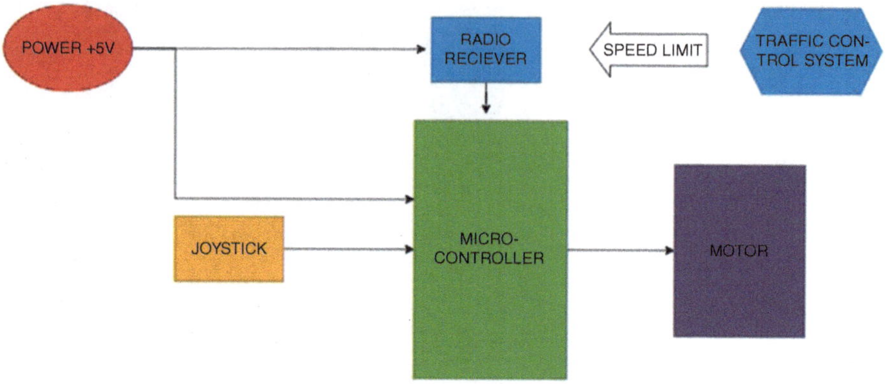

Fig. 13 Vehicle demo block diagram

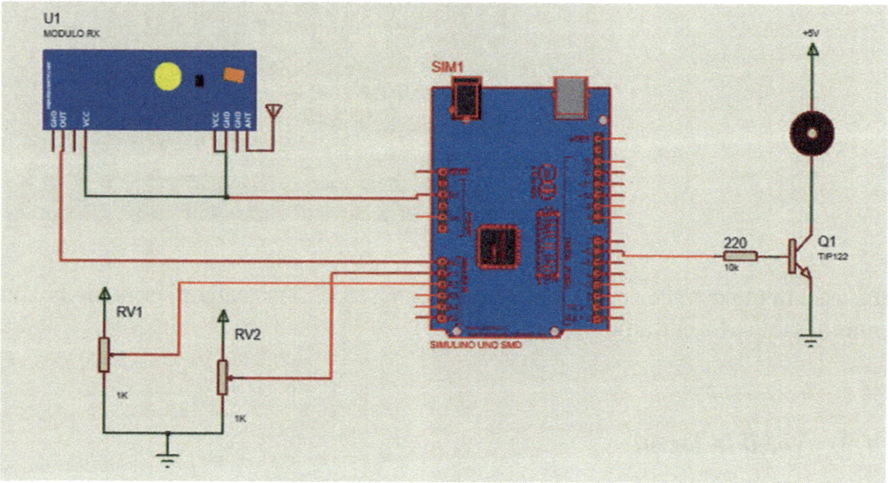

Fig. 14 Vehicle demo circuit schematics

speed of a motor to the broadcasted speed limit. Figure 16 shows an Arduino Uno microcontroller.

Radio receiver. A radio receiver is a device which receives radio waves and convert them into useful information.

We use the 433 MHZ radio receiver to receive speed control signals from the traffic control system. Figure 17 shows a picture of a radio receiver.

Joystick. We use a joystick to emulate a driver's pedal. The joystick sends signals to the microcontroller with the intention of controlling the speed of a motor; just like the driver's pedal, the further the joystick is pushed the greater the speed. The microcontroller is used to filter the joystickssignal to make sure that the broadcasted

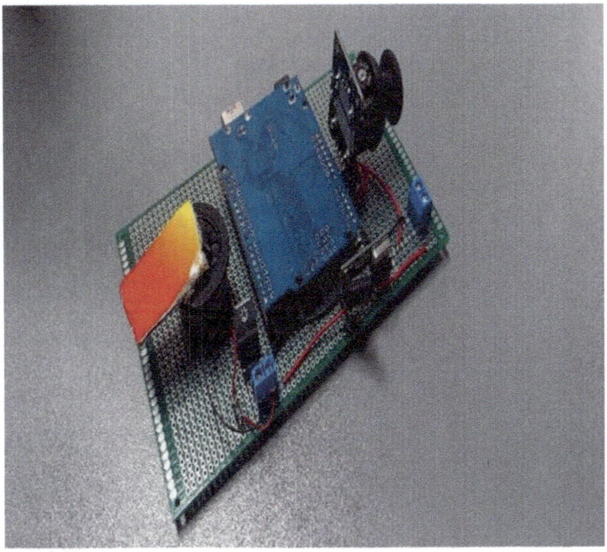

Fig. 15 Vehicle demo circuit

Fig. 16 Arduino Uno

speed limit is not exceeded by the motor even when the joystick (pedal) is pushed to the maximum. Figure 18 displays a picture of a joystick.

Motor. Here a motor is used to demonstrate how vehicle speed can be influenced remotely. The motor's speed is controlled by a joystick but will not be allowed to exceed the set speed limit. Figure 19 shows a picture of a DC motor.

Transistor. A Tip122 transistor is used as a motor driver. By controlling the base voltage of the transistor, we control the motor's speed.

Fig. 17 433MHZ radio receiver

Fig. 18 Joystick

Fig. 19 DC motor

5 Conclusion and Results

The traffic control system demonstrated in this chapter attempts to solve multiple problems regarding traffic congestion and accidents in land transport. Judging by the prototype's operation and response to different faced traffic situations, it is clear that most traffic problems can be solved by a system like this. The prototype's operation is evidence that intelligent traffic management can go a long way in solving long-lived issues in land transportation. Figure 20 shows the complete working prototype.

The fact that the system's nature of operation is not too dissimilar to the operation of existing systems for the most part (both are light based systems), and its ability to also operate as a normal open-loop traffic control system under certain conditions, shows that this system can be easily adapted and installed as improvements to already existing infrastructure in order to lower cost of installation. Installing this system as an improvement to existing light-based systems also help to maintain the existing ISO standards for traffic light luminance, size, and construction as described in ISO16508:1999.

To archive an industrial grade product, we have to use industrial grade components and tools while also considering use cases and factors affecting those tools; hence when transitioning from a prototype to an industrial product, careful selection of robust sensors suitable for outdoor use should be conducted. IR sensors should be replaced with more robust and capable sensors which are not easily affected by the environment; an example of capable sensors would be FCMW radar sensors. Also, the use of a controller with enough input/output interfaces will go a long way in reducing costs and ensuring stability. LEDs should be replaced with lights that

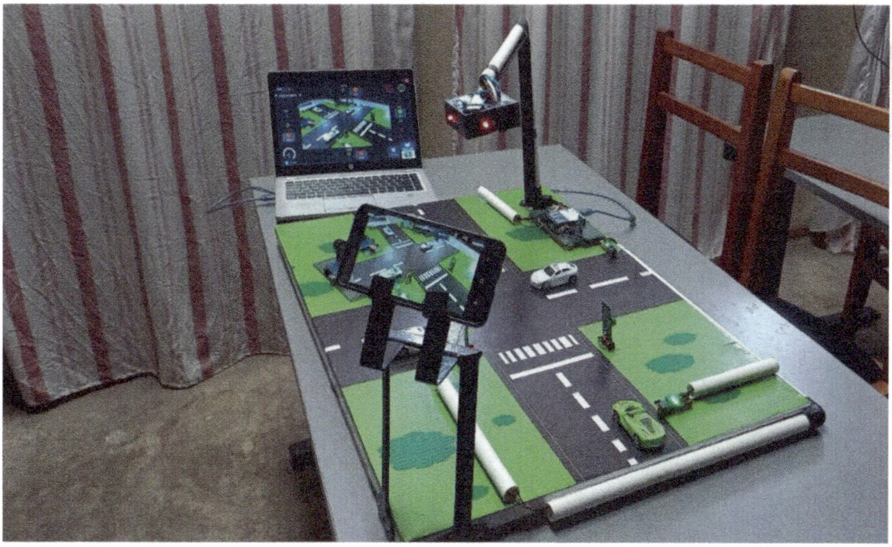

Fig. 20 Complete working prototype

meet ISO standards, and logic level shifting circuits or drivers should be employed in order to drive the suitable lights properly.

6 Future Work

Further attempts to improve this system will be done by employing technologies such as computer vision and machine learning to detect traffic, learn traffic patterns, and recognize traffic violations, as well as count the number of vehicles present in every lane. Techniques such as object detection, anomaly detection, and video analytics can be used in addition to the prototype's functionality to achieve an even more efficient solution. Furthermore, software overriding can be done by the use of IoT infrastructures instead of long serial cables.

References

1. Marcin, L., Bartłomiej, P., Marcin, B., & Piotr, S. (2018). Road traffic monitoring system based on Mobile devices and bluetooth low energy beacons. In G. Carlo (Ed.), *Wireless communications and mobile computing*.
2. Ninad, L., & Koul, S. (2013). Smart traffic management system. *International Journal of Computer Applications (0975-8887), 75*(7), 19–22.
3. Shubhangi, B., Monika, J., & Aditi, P. (2018). Automatic vehicle speed control system. *International Journal of Innovative Science and Research Technology, 3*(1).
4. Amulya, A. M., & Karuna, C. V. (2018). Intelligent vehicle speed controller. *International Research Journal of Engineering and Technology (IRJET), 05*(04), 2537–2540.
5. Nang, H. K., & Chaw, M. N. (2014). Implementation of modern traffic light control system. *International Journal of Scientific and Research Publications, 4*(6), 1–6.
6. Vidhya, K., & Banu, A. B. (2014). Density based traffic signal system. *International Journal of Innovative Research in Science Engineering and Technology, 3*(3), 2218–2222.

Development of a User-Friendly Digital Library Resource Discovery Tool to Mitigate Learners' Technical Hitches

Agrey Kato, Elizabeth Ludovick Temba, Eric W. Steinhauer, Michael Kisangiri, and Shubi Kaijage

1 Introduction

1.1 Background

The advancement of open-source software has led to the need for library resource discovery tools (RDTs) to be developed. As a consequence, libraries move from library automation to resource exploration by discovering various commercial and free information resource software applications [1]. The discovery toolset is based on the central index of the material, object, metadata, full text, or other items on which the search result is based in the library database [2]. The invention layer offers an interface that allows users, supporting keywords entered for this purpose, to seem for and retrieve the results and pick the required content. Therefore, the results generated concentrate on relevance, faceted navigation, and other web-based compatible features [3]. EBSCO Discovery Service, Summon, World Cat Discovery, and Primo Central are a series of index-based commercial discovery tools, while Blacklight, VuFind, eXtensible catalog, and Franklin are incorporated in the open-source discovery interface [4]. These open-source search tools are capable of harvesting content from multiple sources and openly providing access to the content. In essence, for librarians who want to own a Google-like search box, open-source discovery tools have become a de facto option. The goal of this chapter is to develop a user-friendly platform by exploring digital library instruments to

A. Kato (✉) · M. Kisangiri · S. Kaijage
The Nelson Mandela African Institution of Science and Technology, Arusha, Tanzania

E. L. Temba
Tengeru Institute of Community Development (TICD), Arusha, Tanzania

E. W. Steinhauer
Fern Library University in Hagen, Hagen, Germany

J. Marx Gómez et al. (eds.), *Smart and Secure Embedded and Mobile Systems*, Progress in IS, https://doi.org/10.1007/978-3-031-56603-5_33

alleviate the technical hitches of online learners. The researchers suggested that the adaptability approach should be taken into account, based on the guideline approach but concentrating on resource harmonization with the user's requirements and preferences [5]. Therefore, to investigate how the adaptability strategy could improve the usability and accessibility of RDTs, this chapter reviewed in its literature various articles representing the usability issues discovered in various RDTs developed concerning their operations, visual interfaces, and level of navigation from the user viewpoint.

1.2 Adaptations

RDTs Operation concerns: Ex Libris®Primo RDT as evaluated by researchers [5], for users with diverse objectives; the tool has proven to be successful and helps users complete numerous tasks with a limited number of steps. Primo discovery tool allows search findings to be filtered without reentering keywords in different ways. They also noted that Primo allows comparisons to search results through the information tabs found in the title, and provides where appropriate a seamless transfer to external websites but does not take into account users'interests, preferences, and disabilities. An EBSCO Discovery Service (EDS) usability test has defined user friendliness and therefore, the capacity to limit the search results [6]. RDTS operations are rich in functionality that includes methods of alternative search and filtering. For a few users, this may be a source of trouble; the EDS study showed that the different interface features are "overwhelming" or "confusing." Additional EDS issues include an excessive number of clicks to access electronic resources, irrelevant search results, hard-to-understand jargon (for instance, "reviews" for peer-reviewed journals), and restrictions on recognition of language by librarians. Thus, further study endorsed that, aside from the search box, users pay little attention to end-user functionality. Users also are going to be mixed up about the filter/facet functionality in selecting the correct one to minimize the search for the type of resource they need (e.g., when finding out "research documents," under e-books, or audiobook) [1]. The study that has shown the complexity of using Summon library search tool indicated that complex interfaces are the foremost problem [7]. The document suggested that the selection and layout of end-user functions could affect the usability behind tool interfaces. Other researchers [8] found that, having tabs for search alternatives leads to the better discovery of resources rather than drop-down lists therefore, the results examined, recommend that during the development of RTD, the needs, and interests should be taken into account.

RDTs Visual Interface: Studies show that the progressive approach to the disclosure of simple search interfaces can be a solution for RDTs requirements, where the interface illustrates some key start-up functions and then provides more advanced features as requested by the user [9, 10]. Thus, to identify fewer and more meaningful interface features, it will need to consider the following variables. First, it is important to consider the user's information requirements, behavioral descriptions, roles, task models, priorities, and their understanding of search systems [11]. Second, libraries need RDTs to point out instruments to the right people and to help promote the use of library collections to justify their preservation [12]. Thus, the design of RDTs requires that libraries match the preferences, needs, requests, and customs of users. In addition, it is necessary to bear in mind that libraries quickly deploy resources that do not allow for customization. Therefore, as the interface is suited to high contrast, blurring or disappearing text and icons would certainly be a concern for users with low vision disorders [13]. According to the search results presentation, RDTs usually display outcomes amid metaphors and visual indicators, these are considered important for the comparison of search results by usability, which raises the inconsistency of metadata as a problem. The value of technical metadata, also called accessibility metadata that could provide useful information to disabled users (e.g., whether a resource was accessible via a text-to-speech application or behind a paywall) should be underlined [1]. Therefore, the accessibility issues addressed in the above-mentioned literature may generally be narrowly defined as a common interface design phenomenon that causes problems with usability. As a major usability characteristic of library RDTs, an interface with smooth navigation is more likely to be employed to mitigate the above problems [14, 15].

RDTs Level of Navigation: The subsequent section of this literature compares the above-mentioned usability problems with navigation concerns addressed in handling user sources of impediments in a library RDT interaction, either personal or through design features. Most studies were linked to library websites about the accessibility of digital library resources [9, 16]. Several of the articles used automated testing software to review Web Content Accessibility Guidelines (WCAG) for compliance with library websites [17, 18]. Although there are few research projects relating to RDTs in the library areas, as well as studies that take into account the needs of people with disabilities when working with library search tools. Research indicated that people with dyslexia may make spelling errors during typing, therefore, guided search tools should be considered to allow the tolerance of errors and autocomplete wording to mitigate the impact of dyslexia. This is often referred to as an accessibility problem that can impact people who may need various assistive devices with dyslexia and visual impairments. In turn, the appropriateness of background and foreground colors, font style, scale, intensity, and link design were among the accessibility issues reported in the aforementioned article. However, using the fragile or incorrect marking of links relevant to site navigation by creating a list of links for access, this could prevent users with an inability to use an RDT library, thus for screen-reader technology, such as Job Access With Speech (JAWS), this might pose a difficult to users [3]. Even among users with similar conditions, the case mentioned so far can demonstrate the variation in needs and preferences in the use of RDTs; therefore, adaptation approach seems to be a feasible option for improving accessibility and usefulness.

2 Methods

2.1 *RTD Development Approach, Technological Methods, Standards, and Protocols*

With different open-source software, a digital library Resource Discovery Tool (RDT) was developed, this case focused on the library resource discovery procedure, which evaluates the methods in several configurations. This development is essentially a method of finding resource exploration that can be incorporated with any online information retrieval (IR) framework. The work incorporated Blacklight software, an integrated library system (ILS), and a DSpace repository system framework as well as other independent commercial and open-access external databases. Data (in Marc format) for the sample test was exported to the bibliographical database (IndCat into Koha Version 19.11.00) and then to Blacklight. Similarly, resources were extracted from selected institutional repository systems (IR) developed by DSpace software (version 6.3), which were then imported into Blacklight. At different layers and stages of implementation, a number of open-source software protocols and open standard technologies were used within the assembly; see Fig. 1 illustrates the scheme of obtaining bibliographic data from various external sources of discovery.

It includes three layers: the greenstone LAMP architecture (Linux-Apache-MySQL-Ruby on Rails) is provided by Layer-I (core layer), MySQL is included like an electronic database (release 5.7), an Apache web server (version 2.4), a Ruby on Rails programming/scripting language (Ruby version 2.5.8 and Rails version

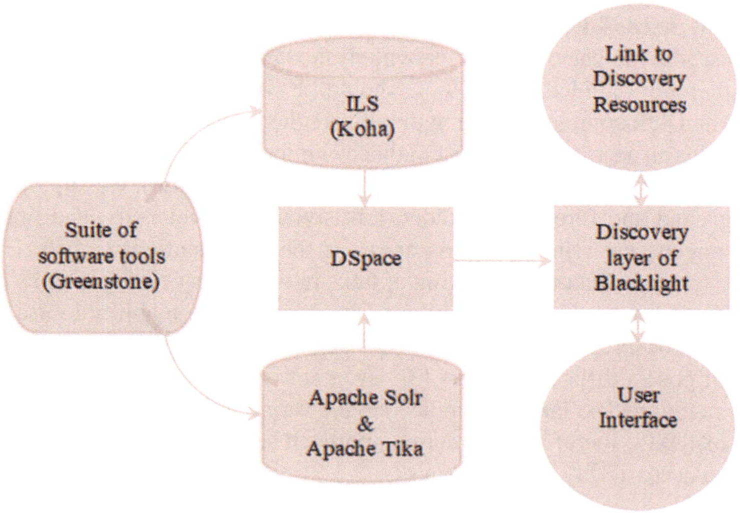

Fig. 1 Functions of the discovery system model

6.0.0) and utilizes Linux Ubuntu-18.04 LTS as an operating system. Layer-II (full-text layer) uses Apache Tika as a full-text extractor (version 1.18) and Apache Solr (version 6.1.0) to index the harvested metadata from various subscribed or external sources. Layer-III (front layer) is just an interface adapted to give users value-added services with Blacklight. As demonstrated in this paper, the discovery system model focuses on the collection of Koha formatted records from machine-readable cataloging (MARC 21) by setting up the ILS's open archives initiative (OAI) compliant function. The seamless integration of a discovery system with the online IR Z39.50 as well as its interoperability is important for its success and protocols when required to be established. Koha OAI-PMH (i.e., PMH stands for the Metadata Harvesting Protocol) is the prime logical method of integrating Blacklight with any ILS whereby the files Koha.ini and config.ini must be configured to sync the Koha driver with Blacklight. The following logical step should be engaged in making changes to Koha, a MARC_local.properties file imported to MARC documents from Koha to Blacklight, by creating a separate section named that source, oai.ini files had to be configured from any OAI-PMH source to collect and index Blacklight data. The harvest is followed by the batch import of the collected records into the invention sheet's indexing process. In Koha, Tag 856u should be loaded in for full-text indexing by uploading full-text documents in any form and scale. Apache Tika must be installed and configured properly for this purpose and the link must be generated within the fulltext.ini file. On top of Koha, the Blacklight layers serve as a major index, an interface, or as an optional portal. The following configuration requires more steps to import DSpace metadata into Blacklight, and to render OAI-PMH compatible with every other repository's framework, for which two files must be synchronized, such as dspace.config file, and the oai.cfg file. To line up an OAI-PMH harvester, a separate DSpace file is recognized in the oai.ini registry. When the machine is linked, it is possible to collect documents from the Blacklight index from an OAI-PMH repository. To better manage, represent, and use data retrieval, the incorporation of the Knowledge Organization System (KOS) into an online IR system is necessary (Clayton & Widener, 2017). The addition of the KOS framework would be important to improve the integration of Dewey Decimal Classification (DDC) into the Blacklight Interface config.ini (in the user interface to invoke alpha browsing), facet.ini (in the user interface to invoke DDC-dependent browsing), and MARC_local.properties (in support of Dewey class number-based indexing). This configuration is able to create modules, thus collecting data from a broad range of relative external sources beyond the boundaries of the library concerned, including access and licensed access, which is not part of the Blacklight area. Users can enable resource search by setting the search API value in the config.ini section of the search tab, and in the searchbox.ini file. A separate section must be generated in the search.ini format after choosing the source. It also supports full-text indexing, and Apache Tika is used as a method for full-text extraction. The setup is a Java-based approach that allows metadata and text from various file types to be extracted by default at a time when full-text indexing of Blacklight is disabled. Then the trail is set in the fulltext.ini file by configuring Apache Tika and commenting on the line requested in the MARC_local.properties file. This evolves also by replacing old technologies such as federated browsing, allowing the emerging worldwide adoption of discovery tools for web-scale discovery services. In relation to its full-text level with advanced recoverability functions, the solution is able to index and search through local content and hosted systems on the level of metadata. However, before selecting the Blacklight applications, the other two open-source platforms, namely, VuFind and Extensible Catalog, were shortlisted for comparison with Blacklight having their differences in technical and architectural functionality variations. Comparisons of detailed criteria/parameters were given, not to demonstrate which instrument performs better than the other, but instead to describe the tool's possible characteristics. As no broad variations are found in the operations or access to metadata or index information, since these tools are contrary to predefined data, therefore, Blacklight was essentially our choice for this model's front layering discovery application. In different configurations, all features were tested and validated with separate search syntax to experience the applicability and utility of the specific software tool. The selection of any tools for exploration depends on their features/parameters because all tools do not support such parameter values at an advanced level. Blacklight advantages over other tools were the use of Ruby with Rails platform as a programming/scripting language in place of PHP with that of VuFind, as Ruby is newer than PHP. The tool provides strong search functionality to the convention-driven rail environment and has made a great development platform for organizations requiring extensive customization. Blacklight has allowed many pleasant objectives to coexist and demonstrate different custom behaviors. Blacklight has been used for MARC-built Solr indexes, Encoded Archival Definition (EAD), Text Encoding Initiative (TEI), Public Broadcasting Core (PBCore), Dublin Core, digital content management (content DM) record exports, and a variety of locally defined metadata standards. This versatility makes Blacklight desirable not only as a front-end library catalog but also as an institutional repository search solution.

3 Results and Discussion

3.1 The Criteria for a Successful System and User Benefits

Libraries are currently involved in digital content presentation, the organization of virtual academic libraries and open access, educational film production and management, providing online access to resources, and mass digitizing of print resources [19]. The presentation of books in e-books, audiobooks, and text creation in PDF, HTML, and EPUB alternatives is one of the leading activities in the digital library environment [20]. In addition, the focus of user engagement with libraries is on library search tools as libraries continue to embrace technology. User interactions have been expanded from basic card catalogs to web-based catalogs, then tools for meta-searching, and finally to web-scale resource discovery tools (so-called

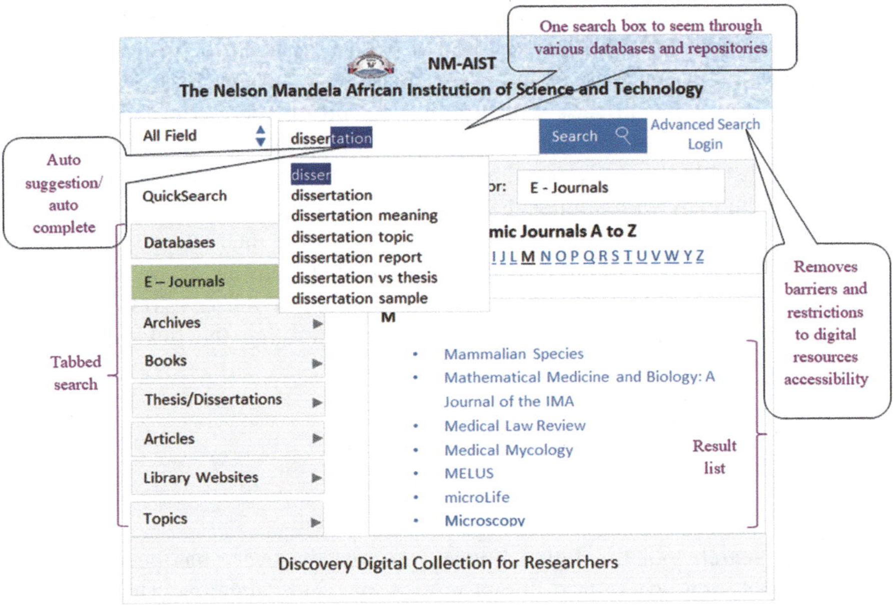

Fig. 2 The library resource discovery tool developed

RDTs) [21]. RDTs are considered as modern library catalogs that provide users with a Google-like search interface, give libraries statistics of their collections, and provide content providers with an alternative platform to encourage the use of resources [22, 23]. Due to its ability to use a single search box to search in-house and remote databases in a manner that is suitable for even experienced users, the RDT has become the preference of library users [24]. RDT, as an open-source product, has advanced search options, filters for search results; ranking results, cloud resource information, search, image cover titles or thumbnails, push technology, i.e., Really Simple Syndication (RSS), and other architectural features. Figure 2 shows a number of significant features in the digital library resource discovery tool that has been developed.

The above-developed discovery tool takes into account adaption issues addressing the usability and accessibility of RTDs. Adaptation has been described regarding enabling simple communication, rapid data discovery, web-based application adjustment to accommodate many users, and solution individualization. In literary works, there are two forms of adaptation techniques, namely, adaptable and adaptive [25]. The adaptive approach is an automated mechanism in which the tool learns the actions of the user from his or her history of interaction and automatically adjusts the interface [26]. As stated by Zimmermann [27], adaptable systems give the user total freedom from his/her point of view to vary the look of the interfaces, but it is a demanding method for users to spend time implementing the modifications. The adaptive process, on the other hand, allows the computer to make improvements on behalf of the user; however, such automatic adjustments can confuse certain users [28]. The benefits and drawbacks of both approaches should be presented from at least two different perspectives in library environments. First, library practice that guarantees sacrosanct privacy will prohibit any information from being obtained from the user. That goes to the point of erasing the log files and personal history automatically [29]. Secondly, profiling people with disabilities would not be realistic because individuals with similar disabilities might have different needs related to accessibility. This meant helping users to decide on the interaction style that best suits their needs. The invention method, constructed from the above perspectives, conveyed an adaptable technique to be our choice for the developed RTD that automatically increases website accessibility by elevating the link contents and navigation of online resources.

4 Conclusion

An online search tool for digital library resource discovery has been developed to allow one-point access to different repositories and databases. The application of RDTs should be responsive to the user needs, as stated in related articles, and as shown in this chapter. Study results show that simple RDTs must be further developed to provide simplification and adaptability to meet the needs of various user groups. This RTD developed addresses issues related to search outcomes, resource description, the use of icons, and fonts that reflect the need to enhance the effectiveness of user's requirements. As a result, the problems of usability and accessibility explored in this work led to the creation of an easier method for knowledge and access discovery for multiple users. RTDs are rich in search interfaces with distinctive features to discover and access online library resource; comparison with other RTDs, the developed RTD removes some actions of verifying the identity of a user or process. On the other hand, the overall effort of this study was focused on adaptation strategies where the adaptable approach is being taken to meet the usability and utility needs of different people with disabilities regarding presentation, information, and interface navigation. The created innovation tool allows users to make their choices about the library's search utilities. Within the longer-term steps, researchers could conduct research to match various designs, which could result in an additional suite of information resource retrieval for anticipated RDT-disabled users.

5 Recommendation

Libraries may prefer a discovery service based on its functionality and content coverage as well as resource management system from vendors based on sets of distinct requirements. Users require a discovery system that excels at providing precise methods for interacting with the library's local collections in a variety of ways. The genre of discovery services will continue to be enhanced to add new functionality and capabilities in response to requests from libraries and users to improve their competitive position. Some useful improvements and enhancements should be in the areas of application programming interfaces, expanding API ecosystem, enhancing social features, rich media materials and collections, research data sets, discovery, and access related to special collections, materials, analytics and altimetrics.

Acknowledgments The discovery tool developed is going to provide resource access to the education community in three different institutions, The Nelson Mandela African Institution of Science and Technology, Mzumbe University, and The University of Dar es Salaam which actively participated. The authors acknowledge the individual contribution of every institution as well as the highly valuable involvement of their library managers; finally, we recognize the German Academic Exchange Service (DAAD)'s financial support.

References

1. Beyene, W. M. (2017). *Metadata and universal access in digital library environments*. Library Hi Tech.
2. Yang, S. Q., & Li, L. (2016). Web-scale discovery services. In *Emerging Technologies for Librarians*.
3. Khan, A., & Qutab, S. (2016). Understanding research students' behavioural intention in the adoption of digital libraries: A Pakistani perspective. *Library Review, 65*, 295–319.
4. Pal, S. K. (2020). Library resources discovery service: Future of the libraries. SSRN Electronic Journal.
5. Brewer, J. (2018). Exploring paths to a more accessible digital future. In *ASSETS 2018 - Proceedings of the 20th international ACM SIGACCESS conference on computers and accessibility*.
6. Chew, B. L., Rahim, M. A., & Vighnarajah, V. (2017). Integration of EBSCO discovery service widget into the learning spaces of LMS. *Asian Association of Open Universities Journal, 12*(2), 137–153.
7. Foster, A. K., & MacDonald, J. B. (2013). A tale of two discoveries: Comparing the usability of summon and EBSCO discovery service. *Journal of Web Librarianship, 7*(1), 1–19.
8. Johnson, M. (2013). Usability test results for encore in an academic library. *Information Technology and Libraries, 32*(3), 59–85.
9. Gaona-Garcia, P. A., Martin-Moncunill, D., & Montenegro-Marin, C. E. (2017). Trends and challenges of visual search interfaces in digital libraries and repositories. *Electronic Library, 35*(1), 69–98.
10. Beyene, W. M., & Ferati, M. (2017). A case for adaptation to enhance usability and accessibility of library resource discovery tools. In *Lecture notes in computer science (including subseries lecture notes in artificial intelligence and lecture notes in bioinformatics)*.
11. Zhang, T., & Niu, X. (2015). The user experience of e-books in academic libraries: Perception, discovery, and use. In *Academic e-books: Publishers, librarians, and users*.
12. Coughlin, D. M. (2015). A framework for evaluating electronic resources. ProQuest Diss. Theses.
13. Beyene, W. M. (2016). Resource discovery and universal access: Understanding enablers and barriers from the user perspective. In *Studies in health technology and informatics*.

14. Crymble, A. (2016). Digital library search preferences amongst historians and genealogists: British history online user survey. *Digital Humanities Quarterly*.
15. Prommann, M., & Zhang, T. (2015). Applying hierarchical task analysis method to discovery layer evaluation. *Information Technology and Libraries, 34*(1), 77–105.
16. Matthews, G., & Walton, G. (2016). *University libraries and space in the digital world*.
17. Osman, A. (2017). Web-accessibility automatic checking tools and evaluation in Saudi Arabia: A systematic. *International Journal of Engineering Science and Innovative Technology, 6*(1), 14–17.
18. Balsells, L. A. C., González, J. C. G., Balsells, M. A. C., & Chamorro, V. A. P. (2017). Web accessibility of public universities in Andalusia | La accesibilidad de los portales web de las universidades públicas andaluzas. *REVISTA ESPANOLA DE DOCUMENTACION CIENTIFICA, 40*(2).
19. Toledo, A. (2017). Open access and OER in Latin America: A survey of the policy landscape in Chile, Colombia and Uruguay. In *Adoption and impact of OER in the global south*.
20. Enis, M. (2013). Accessibility upgrade. Library Journal.
21. Babu, P. B., & Krishnamurthy, M. (2013). Library automation to resource discovery: A review of emerging challenges. *Electronic Library, 31*(4), 433–451.
22. Hanrath, S., & Kottman, M. (2015). Use and usability of a discovery tool in an academic library. *Journal of Web Librarianship, 9*(1), 1–21.
23. Dhamdhere, S., & Lihitkar, R. (2016). Commercial and open access integrated information search tools in Indian libraries. In *E-discovery tools and applications in modern libraries*.
24. Shapiro, S. D. (2014). *Discovery tools as electronic billboards to market your library*. Library Hi Tech News.
25. Arcelli, D., Cortellessa, V., & Leva, A. (2016). A library of modeling components for adaptive queuing networks. In *Lecture notes in computer science (including subseries lecture notes in artificial intelligence and lecture notes in bioinformatics)*.
26. Le, B. P. (2015). Academic library leadership in the digital age. *Library Management, 36*, 300–314.
27. Zimmermann, A., Schmidt, R., Sandkuhl, K., Jugel, D., Bogner, J., & Möhring, M. (2018). Evolution of Enterprise Architecture for Digital Transformation. In *Proceedings - IEEE International Enterprise Distributed Object Computing Workshop, EDOCW*.
28. Paternò, F. (2000). Effective levels of adaptation to different types of users in interactive museum systems. *Journal of the American Society for Information Science and Technology, 51*(1), 5–13.
29. Magi, T. J. (2010). A content analysis of library vendor privacy policies: Do they meet our standards? *College and Research Libraries, 71*(3), 254–272.

IoT-Based Control and Monitoring System of a Solar-Powered Brushless DC Motor for Agro-Machines

Gilbert Minja, Shubi Kaijage, and Jema Ndibwile

1 Introduction

Modern testing has played a major part in attempts to screen and control electrical and mechanical equipment drives. It is possible to observe, control, and collect the dynamic condition of electrical and mechanical devices or machinery drives. To improve the quality of operations, maintenance, and low power usage are used. Several methods for monitoring and controlling current procedures, such as Zigbee, PLC-SCADA, and the IoT are accessible [1].

The Internet of Things (IoT) allows things to be sensed or controlled remotely utilizing existing network infrastructure, allowing for more seamless integration of the real world into computer-based processes, resulting in increased efficiency, accuracy, and economic benefit, as well as reduced human interaction [2]. Hence, a need for a more reliable and sustainable power source, modes of control/automation and monitoring of these machines in areas where there is inadequate or no communication is of a paramount.

1.1 Objectives

To develop a solar-powered control and operation data acquisition system for a brushless DC Motor deployed in Agro-Machines locally made in Tanzania.

G. Minja · S. Kaijage
The Nelson Mandela African Institution of Science and Technology, Arusha, Tanzania
e-mail: minjag@nm-aist.ac.tz

J. Ndibwile (✉)
Carnegie Mellon University — Africa, Kigali, Rwanda
e-mail: jndibwil@andrew.cmu.edu

J. Marx Gómez et al. (eds.), *Smart and Secure Embedded and Mobile Systems*,
Progress in IS, https://doi.org/10.1007/978-3-031-56603-5_34

Identifying requirements for a solar-powered IoT-based System for control and data acquisition for industrial machine drives, developing a solar power unit, control, and data acquisition mechanism for industrial machine drives (BLDC Motors).

This chapter highlights our contribution to the body of knowledge by how we can integrate different components and devices off-the-shelf creating a seamless system that caters to easing operations on a plethora of electrically powered machines.

1.2 Problem Statement

The locally made Agro-Machines that are currently deployed in the off-grid areas require renewable power sources, particularly solar energy. These machines rely solely on manual operations and technical know-how of the operators. Notwithstanding, the crucial parameters monitoring of the core driving entities of the machine's drives such as a motor are inadequate.

A need for more efficient and sustainable power sources, modes of control/automation, and monitoring of these machines in areas where there is inadequate or no communication is of paramount importance.

2 Literature Review

It is important to analyze significant literature linked with the control of BLDC Motors and electric solenoid valves as well as BLDC Motor monitoring and acquisition methods and identify gaps in order to lay the groundwork for the project in the subject.

The BLDC Motors have become more commonly used in industrial applications and instruments than typical DC motors due to attractive qualities such as high efficiency, great torque, incredible speed, low noise, compact area, and long life [3].

Numerous adaptive control methods have been used to regulate BLDCs one being a combination of Fuzzy Logic and PIDs. However, these algorithms are mostly for linear models and are not relevant to nonlinear models since fuzzy control is based on fuzzy logic and fuzzy set theory, thus, too complex to deploy in small-scale systems [4].

The most frequent and essential metrics monitored for assessing the operation of an electric motor in industries are voltage, current, active power, reactive power, and temperature. The significance of monitoring is highlighted since it is dangerous to manage and monitor these devices directly during continuous operation [5].

Rotating electrical drive machines, whether driven by BLDC motors or induction motors, are at the core of most engineering processes, and as they are developed to tighter margins, there is a rising need to monitor their behavior and performance for reliability, efficiency, and sustainability sake [6].

3 Related Work

To come up with the project design, we went through some of the control and monitoring work that had been done with a similar vision of purpose and expected output.

Cristian, Constantin, Zoltan, Adina, and Florica demonstrated the value and utility of using a PLC to regulate and examine mechanical applications in driving engines. In this system design, the motors were controlled using Siemens PLC and SCADA programming [7].

Senthilkumar and others proposed an M2M-based Industrial automation using Advanced Microcontroller and IoT with auto-sensing technology based on deployment of an ARM workstation, where the workstation is used as both controller and server. The system would automatically monitor and control the industrial electrical appliances while giving emergency alerts to authorized personnel without human interference. Acquisitions from machine activities, on the other hand, had to be physically accessed from the ARM controllers, which necessitated the use of technically skilled individuals. Furthermore, when it comes to distribution to Small and Medium Businesses (SMBs), ARM workstations are complex [8]. Both the two designs had a good approach to solving the intended problem, however, we had some limitations on the cost and availability of materials off the shelf from local stores.

4 Materials and Methods

To design and implement the system, the Agile-Scrum System Design Methodology (Fig. 1) was deployed. Since customer demands change so fast, today's industrial environment is defined by complexity. As a result, suppliers are faced with the issue of shortening speed to value while still offering new products that clients expect [9].

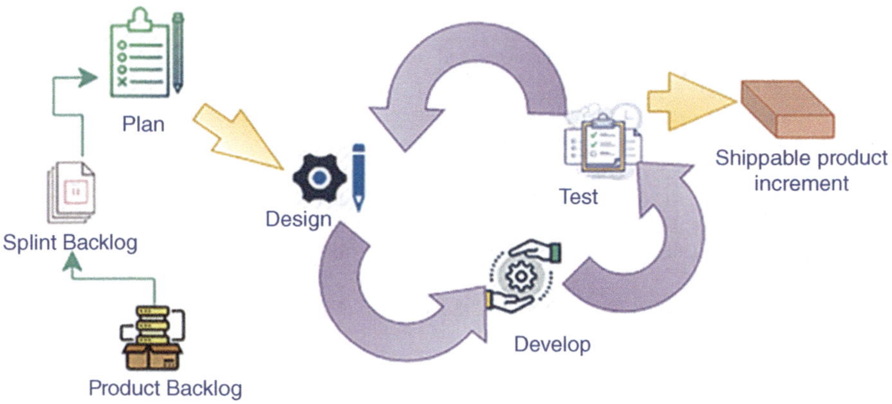

Fig. 1 Agile-Scrum methodology [10]

Seven stages were taken to choose components for the creation of a Motor Control and Data Acquisition Unit (DAU) for the proposed system: Determining the best approach to getting control information from human viewpoints, identifying the control target based on system needs and information to be controlled, determining the control target viewpoint based on determining the best approach to getting control information from human viewpoints, Examination of module conditions in relation to system requirements, listing of module restrictions, and selection of qualified modules to be used in system development based on module type and physics, when compared to an actual physical phenomenon, the module operation level is identified, examination of module conditions in relation to system requirements, listing of module restrictions, and selection of qualified modules to be used in system development.

A two-step data collecting strategy was used to acquire adequate and relevant information for creating the control and monitoring system for a BLDC motor for a machine, utilizing Arduino UNO R3 and Raspberry Pi 3 Model B, and other relevant and widely available components off-the-shelf. The hardware used were grouped as the power supply unit, the control unit, and the data acquisition unit.

4.1 System Requirements

The first step was to gather existing data on the manual control system and the issues it faced, and the second step was to use the data acquired in step one to design and test the control and monitoring system utilizing the components mentioned earlier (Arduino UNO and RPi). The necessary requirements were gathered from the test lab using miniature designs that mimic the real final designed system, where both services and constraints were divided into functional and non-functional demands (see Table 1).

Table 1 The functional and non-functional requirements

Functional requirements	Non-functional requirements
The system shall automate the whole motor and solenoid valve switching process	Security
The system shall have an option for manual or automatic control	Accessibility
The system shall collect motor parameters (voltageand current) and store them in an SD card. The system shall automatically upload data to a client phone once Bluetooth pairing is detected. The system shall stop operations once the batteries are below 48 V	Usability
The created app will be requested to upload the data to a cloud server once the data is on the client's phone	
The system shall be powered by solar energy and have a backup power plan	

5 Results and Discussion

This section summarizes the project's findings and examines the outcomes. It also details the design and execution of a control and monitoring system for a solar-powered BLDC motor for the Agro-Machine.

5.1 System Implementation

The project created a system prototype that operates a BLDC motor externally through the motor's control unit, gathers motor operating data (voltage and current), stores it on an SD card, and passively uploads the same to a cloud storage database. The prototype indicated that the motor control for the operation of the machine was executed and that operation data such as voltage and current were passively communicated to the firebase database for storage and subsequent viewing for later analysis.

The developed control box circuitry represented the interconnect of all building blocks of the control and monitoring system by piecing together the Power supply unit with the DC buck converters, Raspberry Pi 3, Arduino UNO R3, the Relay switches, the cooling fan and the Solenoid connection as seen in Fig. 2.

A motor control and monitoring system's developed circuitry combined all the machine drive building blocks, wireless communication, and programming components into a single module (Figs. 3, 4, 5, 6). Furthermore, within a digital assembly environment, the device could collect significant variations in motor operation conditions such as voltage, current, and frequency, which is advantageous in short or long-time operating systems because a motor mounted at the machine

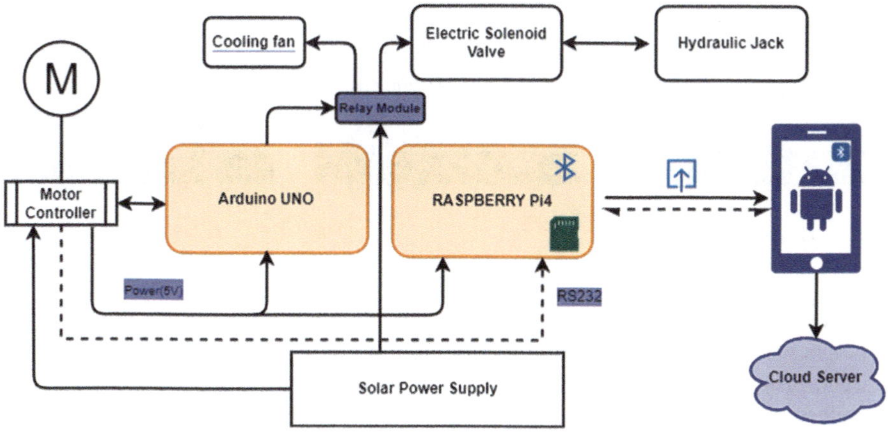

Fig. 2 The block diagram of the motor control and monitoring system

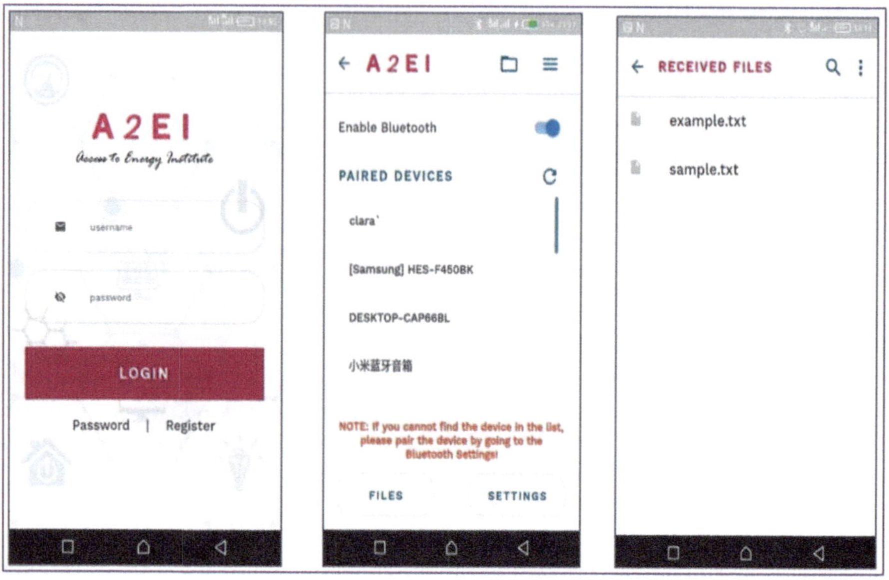

Fig. 3 The Blue app (1)

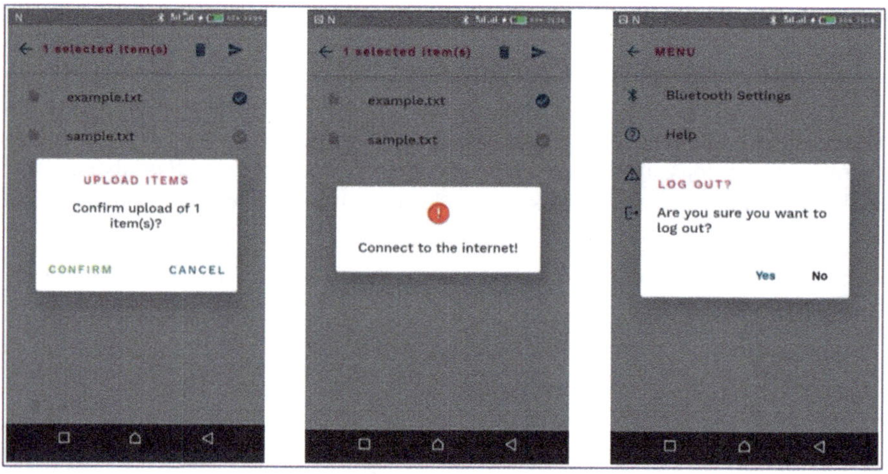

Fig. 4 The Blue app (2)

can have a centrally located means of passively gathering data for reliability and efficiency monitoring. This also illustrates that the system can achieve.

The project's future goal of gathering data and sending out alerts in real time. Wireless monitoring systems, particularly offline "applinks," are valuable tools in monitoring industrial machine drives, especially in areas where there is limited or

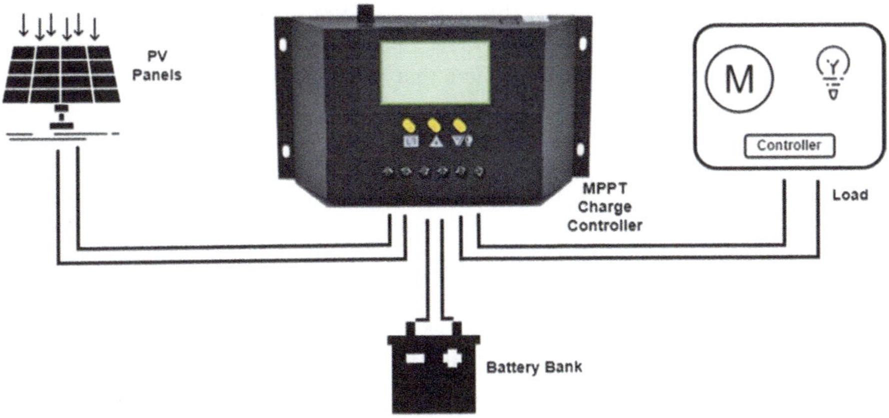

Fig. 5 The power supply unit

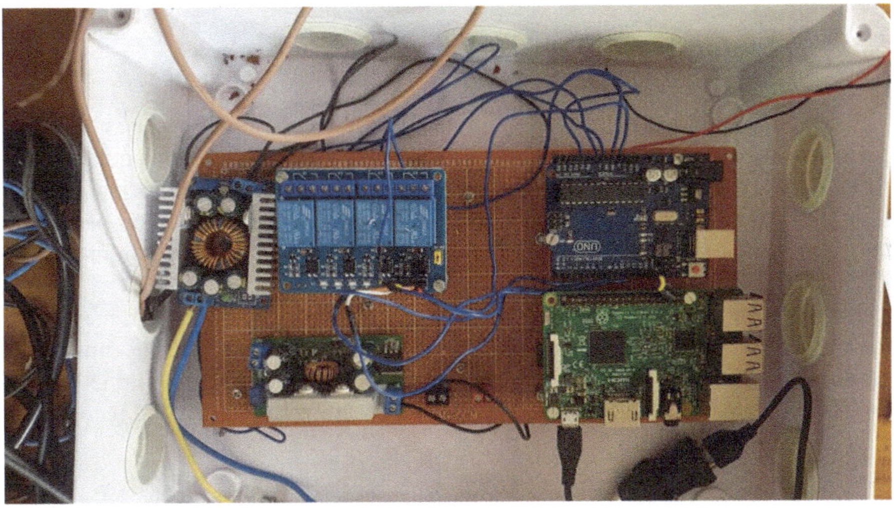

Fig. 6 The implemented circuit

no access to internet services. Their implementation should be simple enough for any engineer to comprehend and utilize.

The development of a data logging application was done using several readily available free tools such as Android Development Studio, Flutter Software Development Kit (SDK), and Firebase for data storage in cloud and source code editor, such as the Visual Studio. Converting locally manufactured agricultural machinery to more advanced machinery through the use of renewable energy and widely accessible machine drives and smart controllers has proven critical to improving the living standards of many local small-scale farmers' communities.

To enhance the system design, this project proposes developing a framework for the fundamental design that all other developers may use as a guide for gathering requirements and implementing a system that would serve their needs.

5.2 The Power Supply Unit

To cater for power needs for the Agro-Machine the photovoltaic solar system (Fig. 5) was implemented as per the needs and requirements. The system produced enough power to run the machine for at least 8 h in a day with enough solar insolation continuously in a 24-hours day without power shortage/outbreak since the system was connected to an 800-Ah battery bank with 200 Ah per cell arranged in series, storing energy to suffice the operation.

5.3 The Data Acquisition Mobile Application

The designed mobile application system that would be accessible via the company's premises, was developed using flutter framework. The mobile app acquires monitoring data from the RPi controller via a Bluetooth communication technology and uploads it to a cloud server for storage and later monitoring. The app-based data collecting tool (Figs. 3 and 4) for system monitoring includes user administration, station management, account settings, and a log dashboard.

The system's privileged users are administrators and respective user's technicians. The administrator has the authority to increase or reduce the number of features to which other parties have access. End-user functionality is limited to self-registration, report uploads to the server, report printing, and password recovery.

6 Conclusion

A control and monitoring system for the solar-powered Agro-Machine was developed with a fully integrated electronic control system as per Fig. 6. Readily available devices/components were deployed to come up with a solar-based power supply unit that would cater to the machine operation. Appropriate programming on timing was attempted to calibrate the information for the machine operation as per requirements.

A four-channel relay module and Arduino UNO R3 microcontroller were successfully interfaced with the rest of the system such as the Solenoid valve and DC buck converters to arrive at the required system. A Raspberry Pi together with the designed mobile application enabled acquisition of crucial motor operation data and storage to the cloud server.

The power supply unit was designed, to embrace solar energy harvesting that is clean, sustainable, and enables operations of the machine for up to 8 h without recharging the batteries. All observations and experimental tests prove that the developed solution suffices the agro-processing activities and control requirements for the machine.

Implementing such a system in the field could significantly boost productivity, saving time, lowering carbon emissions, and allowing operators and small-scale farmers to participate fully in value-chain addition of their produce.

The project addressed three 2030 Sustainable Development Goals in SGD1—Poverty, SGD7—Affordable Clean Energy, and SDG 9—Industrial, Innovation, and Infrastructure.

7 Future Work

Industrial machine drives' control and monitoring involves the definition of control parameters and steps as well as measurement of different machine parameters including voltage, current, and temperature. Due to the limitation of scope, the developed system was designed to control and monitor only a few parameters. For better control of the BLDC motor-powered machine drives, it highly needs the above-mentioned parameters to be considered in a closed-loop system. This system is also limited by the power stored in the solar batteries that cannot run beyond 8 h of constant operation. To increase the operation time To increase the operation time larger Solar PV and battery assembly systems have to be put in place

Fig. 7 Control and monitoring system implemented on Agro-Machine

as well as machine cooling systems, especially for the machines with hydraulic systems. A more insightful and real-time parameters monitoring dashboard system will be a novel addition to the system, this category needs to be considered to ensure industrial data and efficiency of operation of the machine drives are closely monitored to achieve a higher functioning system. In Fig. 7, you can observe the tangible prototype that we created and were actively testing at the site.

References

1. Hemalatha, M. C., Nagarajan, M. R., Suresh, P., Shankar, G. G., & Vijay, A. (2017). Brushless DC motor controlled by using internet of things. *IJSTE-International Journal of Science Technology and Engineering, 3*, 373–377.
2. Ganga, D., & Ramachandran, V. (2018). IoT-based vibration analytics of electrical machines. *IEEE Internet of Things Journal, 5*, 4538–4549.
3. Ibrahim, M. A., Mahmood, A. K., & Sultan, N. S. (2019). Optimal PID controller of a brushless DC motor using genetic algorithm. *International Journal of Power Electronics and Drive Systems ISSN, 2088*, 8694.
4. Somwanshi, D., Bundele, M., Kumar, G., & Parashar, G. (2019). Comparison of fuzzy PID and PID controller for speed control of DC motor using LabVIEW. *Procedia Computer Science, 152*, 252–260.
5. Magdum, A. D., & Agashe, A. (2016). Monitoring and controlling the industrial motor parameters remotely using LabVIEW. In *2016 IEEE International Conference on Recent Trends in Electronics, Information and Communication Technology (RTEICT)* (pp. 189–193). IEEE.
6. Anshory, I., & Robandi, I. (2016, May). Monitoring and optimization of speed settings for brushless direct current (BLDC) using particle swarm optimization (PSO). In *2016 IEEE region 10 symposium (TENSYMP)* (pp. 243–248). IEEE.
7. Cristian, B., Constantin, O., & Zoltan, E. (2014). The control of an industrial process with PLC. In *2014 International Conference on Applied and Theoretical Electricity (ICATE)* (pp. 1–4). IEEE.
8. Senthilkumar, S., Prabakaran, C., Saranya, M., Keerthana, V., Kayalvizhi, S., & Shinthana, S. (2020). M2M based industrial automation using advanced microcontroller and IoT with auto sensing technology. *International Research Journal of Innovations in Engineering and Technology, 4*, 101.
9. Soeteman-Hernandez, L. G., Apostolova, M. D., Bekker, C., Dekkers, S., Grafstrom, R. C., Groenewold, M., Handzhiyski, Y., Herbeck-Engel, P., Hoehener, K., & Karagkiozaki, V. (2019). Safe innovation approach: towards an agile system for dealing with innovations. *Materials Today Communications, 20*, 100548.
10. Van Casteren, W. (2017). The waterfall model and the agile methodologies: A comparison by project characteristics. *Research Gate, 2*, 1–6.

IoT-Based Monitoring and Reporting System for Dosimeter Wearers in Radiation Areas

Avith Habonimana, Devotha Nyambo, Anael Sam, and John Ben Ngatunga

1 Introduction

1.1 Background

Every living thing and every place in the environment are exposed to radiation sources. There are two categories of radiation sources: ionizing and non-ionizing radiation sources. Non-ionizing radiation sources, on the other hand, are non-destructive to human health. In contrast, ionizing radiation sources are harmful to human health when precautions to avoid contamination are not in place [1, 2]. Indeed, individuals' average radiation dose is encountered throughout the environment, not only from natural sources. But also from artificial radiation sources such as experimental or industrial use and medical use, which results in radiation exposures to public members occupationally exposed individuals [3].

Thus, people are exposed to two main primary sources of radiation, natural radiation that encompasses internal radiation, which comes from the human body, and natural environments. In addition, however, there is a secondary external radiation source, which comes from manufactured radiation.

The primary source of manufactured radiation exposure to the community in general and workers in particular, is coming from work and as well as trial

A. Habonimana (✉)
Nelson Mandela African Institution of Science and Technology (NM-AIST), Arusha, Tanzania
e-mail: habonimanaa@nm-aist.ac.tz

D. Nyambo · A. Sam
The School of CoCSE, Nelson Mandela African Institution of Science and Technology (NM-AIST), Arusha, Tanzania

J. B. Ngatunga
Tanzania Atomic Energy Commission (TAEC), Arusha, Tanzania

J. Marx Gómez et al. (eds.), *Smart and Secure Embedded and Mobile Systems*,
Progress in IS, https://doi.org/10.1007/978-3-031-56603-5_35

practice, mainly medical dealing, such as cancer treatment, radiation therapy, nuclear medicine, X-ray machines, and industrial use [4, 5].

It is well known that radiation exposure is harmful to human health because it destroys tissues that compose the human body. That harm include fever, headaches, vomiting that might lead to severe illnesses like cancer, or even death; conversely, people do not care even for individuals working in radiation sites [6]. Due to that, the imperatives for protection from radiation exposure in the workplace were established. The culture of radiation protection is a theme in emergence along with information and awareness of radiation, personal protective equipment, radiation safety practice, education, and training as well [7].

More institutions are involved in radiation safety promotion, but they all aim to achieve the common goal: to keep people informed and safe. The International Atomic Energy Agency (IAEA), the Nuclear Energy Institute (NEI), Nuclear Regulatory Commission (NRC), and Occupational safety and Health Administration (OSHA) are among the organizations that strive and recommend that radiation standards must be followed [8]. Moreover, at the local level, via the declaration which states the use of radiation sources must be regulated to safeguard the public, employees, and the environment from the negative consequences of both ionizing and non-ionizing radiation. Here in the United Republic of Tanzania, the Tanzania Atomic Energy Commission (TAEC) is an institution established by the Tanzania Government by act no. 7 of 2003 [9] to ensure radiation safety via control of peaceful uses of nuclear technology and atomic energy and promoting the application of radiation sources peacefully as well. This can be achieved by inspecting all centers that utilize radioactive sources to monitor the implementation of the Atomic Energy Act and its regulations.

Upon that, TAEC is responsible for tracking and keeping radiation dose perceived by occupational exposure in workplace within the international occupational dose limit, that is 20 millisievert yearly [10]. Furthermore, TAEC realizes that via the Personal Monitoring and National Calibration section, dosimeters (TLDs) are distributed to each radiation worker to record the radiation dose perceived at the time being at the radiation working place.

Despite the efforts, the overall performance for striving for the ionizing radiation health hazard is still needed because the workers wearing dosimeters (passive dosimeters) in radiation sites are not abiding by safety measures ionizing radiation.

It was discovered that improper managing of a personal dosimeter might result in a poor dosimeter wearing exercise among others:

- A worker may put aside the dosimeter.
- An operator might corrupt by radiating the dosimeter using an artificial source.
- An employee should move out within the estimated radiation range and then encounter an overdose outside the radiation departments.

And probably, that can source improper assessment of an individual occupational radiation dose, thereby leading to biased health risk estimation [11].

Hence, the need of being monitored and reported to enhance the strive against the hazards from radiation toward radiation workers. As technology evolves quickly, there is an opportunity for intelligent solutions to overcome radiation hazards, from experimental scale to industrial practice, by using intelligent surveillance and real-time reports of dosimeter users.

Therefore, the main objective of this project was to develop an IoT-based safeguard system capable of monitoring and reporting in real time the non-compliance dosimeter users in radiation departments. To accomplish the main objective of the project, specific activities such as:

1. To identify and analyze the requirements for an IoT-based safeguard system for dosimeter users monitoring and reporting in the area.
2. To design and build an IoT-based safeguard system for dosimeter users to monitor and report on radiation exposure.
3. To validate the developed system.

1.2 Related Works

Studies have been undertaken and have come up with several solutions to overcome radiation hazards.

The University Hospital of King Abdul-Aziz University performed the tracking of the medical radiation employees to know how much their average 12-monthly effective dosage has developed. Nevertheless, the said monitoring was done by using the thermoluminescence dosimeter [10]. Then, while performing their work, staff have to wear the thermoluminescence dosimeters at the proper place, that is, at the chest level, which is the most critical body portion where the maximum radiation is predictable. Yet, it is difficult to know if the supposed wearer has worn it. Unless the closer follow follows each operator is set up, which is also a burden to the manager.

Mohamed [12] surveyed Egypt's awareness and implementation of ionizing radiation safety measures. The finding was that only the completion of radiation safety training was the major predictor of good adherence to radiation safety procedures [12].

A study conducted in the United States about practices in use against radiation protection revealed that as a measure of personal protection, workers wear a one- and two-piece lead apron as well as a thyroid shield [6]. Still, the utilization of dosimeter was inconsistent in half of the cases. Hence personal dose monitoring is not perfectly achieved.

The international project on individual monitoring and radiation exposure levels in interventional cardiology has been conducted an assessment of staff radiation protection levels. And this was done by having an international occupational exposure database [13]. When it comes to the requirement of wearing a personal dosimeter, only 57% of the regulatory bodies specify the number and location of dosimeter for staff wearing. However, about 40% could provide only occupational dose, which induces that adherence to individual monitoring is frequently unachieved. Hence, propose the analysis incorporates monitoring compliance to achieve an accurate assessment of personal dose.

From 2011 to 2017, an evaluation of occupational radiation exposure to external ionizing radiation was performed in Tanzania. The demonstrative method compared the previous results with the fresh yearly collective dose recorded using dosimeters such as effective dose, average effective dose, individual dose distribution ratio, and collective effective dose distribution ratio [14]. Yet the need to look at the way to increase safety in the industrial application was recommended.

In South Korea, a study on the assessment of the working environment and personal dosimeter-wearing compliance of industrial radiographers was conducted. The demonstrative way to monitor individual occupationally exposed radiation dose and keep it under the internationally recommended dose limit was to wear a personal dosimeter. However, the legal personal dosimeter wearing obedience was inspected by relationship examination between recorded dose and chromosome aberration frequency [15].

For two community hospitals, a calculation of occupational radiation doses of medical workers was carried out [16]. The TLDs put on the chest and the collar, ring dosimeters were utilized to estimate dose for the whole body, i.e., Hp (10) dosage, the lens of the eye doses, i.e., Hp (3), and dose for skin, i.e., Hp (0.07) dose, respectively. However, to discover the reason for the high doses, an investigation is normally conducted to ascertain whether a personal dosimeter was accidentally left in the treatment room or not. Conversely, it was impossible to ascertain the unintentional dosimeter exposures and demonstrate compliance with applicable radiation protection measures and personal dose.

A radiation reduction strategy has been conducted, and this was done in pediatric orthopedics patients using the development of non-radiation methods such ultrasound [4]. But workers were not taken into consideration.

Canadian Organization Medical Physicists concentrate on having the same standards for radiation safety regulations in each sector dealing with radiation exposure [17]. However, it did not consider real monitoring and reporting workers while in Jobsite exposure to keep the personal dose with dose limit range.

From the evaluation of the existing system for radiation and radiation workers monitoring, there was a research gap in having an intelligent strategy for monitoring and reporting remotely staff wearing dosimeters in radiation working places.

The present study proved the need to develop an IoT-Based Monitoring and Reporting System for Dosimeter Wearers in Radiation Area. Therefore, a solution incorporating the Internet of Things technology, human body detector, and location sensor was used.

1.3 Significance of the Study

The focus was the remote follow-up of dosimeter wearing, hence witnessing individual dosimeter wearing within the radiation job site. And enabled institutions in charge of personal monitoring dose to get a real-time report for the compliance and non-compliance to the dosimeter uses.

The system will help remove the traditional close follow-up of dosimeter wearing onsite and increase the accuracy in calculating an individual occupational radiation dose, finally reducing the cost related to biased health risk estimation.

2 Data Collection

Data collection, which elicited and linked information based on variables, was done [18]. To fully comprehend and identify the key challenges to be addressed in TAEC headquarters and their sub-quarters. First, the kind of data needed was determined. Then, the sample survey participants were chosen within the TAEC population: heads of different departments, staff of Personal Monitoring and National Calibration Laboratory, and radiation workers. Qualitative methods such as interviewing and document analysis were utilized to gather a thorough understanding of the issue to be addressed. Thereby, data captured feelings, reactions, and insight on non-compliance and compliance to dosimeter wearing.

2.1 System Requirements

The subsequent stage after data elicitation is requirement analysis, system functional and non-functional requirements have been analyzed so as to understand what the proposed system must do and the product's expectations as well. Tables 1 and 2 depict the functional and non-functional requirements of the proposed system.

Table 1 Functional requirements

Requirements	Descriptions
Human body detection	To be assured with the dosimeter wearing the system shall detect the presence of the human body.
Sense location and time	The TAEC managerial officer needs to ensure if the dosimeter wearing is abided with while being or not in the expected working place. Therefore, the system will sense the location and time.
View information about compliance and non-compliance to dosimeter wearing	The system shall output the real-time employees 'behavior by visualizing the mapping web based on desktop computer.
General daily report generation	To have an insight on the statistic view and provide a regular alert to dosimeter wearers, the system will generate a general daily report.

Table 2 Non-functional requirements

Requirements	Descriptions
Security	The system should allow only the authenticated TAEC managerial officer to access the mapping web based so as to check the real-time employees' behavior.
Usability	The system should be user-friendly to TAEC managerial officers.
Performance	The system may handle numerous requests concurrently.
Scalability	The system should allow any improvement/modification to be performed.

2.2 *System Design*

The system design was carried out to evaluate data input, processing, storage, and information output. The developed system was designed into three parts: detection and processing, software, and reporting.

3 Detection and Processing Unit

The detection and processing unit consists of a human body detector, Global Positioning System receiver module (GPS receiver module), and ESP32 Microcontroller. This is to collect information about the compliance and non-compliance to dosimeter wearing and determine the real-time and location of the supposed wearer by human body detector and GPS receiver module, respectively. When all is done, to treat the collected information for further processing. Figure 1 shows the flowchart of the detection and processing unit.

3.1 *Software Unit*

A software unit that is a set of programs that enable the system to perform specific tasks encompasses various instructions and procedures used to generate codes for proper processing, command, and function of the proposed system. In this project, the software unit comprises storage and coding.

The software unit retrieves data on location and time recently sensed by the body detector and location sensor, respectively (Fig. 2). It then compares that new record with the captured and stored information about the expected location. If the comparison results within the range of the predictable location, the system ensures that the person is in the expected place. It subsequently takes that person to the mapping web-based (Fig. 3) and visualizes him/her with a green icon. On the other hand, if the new record is unmatched with the stored expected location, the system confirms that the person is out of the range of the expected location, it also takes

Fig. 1 Flowchart of detection and processing unit

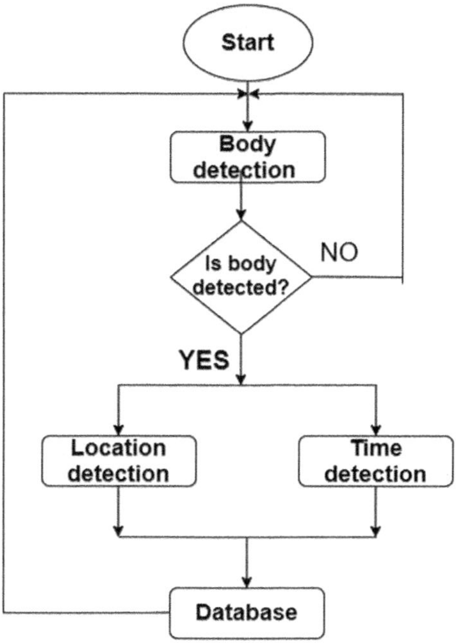

that person to the mapping web-based (Fig. 3) and pictures him/her with a yellow icon.

Lastly, if 10 min elapse without a new record sensed, i.e., nobody sensed, the system knows that the dosimeter is not worn. Therefore, it takes the person from the mapping web-based and places and lists him/her in the text box. Figure 2 illustrates the flowchart of the software unit.

The reporting unit comprises the web-based interface intended to fetch information from the cloud using HTTP protocol and then display it to the desktop computer to visualize the radiation worker's actual behavior. First, the TAEC managerial officer views the worker's comportment by clicking the icon of the dropdown menu list of clients to display the wanted one. Then, he/she promptly grasps the Map on which location is traced and perceives three information, namely workers with their names:

- Wearing the dosimeter and being in the expected place noticeable by a green icon.
- Wearing the dosimeter and being out of the expected place visible by the yellow icon.
- Not wearing the dosimeter and listed in the text box.

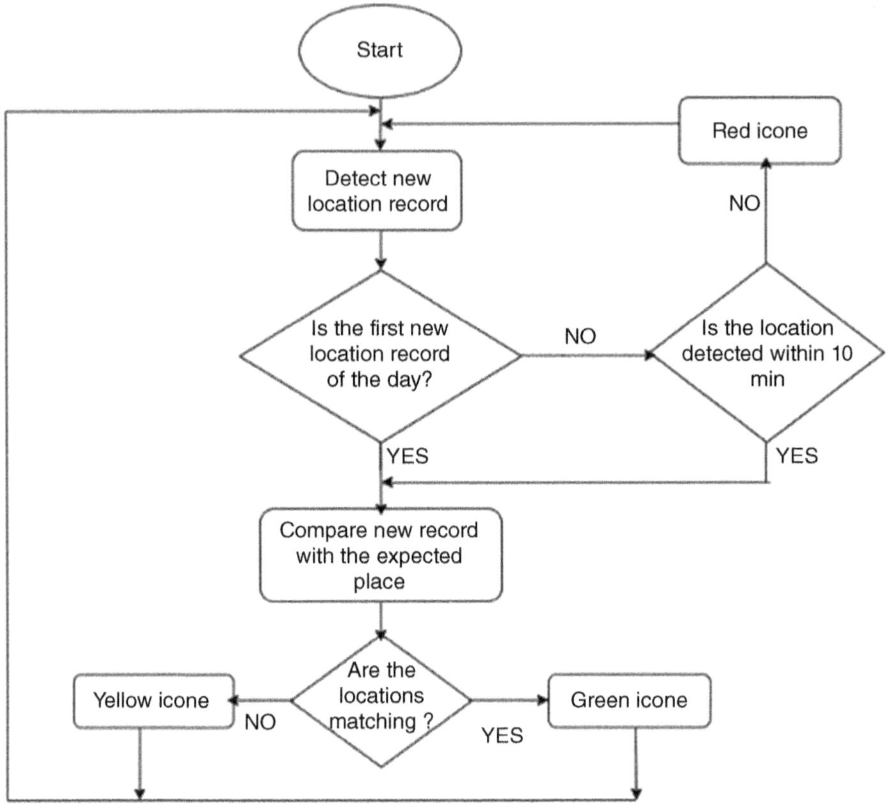

Fig. 2 Flowchart of software unit reporting unit

4 Materials and Methods

The hardware consists of a Thermoluminescence Dosimeter (TLD), Human body detector, GPS receiver module, ESP32-Wroom-32D Microcontroller, and 9 V Rechargeable battery.

A thermoluminescence dosimeter is a device that measures the dose amount of ionizing radiation that is absorbed while working in a radiation area. It is worn on a person's chest to record the radiation dose received.

The Human body detector (the Max30100 Oximeter sensor) helps to observe if the radiation worker has worn the dosimeter or not while performing his/her daily duties.

The Global Position System (GPS) receiver module is a device that tells where a person is by determining a precise location and timing information from a GPS satellite no matter where the user is on the earth. The position determination is based

Fig. 3 Visualization of the mapping functionality of the web application

on the utilization of satellites circling in the space segment that provide a signal that contains coordinates of latitude and longitude.

The ESP32-Wroom-32 Wi-Fi and Bluetooth Microcontroller is a system-on-chip microcontroller with integrated Wi-Fi and dual-mode Bluetooth. It was the brain of the proposed system, the one to receive inputs, process them, provide a relevant command, and finally, send the data to the Webserver where the monitors for further process will retrieve them.

The 9 V rechargeable battery served as the source of low power supply to the entire system.

The main hardware used for developing an IoT-based Monitoring and Reporting System for Dosimeter Wearers in Radiation Areas is depicted in Fig. 4 of the system circuit diagram where inputs and outputs devices from a microcontroller are represented.

Webserver, which is a hardware and software combination that fetches and keeps track of data, served the information to the TAEC manager room. The collection of data through GPS and oximeter sensor after treatment process was a source for determining the individual risk level of radiation by visualizing them through the desktop computer and ensuring if dosimeter was worn or not at exact such time and while being at the expected location. Figure 5 shows a block diagram of the system.

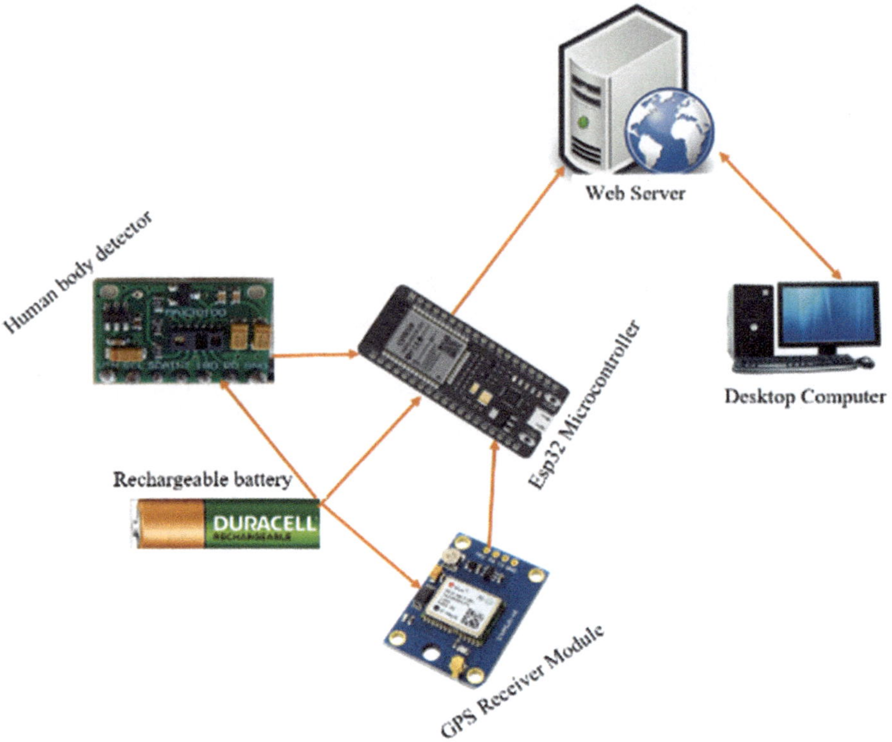

Fig. 4 System circuit diagram

5 Software Requirement and Tools Used

The selection of software and tools used was based on stability since it supports more features and user-friendliness. On the other hand, devices used to develop the web-based focused on the front end, back end [19], and programming editor.

5.1 *Hardware and System Programming*

To develop this project, IoT-Based Monitoring and Reporting System for Dosimeter Wearers in Radiation Areas, the C programming language of text editor Arduino Integrated Development Environment (Arduino IDE) was chosen due to its ease of use and compatibility with boards like ESP32 DevKit v1 ESP32 microcontroller board, NEO-M6 of GPS module, and MAX30100 of oximeter sensor module.

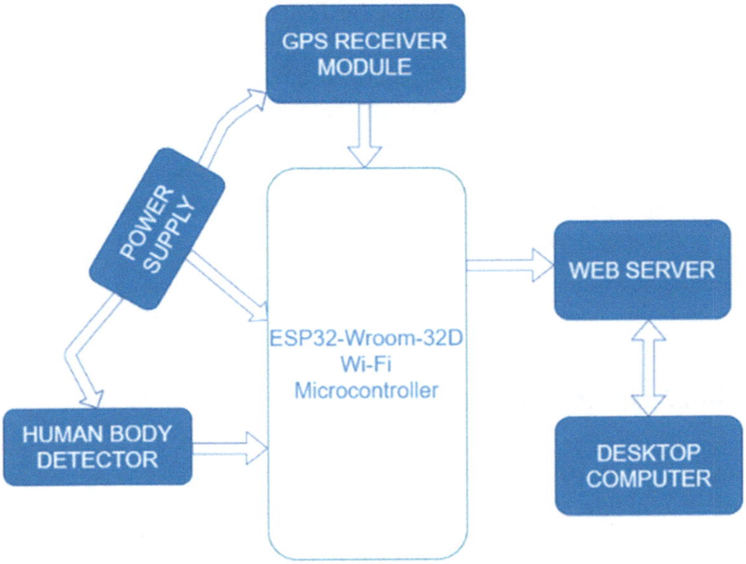

Fig. 5 System block diagram

The Arduino IDE is free software that allows one to create the desired modules by writing the package code in a text editor and subsequently using them to provide instructions to the system.

To program the ESP32 development board, the first thing done was to add the ESP32 Board to Arduino IDE. Afterward, several built-in libraries were included. On the other hand, the non-built-in were imported to and installed in Arduino IDE. Finally, the ESP32 Board is added to Arduino IDE by selecting install ESP32 by Espressif Systems, selecting the tools tab in Arduino IDE, then clicking on Board, lastly Board Manager and installing it from there.

Here are some libraries used for this system:

- TinyGPS++.h for GPS receiver module. This TinyGPS++ library assists in dealing with conveniently getting signals from GPS modules. Among others extracting latitude, longitude, date and time, and even position.
- SoftwareSerial.h for serial communication. This SoftwareSerial library is built-in in Arduino IDE. It provides help to enable serial communication to take place on the other digital pins of the Board other than the serial port when simultaneous data flows are needed. In addition, the softwareSerial is used to replicate the functionality to ensure that any pin on the Board might be exchange serial data with other peripherals.
- HardwareSerial.h for wiring. HardwareSerial library facilitates sending and receiving string over serial.
- EspSoftwareSerial.h for implementation of Arduino serial for ESP32. This EspSoftwareSerial library is not the same as SoftwareSerial, the common library for

Arduino boards; instead, it is mainly for ESP32 boards. The EspSoftwareSerial allows users to convert a few serial ports on the Board using digital pins. This library code adds an encoder and decoder to the two digital pins, enabling them to be used for transmitter and receivers' signals in the same way that a serial port does.

- Arduino IDE supports languages such as C and C++; the system was made utilizing the C programming language. The program's output was displayed in the Arduino IDE's serial monitor window.

The complete system was implemented through the following steps:

5.2 Database Implementation

A database is a structured collection of information to be stored, accessed, and retrieved in a single center to simplify the work. It was used in this radiation worker monitoring and reporting system (RWMR system) to keep all information from Esp32 microcontroller board about wearing behavior and the current location of each supposed dosimeter wearer. Then, it is the storage where the software looks for and retrieves information before displaying them on the web-based. The RWMR database for this system was developed and supported by MySQL database management and PHP script for users' web connectivity. Figure 6 illustrates the table structure of the database used to develop a web based of this system.

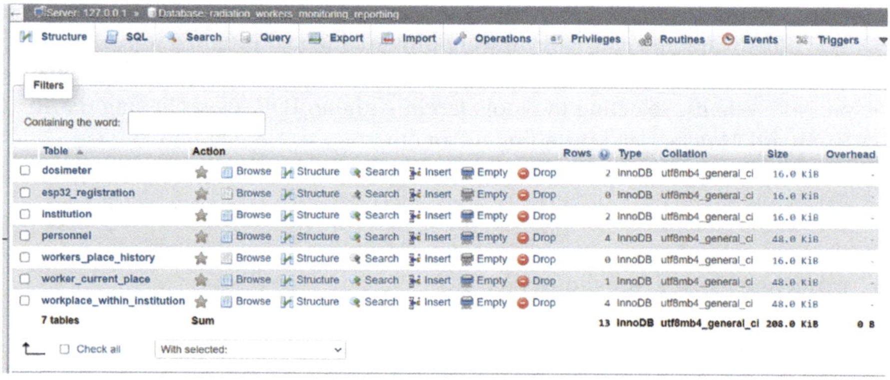

Fig. 6 Radiation worker monitoring and reporting database

5.2.1 Distance Calculation between Two Locations Having Latitude and Longitude Points

In this project, the first point to be considered is the one determined by capturing its latitude and longitude with the help of a smartphone. The second location is the one determined by GPS coordinates.

The distance was calculated using the haversine formula. It is a special formula in spherical trigonometry, that is, to compute geographic distance on Earth without regard for islands, hills, rocks, and other inconvenient factors. The haversine formula calculates the great-circle distance between two points on a sphere given their latitudes and longitudes. It has been proven to be the most accurate method of computing distances between two points on the surface of a sphere utilizing the latitude and longitude of the two points. Therefore, the first location is assimilated to the first point in spherical trigonometry and the second location to a second point.

Here, below is the haversine formula:

$$d = 2r\,\sin^{-1}\left(\sqrt{\sin^2\left(\frac{\theta_2 - \theta_1}{2}\right) + \cos\left(\theta_1\right)\cos\left(\theta_2\right)\sin^2\left(\frac{\gamma_2 - \gamma_1}{2}\right)}\right) \tag{1}$$

where:
d: is the distance between two points.
r: is the radius of the earth.
θ_1 and θ_2: are the latitude of the two points.
γ_1 and γ_2: are the longitude of the two points.

Location Coordinate Capturing

The location coordinates of the institution and the expected workplace for each worker have been captured and stored in the RWMR database in the table named institution table and workplace within the institution, respectively. The capturing was done using a mobile phone with the help of Google Maps. The process is simply done by first launching the Google Map application, secondly, zooming in on the desired location. The subsequent stage is to press and hold on the label of that location, and then the coordinates appear at the top of the Map in the search bar. The last stage is to write down the indicated coordinate. Figure 7 shows the screenshot while capturing location coordinates at Nelson Mandela African Institution of Science and Technology (NM-ASIT) using a mobile phone. The current location on an image is marked by a point labelled with a blue color with a shadow. When you press and hold on to the blue point, the location's latitude and longitude appear in the search bar.

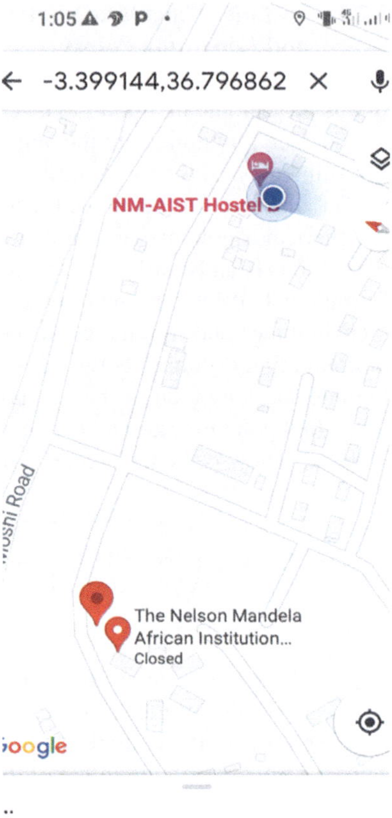

Fig. 7 Location coordinates captured using mobile phone

6 Result

6.1 System Testing Approach

The functionalities of the developed system were tested. The system functioned as expected by detecting the human body and then activating the GPS module to start sensing location, capturing the location's latitude and longitude, and then sending them to the processing unit. If there non-person sensed, the system was able to do not trigger the location sensor to start, and there was no signal sent to the ESP32 microcontroller. Furthermore, data were stored in the RWMR database for later display accordingly to delay setting to avoid interference in data streaming. Lastly, an immediate visualization of live data about workers wearing dosimeters and being within or out of the expected working places was able to be displayed on the web application. Even the ones not wearing dosimeters were listed in the text box with their institution and workplace name. Figure 8 shows an instant visualization of a real-time report about workers' behavior.

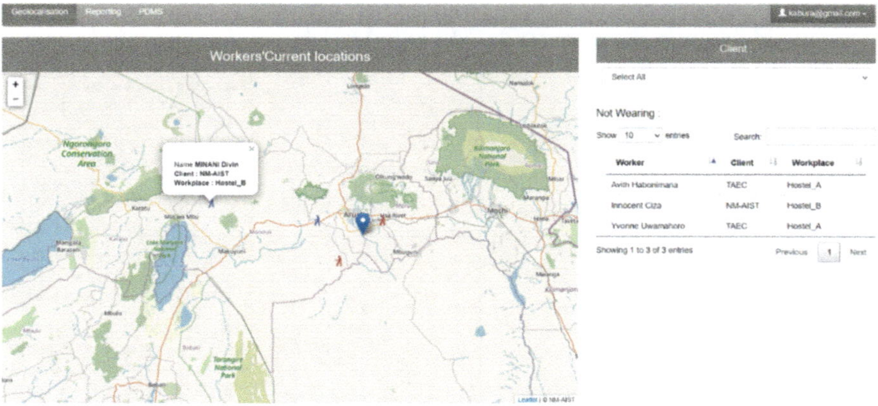

Fig. 8 Visualization of real-time data about dosimeter wearing and not wearing for all institution

In the dropdown menu list of Fig. 8, when the user clicks on the select all, the system is able to output by placing the TAEC institution at the center surrounding client institutions. In Fig. 8, we can see humans stick with blue and red colors and label indicating their details.

The TAEC managerial officer can directly get a general insight into ones wearing dosimeter and ones not wearing. Since the blue color witnesses, the dosimeter wearing while being in the range of the expected working place. Conversely, the red color witnesses wearing dosimeter being out of the expected workplace range, however, in the institution limit. The text box for non-wearing has the capability to show a maximum of ten (10) entries at once. Therefore, there is an option to click on the next button to view the rest or search for the specific worker.

The results testing of human body detection, real-time data streaming while being storing in database, visualization of longitude and latitude captured by receiver module are shown in Figs. 9, 10, and 11.

6.2 *User Acceptance Testing Approach*

The approach of user acceptance testing was performed using the made system. Then, with the actual data, the developed system was tested to prove the features of the developed system. Table 3 illustrates the features of the developed system.

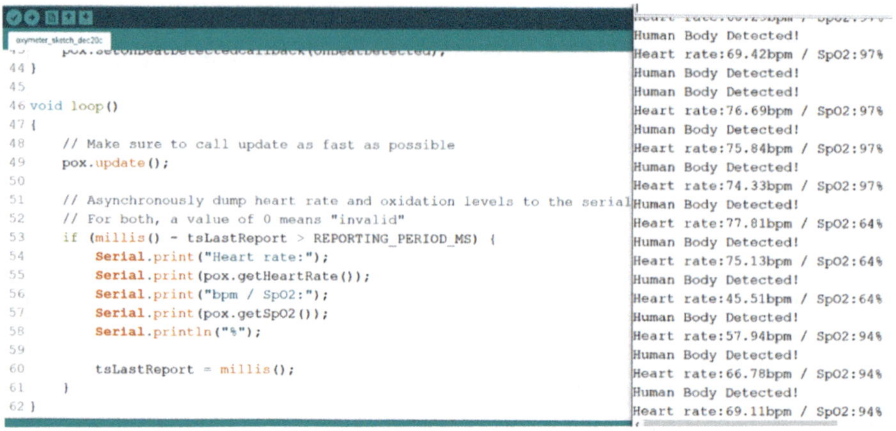

Fig. 9 Signal visualization human body detection

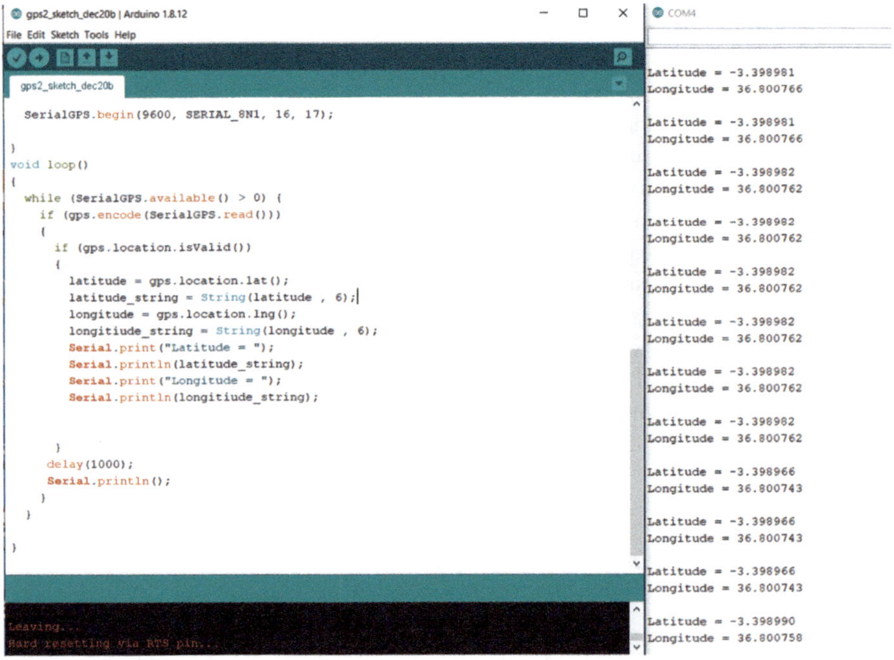

Fig. 10 Visualization of latitude-longitude captured by GPS module

6.2.1 System Validation

System validation of this developed system was performed using functional and non-functional requirements. Tables 4 and 5 depict results on both functional and non-functional requirements validation.

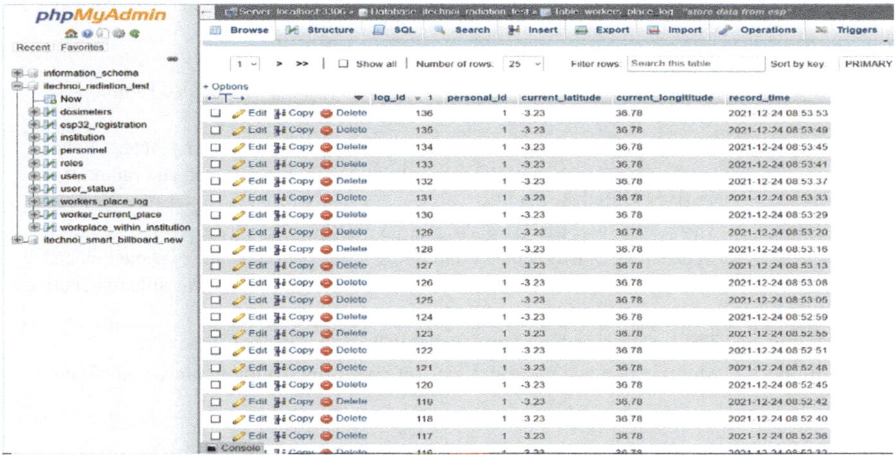

Fig. 11 Visualization of live data stored in database from a webserver

Table 3 Developed system features

Features	Descriptions
Smart dosimeter wearing	The system was able to distinguish the human body from other materials.
Real-time updates	The updates on dosimeter wearing status were timely, human body, and location were detected.
Real-time report	Witness of wearing individual dosimeter within the radiation site was provided.

Table 4 Functional requirements validation results

Requirements	Result descriptions
Human body detection	The presence of the human body was detected.
Sense location	Location's latitude and longitude were sensed and then sent to the processing unit.
View information about compliance and non-compliance to dosimeter wearing	The witness on compliance and non-compliance to dosimeter wearing was timely visualized on the web application.
General daily report generation	The general daily report was to be downloaded or printed.

6.3 Discussion

The experiment conducted from various testing, and also from system functional and non-functional requirements validation proved that dosimeter wearing for radiation workers could be monitored and reported in real time. Hence, reduce or eliminate the effects of non-compliance on dosimeter wearing while being at the radiation site. Figure 8 demonstrates an instant visualization of a real-time report about workers' behavior on dosimeter wearing. Parameters of the human body and

Table 5 Non-functional requirement validation results

Requirements	Results descriptions
Security	The login was allowed for the authenticated users and denied for the non-authenticated ones.
Usability	The system was found with ease to use when one clicks on wanted client, he/she promptly grasps the map where locations are traced and radiation workers with their details.
Performance	The system was found able to handle multiple tasks by reporting radiation workers wearing dosimeter and being within or out of the expected place, even the ones not wearing were reported. In addition, it was able to generate a general daily report.
Reliability	The system was found to be reliable by providing real-time data.
Scalability	Modification and improvement were performed without unwanted effects.

location were monitored utilizing an oximeter sensor and GPS module, respectively. In addition, data updates from ESP32 microcontroller were provided and stored every 10 min in the table of workers' place log of the RWMR database.

The user acceptance testing proved that the system could effectively be utilized in a particular country in the region. Table 3 shows the features of the developed system. Based on the evaluation and observation carried out during system testing, the result gives assurance of the system's accuracy, effectiveness, and affordability.

The system validation was carried out based on functional and non-functional requirements. Tables 4 and 5 illustrate the system's functional and non-functional requirements validation results. It has been proved that from the development point of view, the proposed system was developed accordingly. On another hand, the developed system fulfilled the stakeholders' needs since functions such as human body detection, location sensing, real-time employees' behavior visualization on a map application, and daily reports witnessing the dosimeter wearing were achieved.

7 Conclusion

With the help of wireless technology and the Internet of Things (IoT), we attempted to create an IoT-based monitoring and reporting system for radiation employees while working in areas with high radiation exposures. The aim of the project was attained, the system for real-time employee behavior and remote reporting of the dosimeter wearing was successfully developed.

From the evaluation of the existing system for radiation and radiation workers monitoring, there was a research gap in having an intelligent strategy for monitoring and reporting remotely staff wearing dosimeters in radiation working places. Therefore, this project came out with the development of a locally made radiation workers monitoring and reporting system that allows the TAEC managerial officer to visualize remotely on the mapping web application the radiation workers' behavior on dosimeter wearing and then put in place adequate measures reduction or elimination of radiation hazard.

On the basis of both functional and non-functional requirements, the system validation was completed. It included functions such as human body detection, location sensing, real-time employees behavior visualization on map application, and daily reports witnessing the dosimeter wearing.

Having a smart safeguard system solution for monitoring staff wearing dosimeters in radiation working environments is preferable, as is providing real-time employee behavior and remote reporting, as is the goal of this proposed system. It contributes to overcoming radiation hazards, increasing fimilies income, and allowing workers longevity. If this system is implemented and used effectively, it will make assurance on dosimeter wearing being within or out of radiation site, hence improving radiation safety and increasing health security, also, increase the accuracy in the calculation of an individual occupational radiation dose, finally a reduction of the cost related to biased health risk estimation.

8 Future Works

Due to the project time limitation, this project was not able to develop a mobile application so that to be able to visualize the real-time employee behavior and remote reporting of the dosimeter wearing anywhere. Furthermore, the system can be improved to sense location using Internet-enabled built-in Wi-Fi of ESP32 microcontroller instead of a GPS module. Therefore, the improvement of the system by having a mobile application and sensing location using the ESP32 microcontroller will be an added benefit.

Conflict of Interest

Non conflict of interest to declare.

References

1. OSHA. (2021). Ionizing radiation - Health effects | occupational safety and health administration. Retrieved November 13, 2021, from https://www.osha.gov/ionizing-radiation/health-effects
2. Schauer, D. A., & Linton, O. W. (2009). National Council on radiation protection and measurements report shows substantial medical exposure increase. *Radiology, 253*(2), 293–296. https://doi.org/10.1148/RADIOL.2532090494/ASSET/IMAGES/LARGE/R09AU56C02X.JPEG
3. Cole, P. (2012). Natural and man-made radiation. In *An Introduction to Radiation Protection 6E* (pp. 38–46). CRC Press. https://doi.org/10.1201/b13379

4. Sawyer, J. R. (2021). Radiation reduction strategies in pediatric Orthopaedics. *Journal of Pediatric Orthopedics, 41*, S75–S79. https://doi.org/10.1097/BPO.0000000000001822
5. Shastri, D. D., et al. (2021). Awareness of source of radiation, its hazards and protection among final year MBBS students: A cross-sectional observational study. *International Journal of Anatomy Radiology Surgery, 10*(2), RO24–RO28. https://doi.org/10.7860/IJARS/2021/44872:2628
6. Sethi, S., Barakat, M. T., Friedland, S., & Banerjee, S. (2019). Radiation training, radiation protection, and fluoroscopy utilization practices among US therapeutic Endoscopists. *Digestive Diseases and Sciences, 64*(9), 2455–2466. https://doi.org/10.1007/S10620-019-05564-Z
7. Rose, A., Uebel, K. E., & Rae, W. I. (2018). Interventionalists' perceptions on a culture of radiation protection. *South African Journal de Radiologie, 22*(1), 1–10. https://doi.org/10.4102/SAJR.V22I1.1285
8. SafetyCulture. (2021). What is radiation safety? | SafetyCulture. Retrieved November 16, 2021, from https://safetyculture.com/topics/radiation-safety/
9. TAEC. (2003). Atomic Energy Act no. 7 of 2003 established the Tanzania Atomic Energy Commission (TAEC). Retrieved November 16, 2021, from https://www.taec.go.tz/our-works/
10. Nassef, M. H., & Kinsara, A. A. (2017). Occupational radiation dose for medical Workers at a University Hospital. *Journal of Taibah University for Science, 11*(6), 1259–1266. https://doi.org/10.1016/j.jtusci.2017.01.003
11. Lee, Y., Lee, W. J., Jin, Y. W., & Jang, S. (2021). Interventional radiologists have a higher rate of chromosomal damage due to occupational radiation exposure: A dicentric chromosome assay. *European Radiology, 31*(11), 8256–8263. https://doi.org/10.1007/S00330-021-07883-0
12. Omar, M., Desoky, E. E. A., Elmohamady, B., El-Shaer, A., & Noureldin, Y. A. (2021). Awareness and implementation of ionizing radiation safety measures among urology community in Egypt: nationwide survey. *African Journal of Urology, 27*(1), 1–7. https://doi.org/10.1186/S12301-020-00110-0
13. Padovani, R., et al. (2011). International project on individual monitoring and radiation exposure levels in interventional cardiology. *Radiation Protection Dosimetry, 144*(1–4), 437–441. https://doi.org/10.1093/rpd/ncq326
14. Muhogora, W. E., et al. (2019). Occupational exposure to external ionising radiation in Tanzania (2011-17). *Radiation Protection Dosimetry, 185*(2), 208–214. https://doi.org/10.1093/rpd/ncy297
15. Lee, Y., Seo, S., Jin, Y. W., & Jang, S. (2020). Assessment of working environment and personal dosimeter-wearing compliance of industrial radiographers based on chromosome aberration frequencies. *Journal of Radiological Protection, 40*(1), 151–164. https://doi.org/10.1088/1361-6498/ab4686
16. Osei, E., Nuru, F., & Moore, M. (2020). Assessment of occupational radiation doses of medical radiation workers in two community hospitals. *Radiation Protection Dosimetry, 192*(1), 41–55. https://doi.org/10.1093/rpd/ncaa190
17. Bjarnason, T. A., et al. (2020). COMP report: A survey of radiation safety regulations for medical imaging x-ray equipment in Canada. *Journal of Applied Clinical Medical Physics, 21*(3), 10–19. https://doi.org/10.1002/acm2.12708
18. Dash, B. (2017). Methods of data collection. In *Essentials of Nursing Research and Biostatistics* (pp. 175–175). https://doi.org/10.5005/jp/books/13075_10
19. Bootstrap (front-end framework) - Wikipedia. Retrieved January 04, 2022, from https://en.wikipedia.org/wiki/Bootstrap_(front-end_framework)

The Importance of Soft Skills for Computing Graduates in the Context of the Fifth Industrial Revolution

Rexwhite Tega Enakrire, Brenda Scholtz, and Khulekani Yakobi

1 Introduction

Recent advances in cutting-edge technologies, such as embedded and mobile systems, have demonstrated immense promise for addressing societal and commercial issues [1]. These technologies have made significant contributions to sustainable development in the current knowledge economy. The global state of the post-COVID society of today is a digital one, necessitating a change in managing information in this century [2]. In this digital society, irrespective of the context and organization, competencies have become a crucial component through which organizations thrive in terms of meeting customers' information needs and competing amongst their counterparts or competitors. The digital society has also been impacted by the Fourth Industrial Revolution (4IR), where human beings interact with and make use of different digital technologies such as Artificial Intelligence (AI), robotics, the Internet of Things (IoT), embedded computing, 3D printing, genetic engineering, and quantum computing [3]. These technologies aim to improve service delivery both for citizens and businesses and to provide uninterrupted connectivity irrespective of geographical context [4]. The 4IR is rapidly evolving into the Fifth Industrial Revolution (5IR), where the focus moves from technology and the digital world to the importance of harmonious human–machine partnerships [5]. These partnerships should then positively impact society, by considering the well-being of all humanity and the planet.

R. T. Enakrire (✉) · B. Scholtz
Nelson Mandela University, Gqeberha, South Africa
e-mail: s226229025@mandela.ac.za; brenda.scholtz@mandela.ac.za

K. Yakobi
Mangosuthu University of Technology, Durban, South Africa

J. Marx Gómez et al. (eds.), *Smart and Secure Embedded and Mobile Systems*,
Progress in IS, https://doi.org/10.1007/978-3-031-56603-5_36

In today's world, organizations need to digitally transform and be IT-enabled to render business services with valuable results and to promote organizational growth [6]. The transition to digital workplaces and cities has challenged current practices and demanded the creation of new ones [7]. Soft skills have become even more important in the 5IR era to adequately consider the human element and support human–machine collaboration. The success of Smart Cities is dependent on the dimensions of technology, people, organizations, and sustainability, and on a human-centric view where all stakeholders must be considered to realize the true value of Smart cities [8, 9]. The current knowledge-intensive economy also requires employees to have a positive attitude, critical thinking skills, problem-solving skills, and analytical skills [10].

Computing graduates should be equipped with the required competencies for the digital, data-driven, and smart environments in which they will be employed. Computing as a discipline includes Computer Engineering (CE), Computer Science (CS), Cybersecurity (CSEC), Information Systems (IS), Information Technology (IT), and Software Engineering (SE). The term "Computing Sciences" is sometimes used to refer to both the fields of IS and IT. The lack of Computing competencies is of considerable concern to many private and public organizations today [11]. The study [12] proposed the integration of developing professional skills into an information and communication technology (ICT) curriculum and investigated the impact of this integration on a graduate's competency. The use of the term ICT in their article incorporates the discipline fields of CS, IS, and IT.

Globally diverse studies have identified the necessary competencies for Computing Science, and IT graduates, for example [13, 14]. In countries with an emerging economy, organizations face additional challenges such as high rates of unemployment, a lack of access to natural resources such as water and energy, a lack of skills, and a growing digital divide [5]. Other studies, such as those of [15, 16], have reported that a key competency that is fundamental to organizations for digital transformation is organizational culture adaptability, which leads to increased work efficiency. However, few studies have analyzed these competencies from the perspective of the 5IR with a focus on Computing graduates. There is, therefore, still a gap in research relating to the competencies required of Computing graduates, particularly regarding the new "soft" competencies prompted by the 5IR.

The purpose of this chapter is to address these gaps and answer the following research question: "How does the importance of soft skills in the context of 5IR influence the required competencies of graduates of Computing higher education programmes?" The research was guided by the foundational work conducted by three curricula design projects, namely the IT2017 project [17], the Computing Curricula 2020 [CC2020] initiative, and the Association for Computing Machinery (ACM)/AIS IS2020 project [18]. In all the curricula proposed by these projects, competency models were adopted, which highlighted the transformation from knowledge-based learning to competency-based learning and the constantly expanding need for curricula for Computing Sciences and IT programmes.

A Systematic Literature Review (SLR) was conducted using the Preferred Reporting Items for Systematic Reviews and Meta-Analyses (PRISMA) method proposed by [19]. The focus of the SLR was on the various areas of competencies needed by Computing graduates, specifically the social skills required by the 5IR.

The structure of this chapter is as follows: Sect. 2 describes the research design, including the SLR method that was adopted based on the research questions that guided the study. Section 4 reports on the findings of the SLR and the application of the theory. In the findings, the various competencies specified in the SLR articles as needed by Computing Sciences and IT graduates are identified. These are analyzed according to international curricula, the needs of organizations, and their relevance to 5IR-specific competencies. The paper concludes in the last section by identifying the implications and limitations of the research and outlining opportunities for future research.

2 Research Design and Methods

2.1 Five Steps of the SLR Approach

The SLR method of PRISMA proposed by [19] was adopted to answer the research questions. The first step in this method was to carry out a literature search of research articles, as represented in Fig. 1. Inclusion and exclusion criteria were used to align

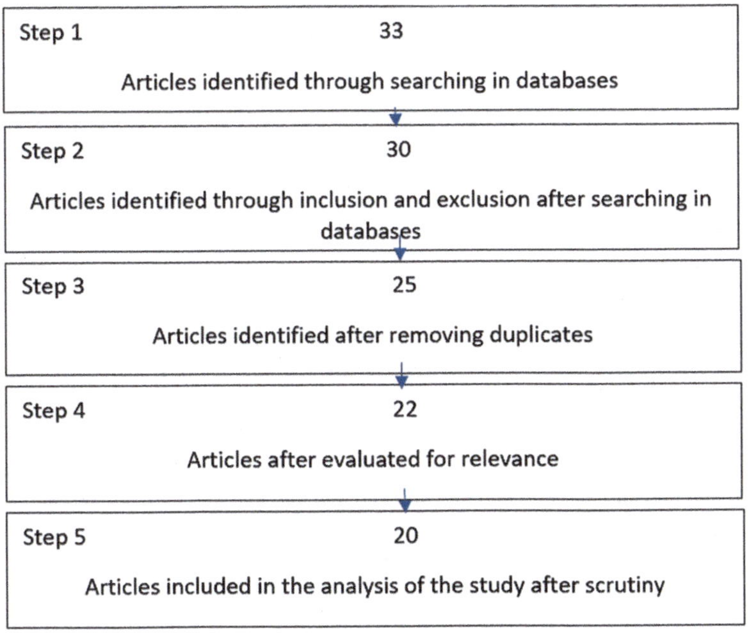

Fig. 1 SLR findings based on PRISMA

the articles with the key variables and themes used in this study. The inclusion criteria were:

- The SLR search strategy was applied to harvest articles from the databases of Google Scholar and Web of Science using the search terms "competencies of computing sciences and "how competencies of computing sciences supported organizations." The assessment of the quality filtration of various articles showed that 20 usable articles remained.
- The online databases used were written in English in Google Scholar and Web of Science.
- Articles were published between 2018 and 2022.

The search identified 33 articles, of which three were removed due to being at a high level, leaving 30 remaining articles. The second stage had to do with the filtering of the 30 articles. The third step was to remove duplicate articles, as some of the articles that appeared in Google Scholar were also present on the Web of Science platform. After removing duplicates, 25 articles remained. In the fourth step, these articles were evaluated for more specific relevance to the study, and three were removed, thus, 22 articles remained. The fifth step involved analysis and detailed screening, resulting in the removal of two more articles, leaving 20 remaining articles. The 20 articles were thematically analyzed to determine the key themes of the competencies of Computing graduates. The research articles used for this paper were freely accessible in the identified online databases. The relevant articles were exported to a folder, where they were analyzed using the qualitative approach of interpretive content analysis of documents proposed in [20].

2.2 Theoretical Context

In the theoretical context, the task teams of the ACM/AIS IS2020 [18] and the CC2020 [21] were the foundational studies adopted in the study. The IS2020 was aimed at IS curricula, whereas the CC2020 considers curricula for computer engineering, CS, IS, IT, and software engineering. Both curricula recommend a competency model for their undergraduate programs. This model was also adopted in the IT2017 curriculum and avoids the use of knowledge alone in establishing curriculum guidelines, which was the foundation of previous curricula [17]. In this model, as shown in Fig. 2, competency consists of the three interrelated dimensions of knowledge, skill, and disposition, where each of these dimensions has a specific measurable meaning [22, 23].

Competencies are key components through which an employee can flourish in an organization [24]. The adequacy of competencies possessed by an individual or employee results in many accomplishments in his/her career, irrespective of the environment. The representation in Fig. 2 illustrates that knowledge is fundamental because it provides perceptions, ideas, and an overview of a discipline [22]. The skill aspect refers to the proficiencies that convert into a distinguished practice through

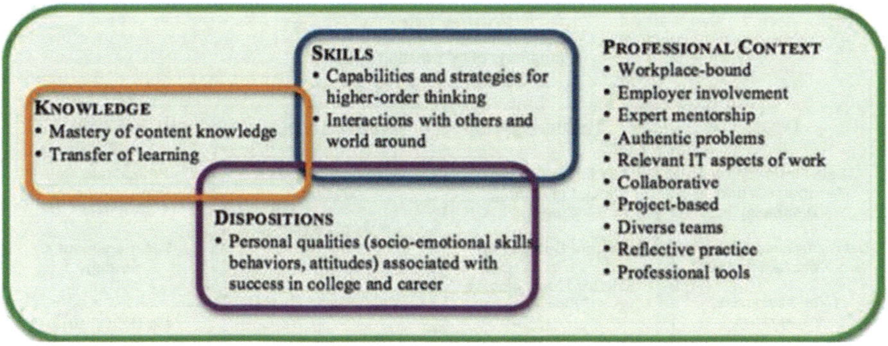

Fig. 2 Competencies = knowledge + skill + disposition [22]

perseverance, time, and hands-on activities. The disposition aspect identifies characteristics of social skills, emotional abilities, behaviors, and attitudes. These attributes are the human element and the ways in which skills are used to bring effective change into the undertaking of an individual's profession. Competencies are drivers of organizational productivity, and without these competencies, employees would not stand a chance of being considered for employment, irrespective of the organization or context.

Academic curricula do not address the need for soft skills (i.e., social, behavioral, and interpersonal skills) adequately, particularly in programs for software engineering [25]. It has long been reported that a superior performer is a professional who possesses both technical and behavioral skills [26]. Soft skills are non-technical skills that permit workers to interact with each other in the organization [27]. The dispositions referred to in competency models such as the IS2020/CC2020 can therefore also be included in the category of soft skills. The six main competency areas in IS2020 are illustrated in Fig. 3 and are:

- Foundations—Foundations of IS.
- Data—Data/information management, including data visualization.
- Technology—IT infrastructure.
- Development—includes Systems analysis and design; and Application development/Programming.
- Organizational Domain—Ethics, use, and implications for society; and IS management and strategy.
- Integration—IS project management and IS practicum (i.e., the project).

Since Computing education at the baccalaureate level may differ slightly from country to country, students should prepare to work in an industry that does not have national boundaries. Therefore, the CC2020 was designed to be flexible for adaptation to various countries and contexts around the world. Table 1 summarizes the six categories of knowledge areas in the CC2020 where competencies are required for all the disciplines (CE, CS, CSEC, IS, IT, and SE).

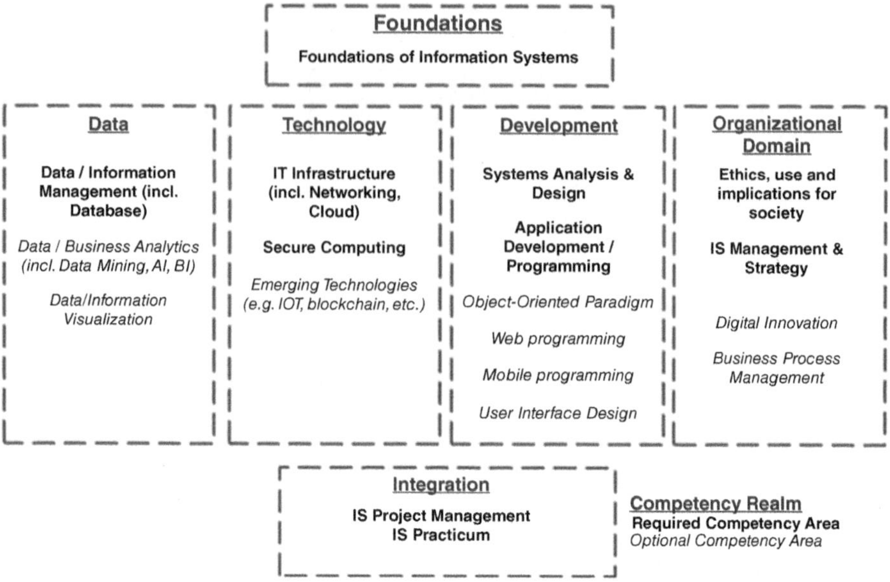

Fig. 3 IS2020 competency areas [18]

These areas are Users and Organizations, System Modeling, System Architecture and Infrastructure, Software Development, Software Fundamentals, and Hardware. The first area of Users and Organizations is the most relevant to social competencies, or soft skills. It emphasizes how users apply social, ethical, and professional practice as well as security policy and management in supporting the organization based on the job specification for which they were employed. For System Modeling, the employee develops models that help define concepts. The concepts are required in the business of developing and advancing IT and software development through job activities carried out daily. The support that the system architecture and infrastructure provide in the operation of systems requires regular overhauling. The Systems Architecture and Infrastructure area includes the technical competencies related to 4IR technologies such as Intelligent Systems, IoT, and embedded systems. These competencies require the support of other areas of software development, software fundamentals, and hardware in organizational activities.

3 Findings

The 20 articles reviewed in the SLR highlighted that an important competency for Computing graduates is digital skills, which relate to the ability of an individual to use any technology [28]. Without digital skills, employees cannot operate any systems that are required for executing tasks in the organization. The acquisition

Table 1 Knowledge areas and competencies for CC2020 [18]

Users and organizations	Systems modeling	Systems architecture and infrastructure	Software development	Software fundamentals	Hardware
Social issues and professional practice Security policy and management IS management and leadership Enterprise architecture Project management User experience design	Security issues and principles Systems analysis and design Requirements analysis and specifications Data and information management	Virtual systems and services Intelligent systems (AI) Internet-of-things Parallel and distributed computing Computer networks Embedded systems Integrated systems Technology Platform technologies Security technology and implementation	Software quality, verification, and validation Software process Software modeling and analysis Software design Platform-based development	Graphics and visualization Operating systems Data structures, algorithms, and complexity Programming languages Programming fundamentals Computing systems fundamentals	Architecture and organization Digital design Circuits and electronics Signal processing

of digital skills by all employees requires continuous training and exposure to computer systems. Digital skills help employees navigate any online workspace [7]. Related to this competency, cited as crucial for CS and IS graduates, is the interactive utilization of systems [29]. With this competency, graduates, having acquired the basic knowledge of Computing Sciences and IS, can effectively and efficiently accomplish tasks without needing any support from anyone in the organization. When employees collectively use technology amidst the application of their knowledge in the workspace, much work is achieved [30]. The complexity of the systems and the tasks that are required make it clear that the individual must be well-rooted in the relevant broad knowledge before its application and use.

The second technical competency required is that of fixing, operating, and maintaining the systems that provide solutions to an organization's operations [31]. IT graduates must also be able to possess competencies for the development of software [32]. Computational skills for problem solving are also crucial for software development [33]. The infiltration of data into society and organizations has necessitated the need to consider appropriate and high-quality curricula on data science in Computing Sciences and IT programs as well as those of other disciplines [34].

The application of soft skills and tacit knowledge by employees can help generate ideas to carry out certain tasks and support the organization. Tacit knowledge is knowledge hidden in the mind or brain [35]. The possession of soft skills enables employees to showcase their competencies where their tacit knowledge is unveiled based on finding solutions to critical problems. Creativity is often required for problem solving and is a key competency of ICT graduates, as are communication (written and oral) skills [13]. Social communicative skills are a key disposition used to interact with all the different stakeholders in different roles in the organization [14]. Cognitive and non-cognitive skills help the employee through proper knowledge application, usage, comprehension, and the development of information systems. Without critical and analytic articulation, employees do not have the competencies needed to solve a specific problem or make decisions in the organization. Cognitive and non-cognitive skills serve as basic knowledge of the application, usage, comprehension, and development of systems [36]. These competencies are crucial when dealing with information modeling, system comprehension, and task execution.

Attitude and willingness are important soft skills since IT staff should help reinvigorate their minds and willingness for self-dedication and selfless service in the organization so that their attitudes align with the goals of the organization [30]. Motivational skills are important for job performance and reflect the self-regulation, dedication, and commitment of the individual [37]. Traits such as willpower, and self-commitment are important for accomplishing tasks in the organization and for personal development [14]. Interpersonal skills and competencies are crucial and include the ability to interact well in social situations and relate well with people [38].

Collaborative and team competencies assist the employee to persevere in working with the team to achieve results even in pressured situations [13]. Working together as a team cannot be overlooked in the organization as it brings uniformity and the cross-fertilization of ideas. To enhance cooperativeness and collaboration, individuals must work together as team members, as the effort of one individual alone cannot bring success and growth to the organization [39]. There are few to no organizations that do not require competencies in teamwork, as without these competencies, it would be difficult to work or function outside your environment and with the people in the organization [40].

Sharing knowledge and brainstorming using soft skills are important for addressing critical problems experienced by CS students [27]. Other studies emphasize the competencies of collaborative learning [41] and quick uptake, which represent the ability to learn and understand easily [42]. The ability to network with people and make decisions is also considered a required competency [43]. Individuals with greater motivational competency [41] are not distracted from the tasks to which they are assigned, even though they might or could be preoccupied with other thoughts or reasonings. Therefore, it is important to develop skills of self-motivation irrespective of the complexity of the tasks assigned to the individuals in the organization.

4 Discussion and Implications of the Study

There is an increasing demand for the skills, knowledge, and dispositions (i.e., competencies) of Computing graduates to meet the needs of the 5IR. These graduates are crucial for organizations to remain relevant, digitally transformed, and human-centric organizations in the 5IR. Educators, therefore, need to design Computing curricula accordingly. The SLR identified competencies from various articles, particularly regarding soft skills. Cognitive and non-cognitive skills were highlighted as crucial in organizations to assist in their transformation, especially for tackling multifarious tasks that need adequate attention [30]. Communication and teamwork competencies are believed to provide value for all stakeholders, particularly in challenging situations where tolerance of one another is required. For employees to be responsive and adaptive in a digitized world, graduates must be able to work in teams, irrespective of the class of the individuals, their background, their knowledge levels, their skills, or their value systems. This teamwork would help to bridge the individual's ability to function adequately [13]. For employees to make a breakthrough in their endeavors, they need to be motivated, and that is why it is imperative to address issues of motivation among employees. Suitable motivational skills relate to self-regulation.

The implication of this chapter is that competencies are critical components through which results and value can be obtained, whether for a private or public organization or individual internal development. The importance of a competency-based approach that carefully considers dispositions or soft skills was highlighted by the goals of the CC2020 Computing Science curriculum, the IS2020 draft document as well as the reviewed literature. No individual or organization could survive the 5IR successfully without the development of the competencies of their employees and the recruitment of the graduates that they employ. One of the most important factors to reflect on is how employees use their diverse skills to solve personal and organizational problems. Becoming more effective and efficient in task accomplishment depends largely on the knowledge, skills, and disposition of employees. These competencies vary from one specific job or task to another and are also related to the exposure and training experienced.

The competencies identified in this chapter are significant since they can guide educators in designing appropriate curricula. If these graduates are not well prepared for employability in terms of acquiring the appropriate competencies to function, it will be difficult for them to progress in their careers. Another consideration for designers of Computing curricula is the influence of 4IR and 5IR on how employees develop and use these competencies to solve personal and organizational problems in the domain of ICT. These competencies can help employees distinguish their roles and opportunities for organizational growth. When evaluating employability, organizations would measure applicants by considering what they could contribute to quality service delivery, transformation, and organizational growth.

5 Conclusion

The findings established that competencies are key components through which employee tasks are accomplished in organizations. Without adequate competencies, employees would not have much effect in terms of adding value to the actualization of work performance. Curricula for Computing graduates need to be addressed in terms of developing graduates who are versatile, human centric, as well as technically savvy, and who can contribute to the goals of digitally transformed organizations. Competencies possessed by employees are believed to increase productivity, sustain prevailing capacity, generate new excellence, enable partnerships, encourage teamwork, and encourage articulation between stakeholders and management teams. It can be concluded that further effort is required to improve the curriculum design of Computing courses. The findings of this research can be used by educators and pedagogical designers to supplement the IS2020 and CC2020 projects, particularly when designing the soft skills or dispositions required in Computing programmes. A limitation of this research is that it was only exploratory, and limited studies were reviewed. However, it provided some insight into the competencies needed for 5IR-ready organizations. Additional research is required to investigate competency-based curricula that have been implemented in Computing programmes in different higher education institutions globally.

References

1. Allen, S. J. (2020). On the cutting edge of the chopping block? Fostering a digital mindset and tech literacy in business management education. *Journal of Management Education, 44*(3), 362–393.
2. Costa, D. G., & Peixoto, J. P. J. (2020). COVID-19 pandemic: A review of smart cities initiatives to face new outbreaks. *IET Smart Cities, 2*(2), 64–73.
3. Schwab, K. (2016). *The fourth industrial revolution*. World Economic Forum.
4. Xu, M., David, J. M., & Kim, S. H. (2018). The fourth industrial revolution: Opportunities and challenges. *International Journal of Financial Research, 9*(2), 90–95.
5. Noble, S. M., Mende, M., Grewal, D., & Parasuraman, A. (2022). The fifth industrial revolution: How harmonious human–machine collaboration is triggering a retail and service [r]evolution. *Journal of Retailing, 98*(2), 199–208.
6. Wessel, L., Baiyere, A., Ologeanu-Taddei, R., Cha, J., & Blegind-Jensen, T. (2021). Unpacking the difference between digital transformation and IT-enabled organizational transformation. *Journal of the Association for Information Systems, 22*(1), 102–129.
7. Vallo Hult, H., & Byström, K. (2021). Challenges to learning and leading the digital workplace. *Studies in Continuing Education, 44*(3), 1–15.
8. Alter, S. (2020). Making sense of smartness in the context of smart devices and smart systems. *Information Systems Frontiers, 22*(2), 381–393.
9. Van der Hoogen, A., Scholtz, B., & Calitz, A. P. (2021). Innovative digitalisation initiatives for smart communities and smart cities in a developing country. In *Resilience, entrepreneurship, and ICT* (pp. 57–78). Springer.
10. Hatziapostolou, T., Dranidis, D., Sotiriadou, A., Kefalas, P., Nikolakopoulos, I. (2018, July). An authentic student research experience: Fostering research skills and boosting the employability profile of students. In: Proceedings of the 23rd Annual ACM Conference on Innovation and Technology in Computer Science Education, pp. 254–259.
11. Gázquez, J. L. R., Delgado, M. V. B., Gras, J. J. O., Lova, J. G., Gómez, M. V. G., & Zbiec, M. (2021). Lack of skills, knowledge, and competences in higher education about industry 4.0 in the manufacturing sector. *Revista Iberoamericana de Educación a Distancia (RIED), 24*(1), 285–313.
12. Herbert, N., Herbert, D., Wapstra, E., Salas, K. D., & Acuña, T. (2021). Integrating the development of professional skills throughout an ICT curriculum improves a graduate's competency. In *Advances in software engineering, education, and e-learning* (pp. 55–67). Springer.
13. Loyalka, P., Liu, O. L., Li, G., Chirikov, I., Kardanova, E., Gu, L., & Tognatta, N. (2019). Computer science skills across China, India, Russia, and the United States. *Proceedings of the National Academy of Sciences, 116*, 6732–6736.
14. Topi, H., Karsten, H., Brown, S. A., Alvaro, J., Donnellan, B., Shen, J., & Thouin, M. F. (2017). MSIS 2016 global competency model for graduate degree programs in information systems. *Communications of the Association for Information Systems, 40*(18).
15. Dewi, P., & Fitrio, T. (2022). The role of adaptive millennial leadership, organizational culture, and competency as a strategy to increase employee performance. *Journal Aplikasi Management, 20*(3), 697–710.
16. Anning-Dorson, T. (2021). Organizational culture, and leadership as antecedents to organizational flexibility: Implications for SME competitiveness. *Journal of Entrepreneurship in Emerging Economies, 13*(5), 1309–1325.
17. Sabin, M., Impagliazzo, J., Alrumaih, H., Tang, C., & Zhang, M. (2018). IT2017 Report: Implementing a competency-based Information Technology program. In: Proceedings of the 49th ACM Technical Symposium on Computer Science Education, pp. 1045–1046.
18. Leidig, P., & Salmela, H. (2020). IS2020 a competency model for undergraduate programs in information systems: The joint ACM/AIS IS2020 task force.

19. Moher, D., Liberati, A., Tetzlaff, J., Altman, D. G., & The PRISMA Group. (2009). Preferred reporting items for systematic reviews and meta-analyses: The PRISMA statement. *PLoS Medicine, 6*(7).
20. Lindgren, B. M., Lundman, B., & Graneheim, U. H. (2020). Abstraction and interpretation during the qualitative content analysis process. *International Journal of Nursing Studies, 108*, 103632.
21. Clear, A., Parrish, A. S. Impagliazzo, J., & Zhang, M. (2019). Computing Curricula 2020: Introduction and community engagement. In: Proceedings of the 50th ACM Technical Symposium on Computer Science Education, pp. 653–654.
22. Impagliazzo, J., & Pears, A. N. (2018). The CC2020 project-computing curricula guidelines for the 2020s. In *2018 IEEE global engineering education conference (EDUCON)* (pp. 2021–2024). IEEE.
23. Clear, A., Clear, T., Vichare, A., Charles, T., Frezza, S., Gutica, M., & Szynkiewhich, J. (2020). Designing Computer Science competency statements: A process and curriculum model for the 21st century. In: Proceedings of the Working Group Reports on Innovation and Technology in Computer Science Education, pp. 211–246.
24. Barkhuizen, N. E., & Gumede, B. (2021). The relationship between talent management, job satisfaction and voluntary turnover intentions of employees in a selected government institution. *SA Journal of Human Resource Management, 19*, 12.
25. González-Morales, D., Moreno de Antonio, L. M., & Roda García, J. L. (2011). Teaching "soft" skills in Software Engineering. In: 2011 IEEE Global Engineering Education Conference (EDUCON) 2011, pp. 630–637.
26. Spencer, L. M., & Spencer, S. M. (1993). *Competence at work: Models for superior performance*. Wiley.
27. Milczarski, P., Podlaski, K., Hłobaż, A., Dowdall, S., Stawska, Z., & O'Reilly, D. (2021). Soft skills development in Computer Science students via multinational and multidisciplinary gamedev project. In: Proceedings of the 52nd ACM Technical Symposium on Computer Science Education, pp. 583–589.
28. Taylor-Smith, E., Smith, S., Fabian, K., Berg, T., Meharg, D., & Varey, A. (2019). Bridging the digital skill gap: Are Computing degree apprenticeships the answer? In: Proceedings of the 2019 ACM Conference on Innovation and Technology in Computer Science Education, pp. 126–132.
29. Kurniawan, F. S., Sariyatun, S., & Widyastono, H. (2022). The utilization of smartphones in the digital era as interactive learning tools for sociology lessons in high school. *Journal of International Conference Proceedings (JICP), 5*(1), 400–407.
30. Gholami, R., Nishant, R., & Emrouznejad, A. (2021). Modeling residential energy consumption: An application of IT-based solutions and big data analytics for sustainability. *Journal of Global Information Management (JGIM), 29*(2), 166–193.
31. Puspitasari, I., & Jie, F. (2020). Making the information technology-business alignment works: A framework of IT-based competitive strategy. *International Journal of Business Information Systems, 34*(1), 59–82.
32. Abrahamsson, P., Salo, O., Ronkainen, J., & Warsta, J. (2017). Agile software development methods: Review and analysis. arXiv preprint.
33. Emara, M., Hutchins, N. M., Grover, S., Snyder, C., & Biswas, G. (2021). Examining student regulation of collaborative, computational, problem-solving processes in open-ended learning environments. *Journal of Learning Analytics, 8*(1), 49–74.
34. Daniel, B., Kumar, V., & Omar, N. (2018). Postgraduate conception of research methodology: Implications for learning and teaching. *International Journal of Research & Method in Education, 41*(2), 220–236.
35. Schrijver, L. (2021). Introduction: Tacit knowledge, architecture, and its underpinnings).
36. Islam, M. A. (2021). Effects of cognitive and non-cognitive skills on employment conditions of the tertiary graduates. *Journal of Service Science and Management, 14*, 530–539.

37. Ruthotto, I., Kreth, Q., & Melkers, J. (2021). Entering or advancing in the IT labour market: The role of an online graduate degree in computer science. *The Internet and Higher Education, 51*, 100820.
38. Charleston, L. J. (2022). STEMfluences: The role of social interaction and scientific identity formation in the successful matriculation of African American males in STEM. In *Young, gifted and missing* (Vol. 25, pp. 53–72). Emerald Publishing Limited.
39. Buchner, J., & Kerres, M. (2021). Students as designers of augmented reality: Impact on learning and motivation in computer science. *Multimodal Technologies and Interaction, 5*(8), 41.
40. Kollee, C., Magenheim, J., Nelles, W., Rhode, T., Schaper, N., Schubert, S., & Stechert, P. (2009). Computer science education and key competencies. In: 9th IFIP World Conference on Computers in Education (WCCE).
41. Yadav, A., Mayfield, C., Moudgalya, S. K., Kussmaul, C., & Hu, H. H. (2021). Collaborative learning, self-efficacy, and student performance in CS1 POGIL. In: Proceedings of the 52nd ACM Technical Symposium on Computer Science Education, pp. 775–781.
42. Teodorescu, M. H., Morse, L., Awwad, Y., & Kane, G. C. (2021). Failures of fairness in automation require a deeper understanding of human-ML augmentation. *MIS Quarterly, 45*(3).
43. Novak, A., Bennett, D., & Kliestik, T. (2021). Product decision-making information systems, real-time sensor networks, and artificial intelligence driven big data analytics in sustainable industry 4.0. *Economics, Management & Financial Markets, 16*(2), 62–72.

Developing an Automated Core Rolling Machine for the Metering Unit's Current Transformer

Rebecca Magomere, Michael Kisangiri, and Silas Mirau

1 Introduction

1.1 Background Introduction

Electricity is the most valuable commodity for socioeconomic and technological advancement. It is simply defined as the flow of charges that can be generated from a multitude of sources, including coal, natural gas, nuclear fission reaction, sunlight, wind, and hydropower. In the United Republic of Tanzania, 45% of electricity produced is generated from hydropower, which produces a large amount of electricity around 1605.86 MW per year [1].

Concerning its uses, electricity can be used for domestic, commercial, or industrial purposes and so, the amount of electricity that reaches the destination is never equal. Determining the source and type of electricity as well as the amount of electricity entering a certain destination is important to prevent downtime and revenue losses caused by electrical power quality events. This can be done by measuring the electrical current using electrical meters provided by the power company. The electric meters differ due to different amounts of electricity in destinations. The electric current of low voltage can be measured using the Amp meter. However, the electrical current of high voltage is measured by using metering units.

The metering unit is composed of two types of transformers which are the Current Transformer (CT) and the Potential Transformer (PT). Potential transformers (PTs) also known as Voltage Transformers (VTs), are used to convert low primary

R. Magomere (✉) · M. Kisangiri · S. Mirau
The School of Computational and Communication Science and Engineering, (CoCSE), The Nelson Mandela African Institution of Science and Technology (NMAIST), Arusha, Tanzania
e-mail: rmagomerer@nm-aist.ac.tz

J. Marx Gómez et al. (eds.), *Smart and Secure Embedded and Mobile Systems*,
Progress in IS, https://doi.org/10.1007/978-3-031-56603-5_37

voltages to the standard 120Vac that most metering devices require as an input voltage signal. Furthermore, PTs are primarily used in a power system to measure high alternating voltage [2]. The current Transformer (CT) is an electrical device that transforms high current to low current and is used to monitor high-voltage lines that connect national power grids [3]. A CT is intended to generate an alternating current in its secondary winding that is proportional to the current measured in its primary winding.

The first stage of CT development involves rolling the core steel to the required dimensions which are inner diameter, plate width, outer diameter, and radial build. After core rolling, the next process is winding the rolled core where the copper wire is used to wind up the rolled core then assembling three current transformers and a potential transformer to make one metering unit.

A quality metering unit lies on the well-made CT's core [4]. As stated above, the core of the metering unit is made by rolling the core steel which is composed of 3% of silicon and 97% of ferromagnetic iron. When rolling the core, the material is not supposed to be scratched and all dimensions have to be exact no gap should be left in circles to avoid failure of the metering unit.

1.2 Problem Statement

Most of the tested metering units at TANELEC have failed to reach the targeted class/quality due to inaccurate dimensions and mechanical imbalance of the rolled core as illustrated in Fig. 1. Consequently, the metering unit is returned for correction during the testing phase which makes the person in charge disassemble the whole metering unit to correct the dimensions of the CT core. This is due to mechanical imbalance which can operate in normal conditions, with faults being uncommon but later resulting in faults in the future [5]. All this is because of the current core rolling process which is manual and tiresome and has made an industry fail to reach the targeted goal of metering units' production per week as shown in Fig. 2. The process also is very dangerous specifically, this is because the endings of the core material used are too sharp hence, they can injure the person rolling it.

In this background, the study conducted focused on automating the core rolling process by ensuring the core of CT is perfect by having accurate dimensions and mechanically balanced. The study also focused on helping TANELEC to meet their customers' demands on time and ensuring the safety of their workers.

1.3 Rationale of the Study

For an industry to win the market, it has to reach customers' demands by delivering the perfect products to customers on time. It has been established that the goal of TANELEC is to manufacture 25 metering units per week whereby in each metering

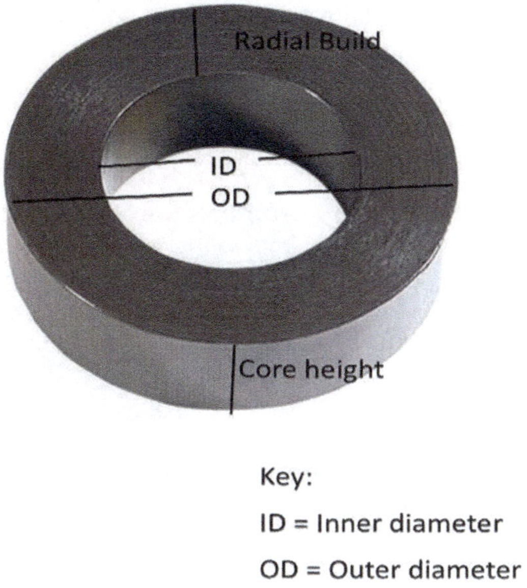

Fig. 1 The ready-made core of the current transformer

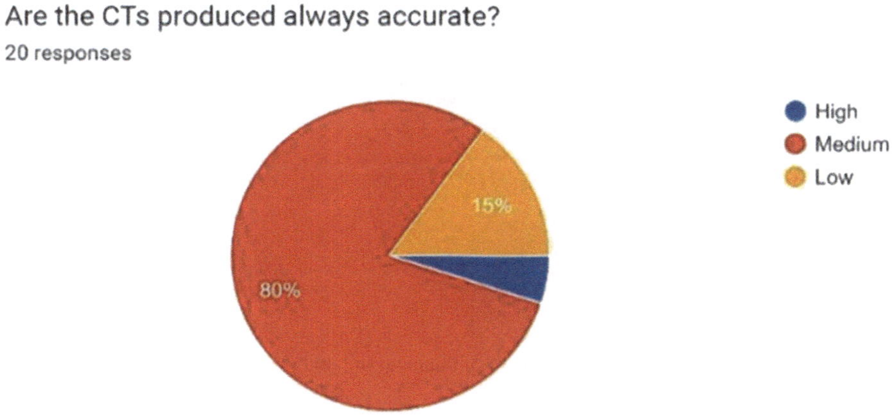

Fig. 2 The responses showing the accuracy of CT produced at TANELEC

unit of three-phase, three CTs are required. Surprisingly, currently, the industry is manufacturing up to ten metering units per week which are away from its goal as indicated in Fig. 3. That means each day, six CTs are manufactured and so only two metering units are made.

The presence of gaps in the core of the transformer causes vibration of the current transformer, especially when the metering unit is used and hence overheats which leads to an explosion of the metering unit. So, for the metering unit to work well, all dimensions have to be accurate and no gap should be in the circles of the rolled core.

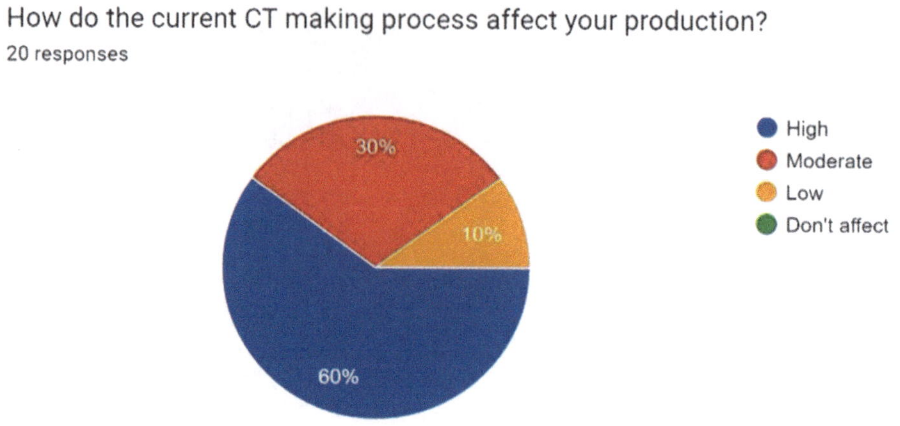

Fig. 3 The responses showing the effects of the manual process on the production of CT

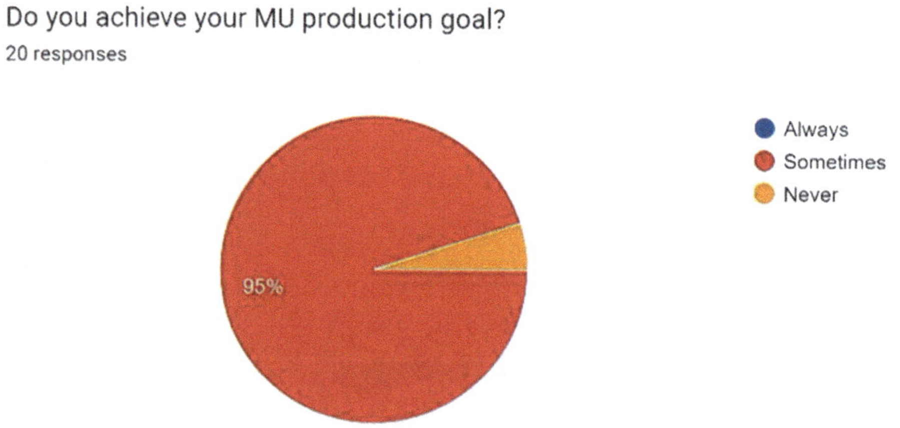

Fig. 4 The responses showing achievement of the metering unit production goal

The core steel used to make CT has a sharp end and it may injure the person rolling it. When a worker is injured, an industry has to work on his treatment. This is because of the current process of making the core of the current transformers (Fig. 4).

2 Literature Survey

2.1 Related Work

Electricity costs in manufacturing have traditionally been considered an overhead cost and have risen dramatically in the manufacturing industry over the last decade, and they can no longer be considered an overhead but rather a valuable resource that must be handled smartly. This is accomplished by collecting data on energy consumed strategically through metering and monitoring. In the context of manufacturing systems, this keynote paper discussed the most recent developments and challenges in electricity metering and monitoring systems and standards [6].

Metering is how the service provided by the Company to the consumer is quantified and measured. The metering unit thus plays a crucial role in the billing of electricity to the consumer. It has therefore been referred to as the "Cash Register" of the company correctly in the interest of fairness to both the Company service provider and the consumer where metering accuracies concern all. Large Power Users (LPUs) have high kVA demand and consume a colossal amount of energy. They are the prominent source of revenue generation. Absolute care must be taken to block all possible sources leading to high Non-Technical Loss [7]. So, the metering unit used to measure electricity in big farms is to be perfect to avoid losses and other electrical dangers. This is well ensured during the manufacturing of the metering unit. This means the metering unit should not have mechanical imbalance which will cause a vibration of the metering unit hence overheating which leads to an explosion of the metering unit.

In recent years, the trends in industrial advancements have been toward digitization. This is due to a variety of factors, including increased accuracy and fewer human errors. The developed system has been implemented in real time. Currently, a manual approach used to roll the core steel of the metering unit's current transformer is slower and more dangerous which takes more time and requires more labor. The automated core rolling machine for the metering unit's CT's main goal is to roll and cut the required core into specified dimensions and required quality. Through this, the industry can meet customers' demands on time with perfect products.

In this industrial era, a lot of work is done on sheet metal to achieve a better surface finish and a high degree of flexibility in the production processes in the industries. Sheet metal is cut and bent into a variety of shapes to ensure adequate demand. In this review, the author is reviewing the previous sheet metal work in which the cutting and bending of sheets were investigated under various conditions. The author suggested pneumatic sheet cutting machines as the most advanced technology to create sheet cutting and bending a quick and easy process [8].

In most small-scale sheet metal industries, sheet metal cutting machines are relied on. The sheet metal cutting machine is primarily a hand-operated machine used in medium and small-scale industries. The goal of this study was to design and develop an automatic sheet metal cutting machine that will save time and money. With the help of a solenoid valve, control timing unit, proximity sensor, and microcontroller, automation in sheet metal cutting machines was implemented [9].

Sheet metal is formed into thin, flat pieces that can be cut and bent into a variety of shapes for use in metalworking. Sheet metal made of iron and other magnetically conductive materials, also known as laminated steel cores, is used in transformers and electric machines. The layout consists of three main procedures. There are three of them: parallel, radial, and triangulation. The primary goal of this study was to investigate the pneumatic control system, double-acting cylinders, the benefits of pneumatic hand-operated valves, and the high-speed blade [10].

Metal detection systems are widely used in a variety of industries for a variety of applications, including segregation. The Arduino Uno microcontroller is used to create a metal detection system for sorting purposes in this project [11]. The goal of this study was to investigate the performance of a metal recognition system using an inductive proximity sensor.

2.2 *Research Gap*

Most of the work done presented the mechanical way of simplifying the process of rolling and cutting metals and wires. This study aimed at automating the whole process of rolling the core steel into the specified dimension at TANELEC during the manufacturing of the current transformer for a metering unit.

The main objective of this study is to develop an Automated Core Roller Machine for Metering Unit's Current Transformer.

3 Results and Discussion

3.1 *Results*

3.1.1 Proposed System

Recognizing the need for an advanced way of producing the current transformers at TANELEC, it was envisaged that the system should be developed that will help the industry reach its goal of metering unit production and reaching a customer's demand on time. This is based on the fact that the automated system performs the CT rolling process at a speed faster than the speed of a person. Additionally, the safety of a person who is rolling the CT core will be highly ensured. More importantly, the dimensions of CT cores will be accurate and hence, reduce the disturbance of disassembling the completed metering units that were found with a fault.

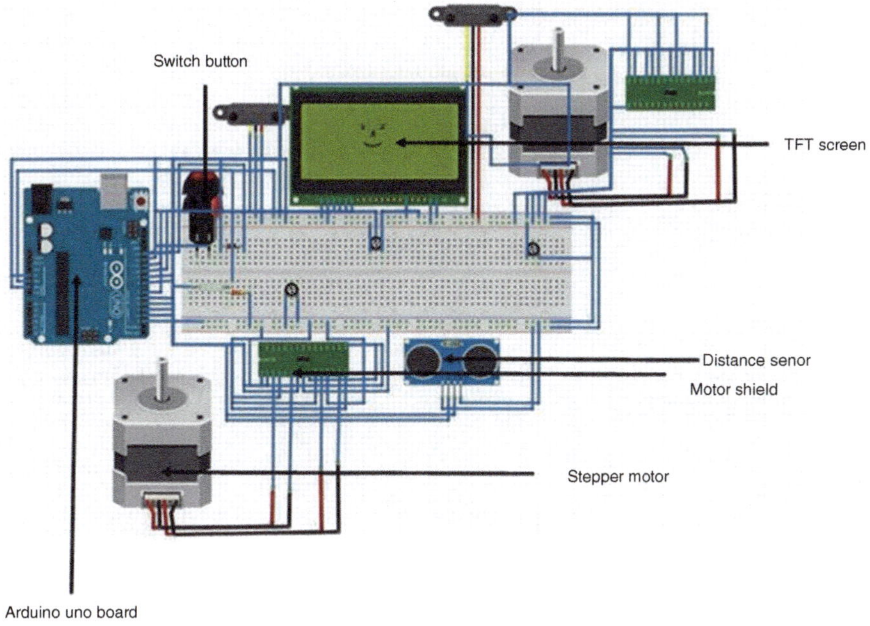

Fig. 5 Breadboard circuit diagram of the developed system

3.1.2 System Description

The system is built on an Arduino UNO board as illustrated in Fig. 5 and it comprises a switch button for switching on and off the machine, and a reed switch that senses the presence of the material to be rolled. The system also comprises of TFT screen that provides a good interaction between the user and the machine. The screen displays an important notification to the user which includes warning alerts like when the material inserted into the machine is not required, prompts from the machine, and the progress of the work. The system has a stepper motor that actuates the roller to perform a rolling process, and keypads that allow the user to insert different commands like the dimensions of the required core, and the number of the cores to be rolled (Fig. 6).

3.1.3 System Performance

An extensive review of the performance of the developed system was performed to compare the speed and accuracy of the developed prototype with the manual operation as shown in Table 1. Sufficient evidence was found which concluded that

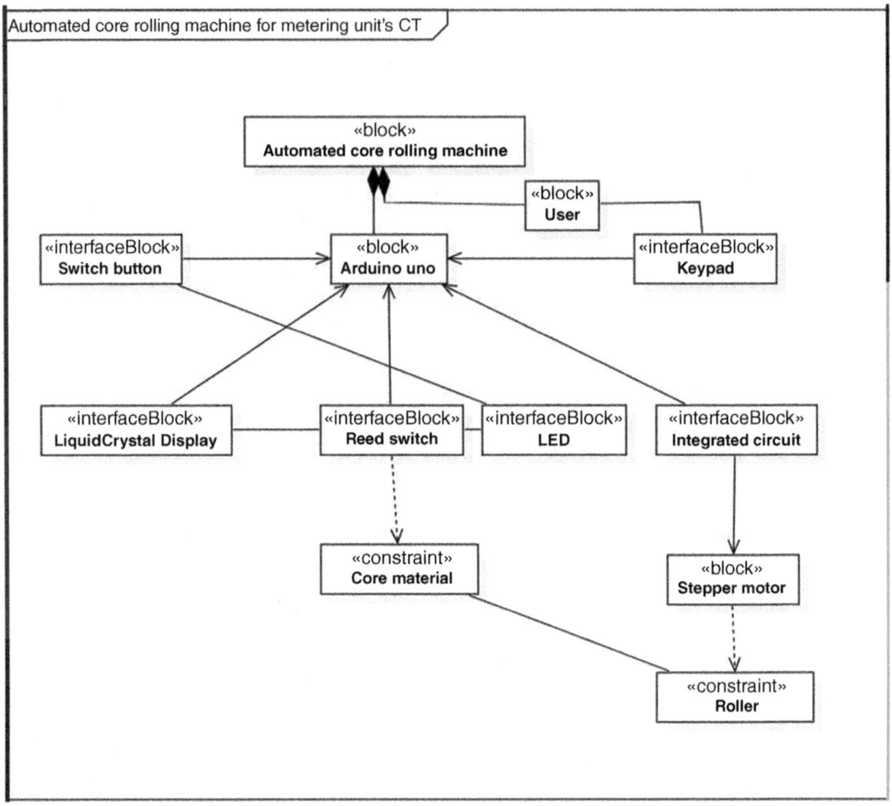

Fig. 6 Block definition diagram

Table 1 Performance comparison between the testing results of the manual way and the developed way of making CT

No.	Testing parameter	Manual way	Developed system
1.	Speed per 2 hours	1 core	120 cores
2.	Accuracy	< 75	>85
3.	Safety	<65	>90

the Automated core rolling machine for the metering unit's current transformer will advance the production of metering units at TANELEC as illustrated in Fig. 7.

3.2 *Discussion*

The developed system can roll 60 cores per hour which increases the rate of production of metering units in the industry and can make the industry grow its market. The system also reduces the mechanical imbalances that could cause an explosion of the metering unit at the site. Also, it reduces the risks that the worker

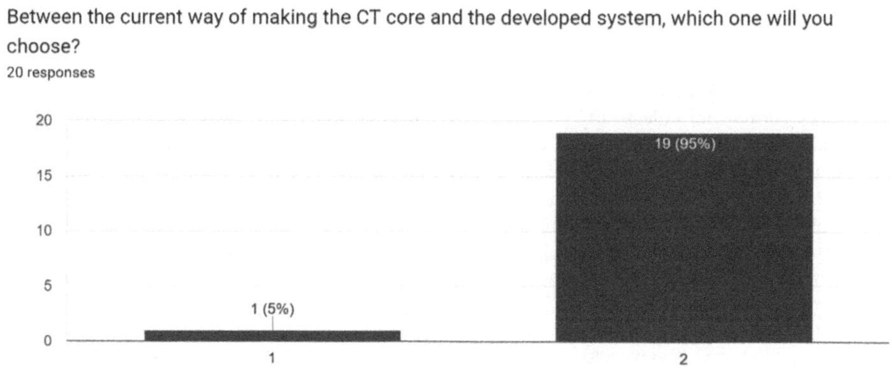

Fig. 7 Responses showing the acceptance of the developed system

could get during rolling because of the sharp ends of the material since the process of rolling will be done by the machine.

4 Conclusion and Future Work

The automation process in an industry is very important for the economic growth of the industry. It is applied to simplify difficult work and take the risks of dangerous processes which, a human being could encounter if he could be doing it by himself. The implementation of this project is one of the applications of Embedded systems in industries. The developed system has seemed to increase the production of the metering units at TANELEC while ensuring the safety of the workers. It has also resulted in the accuracy of the rolling process and has reduced the time for rolling. So, the TANELEC industry can increase the metering units' production and hence meet the customers' demands on time. By using the developed system, the industry can also maximize its profit and win over its competitors in the market of metering unit production compared to the manual system.

For future work, the machine can be made able to insert the material and create tension by itself and be able to cut material when the rolling process of one core is done. In addition, the process of locking the completed core and removing the rolled core can be advanced to reduce human interaction with the system.

Acknowledgments We are gratefully acknowledging the contributions of Eng. Patrick Kivanda, TANELEC, and NM-AIST toward the successful implementation of this work.

References

1. Kichonge, B., Mkilaha, I. S. N., John, G. R., & Hameer, S. (2016). The economics of renewable energy sources into electricity generation in Tanzania. *Journal of Energy, 2016*, 1–8. https://doi.org/10.1155/2016/5837154
2. Bera, S. C., & Kole, D. N. (2009). Study of a modified design of a potential transformer. *S e n s o r s & T r a n s d u c e r s, 105*(6), 56–65.
3. Hassan Mir, S. (2019). Review on smart electric metering system based on GSM/IOT. *Asian Journal of Electrical Sciences, 8*(1), 1–6. https://doi.org/10.51983/ajes-2019.8.1.2340
4. Irwin, L. A. (2010). A high accuracy standard for electricity meters. In *2010 IEEE PES Transm. Distrib. Conf. Expo. Smart Solut. A Chang*. World. https://doi.org/10.1109/TDC.2010.5484291
5. Zhang, T., et al. (2022). Intelligent fault diagnosis of machines with small & imbalanced data: A state-of-the-art review and possible extensions. *ISA Transactions, 119*(March), 152–171. https://doi.org/10.1016/j.isatra.2021.02.042
6. Kara, S. (2011). Glocalized solutions for sustainability in manufacturing. In Glocalized Solut. Sustain. Manuf., pp. 3–4. https://doi.org/10.1007/978-3-642-19692-8.
7. Blokland, P. (2019, June). Tanesco Distribution Engineering Instruction Manual. *Plannng*, Des. Constr. Good, pp. 1–174.
8. Gafer, A. E., & Said, K. M. A. (2019). Intelligent plc system to control wire cutting machine. *International Journal of Engineering Applied Sciences and Technology, 03*(11), 35–38. https://doi.org/10.33564/ijeast.2019.v03i11.007
9. Bharath, R. M. S., Gopal, A., James, I. M., & Sankar, S. L. (2020). Design and development of automatic sheet metal cutting machine. In *AIP Conference Proceedings* (Vol. 2311). AIP Publishing. https://doi.org/10.1063/5.0034349
10. Barman, K., Ali, N., Pulp, M., & Limited, P. M. (2017, December). ICMERE2017-PI-108.
11. Study of metal detection system performance using inductive proximity sensor (Manufacturing) (Hons.) (2020, July). Universiti Teknologi Mara (Uitm), no. July.

Blockchain-Based Crowdfunding Charity Platform

Prithivi Rao Appadoo and Roopesh Kevin Sungkur

1 Introduction

Crowdfunding is the technique of supporting a project or business by acquiring small sums of money from a large number of individuals, generally over the Internet in modern times. Crowdfunding has been around for hundreds of years in several ways but only gained popularity on the internet within the arts and music communities. Crowdfunding has drastically altered the strategy of financing and offers the chance for start-ups to raise funds without much effort and paperwork. However, the system has been discovered to contain some risks and flaws. The beginnings and rising popularity of crowdfunding during the last decade was represented and promoted by the spread of thousands of online crowdfunding platforms throughout the world [1]. One of the main problems in the existing system is that it is centralized meaning that it is run under one central authority and little to no transparency is provided when the transactions are executed under that central authority which leads to a lack of trust and credibility between funders and fundraiser [2]. Additionally, the authenticity of transactions is of utmost importance which can be used as proof of payment and with the central authority, there is no actual statement of the online transaction [3].

In an existing crowdfunding process, information like contract, shareholder list, or other kinds of information are kept on a crowdfunding platform. Within the centralized crowdfunding, there is the involvement of three main parties which are the funders, fundraising, and crowdfunding platform. The bank is the fourth party which acts as a passive member for deposit of cash. Crowdfunding platforms take a percentage out of the funds transferred to fundraisers as a profit. The two

P. R. Appadoo · R. K. Sungkur (✉)
Department of Software and Information Systems, Faculty of Information, Communication and Digital Technologies, University of Mauritius, Reduit, Mauritius
e-mail: r.sungkur@uom.ac.mu

J. Marx Gómez et al. (eds.), *Smart and Secure Embedded and Mobile Systems*,
Progress in IS, https://doi.org/10.1007/978-3-031-56603-5_38

most common funding options adopted by crowdfunding platforms are the "all or nothing" or "keep it all" model. The "all or nothing" model (AON) is implemented on most platforms. This model implies that the target funding must be reached for the project to start out otherwise the funders get back to their investment. Even though the contemporary crowdfunding system has a decentralized nature as compared to the traditional approach of fundraising, most project campaigns are centralized, and therefore controlled by a massive intermediary stand-in as the dependable third party accountable for matching funders and fundraisers [4]. With the implementation of blockchain, the intermediaries are not needed and also the method is innovated with the employment of cryptocurrencies.

2 Literature Review

2.1 *Crowdfunding*

Crowdfunding is described as "efforts by individual entrepreneurs or organizations to fund their projects by soliciting modest donations from large groups of people over the internet without the use of traditional financial intermediaries" [5], or "open calls, mostly on the Internet, for the allocation of financial resources, either as a donation or in return for a future product or some type of reward, to support projects for specified causes" [6]. Crowdfunding is a concept where a group of individuals, known as a crowd, can contribute to a common cause or business they wish to support. The main medium for conducting crowdfunding events is the Internet.

2.2 *Crowdfunding Types*

The different types of crowdfunding are highlighted in the section below [7].

1. Donation-based crowdfunding

Donation-based crowdfunding is a part of crowdfunding whereby a contribution is offered without anticipating any financial gain. Most contributors donate to this type of crowdfunding event as a result of their belief within the cause. Charity and Non-Governmental Organizations (NGOs) use donation-based platforms as mediators to focus on a bigger audience. As an example, several families have benefited from these platforms during the COVID-19 pandemic.

2. Reward-based crowdfunding

Reward-based, also referred to as seed, crowdfunding is the funding of small businesses for the financial needs of several individuals without gaining financial benefits, in return, they acquire products or services. The danger of damages to the business is reduced rather than receiving a financial payoff, the contributors are given the position of spokesperson and ambassadors of the products while receiving products or services.

3. Investment crowdfunding

Investment crowdfunding involves funding of several investors to finance small or startup companies to profit from debt-based or equity-based investments or maybe both. The equity investors are paid off to achieve full ownership and increase income.

4. Crowdlending

Crowdlending is a platform that permits individuals and business firms to acquire a sum from a bunch of people at a fixed interest rate which is at a low percentage. The poor and low-income customers are not neglected because of their financial status and also obtain the facility of a loan.

2.3 Blockchain

Blockchains are anti-tampering and anti-fraud digital ledgers implemented without a central database and a central authority like a bank or company most of the time. They permit transactions of a gaggle of users to be recorded in a shared ledger within that community in order that once published, no changes may be made to the transaction. The popularity of the blockchain technology arose substantially in 2009 through the launch of the first of many modern cryptocurrencies referred to as the Bitcoin network [8]. In view of the fact that Bitcoin was pseudonymous, meaning that users remain unknown but not their account identifiers and every one of their transactions, trust was of great significance.

2.4 Smart Contracts

Alharby and Moorsel [9] stated that a smart contract is a piece of executable code that runs on the blockchain and is used to facilitate, carry out, and enforce the conditions of an agreement between untrusted parties. The principal purpose of a smart contract is to execute the terms of an agreement only when the predefined rules are met. Unlike traditional contracts, smart contracts do not require a third party for execution and enforcement of the terms of an agreement thus lowering the transaction fees.

2.5 Integration of Blockchain and Crowdfunding

Crowdfunding can be substantially improved through the adaptation of blockchain technology. An alternative to a platform that collects donations and distributes them to campaign runners is to use a decentralized platform that administers the funds from donors and, if the campaign is successful, distributes them to the fundraisers or, in other cases, returns the payment to the donors [4]. Additionally, the reach of crowdfunding platforms can be exponentially increased with blockchain technology because of the protection of the rights of investors and accessibility that is provided by digital or smart contracts. The trust and credibility between funders and fundraisers can be gained on the crowdfunding platform with the transparency of the blockchain technology which is incredibly crucial for the success of the campaign and platform itself [10]. Additionally, double spending will be prevented as each verified transaction is unique. Furthermore, the placement of shareholders is not important, they can be from different parts of the globe as shareholders can use e-voting, which is a feature in blockchain, to make decisions. Through the traceability feature, the prospect of identifying black money and money laundering will be increased. In all aspects, blockchain technology-based crowdfunding can bring more discipline to this innovative and more effective form of crowdfunding [11].

2.6 Critical Appraisal of Existing Blockchain-Based Platforms

Nowadays, blockchain is being implemented in a lot of existing systems in numerous fields like education, finance, and health. Concerning blockchain-based crowdfunding platforms, the ones shown in Table 1 are the foremost common ones.

Table 1 Comparative study of existing Blockchain-based crowdfunding platforms

	Swarm	Whirl	Lighthouse
Ease of use	Very good (quick navigation and understanding of the platform)	Quite good (takes some time to be familiar with the platform)	Quite good (takes some time to be familiar with the platform)
Customer reach	Widely available (due to bitcoin technology)	Very wide (socially driven platform)	Widely available (due to bitcoin technology)
Customer support	Pretty helpful	Very helpful	Not very helpful
Non-profit currency	N/A	Karma points	N/A
Cryptocurrency	SWM (Swarmcoin)	ADA (Cardano), BCH (Bitcoin Cash), BTC (Bitcoin), DASH (Dash), EOS (EOS), ETH (Ethereum), KICK (KickCoin), LTC (Litecoin), USDT (Tether)	BTC (bitcoin)
Platform	Bitcoin technology	Ethereum blockchain	Bitcoin technology

3 Proposed Solution

3.1 System Architecture

Figure 1 describes the architecture of the proposed system and how each component works together. Users have to login first to gain access to the website. The programming language for the front-end is React.js and for the backend is Solidity for the smart contracts. The whole system is developed on Visual Studio code.

3.2 Description of System

The blockchain-based crowdfunding system comprises three main parts that work together using the blockchain technology. Even though it is one system altogether, these components can be easily identifiable. These include the Contribution System, the Creation System, and the Blockchain System. It must also be noted that in this system, any user can act as an administrator that creates a campaign and only he/she gets the administrator features for that particular campaign. The whole system is a web-based application. The system is connected to metamask which is the link between the website and the Ethernet network. Users must have an Ethereum account and they must login to their account on metamask to get access to the crowdfunding website.

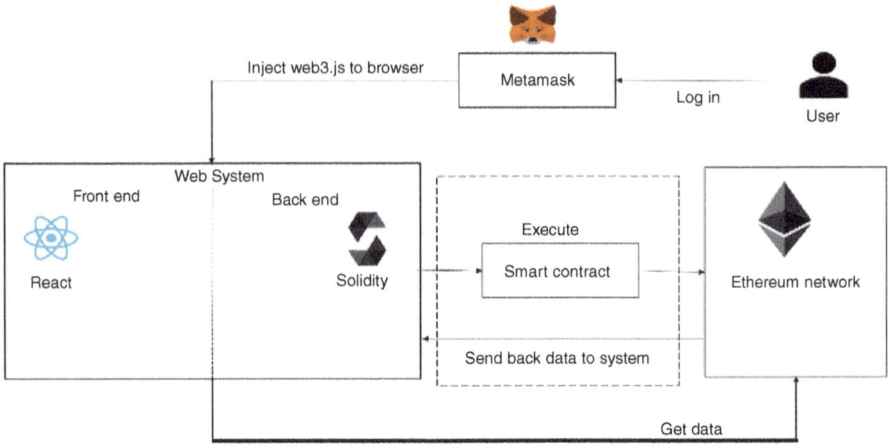

Fig. 1 Architecture of proposed system

3.2.1 The Contribution

Upon successful login on metamask, users will get access to the website where the user can browse through the campaigns and can fund their desired campaign directly on the homepage itself. Another way for contributing is by viewing each campaign for further details where the user can make his/her contributions and look at more information about the campaign and contributions.

3.2.2 The Creation

For this part also the user has to login on metamask which stores private keys to get access to the system where he/she has to click on the create button for a new campaign. Then the user has to fill in details about the campaign and complete the process where a new block will be created. Also, a user cannot contribute to a campaign that he/she has created (Figs. 2 and 3).

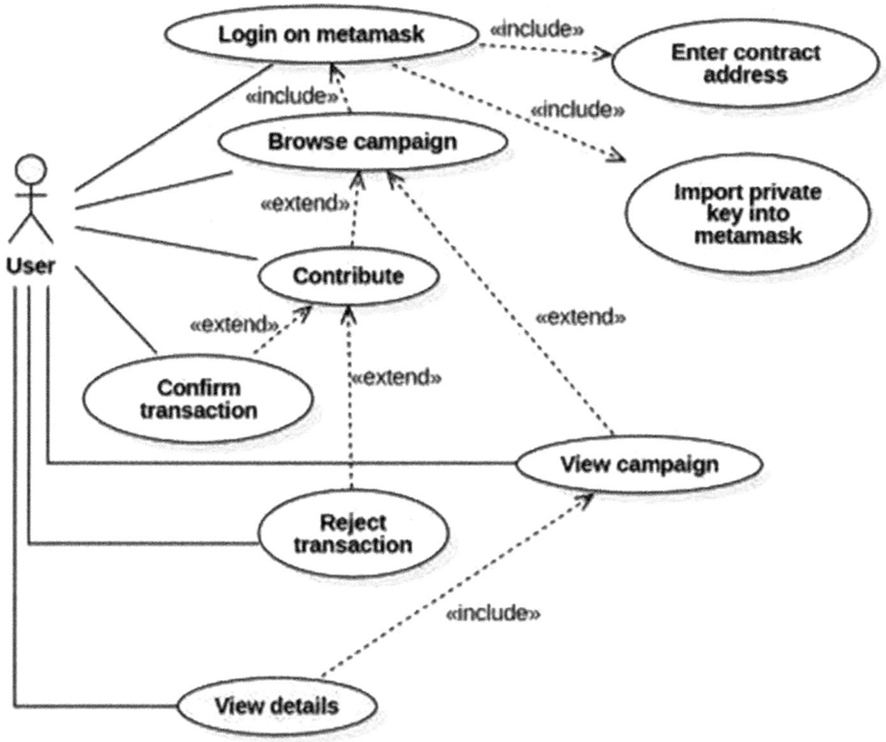

Fig. 2 Use case for contribution

3.2.3 The Blockchain

The functions of the client applications are described in the previous two subsections but in the background is the core of the system which is the blockchain along with its processes. Whenever a user creates a campaign, the details are stored in a block in the blockchain and later the system fetches those details to display them. Additionally, transactions are done using blockchain technology and the information about the contributions are stored on the network (Fig. 4).

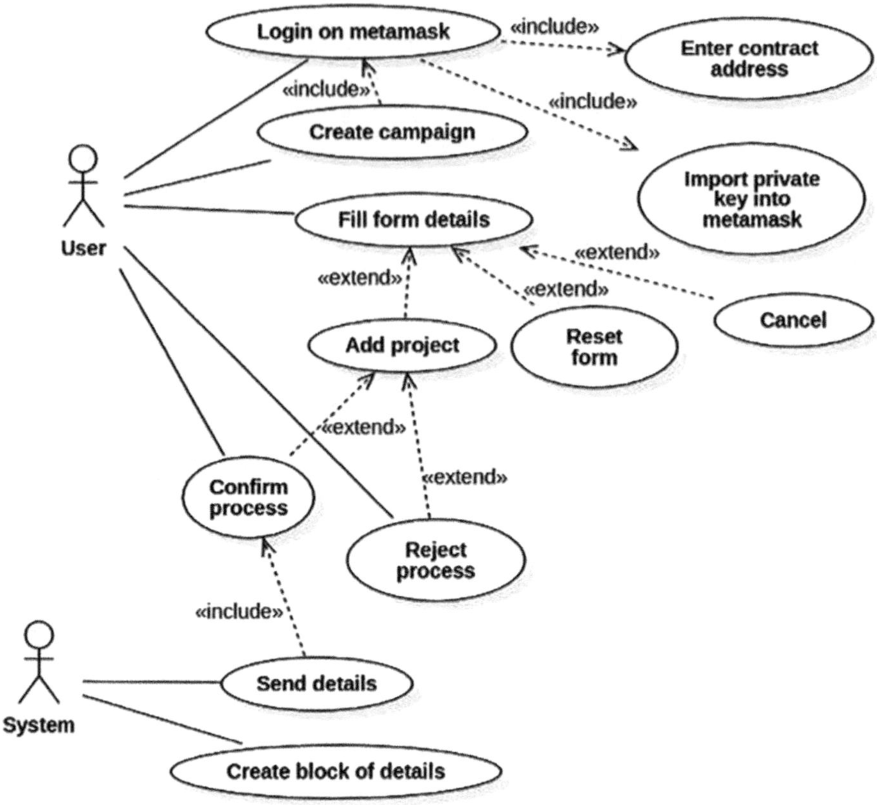

Fig. 3 Use case for campaign creation

4 Implementation and Results

4.1 Implementation Interfaces

This section describes some of the interfaces and features of the proposed system (Fig. 5).

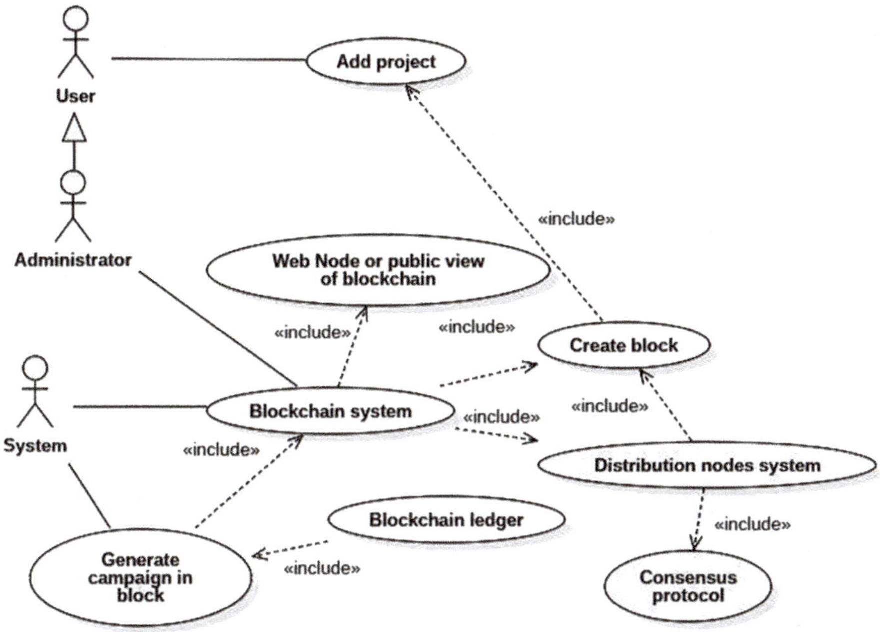

Fig. 4 Use case for blockchain

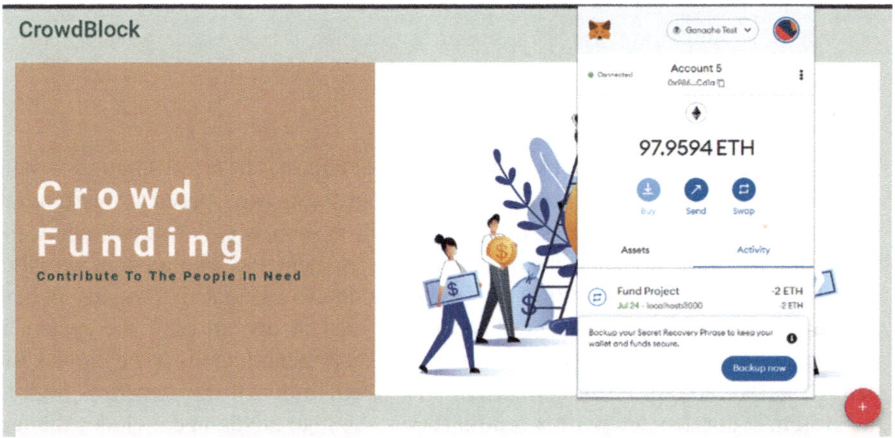

Fig. 5 Homepage of system

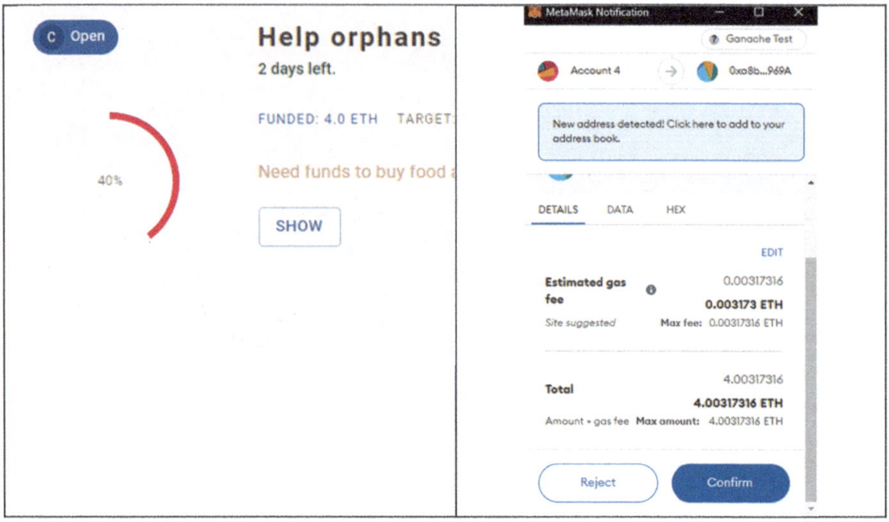

(a) (b)

Fig. 6 (**a**). Help orphans campaign and (**b**) User confirmation transactions

Figure 6(a) shows a campaign "Help Orphans," percentage of funds collected and Fig. 6(b) shows the user confirmation transactions.

5 Conclusion

The aim of this research was to develop a blockchain-based crowdfunding system that would address the inherent limitations of existing web-based crowdfunding applications. A Blockchain-based crowdfunding system was developed using the Ethereum network and this brought a number of benefits. The system provides transparency by allowing everyone to view the details of contributors and is both politically and physically decentralized so the cost of operation of the system is pretty much insignificant. Every transaction is secured and needs to be signed and verified before adding to the blockchain. The availability of the system is high as the system is not dependent on a central server. Another advantage includes the fact that the system can be used anywhere in the world as long as they have an internet connection and an Ethereum account. Future works include the addition of several different cryptocurrencies thus allowing a greater range of users to use the website.

References

1. Shneor, R., Zhao, L., & Flåten, B. (2020). *Advances in crowdfunding*. Springer International Publishing: Imprint: Palgrave Macmillan. https://doi.org/10.1007/978-3-030-46309-0
2. Nguyen, L. T. Q., Hoang, T. G., Do, L. H., Ngo, X. T., Nguyen, P. H. T., Nguyen, G. D. L., & Nguyen, G. N. T. (2021). The role of blockchain technology-based social crowdfunding in advancing social value creation. *Technological Forecasting and Social Change, 170*, 120898. https://doi.org/10.1016/j.techfore.2021.120898. ISSN 0040-1625.
3. Madaan, L., Jindal, D., Kumar, A., Kumar, S., & Naruka, M. S. (2022). Secure and enhanced crowdfunding solution using Blockchain technology. In F. Al-Turjman, S. P. Yadav, M. Kumar, V. Yadav, & T. Stephan (Eds.), *Transforming management with AI, big-data, and IoT*. Springer. https://doi.org/10.1007/978-3-030-86749-2_17
4. Righi, R., Alberti, A., & Singh, M. (2020). Blockchain technology for Industry 4.0. Blockchain secure, decentralized, distributed and trusted industry environment. https://doi.org/10.1007/978-981-15-1137-0.
5. Mollick, E. (2014). The dynamics of crowdfunding: An exploratory study. *Journal of Business Venturing, 29*(1), 1–16. https://doi.org/10.1016/j.jbusvent.2013.06.005
6. Belleflamme, P., Omrani, N., & Peitz, M. (2015). The economics of crowdfunding platforms. *Information Economics and Policy, 33*(C), 11–28. https://doi.org/10.1016/j.infoecopol.2015.08.003
7. Böckel, A., Hörisch, J., & Tenner, I. (2021). A systematic literature review of crowdfunding and sustainability: Highlighting what really matters. *Management Review Quarterly, 71*, 433–453. https://doi.org/10.1007/s11301-020-00189-3
8. Beck, R. (2018). Beyond bitcoin: The rise of Blockchain world. *Computer, 51*(2), 54–58. https://doi.org/10.1109/MC.2018.1451660
9. Alharby, M., & Moorsel, A. (2017). Blockchain based smart contracts: A systematic mapping study. Fourth international conference on computer science and information technology (CSIT-2017), Dubai, UAE. https://doi.org/10.5121/csit.2017.71011.
10. Maia, D. J. H., & Coutinho, E. F. (2022). A blockchain solution for crowdfunding and cost analysis. EATIS'22: Proceedings of the 11th Euro American Conference on Telematics and Information Systems June 2022 Article No.: 8, pp. 1–8. https://doi.org/10.1145/3544538.3544650
11. Mutharasu, J. M., Pandey, U., Rethick, B., Kulkarni, B., & Pawar, M. (2022). A framework for crowdfunding platform using Ethereum blockchain technology. In R. Agrawal, J. He, E. Shubhakar Pilli, & S. Kumar (Eds.), *Cyber security in intelligent computing and communications. Studies in computational intelligence* (Vol. 1007). Springer. https://doi.org/10.1007/978-981-16-8012-0_9

The States Perspective of Blockchain—A Qualitative Content Analysis

Hauke Precht, Tim Siedenburg, and Jorge Marx Gómez

1 Introduction

The blockchain technology has been investigated through several perspectives and lenses. Especially form the point of view of enterprises, this new technology has been analyzed [1–5]. Often, the focus is on potential of blockchain, to disrupt existing business models that will be changed by this technology [6]. But with its disruptive potential and improving adopting rate, the technology is also a relevant topic for governments. On one side, governments are interested in the possibilities of leveraging the technology itself, for example, to enhance citizen services. On the other hands, governments might be concerned considering crypto currencies and their use for money laundering [7]. While both viewpoints are valid, the question arises, what perspective states take when it comes to this novel technology. As mentioned, it can range from adoption, acceptance, or toleration to regulation or even a ban on technology or individual application leveraging this technology.

There is currently a lack of comparison that shows how the most economically strongest countries position themselves overall in the area of blockchain technology. A holistic picture could further help companies to learn about the extent to which their blockchain ideas meet with government approval or rejection. This can help identify, ahead of time, whether government subsidies or regulations are to be expected. This is particularly important for internationally oriented blockchain start-ups that are building their business model entirely on blockchain technology. In this case, it is essential to know which views the economically strongest countries have on blockchain technology.

H. Precht (✉) · T. Siedenburg · J. Marx Gómez
Carl von Ossietzky University of Oldenburg, Oldenburg, Germany
e-mail: hauke.precht@uol.de; tim.siedenburg@uol.de; jorge.marx.gomez@uol.de

J. Marx Gómez et al. (eds.), *Smart and Secure Embedded and Mobile Systems*, Progress in IS, https://doi.org/10.1007/978-3-031-56603-5_39

The goal of this chapter is therefore to analyze the blockchain strategies of the world's six largest economies by Gross Domestic Product (GDP), namely the USA, China, Japan, Germany, the UK, and India [8]. To do so, we analyze official strategy papers and reports, which will be referred to as blockchain strategy papers in the following paper. By doing so, we want to provide insights in the perspective of each country toward blockchain technology. In particular, the aim is to find out whether the views of the individual countries are roughly congruent or whether there are strong divergences. The research question for this paper is therefore: *What are the general views of the world's six most economically powerful countries on blockchain technology?*

2 Methodology

To answer the above-mentioned research questions, the qualitative content analysis according to Mayring [9, 10] is used. In doing so, the work is based on the 12th revised edition from the year 2015, since this corresponds to the latest version. The qualitative content analysis is a flexible research methodology that can be applied on any kind of communication material to structure and analyze its content in a defined and structured way, following pre-defined steps for research purposes. This research method is particularly characterized by the fact that, in contrast to quantitative content analysis, it only takes into account features that are needed to answer the previously specified research questions that are needed [11]. Thereby, often a smaller number of materials are used, which, however, are interpreted in greater detail. In this chapter, we use the summarizing qualitative content analysis in order to reduce the material to be examined to the text passages that are essential for answering the stated research question.

In order to perform this qualitative content analysis, we followed the general process described in [9].

2.1 Determination of the Material

In the first step, we define the material that will be analyzed. As mentioned, in this chapter, we focus on the blockchain strategy paper of the six largest states by GDP. For Germany, the paper entitled *Blockchain Strategy of the Federal Government We Set Out the Course for the Token Economy* with 24 pages is used [12]. For India, its paper entitled "Blockchain: The India Strategy" [13] is used. The USA published a blockchain strategy paper called *Blockchain Technology Overview* [14]. China published its 49-page log blockchain strategy paper in 2018 via the China Academy of Information and Communication Technology and the Trusted Blockchain Initiatives that is called *Blockchain White Paper* [15]. The blockchain strategy paper for Japan is called *Blockchain in Japan* and was also published in

2018 [16] and has 106 pages. Great Britian's blockchain strategy paper was already published in 2016 by the Government Office for Science and is entitled *Distributed Ledger Technology: Beyond Blockchain* [17].

2.2 Determine the Direction of the Analysis

In order to perform the actual analysis, we used the recommended software *QCAmap*[1] that is specifically tailored for a quantitative content analysis, in comparison with, for example, *MAXQDA*[2] [9]. As mentioned above, we will perform a summarizing qualitative analysis to answer our set research question *What are the general views of the world's six most economically powerful countries on blockchain technology?*.

2.3 Selecting the Method and Form of Category Formation

The coding categories that are used to code statements can be inductively or deductively defined. As in this chapter, we aim to analyze content and insights that have not yet been discussed in the literature, we choose to create the categories with the inductive category formation.

2.4 Definition of the Units of Analysis

There are several units of analysis that must be defined when conducting a qualitative content analysis. First, we defined the coding unit, which is the smallest unit of coding, for example, a single word, a phrase, or even a page [9]. As we aim to identify statements with clear meaning, we choose the unit *Clear meaning (seme) in the text*. Next, we defined the context unit, which defines the largest unit of a single material for coding, which in this case is a single blockchain strategy paper. The recording unit is pre-defined when choosing the inductive category formation, meaning the recording unit is always to be considered as the whole set of material available. Further, we defined the *definition of selection criteria* that defines which statements are to be selected. Our definition for selection is the following: *All text passages that provide insight into how the respective state under review views blockchain technology in general or a blockchain application area are to be coded. In addition, text passages that reveal the strategies of the respective state in*

[1] https://qcamap.org

[2] https://maxqda.de

relation to the Blockchain technology as technology in general or toward a specific blockchain application area (e.g., requirement, regulation, or prohibition) are to be coded. Considering the level of abstraction, we created the following definition: *The data material should be coded at a low to medium level of abstraction. Clear strategies and application cases should be specifically named as such.*

2.5 Run Through the Material with Back Checks

We started with coding the blockchain strategy paper of Germany. After roughly 80% of coding of this blockchain strategy paper (13% of the whole material), we re-defined the abstraction level and the definition of selection criteria to better meet our specifications. The new abstraction level is defined as follows: *The data material should be coded at a medium to high level of abstraction. Clear strategies and viewpoints should be named as such.* We also re-defined the definition of selection criteria: *All text passages should be coded that provide insight into how the respective state under investigation views blockchain technology in general or a blockchain application area. In addition, text passages should be coded that reveal which strategies the respective state is pursuing in relation to blockchain technology in general or toward a specific blockchain application area (e.g., requirement, regulation, or prohibition). In addition, principles and framework conditions as well as self-assessments and views of other states are to be recorded.*

2.6 Present and Interpret Results

We present our finding within this chapter while also interpreting and discussing the results in the following sections.

3 States' Perspectives on Blockchain

Based on our performed qualitative content analysis, we will now present the results of statements in the respective category based on the available strategy paper of the respective states. In Table 1, we show the identified categories and the number of statements for each category we identified in each analyzed blockchain strategy paper. In the following subsection, we will provide some highlights and insights within the respective blockchain strategy papers.

Table 1 The number of codings for category for states

The number of codings for category states							
Category	Title	Germany	India	USA	China	Japan	UK
RQ-1-1	High relevance of blockchain technology	4	6	0	7	8	8
RQ-1-2	Opportunities of Blockchain Technology	14	15	2	4	12	41
RQ-1-3	Claim of the blockchain strategy paper/government	9	12	10	2	9	5
RQ-1-4	Climate protection and sustainability	16	0	0	1	0	0
RQ-1-5	Self-assessment/Own prospects	1	3	0	9	42	8
RQ-1-6	Promotion of blockchain technology	8	0	0	10	11	0
RQ-1-7	Use of blockchain technology in government	5	4	0	0	3	4
RQ-1-8	Stability of the financial system investment security	4	0	0	0	2	0
RQ-1-9	Technology neutrality	8	0	2	0	1	0
RQ-1-10	(International) Cooperation	12	1	0	4	20	9
RQ-1-11	IT security, data protection, and consumer protection	10	0	0	5	11	10
RQ-1-12	Regulation of blockchain technology	0	0	0	1	1	2
RQ-1-13	Investigation/piloting of blockchain technology	4	0	0	4	4	4
RQ-1-14	Promoting a blockchain application area	7	0	0	0	11	0
RQ-1-15	Support for start-ups and SMEs	5	0	0	0	13	0
RQ-1-16	Accessibility, transparency, and standardization	6	0	0	15	1	3
RQ-1-17	Investigation piloting of a blockchain application area	10	10	0	0	5	0
RQ-1-18	Measures (were not coded separately)	44	0	0	0	0	0
RQ-1-19	Criticism and neutral objective view of blockchain technology on a scope of application.	2	10	20	12	9	16

(continued)

Table 1 (continued)

The number of codings for category states							
Category	Title	Germany	India	USA	China	Japan	UK
RQ-1-20	Blockchain use-case framework	0	1	1	1	0	1
RQ-1-21	General challenges	1	11	1	10	3	5
RQ-1-22	Consideration of other states	0	0	0	12	2	4
RQ-1-23	Prohibition of a blockchain application area	0	0	0	1	2	0
RQ-1-24	Comparison with other states	0	1	0	10	6	2
RQ-1-25	General criteria framework conditions	0	0	0	1	2	4
RQ-1-26	Proposals recommendations	0	0	1	9	2	11
RQ-1-27	Blockchain application areas in general	3	2	2	2	21	13
RQ-1-28	Regulation of a blockchain application area	3	0	0	1	9	1

3.1 Germany

We coded 176 statements in Germany's blockchain strategy paper. It is notable that with 44 codings, Measures, i.e., ideas to further promote or use blockchain technology, were present throughout the chapter. Similar holds true for the focus on climate protection and sustainability. For example, it is stated as follows: "Particularly with regard to the Federal Government's Climate Protection and Sustainability Goals, it is necessary to carefully weigh up the areas of potential and the risks" [12].

3.2 India

For India, we coded 76 statements. Similar to Germany, also India sees the potential of this technology, but with 11 encoding for RQ1-21, India sees challenges too. Topics such as climate protection, IT security, or data protection are not (yet) mentioned in the strategy paper of India. But also India noticed the chances of this technology, stating, for example, "India can considerably move toward improving the 'Ease of Doing Business' by allowing entities to interact through a trusted medium with a reduced dependency on cumbersome regulatory oversight and compliance" [13].

3.3 USA

The blockchain strategy paper of the USA [14] is 68 pages long and was published in 2018. They discuss mainly on the technology itself, which is shown by 20 codings in RQ-1-19, *Criticism and neutral objective view of blockchain technology on a scope of application*. This explains why, in this coding, statements for only 8 categories were found, and 20 categories have 0 statements. In comparison with other blockchain strategy papers, they did not mention any aspects of promoting a blockchain application area (RQ-1-14) or data protection aspects.

3.4 China

The strategy paper from China has a total of 121 codes. It is noticeable that accessibility, transparency, and standardization were coded particularly frequently. Compared to the strategy papers from Germany and India, this strategy paper also presents a rather critical and neutral view. It is also unusual that China refers to other countries and makes comparisons with them.

3.5 Japan

With 210 marked passages, Japan's strategy paper has the most codes to date. By far the most frequently assigned category is RQ1-5 Self-assessment/Own prospects, with a total of 42 passages. It is clear that this strategy paper relates to a large extent to its own state. The consideration of other countries and comparisons with them tend to recede into the background. Also striking is the high number of codes in the category RQ-27 Blockchain—Areas of application in general.

3.6 Great Britain

The most recently coded blockchain strategy paper from Great Britain has 151 codings with 41 codes clearly focusing on the potential and opportunities of blockchain technology. With 16 codings in the category RQ1-19 Criticism and neutral, objective view of the blockchain technology/on an area of application, however, it also represents objective and critical views. With 10 codes of the RQ1-11 IT security, data protection, and consumer protection category, however, IT security, data protection, and consumer protection also seem to be a relevant criterion for Great Britain.

4 Discussion and Conclusion

The complete coding of 773 coded text passages results in a total of 28 categories, plus 4 main categories. They are split among the respective blockchain strategy paper as follows:

- Germany 176 codings
- India 76 codings
- USA 39 coding
- China 121 codings
- Japan 210 codings
- Great Britain 151 codings

It is clearly evident that the totals of the codes of the respective countries show strong deviations in some cases. It is obvious that these deviations result from the different scopes of the blockchain strategy papers examined. While the German blockchain strategy paper, at 24 pages, is the shortest of the strategy papers examined, this one has the most coded text passages after Japan, with 176. The strategy paper from the USA, on the other hand, is 68 pages long but has only 39 coded text passages. Rather than the number of pages, the differences can be explained by the individual claims of the blockchain strategy papers. For example, while Germany's blockchain strategy is aimed at the goal of presenting its all-encompassing view of blockchain technology and of defining framework, the aim of the U.S. Blockchain strategy paper of the USA is rather to give a comprehensive, technical overview of the blockchain technology. With reference to the research question posed before, we aim to further abstract our categories by forming alternative main categories: *rather positive views*, *rather neutral views*, *rather negative views*. In the alternative main categories for rather positive views, the categories RQ-1-15, RQ-1-1, RQ-1-2, RQ-1-6, RQ-1-7, and RQ-1-14 are present.

All categories that in some way directly or indirectly suggest neutrality toward blockchain technology are considered to be more neutral views of blockchain technology. Categories relating to pilot projects or general investigations of the technology should also be rated as neutral, since the results of such pilot projects lead to both demands and regulations or bans, and such investigations cannot therefore be indefinitely rated as positive or negative. Therefore, in this alternative, main categories are RQ-1-9, RQ-1-13, RQ-1-19, and RQ-1-17.

Direct and indirect prohibitions and regulations of blockchain technology are considered to be rather negative views in this context. Even though it must be mentioned at this point that regulations do not always have to be of a negative nature, regulations can also contribute to making the technology usable and secure in the first place. However, since the strategy papers tended to make less of a statement about regulatory measures, a complete classification of all regulations in this main category is not considered decisive for the overall result. The following subcategories therefore emerge as subcategories for the more negative views of blockchain technology: RQ-1-12, RQ-1-23, and RQ-1-28. With these alternative

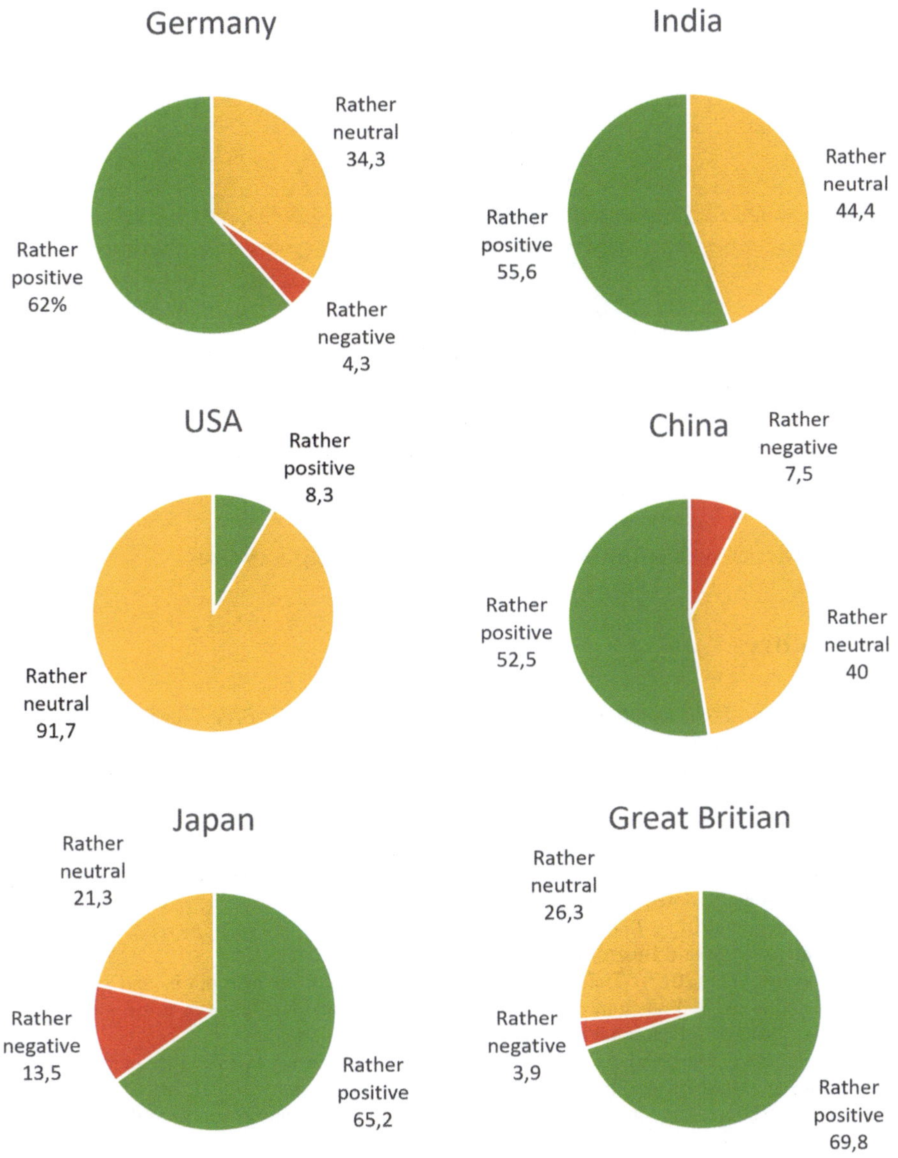

Fig. 1 Overview of perspectives toward blockchain technology by single states

main categories, we can now visualize the current perspective of these states toward blockchain technology, as shown in Fig. 1.

Summed up, the general direction toward rather positive, followed by rather neutral, can be identified, as shown in Fig. 2, thus answering our stated research question.

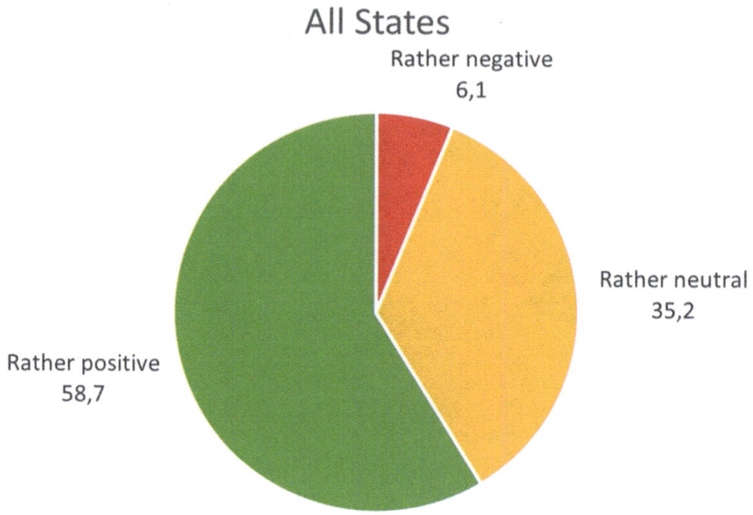

Fig. 2 Overview of perspectives toward blockchain technology in a whole

References

1. *Blockchain 2.0: Einfach erklärt - weit mehr als nur Bitcoin*. FBV FinanzBuch Verlag, 1. auflage ed. (2018).
2. *Blockchain for supply chains and international trade: Report on key features, impacts and policy options: study*. European Parliament (2020).
3. LeadBlockPartners. (2020). Enterprise blockchain 2020: Data driven insights into the uncharted enterprise blockchain world & data economy.
4. Pawczuk, L., Massey, R., & Holdowsky, J. (2019). Deloitte's 2019 Global Blockchain Survey: Blockchain gets down to business.
5. Furlonger, D. (2019). *The real business of blockchain: How leaders can create value in a new digital age*. Harvard Business Review Press.
6. Bussmann, O. (2017). The future of finance: Fintech, tech disruption, and orchestrating innovation. In R. Francioni & R. A. Schwartz (Eds.) *Equity markets in transition* (pp. 473–486). Springer International Publishing.
7. Barone, R., & Masciandaro, D. (2019). Cryptocurrency or usury? Crime and alternative money laundering techniques. *European Journal of Law and Economics, 47*(2), 233–254.
8. Statista. (2021). Ranking der 20 länder mit dem größten bruttoinlandsprodukt (bip) im jahr 2021.
9. Mayring, P. (2015). *Qualitative Inhaltsanalyse: Grundlagen und Techniken*. Weinheim and Basel: Beltz, 12., überarbeitete auflage ed.
10. Mayring, P. (2015). Qualitative content analysis: theoretical background and procedures. In A. Bikner-Ahsbahs, C. Knipping, & N. Presmeg (Eds.) *Approaches to qualitative research in mathematics education. Advances in mathematics education*. Dordrecht: Springer. https://doi.org/10.1007/978-94-017-9181-6_13.
11. Pfeiffer, F. (2018). Qualitative inhaltsanalyse nach mayring in 5 schritten.
12. Bundesministerium für Wirtschaft und Energie. (2019).
13. NITI Aayog. (2020). Blockchain: The India strategy.

14. Yaga, D., Mell, P., Roby, N., & Scarfone, K. (2018). *Blockchain technology overview*. Online. https://doi.org/10.6028/NIST.IR.8202.
15. China Academy of Information and Communication Technology und Trusted. (2018). Blockchain white paper.
16. González, M. (2018). Blockchain in Japan.
17. Government Office for Science. (2016). Distributed ledger technology: beyond block chain: A report by the UK government chief scientific adviser.

Mobility Transition @ Quality of Life (MobiLe)—The Development of a Qualitative Model for Conveying Significant Interdependencies in the Complex Transport System

Herbert Brüning, Alexander Papke, Sreedhar Kokkarachedu, and Jorge Marx Gómez

1 Introduction

A mobility transition is crucial for sustainable development [1], but so far been only insufficiently initiated [2]. A variety of beneficial effects, such as reduced air and noise pollution, reduced consumption of land and other resources, and the positive health effects of active travel, can be achieved through environmentally friendly transportation systems [3, 4]. This approach fits the concept of "cities for people" [5], which offer a high quality of life and thus attractiveness. A famous example of the implementation of such changes is Copenhagen. Though the scale of transitioning the transportation sector is massive, the German Sustainability Strategy [6] states that the focus on reorienting the transportation sector toward sustainability is especially important at a municipal level.

An aggravating factor for the mobility transition is the complexity of the transport system. Participation in traffic is commonplace for almost all people. As a result, many people consider their own experiences to be universal and underestimate the complexity of the entire transportation system. In this, the decision-makers are not fundamentally different from the general population. Therefore, it is necessary to enhance the understanding of system interrelationships, by "laymen" in decision-making positions to achieve a mobility transition. This understanding has to be solid so that system relationships can easily be communicated to the general public—both by the politicians and by the administration. For this purpose, MobiLe provides support in clarifying system correlations. It can be applied to both known and new

H. Brüning · A. Papke
Stadt Norderstedt, Norderstedt, Deutschland
e-mail: Herbert.bruening@norderstedt.de; Alexander.papke@norderstedt.de

S. Kokkarachedu (✉) · J. Marx Gómez
Carl von Ossietzky Universität Oldenburg, Oldenburg, Germany
e-mail: sreedhar.kokkarachedu@uni-oldenburg.de; jorge.marx.gomez@uol.de

J. Marx Gómez et al. (eds.), *Smart and Secure Embedded and Mobile Systems*,
Progress in IS, https://doi.org/10.1007/978-3-031-56603-5_40

elements of the municipal transport system. MobiLe provides a knowledge-based approach as a further basis for decision-making, which supports a mobility transition argumentatively.

If expectations in this approach of "political consulting" will be fulfilled, then politicians of all political groups will use MobiLe to prepare their political debates and decisions. The process of using MobiLe is quite simple. Users select measures of their choice from up to seven action fields within the dynamic mathematical model, check the results of the simulations, and compare them to their policy objectives. This process is further described in Sect. 2. If the results match the objective, MobiLe serves as a professional argumentation base. If the objectives are not achieved yet, the analysis functions can be used to understand where the system is behaving unexpectedly and to influence it efficiently if necessary. However, even if the analysis function is not used (in each case), new simulations can be carried out quickly by changing the control variables, so that optimization can also be achieved playfully. Day-to-day political work is already very time-consuming for voluntary local politics. Thus, the main condition for using MobiLe is to be quick and accessible. To ensure its usability, the model is being developed in a co-creation process with politicians of all parties within Norderstedt. In this process, the administration and scientific partners work out the basic principles and coordinate them with policymakers in an iterative process.

2 Mathematical Model

The development of the cybernetic, qualitatively oriented model takes place in the contest MobilitätsWerkStadt 2025, which is currently being funded by the German Ministry of Education and Research as part of the "sustainable urban mobility" research agenda. For a qualitative mapping and analysis of traffic relationships and developments, system-dynamic sensitivity models [7, 8] are already used in research projects in transport and spatial planning [9–12]. The advantages of these models are the comparatively low data effort and the high traceability by the decision-makers [11, 13].

MobiLe is developed using the principles of the sensitivity model [14]. This approach allows the inclusion of everyday aspects of the transportation system and the cybernetic analysis of resulting interactions [15]. This enables the qualitative consideration of the consequences in the municipal environment, which is missing in conventional quantitative transportation models. As a result, it is feasible to evaluate system changes in a temporally dynamic manner and assess their qualitative influence on the system.

The basic model consists of 16 elements subdivided into seven control, six impact, and three target elements (Fig. 1). The corresponding influence on other variables is examined for each of them. In addition to examining whether influences between different variables exist, assessments were made to verify the strength

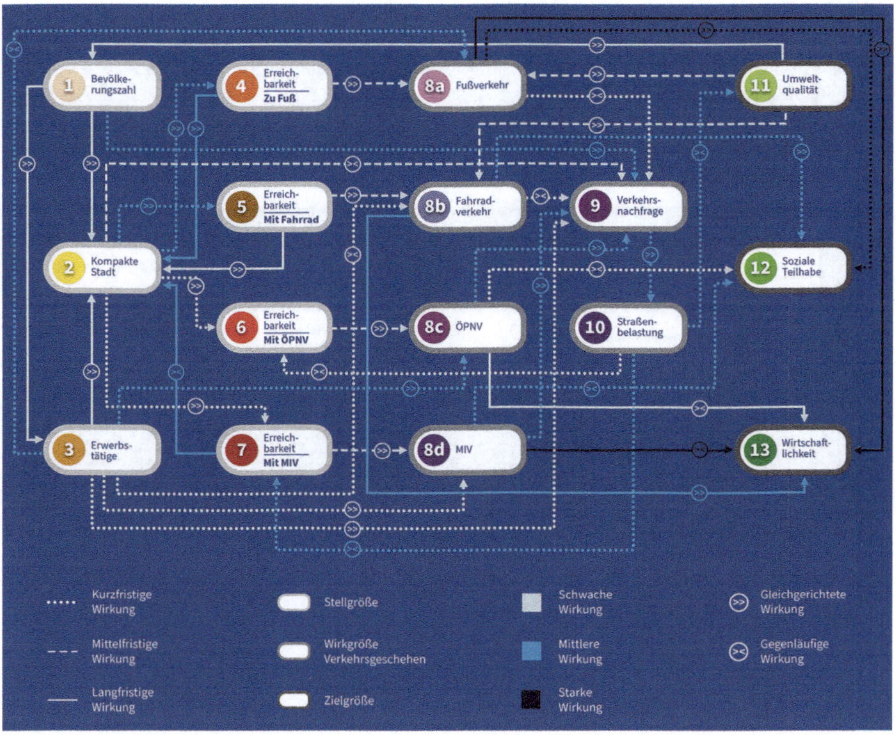

Fig. 1 MobiLe model, development status July 2023 (Source: MOSCHDESIGN)

and the timeframe of those connections and whether they are counter-directional or unidirectional.

The influences found are divided into strong, medium, and weak effects as well as short-, medium- and long-term influences. Users can intervene in the system by selecting measures in each of the seven action fields (Fig. 2). Each field of action contains various measures that have promoting or inhibiting effects. Each of those measures is assigned a technically derived impact strength compared to the other control variables. Based on the sum of the selected measures, a conversion is made into a strong, medium, or weak influence on the affected variables, which is then transferred to the simulation. As a result, the impact of the measures on every element is shown. The model developed in this way enables an assessment of the consequences of implementing a wide range of measures (usually as a combination) within the whole city (initially valid for Norderstedt).

The mathematical model and the associated software are still under development. So far, only small-scale measures have been considered. The first practical tests are currently carried out in Norderstedt. Subsequently, an extension is planned that includes large-scale planning that affect the entire city as a second important application case—such as a new land use plan or a bicycle traffic concept. Since

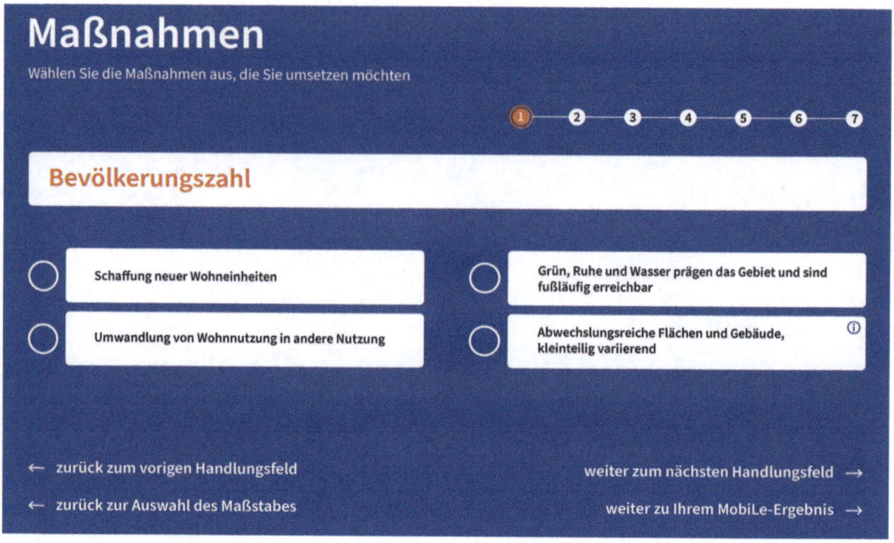

Fig. 2 Web App Design Layout of selecting measures of control variables (Source: MOSCHDESIGN)

this is a qualitative model, the estimates used are not based on concrete statistics but reflect the consensus from the expert assessment of various transport ecologists and scientists, which is supported as far as possible by literature references. This expert impact assessment is gradually being extended to other experts. A side effect of this should be to gather and incorporate more information as early as possible to increase the quality, acceptance, and usability of the model.

To get an insight into the results of dynamic simulations, simple programming in Excel was carried out. This enables to show developments as a sequence of several static simulations, which illustrate not only the direct and indirect effects of system interventions, but also the evolution of the states of the model elements over time. This way, qualitative impact assessments of higher-level strategies (e.g., a promotion of bicycle traffic) can be analyzed. Even these first simple applications show that the model demonstrates some impacts. Among them may also be such effects that cannot be intuitively foreseen by everyone. This in itself offers considerable benefits. The unexpected statements provide important clues to previously unrecognized relationships and provide a gain in knowledge.

The model is initially designed for the city of Norderstedt. It will be usable for many cities of similar size, largely unchanged. In order to derive the greatest possible benefit from the model, transferability to other municipalities is planned from the outset during development. This influences the programming, which has to be developed as open source. This aspect will be discussed in more detail below.

3 Software Development

MobiLe is to be developed as a dynamized digital version of the basic model and its customizing options to represent the municipal transport system accurately and at the same time as simply as possible. At first, it was necessary to investigate which technology is suitable for the implementation of the model. Initial research showed the previously used program GAMMA [16] does not have any public source code or interfaces. Additionally, no other open-source software was found that provides the necessary customization options to carry over the model and the corresponding measures while being easily understandable. Thus, the development of new software was required. For further transferability and easy access, the model is developed completely in-house using well-known and recognized programming languages [JavaScript and TypeScript (Angular)].

The developed software can and will be made available as open-source software to encourage possible adaptations for transferability to other cities/municipalities and to ensure continued use even after the project ends.

The software is designed as a web application. This allows to use the application via the browser across platforms, especially on smartphones and tablets. There is no need to download or install the web application in advance, however; a good Internet connection is required. The development of the web application usually requires less development and maintenance effort compared to similar software [17]. The expansion of the web application as a Software as a Service (SaaS) solution is conceivable as a future business model [18]. In this SaaS solution, the software and IT infrastructure are operated by an external IT service provider and used by the customer as a service.

Initially, this software is developed with a focus on the city of Norderstedt, so the language version of the software is German. Since the software is primarily intended for local governments and the population, special attention must be paid to the user interface (UI). Thus, an intuitive and responsive design of the UI is crucial. For this purpose, an experienced graphic designer (MOSCHDESIGN) supplies the designs and UI elements.

For the development of web applications, different software technologies are used. While the data operations and calculations are performed in the backend, the visualization for this is done by providing the calculation both as a bar chart (Fig. 3), by showing the changes over time in a line graph (Fig. 4) and in the form of a summary of results for the three target variables in figures (Fig. 5). Both the backend and frontend communicate via Restful API. By deploying in Docker-based containers, the application can be hosted quickly and without customization on different IT structures.

During the development of the new software, after a software design is available, various test phases are run through. Thus, evaluation and testing of the implemented software through unit tests, integration tests, system tests, and acceptance tests [19] will be performed through various workshops with the project partners, to which potential users will be invited.

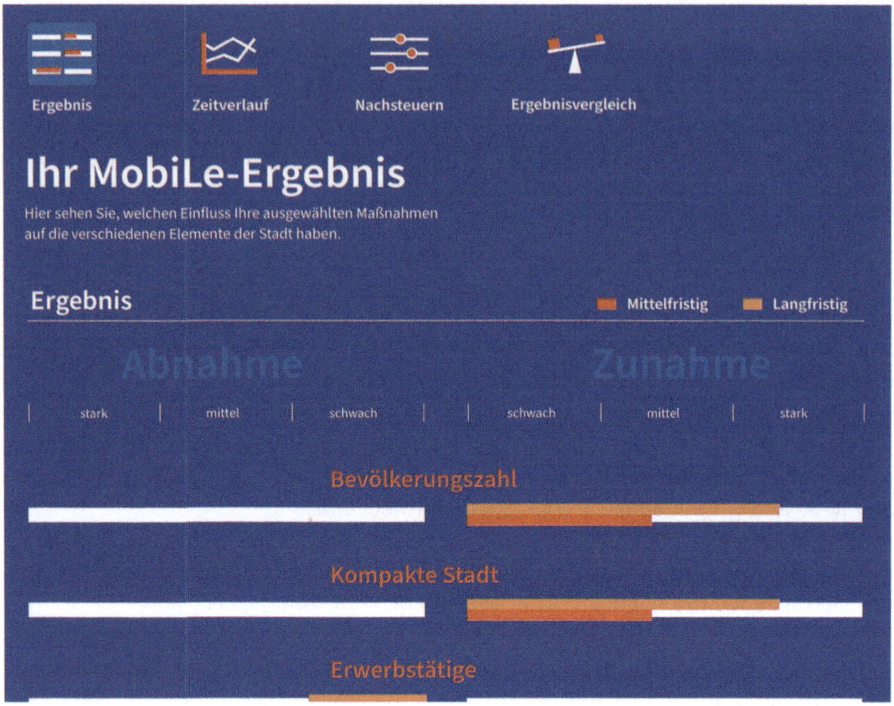

Fig. 3 Overview of the results of a simulation in a bar chart (Source: MOSCHDESIGN)

The developed software is available to the project partners at an early stage, still during development. For this purpose, the software versioning tool GitLab is used, which is hosted by the IT services of the University of Oldenburg. A public GitHub repository has been set up, and the code will be made available to the public for an (test) application. After project completion, the code continues to be available via the repository. In addition, an executable version is hosted at the University of Oldenburg to enable public access. The software has been made publicly available since March 2024. Additionally, there is a development version that is password-protected and used for testing new implementations. Interested municipalities can set up their own version by using the public repository. This capability will likely be established during the life of the project and can be supported by the University of Oldenburg. Applying the software in different municipalities allows for researching the impact of qualitative models on political decision-making and political discussions. Support for external persons in editing and adapting the model after the end of the project is conceivable. The type of support depends on the further course of the project and can therefore only be specified at a later point in time.

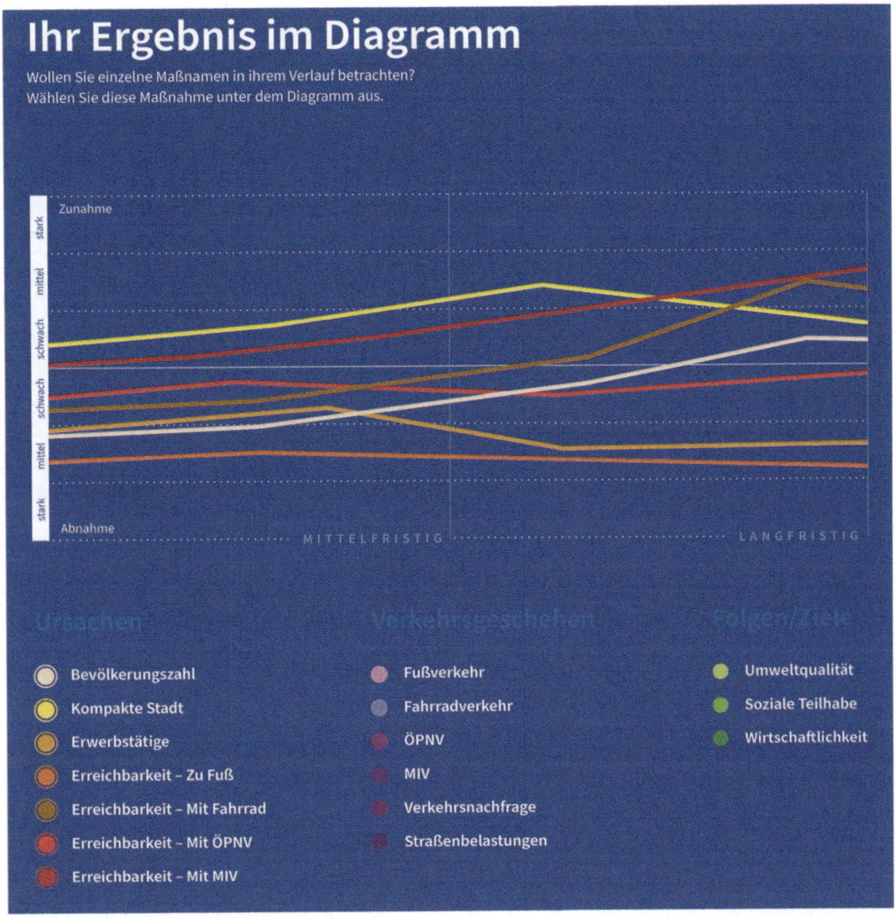

Fig. 4 Line chart showing the results of a simulation for the target variables over time (Source: MOSCHDESIGN)

4 Conclusion

MobiLe is becoming an easy-to-use tool that offers the opportunity to support municipal decisions in the transport system and facilitate the assessment of the consequences of decisions through its knowledge-based approach. Before parliamentary deliberations, traffic-relevant measures can be quickly assessed by checking the modeled influences they will have on the traffic situation in the city. If political goals are not achieved, users can change one or more parameters to find the best option for achieving set goals. This does not restrict the decision-making freedom of politicians but improves the understanding of the impacts of different measures. Expected, this will eventually lead to a better understanding

Fig. 5 Summary of results for the three target variables—including a condensation as a sustainability value (Source: MOSCHDESIGN)

of the complex interrelations of the transportation systems and the city itself and probably to more sustainable approaches.

MobiLe is still a work in progress, and its effects on urban traffic planning and political decision-making need to be assessed. However, the ongoing exchange with policymakers as well as the later involvement of the public will likely lead to an increased acceptance of the new tool. In addition, the use of the tool beyond the end of the project is encouraged. The web application, which is made available as open-source software, can thus make a small contribution to the necessary changes of the transportation system.

5 Declarations

This publication is based on research in the project MobiLe, which is funded by the Federal ministry of Education and Research as part of its Social-Ecological Research funding priority, funding no. 01UV2129A. Responsibility for the content of this publication lies with the authors.

SPONSORED BY THE

Federal Ministry of Education and Research

FONA Research for Sustainability

References

1. Deutscher Städtetag Nachhaltige städtische Mobilität für alle. Agenda für eine Verkehrswende aus kommunaler Sicht. Positionspapier des Deutschen Städtetages (2018).
2. Deutscher Städtetag Monitoring zum Positionspapier "Nachhaltige städtische Mobilität für alle. Agenda für eine Verkehrswende aus kommunaler Sicht von 2018" (2021).
3. Neun, M., & Haubold, H. (2016). The EU cycling economy. Arguments for an integrated EU cycling policy.
4. Colville-Andersen, M. (2020). *Copenhagenize: Der Ultimative Weg zur urbanen Fahrradkultur*. Thiemo Graf Verlag.
5. Gehl, J. (2016). Städte für Menschen. *Städte Für Menschen.*
6. Die Bundesregierung Deutsche Nachhaltigkeitsstrategie. Weiterentwicklung 2021. Abgerufen von https://www.bundesregierung.de/resource/blob/992814/1875176...,2021
7. Vester, F., & Hesler von, A. (1988). Sensitivitätsmodell. 2. unveränderte Auflage, Umlandverband Frankfurt, Frankfurt. *Ökologie Und Planung In Verdichtungsgebieten. Forschungsbericht. Frankfurt Am Main.*
8. Kollosche, I. (2011). Verkehrspolitik und Zukunftsforschung. *Verkehrspolitik.*
9. Köhl, W., Beckmann, K., Heberling, G., Schmidt, R., & Becker, T. (1992). Raumordnungspolitische Anforderungen an eine integrierte Verkehrsplanung und Verkehrsgestaltung. - Forschungsvorhaben im Auftrag des Bundesministers für Raum-ordnung, Bauwesen und Städtebau. Institut für Städtebau und Landes-planung der Universität Karlsruhe (TH), Karlsruhe.
10. Schade, B., Rothengatter, W., & Schade, W. (2002). Strategien, Maßnahmen und ökonomische Bewertung einer dauerhaft umweltgerechten Verkehrsentwicklung. Bewertung der dauerhaft umweltgerechten Verkehrsentwicklung mit dem system-dynamischen Modell ESCOT (Economic assessment of sustainability policies of transport). Umweltbundesamt Berlin (Hrsg.), Berichte 5/02, Berlin.
11. Klönne, M. (2008). Methodik und Prozessgestaltung strategischer kommunaler Verkehrsplanungen. Anwendungsmöglichkeiten von systemdynamischen Modellen zur Bewertung kommunaler Verkehrsstrategien in der Planungspraxis, Aachen.
12. Göllinger, T., & Harrer-Puchner, G. (2020). 40 Jahre Neuland des Denkens: Frederic Vesters programmatische Schrift für eine nachhaltige Zukunft. IöB-Schriften. (Institut für ökologische Betriebswirtschaft (IöB) eV).
13. Harrer-Puchner, G., Wagener-Lohse, G., & Bobsien, A. (2019). Co-developing and implementing measures for a new mobility for municipalities through interconnected thinking & system analysis. *Transportation Research Procedia, 41*, 165–168. https://doi.org/10.1016/j.trpro.2019.09.031.
14. Vester, F. (2015). Die Kunst vernetzt zu denken. Ideen und Werkzeuge für einen neuen Umgang mit Komplexität. - 10. Aufl., Stuttgart. *Ideen Und Werkzeuge Für Einen Neuen Umgang Mit Komplexität.*

15. Vester, F. (1990). *Ausfahrt Zukunft: Strategien für den Verkehr von morgen; eine Systemuntersuchung*. Heyne.
16. TOPSIM Kurzbeschreibung GAMMA – ein PC-Werkzeug für Vernetztes Denken, https://www.topsim.com/gamma/
17. Yaskevich, A. (2021). Mobile web-app Im Vergleich zu anderen Arten von Apps. *ScienceSoft Footer Icon*. https://www.scnsoft.de/blog/mobile-web-app-und-andere-arten-von-apps
18. Schütz, S., Kude, T., & Popp, K. (2013). The impact of software-as-a-service on software ecosystems. In *International Conference of Software Business*.
19. Spillner, A., & Linz, T. (2019). Basiswissen Softwaretest: Aus-und Weiterbildung zum Certified Tester–Foundation Level nach ISTQB@-Standard. (dpunkt. verlag) @Commentjabref-meta: databaseType:biblatex;.

A Proposal to Store Remote Monitoring Sensor Data in a Distributed Manner, Using IOTA Streams and IPFS

Ali Amin Rezaei and Jorge Marx Gómez

1 Introduction

In 2020, the world faced with corona pandemic. One of the consequences was the overloading of the hospitals and medical centers, which led to the exhaustion of the medical resources, and therefore, not all the patients could receive the necessary care. Although most of the patients do not need intensive care, many of them occupied the intensive care resources just to remain under monitoring for potential emergency circumstances. As a result, some patients with more severe symptoms might be deprived unintentionally to receive the level of the care and support they needed.

That might appear contradictory, since all the patients have the right to get monitored but there is not enough resources and facilities in the hospitals for all. This problem can be tackled by enabling patient's remote monitoring through IoT (Internet of Things) sensors/gadgets. Through remote monitoring possibility, still the patients with less severe symptoms can get monitored, while they are not occupying the resources in the medical center. The common way of remote monitoring is through the use of sensors that are connected to the patient's body and Bluetooth or direct WiFi transmitting gathered signals to mobile phone; then through the application, the sensor data will be transferred to medical center for the analysis. What the application does in the background to store data and issuing access control is the subject of the proposed storage method in this research. For the sake of easy calling, we call the proposed architecture in a short form the p2psds-isac (P2P Sensor Data Storage with IOTA Stream Access Control).

A. A. Rezaei (✉) · J. Marx Gómez
Carl von Ossietzky Universität Oldenburg, Oldenburg, Germany
e-mail: ali.amin.rezaei@uol.de; ali.amin.rezaei@uni-oldenburg.de; jorge.marx.gomez@uol.de

J. Marx Gómez et al. (eds.), *Smart and Secure Embedded and Mobile Systems*,
Progress in IS, https://doi.org/10.1007/978-3-031-56603-5_41

IOT sensors can automatically collect health metrics such as heart rate, blood pressure, temperature, and so on. The common practice to store the gathered data is the use of centralized storage system. However, having owned centralized storage needs proper maintenance policy that in most of the cases, beyond the resources and budget of a medical center; therefore, most of the centers would deliver the task to third parties that will be based on cloud infrastructure [15]. Healthcare companies were projected to spend $11.4 billion in 2019 on cloud computing for streamlining health data sharing and driving innovation [24].

However, storing data on the cloud has some disadvantages; since clouds run by third-party companies (like Google, Amazon, Microsoft Azur, and so on), the stored data remain under third-party control. In case of personal medical data, that would violate the privacy rights of the patients. Moreover, the trace of data on the cloud is almost impossible. In the cloud, each chunk of data might be stored in different physical servers, which can be in completely different geographical locations. Therefore for the personal data of the citizens of one country that subjected to the regulations of that country, that might be considered the violation of the privacy and patients' rights.

As mentioned, setting up owned data storage infrastructure in most of the cases is not justified by the cost and available resources of a medical center. Therefore, using cloud storage is considered as a common practice. Even if the costs of running centralized storage are justified, putting the patient's data completely under the control of one authority is the violation of the data privacy and brings about the risk of single point of failure in case of any security breach [3, 13].

Considering the mentioned shortcomings of a cloud-based service to store healthcare data, many scholars proposed alternative architecture to address the mentioned limitations, through application of distributed ledger technology. The spectrum of the proposed DLT-based architectures reviewed in the previous literature reflected in a concise way in this research in the literature review section.

We are required in this research to enable multiple medical center remote monitoring of the patient's symptoms though using IoT sensors. Along our objectives, we aim to address security, privacy, scalability, feeless transactions validation, decentralization, flexibility, easy access, access control, low system throughput, storage efficiency, and availability of the data.

The medical center should be able to subscribe—in a real time—to the published data (sensor values) of the patients, through the app that is controlled by the patients. In case of need, medical center should be able to share data with another medical center—of course with patient's permission.

This research is a research in progress, which at this stage proposes an architecture to address the objectives in the use case, as well as addressing the gap that is reflected in the previous literature. However, it should be noted that p2psds-isac has not been yet implemented; therefore, the implementation comes at the later phase of the research.

In this research after reviewing the literature, we proposed an architecture to store encrypted sensor data off-chain on an IPFS [40]-based peer-to-peer database called OrbitDB [27]. To access the sensor values on OrbitDB [27], the requester needs to obtain the database address and IPFS pubsub id, as well as the key to decrypt data. Obviously, only the authorized users have to be able to obtain these data, which would be in our case the medical center. Another objective that we would like to address through p2psds-isac is the ability to revoke or alter previous issued permissions.

The novelty of this research is that we propose to use IOTA Streams to impose access control; the common practice, which has been found in the previous literature, is to use smart contracts to apply access control; however, avoiding using it provides some advantages, such as reducing transaction delays and decreasing the throughput of the system. The p2psds-isac will be described in more detail in Sect. 3 of this chapter.

The p2psds-isac is mainly based on two available technologies: IOTA Stream and IPFS. IOTA is a public DLT that is based on DAG (Directed Acyclic Graph) [28]. We use IOTA Streams to impose access control. The keys to access the actual sensor values will be stored on IOTA Streams channel—which is a patient-specific channel. After the keys obtained for the authorized users—in our case medical center, the actual encrypted data that are stored on OrbitDB [27] can be decrypted and accessed.

We have some objectives in this research as following: security, privacy, scalability, feeless transactions validation, decentralization, flexibility, easy access, access control, low throughput, storage efficiency, and availability. Based on these objectives, we have choice to make about the technology that we are going to use. Regarding access control, we can use either permissioned blockchain or public one.

We need to have easy open access to join the service and upload the sensor values on the OrbitDB. Open access means that patients should be able to join the system without being part of a specific network. Besides, flexibility and scalability in joining the system are important as well.

1.1 Introducing Related Technologies and Concepts

In this part, the key technologies and concepts that are playing the major roles in the p2psds-isac will be introduced.

1.1.1 IOTA

IOTA is a DLT, based on DAG (Directed Acyclic Graph) data structure. The significance of using IOTA in this architecture is: IOTA provides an open access and based on its protocol design ensures the integrity and immutability of the data. Moreover, transactions on IOTA are feeless; therefore, the application does not need to deal with any cryptocurrency policy—like in Ethereum blockchain that is depending on gas price for issuing smart contract.

Another advantage of using IOTA over other blockchain technologies is the low throughput of the protocol; therefore, by design, IOTA is made to be used by IOT devices. However, in our proposed architecture, we use IOTA just as an access control mechanism to deliver the right key to the authorized requester to decrypt the data that are stored in permissioned IPFS node.

IOTAStreams

While transactions on the IOTA distributed ledger technology (DLT) are inherently immutable, IOTA Streams offers a unique feature that allows for a certain degree of mutability. This is achieved through message linking and message sequencing capabilities provided by IOTA Streams. By leveraging these features, it becomes possible to alter the path to the announce message, which is the initial message that establishes a channel and is created by the channel author. In the context of healthcare applications, patients would be considered the authors of their respective channels. This characteristic of IOTA Streams enables users to modify or amend previous messages within an existing channel, providing a level of flexibility that is not typically associated with immutable DLT transactions [16], therefore being able to replace and change information—such as credentials, while keeping the old message to maintain the integrity of the tangle [16]. The use case of such feature is when patient wants to deprive the access of a party that has already been granted.

In p2psds-isac, the patient as an author creates a channel (create an announce message). This channel has multiple branches. Each branch is devoted to the separate sensor. Each branch through a keyload connects to the announce message. The keyload issued by the author of the channel (in our case patients) can be based on the public key of the subscriber or based on a pre-shared key [17].

1.1.2 IPFS

In IPFS [4] network, content can be found based on its content address—which is the root hash of the content. Therefore, if the content is altered, the hash of the content will change too that would ensure the integrity of the data.

In our application, we proposed p2psds-isac, to ensure the integrity of the data, the hash of the set of blocks of data will be calculated, and then generate a sum. That sum will be registered on IOTA channel, under specific branch—which is related to the specific IoT sensor. After some transmissions of data, the hash will be checked against the hash on IPFS. If the hash that is transmitted on IPFS is the same as the one registered on IOTA network, that ensures the integrity of the data. In this architecture, IPFS [4] network will be used to store sensor data. The sensor data are encrypted, and the key to decrypt them can be accessed through IOTA Streams channel.

IPFS pubsub

IPFS pubsub [37] enables publishing/subscribing [29] pattern in IPFS. It enables publishing messages under the shared channel. The subscriber can subscribe to that specific channel id and receive publishing data (in our case sensor data). Moreover, the IPFS pubsub provides easy, real-time subscription to the published data.

OrbitDB

OrbitDB [27] is a peer-to-peer database, meaning that each peer has its own instance of a specific database. A database is replicated between the peers automatically resulting in an up-to-date view of the database upon updates from any peer. That is to say, the database gets pulled to the clients. The published data will be permanently persisted on the IPFS network.

In the next section, we reflect the related literature review, to define our domain of focus, as well as introducing common practices in the previous literature.

2 Literature Review

There are various domains in healthcare blockchain. Considering our use case, we defined that our domain focus will fall under remote patient monitoring. However, there are various terminologies defining this domain.

In some literature, IoT in healthcare is known as IoHT (Internet of Healthcare Things) and is sometimes interchangeably be used as IoMT (Internet of Medical Things) [35]. Since the advent of the blockchain technology, the application of blockchain in healthcare was the target of many previous researches. As our use case is related to both blockchain and remote patient monitoring, accordingly we define our precise target domain as IoHT and blockchain.

According to [42], the whole system considered in 4 layers:

1. Physical; sensors that attach to the body and record the values
2. Storage, where actual data are stored
3. Access control and verification
4. Application layer that connects layers 1, 2, and 3

Our focus in p2psds-isac lays on layers 2 and 3. By reviewing the literature on these two layers, we grasp a big picture as following:

For the storage layer, either the centralized storage (cloud based) [2, 7, 8, 10–12, 14, 19, 31, 34, 36, 38, 39] was used, or decentralized storage like IPFS [9, 22, 32, 41].

The review of the previous literature showed just a few researches were using blockchain to store the actual data on-chain. The majority of researches—to reduce transactions throughput and to ensure data integrity—used blockchain (on-chain) just to store the hash of the data. The usage of both public blockchain [11, 25, 26, 31, 41] and permissioned blockchain [5, 9, 20–22, 30, 33] recognized in the literature.

The choice of the blockchain technology was mostly dependent on the use case. Two requirements were the key derivatives to use permissioned blockchain: higher data privacy and feeless smart contract [9, 20, 21]. To avoid transaction's costs, the permissioned blockchain based on Hyperledger fabric was applied [5, 20, 21] or less common a private version of the Ethereum blockchain [18, 23, 25].

To the best of knowledge of the authors, just two papers [1, 6]have been found that used IOTA as a DLT choice; however, in none of them, IOTA Streams have been used to issue access control.

To grasp a big picture from the state of the art in this domain, the majority of the previous solutions—to avoid transaction costs, ensure the privacy and integrity of the data—tends to store only the hash of data on-chain on a permissioned blockchain while storing the actual data on the cloud or on IPFS-based network storage. Moreover, the access control is issued, through applying smart contracts.

3 Proposed Architecture

We defined the objectives in our architecture, based on the use-case requirements as well as the gap/shortcoming that discovered in the literature review as mentioned.

The p2psds-isac focused on two layers: storage of sensor data and access control layer. In the following, we describe our approach toward these two layers.

3.1 Access Control Strategy

This research follows a novel approach in providing access control. We use IOTA Streams to create channel structure, in which multiple branches can be issued—with the publishing/subscribing capability. In our case, the patients create a channel with multiple branches possibility. Each branch is dedicated to a sensor that stores the access information of the encrypted sensor values that reside on IPFS-based network. The access would be provided only to the authorized subscriber. The subscription is based on the public address of the subscriber on IOTA network, which the author would be able to issue a keyload on a branch, to allow one or multiple public keys (subscribers) access to the branch. The keyload to the branch can be issued as well based on the pre-shared key that can be exchanged between publisher and subscriber.

Based on IOTA Streams capability, the author is capable of adding or removing the public addresses, which should have access to the branch and therefore issue a new keyload message and link it to announce message. Based on IOTA Stream protocol, the old keyload—although still existed to keep the integrity of the tangle—would be obsolete [16]. In our case, that means, revoking the previously issued access permissions to the specific or multiple subscribers, put it more clear; for example, the patients can revoke the access of a medical center to their sensor value data.

The blocks of data in the branch, which issued after keyload message/block, include the information about database id on OrbitDB, IPFS pubsub id, as well as the key to decrypt sensor values.

Through IOTA Stream, we provide access control. The literature review has been shown: imposing access control through issuance of the smart contract as a common approach. However, in this research to avoid unnecessary transactions, we use IOTA Streams to issue access control. Since we decided to provide an open access, flexibility, scalability, and decentralization, using permissioned blockchain like Hyperledger fabric would not address our requirement. Therefore, we tend to use public blockchain. We need to minimize the validation of the transaction as well as having feeless transaction—not to deal with any cryptocurrency policy. IOTA DLT would provide the feeless transactions; and through applying IOTA Streams, we would be able to impose access restriction.

3.2 Data Storage

We proposed to use peer-to-peer database called OrbitDB on a private IPFS network, to store encrypted sensor values. Since the data on IPFS network fetched based on content id (the hash of the content) rather than ip address, ensures that the stored data are not redundant. Despite that we are storing encrypted data, to further ensure the privacy of data, we would install multiple private IPFS nodes—which would be managed by multiple medical centers; therefore, the risk of unauthorized access will be further reduced.

We will use IPFS pubsub to create publisher/subscriber pattern and enable subscribers—in our case one or multiple medical centers—to listen in real time to the sensor values published by the publisher. At the same time, the values will be stored in the OrbitDB [27] database for the future retrieval.

From what has been explained about these two layers, the following conceptual model (Fig. 1) can be depicted:

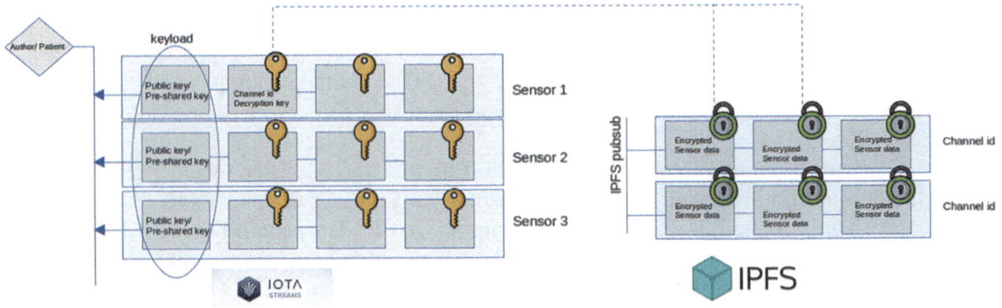

Fig. 1 p2psds-isac (the proposed architecture in the current paper)

4 Conclusion

In the proposed architecture (p2psds-isac), we tried to address the gap, which we discovered from reviewing previous literature. The significance of our solution in comparison to previous literature is that we are able to impose access control through using IOTA Streams without executing smart contract. Avoiding smart contract reduces the unnecessary transactions and therefore decreases transaction delay—which is very important in patient remote monitoring use case. Moreover, using IOTA as a public DLT enables our architecture to provide higher flexibility—to join the system, as well as scalability, in comparison with other solution that uses permissioned blockchain like Hyperledger fabric.

As mentioned in the introduction part, this research is work in progress; therefore, based on the feedback we might receive after implementation, there would be possibilities of further optimization and thus might subject to change.

Acknowledgments This research was supported as part of BLING project, an Interreg project supported by the North Sea Programme of the European Regional Development Fund of the European Union.

References

1. Abdullah, S., Arshad, J., Khan, M. M., Alazab, M., & Salah, K. (2022). PRISED tangle: A privacy-aware framework for smart healthcare data sharing using IOTA Tangle. *Complex & Intelligent Systems, 9*, 1–19.
2. Al Omar, A., Bhuiyan, M. Z. A., Basu, A., Kiyomoto, S., & Rahman, M. S. (2019). Privacy-friendly platform for healthcare data in cloud based on blockchain environment. *Future Generation Computer Systems, 95*, 511–521.
3. Azbeg, K., Ouchetto, O., & Andaloussi, S. J. (2022). BlockMedCare: A healthcare system based on IoT, blockchain and IPFS for data management security. *Egyptian Informatics Journal 23*, 267–277.
4. Benet, J. (2014). IPFS-content addressed, versioned, P2P file system. Preprint. arXiv:1407.3561.
5. Bhawiyuga, A., Wardhana, A., Amron, K., & Kirana, A. P. (2019). Platform for integrating Internet of Things based smart healthcare system and blockchain network. In *2019 6th NAFOSTED Conference on Information and Computer Science (NICS)* (pp. 55–60). IEEE.
6. Brogan, J., Baskaran, I., & Ramachandran, N. (2018). Authenticating health activity data using distributed ledger technologies. *Computational and Structural Biotechnology Journal, 16*, 257–266 .
7. Cao, S., Zhang, G., Liu, P., Zhang, X., & Neri, F. (2019). Cloud-assisted secure eHealth systems for tamper-proofing EHR via blockchain. *Information Sciences, 485*, 427–440.
8. Chen, Y., Ding, S., Xu, Z., Zheng, H., & Yang, S. (2019). Blockchain-based medical records secure storage and medical service framework. *Journal of Medical Systems, 43*(1), 1–9.
9. Dai, H. N., Imran, M., & Haider, N. (2020). Blockchain-enabled Internet of Medical Things to combat covid-19. *IEEE Internet of Things Magazine, 3*(3), 52–57.
10. Dilawar, N., Rizwan, M., Ahmad, F., & Akram, S. (2019). Blockchain: Securing Internet of Medical Things (IoMT). *International Journal of Advanced Computer Science and Applications, 10*(1), 285–286.

11. Dwivedi, A. D., Malina, L., Dzurenda, P., & Srivastava, G. (2019). Optimized blockchain model for Internet of Things based healthcare applications. In *2019 42nd International Conference on Telecommunications and Signal Processing (TSP)* (pp. 135–139). IEEE.
12. Dwivedi, A. D., Srivastava, G., Dhar, S., & Singh, R. (2019). A decentralized privacy-preserving healthcare blockchain for IoT. *Sensors, 19*(2), 326.
13. He, C., Fan, X., & Li, Y. (2012). Toward ubiquitous healthcare services with a novel efficient cloud platform. *IEEE Transactions on Biomedical Engineering, 60*(1), 230–234.
14. Hyla, T., & Pejaś, J. (2019). eHealth integrity model based on permissioned blockchain. *Future Internet 11*(3), 76.
15. 10 Internet of Things (IoT) healthcare examples. (2020). https://ordr.net/article/iot-healthcare-examples. Online, Accessed 27 Apr 2022.
16. IOTA Foundation: IOTA Streams alpha. (2020). IOTA Foundation Blog. https://blog.iota.org/iota-streams-alpha-7e91ee326ac0
17. IOTA Foundation: IOTA Streams Update — September, 2020. (2020). IOTA Foundation Blog. https://blog.iota.org/iota-streams-update-september-2020-c3b8668e231e
18. Islam, A., & Shin, S. Y. (2020). A blockchain-based secure healthcare scheme with the assistance of unmanned aerial vehicle in Internet of Things. *Computers and Electrical Engineering, 84*, 106627.
19. Jabbar, R., Fetais, N., Krichen, M., & Barkaoui, K. (2020). Blockchain technology for healthcare: Enhancing shared electronic health record interoperability and integrity. In *2020 IEEE International Conference on Informatics, IoT, and Enabling Technologies (ICIoT)* (pp. 310–317). IEEE.
20. Jamil, F., Ahmad, S., Iqbal, N., & Kim, D. H. (2020). Towards a remote monitoring of patient vital signs based on IoT-based blockchain integrity management platforms in smart hospitals. *Sensors, 20*(8), 2195.
21. Kumar, M., & Chand, S. (2021). Medhypchain: A patient-centered interoperability Hyperledger-based medical healthcare system: Regulation in covid-19 pandemic. *Journal of Network and Computer Applications, 179*, 102975.
22. Kumar, R., & Tripathi, R. (2021). Towards design and implementation of security and privacy framework for Internet of Medical Things (IoMT) by leveraging blockchain and IPFS technology. *The Journal of Supercomputing, 77*(8), 7916–7955.
23. Malamas, V., Dasaklis, T., Kotzanikolaou, P., Burmester, M., & Katsikas, S. (2019). A forensics-by-design management framework for medical devices based on blockchain. In *2019 IEEE World Congress on Services (SERVICES)* (Vol. 2642, pp. 35–40). IEEE.
24. Meola, A. (2022). IoT Healthcare in 2022: Companies, medical devices, and use cases. https://www.insiderintelligence.com/insights/iot-healthcare. Online, Accessed 27 Apr 2022.
25. Mohanta, B. K., Jena, D., & Satapathy, U. (2019). Trust management in IoT enable healthcare system using Ethereum based smart contract. *International Journal of Scientific & Technology Research, 8*(9), 324–325.
26. Muofhe, M., Dlodlo, N., & Terzoli, A. (2019). An Internet of Things-based system integrated with blockchain to manage patient data in the healthcare sector. In *2019 Open Innovations (OI)* (pp. 97–103). IEEE.
27. orbitdb. (2022). orbit-db. https://github.com/orbitdb/orbit-db. Online, Accessed 21 Sep 2022.
28. Popov, S. (2018). The Tangle. *White Paper, 1*(3).
29. Publish/Subscribe :: libp2p Documentation. (2022). https://docs.libp2p.io/concepts/publish-subscribe. Online, Accessed 21 Sep 2022.
30. Ray, P. P., Chowhan, B., Kumar, N., & Almogren, A. (2021). BIoTHR: Electronic health record servicing scheme in IoT-blockchain ecosystem. *IEEE Internet of Things Journal, 8*(13), 10857–10872.
31. Ray, P. P., Kumar, N., & Dash, D. (2020). BLWN: Blockchain-based lightweight simplified payment verification in IoT-assisted e-healthcare. *IEEE Systems Journal, 15*(1), 134–145.

32. Rifi, N., Agoulmine, N., Chendeb Taher, N., & Rachkidi, E. (2018). Blockchain technology: Is it a good candidate for securing IoT sensitive medical data? *Wireless Communications and Mobile Computing, 2018*, 340–341.
33. Satamraju, K. P. (2020). Proof of concept of scalable integration of Internet of Things and blockchain in healthcare. *Sensors, 20*(5), 1389.
34. Seliem, M., & Elgazzar, K. (2019). BIoMT: Blockchain for the Internet of Medical Things. In (2019 IEEE International Black Sea Conference on Communications and Networking (BlackSeaCom)) (pp. 1–4). IEEE.
35. Sharma, A., Kaur, S., & Singh, M. (2021). A comprehensive review on blockchain and Internet of Things in healthcare. *Transactions on Emerging Telecommunications Technologies, 32*(10), e4333.
36. Srivastava, G., Crichigno, J., & Dhar, S. (2019). A light and secure healthcare blockchain for IoT medical devices. In *2019 IEEE Canadian Conference of Electrical and Computer Engineering (CCECE)* (pp. 1–5). IEEE.
37. Take a look at pubsub on IPFS. (2022). https://blog.ipfs.tech/25-pubsub. Online, Accessed 21 Sep 2022.
38. Uddin, M., Stranieri, A., Gondal, I., & Balasubramanian, V. (2021). Blockchain leveraged decentralized IoT eHealth framework. *Internet of Things, 9*, 1–35.
39. Wang, H., et al. (2020). IoT based clinical sensor data management and transfer using blockchain technology. *Journal of ISMAC, 2*(03), 154–159.
40. What is IPFS? | IPFS Docs. (2022). https://docs.ipfs.io/concepts/what-is-ipfs. Online, Accessed 6 Jun 2022.
41. Xu, J., Xue, K., Li, S., Tian, H., Hong, J., Hong, P., & Yu, N. (2019). Healthchain: A blockchain-based privacy preserving scheme for large-scale health data. *IEEE Internet of Things Journal, 6*(5), 8770–8781.
42. Zaabar, B., Cheikhrouhou, O., Jamil, F., Ammi, M., & Abid, M. (2021). HealthBlock: A secure blockchain-based healthcare data management system. *Computer Networks, 200*, 108500.

GPSR Compliance

The European Union's (EU) General Product Safety Regulation (GPSR) is a set of rules that requires consumer products to be safe and our obligations to ensure this.

If you have any concerns about our products, you can contact us on ProductSafety@springernature.com

In case Publisher is established outside the EU, the EU authorized representative is:

Springer Nature Customer Service Center GmbH
Europaplatz 3
69115 Heidelberg, Germany

Batch number: 10761599

Printed by Printforce, the Netherlands